AF228377

FIGHTING FOR PHILADELPHIA

Forts Mercer and Mifflin, the Battle of Whitemarsh,
and the Road to Valley Forge, October 5-December 19, 1777

Michael C. Harris

Savas Beatie

California

Library of Congress Cataloging-in-Publication Data

Names: Harris, Michael C., 1978- author.
Title: Fighting for Philadelphia : Forts Mercer and Mifflin, the Battle of
    Whitemarsh, and the Road to Valley Forge, October 5-December 19, 1777 /
    by Michael C Harris.
Description: El Dorado Hills, CA : Savas Beatie LLC, 2025. | Includes
    bibliographical references and index. | Summary: "Harris's work is the
    first complete study to merge the strategic, political, and tactical
    history of the complex operations sandwiched between Germantown and the
    arrival of the Continental Army at Valley Forge. Closing his magnificent
    trilogy that began with Brandywine and left off with Germantown, and
    told largely through the words of those who fought there, this is sure
    to please the most discriminating reader and assume its place as one of
    the finest military studies of its kind"-- Provided by publisher.
Identifiers: LCCN 2024060381 | ISBN 9781611217421 (hardcover) |
    ISBN 9781611217438 (ebook)
Subjects: LCSH: Philadelphia (Pa.)--History--Revolution, 1775-1783. |
    Pennsylvania--History--Revolution, 1775-1783. | United
    States--History--Revolution, 1775-1783--Campaigns.
Classification: LCC E233 .H377 2025 | DDC 973.3/33--dc23/eng/20250224
LC record available at https://lccn.loc.gov/2024060381

First edition, first printing

SB

Savas Beatie LLC
989 Governor Drive, Suite 101
El Dorado Hills, CA 95762
Phone: 916-941-6896 / (E-mail) sales@savasbeatie.com

Savas Beatie titles are available at special discounts for bulk purchases in the United States. Contact us for more details.

Printed and bound in the United Kingdom

To the men
who endured the siege of Fort Mifflin

Table of Contents

Table of Contents (continued)

Back Matter

Excerpt from *Brandywine: A Military History of the Battle that Lost Philadelphia but Saved America, September 11, 1777,* by Michael C. Harris

Excerpt from *Germantown: A Military History of the Battle for Philadelphia, October 4, 1777,* by Michael C. Harris

About the Author

List of the Maps

Photos have been placed throughout the book for the convenience of the reader.

Preface

If someone had asked me 20 years ago what book I would someday want to write, my heart would have driven me to this study. I grew up a mile from Fort Mercer and have loved studying coastal defenses since childhood. Memories of visiting Fort Sumter and Fort Delaware led to my undergraduate thesis: "The Evolution of Atlantic Seacoast Defenses of the Delaware River Valley." While the Delaware River story is only part of this book, I feel like *Fighting for Philadelphia: Forts Mercer and Mifflin, the Battle of Whitemarsh, and the Road to Valley Forge, October 5-December 19, 1777* has carried me back to my roots.

When I offered my first manuscript to my publisher, *Brandywine: A Military History of the Battle that Lost Philadelphia but Saved America, September 11, 1777* (2014), I explained that it was only part of the story of the Philadelphia Campaign and there was more to come. *Germantown: A Military History of the Battle for Philadelphia* (2020) picked up where *Brandywine* left off, but I knew a third volume would be necessary to complete the campaign. Now, finally, that book is in your hands. This trilogy is intended as a comprehensive history of the 1777 Philadelphia Campaign.

The latter phase of the Philadelphia Campaign, which begins in the aftermath of the Battle of Germantown and ends with the Continental Army's arrival at Valley Forge, is the least understood. The major fighting at Fort Mercer, Fort Mifflin, and Gloucester along the Delaware River is but lightly covered in most accounts of the war. The Whitemarsh Hills portion of the campaign just outside Philadelphia is a fascinating chess match—a series of thrusts, parries, and brisk engagements but little understood—all while George Washington's own command was being seriously threatened by what is now known as the Conway Cabal. Various monographs on the campaign rarely cover these events chronologically or in sufficient depth, which fosters ongoing confusion about what happened and their importance. Almost none of these important events—and many others—have been examined and put into the context of the larger three-month period at the end of the Philadelphia campaign.

Individual Studies

Several works exist covering bits and pieces of the fighting along the Delaware River. Philadelphia-based historian John Jackson authored three studies: *Fort Mifflin: Valiant Defender of the Delaware*, *The Delaware Bay and River Defenses of Philadelphia 1775-1777*, and *The Pennsylvania Navy, 1775-1781: The Defense of the Delaware*. The Gloucester County, New Jersey Historical Society, produced two early histories of Fort Mercer: Wallace McGeorge's 1909 *The Battle of Red Bank: Resulting in the Defeat of the Hessians and the Destruction of the British Frigate Augusta, Oct. 22 and 23, 1777*, and Frank Stewart's 1927 *History of The Battle of Red Bank With Events Prior and Subsequent Thereto*. A more recent look at Fort Mercer—Lee Patrick Anderson's 1999 *Forty Minutes by the Delaware: The Battle for Fort Mercer*—spills over with undocumented myths. Jeffrey Dorwart provides a solid history of Fort Mifflin in his 1998 *Fort Mifflin of Philadelphia: An Illustrated History*. Garry Wheeler Stone and Paul W. Schopp cover a minor engagement in their recent *The Battle of Gloucester, 1777*. Each of these studies focus on individual elements of the river fighting, but none of them put the subject within the larger context of the river fighting or the Philadelphia Campaign.[1]

Other histories focus on the Delaware River fighting in its entirety. Worthington Chauncey Ford covered this subject in his 1894 article "Defences of Philadelphia in 1777." Samuel Smith's excellent 1970 book *Fight for the Delaware, 1777* and James McIntyre's 2022 *A Most Gallant Resistance: The Delaware River Campaign, September-November 1777* both cover the fighting for control of the river. Unfortunately, none of them place the fighting within the larger context of the campaign or the war in general.[2]

---

1 John W. Jackson, *Fort Mifflin: Valiant Defender of the Delaware* (Norristown, PA, 1986); John W. Jackson, *The Delaware Bay and River Defenses of Philadelphia 1775-1777* (Philadelphia, 1977); John W. Jackson, *The Pennsylvania Navy, 1775-1781: The Defense of the Delaware* (New Brunswick, NJ, 1974); Wallace McGeorge, *The Battle of Red Bank, Resulting in the Defeat of the Hessians and the Destruction of the British Frigate Augusta, Oct. 22 and 23, 1777* (Camden, NJ, 1905); Frank H. Stewart, *History of the Battle of Red Bank: With Events Prior and Subsequent Thereto* (Woodbury, NJ, 1927); Lee Patrick Anderson, *Forty Minutes by the Delaware: "The Battle for Fort Mercer"* (Boca Raton, FL, 1999); Jeffery M. Dorwart, *Fort Mifflin of Philadelphia: An Illustrated History* (Philadelphia, 1998); Garry Wheeler Stone & Paul W. Schopp, *The Battle of Gloucester, 1777* (Yardley, PA, 2022).

2 Worthington Chauncey Ford, "Defences of Philadelphia in 1777," *The Pennsylvania Magazine of History and Biography*. 148 vols. (Philadelphia, 1894), vol. 18, 13; Samuel Steele Smith, *Fight for the Delaware, 1777* (Monmouth Beach, NJ, 1970); James R. McIntyre, *A Most Gallant Resistance: The Delaware River Campaign September – November 1777* (Point Pleasant, NJ, 2022).

To date, three studies focus on the fighting at Whitemarsh. William Buck's article "The Battle of Edge Hill" (1900), John Jackson's *Whitemarsh 1777: Impregnable Stronghold* (1984), and Ray Thompson's *Washington at Whitemarsh: Prelude to Valley Forge* (1974). All three lack documentation and campaign context. Mark Lender's recent examination of the effort to remove Washington as commander in chief in *Cabal!: The Plot Against General Washington* (2019), is a well-written and significant contribution, but it is also non-chronological by its nature, which makes following the campaign difficult.[3]

War Histories

The final three months of the Philadelphia Campaign usually receive minimal coverage in histories of the American Revolution. William Gordon did little justice to this phase of the campaign by dedicating fewer than a dozen pages in his four-volume 1788 history of America's establishment *The History of the Rise, Progress, and Establishment of the Independence of the United States of America*. In just eight pages, Charles Botta covered the same period in his 1845 *History of the War of the Independence of the United States of America*. Botta wrapped up his coverage with this succinct summary: "After a severe and sanguinary campaign of four months, the two armies appeared thus to enjoy some repose, sufficiently protected from the rigors of the season." That same year, Jacob Neff devoted just a single paragraph in his *The Army and Navy of America*. Lord Mahon offered about three pages in his 1858 *History of England*.[4]

George Bancroft's 10-volume 1866 *History of the United States, from the Discovery of the American Continent* reserved just 14 pages for these critical three months. In 1912, British statesman and author Sir George Otto Trevelyan, in his four-volume *The American Revolution*, covered the fighting on the Delaware in just 16 pages, but made

3 William J. Buck, "The Battle of Edge Hill," in *Historical Sketches: A Collection of Papers Prepared for the Historical Society of Montgomery County, Pennsylvania*, 8 vols. (Norristown, PA, 1900), vol. 2, 214-233; John W. Jackson, *Whitemarsh 1777: Impregnable Stronghold* (Fort Washington, PA, 1984); Ray Thompson, *Washington at Whitemarsh: Prelude to Valley Forge* (Fort Washington, PA, 1974); Mark Edward Lender, *Cabal!: The Plot Against George Washington* (Yardley, PA, 2019).

4 William Gordon, *The History of the Rise, Progress, and Establishment of the Independence of the United States of America*, 4 vols. (London, 1788), vol. 3, 1-12; Charles Botta, *History of the War of the Independence of the United States of America*, 2 vols., George Alexander Otis, trans. (Cooperstown, NY, 1845), vol., 2, 55; Jacob Neff, *The Army and Navy of America: Containing a View of the Heroic Adventures, Battles, Naval Engagements, Remarkable Incidents, and Glorious Achievements in the Cause of Freedom* (Philadelphia, 1845), 404-405; Lord Mahon, *History of England from the Peace of Utrecht to the Peace of Versailles, 1713-1783*, 7 vols. (London, 1858), vol. 6, 171-174.

no mention of the fighting at Whitemarsh. Christopher Ward's outstanding *The War of the Revolution*, a two-volume history published in 1952, covers the fighting better than most but does so in just 11 pages. Despite the important size and scale of the engagements, W. J. Wood's well-received and reviewed *Battles of the Revolutionary War, 1775-1781* (1990) spills just a page of ink to cover these three months. Lastly, *Angel in the Whirlwind*, a 1997 book by Benson Bobrick, covers the time after the battle of Germantown in fewer than three pages.[5]

Campaign Histories

John Reed's *Campaign to Valley Forge: July 1, 1777-December 19, 1777* made its appearance in 1965. The study, now considered a classic, stands up well against many later monographs. Unlike most campaign histories, Reed does a solid job of covering the events chronologically: Fort Mercer, Fort Mifflin, Conway's Cabal, and Whitemarsh. The nation's bicentennial saw a resurgence in the publication of books and articles on the battles of the Revolution. Only two dealt in any meaningful way with the final three months of the Philadelphia Campaign. John Pancake's *1777: The Year of the Hangman* covers this time in eight pages with no new conclusions. Historian John Jackson researched and wrote on the British occupation of Philadelphia and the fighting along the Delaware River in his 1979 *With the British Army in Philadelphia: 1778-1778*. Jackson's chronology gets bogged down with chapters on administrative aspects of the occupation interspersed within his campaign narrative.[6]

David Martin's 1993 *The Philadelphia Campaign: June 1777-July 1778* includes 48 pages on the final three months of the campaign but lacks documentation and misrepresents several aspects of the contending forces. Gregory Edgar's 1998 *The Philadelphia Campaign: 1777-1778* relied on undocumented block quotes of campaign participants in his single chapter coverage that fails to mention Whitemarsh. *Philadelphia 1777: Taking the Capital*, Justin Clement's 2007 campaign

---

5 George Bancroft, *History of the United States, from the Discovery of the American Continent*, 10 vols. (Boston, 1866), vol. 9, 429-460; George Otto Trevelyan, *The American Revolution*, 4 vols. (New York, 1912), vol. 4, 250-266; Christopher Ward, *The War of the Revolution*, 2 vols. (New York, 1952), vol. 1, 372-383; W. J. Wood, *Battles of the Revolutionary War, 1775-1781* (Chapel Hill, NC, 1990); Benson Bobrick, *Angel in the Whirlwind* (New York, 1997), 269-271.

6 John F. Reed, *Campaign to Valley Forge: July 1, 1777-December 19, 1777* (Philadelphia, 1965), 249-396; John S. Pancake, *1777: The Year of the Hangman* (Tuscaloosa, AL, 1977), 199-207; John W. Jackson, *With the British Army in Philadelphia* (San Rafael, CA, 1979), 53-163.

study, provides evenhanded coverage before concluding, "the British achieved nothing strategically for all their effort and their tactical successes." Arguably, none of these works did much to further our understanding of the Philadelphia Campaign.[7]

The most recent and well-documented examination of the Philadelphia campaign's conclusion can be found in Thomas McGuire's 2007 *The Philadelphia Campaign: Germantown and the Roads to Valley Forge*. While it has its strengths, the parts read like separate studies on Fort Mercer, Fort Mifflin, and Whitemarsh, and the chapters overlap in campaign chronology, which can be confusing. A lack of quality maps make it more than difficult to understand the ebb and flow of the narrative and the complex actions it attempts to describe.[8]

A New Study

Like Brandywine and Germantown, plenty of primary accounts exist for Fort Mercer, Fort Mifflin, and Whitemarsh to provide solid monographs on each of those actions. Each must be put into the context of the Saratoga Campaign, the Conway Cabal, and the larger Philadelphia Campaign. My hope is this study satisfies those searching for the most recent research coupled with good maps, insightful footnotes, and complete orders of battle. While this book focuses on the larger actions along the Delaware River and at Whitemarsh, lesser-known engagements at Gloucester and Matson's Ford are also covered and put within the overall context of the campaign. The Continental Army's arrival at Valley Forge cannot be appreciated without understanding the complex events that followed Germantown.

Acknowledgments

An undertaking of this magnitude requires the help of many people around the world. If I fail to include your name, please know I appreciate deeply your help in making this book a reality.

---

7 David G. Martin, *The Philadelphia Campaign: June 1777-July 1778* (Conshohocken, PA, 1993), 121-169; Gregory T. Edgar, *The Philadelphia Campaign: 1777-1778* (Bowie, MD, 1998), 71-104; Justin Clement, *Philadelphia 1777: Taking the Capital* (New York, 2007), 88.

8 Thomas J. McGuire, *The Philadelphia Campaign: Germantown and the Roads to Valley Forge*, (Mechanicsburg, PA, 2007).

I would like to collectively thank the staffs at the following repositories: the Historical Society of Pennsylvania, the Library of Congress, the Rush Rees Library at the University of Rochester, the Wisconsin Historical Society, the National Archives, the Massachusetts Historical Society, the Chicago Historical Society, the British Library, the Historical Society of Delaware, Durham University in England, the National Archives of Scotland, the Maryland Historical Society, the Historical Society of Montgomery County Pennsylvania, the Virginia Historical Society, the New York Public Library, the National Library of Scotland, the curator for the United States House of Representatives, Morristown National Historical Park, the William Clements Library, the North Carolina Department of Archives and History, the First City Troop Archives, the University of Virginia Library, the Harlan Crow Library, the Duke University Library, the New York Historical Society, the American Philosophical Society, the British Archives, the Gloucester County, New Jersey Historical Society, and the Canadian Archives.

Historian and author Don Hagist kindly helped verify British source questions and Justin Clement kindly assisted with source searches at Valley Forge National Historic Park. Robert Fanelli deserves thanks for walking the ground at Whitemarsh with me and for fielding my questions. Archaeologist Wade Catts took time to answer my questions and provide material related to the current archaeology being done at Fort Mercer. I also want to thank Roger Williams and Bruce Venter for their support over the years. The staffs at the American Battlefield Trust and the North American Land Trust deserve my appreciation for their support and preservation efforts on the Brandywine Battlefield. Bill Welsch of the American Revolution Roundtable of Richmond, Rob Orrison of Emerging Revolutionary War, and fellow SB author Jason Bohm agreed to read the manuscript and provide constructive criticism. Edward Alexander deserves many thanks for producing the fine maps.

Author and historian Gary Ecelbarger deserves a special thank you. Gary and I met during the Covid-19 pandemic and quickly became friends. Since then, we have coauthored articles for the Journal of the American Revolution, shared resources, and served as a sounding board for each other.

I would like to thank everyone at Savas Beatie for their often overlooked efforts. Their marketing and promotions team is unparalleled. Managing Director Theodore P. Savas was amazingly supportive throughout the process of my previous books and is equally supportive working with me every step of the way on this one. Ted's efforts have opened numerous opportunities, and I thank him and his entire team. MaryBeth Allison helped with the final copyedit, and author liason Sarah Closson helps keep my schedule full with events and appearances.

Lastly, I would be remiss if I did not thank my family. I recently reconnected with my father, Chris Harris, after a number of years. Responsibility for my love of military history lies as much with him as my grandfather. My son, Nate, has been with me along the way since *Brandywine* was released. I pity his history teachers as his knowledge of early America rivals my own. And a special thanks to my wife Michelle who has come along on many of the promotional trips, helped find resources, traipsed many of these long-lost sites of fighting with me, and helped read and edit this work. Every time I find something new on Billingsport, she responds: "You know Ted [Savas] loves himself some Billingsport." All you have done over the years to help keep the house running and my sanity intact is appreciated more than you know, and I love you.

Note on Sources and Methods

This work relies heavily on primary source material. Spelling and grammar acceptable in the 18th century would not pass muster in any classroom today. However, to preserve and distill the flavor of the period, I have refrained from correcting sentence structure and misspellings when directly quoting them. I also have avoided the use of "sic," which interrupts the flow of the narrative. Though a united Germany did not exist in 1777, both "German" and "Hessian" are used interchangeably to identify the various Germanic troops who served with Howe's army. While most of those troops were true Hessians, there were Ansbachers as well.

William Alexander, Lord Stirling

William Alexander (Lord Stirling) was one of Washington's senior commanders. He was born in 1726 in New York. An accomplished mathematician and astronomer, Alexander served during the French and Indian War as an aide-de-camp to Governor Shirley of Massachusetts. Later, while in London, he attempted to claim the vacant title of Earl of Stirling. Although only partially successful in his effort, he was known to most thereafter as Lord Stirling. Once back in the colonies he became the surveyor-general for East Jersey and helped found Columbia University. Stirling held interests in land, iron and trade providing him with social and political influence. His brother-in-law, William Livingston, served as New Jersey's governor during the war. Stirling began the war as a colonel in the New Jersey militia and in 1776 was appointed brigadier general. He was captured in the fighting on Long Island. An exchange was worked out for Montfort Browne, the governor of Nassau in the Bahamas captured in a naval action. Stirling rejoined the colonial effort and served with Washington at Trenton. Stirling had turned in a mixed record thus far in the Philadelphia campaign. His division was caught off guard at Short Hills in northern New Jersey but performed admirably under difficult circumstances at Brandywine. He led the army's reserve division at Germantown and continued in that role at Whitemarsh.

Library of Congress

John Armstrong

He was born in 1717 in Ireland, educated as a civil engineer and emigrated to Pennsylvania to serve as a surveyor for the Penn family. He laid out the town of Carlisle and became the surveyor of Cumberland County. During the French and Indian War he commanded the Pennsylvania contingent on the 1758 Forbes Expedition to capture Fort Duquesne in western Pennsylvania. When the Revolution broke out, he was sent to Charleston to help lay out the defensive works there. However, he returned home to take command of the Pennsylvania militia. His command failed the army at Brandywine and Germantown, but would have a chance to redeem itself at Whitemarsh and Matson's Ford.

Thomas Conway

Irish-born Conway served for 20 years (rising to colonel) in the French army prior to coming to America. Fluent in English and French, he arrived in April 1777. Congress appointed him a brigadier. Conway was a good disciplinarian (which many resented) and battlefield leader and served admirably at Brandywine and Germantown. Disgusted with Washington's leadership, he became embroiled in efforts to replace the commander-in-chief.

Charles Cornwallis

Lord Cornwallis played a major part in the Philadelphia campaign. He was born in London in 1738 and educated at Eton and Cambridge University. He joined the Grenadier Guards in 1756 and attended the military academy at Turin, Italy. Cornwallis served in Germany during the Seven Years' War and later, like William Howe, became a member of the House of Lords.

Although he voted against the Stamp Act and had some sympathy for the colonists, Cornwallis volunteered to serve in America. He took part in the battles of Long Island, the second battle of Trenton, and Princeton. Cornwallis performed well at Brandywine and the Battle of the Clouds. During the Battle of Germantown, he rushed to William Howe's assistance from Philadelphia. After helping clear the Delaware River of Continental resistance, Cornwallis commanded a wing in the Whitemarsh operation.

Francois-Louis de Fleury

He was born in 1749—the scion of a French noble family. Nineteen years later he joined the Regiment de Rouerge. By February 1772 de Fleury rose to major and sailed to America with Phillippe du Coudray four years later. Rebuffed by Congress on arrival, de Fleury joined Washington's army as a volunteer. While serving as a major of engineers he had horses shot from under him both at Brandywine and Germantown. The Frenchman soon provided valuable service along the Delaware.

Joseph Galloway

Prior to the war, Philadelphia aristocrat Joseph Galloway was one of the most powerful politicians in Pennsylvania and a member of the First Continental Congress. Galloway was born to Quaker parents in Maryland. During the years between the French and Indian War and the American Revolution, Galloway (along with Benjamin Franklin) was a prime mover in creating the Assembly Party in Pennsylvania. Galloway rose to become the speaker of the Pennsylvania assembly, and the proprietary family soon lost majority control to the royalists. Once Congress pushed for independence Galloway fled Philadelphia to New York City, where the main British Army was located. Using his social standing, Galloway worked through Ambrose Serle, secretary to Admiral Richard Howe, and gained an audience with General Howe. Howe consulted with Galloway during the planning stages of his campaign to capture Philadelphia. When the British troops began their campaign in the late spring of 1777, Galloway was with them. He recruited local guides who helped Howe at Brandywine and eventually at the Battle of the Clouds and Paoli. Galloway was rewarded with a position in the provisional government of Philadelphia when the British took the city.

Yale University Art Gallery

Horatio Gates

Born in 1728, Gates joined the British army in 1745 and fought during the War of the Austrian Succession. He served in North America during the French and Indian War, where he met George Washington. Soon thereafter Gates left the army and took a land grant in Virginia. He sided with the patriots and Congress commissioned him a brigadier. Gates was serving on the northern frontier when Washington tasked him with stopping Burgoyne's 1777 invasion. His political fortunes rose with the victory at Saratoga while Washington struggled to find success around Philadelphia.

Christopher Greene

Nathanael Greene's cousin was born in Rhode Island in 1737 and became a prominent businessman. He was involved in local politics and the militia, and served during the siege of Boston as a major. Christopher took part in Benedict Arnold's expedition through Maine and was captured at Quebec in December 1775. Following his exchange, he was promoted to colonel of the 1st Rhode Island regiment. He led two Rhode Island regiments in the defense of Fort Mercer.

Library of Congress

Nathanael Greene

Greene was not a healthy man. He was born in 1742 into a Rhode Island Quaker family and suffered a childhood accident that left him with a lifelong limp. He also suffered from asthma and endured a painful spot in his right eye from a smallpox inoculation. None of these issues slowed him down.

Greene sold toys to earn money to buy books and owned an iron fabrication business before the war. After serving in a Rhode Island militia company, he was commissioned a brigadier general in 1775 and given command of the state's troops. His first test was the successful defensive action at Harlem Heights in September 1776, one of the few bright spots of the New York Campaign. Greene's bad advice was responsible for the disaster at Fort Washington, but he redeemed himself by leading a wing of the army well at Trenton and Princeton. He performed well at Brandywine by covering the retreat. Washington trusted him implicitly and gave him nearly half the army

for the assault on Germantown. After failing to save the river forts in New Jersey, Greene led an army wing at Whitemarsh.

Charles Grey

The commander of the 3rd British Brigade was born in 1729 in Northumberland, England. In 1744, Grey purchased a commission as ensign in the 6th Regiment of Foot and took part in suppressing the Jacobite rising the following year. During the Seven Years' War he served as an adjutant on the staff of Duke Ferdinand of Brunswick and was wounded at the Battle of Minden. In 1772, Grey was promoted to colonel and served as aide-de-camp to George III. By the time of the American Revolution, he had three decades of extensive military experience and was considered one of Britain's best commanders. After leading the attack at Paoli earlier in the campaign, he entered the drama again at Whitemarsh.

Alexander Hamilton

The young and opinionated Hamilton was born an illegitimate child (likely in 1755) in the Caribbean. He commanded a New York militia artillery battery throughout the 1776 campaign. His capabilities caught Washington's attention, and the commander added Hamilton to his staff as an aide-de-camp in March 1777. Hamilton's fluency in French helped Washington translate important documents. He served on Washington's staff at Germantown. Washington tasked him with a mission to Horatio Gates.

John Hazelwood

Born in England in 1726, Hazelwood came to America in the 1740s. Settling in Philadelphia, Hazelwood led merchant vessels a decade later and continued to do so when war erupted. When called to duty, he claimed much sailing experience but no combat service. Well-suited to overseeing construction of naval vessels, his ability to fight the British navy remained unclear. Hazelwood's familiarity with the changing shoals of the Delaware River, coupled with the fact that most of the effective elements of the fleet (galleys, floating batteries, and fire ships) were State Navy vessels, made him a wise choice to lead the combined fleet on the Delaware River.

Richard Howe

Gen. William Howe's older brother and commander of the British fleet in North America joined the navy at 13 and served throughout the War of the Austrian Succession and the Seven Years' War. Like his brother, the admiral was not unsympathetic to the American cause, which may have influenced how he employed his naval power. His blockade of the American coast proved ineffective. It was mostly his responsibility to open the Delaware River to British shipping after disembarking his brother's army in northeastern Maryland.

William Howe

Washington's chief antagonist for the 1777 Campaign was born in England in 1729 and entered the army in 1746 as an officer in a dragoon regiment. He fought in the War of the Austrian Succession, commanded the light infantry under James Wolfe during his Canadian operations during the Seven Years' War, and served in Havana. Howe was elected to Parliament in 1761 and went on to train the army's light infantry companies. In June 1775, he commanded the unimaginative assaults at Bunker (Breed's) Hill near Boston, and was elevated to overall command in North America that October. His 1776 New York Campaign nearly (and likely could have) destroyed the Continental army and ended the war. Howe's offensive plan at Brandywine—holding Washington in place while flanking his right—worked to perfection, though he failed to decisively follow up his victory. The control of Philadelphia required the elimination of the American threat along the Delaware River.

Henry Knox

Henry Knox lost two fingers in a musket accident early in life. The native Bostonian

born in 1750 opened a bookstore and became well-read on military issues in general, and ordnance in particular. During the winter of 1775-1776, he orchestrated a daring removal of artillery from Fort Ticonderoga and oversaw its transfer to Boston—a bold success that earned him Washington's gratitude and a promotion to head the Continental artillery.

Knox helped improve the defenses of Connecticut and Rhode Island and was promoted after Trenton to brigadier. During the winter of 1776-1777, Washington commissioned him to raise a brigade of artillery. By 1777 he had been in command of the Continental artillery for more than a year. Knox played but a minor role at Brandywine, but he had Washington's ear. He would speak into it at the most inopportune time with the Chew house in sight at Germantown. Knox remained in command of Washington's artillery when Howe marched out of Philadelphia toward Whitemarsh.

Wilhelm von Knyphausen

Born in Luxembourg in 1716, Baron Wilhelm Reichsfreiherr zu Inn-und Knyphausen became a general in Hesse, but traditionally served the Prussian kings. In 1776, he was sent

to North America as second in command of the hired German troops, and the following year, at age 61, became their overall commander. Knyphausen was instrumental in the assault on Fort Washington on upper Manhattan Island (near the current site of the George Washington Bridge), and performed admirably at Brandywine and the Battle of the Clouds. He and his men were camped west of German- town when the Americans poured out of the fog. He led a wing of William Howe's army when it marched out of Philadelphia toward Washington's army at Whitemarsh.

Marquis de Lafayette

Although baptized Marie Joseph Paul Yves Roch Gilbert du Motier, and was hereditarily Marquis du Lafayette, Baron de Vissac, and Seigneur de St. Romain, he is better known as simply the Marquis de Lafayette.

The native of Chavaniac Auvergne, France, who was born on September 6, 1757, grew to more than six feet tall, a height at that time nearly as imposing as his name. Lafayette's father was killed at the battle of Minden in 1759 during the Seven Years' War. Lafayette moved to Paris with his mother in 1768 to enter the College du Plessis. Two years later, when his mother and grandmother died during the same week, he inherited significant wealth and joined the royal army as a sous-lieutenant in the Kimip Musketeers. Lafayette became a captain in the Noailles Dragoons in 1775.

Fascinated by the upheaval on the other side of the Atlantic, on December 7, 1776,

Lafayette signed an agreement with Silas Deane, the American army commissioner in Paris, to serve as a major general in the Continental Army. The next year he bought his own ship and sailed for America, accompanied by Baron Johann de Kalb and a dozen other French officers. During the 56-day trip, Lafayette studied English. He was wounded at Brandywine, recovered, and rejoined the army in time to play a prominent role.

Alexander McDougall

McDougall was born in Scotland in 1732 and moved to New York six years later. Following a stint as a privateer during the French and Indian War, McDougall became a merchant and importer. By the eve of the Revolution he was an ardent patriot in the protest movement, and began the war as colonel of the 1st New York Regiment. After taking part in the New York campaign in 1776, McDougall's brigade formed part of the force holding the Hudson Highlands early in the 1777 campaign. His brigade joined Washington in time for Germantown. By the time of the Whitemarsh operation, he was in command of a division.

Wikipedia

Wikipedia

Thomas Mifflin

The 33-year-old Mifflin had been appointed quartermaster general of the Continental Army in August 1775. He broke with Washington in late 1776 and helped lead the movement to replace the Virginian as commander of the army. Mifflin's lackadaisical effort in 1777 led to many of Washington's supply problems. The position of quartermaster general necessarily entailed that Mifflin be fully informed of the army's movements, but by 1777 he was often absent from headquarters. His absence hampered the army's mobility and health. Like other senior officers, Mifflin's relationship with George Washington soured as the army struggled against William Howe.

John Montresor

Montresor was born in 1736 in Gibraltar and spent his early life there and on Minorca. During the late 1740s, Montresor attended Westminster School in England and learned the principles of engineering from his father, who was a military engineer. During the French and Indian War, he came to North America with his father and served as an ensign in the 48th Regiment of Foot. After the war, Montresor helped prepare maps of Acadia (a region that today includes parts of Quebec and Maine), the St. Lawrence River, and the Kennebec River in northern New England. The capable engineer designed and built Fort Niagara and Fort Erie.

He was in Boston when the Revolution began and took part in the New York Campaign before accompanying Howe on the 1777 Philadelphia Campaign. Prior to the war, Montresor helped design and build Fort Mifflin on Mud Island, an experience that would prove valuable to Howe later in the campaign. He left behind his memoirs, which were published in the late 1800s as "The Montresor Journals."

Thomas-Antoine de Mauduit du Plessis

The son of a French noble family, du Plessis as a young man traveled to visit the battlefields of Ancient Greece. He joined the French artillery in 1771, and rose to lieutenant three years later. He left France for America at the beginning of 1777, carrying a commission as captain of the artillery. During the early stages of the Philadelphia campaign, du Plessis served as an aide to Henry Knox. His engineering experience proved valuable along the Delaware River.

Casimir Pulaski

Pulaski was born on March 6, 1745, on a family estate near Warsaw, Poland. In the late 1760s he led a partisan force against the Russian army during a series of revolts in his native land. By the age of 23 he was in command of the military arm of the Confederation of Bar, a patriotic movement that sought to evict the Russians from Poland and restore sovereignty to the country. Pulaski was captured by the Russians but managed to flee Poland. He briefly aided the Turks against Russia, did time in a French debtors' prison, and finally emigrated to America.

Pulaski landed at Marblehead, Massachusetts, on July 23, 1777, and caught up with Washington's army on August 21. In the aftermath of Brandywine, Washington appointed him commander of the light dragoon brigade on September 15. His command was largely responsible for screening the front of Washington's army under challenging circumstances.

Samuel Smith

The Pennsylvania native was born in Lancaster County in 1752 and moved to Baltimore with his family. Following education at Carlisle and Elkton, he worked in his father's counting house. Smith traveled extensively in Europe and returned and enlisted in 1776 as a captain in William Smallwood's Maryland regiment in 1776. Smith took part in the battles of Long Island, Harlem Heights and White Plains and retreated with the army across New Jersey. After crossing the Delaware into Pennsylvania in December 1776, he received promotion to lieutenant colonel in the new 4th Maryland Regiment. After fighting at Brandywine, Washington tasked Smith with a steep task: the command of Fort Mifflin.

John Sullivan

The son of Irish indentured servants, John Sullivan was born in 1740 in Berwick in what is now the state of Maine. He studied law and served as a major of militia before the

war. In June 1775 he was appointed brigadier general in the army and took part in the Canadian operations. Sullivan was promoted to major general in August 1776.

The British captured Sullivan during the Battle of Long Island, and General Howe used him as a pawn in the contemplated peace negotiation by sending him as an errand boy under parole to speak with Congress. In September, Sullivan was exchanged for Brig. Gen. Richard Prescott, who had been captured in November 1775. When Gen. Charles Lee was taken prisoner in northern New Jersey, Washington put Sullivan in command of Lee's division, and he performed well at Trenton. Sullivan's conduct was under question after actions at Staten Island and Brandywine, but he fully intended to redeem himself at the head of one of Washington's four columns in the attack against Germantown. Sullivan commanded one of Washington's wings during the Whitemarsh operation.

Simeon Thayer

Born in Mendon, Massachusetts on April 28, 1738, Thayer began his military service in the Army of Observation outside of Boston in April 1775. He took part in the ill-fated march on Quebec under Benedict Arnold and was captured during the unsuccessful attempt to storm the city on December 31, 1775. Following his exchange, Thayer received a major's commission in the 2nd Rhode Island Regiment. His star rose during his service in the Delaware River forts.

James Varnum

Varnum was born in 1748, graduated from Rhode Island College, and became a lawyer in 1771. By 1774 he was a militia colonel and participated in the Lexington alarm that marked the opening fighting of the war. Although colonel of the 1st Rhode Island Regiment by May 1775, he had played only a minor role thus far in the war. During the army's reorganization after 1776, Varnum was made brigadier on February 12, 1777. His would be a major part in the Delaware River operations.

Carl von Donop

Born to nobility in 1732 and blessed with valuable connections in the European courts, von Donop was the personal adjutant to the Landgraf of Hesse-Kassel and served during the Seven Years' War. When the British government hired Hessian troops for the American Revolution, he was made commander of the grenadiers and jaegers dispatched to fight in the rebellious colonies.

Von Donop fought throughout the New York campaign (Long Island, Kip's Bay, and Harlem Heights). He was the senior officer in New Jersey in late 1776 when his warnings of a pending attack were brushed aside by Gen. James Grant. Von Donop fought well at Brandywine. His task in the much smaller affair at Red Bank to control the Delaware River forts would extract a high price.

George Washington

Washington was born in Virginia on February 22, 1732. In 1749, he was appointed the official surveyor for Culpeper County, and in that capacity helped lay out the town of Alexandria. Washington was commissioned a major in the Virginia militia in 1752.

The following year the governor, under orders from King George II, sent him to deliver an ultimatum to the French in the Ohio Valley. It was Washington who ordered the shots fired that opened the global Seven Years' War in the colonies. He was promoted to lieutenant colonel, fought in the battle at Fort Necessity in the Pennsylvania back country in July 1754, and was an aide-de-camp to Gen. Edward Braddock during the catastrophic expedition to the forks of the Ohio River. Washington was elected to the Virginia House of Burgesses in 1758 and married widow Martha Custis the following year.

After Lexington and Concord Congress named Washington commander-in-chief of the Continental Army. He was 45 years old during the 1777 campaign. Modern perception imagines Washington as a gray-haired old man leading troops into battle. In fact, he pulled back his dark reddish-brown hair into a queue and powdered it white (he never wore a wig) during the Revolution. He was a formidable man—tall, strong, and robust. His poor generalship early in the war nearly trapped the army on Long Island, but his bold, unexpected strikes at Trenton and Princeton demonstrated his ability in the field. He was in desperate need of a decisive battlefield victory in the 1777 campaign, but was defeated by

Howe at Brandywine and Germantown. Washington would be simultaneously pulled in several directions, politically and militarily, in the final phase of the challenging Philadelphia Campaign.

Anthony Wayne

The bombastic Wayne was born in Chester County, Pennsylvania, in 1745. He attended an academy for two years, became a prosperous tanner, and spent a year as a surveyor. He later became a colonel of the 4th Pennsylvania Battalion. Wayne took part in the Canadian expedition and was put in command of Fort Ticonderoga.

In February 1777, Wayne was promoted to brigadier general while commanding a portion of the Pennsylvania Line at Ticonderoga, and then joined the army at Morristown. He was placed in command of the First Pennsylvania Brigade of Benjamin Lincoln's division, and when Lincoln was detached to serve under General Horatio Gates during the Saratoga Campaign, the 32-year-old Wayne assumed temporary command of the division.

Wayne performed well along Brandywine Creek but was surprised and embarrassed by the slaughter at Paoli. The stain of that massacre hung over him like a gray cloud as he and his men marched with John Sullivan's column toward Germantown on the night of October 3, 1777.

Wayne continued to lead an infantry division as the army took up a strong position at Whitemarsh.

The Origins of the 1777 Campaign

The American Revolution was entering its third year by spring 1777. Most of the prior year was a disaster for American hopes. While the fledgling Continental Congress declared independence from Great Britain that summer, the year also witnessed the failed attempt to make Canada the fourteenth colony, the loss of New York City to British occupation, and the rapidly disintegrating Continental Army's retreat across New Jersey late in the year. As Christmas approached, Gen. William Howe and the British army settled into winter quarters under the mistaken belief that victory was at hand and would be quickly achieved with the spring thaw.

General George Washington, commander of the nascent American army, had different plans. In a daring raid, Washington crossed the Delaware River and defeated the Hessian garrison at Trenton, New Jersey, the day after Christmas. About a week later, Washington stunned the British high command with a successful maneuver again at Trenton, followed by a second victory at Princeton. The patriot victories forced Howe to withdraw his scattered outposts into the New York City area and allowed Washington to move the remnant of his army into the mountains around Morristown, New Jersey, for the balance of the winter. As Washington began the process of rebuilding the Continental Army, William Howe set about deciding his course of operations for 1777.

British Planning

As early as 1775, British strategy revolved around isolating New England, viewed as the core of the rebellion, from the other colonies. If the British seized the Hudson River-Lake Champlain corridor, New England would lose its physical connections and support from the rest of the colonies. Phase one occurred the next year when the British seized New York City. If successful, at least theoretically, Howe could move north along the Hudson River, meet a force coming south from

Canada, and together strike east into Massachusetts. After the relatively easy capture of New York City, Howe proposed moving up the Hudson—which was in line with Great Britain's original strategic thinking.

Late in November 1776, Howe sent a proposal to Lord George Germain, the Secretary of State for the American Department. He wanted a 10,000-man army to penetrate Massachusetts from Rhode Island and an additional 10,000 men to start moving north along the Hudson. Some 8,000 troops would remain in New Jersey to block the remnant of Washington's army. Howe hoped this small force could keep Washington busy while the other two strong columns executed the New England strategy. It was a bold plan designed to bring an end to the war by the close of 1777. With the Americans reeling on all fronts in November 1776, Howe's plan appeared achievable.[1]

While Lord Germain believed the destruction of the Continental Army was the key to victory, Howe believed the occupation of colonial territory was the ticket to success. The more territory that came under British control, the easier it would be for more Loyalists to regain control of provincial affairs and restore crown authority. To achieve victory, Howe intended to move through the countryside with "impressive strength through centers of rebellion, relying upon overawing the disaffected, animating the loyal, and demonstrating to the wavering the futility of resistance." Howe's thoughts on war contrasted sharply with Washington's. The Virginian was willing to lose territory and cities if it meant preserving his fighting strength.[2]

Howe changed his thinking by late December when Washington, beaten and despondent, fled west across New Jersey. Rather than shift units into the Hudson River valley, Howe gave pursuit. By December 20, the British had pushed the Americans across the countryside until Washington crossed the Delaware River into Pennsylvania. The ease with which the British occupied New Jersey caused Howe to change his strategy. Rather than move up the Hudson, he set his eyes on capturing Philadelphia—a seemingly easy target. Washington, who was perhaps at the nadir of his military career, would be forced to defend the American capital, lured into battle and handily defeated. The defeat and occupation of the capital

---

1 John Stockdale, ed., *The Parliamentary Register; or, History of the Proceedings and Debates of the House of Commons: Containing an Account of the most interesting Speeches and Motions; accurate Copies of the most remarkable Letters and Papers; of the most material Evidence, Petitions, &c laid before and offered to the House, During the Fifth Session of the Fourteenth Parliament of Great Britain*, 17 vols. (London, 1802), vol. 10, 362.

2 John F. Luzader, *Saratoga: A Military History of the Decisive Campaign of the American Revolution* (New York, 2008), xxii, 2-3.

would achieve ultimate victory, or at least Howe believed as much. To capture the enemy capital, per traditional European strategy, was to practically win the war.

British leadership remained convinced the Loyalists of North America would rise up and support the British government if given the opportunity to do so, and Philadelphia was believed to be a hotbed of Loyalism. Joseph Galloway, the former speaker of the Pennsylvania Assembly, convinced Howe that the Loyalists of Philadelphia would indeed rush to his support. Galloway told the general that as much as 90 percent of Pennsylvanians were loyal to the Crown and would rise to support Great Britain. That grand claim was grandly false, but Howe believed it. The inhabitants of the Middle Colonies, he wrote, were "disposed to peace, in which sentiment they would be confirmed, by our getting possession of Philadelphia, I am, from this consideration, fully persuaded, the principal army should act offensively on that side, where the enemy's chief strength will certainly be collected."[1]

And so William Howe abandoned the Hudson River plan before it began. Unaware of the new strategic twist, the northern army under British General Guy Carleton would continue as planned. Howe did not believe Carleton could reach Albany, New York, before September. That would give Howe plenty of time to defeat Washington, swoop into Philadelphia, and return to the Hudson River to help Carleton. To Howe, the capture of Philadelphia trumped all else.

Howe's strategy, explained historian Richard Ketchum, demonstrated an "unwillingness to recognize that the capture of Philadelphia, beyond its potential psychological impact on rebels and loyalists, could not in itself determine the outcome of the war." It's capture, Ketchum argued, "in strategic as well as geographic terms . . . led nowhere." For Howe to win in 1777, he "must destroy Washington's army, and seizing a piece of real estate—no matter how valuable—was no way to achieve that." The double defeats at Trenton and Princeton arrived just after Howe's shift in strategic thinking. Despite the setback, he remained convinced moving on Philadelphia, and not the Hudson River plan, was the key to the final campaign.[2]

Unbeknownst to Howe, John Burgoyne had returned to London during the winter of 1776-77 with orders from his commander, Guy Carleton, to report on the needs and intent of the northern army. During the voyage across the Atlantic, Burgoyne jotted down notes and took the liberty to elaborate upon Carleton's ideas

---

1 Stockdale, *Register*, vol. 10, 371.

2 Richard M. Ketchum, *Saratoga: Turning Point of America's Revolutionary War* (New York, 1997), 59.

for 1777. Once in London, Burgoyne met with Germain and King George III. The primary objective of his army would be the capture of Fort Ticonderoga. Thereafter, argued Burgoyne, the "sole purpose of the Canada army [was] to effect a junction with General Howe, or after co-operating so far as to get possession of Albany and open communication to New York, to remain upon the Hudson's river, and thereby enable that general to act with his whole force to the southward." Burgoyne, throughout the planning process, assumed he would eventually form a juncture with Howe. King George III agreed with Burgoyne's plans, stating that his "force [should move] down to Albany & Join at that [with Howe's army]." In March of 1777, Burgoyne received orders to lead the Canadian army south along the Lake Champlain-Hudson River corridor and form a junction with Howe. These orders were in line with the plan to isolate New England. Once Burgoyne reached Albany, he was to "put himself under the command of Sir William Howe." No matter what complications Burgoyne may encounter along the way, he was to never lose sight of the "intended junction with Sir William Howe as their [Burgoyne's army] principal objective." Germain promised to inform Howe of Burgoyne's orders, but that communication never took place. Burgoyne went into the campaign assuming Howe would stick to the original plan and clear the lower Hudson River valley. It was a fatal mistake.[3]

Although Germain never sent a copy of Burgoyne's orders to Howe, the longstanding Hudson River plan was of course familiar to Howe, who sent dispatches to Lord Germain informing him of his change in objective. Burgoyne never learned of this change in plan. Germain needed to reconcile the issue. "It is clear that Lord George expected the armies to join, that he assumed Howe understood the general plan, and that he believed Howe could take Philadelphia and join Burgoyne in a single campaign." Most historians lay blame for the failures of 1777 at the feet of Lord Germain. However, they fail to consider the limitations of 18th century communication. Germain was forced to rely on face-to-face contact with his subordinates or dispatches sent back-and-forth across the Atlantic Ocean. Sending an inquiry, waiting for a written response, and then the necessary return trip could take up to two months. By the time a letter or order arrived, the facts on the ground were almost always outdated. Germain had no personal contact with Howe during this period. While both Burgoyne and Henry Clinton (a subordinate from Howe's army) returned to London during the winter, Germain viewed the information and opinions of these self-serving officers with caution.

---

3 Piers Mackesy, *The War for America: 1775-1783* (Lincoln, NE, 1964), 115.

When King George III approved Burgoyne's revision of the Hudson River plan and approved Howe's Philadelphia thrust, it was Germain's duty to point out the contradictory orders to the King, or at least inform the two principal generals of the 1777 campaign of the difference between their orders. Burgoyne's advance was made with the full understanding that Howe would support him, but not until he reached Albany.[4]

Howe's blind ambition to capture Philadelphia would play a major part in the disaster that would befall Burgoyne in the fall of 1777 at Saratoga. One historian has argued, however, that "it would be mistaken to assume that Howe sacrificed Burgoyne either through indifference or stupidity." Howe had no enthusiasm for the New England plan, but "a lack of enthusiasm for it . . . leaves the impression that the failure of the government to send Howe reinforcements as numerous as he wished put him in a mood prejudicial to a sympathetic handling of the problem presented by Burgoyne's advance." Howe previously requested additional troops so he could both attack Philadelphia and support the Hudson River operations. Despite his obsession with Philadelphia, Howe took an inordinate amount of time to achieve his now primary goal, but by then Burgoyne's fate was already sealed.[5]

By spring 1777, the British high command knew of Howe's intentions, approved his plans, and realized he might not return in time to help Burgoyne. In a long letter to Germain, Howe believed Washington would be forced to move south and defend Philadelphia. If he was wrong and Washington moved up the Hudson River Valley, Howe would turn around and follow him. Several weeks later, events proved Howe correct. Washington was forced to block Howe from gaining Philadelphia and played no role in the Hudson River operations.[6]

The 1776 campaign demonstrated that Howe was unwilling to conduct a purely military assault to annihilate Washington's army. He chased, pushed, and kept up pressure without a final blow to the weakened army. Lord Germain preferred a scorched-earth policy as he reasoned the rebellion would not end until they eliminated the main rebel field army. To Howe's way of thinking, such brutality would only further alienate the Americans and set the stage for future civil

---

4 Ira D. Gruber, *The Howe Brothers & the American Revolution* (New York, 1972), 187-188.

5 Troyer Steele Anderson, *The Command of the Howe Brothers During the American Revolution* (New York and London, 1936), 272-273.

6 Stockdale, *Register*, vol. 10, 414-415. For more information and details on William Howe and British strategy in 1777 as well as the options facing George Washington that year, refer to my first book on the Philadelphia campaign: *Brandywine: A Military History of the Battle that Lost Philadelphia but Saved America, September 11, 1777* (El Dorado Hills, CA, 2014).

wars even if they achieved victory. Winning the hearts and minds of the people was more important than military extermination. Howe intended to "use persuasion in conjunction with demonstrated military might, employing their martial resources to prod the rebels into renewing their allegiance to the Crown." Capturing the capital, he believed, would achieve this with no change to his strategy.[7]

Washington's Strategy

Congress's choice of George Washington to lead the first American army was curious, at best. The Virginia planter never commanded more than a regiment or two in combat, though he had exercised limited departmental command during the French and Indian War. Despite a personal desire to have done so, Washington never served as a British regular, nor did he attend any of the military schools in Europe. Faced by some of the best military professionals of the 18th century, Washington's learning curve needed to be steep. Despite his victories at Trenton and Princeton, Washington had been battered, beaten, and out-generaled throughout 1776.

Washington soon came to realize that it would take time to mold the Continental Army into a force that could stand toe-to-toe with British regulars. He would spend most of the war avoiding pitched battles—especially offensive ones. While this strategy kept his army intact for the long haul, Washington still needed a strategy to defeat the British. The Continental Army could have waged a guerilla war with smaller forces and slowly drained away British strength. Congress, however, whose members had to answer to their constituents, wanted every colony and every major city defended with a standing army. While politically viable, this strategy would have spread Washington's limited manpower thin and guaranteed overall defeat. With limited options available, Washington needed a plan that would be effective with his sparse resources.[8]

Washington became best known for implementing something of a Fabian-style of warfare. While Washington preferred a large professional army and constantly begged Congress for one, he was a realist. The relatively small army he was given was easier to supply and could move more rapidly than their British and Hessian counterparts. When not on the defensive, Washington could attack rapidly

---

7 James Kirby Martin & Mark Edward Lender, *"A Respectable Army": The Military Origins of the Republic, 1763-1789* (West Sussex, United Kingdom, 2015), 51-52.

8   David Hackett Fischer, *Washington's Crossing* (Oxford, 2004), 79-80.

and retreat even more quickly. In this manner he could prevent heavy casualties, maintain his army, and always live to fight another day. By avoiding major battles and using the wilds of North America, Washington hoped to frustrate the British army by making the war too expensive for Great Britain to maintain. Still, Washington harbored a desire to wage a classic battle with the British on equal terms. He hoped to maintain and train the Continental Army through stall tactics until his men were ready to fight on Washington's terms. Washington described his strategy as "time, caution, and worrying the enemy until we could be better provided with arms and other means, and had better disciplined troops to carry on."[9]

The longer the war continued, the more unpopular it became in Parliament and with the people back home. The financial costs were staggering and rising. British leadership hoped to bring the conflict to a conclusion in 1777. In contrast, Washington believed the British government would tire of losing men and material, of the rising costs of the war, and of the increasing criticism of the opposition party. Time was on his side.

The lesson of 1776 was that the fledgling American army was not capable of traditional warfare—yet. In 1777, Washington would rely on defensive warfare, daybreak assaults, sneak attacks, and trickery. It was a strategy of guerilla warfare, known as partisan warfare or at the time, petite guerre.

When the spring campaign season dawned, Washington was in a quandary because he did not know Howe's strategic goals. His opponent had many options because of the large Royal fleet commanded by his brother, Adm. Richard Howe. With few ships of his own, Washington's options were limited. Howe could use his fleet to move north up the Hudson River, jump to any number of ports along the American coastline, or could move directly overland to Philadelphia, picking up where the previous campaign ended. Limited options and manpower forced Washington into a reactive strategy. His defensive positions around Morristown placed him in position to block the overland route to Philadelphia. If Howe pushed north along the Hudson to meet the British force from Canada, Washington would follow him and harass his rear. If Howe chose to completely change the field of operations using the British fleet, Washington would be forced to wait and see where the British army appeared before reacting.

---

9   Fischer, *Crossing*, 79. This Fabian strategy was named for Fabius Cunctator, a Roman general who had fought a delaying campaign against the Carthaginians. James Thomas Flexner, *Washington: The Indispensable Man* (Boston, 1969), 131.

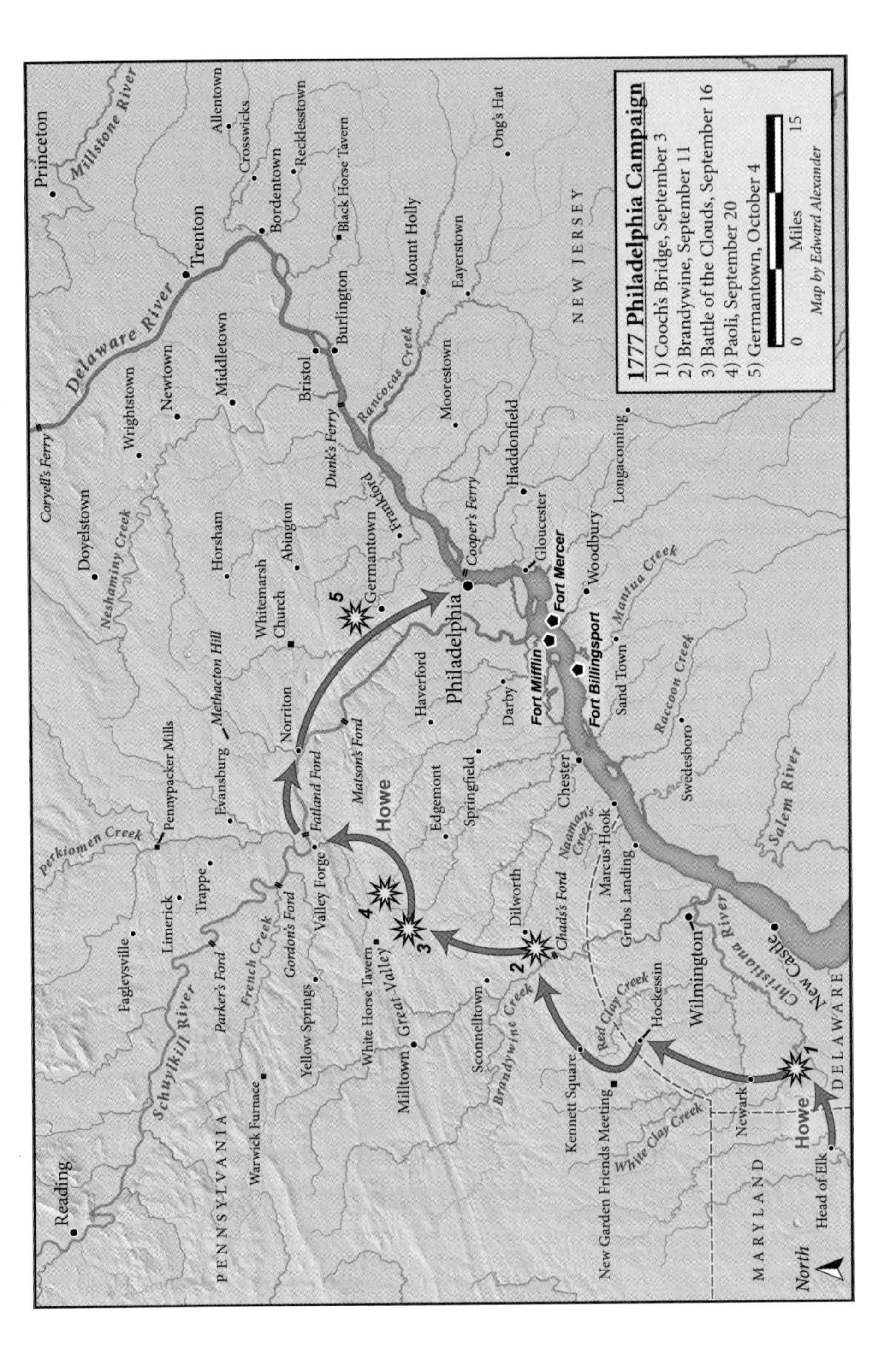

1777 Philadelphia Campaign
1) Cooch's Bridge, September 3
2) Brandywine, September 11
3) Battle of the Clouds, September 16
4) Paoli, September 20
5) Germantown, October 4
Map by Edward Alexander
0   Miles   15

North

PENNSYLVANIA
NEW JERSEY
MARYLAND
DELAWARE

Reading
Princeton
Millstone River
Allentown
Crosswicks
Recklesstown
Bordentown
Trenton
Black Horse Tavern
Burlington
Mount Holly
Eayerstown
Delaware River
Coryell's Ferry
Doyelstown
Wrightstown
Newtown
Middletown
Bristol
Rancocas Creek
Moorestown
Ong's Hat
Neshaminy Creek
Dunk's Ferry
Frankford
Germantown
Abington
Horsham
Whitemarsh Church
Methacton Hill
Cooper's Ferry
Haddonfield
Longacoming
Gloucester
Woodbury
Fort Mercer
Pennypacker Mills
perkiomen Creek
Evansburg
Norriton
Fatland Ford
Matson's Ford
Howe
Philadelphia
Haverford
Darby
Fort Billingsport
Mantua Creek
Sand Town
Schuylkill River
Trappe
Limerick
Fagleysville
Parker's Ford
French Creek
Gordon's Ford
Valley Forge
Edgemont
Springfield
Fort Mifflin
Marcus Hook
Naaman's Creek
Raccoon Creek
Swedesboro
Warwick Furnace
Yellow Springs
White Horse Tavern
Great Valley
Milltown
Dilworth
Chester
Chad's Ford
Grubs Landing
Sconnelltown
Brandywine Creek
Red Clay Creek
Hockessin
Wilmington
Christiana River
Salem River
Kennett Square
New Garden Friends Meeting
White Clay Creek
Newark
Howe
New Castle
Head of Elk

Howe

3
4
2
1
5

Chapter 1

The Philadelphia Campaign

June – October 1777

"[William Howe] can neither support his Army in Philada if he is cut off from comm[u]nication with his ships, neither can he make good a Retreat should any accident befall him."[1]

— Gen. George Washington, September 29, 1777

After his successes at Trenton and Princeton in late December 1776 and early January 1777, Gen. George Washington spent the next six months in the Watchung Mountains around Morristown, New Jersey, building a new army nearly from scratch following the expiration of his one-year enlistments. During that long and arduous process, Washington harassed British outposts scattered across northern New Jersey in a series of raids and skirmishes. Fortunately for him, British Gen. William Howe was more concerned with strategic planning than with what he considered the minor doings of the Continental Army.[2]

---

1 Philander D. Chase & Edward G. Lengel, eds., *The Papers of George Washington, Revolutionary War Series*, 30 vols. (Charlottesville & London, 2001), vol. 11, 347.

2 For more information on the opening months of the campaign as well as the Battle of Brandywine, refer to my first book on the Philadelphia campaign: *Brandywine: A Military History of the Battle that Lost Philadelphia but Saved America, September 11, 1777* (El Dorado Hills, CA, 2014). A more generalized overview of the campaign can be found in Michael C. Harris, "The Empire Strikes Back:

The small-scale raids and skirmishes between January and June 1777 were the only military operations in that region. The revolution had devolved into something more closely resembling a guerilla war than the more traditional European-style of combat. This respite gave Washington the time and space he needed to rebuild his weakened army. The buildup of stress during this extended low-intensity war boiled over into the savageness exhibited later in the campaign—especially at Paoli.

General Howe mostly ignored Washington's movements during this period and made little effort to open the 1777 campaign season. He openly desired to capture Philadelphia as rapidly as possible and return to New York to join forces with Gen. John Burgoyne and the northern army, yet demonstrated scant urgency to put any plan in motion.

June 1777

Howe finally lurched into action that June. The British commander decided his best bet was to attempt the overland route to Philadelphia in the hope of luring Washington down from his mountain stronghold. Defeating Washington in New Jersey and then marching to Philadelphia offered Howe the best chance to take the colonial capital and leave in time to aid Burgoyne in New York. The delay in opening the campaign triggered some dissatisfaction within the British officer corps. The army had failed to move weeks earlier when the winter rains stopped, and the warmer weather had dried the roads. By the time Howe moved into northern New Jersey, it was already June 13.[3]

To the disbelief of officers in both armies, Howe moved thousands of troops ten miles, went into camp, constructed earthworks . . . and waited. Howe no longer intended to move toward Philadelphia through New Jersey but would instead attempt to draw Washington down from the high ground and offer battle on the relatively flat country east of the Watchung Mountains. No one believed Washington's force formidable, including Washington himself, who refused to allow himself to be drawn into a battle he could not win. By remaining idle during

Philadelphia Campaign 1777," in Edward G. Lengel, ed., *The 10 Key Campaigns of the American Revolution* (Washington, DC, 2020), 111-28, or Michael C. Harris, *The Philadelphia Campaign 1777* (Havertown, PA, 2023).

3 For a full discussion on the timing and maneuvers and their effect on the northern campaign, see generally Luzader, *Saratoga.*

weeks of good weather, however, Howe effectively removed his army from the active war effort. A flummoxed Howe was on his way back to New Brunswick by June 19, with elements of the Continental Army skirmishing fitfully with his rear guard.[4]

On June 22, Howe retired to Amboy, New Jersey, to load his army and its baggage for the voyage to the Delaware River. The Americans continued pressing Howe's rear guard. Washington's willingness to come down off the high ground and pursue the retreating enemy, however, provided Howe with the opportunity he sought. The Continental Army was on more engageable terrain, and Howe saw his opportunity. On June 25, he turned and assaulted Maj. Gen. Lord Stirling's isolated and heavily outnumbered American division of some 2,500 men. Stirling waged a well-crafted fighting withdrawal and took up a strong defensive position in the area of Ash Swamp and Scotch Plains. The British pushed hard and forced Stirling's command back toward Westfield. With his men suffering under an intense sun, Howe called off the pursuit and ended the fighting. The defensive combat cost Stirling roughly 100 casualties, in addition to 70 men and three cannons captured. British losses totaled just five killed and 30 wounded. The Battle of Short Hills bought precious time for Washington to move the balance of his army into the hill country, once again denying Howe the opportunity of the larger battle he craved. Howe returned to Amboy on June 28, his attempt to defeat Washington in northern New Jersey at an end.

Washington fully expected Howe to use the British fleet to change the field of operations—but where would those ships carry his army? On June 30, Howe removed the last of his troops from New Jersey and returned to Staten Island, New York. He and his men were back where they had started nearly a year earlier before attacking New York City. The city and its environs, together with Newport, Rhode Island, remained under British control, but Howe's withdrawal left Washington in complete control of New Jersey.

July 1777

Early July found most of Washington's Continental Army back in the mountains around Morristown. The position provided Washington with the

4 Although Howe's move appears baffling, he likely never intended to assault Philadelphia by marching through New Jersey, and believed it was worth an effort to bring Washington to battle quickly.

option of shifting north to block the Hudson River, or south to protect Philadelphia. The next move remained with Howe. Determined to use his fleet to reach the capital, on July 8, the British general began the arduous process of loading his army onto transport ships. Howe believed he could ascend the Delaware River, gain Philadelphia, and still aid Burgoyne in upstate New York in a timely fashion. He also believed moving by sea would freeze the Americans in place until Washington realized where Howe headed. On the second point, he was correct.

By the time Howe finished loading on July 9, he had some 260 ships with 20,000 soldiers, support personnel, artillery, horses, and everything else needed to launch a major campaign. Rather than depart immediately, however, he once more delayed, leaving his men and animals bobbing in the harbor for several days in tight quarters aboard hot stuffy transports.

Washington knew Howe was loading ships for a campaign and decided to get a jump on him by moving to the New Jersey-New York border in anticipation of an ascent up the Hudson. The army moved north on July 12. Eight days later Howe ordered the large British armada to sail out of New York harbor, leaving behind Gen. Henry Clinton and the city's garrison of 7,400 troops. American observers along the New Jersey coast speculated the fleet turned south, but at this point Howe's target remained an open question. The lack of a Continental Navy hampered Washington and forced him to rely upon spotters scattered along the coastline to locate the ships and relay information. Until reliable intelligence arrived, Washington had no choice but to mark time in northern New Jersey.

Howe's voyage promised to be long and slow, for the prevailing summer winds along the Atlantic coast tend to blow north, impeding the fleet's southern direction. The journey was a miserable experience for man and beast alike. In addition to the stifling heat and humidity, brisk winds buffeted the ships. Frequent late afternoon thunderstorms added to the misery of the passengers. The weather proved so uncooperative that it took the fleet a week to travel only 150 miles to Cape May, New Jersey. Washington, meanwhile, concentrated near Ramapo on the New York-New Jersey border, a position from which he could march north to the Hudson Highlands or move rapidly to Philadelphia.

On July 26, spotters along the New Jersey shoreline sighted a large portion of the British fleet heading south near Little Egg Harbor, New Jersey. Washington began to hedge his bets and inched toward Morristown with four of the army's five divisions. The Continentals headed for three separate fords on the Delaware River to expedite the crossing into Pennsylvania, if warranted. When news of the fleet found its way to Washington, little doubt remained of Howe's destination. On July 28, Washington's leading elements reached the Delaware.

The final days of July arrived with the British fleet tacking into the Delaware Bay to assess the current conditions and intelligence about Washington's army. When the news reached Washington about 24 hours later, he ordered the army to cross into Pennsylvania to block a move against Philadelphia. Almost simultaneously, the Howe brothers made perhaps the most critical decision of 1777.

At 10:00 a.m. on July 30, Capt. Andrew Hamond reported to Adm. Richard Howe's flagship HMS *Eagle* to meet with the Howe brothers. One of the first questions posed involved whether the naval officer knew the location of Washington's army. The Rebels, replied the captain, crossed the Delaware heading for Wilmington. His intelligence source remains unknown but was untrue. Only two brigades had crossed the river; the rest of Washington's army remained strung out across northern New Jersey. Howe's most recent dispatch to Lord George Germain, Secretary of State for the American Department, however, stated that he would ascend the Delaware River only if Washington remained in northern New Jersey. If he entered Pennsylvania, Howe would ascend Chesapeake Bay. Hamond's inaccurate report made Howe's decision for him.[5]

Hamond also told the Howes that Americans constructed fortifications along the shores of the Delaware and placed various obstructions in the river to halt the fleet. These river defenses and a small naval militia were of trifling concern. Apparently, the most important city in North America remained essentially undefended. Although Hamond informed William Howe Washington's army was west of the Delaware River, little if any of the Continental Army had yet to arrive in Philadelphia. A clear and open path for the British to the American capital existed.

Despite easy access to Philadelphia, approximately 90 miles by ship, Howe decided to sail south to Chesapeake Bay, where he could put his troops "ashore without molestation, have time to recover the Horses after the fatigue of the Voyage before they entered Service, and where the Transports could remain in perfect security." The move, he also stressed, would threaten backcountry settlements. The fleet headed back to sea on July 31. Howe later claimed the move farther south benefitted John Burgoyne by drawing Washington away from the Hudson River Valley. In reality, the moment Howe gave the order to steer toward the Chesapeake, he eliminated any reasonable possibility of aiding Burgoyne.[6]

---

5 Harris, *Brandywine*, 83-84.

6 Denys Hay, "The Denouement of General Howe's Campaign of 1777," in *English Historical Review*, vol. 74 (1964), 504.

August 1777

By the beginning of August, the British fleet was moving south along the Delaware coast. The move left Washington with a conundrum. Was Howe making for the Hudson River or was his objective one of the major port cities farther south, like Charleston or Savannah?

On August 10, Washington shifted the army to the banks of Neshaminy Creek north of Philadelphia and closer to the Delaware River in case he needed to rush back to the Hudson Highlands. Little more could be done until definitive intelligence arrived, confirming the location of Howe's fleet. Washington may well have smiled had he known the British fleet reached the entrance to the Chesapeake Bay after suffering through terrible storms. Fresh food and water ran out on many transports and horses died by the score. When definitive news of Howe's location, if not his army's condition, arrived on August 22, Washington scrambled to move the scattered elements of his army into a position to confront Howe south of Philadelphia. Washington started inching toward northern Delaware to block Howe.

The British fleet anchored near the mouth of the Elk River in the upper reaches of the Chesapeake Bay. Howe would approach Philadelphia from the southwest. Several creeks and rivers, including the Red and White Clay, the Brandywine, and the Schuylkill, would slow Howe's approach to the city. Washington remained concerned Howe might march into the American interior and threaten the major supply depots at Lancaster or Reading. He had no real choice: he would have to advance toward Howe.

On August 24, Washington paraded his army through Philadelphia en route to Delaware to block Howe's approaches to the city. The next morning, Washington crossed into the state with two divisions and camped along Naamans Creek. At about the same time, Howe began offloading troops into northeastern Maryland. Other than meeting some local militia Howe easily brushed aside, his landing proved uneventful.

With Howe now ashore, making a connection with the Delaware River by land became imperative. A good supply of land transportation plagued the British throughout the war. The death of so many horses during the voyage compounded Howe's logistical concerns. British armies needed to operate near navigable rivers so the Royal Navy could easily resupply them. As one recent historian put it, "The insecurity of overland communications restricted an army's maximum operational range to about fifteen to twenty miles from navigable water." This operational conundrum affected Howe's decision-making throughout the campaign. A landing in northern Delaware at the end of July would have given him a connection with the Delaware River. Now that he was back on land, Howe had no choice but to operate near and along the Delaware, which eviscerated the reason he provided for delaying the campaign for another month by shifting his army farther south.[7]

Howe stripped the countryside in northeastern Maryland in search of needed supplies, including fresh horses and reinforcements. Food he could find; more troops were another matter. Contrary to his belief, Loyalists showed little interest in flocking to his standard. Howe later claimed the real reason he could not support Burgoyne's army was the failure to recruit Loyalist support. Excuses for abandoning Burgoyne grew larger with each telling.[8]

September 1777

By the beginning of September, Howe's men itched for action. They spent several weeks cooped up on ships and the last several days conducting a frustrating advance into northeastern Maryland. Thus far Howe had missed opportunities for a pitched confrontation, but the campaign season was winding down and the British had precious little to show for it.

Washington placed an outpost in northern Delaware at Cooch's Bridge on the Christiana River, which Howe needed to cross to reach Washington's main army. He attacked the position on September 3, pushing jagers and light infantry in a series of flanking movements against Americans under William Maxwell. The fighting lasted seven hours before Maxwell's men ran out of ammunition and fled across the bridge back toward Wilmington, leaving the British in command of the banks of the river. The fitful fighting carried Howe one step closer to Philadelphia and was the largest land engagement in the history of Delaware. Once he achieved this success, however, Howe settled down for another five days to strip the countryside of supplies. Feeding his army was imperative, and providing for it in a hostile land was a constant problem.[9]

---

7 Matthew H. Spring, *With Zeal and With Bayonets Only: The British Army on Campaign in North America, 1775-1783* (Norman, OK, 2008), 35.

8 Stockdale, ed., *Register*, vol. 10, 418.

9 William Maxwell was born in Ireland about 1733 and lived in New Jersey by 1747. He served as a militia officer during the French and Indian War and took command of the 2nd New Jersey Battalion when the Revolution erupted. He served as a member of the New Jersey Provincial Congress in 1775-1776 and in the Canadian Expedition in 1776. Appointed brigadier general in October 1776, Maxwell took part in Washington's successful late December campaign. He made a

Following Cooch's Bridge, Washington convinced himself Howe would take the main road into Wilmington and deployed his army behind the Red Clay Creek with a defense-in-depth. Howe utilized flanking attacks at Long Island, White Plains, Short Hills, and Cooch's Bridge and had never tried a frontal assault, so Washington's thinking remains a mystery. Given his history, Howe's next move was entirely predictable. On September 8 he gained the Pennsylvania border ahead of Washington, and by late morning the bulk of his army was camped on the hills around Hockessin, Delaware—well above Washington's right flank.[10]

The outgeneraled Washington scrambled to get his army in motion and into a blocking position to protect Philadelphia. In the middle of the night, the Virginian pulled the Continental Army from northern Delaware, marched north, and the next day began moving into positions on the east side of the Brandywine River near Chads's Ford in Pennsylvania.[11]

On the evening of September 9, Howe moved north, parallel to Washington's position, and camped at Kennett Square six miles west of Washington at Chads's Ford. Washington had spent the long summer months using militia and other troops to hinder British movements while seeking a favorable opportunity to make a stand. The terrain along the Brandywine River provided him with that opportunity. The battle that followed would be the longest and largest single-day engagement of the war. It is also a study of contradictions.

Washington hoped a stout defense along the rolling terrain hugging the Brandywine and its various crossings would block access to Philadelphia by preventing the British from gaining the east bank. Although he had his troops in position east of the Brandywine for a full day before the fighting began, Washington somehow failed to gather the intelligence he needed to execute his battle plan. He intended to use the river to block Howe's advance yet remained almost completely ignorant of the surrounding terrain and road network and failed to identify and guard all the possible crossings. Even more alarming, no one in a

---

reputation for himself during the skirmishes in northern New Jersey during the winter and spring of 1777 and Washington gave him the command of the light infantry that August, with whom he served at Cooch's Bridge and Brandywine. The light infantry brigade was soon disbanded, and Maxwell lost his independent command. Michael C. Harris, *Germantown: A Military History of the Battle for Philadelphia, October 4, 1777* (El Dorado Hills, CA, 2020), xv.

10 Harris, *Brandywine*, 140-145.

11 Chads's Ford is named for John Chads, the local property owner prior to his death before the war. The name morphed into Chadds Ford in the 19th century.

position of authority thought to speak to the locals serving in the ranks of the Continental Army.

While Washington prepared for battle with little terrain knowledge and even less help from the nearby residents, William Howe made his plans with the advantage of both. Pennsylvania loyalist Joseph Galloway and others provided Howe with everything he needed to know about terrain conditions and the road network. Washington's position east of the Brandywine limited Howe's options. A frontal assault against the American positions would be too costly and the men hard to replace. Instead, Howe determined to shove a diversion against the center of Washington's position to pin him in place and throw a heavy left hook in the form of a flanking march to turn his enemy out of his position.

Howe had used this tactic repeatedly and recently against Washington, but the Virginian had not yet taken the lesson to heart and was consistently unprepared for Howe's predictable maneuver. Wilhelm von Knyphausen's division moved ahead and staked Washington in place. A short time later, General Lord Cornwallis surprised the Americans by appearing beyond their vulnerable right flank. Washington discovered the move too late to prevent it. To his credit, he shifted the bulk of his army to oppose the flanking operation and conducted a dogged defensive action that cost Howe dearly. British success at the Brandywine can be evenly credited to his good generalship and Washington's failures.[12]

The tactical defeat cost the Continental Army about 1,300 casualties (300 killed, 600 wounded, and 400 missing/captured). Washington's poor use of scouts and the conflicting intelligence they produced haunted him throughout that long day. Given the trying circumstances, the Americans fought remarkably well. Howe, on the other hand, gathered accurate information about local terrain despite operating in hostile territory. He based his flanking maneuver on that intelligence, and it worked almost to perfection. His veteran British and Hessian troops performed well and did all Howe asked of them. Knyphausen's division played its diversionary role exceedingly well, deceiving Washington through most of the day as to Howe's true intentions. Cornwallis's division executed a grueling flank march, deployed, and broke the American lines in what eventually evolved into a frontal assault. British losses approached 600, with 93 killed and nearly 500 wounded.

12 For a full discussion of the battle and its results, see Harris, *Brandywine.*

Fortunately for the Americans, a lack of mounted troops hampered Howe and prevented him from pursuing his defeated enemy.[13]

The realities of campaigning made it difficult for Howe to interfere with Washington's efforts to regroup in the immediate aftermath of the battle. For four days, Howe kept most of his exhausted army on the battlefield rather than launch it in a vigorous pursuit. The soldiers endured a long tedious voyage, hard marching, and prolonged combat with sustained casualties. Howe needed to establish a bridgehead at Wilmington, Delaware, to evacuate the injured, the seriously ill, and the collected provisions to a safe garrison town. Insufficient wagons and the paucity of healthy horses hampered operational ability, and it took several days to accomplish these tasks.[14]

Washington needed to find fresh defensive ground to protect Philadelphia from Howe's victorious army. The only remaining natural barrier was the Schuylkill River. The Continentals left Chester and crossed into the outskirts of Philadelphia near Germantown. Moving the army north of the Schuylkill River put Washington behind the last natural barrier between the British and Philadelphia. The river was swift-flowing but shallow in many spots. As a defensive barrier, it was less than ideal. Defending the numerous fords across the Brandywine proved almost impossible, and the fords along the Schuylkill were even more spread out. Moving into the Germantown area left Washington with a vexing challenge. The Delaware and Schuylkill Rivers form a peninsula, at the tip of which sat Philadelphia. He felt duty-bound to defend the capital, but he could not leave the critical supply depots in the back country unprotected. Moving northwest to protect the depots would expose the city. Moving into position to protect Philadelphia exposed the supply centers upon which his army depended. The loss at Brandywine made protecting the American capital nearly impossible. The choice eventually became clear: protecting his storehouses took precedence over the most important city in North America. Washington hoped to recross the Schuylkill River and engage Howe before the British could approach Philadelphia or the backcountry supply centers.

Most of Howe's army, meanwhile, remained idle. An aggressive pursuit of Washington's defeated army would have maintained the momentum, forced additional fighting on his terms, and likely crushed or further dispersed the Americans. Howe could have crossed the upper fords on the Schuylkill River with ease, cutting Washington off from his crucial supply depots. Earlier in the

---

13 Harris, *Brandywine*, 368.

14 Spring, *With Zeal*, 269.

campaign, Howe told Lord Germain he took the long route up the Chesapeake Bay so he could threaten those American storehouses, but his continued lethargy gave Washington the time he required to block access to them. Like his propensity for flanking operations, Howe had a history of unenthusiastic follow-through after successful battles. Brandywine's aftermath was no different.

Washington's army left the Germantown area on September 14 and recrossed the Schuylkill. The move into the Great Valley stretched along three miles of the Lancaster Road and blocked access to the river. The Americans took a roundabout route to get there but were now just ten miles from where they had fought at Brandywine four days earlier. The Great Valley protected the approaches to the Schuylkill, but did not protect Philadelphia along the Delaware River, which was still vulnerable to the British navy making its way toward the waterway after backtracking from the Chesapeake Bay.[15]

While Washington contemplated how best to defend Philadelphia and weaken the British, information reached Howe prompting action. The American army was within reach, and Howe intended to move on it. On the night of September 15, he issued orders for the army to march into the Great Valley the next day. Rain had already moved into the area, turning the rutted dirt roads of Chester County into a dense paste through which thousands of soldiers tramped. What Howe seems not to have known is that on the morning of September 16, Washington's army moved from the Lancaster Road and ascended the South Valley Hill to block Howe from the Schuylkill River. The armies were once more on a collision course, and only five days after the conclusion of the largest battle of the American Revolution.

As the British columns came together at Goshen Meetinghouse, Washington began moving into position on the South Valley Hill. The Continentals maneuvered in two columns south from the Lancaster Road to deploy along the crest of South Valley Hill to block Howe's advance. Howe and Cornwallis moved north in two columns up South Valley Hill as well. The two armies were marching toward each other.

The British easily pushed the lead American elements off South Valley Hill. Washington quickly formed a line on the southern slope of North Valley Hill about three miles north of where the two separate actions known as the "Battle of the Clouds" occurred. As the name suggests, wind-whipped rain rendered ammunition useless. If the Americans were attacked, they would have no choice but to rely on

---

15 For a full discussion of the weeks following the Battle of Brandywine and the Battle of Germantown see Harris, *Germantown*.

bayonets—an unpalatable option that would give the British a distinct advantage. Howe's men also found the weather unbearable. As a result, other than some skirmishing and muddy maneuvering, the "Battle of the Clouds" ground to a muddy halt without a major clash of arms. To the dismay of Howe and his subordinates, the driving rain of a nor'easter prevented any exploitation of initial success.

Washington ordered his army to move to Yellow Springs, ten miles distant on the other side of North Valley Hill. Once there, the Americans dropped onto the soggy ground with little or no shelter from the cold driving rain. Most had thrown away their blankets during the retreat from Brandywine and lacked even meager cover. While the Americans were slogging through that miserable night, the British took up camp wherever they happened to be when the action stopped. If Howe delayed his pursuit, as he had after Brandywine, perhaps Washington would have enough time to move into a blocking position north of the Schuylkill.

The early hours of September 17 found Washington's waterlogged army essentially defenseless, its members exhausted by their recent travails and in a foul mood. No option remained open to Washington but to distance his army from the British and find a new source of ammunition and other badly needed supplies. He decided on Warwick Furnace in northwestern Chester County, where he could rest and refit. Anthony Wayne's Pennsylvania division remained behind to screen the rear of the army and keep a close watch on Howe.

After waiting out the rain, Howe moved on September 18 to a new position stretching for three miles along Swedesford Road facing Valley Forge. He intended to cross the Schuylkill, but, like every waterway in the region, it was above flood stage. Washington knew his opponent wanted to move north of the river and hoped to use the barrier to his advantage and make Howe pay for the effort. General Wayne received orders to march his division into the British rear. By this time the heavy rain had turned the Schuylkill into a rushing torrent, so Howe set his sights on Continental supply depots south of the river. Three miles down the Valley Creek from the British camp sat Valley Forge, an ironworks and American storehouse. The storehouses there were convenient locations for finished goods and flour ground at local mills. Washington's aide Alexander Hamilton, together with Henry "Lighthorse Harry" Lee and a handful of dragoons, made for Valley Forge to rescue the supplies stored there. The task proved impossible because Howe beat them to it. Without any serious opposition, the British easily captured 4,000 barrels of flour and other items, such as soap, candles, kettles, tools, axes, and more. The loss of the supplies was a severe blow, but the British now controlled a critical junction, explained Lee, "with roads leading to Reading, the French Creek iron region, Lancaster, and several Schuylkill River fords."[16]

The next day, September 19, General Wayne marched his 2,200-man column out of Yellow Springs back into the Great Valley onto Lancaster Road. After passing the Admiral Warren Tavern, the Pennsylvania general halted at the Paoli Tavern 10 miles east of Yellow Springs and just two miles behind the British camp at Tredyffrin. Howe's army found itself in a vulnerable position. Overflowing creeks and rivers blocked its front, various roads exposed its flanks, and heavy woods clogged its rear. Wayne's Pennsylvania division threatened any British retreat. Wayne moved his division back up the road toward Admiral Warren Tavern before turning left "and took Post on some high Ground above the Warren Tavern on the Lancaster Road" and made camp in an open field surrounded by woods with roads passing on both flanks. The British were fully aware that Wayne was in proximity, but did not yet know his precise whereabouts.

While the British were moving and Wayne was shifting to a new camp, Washington crossed north of the Schuylkill at Parker's Ford with his main army into a blocking position above its many crossings. With Wayne behind the British, Washington hoped to catch the enemy in a pincher movement and force Howe to fight on his own terms. Most of the army camped along the east side of Perkiomen Creek after a grueling 29- mile march. No one in either army had any knowledge yet that General Horatio Gates had defeated General Burgoyne at Freeman's Farm the same day in upstate New York. The consequences of Howe's decision to campaign for possession of Philadelphia instead of moving north to join forces with Burgoyne would soon be obvious to all.[17]

Washington's decision to increase the distance between his main body and Wayne left the latter without immediate support and with Howe's army between him and Washington. Wayne was not too concerned because he believed Washington would march back into the Great Valley once the army had been resupplied. Washington had sent a dispatch to Wayne informing him of his new

16 Lighthorse Harry Lee was the father of famed Civil War general Robert E. Lee. The young and opinionated Alexander Hamilton was born an illegitimate child in the Caribbean. He commanded a New York militia artillery battery throughout the 1776 campaign. His capabilities reached Washington's attention, and he added Hamilton to his staff as an aide-de-camp in March 1777. Hamilton's fluency in French helped Washington translate important documents. Henry Lee, *Memoirs of the War in the Southern Department of the United States* (Philadelphia, 1812), vol. 1, 91.

17 Freeman's Farm was part of the Saratoga Campaign (June 14 to October 17, 1777), which is widely recognized as a major turning point of the Revolutionary War. For more on this campaign and its leadership, see, generally, Luzader, *Saratoga.*

plans, but neither general knew that a British patrol had intercepted it, leaving both in the dark as to the true nature of the danger. Now with the advantage of interior lines, Howe had the opportunity to turn against Wayne and defeat him.

The Continentals moved from their camp along the Perkiomen Creek the next day to tramp between 10 to 15 miles to take up positions along the Schuylkill on a seventeen-mile front stretching from Parker's Ford to Swedes' Ford. Just as he had at Brandywine, Washington spread his army thin along a wide front to keep the British from crossing a natural barrier. Howe now faced American forces of varying strength on multiple sides. Despite his defeat at Brandywine and the near disaster at the Battle of the Clouds, Washington had once more managed to seize the initiative. Temporarily at a loss on how to proceed but hell bent to take Philadelphia, Howe pondered how to cross the Schuylkill.

Howe had decided before moving the main army to the Valley Forge area that he needed to deal with General Wayne's isolated command, and he tapped Maj. Gen. Charles Grey to lead the operation. Grey intended to achieve complete surprise and ordered his men to remove their flints to prevent a musket from accidently discharging. They would perform their dirty work with bayonets, in the dark. When videttes rode into Wayne's camp and spread word of the British advance, Wayne formed his division on the parade ground facing north. His plan was to move his division across the fields and get his men on the road to the White Horse Tavern before the British could strike. Fitful small arms fire echoed in the distance: the British were approaching Wayne's right flank. Nothing of substance could be seen in the darkness. The Pennsylvanian ordered his command to file left (west) and head toward the tavern.

Before his foot soldiers could move, however, Wayne needed to extricate his guns and wagons. One of the artillery pieces overturned, blocking the escape route. The timing was unfortunate. Having overwhelmed Wayne's pickets, British light infantry began sweeping into Wayne's camp. Panic began taking hold. The 2nd Light Infantry Battalion swarmed through the tents and campfire sites and surrounded the rear of the stalled column. Confusion spread through the Pennsylvania ranks. Farther up the stalled column men scattered to save themselves, climbing fences and scampering into the woods. The pursuing British foot soldiers caught many atop the fences and bayonetted them. The atrocities committed by Grey's troops marked the horrific affair in history as the "Paoli Massacre." Pockets of Pennsylvanians attempted to stem the crimson tide from behind the stout fences, but nothing they could do stopped the surge of British Regulars pouring through the camp.

Despite the close-quarter fighting and darkness, the British assault force lost only three men killed and nine wounded and rounded up between 70 and 80 prisoners, many of whom had multiple stab wounds. The horrific condition of the wounded and the mutilated bodies of the dead infuriated the survivors, who swore to gain revenge in their next fight. Howe planned to cross the Schuylkill, so Grey did not initiate a pursuit and returned to the British camp, leaving the American dead and many of the wounded in the fields where they fell.[18]

Despite being taken by surprise, Wayne managed to extract most of his division, including all four of his precious artillery pieces. His losses, though, were fairly heavy with about 300 killed, wounded, and captured, or about 15 percent of his strength. The darkness that shielded Grey's men and added to the terror of the suddenness of the bayonet attack in some ways aided the Continentals. Grey did not know the precise location of Wayne's camp, and maneuvering men at night under a light rain was a confusing endeavor that helps explain why Wayne managed to extract so many of his troops.

Washington now faced a Hobson's Choice: the storehouses at Reading needed to be protected, but doing so meant uncovering Philadelphia, which, politically speaking, could not be surrendered without a fight. Should he give up the supply depots of the Pennsylvania backcountry, or protect them and allow the colonial capital to fall without another battle? If he shifted troops to guard the city, Howe could move and seize the iron manufacturing region to the west. The American army was poorly supplied and could not survive long without food, ammunition, and other resources. A glance at a map made it obvious that Howe could move rapidly west, capture the Continental supply centers, and still return for Philadelphia and perhaps win both major prizes. Howe held the winning hand. Philadelphia was all but lost.

Convinced Reading was Howe's immediate objective, Washington pulled away from the river fords on the evening of September 21 and shifted his army westward to better protect the vulnerable supply center. The risky move exposed the lower fords of the Schuylkill River to the British. With Washington moving west away from the fords, the British army crossed to the north side of the Schuylkill unopposed at Fatland and Richardson's fords under a bright moonlight that made for a challenging, but not difficult, passage. The British were now firmly positioned

---

18 Friedrich von Muenchhausen, *At General Howe's Side: 1776-1778: The Diary of General William Howe's aide de camp, Captain Friedrich von Muenchhausen*, trans. Ernst Kipping, ed. by Samuel Steele Smith (Monmouth Beach, NJ, 1974), 34.

between Washington's army and Philadelphia. Howe held every strategic card except one: he desperately needed to be resupplied by the British fleet. The army officer, however, did not have a full understanding of the difficulties facing his naval officer brother.

After the victory at Brandywine, Admiral Richard Howe needed to move the frigates and supply ships to the mouth of the Delaware. It took several weeks before the fleet could return to the Delaware from the Chesapeake. At the outset of the campaign, Admiral Howe had waited at the Elk River for word of his brother's progress. News of his victory at Brandywine did not arrive until September 13. The admiral acted immediately by detaching the *Isis*, a 50-gun ship-of-the-line, for the Delaware River with a dozen supply ships jammed with food and ammunition for his brother's army and ordered the rest of his fleet to follow.[19]

On September 25, Howe marched his army 11 miles into Germantown, just five miles from Philadelphia. While Washington contemplated his next move, Howe maneuvered to march into Philadelphia unopposed the next day. Charles Cornwallis received the honor of leading a column of troops into the city to occupy and garrison the colonial capital. He selected about 3,000 troops for the honor and set out from Germantown. Thus began what would turn into a nine-month occupation, one month and one day after Howe landed his army on the Elk River. The campaign that had begun that June consumed nearly three months, captured Philadelphia, and abandoned Burgoyne to his fate.

So long as the British could gain and maintain control of the Delaware River, Philadelphia would remain in the hands of the Crown. If they could not navigate the Delaware at will, they would lack sufficient supplies to remain in place and would almost certainly have to evacuate the capital. Howe "can neither support his Army in Philada if he is cut off from comm[u]nication with his ships," concluded Washington, "neither can he make good a Retreat should any accident befall him."[20]

On September 26, Washington moved to Pennypacker's Mills, ten miles closer to Philadelphia but still more than 20 miles outside the capital. The exhausted Continentals established their new camps having marched 140 miles in just the past 11 days. Only now did news arrive of Burgoyne's defeat at Saratoga in upstate New York. Washington used the news to raise the morale of his army by ordering

---

19 The *Isis* was commanded by Capt. William Cornwallis, the younger brother of Charles Cornwallis.

20 Chase & Lengel, eds., *The Papers of George Washington,* vol. 11, 347.

artillery salutes and extra rum rations. The inspiring victory made the naturally aggressive Washington more eager than ever to match the exploits of Horatio Gates's northern army and strike his own decisive blow. But when and where?

September 1777 ended with Howe in Philadelphia moving to open the Delaware River, the British fleet poised to sail up it and supply him, and Washington about 20 miles northwest of the city seeking an opportunity to strike. It had been a difficult month for the Americans. Despite fighting well at Brandywine, poor intelligence and tactical mistakes resulted in a defeat and the loss of hundreds of men. The aborted Battle of Clouds five days later risked the army and could well have led to its destruction if rain had not interceded to save it. Wayne's Pennsylvania division was roughly handled at Paoli, Philadelphia fell, and Congress scampered off to York, Pennsylvania. Problems boiled over within the officer corps. John Sullivan was investigated by Congress for misconduct at Brandywine, Wayne sought a court of inquiry for actions at Paoli, and the army's senior brigadier general, William Maxwell, was removed from his independent command.[21]

Washington knew the Continental Army could not sit outside Philadelphia and wait for winter or remain idle and receive an attack on Howe's terms. The Virginian understood seizing the initiative and determined to take it.

October 1777

The Continental Army was on the move again on October 2. This time, the men tramped four miles beyond the crossroads in Worcester Township onto Methacton Hill. The high ground provided an excellent viewing platform toward Philadelphia and a strong defensive position. The Rebels were now fewer than 20 miles from the city limits and about half that to Germantown. Rumors of the American advance and offensive plans trickled into British headquarters. Howe was now isolated from his Tory spies in the countryside and could not verify such reports. Washington's dragoons and militia patrols cut off access to the city by anyone outside the British lines.

The American commander estimated that Howe's army had thus far lost between 1,000-2,000 men during the entire campaign. With nearly 6,000 scattered

---

21 York was chosen by Congress since it was close to the edge of Pennsylvania civilization. The town was a four day march from Philadelphia, thus providing plenty of time to flee should the British army move inland.

across the Delaware River Valley, remaining British forces in Germantown might number as many as 8,000. On paper, Washington counted nearly 17,000 bayonets. But the army bled stragglers and knots of deserters throughout the campaign, and hundreds more were left behind to guard encampments and wagons. Washington was moving at least 15,000 men into a fight.

It took less than two days for Washington to plan his daring assault on the enemy garrison holding Germantown. He would rely on surprise, which required a great deal of discipline, coordination, and good luck. Washington intended to divide his army into four columns that would meet on the northern and western edges of Germantown simultaneously at 5:00 a.m. The columns would move silently through the darkness for 14 to as many as 20 miles over four separate poorly marked roads. Washington had learned through hard experience that a stand-up fight against the British was a losing proposition. His preferred tactic was to strike isolated enemy detachments, such as the depleted force at Germantown. The plan was as bold as it was complicated and risky—especially for an army like Washington's.

Warning of the approaching American assault reached the British high command with at least two hours to prepare to receive it. Not all the men at the front received the warning, including the outposts that would be hit first; others failed to believe it. Once the engagement began, the British light infantry experienced a complete breakdown of discipline and superior American numbers overwhelmed them. Thomas Musgrave's decision to save his regiment by moving into Cliveden rather than surrender on the spot or rout with the rest ultimately proved fatal to Washington's attack. Once the rallying began, Generals James Grant, Charles Grey, and James Agnew moved their brigades forward and pushed the Americans out of Germantown.[22]

Washington had learned from Trenton that his army could achieve surprise over the enemy by daring to do the unexpected. By the aftermath of Brandywine, he firmly believed his troops could undertake a more complicated task. Perhaps the most surprising achievement that day was that all four columns arrived where

---

22 Widely disliked by the Americans for advocating draconian measures against the colonists, British Gen. James Grant was a veteran of the Seven Years' War in North America and former governor of Florida. After serving in the colonies before the Revolution he rose to command the 55th Regiment of Foot. In 1776, he served General Howe as a division commander during the New York campaign and played a key role in the Long Island fighting. Grant played a minor role at Brandywine (though his writings imply otherwise) but commanded one-half of the army at Germantown.

expected. Despite poor communication and the lackluster performance of Casimir Pulaski's horsemen, who failed to maintain contact between the four columns, they also arrived almost simultaneously with the balance of the attacking columns.

The responsibility for the final tactical defeat rested with Washington. Once the American strike forces arrived and the British line was collapsing, the pivot point of the battle centered on Cliveden, where Musgrave's men were holed up inside. Rather than make his own decision, Washington held an impromptu council of war during which Henry Knox, his artillery commander, insisted on neutralizing the troops inside the house before they could continue driving south into Germantown. The tactically flawed decision tied up hundreds of men and several commands that would otherwise have continued the attack and kept the British off balance. Washington's decision turned the initiative over to the enemy. Men like Timothy Pickering argued against the move, but Washington ordered the successful assault stopped while Lord Stirling's reserve division deployed to eliminate Musgrave's bastion. Stirling's fresh units may well have proven decisive in overwhelming the British camps deeper in Germantown. Instead, the men under Wayne and Sullivan well to the front heard firing in their rear, believed they were flanked, and reversed course—a chaotic withdrawal during which Americans fired into one another. The time wasted around Cliveden and withdrawal of the two divisions in the middle of the American assault gave the British the time they needed to regroup and turn the tide of the battle.[23]

The well-trained veteran British troops pushed back the confused and inexperienced Continentals and regained the lost ground, freeing Musgrave's men from Cliveden and driving the Americans off the field. The rank-and-file Americans had done their duty and performed heroically. Choices made at the highest levels failed them. Just as poor intelligence had doomed the Americans at Brandywine, poor tactical decisions did the same at Germantown.

With the Battle of Germantown behind him and Washington in retreat, William Howe turned his attention to the Delaware River. It was time to clear the obstacles blocking the Royal Navy from docking at, and supplying, Philadelphia.

---

23 Timothy Pickering was the senior staff officer traveling with Washington's Continental Army. He rose to the rank of colonel in 1774. Pickering's "Plan of Discipline" was widely used in the army until it adopted Baron von Steuben's manual in 1778. Pickering took part in the Lexington alert in 1775 and in the New York and New Jersey campaigns through early 1777. His service brought the 32-year-old to the attention of Washington, who appointed Pickering to his top staff position, adjutant general, on June 18, 1777.

Chapter 2

The Delaware River Defenses

June-October 1777

"Sorry to hear that you found Matters so much out of order at Fort Mifflin. Much must depend upon your activity and that of other Officers in Garrison."[1]

— Gen. George Washington—October 1, 1777

Following the fight at Germantown, British occupation of Philadelphia depended on controlling and navigating the Delaware River to keep open their line of supplies. The campaigning that followed cannot be understood without a full appreciation of the state of American defenses along the river.

The Delaware runs generally north-south dividing New Jersey to the east from Pennsylvania and Delaware to the west. The Schuylkill River flows east through Pennsylvania and empties into the Delaware just south of colonial Philadelphia.

Pre-Revolution River Defenses

The Dutch West India Company first fortified the Delaware River as early as 1626. Constructed opposite the mouth of the Schuylkill River on the New Jersey

---

1 Chase and Lengel, eds., *Papers*, vol. 11, 364.

shore, Fort Nassau consisted of a fortified storehouse surrounded by a strong wooden palisade with bastions for small iron cannon. The fort's guns were not big enough to reach the main river channel or the mouth of the Schuylkill River. The fort was never provided with a permanent garrison, and the Dutch abandoned it in 1651.[2]

Peter Minuit claimed the Delaware River for Sweden in 1638, which soon built several earthworks. Minuit constructed Fort Christina at the mouth of the Christiana River, which flows easterly through the state of Delaware before emptying into the Delaware River near modern Wilmington. Later, Johan Printz built Fort Nya Korsholm on Province Island at the mouth of the Schuylkill River and Fort Elfsborgh on the New Jersey side of that waterway. The tiny kingdom of Sweden, however, refused to commit the resources necessary to maintain these forts.[3]

Peter Stuyvesant constructed a palisaded Fort Beversreede on the Schuylkill near the present Platt Bridge in Philadelphia. He soon abandoned it and Fort Nassau and constructed Fort Casimir near modern New Castle, Delaware. The fort contained four bastions, batteries of cannon mounted on ship carriages, and two lines of wooden palisades. When Stuyvesant departed with the fleet for New York, the Swedish captured the Dutch garrison, but Stuyvesant returned in 1655 to recapture the post for the Dutch.[4]

The British made a push to seize the region in 1664 when an expedition captured Fort Casimir. Soon William Penn arrived to develop the land on both sides of the river for Quaker settlement and construction on what would become Philadelphia began in 1681. American colonists and British officials long recognized Philadelphia's importance as a riverine port, but the pacifist attitudes in the Quaker governing body of Pennsylvania often disrupted efforts to construct defensive fortifications. An unofficial militia organization started by Benjamin Franklin called The Philadelphia Associators constructed the earliest river defenses. During the War of Austrian Succession in the 1740s, Spanish and French soldiers landed near New Castle, Delaware, and pillaged the surrounding countryside. The Associators constructed a 27-gun battery along the waterfront

---

2 Dorwart, *Fort Mifflin*, 7. The fort was located at the southernmost riverfront of modern Gloucester City, New Jersey.

3 Dorwart, *Fort Mifflin*, 8. Fort Elfsborgh was located near modern-day Elsinboro, New Jersey.

4 Ibid.

just south of Old Swede's Church in Philadelphia, but within twenty years the battery fell into disrepair.[5]

By 1770, Pennsylvania Governor John Penn appreciated the vulnerability of Philadelphia and requested Gen. Thomas Gage, commander of British forces in North America, to help improve the city's defenses. Gage sent Capt. John Montresor of the Royal Engineers to Philadelphia to do just that. Montresor arrived in April 1771 and reviewed "a sketch of that part of the River where Mud Island is situated, being as their [governor's] the proposed spot for fortifying." The engineer proposed a star-shaped fort capable of mounting 38 guns. Mud Island was aptly named because it flooded frequently. Any construction would require deep piles for a firm foundation, but the 40,000-pound price tag proved unacceptable to the Pennsylvanians.

The colonial government approved less than half that much to purchase the island from Joseph Galloway and construct a fortification. Montresor traced the lines for the proposed work on the island and returned to New York City in June 1772, turning over construction to Lt. Elias Myer of the 60th Royal American Regiment. After several delays and disagreements, the fortification on Mud Island was partially constructed with a single stone wall facing south downriver with no piles supporting the foundation. Without a foreign threat, the Provincial Assembly quietly refused to continue supporting the endeavor.[6]

The American Revolution Begins

Soon after war erupted on the greens of Lexington and Concord in 1775, the Pennsylvania Committee of Safety sent a delegation to inspect the state of the Delaware River defenses. Lewis Nicola authored the delegation's report. "I am sorry to say any effectual defense thereof [the river], so as to protect this city from an insult by water," concluded Nicola, "appears to me very difficult, tho' not impossible." The high cost "of doing it to good purpose," however, "will be thought too heavy." Because of the costs involved, the Committee of Safety decided to construct shallow-draft vessels to support the primitive land batteries rather than improve or construct substantial land defenses. Counterparts in New

---

5 Dorwart, *Fort Mifflin*, 9-10; McIntyre, *A Most Gallant Resistance*, 18.

6 John Montresor, "The Montresor Journals," ed. G. D. Delaplaine, in *Collections of the New York Historical Society for the Year 1881* (1882), 414-417; McIntyre, *A Most Gallant Resistance*, 20; Dorwart, *Fort Mifflin*, 16.

Jersey soon committed to assisting Pennsylvania in preparing the river defenses. In August 1775, the Committee tasked Robert Smith (a Philadelphia architect and carpenter) with placing river obstructions known as *cheveaux-de-frise* in the Delaware to assist the shallow-draft vessels. By that fall, the Committee determined additional earthworks were required in both New Jersey and Pennsylvania to protect the sunken *cheveaux-de-frise* from British attempts at removal.[7]

The defenses at Mud Island remained rudimentary at best, but by December 1775, an artillery garrison of 90 men under Capt. Thomas Proctor was present. Had the British attacked Philadelphia in early 1776, Proctor could not have offered much resistance. His artillery pieces lacked carriages and remained unmounted. His command lived in the Pest House on Province Island with the Fort Mifflin barracks incomplete. By the end of the year, Col. John Bull's Pennsylvania militia battalion reinforced Proctor's garrison. Foreshadowing the problems to come, an inspection recommended to the Committee of Safety "their hearty consent to the Board's erecting any works on the Province Island that they may think proper and necessary for the defense" of Pennsylvania. Sensing a need for professionals to help with the river defenses, Benjamin Franklin wrote to Charles Dumas on December 12: "We are [in] great Want of good Engineers . . . acquainted with . . . fortifying of Sea-Ports." Luckily for Philadelphia, much of the first two years of the war were confined to the northern colonies and Canada. Time, at least for now, was on their side, but would they use it effectively?[8]

During January 1776, the Committee of Safety sent a delegation to inspect New Jersey for fortification sites. The report was less than favorable. "In our opinion, that it is not adviseable, because any part of Billingsport or Red Bank is at too great a distance from the Chevaux de Frize, for either Friends or enemys to annoy with certainty any Boats, &c., that may be stationed at them. And if a Fort were built at either of those places," the report continued, "the Enemy could land above or below it, without any difficulty . . . and oblige our people to spike their Cannon and quit the Fort, or submit to be made prisoners, & the very means of our

7 Samuel Hazard, ed., *Pennsylvania Archives: Selected and Arranged from Original Documents in the Office of the Secretary of the Commonwealth*, Series 1, 12 vols. (Philadelphia, 1853), vol. 4, 635; McIntyre, *A Most Gallant Resistance*, 22-29. *Cheveaux-de-frise* were spiked obstacles, usually hardened wood, to stop cavalry on land and ships on the water.

8 McIntyre, *A Most Gallant Resistance*, 38-42. *Minutes of the Provincial Council of Pennsylvania, From the Organization to the Termination of the Proprietary Government*, 10 vols. (Harrisburg, PA, 1852), vol. 10, 371. William Bell Clark, ed., *Naval Documents of the American Revolution*, 13 vols. (Washington, D.C., 1968), vol. 3, 74.

defence be made to operate against us, or at least, be dismantled." The delegation suggested a mobile defense force that could quickly erect a battery along the shoreline as needed instead.[9]

An early warning to the vulnerability of the Delaware River arrived on March 25, 1776, when the HMS *Roebuck* entered Delaware Bay searching for prizes. While no engagement occurred, the weakness of the area was clear. Work on the fortifications at Billingsport and Red Bank had not yet started. Only some *cheveaux-de-frise* sat in the river around Mud Island and Billingsport, a weak and ineffective conglomeration of vessels known as the Pennsylvania Navy bobbed about, and the fortification with a weak garrison, incomplete yet defiant, stood on Mud Island. The *Roebuck* returned to the Delaware Bay a month later accompanied by the *Liverpool*. The warships remained several days gathering supplies along the Delaware shoreline, the defenders incapable of interfering with powerful Royal Navy ships. On May 8, a mixture of Continental and Pennsylvania naval vessels moved downriver to engage the British for two hours of fitful fighting. The next day, the resupplied American flotilla returned and boldly reengaged—this time hitting the *Roebuck* some 40 times in four hours of fighting.[10]

Two months later, one day after declaring independence, two members of Congress purchased 96 acres in Billingsport, New Jersey, to construct an earthwork to protect the *cheveaux-de-frise* located near there.[11]

The Philadelphia Campaign

Early in the campaign, the Delaware River defenses played only a minor role in the decision-making of both armies. In July 1777, the Continental Congress appointed Philippe Charles Trouson du Coudray and Gen. Thomas Mifflin to examine the state of the obstructions and forts. There was much to do. Du Coudray concluded the fortification at Billingsport required several changes and a garrison of 2,000 troops. In addition, a battery needed to be added on the Pennsylvania shore opposite Billingsport to provide a crossfire on the river. Fort

---

9 *Minutes of the Provincial Council of Pennsylvania*, vol. 10, 474-475.

10 McIntyre, *A Most Gallant Resistance*, 59-70.

11 Ibid., 55. Billingsport is named for Edward Bylling, one of the proprietors of West Jersey. The government paid 650 pounds for the 96-acre farm of Margaret Paul and Benjamin Weatherby. Douglas B. Mooney & Ingrid Wuebber, "Archaeological Investigations of Revolutionary War Fort Billingsport: Paulsboro, Gloucester County, New Jersey" (Burlington, NJ, May 2009), 7.

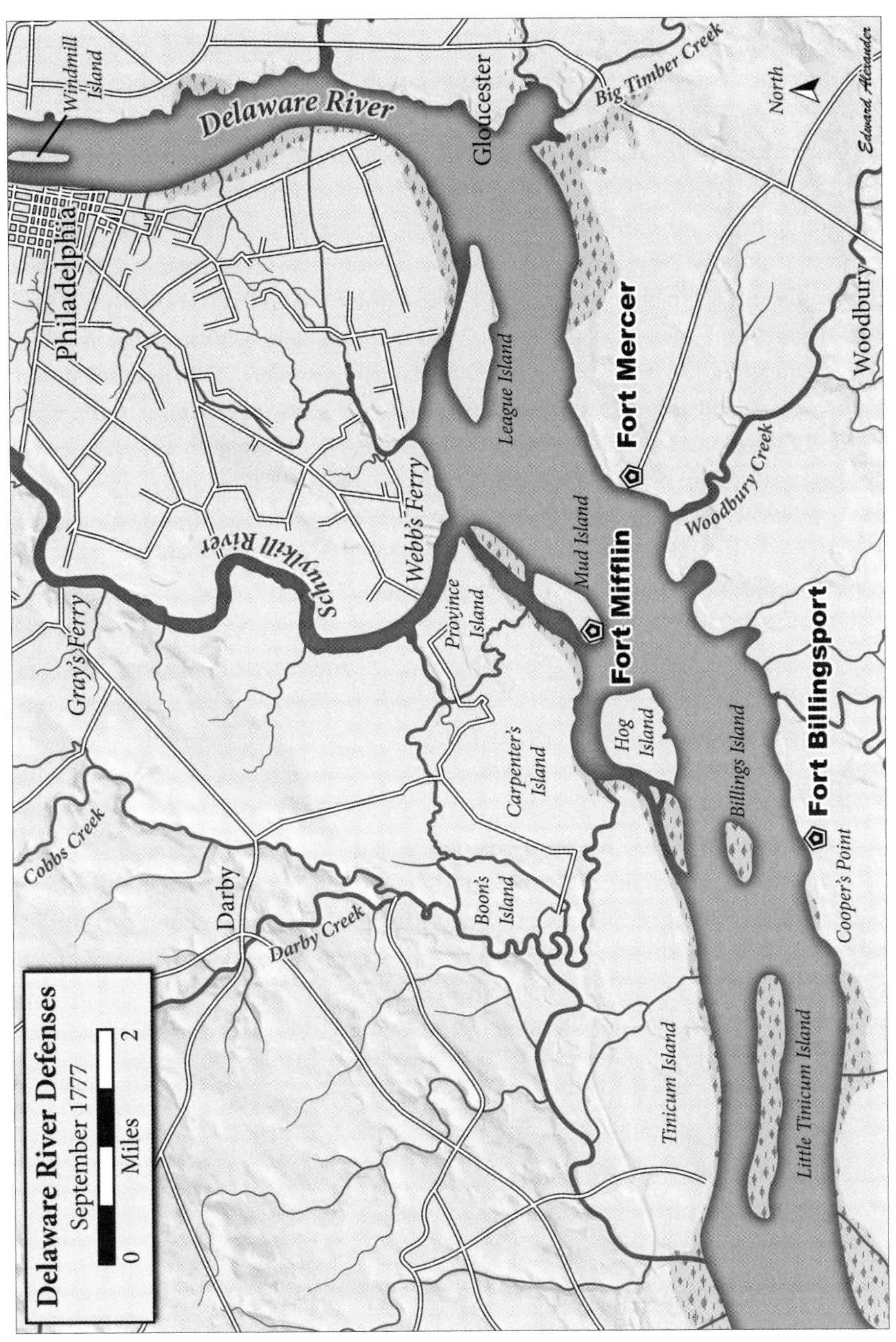

Delaware River Defenses
September 1777
Miles
0
2
Windmill Island
Delaware River
Gloucester
Big Timber Creek
North
Edward Alexander
Philadelphia
League Island
Fort Mercer
Woodbury
Schuylkill River
Webb's Ferry
Mud Island
Fort Mifflin
Woodbury Creek
Gray's Ferry
Province Island
Hog Island
Billings Island
Fort Billingsport
Cobbs Creek
Carpenter's Island
Cooper's Point
Darby
Boon's Island
Darby Creek
Tinicum Island
Little Tinicum Island

Mifflin's guns, he added, were incapable of preventing passage on the river. Du Coudray emphasized focusing on the *cheveaux-de-frise* to bar enemy access.[12]

At the end of July 1777, when William Howe entered the Delaware Bay with his armada, the British commander made the fateful decision to return to sea without attempting to make a landing somewhere along the river. There was little at that time to oppose his direct access to Philadelphia. The fortification at Billingsport on the New Jersey side remained incomplete and unmanned, and Fort Mercer had yet to be built. On the Pennsylvania side of the water, Fort Mifflin held a weak garrison of Pennsylvania militia, and incomplete redoubts existed on Bush Island and along Darby Creek on the Pennsylvania shoreline. The only real threats to the British were American naval elements and the stake obstructions in the river. With Washington's army still in northern New Jersey, there was no serious obstacle to Howe landing in northern Delaware or near Chester, Pennsylvania. Instead, he chose to return to sea and the Chesapeake Bay. It was not until six weeks later, after the Battle of Brandywine, that anyone seems to have given any serious consideration to strengthening the river defenses.[13]

Two days after the battle at Brandywine, Washington expressed his general views to Thomas Wharton, Jr., president of the Pennsylvania Assembly. "As I am well apprized of the importance of Philadelphia you may rest assured that I shall take every measure in my power to defend it," he explained, "and I hope you will agree with me that the only effectual Method will be to oppose General Howe with our whole united Force." Local forces, he added, must be pressed into action. Washington also offered his thoughts on the state of the river defenses. "In my opinion, the River would be sufficiently secured against any sudden attacks by Water only, if the City Artillery Companies [militia] were thrown into Fort Mifflin, and all the Vessels of War of different kinds drawn up behind the Chevaux de Frize," he observed. "I have given orders to Colo. [Joseph] Penrose [of the Pennsylvania Militia] to overflow the Grounds upon Province Island, which will render it impossible for the Enemy to approach the Fort in the Rear and raise Batteries against it."[14]

While Washington fretted over how best to keep Howe out of the capital, Thomas Wharton worried about the precarious state of the river defenses.

---

12 McIntyre, *A Most Gallant Resistance*, 82.

13 The Darby Creek redoubt stood on Tinicum Island and contained a four-gun battery. The redoubt on Bush Island consisted of two 18-pounders. McIntyre, *A Most Gallant Resistance*, 100-101.

14 Chase and Lengel, eds., *Papers*, vol. 11, 222.

Washington had stripped the river of nearly every available Continental soldier and militiaman to reinforce the main army. By September 5, only 80 men remained at Billingsport, 45 at Fort Mifflin, and none at Fort Mercer, the Bush Island redoubt, or the Darby Creek redoubt. The three rows of *chevaux-de-frise* jamming the river between Fort Mifflin and Fort Mercer were next to useless without riflemen and artillery to make them truly effective. Washington wanted to improve the various redoubts and forts along the Delaware, but believed "if we should be able to oppose Genl Howe with success in the Field, the Works will be unnecessary."[15]

Once Philadelphia fell on September 26, Washington decided to focus on the river to cause as many problems as possible for the British. If he could bar water access to the Royal Navy, he might be able to starve Howe's army into submission much as he had done at Boston two years previously. To solidify the waterborne command on the Delaware, Washington placed Commodore John Hazelwood of the Pennsylvania State Navy in charge of the combined State and Continental fleets. The Continental Board of Admiralty told Capt. Charles Alexander, the Continental naval officer Hazelwood superseded, "the Fort and the passage of the River if bravely and properly defended, the possession of Philada will probably turn out to be the ruin of the British Army." Washington hoped Hazelwood would unify and energize the fragmented elements defending the river, but Continental officers distrusted and looked down upon State officers.[16]

Washington wanted Hazelwood to remove 200 to 300 men from his ships to garrison Fort Mifflin on Mud Island just south of Philadelphia. There were no Continentals or militia garrisoning the stronghold, so sending seamen who could operate the guns made sense. Washington, however, was unaware that many of Hazelwood's small ships sat bobbing at anchor because they did not have enough men to operate them. Stripping bodies off stationary ships to garrison a fort was out of the question. Washington next requested all boats be gathered under colonial control to better respond to any attempts against the fort. Fort Mifflin was on an island, so the approaching British army would be unable to occupy the fort without boat access. "If we can stop the Enemy's fleet from coming up & prevent them from getting Possession of the Mud fort, & they take Possession of the City & our Army moves down upon the back [of the city]," Washington informed the

---

15 Jackson, *Pennsylvania Navy, 1775-1781*, 118-119, 121; Chase and Lengel, eds., *Papers*, vol. 11, 213.

16 Smith, *Fight for Delaware*, 6; Charles Oscar Paullin, ed., *Out-Letters of the Continental Marine Committee and Board of Admiralty: August, 1776-September, 1780*, 2 vols. (New York, 1914), vol. 1, 159; Jackson, *Navy*, 121-122.

commodore, "it will be the most effectual method of ruining General Howe's Army. . . . If you think it necessary for the Security of the Fort to lay the Island under water," he added, "let it be done immediately."[17]

Washington placed Col. Henry D'Arendt in command of Fort Mifflin and ordered Lt. Col. Samuel Smith of the 4th Maryland Regiment to garrison the fort with a detachment of Continentals. D'Arendt, a man of exceptional engineering ability and a logical choice for the assignment, was ill and would not arrive at the fort for some time. "If it [reinforcement] succeeds and they with the Assistance of the Ships and Gallies should keep the obstructions in the River," wrote Washington to Continental Congress President John Hancock, "General Howe's Situation in Philada will not be the most agreeable, for if his supplies can be stopped by Water it may be easily done by land. To do both shall be my utmost endeavor, and I am not yet without hope that the acquisition of Philada may, instead of his good fortune, prove his Ruin." Keeping the fort in American hands, he added, was "of very great Importance." Knowing that squabbles between the branches were common and detrimental to the cause of liberty, Washington appealed to the army and navy commanders to work together to maintain control of the Delaware. "Let us Join our Force & Operations both by land & Water in such a manner as will most effectually work the Ruin of the Common Enemy, without confining ourselves to any particular Department," he urged.[18]

With Philadelphia in hand, Howe needed to keep the Continental Army at bay while his own command, with the assistance of the British fleet, endeavored to open the river to provide provisions and supplies to his army. It would not be an easy task. The same day the British occupied Philadelphia (September 26), Lt. Col. Samuel Smith's detachment of Continentals from Washington's main army arrived at Fort Mifflin. Smith's command of 200 officers and men joined roughly 60 invalids already stationed there. Just reaching the post required a roundabout route since the British army blocked the main roads. What he discovered upon his arrival shocked him.

"[E]very-thing in the utmost Confusion, not as many Cartouches [gun cartridges] as will last one day," wrote Smith to Washington, "& the very necessary

17 The Pennsylvania Navy consisted of a conglomeration of vessels of varying sizes raised by the Pennsylvania Assembly to defend the Delaware River. They answered to the Assembly, not the Continental Congress. Jackson, *Fort Mifflin*, 24; Chase and Lengel, eds., *Papers*, vol. 11, 303. Dikes along the shore of Mud Island "kept" the river water out of Fort Mifflin. If the dikes were cut, water could flood the island and make occupying the fort pointless.

18 McGuire, *Campaign*, vol. 2, 137; Chase and Lengel, eds., *Papers*, vol. 11, 302-303.

Cartouches for the Block houses not sufficient for an hour: 60 untrained Militia, are all the artillery men in the Fort, the provisions almost out." Smith's reference to "60 untrained Militia" referred to men under Col. Lewis Nicola known as the Corps of Invalids. This official Continental Army unit was established the previous summer to garrison posts with troops unfit for field duty, thus freeing up combat units. Smith was also shocked to find not a single engineer, artillery officer, or artillery crew in the fort. He arrived with three officers—Majors Robert Ballard of Virginia, Simeon Thayer of Rhode Island, and Capt. Samuel Treat of New York—but only the latter was an artilleryman.[19]

The Pennsylvania Navy under Commodore Hazelwood assembled several watercraft near Fort Mifflin to prevent the approach of the Royal Navy. This flotilla contained the Continental frigate *Delaware*, the 32-gun frigate *Montgomery*, the 8-gun sloop *Fly*, a floating battery, several gondolas, and fire ships. "If the garrison at the fort will hold out a few days perhaps Mr. Howe may repent his going into Ph[iladelphi]a," offered Congressman Charles Carroll to his father. "General Washington is assembling & collecting troops from all sides. His army is much broken down with their late marches, but a few days rest I hope will revive their strength & spirits."[20]

The Loss of the *Delaware*

The sound of cannon fire rolling across the waters of the Delaware greeted the citizens of Philadelphia on the morning of September 27. Unaware General Cornwallis had entered the colonial capital, Commodore Hazelwood issued orders to Capt. Charles Alexander of the Continental frigate *Delaware* to "Do Every Thing in your Power, with the Force with you, to annoy the Enemy should they attempt to Come in to our City, & should you see them preparing any works for Cannon or

19 McGuire, *Campaign*, vol. 2, 137 & 184. Smith's troops and everyone who arrived thereafter had to march to Bristol, and from there cross the river to Burlington, New Jersey, move south through Haddonfield to either Gloucester or Red Bank and be ferried over to Fort Mifflin. Smith's men crossed into New Jersey at Dunk's Ferry, just south of modern Neshaminy State Park. Chase and Lengel, eds., *Papers*, vol. 11, 334; Robert K. Wright, Jr., *The Continental Army* (Washington, D.C., 1983), 136. Simeon Thayer, born in Massachusetts on April 28, 1738, began his military career outside Boston in 1775, as a militia lieutenant. After serving in the unsuccessful attempt to capture Quebec, Thayer found himself a British prisoner. Once exchanged, he became major of the 2nd Rhode Island Regiment where fate would place him at Fort Mifflin in the closing days of the siege.

20 Jackson, *Navy*, 123; Paul H. Smith, et al., eds., *Letters of Delegates to Congress* (Washington, 1981), vol. 8, 17.

Modern view of Dunk's Ferry looking from New Jersey. *Author*

Hauling Cannon near the river." He added, "you are in that case to send a Flag on shore & warn them if they do not desist in making any preperations of Fortifying any where, that you will in that case fire on the City." Hazelwood left "the Conduct & management of the whole" to Alexander's "prudent & effectual management."[21]

The combined Continental and State fleet that morning consisted of the 24-gun *Delaware* and her 150-man crew in the lead, together with the 24-gun State Guard ship *Montgomery*, the Continental 8-gun sloop *Fly*, and five single-gun row galleys. When the *Delaware* rounded Gloucester Point, British drummers alerted the garrison and Royal artillerymen and grenadiers of the 1st British Battalion formed to prepare for whatever was coming their way.[22]

Captain-Lieutenant Francis Downman was in command of the British artillery at the southern edge of the city—a six-gun battery consisting of four 12-pounders and two Royal howitzers. The earthwork underway to hold his half-dozen guns remained unfinished, and only two of the 12-pounders were in place that morning.

---

21 Samuel Hazard, ed., *Pennsylvania Archives: Selected and Arranged from Original Documents in the Office of the Secretary of the Commonwealth*, Series 1, 12 vols. (Philadelphia, 1853), vol. 5, 637. The September 27 order is headlined "Off Fort Mifflin." The course of the river and surrounding terrain blocked Hazelwood's view of the occupation, which explains why he sent Alexander to investigate the situation.

22 McGuire, *Campaign*, vol. 2, 30; Jackson, *Navy*, 123.

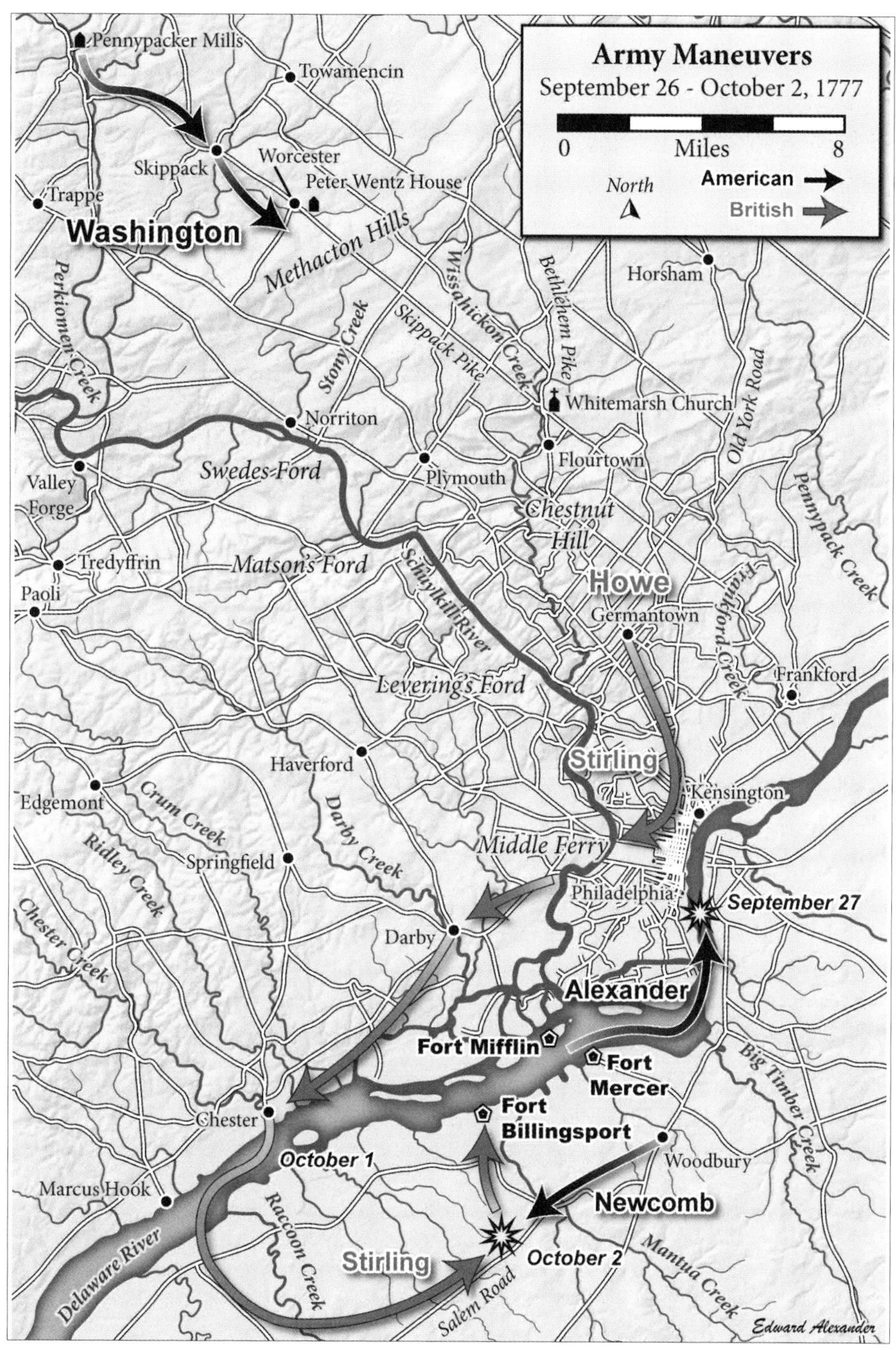
Army Maneuvers
September 26 - October 2, 1777
0 Miles 8
North
American
British
Pennypacker Mills
Towamencin
Skippack
Worcester
Peter Wentz House
Trappe
Washington
Methacton Hills
Horsham
Perkiomen Creek
Stony Creek
Skippack Pike
Wissahickon Creek
Bethlehem Pike
Whitemarsh Church
Norriton
Flourtown
Old York Road
Valley Forge
Swedes Ford
Plymouth
Chestnut Hill
Pennypack Creek
Tredyffrin
Matson's Ford
Howe
Paoli
Schuylkill River
Germantown
Frankford
Levering's Ford
Frankford Creek
Haverford
Stirling
Kensington
Edgemont
Crum Creek
Darby Creek
Middle Ferry
Ridley Creek
Springfield
Philadelphia
September 27
Chester Creek
Darby
Alexander
Fort Mifflin
Fort Mercer
Big Timber Creek
Chester
Fort Billingsport
Woodbury
October 1
Newcomb
Marcus Hook
Raccoon Creek
Stirling
October 2
Mantua Creek
Delaware River
Salem Road
Edward Alexander

Facing Page: "A survey of the city of Philadelphia and its environs shewing the several works constructed by His Majesty's troops, under the command of Sir William Howe, since their possession of that city 26th. September 1777, comprehending likewise the attacks against Fort Mifflin on Mud Island, and until it's reduction, 16th November 1777." *LOC*

His remaining four pieces, deployed along the riverbank, were completely exposed. The army's chief of artillery, Gen. Samuel Cleaveland, ordered Downman "not to fire at the ships until they fired at me," recorded the captain-lieutenant in his journal, a directive that made him "extremely uneasy." Two light 6-pounders attached to the 1st Battalion of British Grenadiers raced, bumped, and jostled their way to the river to bolster the waterfront. Downman found a good spot for one gun and instructed Lt. George Wilson, the commander of the other light fieldpiece, to move his weapon about 150 yards to a wharf that offered a good firing position. Wilson, who had performed well at Brandywine, raced south downriver to the lower end of the shipyards, manhandled the piece onto the end of a wharf jutting 50 yards into the river, and trained his piece in the direction of the approaching warships.[23]

Downman, under orders to hold his fire, watched with nervous trepidation as the enemy flotilla edged closer to his position. "The situation was disagreeable," recalled the officer, "for the largest ship was within 400 yards, and in another tack or two would have been alongside our guns." Lieutenant Wilson was unaware of Cleaveland's order because Downman failed to inform him. When the *Delaware* moved within range Wilson ordered his crew to open. He managed to get off two shots before Downman ordered him to cease fire. Captain Alexander concluded it would be "prudent & effectual" to defend himself and ordered the *Delaware's* 12-pounders to reply. Within seconds the guns discharged blasts of grapeshot screaming toward the wharf, forcing Wilson and his gunners to dodge the deadly iron rounds. Wilson's pair of shots and Alexander's reply was an open invitation for everyone to join in.

Downman's guns along the waterfront thundered and recoiled, their iron balls arcing their way 400 yards in the air or plunging harmlessly into the muddy water

23 F. A. Whinyates, ed., *The Services of Lieut.-Colonel Francis Downman, R.A. in France, North America, and the West Indies, Between the Years 1758 and 1784* (Woolwich, 1898), 36; McGuire, *Campaign*, vol. 2, 31. Samuel Cleaveland rose through the British artillery ranks. He commanded the First Royal Artillery Company in India in 1748. After helping capture Havana in 1762. Cleaveland was promoted to major and transferred to the 4th Battalion Royal Artillery. He came to North America with the battalion and served as Howe's artillery chief.

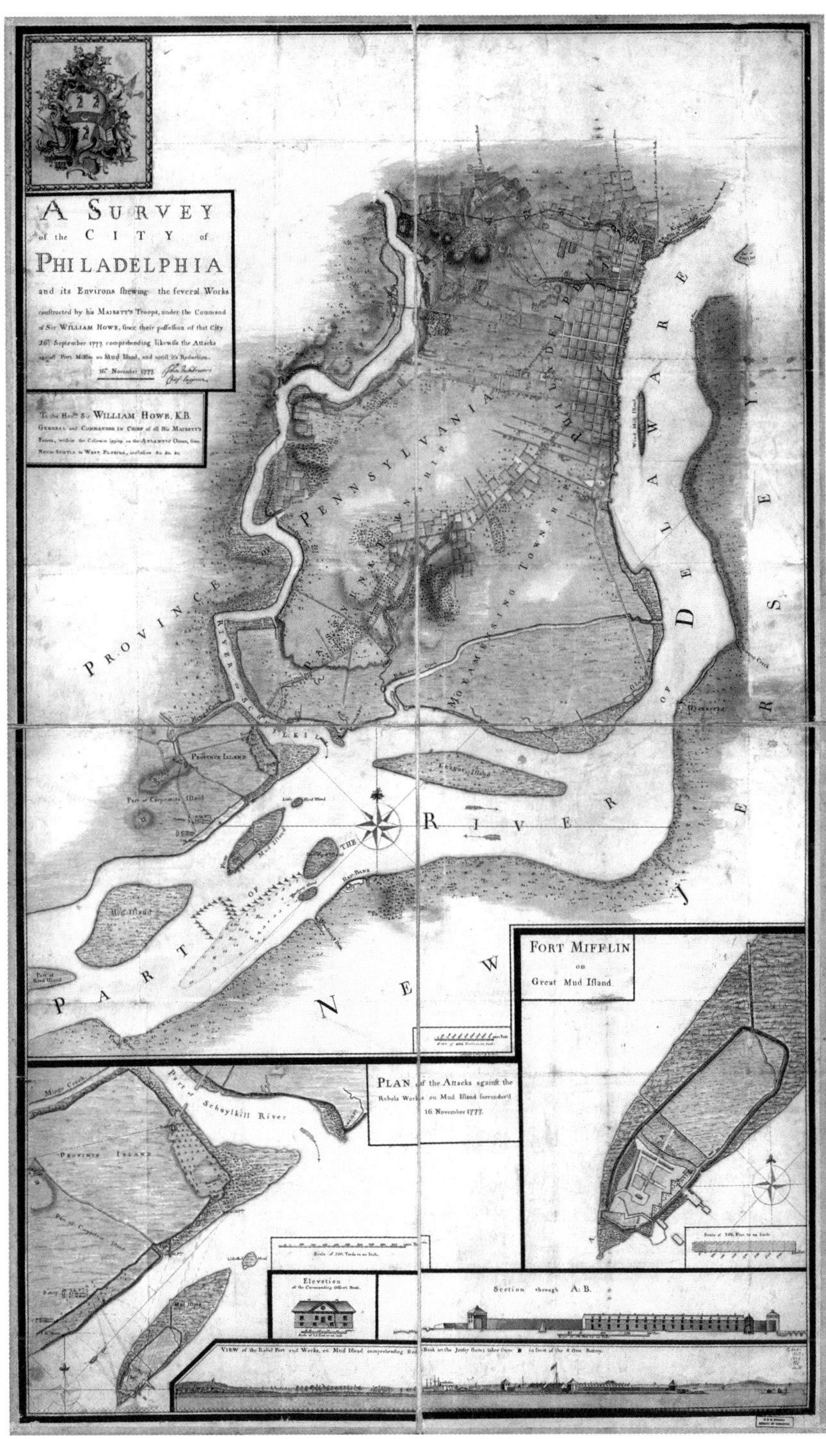

near the hulls of the enemy ships, which hurled in reply a mixture of 12-, 18-, 24-, and 32-pound shot. When Wilson realized the dozen rounds he brought with him were gone, he ran back up the wharf in search of more, leaving his gun without an officer. Exposed on the wharf to a fire that could kill or maim the entire gun crew with a single blast, Wilson's gunners abandoned the piece until Capt. James Moncrieff ordered them to return and extricate the gun. By the time Wilson returned, his men and his gun had disappeared.[24]

Those aboard the *Delaware* felt anything but secure as British rounds began striking the frigate. "We opened upon them and the artillery [was] extremely well directed against the *Delaware*," wrote Howe's chief engineer John Montresor in his journal, a ship he described as the enemy's "best Frigate." To the dismay of Captain Alexander and his crew, their warship—to use Montresor's words—"got somewhat grounded." Montresor continued: "She was 2 or 3 times on fire owing to one of our shot having drove through her caboose [cook house], it not being easily extinguished." Flaming embers flew in every direction and spread small deck fires that threatened to engulf the ship. Confusion mounted on the *Delaware* as Alexander attempted to turn his ship about. Amid the chaos, his sailors mismanaged the sails as a British howitzer round crashed through the foredeck near the bow, setting the hull ablaze. Confusion abounded and the men, recalled Downman, neglected "the management of the sails, and she ran aground" on the lower end of Windmill Island within 250 yards of the barking British guns. Alexander's crew tried to return fire as best they could, but were simply overwhelmed by the sheer weight of British metal. With his ship stuck fast and portions of it in flames, Alexander had little choice but to strike her colors. By the time he performed that act, one crewman had died and six others out of his 152-man crew had been wounded.[25]

---

24 Whinyates, *Services*, 37; McGuire, *Campaign*, vol. 2, 31-32. Six months later, Lt. George Wilson was court- martialed for "misbehaving himself before the Enemy by improperly quitting his Post on the 27th Sept. 1777." Despite several heroic actions before and after September 27, Wilson was found "Guilty of unofficer-like conduct in leaving his gun twice, which was not from fear or cowardice, based on the supporting testimony of his character, but was nevertheless improper." His sentence was a reprimand before the Brigade of Royal Artillery. British War Office, Judge Advocate General Office, Court Martial Proceedings and Board of General Officers' Minutes: WO71/86, March 31-April 1, 1778.

25 Montresor, "Journals," 459; Whinyates, *Services*, 37; McGuire, *Campaign*, vol. 2, 33. Windmill Island was a long, narrow mud flat home to a single windmill and wharf in the middle of the river. Smith, *Fight for Delaware*, 7.

The British immediately dispatched a boat with 10 grenadiers, together with engineer Capt. James Moncrieff and several carpenters, to take possession of the ship and extinguish the fires. Once aboard, the carpenters swung axes, cut away the burning parts of the ship, and tossed them into the river. The British loaded the Continental sailors into the boat, took them ashore near Old Swedes Church, and marched them to jail near the State House. Captain Alexander, the *Delaware's* commander and the fleet's senior Continental officer, was among the prisoners.[26]

While neutralizing the *Delaware*, the British artillery turned its collective attention to the other ships that were now rapidly withdrawing. The *Fly* took repeated hits, had her foremast shot away, and suffered four killed and six wounded. She ran aground on the New Jersey shore. The *Montgomery*, reported British officer John Andre did not venture "near enough to receive much damage [and] returned to her station near Mud Island." The American schooner *Mosquito* would later try to run the gauntlet from upriver past the city but was fired on by the British battery deployed at the upper end of town, struck at least once, and forced aground along the New Jersey shoreline. Her precise fate thereafter remains a mystery.[27]

This hour-long fight around the shipyards of Philadelphia marked the beginning of fighting for control of the Delaware River that would consume the next two months. Despite the capture of the *Delaware* and ease with which the British turned back the American warships, Howe worried that the river forts and obstructions were likely to cause grave long-term injury to his army. "She is an acquisition & a great security to the Town," admitted Gen. James Grant, referring to the captured frigate *Delaware*, but "those Rebell ships & Gallies, the Fort upon Mud Island & the Chevaux de Frize which they have sunk in the River prevent the Fleet getting up, retard our operations—obstruct our supplys & are likely to give much trouble." Grant was right. The British now controlled a warship at

---

26 McGuire, *Campaign*, vol. 2, 34.

27 Despite his poor performance and the fact that he never received another assignment, Alexander never faced a court of inquiry. Many of the captured crewmen from the *Delaware* chose to serve the British rather than rot in jail or die inside the hulk of a prison ship. Jackson, *British Army*, 289; Jackson, *Navy*, 127; McGuire, *Campaign*, vol. 2, 34; John Andre, *Major Andre's Journal: Operations of the British Army under Lieutenant Generals Sir William Howe and Sir Henry Clinton June 1777 to November, 1778 Recorded by Major John Andre, Adjutant General* (Tarrytown, NY, 1930), 53. The *Fly* was refloated that night and returned downstream to the fleet. Jackson, *Navy*, 124. Once British engineers completed the river battery near Kensington, near the modern intersection of Richmond Street and Girard Avenue, they towed the captured *Delaware* there for repairs. Smith, *Fight for Delaware*, 7; Reed, *Campaign*, 203.

Philadelphia stronger than any other vessel the Americans could muster, but the American obstructions blocked the fleet and the delivery of supplies, without which the British army was in grave peril. The capture of the *Delaware*, however, allowed Howe to safely ferry troops to New Jersey to conduct foraging or military operations. With access to New Jersey (i.e., north of Fort Mifflin) assured, he set his eyes on breaking through the American river defenses by assaulting the unfinished American defensive point at Fort Billingsport, New Jersey, about two miles below Fort Mifflin and on the opposite bank of the river.[28]

Lord Cornwallis's quick move into Philadelphia the previous day prevented the Americans from removing or hiding all the river boats as Washington intended and had instructed. As a result, the British accumulated about 50 of various types. One, a large wooden flat-bottomed double-ended Durham boat, was found in Frankford Creek and others were discovered in the marshes south of the city and on Windmill Island. The capture of the frigate, together with 50 additional vessels, offered Howe a host of possibilities.[29]

On the day the *Delaware* surrendered, elements of Admiral Howe's British fleet re-entered Delaware Bay. With his brother's fleet finally approaching, General Howe knew the time had arrived to reduce or destroy the American defenses blocking the Delaware River. With American quartermasters stripping resources from the region surrounding Philadelphia and army patrols blanketing the area, it was getting progressively harder to obtain sufficient forage and provisions from the countryside to supply his army. Winter was coming, and the Delaware River would begin to freeze in early December. If he was going to maintain his grip on the colonial city, Howe needed to open the river to his supply ships soon.

On September 29, engineer Capt. Archibald Robertson, together with Cornwallis, rode to the mouth of the Schuylkill River to study Fort Mifflin from its land side. They arrived opposite Province Island "but did not cross [to] it, the land so low [flooded] we could not see it." To the young engineer and combat general, it was apparent that approaching the fort from the western land approaches was not going to be easy.[30]

---

28 James Grant to Harvey October 20, 1777, in James Grant Papers, National Archives of Scotland, Edinburgh.

29 Jackson, *Navy*, 125.

30 Archibald Robertson, *Archibald Robertson, Lieutenant General Royal Engineers: His Diaries and Sketches in America, 1762-1780*, ed. Harry Miller Lydenberg (New York, 1930), 151.

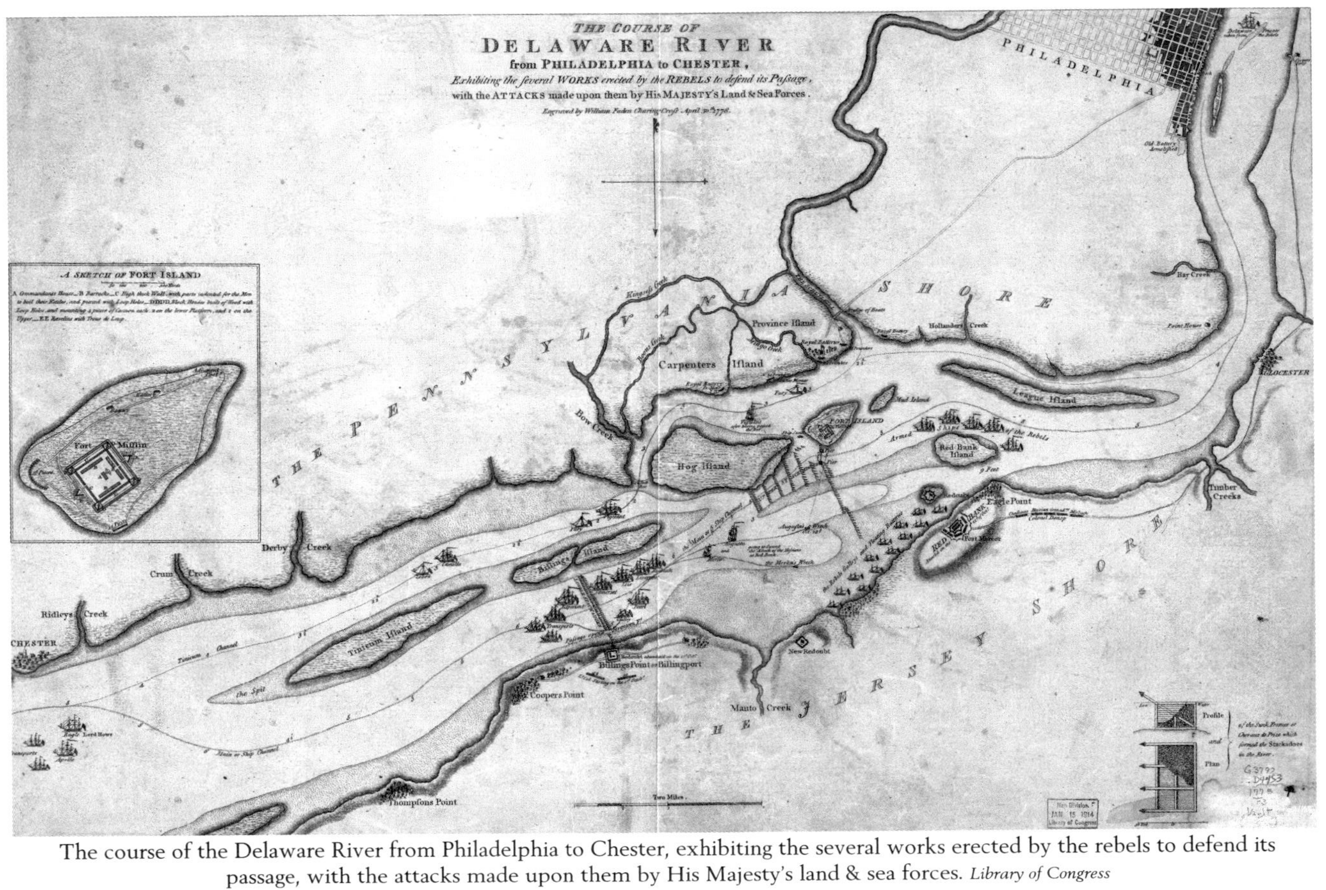

The course of the Delaware River from Philadelphia to Chester, exhibiting the several works erected by the rebels to defend its passage, with the attacks made upon them by His Majesty's land & sea forces. *Library of Congress*

Washington remained upbeat about his chances of holding the river and beating Howe as the calendar turned to October. The seat of the American government had fallen, but Congress reestablished itself in the Pennsylvania backcountry. The army's major supply depot in Reading remained intact. If the war had demonstrated anything, occupying a city meant little in a sprawling multi-colony revolution. The British once occupied Boston but were eventually forced to abandon it. New York was lost to the British, but the war continued. Occupying a major city in the Americas meant much less than it did on the European continent.

The maneuvering and fighting at Brandywine and Germantown settled the initial fate of Philadelphia, but now it all came down to one simple question: Who would control the Delaware? The primary defenses there consisted of three forts: Mercer (on the east bank of the river at Red Bank in New Jersey); Mifflin (directly across from Mercer on a mud island on the Pennsylvania shore); and Billingsport, two miles downstream on the same side of the river as Mercer. Three lines of *chevaux-de-frise* blocked the river and the placement of the forts protected these river obstructions. The Americans operated all of these by the beginning of October, and each depended on the others for success.

Chevaux-de-frise

These obstructions comprised large stone-filled log bins sporting 29-foot iron-tipped logs jutting outward and facing downriver. Heavy wrought iron chains connected the bins. These obstructions were especially effective against the deep-draft vessels of the Royal Navy. The Delaware was notorious for shifting channels, shoals, sandbars, and mud islands that appeared and disappeared, making the waterway a navigational nightmare.

The Americans placed the *chevaux-de-frise* in two different areas. The channel passage between Billingsport and Billings Island was narrow, though deeper than the channel at the second line of defense between Mud Island and the New Jersey

Chevaux-de-frise recovered from Delaware River after Superstorm Sandy, at the Brandywine Battlefield visitor center. *Author*

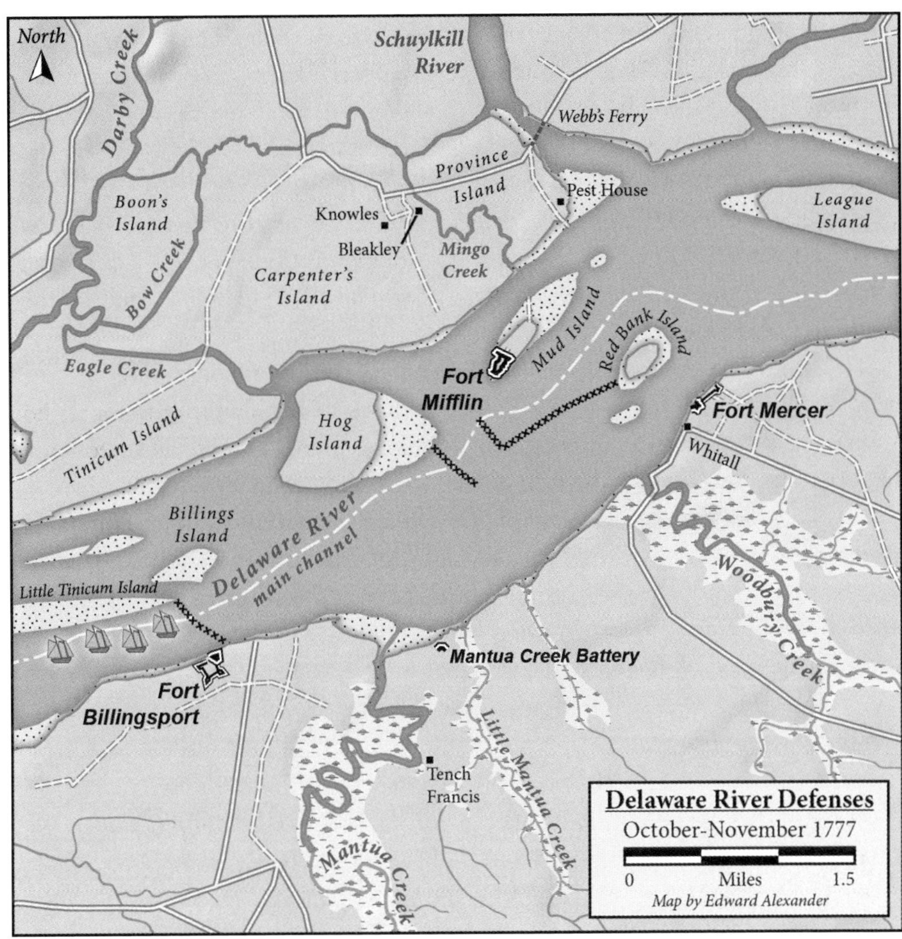

shore. The wider channel near Mud Island contained two sand bars creating a main channel between Hog and Mud islands on the west and a large shoal to the east. East of the shoal, a secondary channel with another sandbar existed near the New Jersey shore.

Any eighteenth-century ship could navigate the main river channel near Mud Island, while the slightly shallower channel at Billingsport often gave navigators fits. Of the blocking *chevaux-de-frise*, 24 were placed in two irregular lines at Billingsport, and another 43 were located near Mud Island in four groupings.[31]

---

31 Jackson, *Navy*, 353-361.

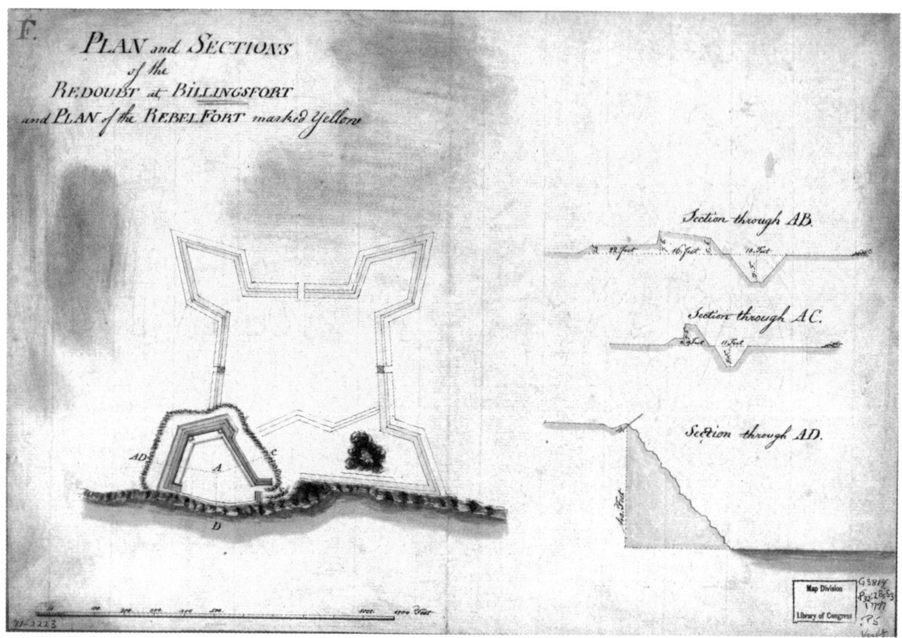

Plan and Sections of Redoubt at Billingsport. LOC

Fort Billingsport

Tasked with defending the lower 24 *chevaux-de-frise*, Fort Billingsport was the farthest fortification from Philadelphia and the least defensible because it was unfinished, undermanned, and poorly designed. As noted earlier, the 96-acre parcel was purchased by the Pennsylvania Committee of Safety at the narrowest point of the Delaware River below Philadelphia with money authorized by the Continental Congress on July 5, 1776. It was the first land purchase ever made by the United States. Coupled with the fortification, *cheveaux-de-frise* placed in the river stretched from Fort Billingsport to Billings Island. The Pennsylvania State Navy had orders to patrol the channel running west of Billings Island.[32]

The Pennsylvania Committee of Safety requested George Washington send an engineer to design the earthwork. Washington responded on June 17, 1776: "I am under the necessity of Informing you It is out of my power at this time to comply with the request made by your Honourable body. The many Important works

32 Mooney & Wuebber, "Archaeological Investigations," 7.

View looking downriver from the site of Fort Billingsport, New Jersey. *Author*

carrying on for the defence of this place [New York] against which there is the highest probability of an Attack being made in a little time, will not allow me to spare from hence any person who has the least skill in the business of an Engineer."[33]

Military engineer Thaddeus Kosciuszko, a Polish national educated in French military schools, caught the revolutionary zeal and made for the colonies in 1776. By October 1776, he was assigned to lay out the fort. Thinking in European terms, with plenty of manpower, Kosciuszko designed a four-sided earthen redoubt with a bastion at each corner. Each side stretched seven hundred feet with walls 7 ½ feet high. A surrounding ditch added 18 feet of width and nine feet of depth for defense. The land side would prove to be the fort's Achilles' heel. Simply put, Kosciuszko's fort was too large for the men and guns available. Washington acknowledged as much in a letter to the Pennsylvania Board of War on April 14, 1777. "I am afraid from the Situation of Billingsport, that the Works which you are constructing there, cannot be supported, if an attack is made upon it by land," he observed, "and I should therefore think, that a small work with a few pieces of heavy Cannon, would be all that would be necessary. You may depend, that no Attack will ever be made by Shipping alone." The Americans would need at least

33 John D. Fitzpatrick, ed., *The Writings of George Washington from the Original Manuscript Sources, 1745-1799*, 39 vols. (Washington, D.C., 1932), vol. 5, 153-154.

1,000 men to adequately defend the post and all the artillery positions focused on the river approaches—to the neglect of a proper land defense. Kosciuszko's original design included an unfinished square fort on 15 acres with a bastion on each corner and five cannon (four 9-pounders and one 12-pounder).[34]

The fort's layout went through several important changes during 1777. By the end of September, engineers had reduced the footprint with just the northeast bastion converted into a redoubt with abatis placed on the landward side. Despite this key reduction, the garrison remained undermanned. Two floating batteries holding 18-pounders (one with nine guns and the other with ten) were anchored near Billings Island. American engineers hoped the "land being very low and narrow, these batteries will be able to produce above it, a formidable fire against the frigates, which may present themselves, to attack the Line of cheveaux de frize, opposite to Billing's port," explained French engineer Philippe du Coudray on August 6.

The fort failed to impress Nathanael Greene, one of Washington's finest field generals. "There have been prodigious sums of money expended on that place," he informed the Virginia commander on August 7, 1777, "[yet the] fortress renders the approaches easy, the enemy can make good their landing a little below the work— the ground is very favorable but a small distance from the fort to open Batteries."[35]

On September 29, Washington ordered the Pennsylvania militia garrisoning Billingsport and "any Stores there" removed to Fort Mifflin, together with the destruction of the works at the ill-designed bastion. A lack of manpower and the fear exhibited by the Pennsylvania Navy at the very suggestion delayed its execution. As far as the Pennsylvania Navy was concerned, Billingsport was the key to the entire river defense.[36]

34 Mooney & Wuebber, "Archaeological Investigations," 7. Fitzpatrick, ed., *The Writings of George Washington from the Original Manuscript Sources*, vol. 7, 411; McIntyre, *A Most Gallant Resistance*, 82-83.

35 McIntyre, *A Most Gallant Resistance*, 120-121; Ford, "Defences," 13; Nathanael Greene to George Washington, August 7, 1777, Washington Papers online, Library of Congress, series 4, General Correspondence, accessed February 5, 2017.

36 Chase and Lengel, eds., *Papers*, vol. 11, 347. The precise order for the destruction of the post does not appear in Washington's papers, but a reference to such an order can be found in Lt. Col. Samuel Smith's letter to Washington on September 27. Ibid., 338-344.

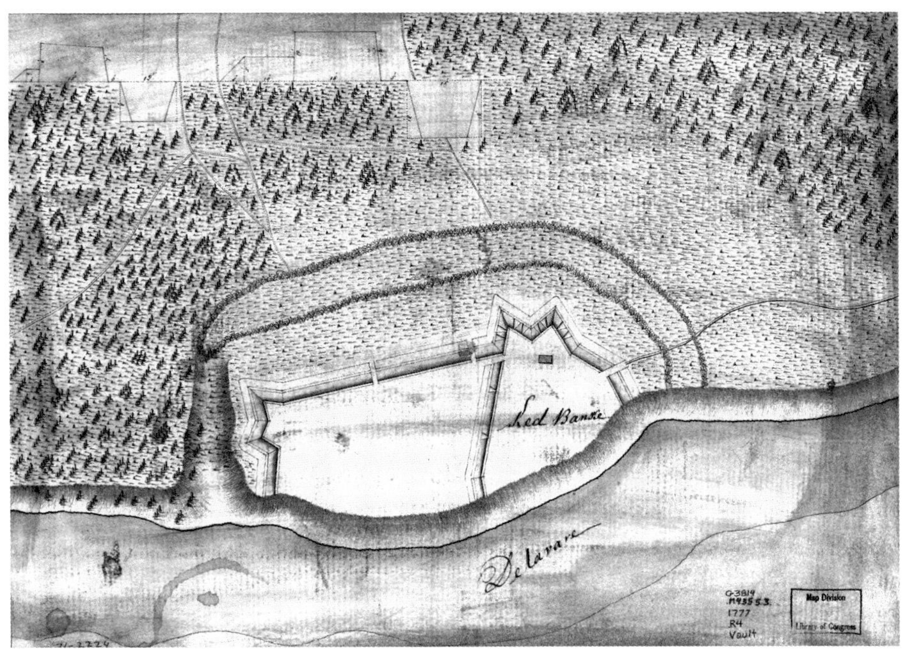

"1777 map of Fort Mercer at Red Bank." East is at the top. *LOC*

Fort Mercer

Two miles upriver on the same side of Billingsport sat Fort Mercer, the best constructed of the trio of forts. This massive fortification loomed over Quaker farmer James Whitall's 196-acre property at Red Bank. Built in stages spanning six months and named after Gen. Hugh Mercer, who was killed at the battle of Princeton earlier that year, Fort Mercer sat at the top of a steep bank 30 feet above the river.

Colonel John Bull of the Pennsylvania militia had supervised its construction, which was completed in early July 1777. Its earthen walls stretched 320 yards long by 50 to 75 yards wide and boasted 14 cannons with bastions (projections built at an angle to the wall to offer covering fire) on the landward corners. Workers cleared trees for 400 yards on the fort's three land sides, though the thick woods beyond that distance would shield any approaching threat. "Fort Mercer was asymmetrical, unbalanced, and utterly utilitarian, obviously assembled by a hodgepodge of well-meaning amateurs with neither training nor taste," was how one modern historian described it. Although designed to hold a garrison of some

The James Whitall House. *Author*

1,500 men, General Washington could never send anywhere near that many men to defend it.[37]

Fort Mifflin

The location and importance of Fort Mifflin destined it to play a major role in the campaign. Erected on a mud flat surrounded by a swamp, workers constructed the fort with logs, ship spars, and pine rafts set in the thick muck—the same material that filled its ramparts and dikes. British engineers began work on the fort in 1771, under the guidance of John Montresor, who was now serving as Howe's chief engineer. They never completed the project. Mud Island, on which the fort stood, was 400 yards long and 200 yards across at its widest point, one of many similar islands lining the Delaware near the mouth of the Schuylkill. Loyalist Joseph

37 McGuire, *Campaign*, vol. 2, 140; McIntyre, *A Most Gallant Resistance*, 83. It is hard to visualize the original structure today. Most of the earthwork has washed into the Delaware through natural erosion. There are recreated ditches and, because of the erosion, the 1748 Whitall House sits much closer to the river than it once did. By 1900, little was left of the earthworks. "Along the eastern shore of the Delaware, among the trees and beneath the undergrowth, we can trace a rounded ridge, a tangle-hidden ditch and a few hillocks—all that is left of the old fort at Red Bank." Alfred M. Heston, "Red Bank: Defence of Fort Mercer," paper read before the Monmouth County, NJ Historical Association July 26, 1900. The original fort extended north beyond the modern park boundaries to the present Monument Avenue which follows the original gully at the north end of the fort. Jackson, *Navy*, 151.

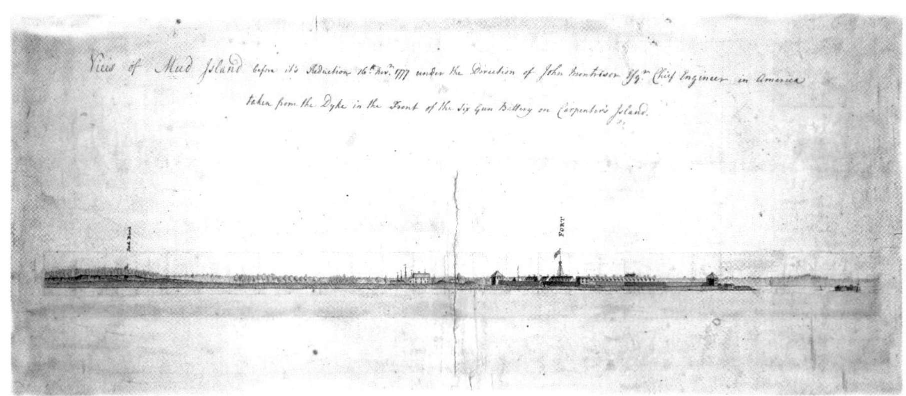

View of Mud Island before its reduction. *LOC*

Galloway, who owned the island in 1771, sold it to the province so the English could build the defensive work there. When winter weather ground the effort to a halt in November 1773, the Pennsylvania Assembly refused to continue funding the project and work never resumed. The failed building program left behind a barracks and a zig-zag wall of gray stone facing the river. Two years later in 1775, the Pennsylvania Assembly established a committee to examine the river defenses. The Americans added the mud and earth parapets and two additional barracks after the start of the Revolution. By 1777, additional barracks sat along the western and northern walls. An officer's barracks sat across the parade ground near the south wall. The only viable way to reinforce or supply the fort was to ferry men and provisions in from the New Jersey side of the river.[38]

Mifflin barely deserved to be called a fort when Lt. Col. Samuel Smith assumed command. While it looked imposing, it was an engineering monstrosity impossible to defend. A line of pine log palisades, each 15 inches thick, extended along the northern and western perimeter and joined the stone wall on the east and south. A poorly conceived battery built in front of the south wall left it open on the east to enfilade and ricochet fire from enemy warships. Engineers dug a ditch on three sides but left the southern side exposed. Wooden blockhouses in the northeast, northwest, and southwest corners left the southeast side exposed to enemy rounds. A floating chain extended along the western side of the fort to prevent landing parties from launching an assault from the Pennsylvania side, and a line of *chevaux-de-frise* blocked the river between Mud Island and Fort Mercer. At high tide

---

38 McGuire, *Campaign*, vol. 2, 182.

much of the island became submerged, and the entire island, including the fort, could be flooded by cutting the dikes on the western side of the island.[39]

Together, Smith and Commodore Hazelwood examined the 600-yard back channel between the fort and Province & Carpenter's islands and the potential problem posed by the vexing geography. The two islands, along with much of the land at the mouth of the Schuylkill River, were diked to keep the water out and create a large meadow. Separated by nothing more than small tidal streams, at ground level the pair of islands appeared to be part of the mainland. Aghast at the danger posed to Fort Mifflin if the British seized either island, Smith related his concern to Hazelwood. The confident naval officer waved away Smith's apprehension by replying that "a musquito could not live there under the fire of my guns." Smith disagreed. The difference of opinion between the Army and Navy regarding how best to defend Mifflin, as well as the other forts, was just beginning.[40]

On October 1, William Howe ordered Royal Engineer Montresor to oversee the construction of gun emplacements on Carpenters' and Province Islands to bombard Fort Mifflin. With Mifflin still controlling river access to the city, Howe was forced to conduct intermittent communication with the fleet over a long and unsecure land route that required a heavy dispersal of troops. Until the British could reduce the American river defenses, the victualling of the army would be impossible. Fort Mifflin had to be eliminated.

While Washington contemplated an assault on Germantown on October 3, Captain Montresor, together with an officer and 20 grenadiers, crossed to Province Island in two skiffs to survey the high ground and flooded marshes near Mifflin. The scouting operation was no secret, and the reconnaissance prompted the Americans to abandon the island, including the Pest House, the hospital for contagious diseases they had established on its northern end. The evacuation of Province Island cleared the way for a British assault on Mud Island and Fort Mifflin.

---

39 Jackson, *Navy*, 156-157.

40 McGuire, *Campaign*, vol. 2, 184; Smith, *Fight for Delaware*, 13. The back channel is now filled and Mud Island as a distinct entity is no longer visible. Much of this area is covered by the Philadelphia International Airport. Samuel Smith, "The Papers of General Samuel Smith," *The Historical Magazine and Notes and Queries, Concerning the Antiquities, History and Biography of America* (2nd series, no. 2), February 1870, vol. 7, 86.

The view looking west from the British landing site south of Billingsport. *Author*

The Fall of Fort Billingsport

On the studied advice of Capt. Andrew Hamond of the HMS *Roebuck*, General Howe decided to move first against the southernmost enemy position on the river: Billingsport. He assigned the task on September 28 to the 10th and 42nd Regiments of Foot, nearly 1,000 troops under Lt. Col. Thomas Stirling, together with a pair of six-pounders from the 3rd British Brigade. Stirling's column left the encampment at Germantown and arrived that evening at the Middle Ferry on the Schuylkill, tramped into Chester on the morning of September 29, and met up there with two battalions of the 71st Highlanders, which came up from Wilmington, Delaware, to protect the depot being established there. The plan called for Stirling's column to cross the Delaware in long boats, march inland, turn north, and seize the unfinished fort, which would effectively remove the first line of obstructions blocking the river.[41]

October opened with Stirling's detachment ferrying across the Delaware. According to the Master's Journal of the *Roebuck*, at 9:00 a.m. the signal went out "to embark in boats [Stirling's command] and afterwards the boats were employed landing Troops in the Jerseys." The troops landed at Paul's Point on Raccoon Creek just south of the present Commodore Barry Bridge. Once organized, they

41 McGuire, *Campaign*, vol. 2, 46; Reed, *Campaign*, 206-207. Following the debarkation of the army at Head of Elk, Hamond was sent back to the Delaware River with a small flotilla of supply ships to await William Howe's arrival in Philadelphia. W. Hugh Moomaw, "The Naval Career of Captain Hamond, 1775-1779," PhD dissertation, University of Virginia, 1955, 357.

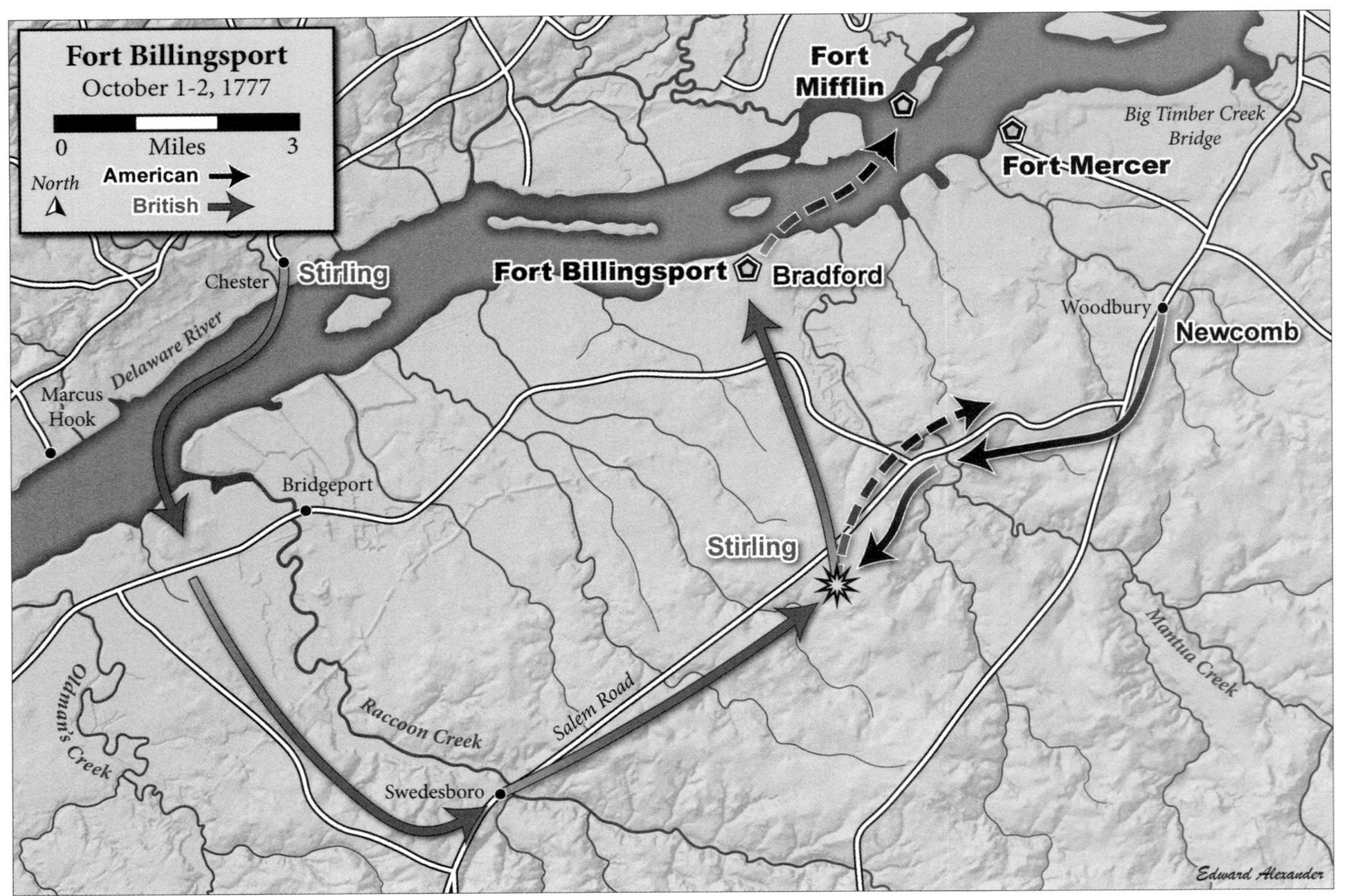
Fort Billingsport
October 1-2, 1777
0   Miles   3
North
American
British
Stirling
Chester
Fort Mifflin
Big Timber Creek Bridge
Fort Mercer
Fort Billingsport
Bradford
Woodbury
Newcomb
Delaware River
Marcus Hook
Bridgeport
Stirling
Oldman's Creek
Raccoon Creek
Salem Road
Swedesboro
Mantua Creek
Edward Alexander

pushed east from the landing site on the present Center Square Road, and then north on the present Kings Highway. New Jersey Line officer Joseph Bloomfield, who was recovering from a severe Brandywine wound in Swedesboro, New Jersey, got lucky the night of October 1 when the British came knocking. "Their light horses came twice to the house where I lay after the Doctor, who was a Militia Colonel & an active man agt. them but not knowing I was in the house I fortunately escaped their search."[42]

Washington had known for some time that the Billingsport position was weak and had issued an order (probably on September 27) for Col. William Bradford of the Pennsylvania Militia to assume command of the Pennsylvania militia troops garrisoning the position. To Bradford's surprise, he arrived on September 29 to discover that Brig. Gen. Silas Newcomb of the New Jersey Militia, who he thought was in charge there, was not in the fort at all. Instead, Newcomb had taken one of its guns and his 300 New Jersey troops with him. Billingsport was essentially an unmanned and demoralized post. "I there found Col. Will of the 4th Battn [Pennsylvania militia] with about 100 men, & Captn Massey['s] Company of Artillery which was reduced by desertion to 12 men," Bradford penned to Pennsylvania President (governor) Thomas Wharton. "After I got in was reinforced by 100 Jersey Militia and the next day with about 50 more," sent by Newcomb.[43]

Newcomb, explained one modern historian, was "never where he should be, and indecisive in the extreme. A very pious and well-meaning individual, he should never have been entrusted with a military command." Washington discovered precisely that earlier in the war and had removed Newcomb from command of the New Jersey Line. "Notwithstanding I believe that Colo. Newcomb is a Gentleman of great goodness and integrity, and cannot entertain the Slightest doubts of his Bravery," explained Washington, "yet I am persuaded that he is not equal to such a

---

42 Michael J. Crawford, ed., *Naval Documents of the American Revolution*, 13 vols. (Washington, D.C., 1996), vol. 10, 13; Reed, *Campaign*, 207; Joseph Bloomfield, *Citizen Soldier: The Revolutionary War Journal of Joseph Bloomfield*, eds. Mark Edward Lender & James Kirby Martin (Yardley, PA, 2018), 129.

43 Hazard, et al, eds., *Archives*, Series 1, vol. 5, 644; Letter, Silas Newcomb to William Livingston, October 4, 1777, William Livingston Family Collection, Reel 1, Massachusetts Historical Society, Boston, MA. William Bradford was the grandson of the William Bradford, who had introduced printing to the colonies. A publisher before the war, Bradford was wounded at Princeton while serving with the Pennsylvania Associators. By 1777, Bradford was Chairman of the State Navy Board of Pennsylvania. William S. Stryker, *The Forts on the Delaware in the Revolutionary War* (Trenton, NJ, 1901), 8.

Command.—Many qualities, independent of personal Courage, are requisite to form the good Officer."[44]

On October 4, the day of the Germantown battle, General Newcomb wrote what was the equivalent of a battle report to Gov. William Livingston of New Jersey. On September 29, he explained, he had made his headquarters at Woodbury, seven miles northeast of Billingsport, rather than at the fort itself. He then posted "A guard of about 50 men at Big Timber creek bridge; with a sergts. guard at each of the ferries [Coopers and Gloucester] to serve as piquet, & to prevent any boats going over to the enemy." The militia officer also placed "a guard of about 40 men at Thompson's point, 4 miles below Billingsport . . . about 150 men I sent to Billingsport [to assist Col. Bradford in the defense of the fort] . . . reserving only a small guard at Woodbury."[45]

On the evening of October 1, continued Newcomb, "I was informed that a party of the enemy was landg on this shore, opposite Marcus Hook. Their number said to be about 400." The New Jersey officer decided it was better to advance and engage them as far from the fort as possible and he did precisely that. "Immediately called in my out guards & marched to a Height, on the Salem Road, about 15 miles below Philada and about 3 ½ miles from Billingsport [near modern Mount Royal]," he explained to the governor.[46]

Lieutenant Colonel Stirling, meanwhile, advanced inland with his column where he spotted the militia deploying to oppose him. "About 9 in the morning . . . the Enemy advanced within a few hundred yards of where we were drawn up, with 2 or 3 field pieces," wrote Newcomb, "when a pretty brisk fire, from both sides, issued—we now discover their numbers to be greatly superior to what they had been represented." To Newcomb's dismay, he was not facing 400 men but "not less than 1500." The Americans watched as Stirling shook out "strong flanking parties" to turn Newcomb's militia line. The tactic may have driven back the heavily outnumbered New Jersey men, or, as Newcomb later claimed, "We might soon have been surrounded, I thought it prudent to retreat, which we did in tolerable good order, keeping up a constant fire in our rear."

The recovering Joseph Bloomfield, who had only narrowly escaped being captured, held nothing but disdain for the militia effort. "This old granny of a Genl.

---

44 Jackson, *Navy*, 133; Fitzpatrick, *Writings of Washington*, vol. 7, 134.

45 Letter, Silas Newcomb to William Livingston, October 4, 1777.

46 Ibid.

[Newcomb] pretending with 300 undisciplined Men to make a stand, but soon retreated helter skelter with his Men, who eminently distinguished themselves by the swiftness of their heels."[47]

Stirling drove Newcomb past the intersection of Salem Road and the road leading west to Fort Billingsport, about 3 ½ miles distant, and up to Mantua Creek, which Newcomb crossed before turning to make a stand. The British crossed after him and a short engagement followed. With the pesky militia out of the way, Stirling decided to ignore the New Jersey defenders and turned his attention westward toward the fort. Newcomb extricated his men from a tight spot and withdrew to Woodbury, New Jersey, just a short march from Fort Mercer. The militia general had the foresight to move valuable stores from Billingsport to Woodbury, saving them from the hands of the enemy. "I believe we had none killed, nor many badly wounded," he informed the governor, though "several are missing, but I believe they are mostly, if not all, gone home. The enemy had 3 or 4 killed at Mantua creek bridge. I have at present," he concluded, "not quite 300 men under my command; & as it is impossible to get any more, under the old Militia law." Years later, militiamen Charles Simpkins testified in his pension application that "two of our men were wounded and nine taken prisoners." Simpkins claims he killed two British soldiers and that Newcomb's horse was wounded in the rump and "he saw the blood run down the horse's tail."[48]

Colonel Bradford of the Pennsylvania Militia, meanwhile, heard the fighting from inside the unfinished fort and knew he could not resist a serious effort to take it. Two guard boats commanded by Lieutenants Dennis Leary and William Barney of the Continental Marines rowed in to rescue the garrison and salvage moveable supplies. Bradford "ordered the People into Boats and sent most of them to Fort Island [Mifflin], spiked up all the Cannon we could not carry off, and set the Barracks & Bake House on Fire, but the Dwelling House somehow escaped." After sending away the small garrison, Bradford remained behind with Capt. Isaiah Robinson of the brig *Andrea Doria* to determine the size of the British force.

47 Letter, Silas Newcomb to William Livingston, October 4, 1777; Bloomfield, *Citizen Soldier*, 129.

48 Smith, *Fight for Delaware*, 10. Salem Road is the modern Kings Highway. Letter, Newcomb to Livingston, October 4, 1777. The action between Stirling and Newcomb was in present-day Clarksboro, New Jersey. Revolutionary War Pension and Bounty-Land-Warrant Application Files (M804) [RWPF], Record Group 15, Records of the Veterans Administration, National Archives, Washington, D.C., file R9588. Newcomb's seemingly poor decision to take the fight to the British outside the walls of Fort Billingsport, may have been the right decision. Rather than be bottled up in the fort and forced to surrender or withdraw to Pennsylvania, his New Jersey militia remained a viable force to harass the Hessian approach to Fort Mercer three weeks later.

"About 12 o'clock the Enemy came on so close thro' a corn field that they were not more than 30 yards from us, and began to fire on us before our Boat put off the shore," reported Bradford, and "we returned the fire with 6 muskets we had on board, and a Guard Boat we had with us also fired on them, and all got off, one man only being wounded."[49]

Lieutenant Colonel Stirling's men moved in to occupy the vacant fort while American row galleys shelled the position. Four British warships supporting the operation from downriver arrived and opened on the troublesome American vessels, driving them back upriver. The embarrassing affair convinced several American seamen to desert to the British, which prompted British Capt. Andrew Hamond of the *Roebuck* to offer pardons to the entire American fleet. Commodore Hazelwood vowed that evening in response to the offer that "he should defend the Fleet to the last, and not give them up, and was not afraid of all the Ships they could bring, and desired they would send no more such flags."[50]

With British forces now occupying the region, the wounded Major Bloomfield was whisked away. "In the midst of the fray I was carried off & narrowly Escaped their pursuit, takeing 10 Miles into the pines of Gloucester County where I lay this Night at a Tar kill hut, miserably Accomodated, seeing the Moon & stars all night. However, being no astronmr. I made but few observations."[51]

The loss of Billingsport meant the loss of the first line of *chevaux-de-frise* river obstructions. The British Navy began removing the obstructions immediately, but the tedious process required three weeks to complete. According to the October 4 journal entry of the HMS *Pearl*, "all the Masters & Pilots in the Squadron were sent with two Boats from each Ship to remove the Chiveaux de frize. . . . At 3 PM two of the Enemies Galleys came down and lay in shore & fired several Guns." Howe, meanwhile, ordered the gun carriages, artillery platforms, and barracks destroyed and the unfinished earthworks leveled at Billingsport.[52]

Like a line of dominoes, the fall of Billingsport exposed Fort Mercer just to the north to any aggressive British commander willing to make the effort. Loyalist Joseph Galloway later insisted Stirling's request for permission to advance on Fort Mercer was denied. "Colonel Stirling saw the necessity of forming a post at Red

<hr>

49   Charles R. Smith, *Marines in the Revolution: A History of the Continental Marines in the American Revolution 1775-1783* (Washington, D.C., 1975), 126; Hazard, et al, eds., *Archives*, Series 1, vol. 5, 644.

50   Smith, *Fight for Delaware*, 10-11.

51   Bloomfield, *Citizen Soldier*, 129.

52   Crawford, ed., *Naval Documents*, vol. 10, 39.

Bank, not yet occupied by the Rebels . . . Colonel Stirling desired permission to take possession of Red Bank—but it was not granted him." What General Howe seems not to have known was that Fort Mercer and Bush Island were ungarrisoned, the cannon and the works without a caretaker except for a few laborers at the former location. If Stirling had advanced and occupied Mercer, the Americans would have had no choice but to immediately evacuate Fort Mifflin on Mud Island.[53]

The unhappy news that Billingsport had fallen to a British strike reached Washington quickly. The Virginian ordered it abandoned, but "Our Reason for not dismantling Billingsport," explained Lt. Col. Samuel Smith the day after it fell, "was the great discontent in the State fleet who already are much scar'd & from whom the greatest desertions of Captains, Lieuts. & men has been. So general a discontent and panic run through that part of the fleet that neither Officer nor men can be confided in," he continued, "they conceive the River is lost if the enemy gets possession of Billingsport nothing can convince them of the contrary & I am persuaded as soon as that fort is taken that almost all the fleet will desert." Bradford's sudden appearance at Fort Mifflin with the remnants of the Billingsport garrison triggered a panic in Smith's command. Responding to Smith's concerns at Fort Mifflin but needing to reassure him of that fort's importance, Washington responded to Smith's dispatches. Washington was "sorry to hear that you found Matters so much out of order at Fort Mifflin. Much must depend upon your activity and that of other Officers in Garrison."[54]

With the Billingsport threat eliminated and the Battle of Germantown behind him, William Howe was ready to turn his full attention to opening the Delaware River to the Royal Navy.

---

53 Reed, *Campaign*, 207-208; Joseph Galloway, *Letters to a Nobleman on the Conduct of the War in the Middle Colonies* (London, 1779), 79-80.

54 Chase and Lengel, eds., *Papers*, vol. 11, 364.

Chapter 3

The Aftermath of Germantown

October 5-19, 1777

"I found it adviseable to remove to Philadelphia, to expedite the reduction of Mud Island, which proved to be more difficult than was at first supposed."[1]

— Lt. Gen. William Howe, British army commander, April 29, 1779

The day after the battle at Germantown dawned warm and dry. Elements of the defeated Continental Army trickled into camps spread across the countryside "in troops and singly with their wagons." It was a trying time for men in the ranks and civilians alike. Rev. Henry Muhlenberg, the leader of Lutheranism in America living in Trappe, Pennsylvania, complained the arriving soldiers were "tired, hungry and thirsty. They will consume all that is left."

Every man in Washington's army needed rest, but for many the luxury remained out of reach. "Small parties of Horse are . . . to be sent up the different Roads above the Present encampment of the Army as much as 10 Miles in order to stop all Soldiers and turn them back to the Army," announced officers as they read Washington's general orders circular to their men the day after the battle. "The Commander in Chief returns his thanks, to the Generals and other officers and

---

1 *The Narrative of Lieut. Gen. Sir William Howe, in a Committee of the House of Commons, on the 29th of April, 1779, Relative to His Conduct, During His Late Command of the King's Troops in North America: to Which are Added, Some Observations Upon a Pamphlet, Entitled, Letters to a Nobleman* (London, 1780), 19-28.

men concerned in yesterday's attack . . . for the spirit and bravery they manifested in driving the enemy from field to field. The enemy are not proof against a vigorous attack, and may be put to flight when boldly pushed. This they will remember."[2]

Much needed reinforcements were on their way to join the beleaguered army. The 1,200-man Rhode Island Brigade under Brig. Gen. James Varnum, detached from the Northern army in the Hudson Highlands, reached Coryell's Ferry on the Delaware River en route to reinforce Washington. The approach of Varnum's Continentals heartened the Virginia commander, but news that Daniel Morgan's rifle corps would not be returning anytime soon—if at all—dampened his mood. Washington had disbanded the light infantry brigade in late September, and the Pennsylvania militia, incapable of effective scouting, disappointed. Washington desperately needed Morgan's men with him. Horatio Gates, the commander of the Northern army in New York, however, was reluctant to return them and informed the Virginian as much in an October 5 letter. After describing the proximity of the armies and the likelihood of a significant battle, Gates added, "In this Situation, Your Excellency would not wish me to part with the Corps the Army of General Burgoyne are most Afraid of. From the best Intelligence he has not more than Three weeks provision in Store."[3]

While Washington saw to the needs of his army, those of his soldiers unfortunate enough to fall into British hands at Germantown found themselves jammed into the Walnut Street Jail in Philadelphia and the State House (Independence Hall) across the street. The latter served as a guardhouse, officers' prison, and hospital. In order to keep Washington apprised of British activities, Thomas Mifflin, the army's quartermaster general, established a spy ring prior to the British occupation. Both Howe and Washington often allowed citizens to pass into the countryside to obtain flour. The humane gesture provided Washington with valuable information about conditions in the city.[4]

---

2 Henry Melchior Muhlenberg, *The Journals of Henry Melchior Muhlenberg*, Theodore G. Tappert and John W. Doberstein, trans., 3 vols. (Philadelphia, 1958), vol. 3, 83; Chase and Lengel, eds., *Papers*, vol. 11, 391-392. The Reverend Henry Muhlenberg was the father of Peter Muhlenberg, a brigade commander in Washington's army.

3 Chase and Lengel, eds., *Papers*, vol. 11, 391-392.

4 McGuire, *Campaign*, vol. 2, 134; John A. Nagy, *Spies in the Continental Capital: Espionage Across Pennsylvania During the American Revolution* (Yardley, PA, 2011), 63; Reed, *Campaign*, 210. Following the battle of Germantown, Maj. John Clark of Nathanael Greene's staff managed the spy operations, assisted by Capt. Charles Craig, Capt. Allen McLane, Pvt. William Dunwoody, and Cadwalader Jones. After serving as a scout and courier in 1776, McLane raised a troop of horse in

*   *   *

Whatever the conditions in the city, the British were now firmly in control of Philadelphia. Washington was no longer in a position to recapture it or drive away the British army. As Howe rightly feared, Washington's strategy turned instead to starving out the occupiers. Nearly everything Howe's army needed—including military equipment, medical supplies and food—remained stored in the holds of British ships stuck downriver near Chester, Pennsylvania. The rows of *cheveaux-de-frise*, supported by Forts Mercer and Mifflin, blocked the Royal Navy from ascending the river.

Regrouping

While Howe pondered how to implement a strategy to open the waterway, he ordered a column of artillerymen, a grenadier battalion, and the 23rd Regiment of Foot to Chester about 15 miles distant to bring back supplies by land. The expedition returned with two eight-inch mortars, two eight-inch howitzers, 400 eight-inch shells, and 500 barrels of pork. "Up to now the army had obtained its provisions with great risk and much inconvenience," noted jaeger Capt. Johann Ewald in his journal, "for they had been transported from Chester to Philadelphia in flatboats manned by armed sailors along the bank of the Delaware under cover of dark nights, in spite of enemy vessels. Should such a convoy be taken by the enemy, the army would be exposed to the greatest privation." Establishing a protected land route would negate having to deal with the risky water route.[5]

When the British evacuated Billingsport on October 5, they left behind the American cannon but burned the platforms, gun carriages, buildings, and other items of value. "Every Thing that would take Fire is burnt," reported Lt. Col.

January 1777 and received a captain's commission. With these men, McLane scouted British positions around Philadelphia and led spying activities. Thompson, *Whitemarsh*, 43.

5 Reed, *Campaign*, 241; Jackson, *Fort Mifflin*, 30; Johann Ewald, *Diary of the American War: A Hessian Journal: Captain Johann Ewald*, ed. and trans. by Joseph P. Tustin (New Haven, CT, 1979), 96-97. Johann Ewald was a jaeger captain who played a major role at Brandywine and was in action again at Germantown. He entered the military at age 16 during the Seven Years' War and fought across modern-day Germany and was wounded in the leg in 1761. A drunken argument in 1770 led to a duel with a friend and the loss of his left eye, which he covered with an eye patch. Ewald was promoted to captain in 1774 in the Hessian Jaeger Corps. He arrived in America during late summer in 1776, where he established himself as a good and dependable officer. His jaeger company had been engaged in fighting around New York the previous year.

Samuel Smith, the commander of American forces at Mifflin, to Washington on October 7. In other words, Billingsport was now essentially useless to the Continental Army for harassing British shipping. The British moved their supply base from Wilmington, Delaware, to Chester, Pennsylvania. With the threat of Billingsport's guns eliminated, the Royal Navy began the tedious process of removing the *chevaux-de-frise* crossing the shipping lane west of Billingsport. In time, the British fleet could achieve Howe's goal of threatening Fort Mifflin.[6]

Washington's strategy to tighten the logistical noose around Philadelphia now hinged on holding Forts Mifflin and Mercer. If the Americans could maintain and protect the *chevaux-de-frise* blocking the river between the forts, the British supply ships would never make it to the city. Doing so, however, required the close cooperation of the army and naval forces, which past experience had demonstrated to be nearly impossible. "The state of our Water defence on the Delaware, is far from being as flattering, as could be wished," Washington told Congress three days after Germantown. On October 6, Lt. Col. Samuel Smith observed the dire need to garrison Red Bank, the location of Fort Mercer: "The Commodore and other Officers of the Navy think Red Bank of the utmost Consequence. I think from the Situation 400 Men might defend it with the Assistance which might be given from the fleet."[7]

The day before Washington wrote Congress, Admiral Howe, the general's brother, arrived with elements of the British navy and anchored between New Castle, Delaware and Reedy Island near Chester. In addition to his flagship HMS *Eagle*, the fleet included the warships HMS *Vigilant* and *Isis*, together with transports carrying "some Articles of Provisions and Military stores likely to be the soonest wanted for the Army." Admiral Howe immediately moved upriver for a meeting with Capt. Andrew Hamond of the HMS *Roebuck*, who spent the previous weeks gathering intelligence while keeping a watchful eye on the Delaware.[8]

---

6 Chase and Lengel, eds., *Papers*, vol. 11, 425; Hazard, et al, eds., *Archives*, Series 1, vol. 5, 648; Dorwart, *Fort Mifflin*, 36.

7 Dorwart, *Fort Mifflin*, 33; Chase and Lengel, eds., *Papers*, vol. 11, 414 & 417.

8 Quoted in Smith, *Fight for Delaware*, 11; Gruber, *Howe Brothers*, 248-249. The *Vigilant* was a privately owned merchant ship purchased by Admiral Howe in early 1777. He converted her into a large seaworthy battery mounting 14 guns. The HMS *Vigilant* had her regular compliment of guns replaced with one 24-pounder, nine two-pounders, and six four-pounders, all mounted on a single side. As a result of these modifications, she drew less than 12 feet of water. This would allow her to get into the back channel separating Fort Mifflin from Province and Carpenters islands. Arthur S.

For reasons that remain unclear, instead of moving north to take the unmanned Fort Mercer after capturing Billingsport, Lt. Col. Thomas Stirling with the battalion companies of the 10th and 42nd regiments returned to the west side of the Delaware and moved back to Chester to escort a provision train into Philadelphia. According to American Capt. Samuel Massey of the Pennsylvania militia, Stirling's troops rounded up cattle in the surrounding countryside and drove them to "Palmer's Point (where they landed) & reembarked their Troops for the Pennsylvania Shore . . . after their Reembarkation an enterprizing Company of Jersey Artillery & Militia . . . followed the British to Palmer's point & finding the Troops reembarked & a small part of ye Detachment left behind for the preservation [protection] of the Cattle (the Americans) fell upon them And possess'd themselves of the Provision."[9]

Several military movements of varying significance unfolded nearly simultaneously. In a half-hearted attempt to relieve John Burgoyne's embattled command in upstate New York, Henry Clinton, the British commander of the New York garrison, led an expedition up the Hudson River from New York City on October 3. While the British fleet was bobbing in the Delaware River below Philadelphia, Clinton captured Forts Montgomery and Clinton below West Point, New York. He made little effort thereafter to relieve Burgoyne and withdrew British forces from the Hudson River forts on October 26 so that he could send reinforcements to Howe's army from the New York garrison.

While this was transpiring, the American fleet in the Delaware launched an ineffective attack against British shipping. Galleys, small ships that relied on oars for propulsion, fired on the British working to remove the *chevaux-de-frise*, but the range was too far to be effective. The Americans next carried out plans to block the

---

Lefkowitz, *George Washington's Revenge: The 1777 New Jersey Campaign and How General Washington Turned Defeat into the Strategy that Won the Revolution* (Blue Ridge Summit, PA, 2022), 233.

9 Jackson, *British Army*, 27, 53 & 59; Samuel Massey, "Journal of Captain Samuel Massey 1776-1778," *Bulletin of the Historical Society of Montgomery County Pennsylvania*, John F. Reed, ed., 39 vols. (Norristown, PA,1976), vol. 20, no. 3, 231. No primary source has come to light to explain why the British abandoned Billingsport. Samuel Smith, *Fight for the Delaware*, 11, claims the force was ordered back to Pennsylvania when a foraging party was harassed by New Jersey militia some thought might overwhelm the isolated garrison. Another secondary source implies the two British regiments had orders to return to the main army once they destroyed Billingsport. The entire operation is something of a mystery considering the British reoccupied the position in late October. Reed, *Campaign*, 41-42.

openings in the obstructions made by the British by stripping everything of value from the brig *Vesuvius* and sloop *Strombello* and sinking them to fill the gaps.[10]

Supply Problems

While the British continued their efforts to open the Delaware, Washington responded to Howe on October 6 regarding the treatment of civilians. "I am happy to find you express so much sensibility to the sufferings of the Inhabitants, as it gives room to hope, that those wanton & unnecessary depredations which have heretofore in too many instances marked the conduct of your Army, will be discontinued for the future," chastised the Virginian. It was not only Howe's army that was suffering from a shortage of provisions. The plight of the population in Philadelphia concerned the American commander, but larger matters were at hand: he had to cut Howe off from the outside world. Washington ordered his militia to establish posts in Bucks County north of the city "upon the different Roads" leading into it "as near philada as they possibly can and pay particular attention to stopping all persons from going in with marketing," explained Washington. "If any are taken coming out of the town from whom any particular information is obtained . . . report it to me. If any persons leave the Country and go in to the Enemy their Horses and Cattle should be immediately secured for the public & sent to this Army, leaving their Milch Cows and a horse or two to draw wood &ca for support of their familie."[11]

Invaluable intelligence reached Washington that provisions were growing scarce in Philadelphia. When he learned wagons were being regularly dispatched to Chester to haul supplies from the fleet, he employed Pennsylvania militia to harass the supply line along the Great Chester Road south of the city. These militiamen patrolled a line stretching from Vandering's Mill on the Schuylkill to Grubs Landing between Marcus Hook and Wilmington on the Delaware River. On October 8, militia commander John Armstrong received orders to send 600 men "across the Schulkill, with directions to keep himself in such a situation as will be most convenient for interrupting the enemy's intercourse, between Philadelphia

---

10 Israel Putnam's decision to dispatch three brigades to Washington in September left his department with only General Samuel Parsons's 1st Connecticut Brigade as a mobile field force, the 5th New York Regiment, part of Lamb's artillery, and some New York militia to garrison the forts. Maj. Gen. Sir Henry Clinton took advantage of this weakness and moved against them. Wright, *Army*, 118; Reed, *Campaign*, 271.

11 Chase and Lengel, eds., *Papers*, vol. 11, 405, 408-409

and Chester &c.—He [Gen. James Potter] is to take every method to keep himself well acquainted with what is doing, and to embrace every opportunity of cutting off the convoys and intercepting the dispatches passing between their army and shipping; and to use every method to prevent their getting supplies from the country around them."[12]

On October 7, the same day Burgoyne lost the second battle of Saratoga (Bemis Heights) that sealed his fate on the battlefield, British engineer Captain Montresor scouted Province Island opposite and north of Fort Mifflin. The Pennsylvania Navy promptly dispatched a pair of galleys into the mouth of the Schuylkill to force the engineering party away. Work on the island could not continue until the pesky vessels were dealt with, but crossing the Schuylkill to reach the island was difficult and vulnerable to attack. Was there a land route to supply Province Island? Bridging the river at Webb's Ferry offered Montresor a good option. Before that could happen, fortifications would have to be erected to protect the crossing site.[13]

Delaware River Defenses

By this time Washington was more than a little concerned about the Pennsylvania Navy. The failure at Germantown left Howe holding Philadelphia and required Washington to maintain the Continental Army north of the city to prevent his enemy from launching excursions against supply depots in the Pennsylvania backcountry. Controlling the Delaware was the game, and that meant keeping the British fleet below the *chevaux-de-frise*. Almost overnight, the naval elements and river forts assumed an oversized role in American strategy. But the water arm lacked effectiveness and, given its high desertion rate, housed men

---

12 Ibid., 429. The reorganization of the American army, meanwhile, continued apace. A battalion of Virginia militia under Col. William Rumney arrived and was assigned to Charles Scott's brigade. John Laurens, a 22-year-old acting as a volunteer aide to Washington, received the position permanently. The effectiveness of buckshot at Germantown had not passed unnoticed, and Washington issued orders to put buckshot in every cartridge. Ibid., 404. Like his father, the President of the Continental Congress, John Laurens, was devoted to the commander in chief. Born in 1754 in Charleston, South Carolina, educated in Geneva, Switzerland, and fluent in French, Laurens joined Washington's staff as a volunteer aide-de-camp in August 1777. Christian McBurney, *George Washington's Nemesis: The Outrageous Treason and Unfair Court-Martial of Major General Charles Lee during the Revolutionary War* (El Dorado, CA, 2020), 266.

13 Webb's Ferry was located near where I-95 crosses the Schuylkill River today. Montresor, "Journals," 463.

suspect as to their loyalties. "Am sorry to find so dastardly a spirit prevailing in the Navy," he wrote Lt. Col. Samuel Smith, the commander of Fort Mifflin, on October 7. "I hope there will still be good men enough left to defend the Fort and obstructions till we can give them a decisive stroke by land." On the same day he wrote Smith, Washington informed Commodore Hazelwood, "you will do all in your power to keep possession of the Ground [Fort Mercer in New Jersey], should the Enemy attempt to take it."[14]

Fortifying the position opposite Fort Mifflin became the next item of business. Fort Mercer, guarding the Delaware River from the New Jersey shoreline, however, still needed a viable garrison. Washington ordered Christopher Greene, a 40-year-old colonel and distant cousin of Nathanael Greene, to take command of Mercer with his 1st Rhode Island and Col. Israel Angell's 2nd Rhode Island regiments that had arrived at Coryell's Ferry above Trenton on the Delaware. "With the assistance of this Force upon the land, I hope you will be enabled to keep your Station with your fleet, and if you can do that," he informed Hazelwood, "I have not the least doubt but we shall by our operations by land and Water oblige the Enemy to abandon Philada." The Rhode Islanders realized the importance of their assignment. "When Genl Washington left [Philadelphia] he took care to poste a Garrison [Lt. Col. William Smith's command] in Fort Mifflin," wrote the 2nd Rhode Island's Sgt. Jeremiah Greenman in his diary. It was "not as strong as the importance & exigence of the place did require," he added, "but such as the Army could afford." Howe, meanwhile, remained active. His British warships pushed aside the sunken American hulls and reopened a passage through the *chevaux-de-frise* near Billingsport.[15]

The British began construction on a small battery designed to hold medium 12-pounders to protect Webb's Ferry on the northern shore of the Schuylkill. "Before it was finished 3 rebel Galleys came … [and] fired grape 3 inch shot, which we did not return, until our Battery was completed," noted Montresor in his journal on October 8. Charles Cornwallis dispatched Maj. John Vatass's 10th Regiment of Foot, which arrived in Philadelphia after participating in the Billingsport operation, to protect the laborers. The British attempted to ferry the infantrymen into

---

14 Chase and Lengel, eds., *Papers*, vol. 11, 421-422 & 425; Dorwart, *Fort Mifflin*, 33.

15 Jeremiah Greenman, *Diary of a Common Soldier in the American Revolution 1775-1782*, Robert Bray & Paul Bushnell, eds. (DeKalb, IL, 1978), 79. Washington continued to order troops down from the Northern theater to reinforce his army. Jackson's Additional Continental Regiment was ordered to march from Boston to Pennsylvania on October 7. Wright, *Army*, 215.

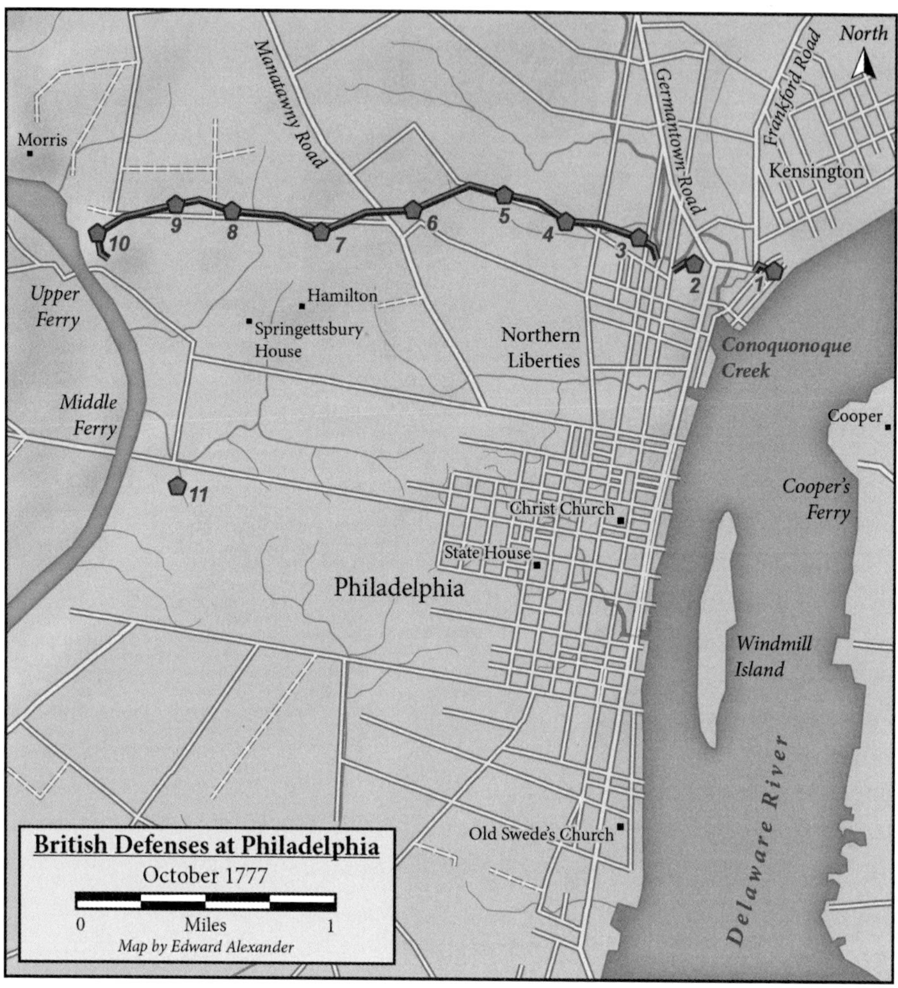

position, but American naval fire (which wounded several of the men), combined with the incoming tide, made landing them impossible. The British needed a foothold on Province Island not only for operations against Fort Mifflin, but also to protect Howe's tenuous supply line along Darby Road (the route to Chester) south of the city.[16]

Howe also wanted more and stronger fortifications to better protect against the irksome American militia infiltrating his army's vital supply routes. Montresor was tasked with erecting redoubts on the city side of the Schuylkill River to cover

16 Jackson, *Navy*, 142; Montresor, "Journals," 463.

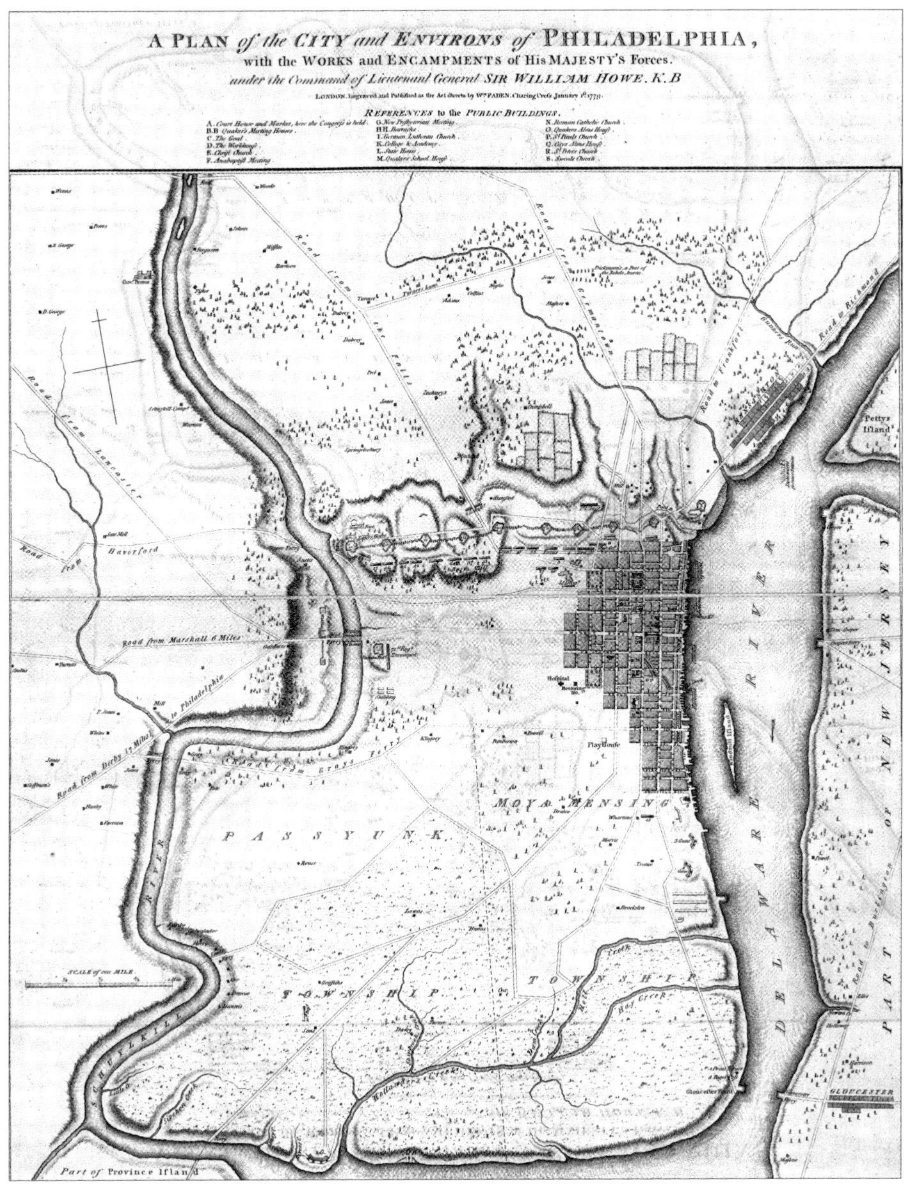

Plan of Philadelphia showing the British works and encampments north of city. *LOC*

the Middle and Grey's ferries, additional fortifications on the other side of the river, and the construction of a bridge at the Middle Ferry. It was a lot of work, and the civilian labor force available to the British engineers was limited and stretched all too thin.

More than a week earlier on September 28, Captain Montresor and Lord Cornwallis had surveyed the terrain in the Northern Liberties selected by the engineer for a line of fortifications. The new defensive front, which could be manned with detachments from the main army, would free up the bulk of Howe's command for operations against the Delaware River forts. The line, Montresor explained to Cornwallis, would require 10 redoubts along with two demilunes and a ravelin, with a front covered by a ditch and abatis and the escarpment of the earthworks fraised—meaning pointed stakes driven into the ramparts in a horizontal or inclined position. Cornwallis agreed and work began. When the line was finished around October 18, it stretched from below Kensington to a hill along the Schuylkill River called Fairmount overlooking the Upper Ferry—a distance of more than two miles.[17]

The Continental Camp

On October 8, Washington moved his entire army from along Perkiomen Creek at Pennypacker Mills, ten miles into the vicinity of Towamencin Township, a region populated by Dutch, Swiss, Welsh and German residents. The movement placed his Continental army just 16 miles northwest of General Howe's garrison at Germantown. The Americans were now closer to reinforcements coming down from the north, and reinforcing the critical river forts was now that much easier.[18]

---

17 One redoubt was constructed at each road leading into the city. Eventually, two additional advanced redoubts were added to the plan 250 yards north of the main defensive line. Jackson, *British Army*, 3. The upper ferry is the location of today's Spring Garden Street Bridge, the Middle Ferry is today's Market Street Bridge, and Lower (or Gray's) Ferry is today's Grays Ferry Avenue Bridge. Ricardo A. Herrera, *Feeding Washington's Army: Surviving the Valley Forge Winter of 1778* (Chapel Hill, NC, 2022), 64. Once completed, the line of defensive redoubts stretched from the Delaware River to the Schuylkill River roughly along modern Spring Garden Street. The redoubts were numbered from east to the west. The final armament varied for each redoubt as follows: Redoubt #1 (two 18-pounders, two 4-pounders, and two 5 ½-in. howitzers); Redoubt #2 (two 12-pounders); Redoubt #3 (6-pounders); Redoubt #4 (two 8-pounders); Redoubt #5 (two 12-pounders); Redoubt #6 (two 6-pounders); Redoubt #7 (two 12-pounders, one 5 ½-in. howitzer); Redoubt #8 (two 6-pounders); Redoubt #9 (two 12-pounders); Redoubt #10 (two 18-pounders). Bob Ruppert, "Fortifying Philadelphia: A Chain of Redoubts and Floating Bridges," *Journal of the American Revolution*, February 18, 2015, www.allthingsliberty.com, accessed 21 April 2023.

18 Thomas J. McGuire, *Battle of Paoli* (Mechanicsburg, PA, 2000), 257. The army moved down Skippack Pike, turned left onto Forty Foot Road, and camped near North Wales Road (modern Sumneytown Pike) north of the pike on the Frederick Wampole farm. The next day, Washington established his headquarters at Wampole's home. McGuire, *Campaign*, vol. 2, 133. The house was destroyed in 1881, and only the barn foundations are said to be original. Reed, *Campaign*, 249.

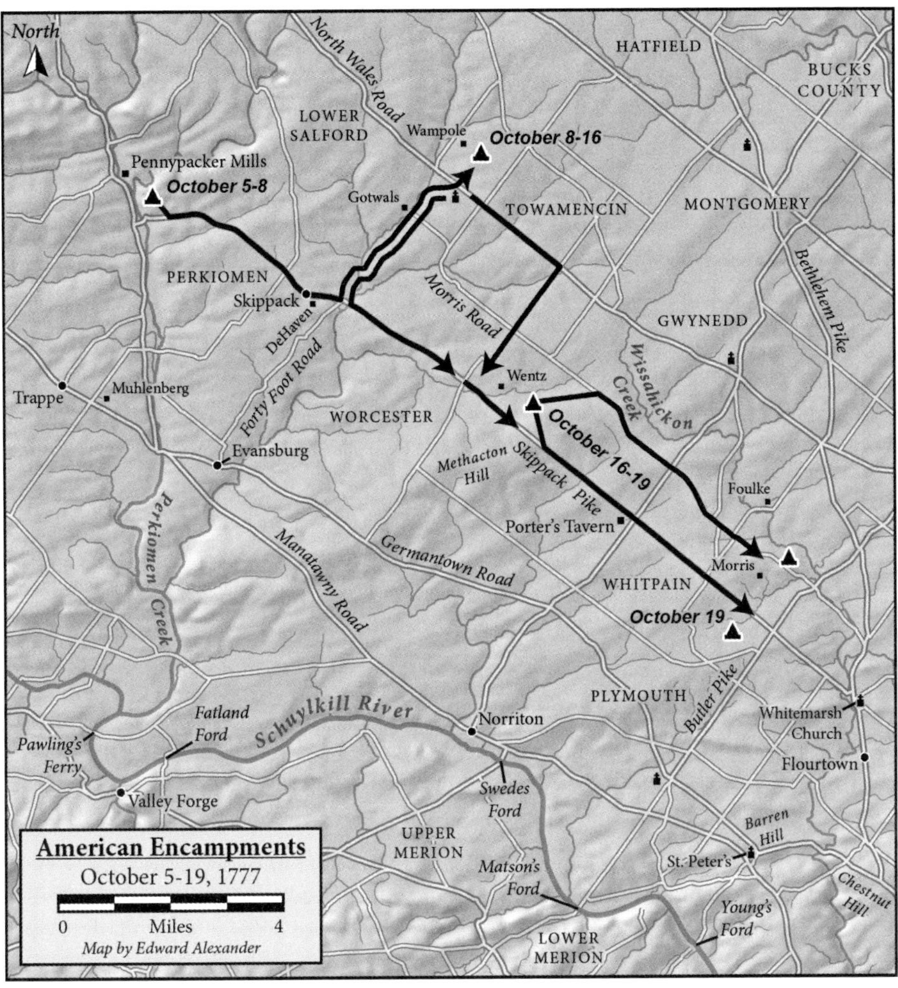

For some observers, Washington and his army were not doing enough. Congressman Charles Carroll expressed concern about the army's lack of professionalism. "It is evident that our men do not want resolution, but they want discipline," argued the politician in an October 8 letter. "[I]f they could have been rallied after the repulse from Chew's house & had renewed the attack when the fog cleared away [at Germantown], it is more than probable that the Enemy rather than risk another onset would have retreated to Chester," he continued, demonstrating his complete lack of understanding of both the course of the battle and the British army. "Soldiers can not be formed on a sudden, but were our officers better, they might be sooner formed." Carroll changed his concern to inflation and the growing cost of the war: "I am apprehensive the want of money, I mean of good money, will subject us to great difficulties & Such I fear as we shall find almost insurmountable." Others disagreed. Richard Henry Lee remained confident. "Another such battle as the last," he predicted to Patrick Henry, "will totally unfit Gen. Howe for pursuing further hostilities this campaign, and again possess us of Philadelphia."[19]

Washington found himself far too busy to stop and react to criticism from politicians safely away from the front. As the decisive confrontation played out along the Delaware River, word arrived that Francis Nash succumbed to his gruesome Germantown wound on October 8. Aides had carried the mortally wounded general on a litter to Porter's Tavern on Skippack Pike, then to the DeHaven house in Skippack Township, and finally to the Adam Gotwals home on Forty Foot Road near the army's new camp in Towamencin Township. Washington had sent his personal physician, Dr. James Craik, in an attempt to save Nash, to no avail.[20]

The same day Nash died, Thomas Mifflin, the army's quartermaster general, accused of embezzlement and often absent from his duties, submitted his resignation in a flurry of frustration over not getting a field command. Congress refused to accept his resignation as major general, but did allow him to resign as quartermaster general. Washington could not fill his position until finding a suitable replacement, but that did not stop Mifflin from leaving the army and his duty for his home in Reading, Pennsylvania. A debate was raging in Congress about whether a standing army was more effective and efficient than smaller armies raised and supplied by individual states. The body elected Mifflin to serve on the Board of War created to resolve the question and picked Mifflin's deputy, Henry Lutterloh to run the quartermaster department in Mifflin's place.[21]

---

19 Smith, et al., eds., *Letters*, vol. 8, 73; Richard Henry Lee, *The Letters of Richard Henry Lee, 1762-1778*, 2 vols. (New York, 1911), vol. 1, 326.

20 The Gotwals home was a little over a mile southwest of the Sumneytown Pike intersection.

21 John A. Nagy, *Rebellion in the Ranks: Mutinies of the American Revolution* (Yardley, PA, 2008), 58. Henry Lutterloh was appointed deputy quartermaster general for the main Continental Army on July 1, 1777. Congress created the Board of War in June 1776. The Board was originally designed to support the Continental Army, not manage its operations. According to historian Mark Lender, there was no provision for the Board to "assume a direct role in logistics, strategic planning, training, field operations, or other daily activities." Washington reported directly to Congress, not to the Board. Lender, *Cabal!*, 111.

Delaware River Defenses

Plans along the waterfront continued apace. Commodore Hazelwood sent nine galleys into the Schuylkill River on the morning of October 9 to reduce the British battery at Webb's Ferry. The noisy distraction prompted the British to dispatch an engineer with 100 grenadiers onto Province Island to shield the increasingly exhausted force of paid civilians working to erect the battery. The fleet disrupted this work by throwing grapeshot into the position that killed a grenadier and wounded three others but withdrew after failing to make any significant headway. A floating American battery and two armed brigs anchored in the Schuylkill's mouth off Little Mud Island for a renewed bombardment the next morning.[22]

Howe's aide, Capt. Friedrich von Muenchhausen, ventured down to the river from Germantown "to see the newly erected battery, and had the pleasure to see not only Mud-Fort [Fort Mifflin] and Province Island, but also the entire American Navy, which was in clear view," recorded the officer. "All ships flew very large flags." Engineer John Montresor reported during the night completing stockpiling supplies at Webb's Ferry for erecting batteries directly opposite Fort Mifflin: "2 medium 12 pounder, two 8 inch Howitzers, and 2 Eight Inch mortars, and 100 rounds to each . . . a Detachment of Three hundred Grenadiers and one Field 6 Pounder." Montresor gathered a large quantity of timber, together with tools and 400 fascines for the effort.[23]

Cutting off supplies to Howe's army weighed heavily on many Continental decision-makers, including John Hancock, president of the Continental Congress. "The absolute Necessity of cutting off all Supplies and Intelligence from the Enemy in and near the City of Philada and thereby preventing any Intercourse between them and the disaffected in the State of Pennsylvania and elsewhere," he informed Washington on October 9, "has induced the Congress to . . . authorize you to sentence by Court Martial any Person convicted of either of the above

---

22 Reed, *Campaign*, 276.

23 Jackson, *Navy*, 143; Von Muenchhausen, *At Howe's Side*, 40. Elizabeth (Betsy) Griscom Ross had been contracted to make flags for the Pennsylvania Navy in May 1777. While the true design and look of these flags remains inconclusive, these were likely the flags von Muenchhausen observed. Montresor, "Journals," 463.

mentioned Offences, or of acting as a Guide or Pilot, to suffer Death or such other Punishment as may be thought adequate."[24]

Despite the importance of the Delaware operations, Washington's subordinates accomplished little in slowing the efforts of British engineers intent on taking Fort Mifflin. American batteries in Mifflin and from fleet assets positioned in the mouth of the Schuylkill River opened fire once again on the British positions to no effect on the morning of October 10. The British finished a battery west of Mifflin on Carpenter's Island and another, recorded Captain Montresor, with an eight-inch howitzer and eight-inch mortar, was begun "250 yards from the enemy's floating battery, and 500 yards West of the Fort on a dyke in an overflowed meadow."[25]

Creating the necessary gun platforms proved more difficult than anticipated because the Americans cut the dikes on Province and Carpenter's islands creating knee-deep swamp-like conditions precisely where the British needed to emplace their guns. The dikes themselves became the only viable place remaining to build them, which left them exposed to enemy fire. Moving the guns onto Carpenter's Island proved both laborious and dangerous. One artillery-hauling raft crew, explained Royal Artillerymen Francis Downman on October 11, "went to the bottom in an instant, with several men and horses, and one of each was drowned." The British dragged another artillery piece "up to the battery through a mile of mud and water, for the whole island is a flat, and from rain, and the rebels cutting the embankment, the whole was nearly under water," continued the artilleryman. The Americans had only one gun in Fort Mifflin positioned to return fire against the ongoing British operations, but lacked adequate ammunition for the 32-pounder to do so.[26]

24 The offenses under discussion included providing supplies and any other material aid to the British. Chase and Lengel, eds., *Papers*, vol. 11, 461. While the drama along the Delaware River continued, Francis Nash was buried with full military honors at 10:00 a.m. on October 9 at Towamencin Mennonite Meeting House. "All Officers whose Circumstances will admit of it, will attend and pay respect to a brave Man who died in defence of his Country," ordered Washington. Chase and Lengel, eds., *Papers*, vol. 11, 452.

25 Montresor, "Journals," 464

26 McGuire, *Campaign*, vol. 2, 187; Whinyates, *Services*, 40; Reed, *Campaign*, 276-277.

The Continental Camp

Not all members of Congress expressed displeasure with the condition of the Continental army. "Our army is in excellent spirit, satisfied they can beat the enemy, and keen for another opportunity of trying," assured an anonymous congressman, and "they will probably be indulged in a few days." Major Henry Miller of the 1st Pennsylvania Regiment agreed: "Our army is in higher spirits than ever, being convinced from the first officer to the soldier, that our quitting the field [at Germantown] must be ascribed to other causes than the force of the enemy: for even they acknowledged that we fled from victory. We hope to meet them soon again, and, with the assistance of Providence, to restore our suffering citizens to their possessions and homes." Doctor Benjamin Rush vehemently disagreed with these opinions and had nothing good to say about the army's commander, his staff aides, or his top generals. "The commander-in-chief at this time [is] the idol of America—governed by Genl [Nathanael] Greene—Gen. [Henry] Knox & Col. [Alexander] Hamilton, one of his aids, a young man of 21 years of age," he seethed to his diary. Washington, continued Dr. Rush, has "4 Major Generals—Greene, Sullivan, Stirling & Stephen. The 1st a sycophant to the general, timid, speculative, without enterprise; the 2nd, weak, vain, without dignity, fond of scribbling, in the field a madman. The 3d, a proud, vain, lazy, ignorant drunkard. The 4th, a sordid, boasting, cowardly sot."[27]

While politicians carped and at least one doctor slandered his officers, Washington worked to improve the discipline of his army. "It is not for every officer to know the principle upon which every order issues, and to judge how far it may, or may not be dispensed with, or suspended, but their duty to carry them into execution with the utmost punctuality and exactness," directed the Virginian in general orders that went out on October 10 referencing mistakes made at Germantown. "They are to consider, that military movements are like the working of a clock, and will go equally regular and easy, if every officer does his duty, but

---

27 *North Carolina Gazette*, October 31, 1777; "A Memoir of General Henry Miller," Henry Miller Watts, ed., in *The Pennsylvania Magazine of History and Biography*, 148 vols. (Philadelphia, 1888), vol. 12, 427; S. Weir Mitchell, ed., "Historical Notes of Dr. Benjamin Rush, 1777," *Pennsylvania Magazine of History Biography*, 148 vols. (Philadelphia, 1903), vol. 27, 147; McGuire, *Campaign*, vol. 2, 133. It is unclear why Dr. Rush held such passionate feelings against these officers. Rush was born outside of Philadelphia in 1745 and attended West Nottingham Academy, the College of Philadelphia, and Edinburgh University. In 1777, he received appointment to surgeon general of the middle department of the Continental Army.

without it, be as easily disordered; because neglect from any one (like the stopping of a wheel) disorders the whole."[28]

Carpenter's Island

On the morning of October 11, the motley American fleet, supported by the artillery at Fort Mifflin and a landing party of some 70 men, launched a combined operation to assault Carpenter's Island adjacent to Province Island and northwest of the fort. The landing party stormed the British battery position after a two-hour bombardment. Few of the attackers had any idea their effort would bag scores of enemy soldiers at little cost and trigger the enemy to launch a court-martial inquiry into how such a thing occurred.

"Fifty of the enemy landed, under the cover of their Gallies, moved to the right of the Front of the battery and then got behind trees and banks to shelter themselves," explained British Matross (gunner's mate) Donald MacLean. "The men in the battery, upon seeing these men land, and the fire upon them being very heavy, one of them being killed and another wounded, they got up, rather in confusion."

"What shall we do?" yelled Ens. Richard Hankey to Capt.-Lieut. Robert Blackmore, "We shall all be killed if you don't strike or put up a flag of distress!"

In the heated debate that followed, "Capt. Blackmore asked the men in general, what they thought of it," as if such a weighty military matter was to be decided by majority vote. Someone shoved the flag into the hands of a grenadier named Blakeney, continued MacLean, and "desired him to hoist it, & he was going to do it." Aghast at what was transpiring, MacLean "beg'd for God's sake that he would not do it yet, and took it out of Blakeney's hand." An infuriated Ensign Hankey yelled, "Is there no Grenadier or other Man here, that will shoot that Artillery Man [MacLean]?" There was not, and "Blakeney got upon the Gun and hoisted it."[29]

---

28 Chase and Lengel, eds., *Papers*, vol. 11, 471-472. The army was resting in Towamencin Township when it was reinforced with Brig. Gen. Jedidiah Huntingdon's Connecticut Brigade by October 11. "Huntington Papers: Correspondence of the Brothers Joshua and Jedidiah Huntington During the Period of the American Revolution," in *Collections of the Connecticut Historical Society*, 31 vols. (Hartford, CT, 1923), vol. 20, 373.

29 Chase and Lengel, eds., *Papers*, vol. 11, 489; British War Office, Judge Advocate General Office, Court Martial Proceedings and Board of General Officers' Minutes: WO71/84, October 16-25, 1777.

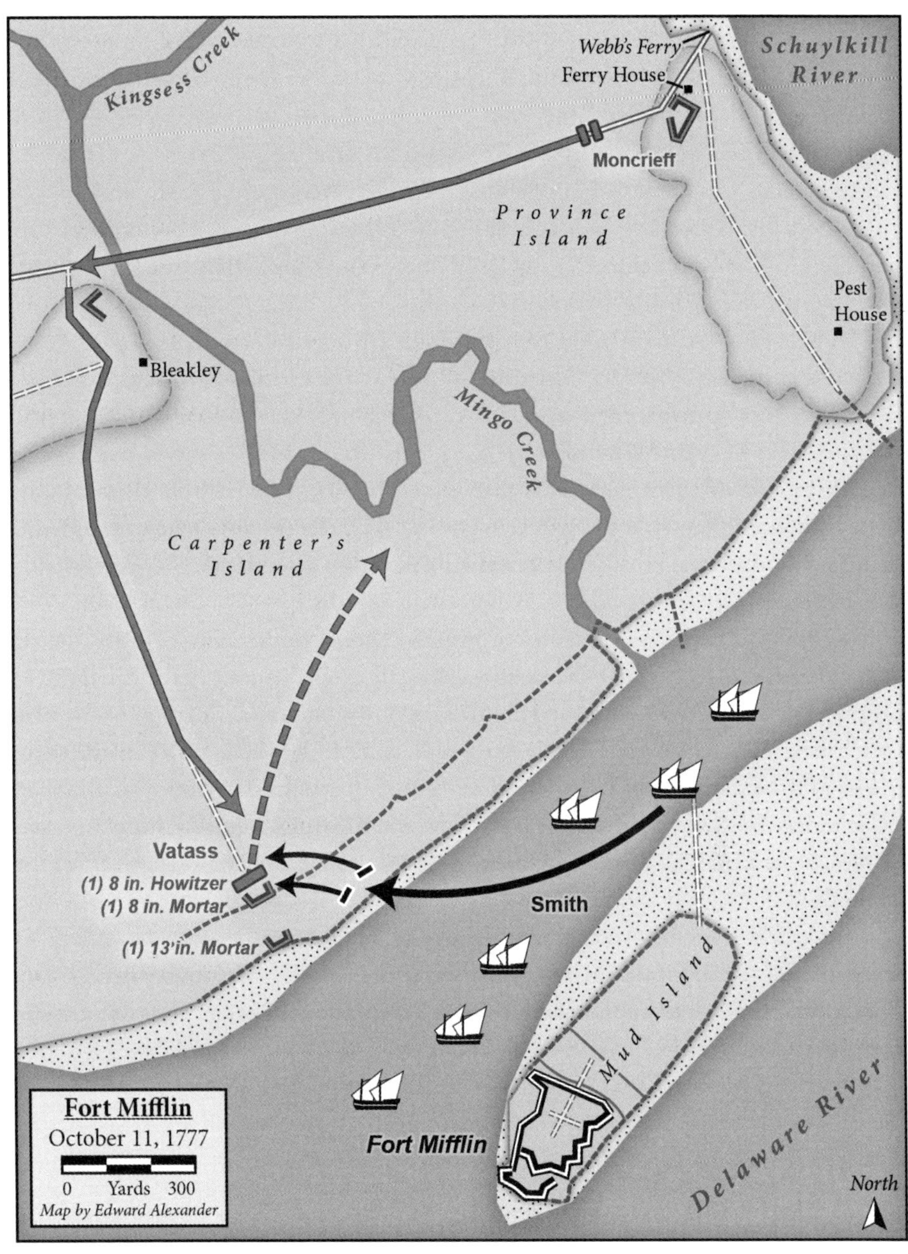

"Six or Seven boats immediately came on shore, in the front of the battery, and a small party [of Americans] came up to the battery, and carried the officers and men [away as prisoners]," recalled MacLean. William Finch, a lieutenant in the 27th Regiment of Foot, together with Ensign Richard Hawkins of the 57th Regiment of Foot and 56 enlisted men, surrendered out of a detachment of 300-400. The prisoners were members of the British 1st Grenadier Battalion and represented the 10th, 17th, 23rd, 27th, and 28th Regiments of Foot. Four others were Royal artillerymen. Major John Vatass and Capt.-Lt. Robert Blackmore of the 10th Regiment of Foot were court-martialed for their role in the embarrassing affair.[30]

Surrender was the last thing the Royal Artillerymen wanted to do under those circumstances. According to MacLean, they "saw some of our people coming up, and therefore drop'd behind, as much as [they] could, and whilst the enemy were hurrying the Men [British prisoners] into the boats . . . by jumping over [Mingo] creek made [the] escape." Engineer Capt. James Moncrieff led a rescue party of 50 Hessians grenadiers over to Carpenter's from Province Island. When Moncrieff and the reinforcements drew near, the captain boldly called "out to the English Soldiers, who were then Prisoners, to quit the Enemy, and stand on one side, as he intended to fire on them, and then called out to the Enemy, who were already in the Boats, and out of reach of the Guns, to go off." The rescue party managed to free a handful of prisoners, but the Americans managed to row the rest to Fort Mifflin and captivity.

Moncrieff's demand outraged Fort Mifflin's commander, who believed the act violated the rules of war. "Notwithstanding they had surrendered themselves prisoners & the party who rescued them came down under the sanction of the Flag then Flying, I conceive your Exclly has a right to demand them, or to charge them to Genl Howe," urged Smith to Washington later that same day. Smith summed up the action by reporting, "We attacked it with the Floating Batteries, Block houses, Gallies, & 32 Pounder from the Battery & in short time obliged them to hoist the white flag."[31]

The effort cost the Americans just two killed and another five wounded. As these events played out on the western shore of the Delaware River, Col. Christopher Greene marched 35 miles with his regiment to reach Fort Mercer late in the evening.[32]

---

30 British Court Martial Records, October 16-25, 1777.

31 British Court Martial Records, October 16-25, 1777; McGuire, *Campaign*, vol. 2, 138 & 189-190. Maj. John Vatass, commander of the 10th Regiment of Foot and Capt.-Lieut. Robert Blackmore would be court martialed for the surrender. Vatass was found guilty on October 25 and resigned from the army five days later. Blackmore was also found guilty and ordered cashiered from the service. Chase and Lengel, eds., *Papers*, vol. 11, 489.

32 Howard H. Peckham, ed., *The Toll of Independence: Engagements & Battle Casualties of the American Revolution* (Chicago, 1974), 43.

Fort Mercer

While marching across Bucks County with the 1st and 2nd Rhode Island regiments to join Washington, Col. Christopher Greene received orders to take his 1st Rhode Island and man Fort Mercer, leaving the 2nd Rhode Island temporarily behind in Bucks County. Washington hoped New Jersey militia would augment the fort's garrison so he could use Colonel Angell's 2nd regiment elsewhere. The New Jersey militia quickly disappointed Washington, which required Angell to hasten on to rejoin Greene.

Greene's men, meanwhile, tramped 35 miles and arrived at Mercer late in the evening on October 11. Greene received orders on October 8 to cooperate with Lt. Col. Samuel Smith at Fort Mifflin and Commodore Hazelwood of the Navy "in every measure necessary for the defence of the obstructions in the river and to counteract every attempt the enemy may make for their removal." The Continental and Pennsylvania navies combined to form a motley conglomeration of vessels wholly incapable of dealing with the British navy. They needed every ounce of support Forts Mifflin and Mercer could provide, just as the forts needed the merged fleet. Captain Thomas-Antoine de Mauduit du Plessis, who had rushed the Chew house with John Laurens at Germantown to set fire to the doors, had extensive training with artillery and was dispatched to the river forts as artillery commander. Washington directed Hazelwood to "afford him [du Plessis] every Assistance of Cannon and Stores, and if he should want a few Men to work the Guns, I beg he may have such as have been used to it." Washington also expected the young French captain to provide Colonel Greene at Fort Mercer any engineering or other assistance necessary.[33]

Mercer needed a garrison 3,000 strong to hold it, but when Colonel Greene reached the fort, he found only a small force of New Jersey militia commanded by Col. Elijah Hand. His own 1st Rhode Island boasted but 252 men and Capt.-Lt. David Cook's Continental Artillery company just 65 more. All told, the defenders numbered no more than 400 men. General Silas Newcomb of the New Jersey

---

33 McGuire, *Campaign*, vol. 2, 138. To get to Fort Mercer, Greene marched down the Pennsylvania side to Bristol, crossed the Delaware to Burlington, New Jersey, and marched south to the position. Reed, *Campaign*, 269-273; Chase and Lengel, eds., *Papers*, vol. 11, 422, 437. The Pennsylvania State Navy contingent consisted of 13 galleys (oar-power), 20 half-galleys (oars and sail), and numerous other smaller craft. The Continental Navy contingent consisted of one brig, five sloops, a schooner, and a few smaller craft. None of these were a match for a British ship-of-the-line. Many only bore a single gun. The main advantage they had was light draft and maneuverability outside the shipping channels.

militia (the same officer involved in the loss of Billingsport nine days earlier) had orders to reinforce Greene with 150 additional troops, but whether they would even arrive was unknown. The newcomers pitched their tents outside the walls with a command tent erected inside for Greene and his staff.[34]

"Upon Col. Greens arrivle the works were in no state of defence being so large as to require 3,000 Men badly laid out & not finished," explained Rhode Island chaplain Ebenezer David. French staff officer Marquis de Chastellux visited the site three years later in 1780 and agreed: "The Americans, little practiced in the art of fortification, and always disposed to undertake works beyond their strength, had made those of Red Bank too extensive." French artilleryman Capt. du Plessis-Mauduit fully agreed. Disgusted by what he found when he arrived, he organized a major construction operation with Colonel Greene to somehow make Mercer defensible.[35]

Without enough troops to man Mercer, du Plessis-Mauduit abandoned the rectangular northern extension and concentrated the garrison in the lower redoubt. The Frenchman ordered an east-west earthen wall erected near the lower redoubt to make it defensible from all sides, and the earth berms planked to prevent dirt from filling the ditch, also denying attackers handholds or footholds. According to de Chastellux, the foreign gunnery officer altered the works "by making an intersection from east to west, which transformed them into a sort of large redoubt of approximately pentagonal shape." Short on tools, Colonel Greene ordered his men to call upon nearby residents for whatever they needed, and to confiscate anything the owners refused to provide.

The hard work paid off by transforming Mercer into a smaller and more defensible position with a "good earthen rampart with pointed stakes projecting from below the parapet . . . a ditch, and an abatis in front of the ditch, constituted the whole strength of this post, in which were placed three hundred men, and fourteen pieces of cannon," concluded de Chastellux. According to Hessian Pvt. Johann Dohla's diary, who visited the site later in the campaign, the Americans also built an underground magazine and filled it with "flour, bread, meat and rum." The changes to the fort came at a cost: the Continentals demolished Quaker Whitall's

---

34 Smith, *Fight for Delaware*, 16; Jackson, *Navy*, 149, 153-154 & 439.

35 Ebenezer David, *A Rhode Island Chaplain in the Revolution: Letters of Ebenezer David to Nicholas Brown 1775-1778*, Jeannette D. Black & William Greene Roelker, eds. (Providence, RI, 1949), 52; Marquis de Chastellux, *Travels in North America in the Years 1780, 1781 and 1782*, 2 vols. (Chapel Hill, NC, 1963), vol. 1, 157.

family farm buildings just south of the fort's walls for wood and cut down his fruit trees to make sharpened stakes.[36]

The River War Continues

News arrived at Washington's headquarters that Gen. Henry Clinton had captured Forts Clinton and Montgomery in the Hudson Highlands. The loss of fixed positions was unsettling, and he knew Mercer and Mifflin could suffer the same fate. Washington, however, had no choice but to remain focused on holding the Delaware and maintaining control of the two forts.

Lieutenant Colonel Smith, meanwhile, conducted another joint attack near Fort Mifflin on October 12. After shelling the British battery on Carpenter's Island south of Mingo Creek "with a heavy cannonade, from the Fort, Floating Batteries and Gallies," recorded engineer Capt. John Montresor in his journal, the position was stormed by about 500 men from the fort's garrison "in the front and 2 flanks of the Battery with Bayonets fixed." The battery's small 50-man Hessian-British garrison, commanded by a Hessian captain, "received it with a well directed fire of musketry" that lasted about three-quarters of an hour, while "the rebels conceal[ed] themselves under the Dyke and behind trees and bushes."[37]

Alerted by the noisy attack, "Major [William] Gardiner with 50 Grenadiers [of the 2nd Grenadier Battalion] moved from his post [on Province Island] to outflank the rebels and the battery," continued Montresor, "which he succeeded in . . . during which the detachment of the battery kept up a smart fire." Unable to take the position, the Americans fell back after losing two killed and five wounded. Among the latter was 20-year-old Sgt. Wardwell Green of the 1st Rhode Island, who "received a musket ball which entered near his throat and passed through his left shoulder." The American commander grasped the difficulties posed by the vexing terrain. "I am sorry your attempts to get possession of the enemy's batteries

36 Chastellux, *Travels in North America*, vol. 1, 157; Johann Conrad Dohla, *A Hessian Diary of the American Revolution*, Bruce E. Burgoyne, trans. & ed. (Norman, OK, 1990), 59. Du Plessis added at least two fougasses to Fort Mercer's defenses—one along the east face and the other near the southeast face of the fort. A fougasse is a simple explosive device made by digging a hole in the ground or constructing a crater in a pile of stone and filling it with black powder and a projectile, such as a rock. It was exploded by a fuse made of gunpowder packing a cloth or leather tube that was waterproofed with pitch. A fougasse could also be exploded with a gun lock connected to a trip wire. The fuse was lighted when the enemy approached to ignite the main charge, sending a lethal blast of rock or debris into the air as shrapnel. Lefkowitz, *Washington's Revenge*, 211.

37 Reed, *Campaign*, 256-257; Jackson, *Navy*, 145; Montresor, "Journals," 465.

have hitherto failed," sympathized Washington in an October 14 letter to Smith. "I hope your future endeavours may be more successful."[38]

Captain Andrew Hamond of the Royal Navy, meanwhile, managed to remove another frame from the line of *chevaux-de-frise* near Billingsport. Commodore Hazelwood responded by sending down "two Chains of Fire Rafts to drive them from that Place, and a heavy Cannonade ensued with the [HMS] *Roebuck* [Hamond's ship]," reported Col. William Bradford of the Pennsylvania militia. "[T]he Commodore obliged them [the British] to quit their Station and fall down the River."[39] The journal of the HMS *Vigilant* recorded the game of parry and thrust:

> Guard Boats gave the Alarm that the enemys fire rafts were coming down, and in 5 minutes after we saw them all in ablaze dropping down with the Tyde, directly athwart the Ships, and covered by their Galleys & Gun Boats, who kept a constant fire of Grape Shott on the Rafts to prevent our boats Towing them clear of the Ships, Our Ships also kept a fire on their Galleys, and Gun Boats, which prevented their advancing nearer, and then our Boats Towed the fire Rafts clear of the Ships, and grounded them on little Tinicum Island.[40]

A small fascine battery under Capt. Samuel Hugg of the New Jersey militia bolstered Hazelwood's efforts. Despite previous British efforts to render the American position at Billingsport unusable, Hugg deployed in the fort's ruins and launched iron rounds to help drive the enemy away from the obstructions they were so desperate to clear.[41]

The British began constructing another battery for two 18-pounders near the Pest House on Province Island not far from the mouth of the Schuylkill River. Work in the flooded and muddy terrain was exceedingly difficult. Gun positions to assist the navy in opening the Delaware were vitally important for Howe, but completing the line of defensive redoubts north of Philadelphia was also vital so he could safely remove the garrison from Germantown. With the Schuylkill and Delaware rivers on the east, south, and west sides of the city, a finished line of

---

38 Montresor, "Journals," 465; Peckham, ed., *Toll*, 43; Revolutionary War Pension and Bounty-Land-Warrant Application Files (M804) [RWPF], file W23161; Chase and Lengel, eds., *Papers*, vol. 11, 509. Throughout this period men were ferried back and forth between the forts for various operations and to serve as replacements.

39 Hazard, et al, eds., *Archives*, Series 1, vol. 5, 668.

40 Crawford, ed., *Naval Documents*, vol. 10, 147.

41 Jackson, *British Army*, 59; Jackson, *Navy*, 141.

redoubts to the north would make Philadelphia a veritable island. On October 13, Captain Montresor complained in his journal about the lack of progress on the works, noting that "the redoubts for the defence of Philadelphia continued on, though slowly, as none but Inhabitants are employed on it, and that at 8 shillings per day and Provisions."[42]

Conditions in Fort Mifflin on Mud Island were nearly as bad for the Americans as laboring on flooded Province Island was for the British. The island was cold and damp and the men poorly equipped. "Chief reason of my Men being so very sickly is their want of Cloathing & Blankets," observed Samuel Smith to Washington on October 14. "I have at least 60 of this small number without Breeches many of whom have scarce . . . enough to cover their Nakedness, never were poor wretches in such a Situation as they are." Smith knew Fort Mifflin needed improvements and he had the men begin building traverses in the water battery and surrounded the fort with wolf-holes filled with vertical stakes to deter British land assaults.[43]

The Continental Camp

The campaign along the river continued while a different type of battling unfolded in the American encampment, where several senior officers faced rebuke for their actions in the field. On the same day Lieutenant Colonel Smith complained about the sickly condition of his men, a Court of Inquiry convened, examined Gen. Anthony Wayne's conduct at Paoli, and exonerated him of any malfeasance. The Pennsylvanian remained angry about the testimony provided by some of his subordinates and demanded a full court martial proceeding. John Sullivan, William Maxwell, and Adam Stephen would face similar proceedings in the coming days.[44]

---

42 Reed, *Campaign*, 280. The Pest House on the northern end of the island was the hospital for contagious diseases. Jackson, *British Army*, 53; Montresor, "Journals," 465. On October 13, William Howe wrote to Gen. Henry Clinton in New York ordering reinforcements be sent to his army. The rigorous campaign and battle casualties had reduced his effective force to about 12,000—nearly 3,000 fewer than he had at Brandywine. British Archives, CO 5/253, Precis of documents relating to military operations against the revolted colonists.

43 Chase and Lengel, eds., *Papers*, vol. 11, 511; Jackson, *Navy*, 153; Reed, *Campaign*, 278-279.

44 Wayne requested the court martial eight days later, which also cleared him of any wrongdoing. Chase and Lengel, eds., *Papers*, vol. 11, 482. For a full account of the Wayne court martial, see McGuire, *Paoli*. Another addition from the northern army, Malcolm's Additional Continental Regiment was assigned to Thomas Conway's 3rd Pennsylvania Brigade this day.

The early warning signs of what would erupt into what is known as the Conway Cabal began when some officers began angling for Thomas Conway's promotion to major general. Benjamin Rush penned a letter to John Adams on October 13 extolling Conway's virtues. "He is moreover the idol of the whole Army. Make him a Major General if Nothing else will detain him in your Service. . . . Some people blame him for calling some of our Generals fools—cowards—and drunkards in public company. But these things are proofs of his integrity, and should raise him in the opinion of every friend to America."[45]

The River War

By the middle of October, the garrison at Fort Mifflin numbered 175 officers and men including militia. French engineering officer Maj. Francois-Louis de Fleury, a 28-year-old recently recovered from a wound suffered at Germantown, arrived to help Lieutenant Colonel Smith better defend Mifflin. On the 14th of the month, British warships widened the gap in the lower chevaux-de-frise near Billingsport and marked it with buoys so ship captains would know where the obstructions ended. The 100-foot gap doomed Fort Mifflin.[46]

With four batteries now erected along the dikes of Province and Carpenter's islands, the British opened fire on Mifflin on October 15. "As soon (after daybreak) as the Fog was dispelled, which was about 7 o'clock [AM] the 4 Batteries . . . opened upon the rebel Fort and marine [naval ships]. . . continued to throw a shell or Howitzer about every ½ hour during the course of the night," recorded Captain Montresor. An 18-pound shell from the American floating battery arced through the sky and exploded, killing an artilleryman and wounded three others in the British battery near the Pest House. The warships HMS *Roebuck* and *Vigilant* joined the bombardment from below the obstructions between Forts Mifflin and Mercer.[47]

"The enemy opened . . . two gun batteries and a mortar battery on the fort. They threw about thirty shells into it that afternoon, without doing much damage," wrote Thomas Paine in a letter to Ben Franklin three months later. "The ground

---

45   Robert J. Taylor, ed., *Papers of John Adams*, 20 vols. (Cambridge, MA, 1983), vol. 5, 315-316.

46   McGuire, *Campaign*, vol. 2, 185; Jackson, *Navy*, 145-147; Smith, *Fight for Delaware*, 11.

47   Montresor, "Journals," 466; Smith, *Fight for Delaware*, 14; Reed, *Campaign*, 281. That same day, the British breached the second row of *cheveaux-de-frise* off Billingsport. Moomaw, "Career of Hamond," 360.

being damp and spongy," he added, "not above five or six burst, and not a man was killed or wounded." Joseph Plumb Martin of the 4th Connecticut found himself stationed in the fort a few weeks later and described the effect of the island's "spongy" mud of which Paine wrote. "I have seen the enemy's shells fall upon it and sink so low that their report could not be heard when they burst, and I could feel a tremulous motion of the earth at the time," explained Martin. "At other times, when they burst near the surface of the ground, they would throw the mud fifty feet in the air." According to Maj. Silas Talbot of Greene's 1st Rhode Island, the British "cut the fusees of the bombs such a length, as to make the shells burst in the air, over the heads of the garrison, and fall in pieces among the soldiers," but the iron bombardment caused "more Fear than Damage." Knowing Fort Mercer served as Mifflin's lifeline, Washington instructed Colonel Greene to "be watchful on every quarter, and industrious in stopping every avenue by which you are assailable."[48]

The Continental Camp

William Maxwell was drunk and woefully incompetent at Brandywine and the Battle of the Clouds while in command of the Light Infantry Brigade—at least that was the accusation leveled by Lt. Col. William Heth of the 3rd Virginia. Heth served in that organization during that time under Maxwell's command (and had the added misfortune to serve under the hapless Adam Stephen at Germantown). Maxwell denied the charges and appeared at Nathanael Greene's headquarters on October 15 for the Court of Inquiry, which soon turned into a full court martial. Maxwell would be acquitted less than three weeks later. The same day the court began, news reached Washington of General Gates's stunning October 7 victory at Bemis Heights in the Second Battle of Saratoga.[49]

---

48 "Military Operations near Philadelphia in the Campaign of 1777-8," *The Pennsylvania Magazine of History and Biography*. 148 vols. (Philadelphia, 1878), vol. 2, 290-291; Joseph Plumb Martin, *Private Yankee Doodle*, George F. Scheer, ed. (Fort Washington, PA, 2000), 87; Silas Talbot, *An Historical Sketch to the End of the Revolutionary War, of the Life of Silas Talbot, Esq. of the State of Rhode-Island, Lately Commander of the United States Frigate, the Constitution, and of an American Squadron in the West-Indies* (New York, 1803), 28; Francois Louis Teisseydre, Marquis de Fleury to Alexander Hamilton, October 17, 1777, Abstract and Journal on Fort Mifflin Siege, Washington Papers online, Series 4, General Correspondence, Library of Congress, Washington, DC; Chase and Lengel, eds., *Papers*, vol. 11, 519.

49 Harry M. Ward, *General William Maxwell and the New Jersey Continentals* (Westport, CT, 1997), 80-82.

While Maxwell was busy seeking justice, Washington was preparing to move his army. On the morning of October 16, he roused his command and marched it five miles from Towamencin Township back to its old camp in Worcester Township on Methacton Hill, where he set up his headquarters once more at the home of Peter Wentz, Jr. The army was now back on the ground from which it had launched the surprise assault on Germantown just twelve days earlier. "One motive for coming here," wrote the Virginian to John Hancock that same day, "is to divert the Enemy's attention and force from the Forts." The results from the Court of Inquiry into John Sullivan's actions on Staten Island and Brandywine were announced during the march to the old camp grounds. The man Dr. Rush described as "weak, vain, without dignity, fond of scribbling, [and] in the field a madman" was acquitted of all charges.[50]

British Philadelphia

Howe's army was scattered across the Delaware Valley since the Battle of Brandywine and subsequent occupation of Philadelphia. Its wide dispersal nearly proved a fatal mistake at Germantown. The British commander fully realized his mistake and began concentrating his far-flung elements on the same day Washington moved. The garrison in Wilmington, Delaware, under Col. Johann August von Loos, who commanded his own Hessian Combined Battalion and the von Mirbach Regiment, destroyed the redoubts around the town, climbed aboard vessels near Christiana Creek, and landed at Chester, Pennsylvania. A convalescent unit of sick and wounded from Brandywine led by Lt. Col. William Medows (who had suffered a serious wound during the attack on Birmingham Hill) accompanied the move.[51]

---

50 The army was split to facilitate the movement. One-half returned down Forty-Foot Road to the Skippack Pike before turning left and heading back into the Methacton Hills. The other half marched straight down Sumneytown Pike before turning right onto modern Route 363 to return to the Methacton area. Chase and Lengel, eds., *Papers*, vol. 11, 528. See Harris, *Brandywine*, 415-427 for more on Sullivan's court martial. Mitchell, ed., "Historical Notes," 147.

51 McGuire, *Campaign*, vol. 2, 144. The Combined Hessian Battalion contained the men from the von Lossberg, von Knyphausen, and Rall regiments who had survived the various actions around Trenton the previous December.

The River War

Washington's shift to the new camp did little to interrupt the British efforts to clear the Delaware River. The attenuated British supply line from Chester to Philadelphia limited Captain Montresor's gunners to only ten rounds a day against Mifflin. This lack of fixed ammunition slowed down the rate of British artillery fire against Fort Mifflin to a fitful and ineffective effort, observed Montresor on October 16. The engineer hinted that Howe needed to change his plans if he wanted to conquer the Delaware defenses. The British captain may have deemed the artillery fire light, but inside the fort, French nobleman and engineer Maj. Francois de Fleury might not have agreed. One shell burst nearby while he was writing a letter, the blast from which "just now drives me from my Table."[52]

The engineer was also painfully aware there were not enough civilian workers available for him to push his various projects to completion, including reinforcing the batteries on Province and Carpenter's islands, building the redoubts to protect the supply route to Chester, and erecting the redoubts in the defensive line north of Philadelphia. The few workers at hand often had to stop whatever they were working on to help artillerymen unload wagons. Repairing the bridge at Gray's Ferry also served to delay work on the Province Island batteries. These shortcomings served to exacerbate the weakness inherent in the light caliber artillery pieces fitfully discharging toward Fort Mifflin. The small balls could not inflict serious damage, and what minor damage they caused, the Americans repaired each night. Montresor needed the big 24- and 32-pound pieces from the British fleet to improve their chances against the American fort. Montresor spilled out his difficulties into his journal. "The Nights as well as the situations very unfavorable as the moon during the whole time rose early and clear & subject to discover us," he complained. "After wading along Causeways, through Cuts in the Meadows and Bog Holes and reaching the spot to work on—we had to fill the Ditch in the rear of a small Dyke with fascines even to get a footing to work. This Season . . . the Waters are in general higher & the spaces they leave slippery and miry."[53]

General Howe lost his patience with the slow progress along the Delaware. Philadelphia needed to be secured, and the river opened if his army was going to maintain itself there for the winter. Howe summoned General Cornwallis, his chief

---

52 Montresor, *Journals*, 467; De Fleury Fort Mifflin journal.

53 Dorwart, *Fort Mifflin*, 38; Montresor, "Journals," 133.

of artillery Samuel Cleaveland, and Montresor to his headquarters in Germantown. Any patience Montresor once had with Howe was lost during this council. Howe, who wanted to know how much longer it would take to finish the defensive redoubts so he could leave Germantown, chastised his engineers by complaining that three weeks elapsed, and nothing had been done. Montresor jotted down his thoughts on mistakes made during the war before asking: "Why [didn't Howe] come to Philadelphia, at least nearer to it, after the possession of it, and open the communication [with the fleet], in stead of three weeks at Germantown?" Two days later Howe would do just that by moving into Philadelphia himself.[54]

Whitemarsh Expedition

As John Burgoyne was surrendering his Army from Canada at Saratoga on October 17, Anthony Wayne was leading an expedition northwest of Philadelphia to distract the enemy. The Pennsylvanian marched the 2nd and 5th Virginia Regiments and the Pennsylvania State Regiment out of the camp on Methacton Hill southeast to Whitemarsh Township about eight miles away. Once there, he built large fires to keep the enemy guessing before marching back to his camp. Wayne's move did not pass unnoticed. "General Grey, with the 2nd Light Infantry, the 33rd, 64th and 44th Regiments," recorded the general's aide John Andre, "marched at about 10 o'clock in the morning [the same day] towards Whitemarsh Church." General Grant also set out about the same time on the Skippack Road with the 1st Light Infantry and 5th, 23rd, 42nd and 55th Regiments of Foot. According to Andre, the two columns met at Whitemarsh and, other than the dragoons giving chase "to a party of Rebel Cavalry," returned without bringing Wayne's men to battle. "The whole matter," summarized one historian, "was simply a little fun and annoyance on Wayne's part, and a waste of time and energy on that of the British."[55]

---

54 Jackson, *British Army*, 54; Montresor, "Journals," 138.

55 Reed, *Campaign*, 262-263; James McMichael, "Diary of Lieutenant James McMichael, of the Pennsylvania Line, 1776-1778," *The Pennsylvania Magazine of History and Biography*, 148 vols., William P. McMichael, ed. (Philadelphia, 1892), vol. 16, 154; Andre, *Journal*, 59. It is not clear why Wayne led three regiments from Nathanael Greene's division rather than some of his Pennsylvania regiments for this operation. Likewise, it is unclear why Greene did not lead this operation.

The Continental Camp

The early Conway Cabal rumblings reached Washington's ears while the army was camped on the Methacton Hills. Congress, the Virginian learned, "has appointed Brigadier [Thomas] Conway to be Major Gen[e]ral in this Army." The move angered him. "It will be as unfortunate a measure, as ever was adopted." Washington clarified his views of the man to Richard Henry Lee on October 17: "General Conways' merit then, as an officer, and his importance in this Army, exists more in his own imagination than in reality; for it is a maxim with him to leave no service of his own untold nor to want any thing to detract from any merit he possesses." Congress's meddling with his army's command structure was so frustrating for Washington that the stoic Virginian hinted at resignation. "I have been a Slave to the service: I have undergone more than most men are aware of, to harmonize so many discordant parts but it will be impossible for me to be of any further survice if such insuperable difficulties are thrown in my way." Washington's anger and displeasure with subordinates and Congress was just beginning.[56]

In York, Pennsylvania, the delegates approved a reconfigured Board of War consisting of three permanent members and a clerical support staff. The board's responsibilities included supervising recruitment, managing prisoners, and producing weapons. This new Board of War became the only authority with the power to get the supplies and manpower from the individual states to the Continental Army under Washington. Two of the permanent members included former Quartermaster General Thomas Mifflin and former Commissary General Joseph Trumbull. Timothy Pickering, Washington's adjutant general, would soon leave to serve with Mifflin and Trumbull.[57]

The River War

The same day he wrote Congressman Lee, Washington sent off a letter to Thomas Wharton of the Pennsylvania Supreme Executive Council. "Without the free Navigation of [the] Delaware, I am confident that Genl. Howe will never remain in Philadelphia," he explained, "and I am as confident that had I a sufficient

---

56 Chase and Lengel, eds., *Papers*, vol. 11, 529-530.

57 Wright, *Army*, 121-122; Erna Risch, *Supplying Washington's Army* (Washington, D.C., 1981), 12. Lender, *Cabal!*, 114.

force to afford as much assistance to the Forts upon [the] Delaware as their importance deserves, that he would not be able to possess them. I have spared as many of the Continental Troops as I possibly can, without endangering the safety of this Army." As the Virginian was dipping his quill and inking the page, the fitful bombardment of Mifflin continued. The guns may have been light artillery pieces, but the balls were large enough to kill two men when a shell hit the barracks.[58]

The next day, October 18, Colonel Angell's 2nd Rhode Island joined Colonel Greene's 1st Rhode Island at Fort Mercer. After marching 70 miles in two days to reach the fort, Angell's regiment paused in Haddonfield, New Jersey, to draw provisions. Newcomb's New Jersey militia had proven less than worthless in helping hold the forts, and the arrival of reinforcements, including 1,100 Virginia militia under Col. William Rumney to the Continental Army, increased Washington's confidence enough to detach the 2nd Rhode Island to help garrison Mercer. The two Rhode Island regiments included many seamen, who Christopher Greene quickly shuttled into service with the naval fleet to fill vacancies from desertions. The arrival of Angell's command coincided with the raising of an "American Flag . . . at Red Bank," observed Philadelphia resident Robert Morton. Lieutenant Colonel John Green's 200 men from the 1st Virginia arrived with the Rhode Islanders and split off to reinforce Fort Mifflin. Green's arrival created a command problem since he outranked Lieutenant Colonel Smith. Washington resolved the potentially vexing problem by asking the sick Col. Henry d'Arendt (Mifflin's actual commander) to physically take charge of the fort.[59]

The Continental Camp

October 18 marked a memorable day for Washington's army when a circular arrived announcing the stunning victory over Burgoyne in upstate New York. "The General has his happiness completed relative to the successes of our northern Army," began the announcement. "On the 14th instant,"

General Burgoyne, and his whole Army, surrendered themselves prisoners of war—Let every face brighten, and every heart expand with grateful Joy and praise to the supreme

---

58 Hazard, et al, eds., *Archives*, Series 1, vol. 5, 679; Jackson, *Navy*, 164.

59 Greenman, *Diary*, 80; Smith, *Fight for Delaware*, 16; Reed, *Campaign*, 253 & 273; Robert Morton, "The Diary of Robert Morton," *The Pennsylvania Magazine of History and Biography*, 148 vols. (Philadelphia, 1877), vol. 1, 19; Dorwart, *Fort Mifflin*, 38. Col. Henry d'Arendt, was recuperating from an illness and had yet to assume command.

disposer of all events, who has granted us this signal success—The Chaplains of the army are to prepare short discourses, suited to the joyful occasion to deliver to their several corps and brigades at 5 O'clock this afternoon—immediately after which, Thirteen pieces of cannon are to be discharged at the park of artillery, to be followed by a feu-de-joy with blank cartridges, or powder, by every brigade and corps of the army, beginning on the right of the front line, and running to the left of it, and then instantly beginning on the left of the 2nd line, and running on to the right of it where it is to end. The Major General of the day [Adam Stephen] will superintend and regulate the feu-de-joy.[60]

"We had . . . a feu de joy through our whole army on the Occasion," exclaimed David Griffith, chaplain of Lieutenant Colonel Heth's 3rd Virginia. "Burgoyne was reduced to the most deplorable Situation—His Troops were deserting fast, and they were almost Starved for want of Provisions. They had hardly any thing to Subsist on but Boiled Corn for Several Days before they surrendered." With Burgoyne no longer a threat, Washington recalled most of the Northern army south to Pennsylvania. "When my last to you was dated I know not," wrote an exhausted Washington to his brother, "for truely I can say, that my whole time is so much engross'd that I have scarce a moment (but sleeping ones) for relaxation, or to endulge myself in writing to a friend." Morale remained high in Washington's army. "Our army is now [in] exceedingly good spirits," wrote Surgeon James Wallace of the 2nd Virginia in an October 12 letter. "We increase every day with the militia from Virginia, we have rec'd a reinforcement of about 1500 Continental troops from New England."[61]

Hugh McDonald of the North Carolina Line, part of Washington's army, recorded some of the day's incidents. "We rejoiced with great shouting and firing all day, our officers being more joyous than the common soldiers and I think more so than was necessary—prancing and capering about everywhere on their horses, and in all places in the camp, among the artillery as well as the infantry." Many

---

60 Chase and Lengel, eds., *Papers*, vol. 11, 541. A feu-de-joy is celebratory gunfire described as a "running fire of guns." Soldiers fire into the air sequentially in rapid succession creating a cascading sound from the blank cartridges.

61 Letter, David Griffith to Hannah Griffith, October 19, 1777, David Griffith Letters, Virginia Historical Society, Richmond, VA.; Chase and Lengel, eds., *Papers*, vol. 11, 551; Letter, James Wallace to Michael Wallace, October 12, 1777 in Horace Edwin Hayden, *Virginia Genealogies: A Genealogy of the Glassell Family of Scotland and Virginia, Also of the Families of Ball, Brown, Bryan, Conway, Daniel, Ewell, Holladay, Lewis, Littlepage, Moncure, Peyton, Robinson, Scott, Taylor, Wallace, and Others, of Virginia and Maryland* (Wilkes-Barre, PA, 1891), 707. The Continental troops were Varnum's Rhode Island brigade.

excited officers hurt themselves. "The result of this irregular bustle was many a hard fall from their horses, which were scared by the thundering of the artillery while riding by it, especially by our artillery from Carolina as we discharged our cannon." Lord Stirling, he continued, "was riding near our artillery on a likely bay mare, which, springing sideways from under him, gave him a very bad fall. After lying for some time, he got up and shook himself like a great water dog, acknowledged himself not hurt, but walked away directly to his quarters and left off his folly for that night."[62]

As far as Capt. Peter Priest was concerned, October 18 was a day to forget. According to Col. Martin Pickett of the Virginia militia, Priest "got Slightly wounded by Accident from one of our own guns which went of[f] Struck the Lower part of his testikles I think but skin deep & went through one side of his Peanus which I hope he will soon get well of without any damage to his reputation."[63]

The River War

While the Americans celebrated, the British erecting batteries opposite Fort Mifflin struggled against odds almost as hopeless as those faced by Burgoyne. They worked in meadows flooded with water waist deep by dikes shot away by American artillery, leaving the muddy Delaware to overflow completed gun platforms. General Howe paid a personal visit to get a better idea of what was transpiring and was shocked at what he discovered. His inspection left no doubt that he needed a change in strategy. "The lightness of our Artillery and the shortness of our ammunition not making the instant impression the Commander-in-Chief wished and expected," penned a pleased Montresor, "he this day at 1 o'clock altered his present Plan." The warships would move beyond the *chevaux-de-frise* and help assault Fort Mercer.[64]

---

62 Hugh McDonald, *A Teen-ager in the Revolution: Being the recollections of a high-spirited boy who left his Tory family at the age of fourteen and joined the Continental Army* (Harrisburg, PA, 1966), 12. Stirling, who was hurt more than he let on, retired to Reading, Pennsylvania, to recover.

63 Letter, Martin Pickett to William Edmonds, October 18, 1777, Martin Pickett Letters, Virginia Historical Society, Richmond, VA; Chase and Lengel, eds., *Papers*, vol. 11, 551. Whether Captain Priest's manhood suffered a permanent reputational disfunction remains a mystery.

64 Jackson, *British Army*, 60; Montresor, "Journals," 467.

Germantown Abandoned

William Howe needed more than ships to assault Mercer: he needed manpower, and his change in strategy signaled the end of the occupation of Germantown. To free up troops, he withdrew his units from the battle-scarred village on October 19 and concentrated his army in Philadelphia. He waited to do this until the line of redoubts north and west of Philadelphia were nearly complete—meaning fewer troops would be needed to block Washington's access to the city. Howe needed men to assault the river forts, and occupying Germantown at this time was pointless. He intended to winter in the former colonial capital, and he wanted his men safely in the city before the cold weather arrived. He also intended to personally supervise operations along the river. His subordinates had failed him there, and time was of the essence. "I found it adviseable to remove to Philadelphia, to expedite the reduction of Mud-Island [Fort Mifflin], which proved to be more difficult than was at first supposed," he later testified to Parliament. "To this end the possession of Red-Bank [Fort Mercer] on the East side of the Delaware engaged my attention. . . . It has been asserted, that an early possession of Red-Bank must have immediately followed by the reduction of Mud-Island, to which I in some measure agree."[65]

Once the move from Germantown was complete, Howe positioned the British right wing north of Philadelphia along the Delaware River behind Kensington, and his left west of the city behind the Morris country house on the Schuylkill River. Howe's new line covered a front 2 ½ miles long. This well-manned and relatively short position allowed him to detach units for use elsewhere, if needed. Most of the troops camped behind the defensive line or in the old barracks in the northern part of the city, while many officers took over civilian homes. While the army was taking up its new position, Col. Johann August von Loos arrived at Gray's Ferry on the Schuylkill with the former Wilmington garrison of 1,500 troops.[66]

The River War

Lieutenant Colonel Samuel Smith, meanwhile, ordered his Fort Mifflin batteries to open on the British gun positions across the back channel. "The rebels opened all their batteries and blockhouses upon us; their grape shot came so thick

---

65 Reed, *Campaign*, 264; Jackson, *British Army*, 61; *The Narrative of Lieut. Gen. Sir William Howe*, 19-28.

66 McGuire, *Campaign*, vol. 2, 144 & 149; Reed, *Campaign*, 264.

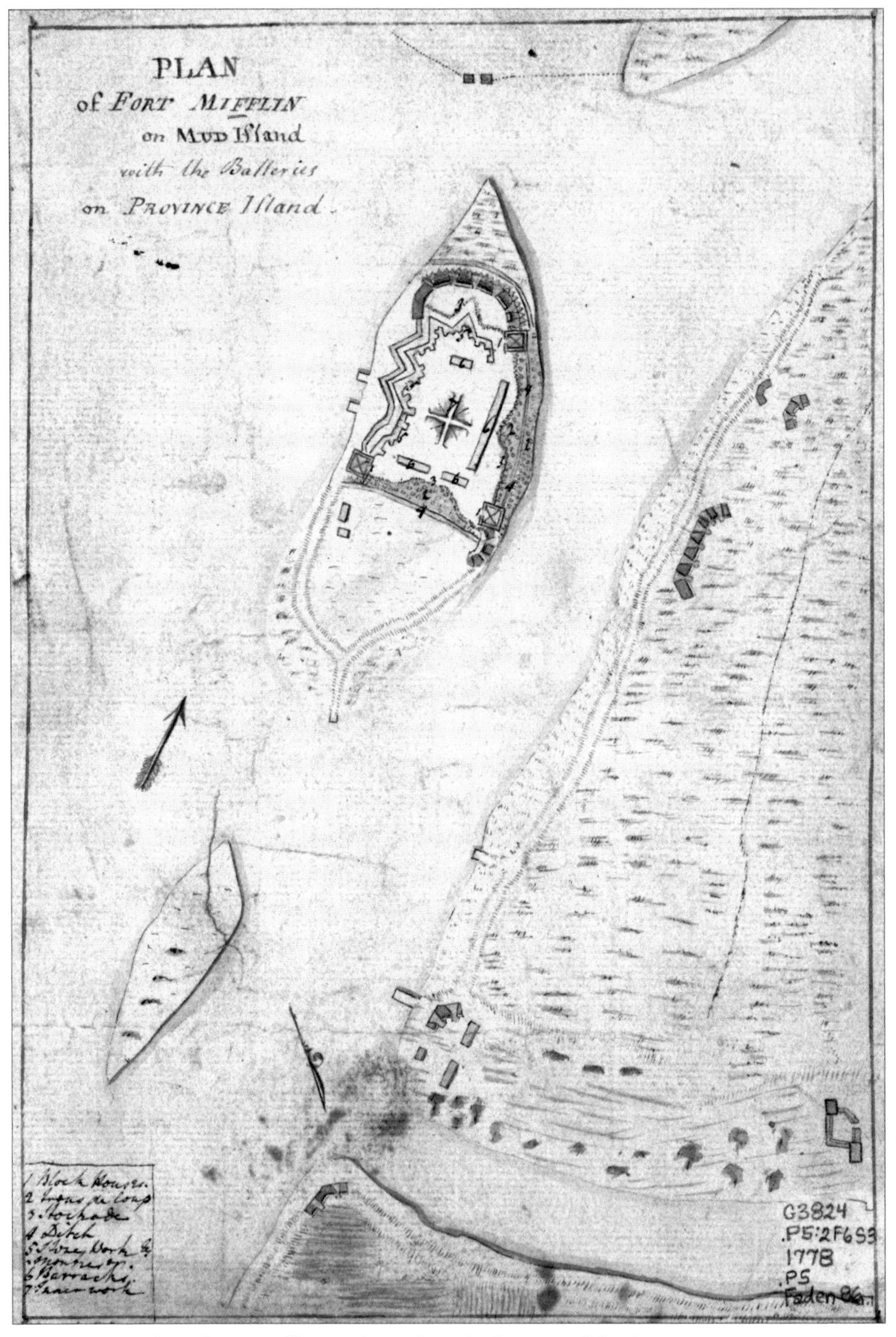

Plan of Fort Mifflin, with north at the bottom of the drawing. *LOC*

that we could not stand to our guns," recorded Royal artilleryman Francis Downman. One of Downman's return rounds scored a direct hit—"set fire to a quantity of powder in the fort." Smith confirmed the strike to Washington the next day: "A red hot ball entered our Laboratory, where were t[w]o boxes of ammunition (about 30 cartouches) which blew up the barracks." Without Captains George Walls and James Lucas of the 4th Virginia "putting out the fire," the round "would have done much more damage."[67]

Despite the damage, de Fleury continued improving Mifflin. By October 19, he raised a bank in front of the palisaded west wall, joined the barracks with ditches, and loopholed each window opening. The Americans also constructed a redoubt in the center of the parade of earth and timbers with barrels of sand and surrounded by a ditch. If necessary, this redoubt would serve as the final defensive position.[68]

The Rhode Island garrison, meanwhile, remained hard at work on du Plessis's insistent changes to Mercer. "Soldiers went to wrk and workt all night on our fort, as we Expected an attack that night or in the morning," Colonel Angell recorded in his diary. Sergeant John Smith of the 1st Rhode Island concurred by noting in his diary how they "went to work on the fort to fortifying the same until Day Light."[69]

The Continental Camp

As Howe withdrew from Germantown, Washington once more had the Continental Army on the move. He shifted his command five miles into Whitpain Township—a mere 15 miles from Philadelphia. Fooled earlier in the campaign by a supposed British withdrawal followed by a swift and deadly attack, Washington was determined not to be duped a second time.

When war reached that part of Pennsylvania in late September, the Daniel Wister family, including daughter Sally, sought refuge at the Foulke farm in the Pennllyn section of Gwynedd Township east of Washington's destination. That morning, Sally Wister's cousin "came running into the room, and said there was the greatest drumming, fifing, and rattling of wagons that she had heard," recorded

---

67 Whinyates, *Services*, 42. Chase and Lengel, eds., *Papers*, vol. 11, 565-566.

68 Jackson, *Fort Mifflin*, 38.

69 Israel Angell, *Diary of Colonel Israel Angell: commanding the Second Rhode Island continental regiment during the American revolution 1778-1781*, Edward Field & Norman Desmarais, eds. (Providence, RI, 1899), n.p. John Smith, *"Thro Mud & Mire Into the Woods": The 1777 Continental Army Diary of Sergeant John Smith*, Bob McDonald, trans., www.revwar75.com/library/bob/smith.htm.

Sally. The grand display was the left wing of the Continental Army tramping down Morris Road half a mile distant. Teenager Sally could not help but sneak a peek.[70]

Maryland militia commander William Smallwood, an Eton College of England graduate and French and Indian War veteran, would make his quarters in their home. Sally was smitten by her new companions. "His Generalship came with six attendants, which compos'd his family, a large guard of soldiers, a number of horses and baggage-waggons," wrote the excited young lady. "When we were alone our dress and lips were put in order for conquest, and the hopes of adventures gave brightness to each before passive countenance. . . I am going to my chamber to dream, I suppose, of bayonets and swords, sashes, guns, and epaulets."[71]

While general officers protected some residents, other civilians suffered terrible hardships because of the American army's occupation. Many years later, Abraham Shoemaker took a few minutes to recall the deeply unpleasant experience at his Gwynedd Township home. "Soon after the Army arrived in our neighbourhood, we suffered very much from the depredations of foraging parties who carted away our Hay and drove off all our Cattle for the subsistence of the Army, not leaving us a Cow to give Milk for the support of a family of small Children," complained Shoemaker, "and if we bought a fresh one she was immediately driven off again."[72]

---

70 The army marched in two columns. The left wing under Nathanael Greene down Morris Road and the right under Washington down Skippack Road. Wayne's, Sullivan's, and Stirling's divisions camped west of Skippack Pike on Prophecy Creek above Butler Pike. The divisions under McDougall (Connecticut troops) and Stephen camped along Morris Road above Butler Pike. Irvine's Pennsylvania militia brigade was with Greene, and Smallwood's Maryland militia was with Sullivan. The artillery park was across Lewis Lane from Washington's headquarters. Jackson, *Whitemarsh*, 8. Washington made headquarters at Dawesfield, named for its builder, Abraham Dawes. James Morris, who married one of Dawes's daughters, owned the 1736 structure in 1777. The house still stands on Lewis Lane between Skippack Pike and Morris Road in Whitpain Township. The original house faced south but was later enlarged with wings added at right angles to the original west wing reorienting the house to the west. Reed, *Campaign*, 266.

71 Reed, *Campaign*, 265; McGuire, *Campaign*, vol. 2, 145; Sally Wister, *Sally Wister's Journal: A True Narrative Being a Quaker Maiden's Account of her Experiences with Officers of the Continental Army, 1777-1778*, ed. Albert Cook Myers (Philadelphia, PA, 1902), 74-81. William Smallwood commanded the Maryland battalion in 1776, which suffered heavy losses on Long Island. He was wounded twice at White Plains (October 1776) and promoted to brigadier and given command of the 1st Maryland Brigade. Washington detached him early in the campaign to raise Maryland militia. His command played a small part in the Battle of Paoli before he was tasked with leading a column of his own militia and those of New Jersey into the attack against Germantown.

72 Mary Foulke Morrisson, "Reminiscences of the Year 1776," *The Pennsylvania Magazine of History and Biography*, 148 vols. (Philadelphia, 1966), vol. 90, 520-521. The Marquis de Lafayette rejoined the army that day after recovering from his Brandywine wound in Bethlehem.

Starvation?

Once the Germantown garrison and Wilmington column moved into Philadelphia, Howe had 18,000 military personnel and 25,000 civilians in need of food and other supplies. If the river remained closed much longer, the population faced the very real prospect of starvation. They needed to eliminate the river forts.

The fleet remained unable to ascend the river to the city's wharves, so Howe made do with supply trains hauling provisions from Chester. He sent a column of the Brigade of Guards, the 71st Highlanders, 27th and 28th Regiments of Foot, and some Hessian units (approximately 3,000 men) to Darby to wait for the provisions and guard the trains. The small hamlet sat between the forks of Cobb's Creek five miles from Philadelphia. The overworked British engineers built a floating bridge across the Schuylkill to expedite access to the city from Chester.

News of enemy operations between Chester and Philadelphia prompted the aggressive Washington to act, and he decided to strike the enemy supply lines. Nathanael Greene would lead the force. "General Greene was ordered to pass the [Schuylkill] river to attack them, but a heavy shower coming up before he reached the river, he returned as he had been directed in case of rain," recalled Joseph Reed, Washington's former adjutant general. "A council was then held, and a majority being of the opinion that it was not yet too late." Washington deemed the mission too important not to try again. This time, McDougall's Connecticut brigade and Maxwell's New Jersey brigade would cross the Schuylkill and march for Darby to intercept the British supplies while the divisions of Greene and Sullivan moved into Germantown the next morning to distract the British.[73]

With the American forts and naval elements continuing to block British naval access to Philadelphia, and Washington ordering parts of his main army to interdict British supply routes, William Howe needed to act. The next day, he ordered a Hessian force to cross into New Jersey and eliminate the threat at Fort Mercer.

---

73 Joseph Reed served as Washington's adjutant general during the Trenton/Princeton campaign but turned down a brigadier's commission in 1777. He held no official rank that fall. William B. Reed, *Life and Correspondence of Joseph Reed, Military Secretary of Washington, at Cambridge; Adjutant-General of the Continental Army; Member of the Congress of the United States; and President of the Executive Council of the State of Pennsylvania*, 2 vols. (Philadelphia, 1847), vol. 1, 328; McGuire, *Philadelphia*, vol. 2, 149-150.

Chapter 4

The River War Escalates

October 20-22, 1777

"We turnd out Early in the Morning & struck tents & Cleared away for an attack &
Every man at work to strengthen our Selves."[1]

— Sgt. John Smith, 1st Rhode Island Regiment, October 22, 1777

Darby Expedition

As ordered the previous day, Alexander McDougall led his own Connecticut brigade and William Maxwell's New Jersey brigade out of the army's camp at Whitpain on the afternoon of October 20 to cross the Schuylkill River and intercept the British supply line south of Philadelphia. Pennsylvania militia officer James Potter reported to Washington that a British force had been sent south of Gray's Ferry to cover a supply convoy. It was McDougall's mission to intercept that convoy.[2]

"We marched from camp just before night as light troops, light in everything, especially in eatables," remembered Joseph Plump Martin of the 4th Connecticut

---

1 Smith, *Diary*, http://www.revwar75.com/library/bob/smith.htm.

2 Alexander McDougall was promoted that same day to major general. His column marched down Butler Pike to Plymouth Meeting, turned left onto Germantown Road, and marched up Barren Hill.

Regiment. The column marched nine miles and forded the Schuylkill near Barren Hill. "About ten o'clock in the evening, we forded the Schuylkill where the river, included a bare gravelly island, or flat, which we crossed, was about forty rods wide, as near as I could judge, and the water about to the waist," continued Martin. The October air chilled the men. "The water which spattered onto our clothes froze as we passed the river. Many of the young and small soldiers fell while in the water and were completely drenched." Connecticut officer Jonathan Todd explained to his father. "Those Nights we Forded it [the Schuylkill] were by far the severest we have had this year. The Ground was froze hard…Ice to be found in some places—how the Soldiers stood it seems a Mystery . . . some of the men fell down all under water as it was darke & stonny Bottom." Still, he marveled, "the men forded the River with a Cheerfulness & Alacrity that would have Reflected the Greatest Honor on the Oldest Veteran Troops."[3]

Emerging from the river bottom, the men found themselves in Lower Merion Township. Joseph Martin grumbled about the experience. "All of a sudden we were ordered to halt. We were, to appearance, in an unfrequented road, cold and wet to our middles, and half starved. We were sorry to be stopped from traveling, as exercise kept us warm in some degree." The men "endeavored to kindle fires, but were ordered by the officers to immediately extinguish them, which was done by all except one, which having been kindled in a hollow tree could not be put out." Martin "got so near to this that I could just see it between the men's legs, which was all the benefit that I derived from it." Colonel Elias Dayton, commander of the 3rd New Jersey, recalled that many of the men were barefooted "and the night by far the coldest this season." Dayton was "much distressed on their account, and they complained much of the hardship." As the night wore on, the men stood shivering in the road awaiting orders.[4]

3 Martin, *Private Yankee Doodle*, 75-76; Revolutionary War Pension and Bounty-Land-Warrant Application Files (M804) [RWPF], file W2197.

4 Martin, *Private Yankee Doodle*, 76. The modern road from Barren Hill Church to the ford is called Harts Lane. The island described by Martin still exists. Modern Young's Ford Road follows the historic route on the opposite side of the river. The American column halted near modern Gladwyne. Elias Dayton, "Papers of General Elias Dayton," in *Proceedings of the New Jersey Historical Society* (Newark, NJ, 1864), vol. 9, 186.

The River War

William Howe, meanwhile, remained in a desperate position. His situation in Philadelphia worsened by the day. The army's military and medical supplies, as well as much of its food, remained in the holds of ships anchored down by Chester. Despite their victories at Brandywine and Germantown, the Crown's forces found themselves in something of a noose. The Delaware River forts on Mud Island and Red Bank kept Lord Howe's fleet out of the city. Washington was slowly tightening the rope.

Colonel Henry d'Arendt finally arrived to take command of Fort Mifflin. Lieutenant Colonel Samuel Smith and Major de Fleury provided the colonel with a tour of the fort. When they came to the scene of the burned-out laboratory, the newly arrived officer inquired as to its cause. "It has been blown up twice; and the enemy's fire is frequently directed at it," explained Smith and de Fleury. To the shock of both men, Colonel d'Arendt "immediately sprang into one window, and out the other, and got clear of the block-house." The stunned de Fleury blurted, "Oar Dieu! C'est un poltroon!" ["By God! He's a complete coward!"] Smith agreed. "Yes, and we must frighten him away from the Fort," he responded to the French engineer, "or he will do more injury than good." Later in life, Smith described d'Arendt as "Prussian, a very military-looking man, six feet high, and elegantly formed. Indeed, his whole appearance was that which would commend him to a command, where personal bravery was not required." D'Arendt shirked his responsibilities when he fled to the relative safety of New Jersey, where he commanded Fort Mifflin from afar. The disgusted Smith, left to make decisions in Fort Mifflin as the senior officer present, submitted his resignation to Washington in disgust. He would remain on duty, however.[5]

Having removed enough of the *chevaux-de-frise* obstructions near Billingsport, the British ships *Roebuck*, *Liverpool*, and *Pearl* warped through the opening and anchored near Billings Island on October 20. As a portent of what lay ahead, the *Roebuck* and *Liverpool* ran aground doing so.

Later in the day, the *Vigilant*, *Zebra*, and *Camilla* passed through the same obstructions and anchored off Hog Island. Commodore Hazelwood responded by sending some American galleys to drive away the British ships. According to the *Vigilant's* journal, "the Fort at Mud Island fired at us, and the [American] Galley's rowed over from Red Bank to Assist the Fort, we returned their fire, as we dropped

5 Smith, "Papers," 88; Chase and Lengel, eds., *Papers*, vol. 11, 565.

down, all the Damage the[y] did us was Sinking a Flat Boat and breaking some Oars . . . the *Camilla* being with us got aground also." The journal kept by the *Zebra* confirms "at 4 Came down 13 Rebel Gallies & fired on the . . . *Vigilant* in this Channel which fire was returned." These British vessels moved into position for the planned naval bombardment of Fort Mifflin the next day.[6]

Soldiers at Fort Mifflin working the British batteries endured nothing less than misery. The Delaware River beyond Philadelphia is a tidal estuary, and the *chevaux-de-frise* disrupted the natural course of the river. As a result, human and animal waste from 25,000 civilians and 20,000 recently arrived personnel with William Howe's army flowed into the river and downstream toward Fort Mifflin. Some 200 ships with 5,000 crewmen anchored below Chester adding their own waste to the river. The tide rose and fell twice a day, pushing the river and its contents back upriver—a churning swirl of filth and stench that swept across Mud, Province, and Carpenter's islands. The living and working environment for these soldiers was anything but pleasant.[7]

British Philadelphia

American officers captured at Brandywine, Germantown, and other minor actions in the region remained confined on the second floor of the Pennsylvania State House. One of them was Lt. Col. Persifor Frazer of the 5th Pennsylvania, snatched by the British from a tavern the morning of the Battle of the Clouds. On the morning of October 20, his wife Mary ("Polly") set out with their nine-year-old daughter Sally to take him provisions. Polly and Persifor had four children and Polly was three months pregnant with their fifth. "Every thing—flour, eggs, chickens, meat, butter, cheese—was packed in large strong home-made tow linnen wallets and saddle bags, and these were thrown across the saddle, the ends projecting far on each side of the horse." Sally sat atop the baggage as mother and daughter set out with two horses from Thornbury Township in Chester County for the 20-mile trip into Philadelphia.[8]

The two were descending the hills into Darby when a Pennsylvania militia officer stopped them in the gathering dusk. Polly "rebuked him for his

---

6 Jackson, *Navy*, 171; Crawford, ed., *Naval Documents*, vol. 10, 228-29.

7 McGuire, *Campaign*, vol. 2, 191.

8 The Pennsylvania States House is today's Independence Hall. Persifor Frazer, *General Frazer A Memoir Compiled Principally from his Own Papers by his Great-Grandson* (Philadelphia, 1907), 162.

impertinence, which she said was unworthy the uniform he wore." Unfazed, the officer refused to let go of the horse's bridle while demanding Polly produce her pass. "Upon reading it, he seemed much mortified, asked her pardon, and rode off very fast," recorded Frazer's memoir. The two continued down the Darby Road past the Blue Bell Tavern at Cobb's Creek toward Gray's Ferry in the dark, passing Hessians cutting wood along the way. Surprisingly, they crossed the floating bridge at the ferry and arrived at the tavern at the Sign of the Conestoga Wagon on High Street near Benjamin Franklin's house. The tavern keeper, "Mrs. Jenkins," provided them with a place to sleep and promised to get a pass from William Howe to visit Persifor. The dangerous trip was worth the risk, and Polly saw her husband the next day.[9]

Fort Mercer Expedition

As McDougall's men shivered in the morning air, soldiers labored in filth near Fort Mifflin, and Polly ventured to see her husband. William Howe decided the time had arrived to eliminate Fort Mercer on the New Jersey side of the Delaware River. Howe understood Fort Mifflin was the key to the American river defenses, but Fort Mercer was Mifflin's lifeline. If the British occupied Mercer, Mifflin's garrison could be starved out.

The fighting thus far had bloodied and worn down most of Howe's regulars. The elite light infantry and grenadiers had suffered severely at Brandywine and Germantown and by mid-October were incapable of conducting independent operations. South of Philadelphia protecting Howe's lone supply line, however, sat the relatively fresh British Brigade of Guards. With the exception of the Hessian jaegers, who had fought well and often in several actions throughout the campaign, the Hessian infantry and grenadiers remained mostly unused and fresh. According to an October 13 British Army return, 3,112 Hessian troops stood combat-ready.[10]

Many Hessian officers were still humiliated by the loss at Trenton the previous year and itched for the opportunity to redeem their reputation. The command of the Fort Mercer operation was assigned to Col. Karl Emil Count von Donop, an outspoken officer who often irritated General Howe. He would later testify to Parliament that von Donop "earnestly intreated Lord Cornwallis . . . to express his

---

9 Ibid., 162-163. The tavern was located between Third and Fourth Streets. McGuire, *Campaign*, vol. 2, 224-225. High Street (today's Market Street) was the main east-west business thoroughfare.

10 Jackson, *Fort Mifflin*, 42; British Archives, CO 5/253.

wishes for an opportunity to signalize himself, and the Hessian troops under his command." Colonel Friedrich von Wurmb, commander of the Leib Regiment, reported several months later that von Donop "made enemies of General Howe and all the English generals with his sarcastic letters and sharp tongue. Among other things, he openly said that the marches made by General Howe on the last expedition could have been done better by an ensign. General Howe naturally didn't appreciate this." Von Donop also criticized Howe's Delaware River operations. "As the siege of Mud Island was being undertaken, Donop openly said this was incorrect," continued von Wurmb. "Red Bank [Fort Mercer] should be taken first. He wished General Howe would permit his brigade to undertake it and requested it personally from the general. General Howe," thought von Wurmb, did not think von Donop would attempt it "because it couldn't be taken, and if he did try, Donop would be the laughing stock. Donop sensed this [and] tried it."[11]

One British artillery officer grasped the importance of the mission. "It is absolutely necessary that we be in possession of this fort for it not only protects their vessels, but also would annoy our shipping very much in passing whenever we are lucky enough to get over their *chevaux-de-frise*, and it likewise commands Mud Island," explained Captain-Lieutenant Francis Downman, "so that we should take Mud Island, unless we had this fort also we should be very much disturbed from it."[12]

To take the fort, Von Donop assembled all three Hessian grenadier battalions and the von Mirbach infantry regiment, some 2,200 men or roughly two-thirds of available Hessian troops. Lieutenant Colonel Ludwig von Wurmb's Hessian jaeger battalion joined the grenadiers and infantry, and eight Hessian 3-pounders attached to the regiments. Von Donop requested two British howitzers for their arcing fire ability. Howe's chief of artillery asked Captain-Lieutenant Francis Downman to "take command of two 5 ½" howitzers ordered for immediate service." Though not directed to do so, "the General hoped I [Downman] would go as the service required a good officer." As Downman soon discovered, he and his men "were the only English on this duty." The jaeger commander, von Wurmb, lacked confidence the operation would be a success. "The colonel [von Donop] told me he had orders

11 McGuire, *Campaign*, vol. 2, 153-154; *Narrative*, 28; Letter, Col. Friedrich Wilhelm von Wurmb to Gen. von Jungkenn, February 7, 1778, Henry Retzer and Donald Londahlsmidt, eds., "The Philadelphia Campaign, 1777-1778: Letters and Reports from the von Jungkenn Papers. Part 2-1778," *Journal of the Johannes Schwalm Historical Association*, 26 vols. (Pennsauken, NJ, 1999), vol. 6, no. 3, 36.

12 Whinyates, *Services*, 43.

to go to Jersey and take Redbank. I asked him what instructions he had, he said none; he was told to improvise."[13]

While the Hessians were attacking Fort Mercer on the land side, William Howe hoped British warships would pass the *chevaux-de-frise* at Billingsport by October 21 and lend weight to the assault. Admiral Richard Howe hoped to use the Hessian attack on Mercer as a distraction to push the *Vigilant* into the back channel "to arrive and act upon the rear and less defensible part of" Fort Mifflin. Entertaining optimism for the river operation, Howe ordered British grenadiers to simultaneously storm Fort Mifflin from Province Island.[14]

Darby Expedition

As the Howe brothers planned the operation to open the Delaware River, Alexander McDougall's Continentals south of the Schuylkill River reversed course. The Connecticut and New Jersey soldiers must have questioned the previous night's march when ordered to re-cross the Schuylkill and move back up Barren Hill the morning of October 21. According to Joseph Plump Martin, "About an hour before day we dashed through the river again, at the same place at which we had crossed the preceding evening, and I can assure the reader that neither the water nor weather had become one degree warmer than it was then." When General Washington learned the size of the British force on the Darby Road, he realized he needed to enlarge McDougall's column. As the day wore on, Washington reinforced McDougall with Thomas Conway's 3rd Pennsylvania Brigade and the 1st and 8th Connecticut regiments. Brigadier General James

13 McGuire, *Campaign*, vol. 2, 154; Whinyates, *Services*, 43. A secondary source claims von Donop requested more British artillery. When told the British would take the fort if he could not, von Donop supposedly snapped, "Tell your general that Germans are not afraid to face death!" No contemporary account has been found to verify this account. Edward J. Lowell, *The Hessians and the Other German Auxiliaries of Great Britain in the Revolutionary War* (Gansevoort, NY, 1997), 204. Col. Johann von Loos certainly sensed the British arrogance. "General Howe and others did not treat him [von Donop] right. The British are arrogant, jealous, and obsessed with their *savoir Militaire*." Letter, Col. Johann August von Loos to Gen. von Jungkenn, October 30, 1777, Henry Retzer and Donald Londahlsmidt, eds., "The Philadelphia Campaign, 1777-1778: Letters and Reports from the von Jungkenn Papers. Part 1-1777," *Journal of the Johannes Schwalm Historical Association*, 26 vols. (Pennsauken, NJ, 1998), vol. 6, no. 2, 21; Letter, Lt. Col. Ludwig Johann Adolph von Wurmb to Maj. Gen. Friedrich Christian Arnold Jungkenn, October 25, 1777, Donald Londahlsmidt, ed., "German and British Accounts of the Assault on Fort Mercer at Redbank, NJ in October 1777," *Journal of the Johannes Schwalm Historical Association*, 26 vols. (Scotland, PA, 2013), vol. 16, 13.

14 Jackson, *British Army*, 63; *Remembrancer; or, Impartial Repository of Public Events for the Year 1777* (London, 1778), 429.

Varnum commanded the fresh Connecticut regiments; Brig. Gen. Jedidiah Huntingdon also arrived. With McDougall commanding the expedition, Huntingdon took command of the Connecticut brigade (which McDougall had led at Germantown). Washington issued new orders for the reinforced column. "The whole party was ordered to march and attack the enemy in their posts precisely fifteen minutes after five o'clock" the next morning wrote Col. Elias Dayton. After waiting until dark, McDougall's column crossed the same Schuylkill ford used the previous night, but this time continued all the way to Merion Meetinghouse before halting at 3:00 a.m.[15]

The column marked time until James Potter's 1,000-man Pennsylvania militia brigade joined them. McDougall now commanded 4,000 men of Washington's available force. The choice of Alexander McDougall, a non-division commander, to lead one-quarter of the army is mysterious. Adam Stephen, John Sullivan, and Anthony Wayne remained under a cloud and faced court proceedings for actions earlier in the campaign and Lord Stirling continued to recover from his horse fall, but the capable Nathanael Greene was available. Greene should have commanded the column.

Instead, Greene with his own and John Sullivan's divisions (some 3,200 men) moved to the outskirts of Germantown in an attempt to divert British attention from McDougall's mission. The divisions "set off about nine at night" the previous day "and halted at daybreak between Germantown and the city," reported Thomas Paine (an aide to Greene) to Benjamin Franklin. Greene established his line along Three Mile Run near Rising Sun Tavern a mere four miles outside the city. Minor skirmishing erupted with British pickets on Fair Hill. Greene was waiting in position for the sounds of McDougall's attack, which was the signal to move closer to Philadelphia and increase British concern.[16]

Washington detached so many units from the main army that the force camped around him at Whitpain the morning of October 21 was a shadow of what he had led into Germantown just 17 days earlier. The 6,000 men left with Washington included Anthony Wayne's and Adam Stephen's divisions, the North Carolina

---

15 Martin, *Private Yankee Doodle*, 76; McGuire, *Campaign*, vol. 2, 150. The two Connecticut regiments marched south with James Varnum. While Varnum's two Rhode Island regiments were ordered to Fort Mercer, the 1st and 8th Connecticut joined Washington's main army. Dayton, "Papers," 186. The column headed up modern Young's Ford Road to Old Gulph Road before bearing left. Old Gulph Road took them to the Lancaster Road (modern Montgomery Avenue in Narberth). After turning left, the column halted just to the east at Merion Meetinghouse.

16 "Military Operations," 291.

Brigade (temporarily under Col. Alexander Martin), William Smallwood's Maryland militia, and elements of the Pennsylvania militia, Continental Dragoons and Henry Knox's artillery.

Unbeknownst to the American commander, Benjamin Rush wrote to John Adams on October 21 in an attempt to undercut Washington's leadership. Horatio Gates, argued Rush, was "on the pinnacle of military glory—exulting in the Success of Schemes planned with wisdom, and executed with vigor and bravery—and above all see a country saved by their exertions." Washington, meanwhile, "outgenerald and twice beaten . . . forced to give up a city the capital of a state. . . . If our Congress can witness these things with composure, and suffer them to pass without an enquiry I shall think we have not Shook off monarchical prejudices, and that like the Israelites of old we worship the work of our hands."[17]

The Fort Mercer Expedition

While McDougall awaited reinforcements on Barren Hill, Lt. Col. Charles Simms arrived at Fort Mercer with 120 men of the 6th Virginia. Under orders to reinforce Mifflin, Christopher Greene dispatched them across the river. The reduced footprint of Fort Mercer had essentially made them redundant there.[18]

As Simms's men rowed across the Delaware, Col. Carl von Donop's Hessian force assembled before dawn at the Arch Street Ferry in Philadelphia. The previous night, Admiral Howe sneaked 12 flatboats up the back channel west of Fort Mifflin for Hessian use. The flatboats offered the only viable means of sending an assault column across the river into New Jersey to capture Mercer. According to Capt. Friedrich von Muenchhausen, moving the boats up from the fleet nearly backfired. "This proved to be almost disastrous because one of our pickets, not having been informed of the expected arrival of the flatboats, fired on them. This alarmed the rebel ships and the forts," explained von Muenchhausen, "so they fired a few cannon shot towards our flatboats, which, fortunately, were almost all the way up the river."[19]

---

17 Taylor, ed., *Papers of Adams*, vol. 5, 316-317.

18 Simms left the Continental camp on October 19, crossed the Delaware River at Bristol, Pennsylvania, marched through Moorestown, New Jersey, to Red Bank and was ferried to Fort Mifflin. Stryker, *Forts on the Delaware*, 13.

19 Jackson, *Fort Mifflin*, 43; Von Muenchhausen, *At Howe's Side*, 40-41.

"Flat boats were standing ready and each one took on from 50 to 60 men," recorded Lt. Heinrich von Feilitzsch of the jaegers. "It was still dark when we got out into the middle of the Delaware." It did not take long for patrols from the American fleet to discover the operation. "We were shelled with cannonfire, double hooks and musket fire," admitted von Feilitzsch. Hessian adjutant Friedrich Werner remembered "a few musket shots were fired at us" from the New Jersey militia. The captured *Delaware* soon arrived to escort the flat boats and "the enemy fire diminished somewhat." Not only had American fire slowed the crossing, "the sailors had to row very hard against the tide." As a result, von Feilitzsch remembered "many boats missed this ferry [the cleared section of riverbank for Cooper's ferry] in the darkness and got into the reeds and rushes, and got stuck, and the crew was obliged to jump out, and wade through the water up to the neck for a long way." By daybreak, the Hessian jaegers unloaded at Cooper's Ferry, pushing back New Jersey militiamen to secure the roads and protect the landing for the Hessian infantry. It proved a difficult and uncomfortable task. "A violent wind came up, which was the more harmful to us, because we were completely wet and had perspired, and now still had to wait several hours for the infantry," concluded von Feilitzsch.[20]

By 2:00 p.m., with jaegers leading the column, the Hessian force marched into the New Jersey flatlands through forests that blazed with autumn colors. About a mile into the march, a smattering of gunfire erupted when advance elements discovered New Jersey militia at the Cooper River Bridge. According to Ludwig von Wurmb, "100 Rebels . . . retired into the woods and disquieted our march on all sides." New Jersey militiamen from Salem and Cape May Counties pestered the Hessian column. Johann Ewald pursued them "up to the end of a wood, where I discovered several hundred men on both sides of Cooper's Creek, with whom I

---

20 "Report of First Lieutenant Friedrich Wilhelm Werner, 25 October 1777," Donald Londahlsmidt, ed., "German and British Accounts of the Assault on Fort Mercer at Redbank, NJ in October 1777," *Journal of the Johannes Schwalm Historical Association*, 26 vols. (Scotland, PA, 2013), vol. 16, 5. Cooper's Ferry was just upriver from today's Camden Aquarium. Heinrich von Feilitzsch, *Journal of several Campaigns in America by Heinrich Earl Philipp von Feilitzsch Prussian Lieutenant of the Ansbach Feldjager*, manuscript located in the Harlan Crow Library, Dallas, Texas, 110-111. Some 300 New Jersey militia under Brig. Gen. Silas Newcomb supported Christopher Greene's garrison at Fort Mercer—the same New Jersey general who had ultimately failed in his attempt to defend Billingsport 18 days earlier. The Cape May and Salem County Regiments were at Cooper's Ferry with a small detachment of light horse. The 2nd Cumberland County Regiment watched Haddonfield and the 1st Cumberland County Regiment was with Newcomb in Woodbury. The Gloucester County Regiment was split between Woodbury and Gloucester—where there was also an artillery detachment. Smith, *Fight for Delaware*, 17.

skirmished until about four o'clock in the afternoon, after which time they withdrew." The brisk skirmish allowed von Donop to continue "his march with his corps" toward Haddonfield.[21]

Militia harassment and the notoriously slow Hessian marching pace brought the fitful advance to a crawl. Von Donop moved about four miles farther inland to Haddonfield hoping to deceive the Americans as to the true purpose of his mission. "A Negro guide, whom Gen. Howe sent along, showed us a hidden route," remembered von Wurmb. Howe actually sent two guides, "One a negroe, the other a whiteman." According to Capt. Samuel Massey of the Pennsylvania militia, "The Negroe [Dick Ellis] proved to be the property" of Maj. William Ellis of the New Jersey militia and "had deserted from his Master." The white man "many persons knew as a Butcher by the Name of [John] McIlvaine" that was recommended to William Howe as being well acquainted with the New Jersey roads, "he being a Butcher used to travel the Jersey for Cattle."[22] The Hessians spent the night camped on the hills near Haddonfield—ten miles from Fort Mercer.[23]

Throughout the day, messages dispatched from the New Jersey militia reached Christopher Greene at Fort Mercer notifying him of Hessian progress. The Rhode Islanders committed every available moment to improving Mercer's defenses. Sergeant John Smith of Greene's regiment recorded the events in his journal: "we

---

21 "Report of Werner," 5; Letter, von Wurmb to Jungkenn, October 25, 1777, 13; Ewald, *Diary*, 97. Ewald's skirmish likely took place where Route 130 today crosses the Cooper River. Two jaegers were wounded. "Diary of Second Lieutenant Carl Friedrich Rueffer," Donald Londahlsmidt, ed., "German and British Accounts of the Assault on Fort Mercer at Redbank, NJ in October 1777," *Journal of the Johannes Schwalm Historical Association*, 26 vols. (Scotland, PA, 2013), vol. 16, 9.

22 Jackson, *British Army*, 63. From Cooper's Ferry in modern Camden, the Hessians marched roughly over what is now Haddon Avenue to get to Haddonfield. Letter, von Wurmb to Jungkenn, October 25, 1777, 13; Massey, "Journal," 234. William Ellis was the cousin of Col. Joseph Ellis, colonel of the 2nd Gloucester County militia regiment. Guides Ellis and McIlvaine were later executed for aiding the British effort. On October 31, Christopher Greene ordered they "be hang'd tomorrow Morning 10 o'clock. A Gallows will be Erected this afternoon for that Purpose. The Garrison will attend this execution of ye Criminals between ye Fort & Ye Brick House under Arms at ye time appointed." Orderly Book of Colonel Christopher Greene in Louis B. Moffett, ed., *Year Book for 1928: The New Jersey Society of Pennsylvania* (1929), 51.

23 Von Donop stayed in the home of John Gill, whose sister Sarah Whitall lived in the house adjacent to Fort Mercer. According to one account, Gill alerted his sister to the Hessian mission, but no primary evidence has been found to support this claim. The Gill house stood on the site of the present-day Historical Society of Haddonfield. McGuire, *Campaign*, vol. 2, 156. The Hessians bivouacked just north of Indian King Tavern (see photo on page 104) along the Cooper River, where Hopkins Pond is today. The millpond was not created till 1789, so it did not exist during the Hessian stay. Jackson, *Navy*, 173.

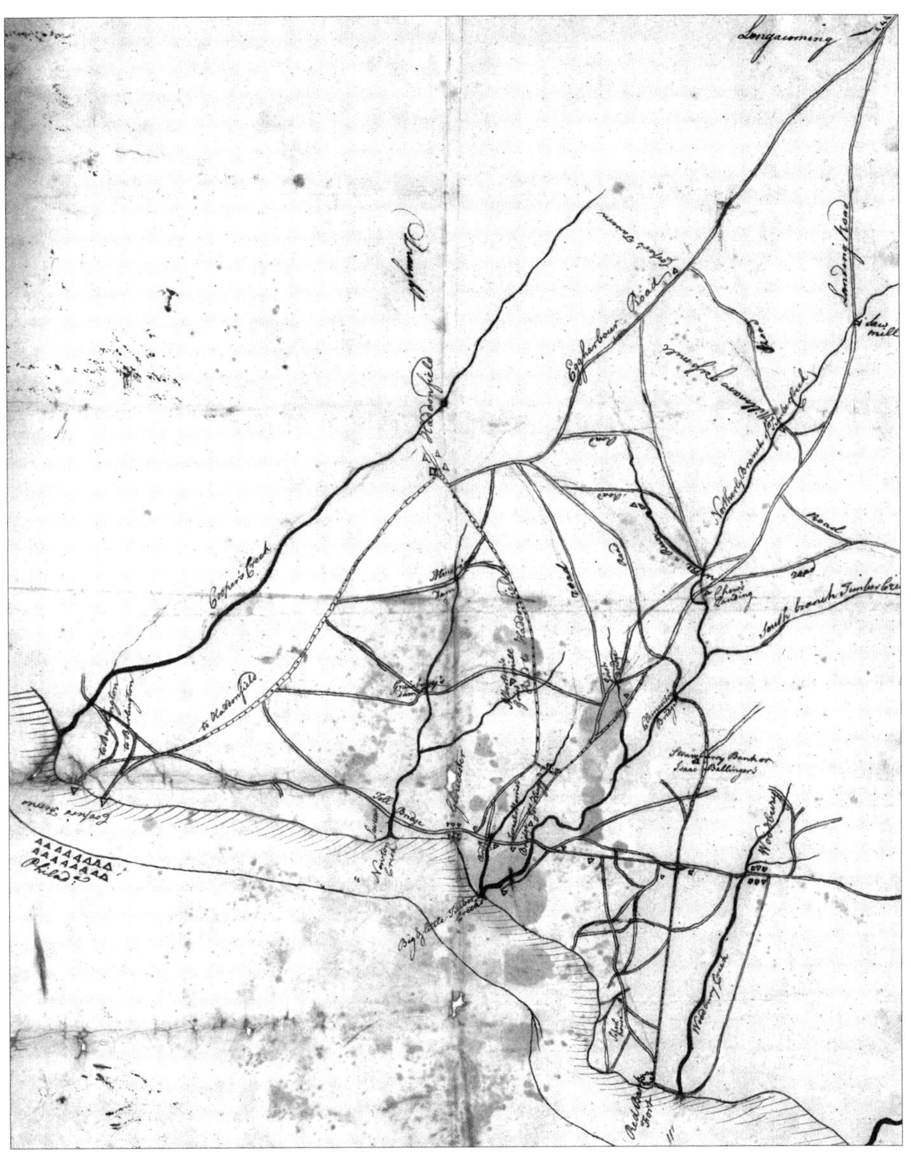

Draft of Roads in New Jersey Showing Hessian Route to Fort Mercer. East is at the top. *LOC*

were Inform'd that a Party of Regulars [Hessians] had Landed at [Cooper's] ferey to attacke our fort—we Remov's all our tents & baggage into the Citidale [Fort Mercer] & Every man was Emplyd at worke on the fort to fortify the same— between 3 & 4 oClock 300 more troops [New Jersey militia] Came here to

Indian King Tavern, Haddonfield, NJ. *Author*

Reinforce us—we Cut Down an orchard by the fort & hald trees Round the fort to Keep off the Enemy."[24]

24 Smith, Diary, http://www.revwar75.com/library/bob/smith.htm.

British Philadelphia

While waiting to see her father, Polly Frazer and her daughter Sally likely saw some of the Hessian troops waiting to cross the river into New Jersey. "The sun just rising shone on their arms and uniforms and made a brilliant sight," Sally would recall. "I hated them so, and was so indignant that I screamed and stamped and cried with rage." After resting from the exhausting journey of the previous day, Polly and her daughter left the tavern on Market Street and walked two blocks to the Pennsylvania State House holding a pass from William Howe. The prisoners could exercise in the hall where a screen extended from the ceiling to within a couple feet of the floor, dividing them from the rest of the building. Sally recalled "Several gentlemen were walking backward and forward as we entered and I instantly distinguished my father's feet and legs. . . . The screen being removed I saw and talked with my Father through the grating." After their brief visit, the two Frazer women began their long trek back to Chester County. Their timing was fortunate. They crossed the floating bridge at Gray's Ferry not long before the British abandoned their camp just to the south and removed it.[25]

A trickle of supplies continued to come into Philadelphia to feed the British army, the American prisoners, and the remaining civilians. Flatboats from the British fleet sneaked foodstuffs up the back channel to Philadelphia at night. According to Capt. John Andre, aide to General Charles Grey, "With respect to provisions, the Army was singularly situated; they were brought once or twice by land from Chester." Since then, "the flat boats bringing them past the fort [Mifflin]; the boats had never yet been insulted [attacked]." Fort Mifflin's on-site commander, Samuel Smith, knew about the British relief efforts. "On a calm night [the Americans] could hear the dip from the muffled oars, carrying up provisions," recalled Smith, who requested that Commodore Hazelwood block the channel with his vessels. Hazelwood balked at the idea, claiming the British warships could knock out his tiny ships with a single shell. "Yes," Smith responded, "and one falling on your head or mine will kill, but for what else are we employed or paid?"[26]

25 Frazer, *A Memoir*, 163-164.

26 Andre, *Journal*, 61; Smith, "Papers," 87. Also occurring on this busy October 21, more British ships snaked their way through the *chevaux-de-frise* line at Billingsport. During the process, the *Isis* and *Cornwallis* stuck fast to sand bars and remained aground overnight. Smith, *Fight for Delaware*, 24.

The Darby Expedition

In the pre-dawn hours of October 22, McDougall marshalled his column into position and prepared to attack the British troops protecting the supply line along modern Woodland Avenue between Blue Bell Tavern and Gray's Ferry. The Americans ordered themselves roughly parallel to the British camp line. Maxwell's New Jersey brigade formed on the American right; Conway's Pennsylvania troops came next, followed by Varnum's two regiments. Huntingdon's Connecticut brigade deployed on the left. Potter's militia remained in reserve. The formidable one and one-half mile-front stretched from the Schuylkill River to Cobbs Creek. "Our Troops were drawn up in a Battalion of a mile in Length Supported by solid colums & Field Piecess they made a very Martial appearance," boasted Connecticut officer Jonathan Todd two weeks later.

The roughly 4,000 Americans outnumbered the 2,500 British troops and, at least thus far, held the element of surprise. The Germantown veterans in McDougall's force yearned for another chance at the British. The sun was just beginning to rise when McDougall ordered the line forward, "but to our very great astonishment and mortification the enemy had in the preceding night moved all over into Philadelphia, and broken up the bridge which they had over the Schuylkill," recalled a disappointed Elias Dayton. The enemy departed so secretly, continued Dayton, "that the inhabitants that lived within one hundred yards of their lines knew nothing of their flight."[27]

"We Burnt their Huts &c. when we got nigh their Encampment our men were drawn up with as much expectation of action as tho' it had really Begun," Ens. Jonathan Todd of the 7th Connecticut wrote his father. "Never was more Calmness & firmness seen in Troops—altho' the[y] Expectd no Quarters if they fell into the Enemys hand they marchd with Undauntd resolution to attack their Lines." Regardless of the expedition's result, the men remained confident. "Altho' we did not accomplish the Errant we went upon," explained Ensign Todd, "We

---

27 McDougall's column turned right onto Merion Road and moved through modern Overbrook across portions of modern 69th Street and Long Lane to the vicinity of Blue Bell Tavern at the intersection of modern Woodland Avenue and Island Avenue. The line likely formed near modern Springfield Avenue and stretched across the grounds of Mt. Mariah Cemetery. Dayton, "Papers," 186-187; Revolutionary War Pension and Bounty-Land-Warrant Application Files (M804) [RWPF], file W2197. Howe's floating bridge was removed from Gray's Ferry and moved to the Middle Ferry.

taught Brittain that we Could Ford Rivers & march Night after Night & Endure hardships & Fatigues Equal to her Troops or Mercenaries."[28]

McDougall's position on the Darby Road threatened General Howe's only line of supply. His 4,000 troops were a mere four miles from Fort Mifflin and behind the British batteries that were bombarding the fort daily. McDougall held several tactical options. New to independent command and far from the support of the main Continental army, however, he had no orders about what to do in that situation. As a result, McDougall started marching back to the main American camp at Whitpain just as Carl von Donop's Hessian column approached Fort Mercer.[29]

A Jonas Cattell Warning?

According to a New Jersey tradition, a patriot sympathizer named Jonas Cattell ran from Haddonfield to Fort Mercer to warn Christopher Greene of the impending Hessian attack. The story originates in an 1846 Issac Mickle story in *The Constitution, and Farmers' and Mechanics' Advertiser*. Mickle claims he "procured" the war account "from Jonas Cattle [Cattell]." Cattell, who was 88 years old in 1846, died three years later. Mickle's secondhand account claims Cattell and others, "were taken prisoners, and forced to stay all night," in Haddonfield prior to the assault on Fort Mercer. The next morning, Cattell "slipped quietly away, and started immediately for Red Bank, to give notice of the approach of the enemy." After moving through the woods and trails, he arrived at Fort Mercer and was introduced to Greene, "to whom he gave the information, that the enemy were on their way, and would arrive there in the course of the day to attack them."[30]

Many secondary sources summarize the story, though none provide a primary source for the tale. Frank Stewart's 1927 history of Red Bank, which has Cattell crossing "Big Timber Creek at Isaiah Marple's," claimed he gave "the first warning at the fort." Stewart concluded with another unsubstantiated claim: "[I]t was well known and expected for over two weeks that an attack would be made." Cattell

---

28 Revolutionary War Pension and Bounty-Land-Warrant Application Files (M804) [RWPF], file W2197.

29 Darby Road is modern Woodland Avenue.

30 *The Constitution, and Farmers' and Mechanics' Advertiser*, March 10, 1846.

later claimed he "gave the first information about the Hessians, that Col. Greene called the men to arms and ordered the militiamen to leave."[31]

John Jackson, historian and chronicler of the Pennsylvania Navy and the Delaware River defenses also related the legend: "As the last of the Hessian column disappeared down the road, the prisoners were released. One suspect, Jonas Cattell, an enterprising young man, immediately departed to warn Colonel Greene. Cattell avoided the Hessian line of march and arrived at Fort Mercer shortly before noon where he advised Greene that Donop would reach the vicinity of the fort in minutes." Jackson included more detail in his history of the Pennsylvania Navy:

> Cattell avoiding the line of march of the Hessians, he reached Timber Creek and discovered that all boats along the stream had been scuttled to prevent Tories or Quakers from taking produce to the British at Philadelphia. He pushed off in a boat partially filled with water and safely crossed, although his boat sank when he reached the other side of the creek. Heading for the fort, he arrived before noon and advised Greene that the Hessians could be expected soon.[32]

Historian Gregory Edgar gave a version of this tale in his history of the campaign. "Circling around the Hessian columns' flankers, he [Jonas Cattell] managed to reach and warn the garrison by noon. The fort's commandant was not sure, though, whether this enemy force intended to attack his fort, or was simply foraging; he had heard that Howe's army was becoming desperate for food supplies," added Edgar, "so he dispatched a few men to reconnoiter." Writer Lee Patrick Anderson noted that other warnings reached Greene, but claimed, "His information was however, vital because it was the last received."[33]

All of these stories become immediately meaningless after reading Jonas Cattell's pension application, submitted to the government 23 years prior to Isaac Mickle's 1846 newspaper article. Cattell was a New Jersey militia member and part of the militia contingent serving under Christopher Greene in Fort Mercer before the battle. "I was in the Service at the time of Battle of Red Bank," he wrote in his application, "and was in the fort the same day, but Col Green turned us all out *before the Battle* [emphasis added]." Sometime during the morning of October 22, Greene

---

31 Stewart, *Battle of Red Bank*, 10.

32 Jackson, *Fort Mifflin*, 43; Jackson, *Navy*, 173.

33 Gregory T. Edgar, *The Philadelphia Campaign: 1777-1778* (Bowie, MD, 1998), 78; Anderson, *Forty Minutes*, 75-76.

ordered the New Jersey militia to leave to provide more room within the fort's limited interior for his Rhode Island Continentals. Cattell's own admittance to being at the fort that morning with the militia precludes the possibility that he ran from Haddonfield in the early morning hours to warn the Americans. It is just as revealing that there is not a syllable in the pension application regarding his supposed marathon run from Haddonfield to Fort Mercer to warn Greene.[34]

Someone, however, did warn Greene of the pending attack. There are two who could have done so. One, 15-year-old militiaman Richard Tice, noted the following in his pension application: "When the object of the Hessians was fully understood, Col. [Joseph] Ellis sent this declarant as the bearer of despatches to Col. Green[e] at the Fort at Red Bank." The messenger could also have been Cornelius Sullivan, who claimed in his pension application that he was sent "as an Express to Col. Green at Redbank Fort" and "was obliged to remain at the Fort one day as it was surrounded." It is also possible both were telling the truth.[35]

The March to Fort Mercer

Wednesday, October 22 dawned with the Whittall family (owners of the land around Fort Mercer) going about their daily routine unaware of the approaching storm soon to rage adjacent to their home. "Ye Boys and myself hung a gate in ye meadow and John and I went to finish ye stacks (hay)," recorded Job Whittall in his diary. Then they "got our horses and wagon and loaded it with goods. Ye reason was because ye English troops were close by." Sometime that morning Capt. Felix Fisler sent a dispatch warning Colonel Greene of the Hessian advance. Likely sensing the commotion at the fort, the Whittalls prepared for the worst. Try as they might, they were unable to save all their livestock. "We drove away 21 head, 8 fat, 4

34 Revolutionary War Pension and Bounty-Land-Warrant Application Files (M804) [RWPF], file S2421. Cattell's son also related in the pension application a tale that occurred at Fort Mercer. "Here a Circumstance occurred that his father often spoke of it was about a camp Kettle belonging to a Company that lay at Red Bank at the time, Jonas took the Camp Kettle which contained their meat, and hung it up at the top of a hickory tree, when it was ascertained that the meat and kettle were gone, a good deal of disturbance was made by the company, the Col. was informed of it, and when the Kettle was discovered hung up in the tree, it was immediately charged upon Jonas, it being thought that he was the only man in Camp that could have put it there, the Col obliged Jonas to go up and get it and restore it to the Owners, and Jonas very narrowly escaped a flogging."

35 Revolutionary War Pension and Bounty-Land-Warrant Application Files (M804) [RWPF], file S28912; Revolutionary War Pension and Bounty-Land-Warrant Application Files (M804) [RWPF], file S1258.

cows, one pair oxen, 3 steers, 1 heifer and 3 calves to Uncle David Cooper and stayed all night. This same day ye people in ye Fort drove from Father and me 47 sheep into ye fort."[36]

Around the same time McDougall discovered the empty British camp near Gray's Ferry, von Donop began marching his Hessians to Fort Mercer. He had failed to keep his mission much of a secret. Continental commissary officer Charles Stewart wrote to Washington at 11:00 a.m. from Haddonfield: "The Enemy left this at half after 4 OClock this morning . . . and says they will this day take Fort Mercer." Haddonfield's residents certainly knew von Donop's destination.[37]

Alerted to the coming danger, Christopher Greene prepared his garrison. "We turnd out Early in the Morning & struck tents & Cleared away for an attack & Every man at work to strengthen our Selves—we sent Partys out to fetch in all the stock & horses into the fort which was Done," recorded Sgt. John Smith in his diary. Colonel Israel Angell of the 2nd Rhode Island confirms the garrison continued working "Dilligent on our works until the after Noon about one oClock, when the Enemy Arrived within musket Shoot of our fort."[38]

Von Donop's planned route utilized Kings Highway to cross Big Timber Creek near modern Westville. Not long after departing Haddonfield, recorded Hessian adjutant Lt. Friedrich Werner, the column came to Newton Creek, "over which there was a bridge, which in its condition could not be used. One of its timbers was broken, and another was missing." The artillery could not cross the 18-foot-wide creek without the bridge. "At once two trees were felled to make new timbers, the existing planks were laid on, the fences torn up and also used for the floor, so that within a quarter of an hour the bridge was fit to be used by the wagons [artillery], all of which passed over it."[39]

After continuing west, the column bore to the south to cross the marshy banks of Little Timber Creek around 9:00 a.m. Johann Ewald described "a dam of several hundred paces" extending across the creek on which were "two wooden bridges." Ewald was surprised they "did not leave here at least one jager company to retain the mastery of this pass, since, after all, the success of our expedition was not yet

---

36 Job Whittall, "Job Whitall's Diary," Frank H. Stewart, ed., *Notes on Old Gloucester County, New Jersey*, 2 vols. (Camden, NJ, 1917), vol. 1, 258-259.

37 Chase and Lengel, eds., *Papers*, vol. 11, 581.

38 Smith, Diary, http://www.revwar75.com/library/bob/smith.htm; Angell, *Diary*, n.p.

39 "Report of Werner," 5-6. The first bridge incident took place where Kings Highway and Chews Landing Road intersect.

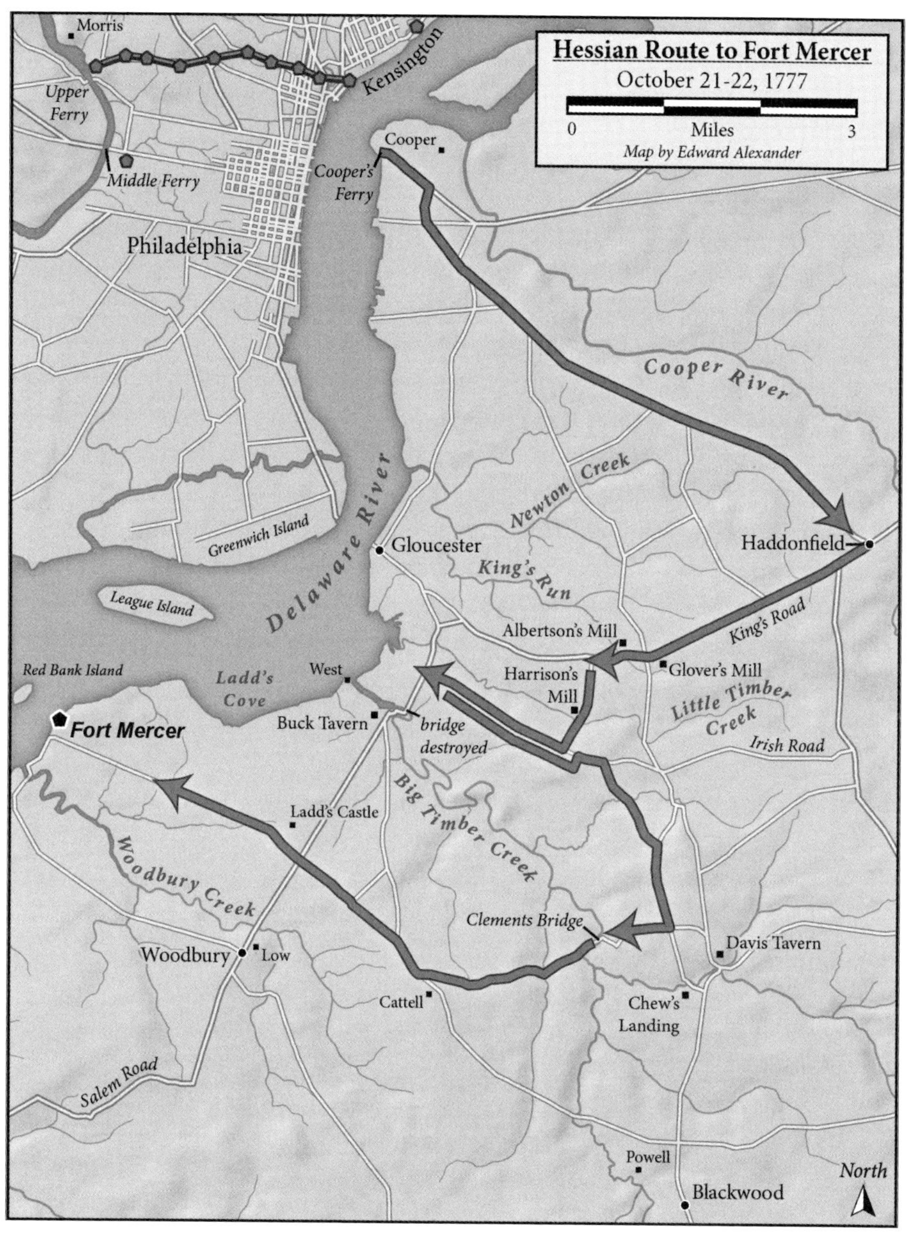
Morris
Upper Ferry
Middle Ferry
Philadelphia
Kensington
Cooper's Ferry
Cooper
Hessian Route to Fort Mercer
October 21-22, 1777
0
Miles
3
Map by Edward Alexander
Cooper River
Newton Creek
Haddonfield
Greenwich Island
Gloucester
King's Run
League Island
Albertson's Mill
King's Road
Glover's Mill
Red Bank Island
Ladd's Cove
West
Harrison's Mill
Little Timber Creek
Delaware River
Fort Mercer
Buck Tavern
bridge destroyed
Irish Road
Ladd's Castle
Big Timber Creek
Woodbury Creek
Clements Bridge
Davis Tavern
Woodbury
Low
Cattell
Chew's Landing
Salem Road
Powell
Blackwood
North

assured." Ewald was worried that Washington might send a column into New Jersey to attack their rear. The Hessians, meanwhile, approached Big Timber Creek near modern Brooklawn. New Jersey militia under Capt. Felix Fisler, however, had destroyed the bridge, forcing the Hessians into a long detour.[40]

Von Donop now needed to move east and try another span across Big Timber Creek. According to jaeger commander Lt. Col. Ludwig von Wurmb, they marched to another crossing point, "or, if it were wrecked [too], to go upstream until the creek could be crossed." The Hessians ended up crossing Clements Bridge, which "was passed with little resistance by the entire corps," according to Hessian quartermaster Lt. Col. Johann von Cochenhausen. Silas Newcomb had somehow failed to place any militia at this crucial bridge or destroy it. Had he destroyed Clements Bridge, the Hessian access to Fort Mercer would have required yet another detour and longer march.[41]

Once across Big Timber Creek, the Hessian column moved through wooded land. Lieutenant Carl von Bultsingsloewen of the von Mirbach Regiment described the march here as moving along "unknown sneaky lanes." Ludwig von Wurmb recalled "the area we passed through was all woods with only an occasional house and quite level except for the last three miles from Redbank where the ground began to rise."[42]

40 Ewald, *Diary*, 97. This dam was located just east of the present Bell Road in Mt. Ephraim. The dam belonged to Capt. William Harrison, who owned a 514-acre plantation running along both sides of the creek. The column turned right onto Browning Road. The Hessians learned of the destroyed bridge over Timber Creek during the approach to the Old Salem Road not far from today's Brooklawn Circle. Stewart, *Battle of Red Bank*, 10. The bridge was located near the Buck Tavern in modern Westville, several hundred feet above the present bridge (Route 47 or Broadway Bridge). The original bridge was located approximately at the terminus of modern Old Salem Road.

41 Letter, von Wurmb to Jungkenn, October 25, 1777, 13. Learning of the destruction of the bridge, von Donop turned around. They moved back down Browning Road and turned right onto a road roughly along present Black Horse Pike before turning onto present Clements Bridge Road and crossing Big Timber Creek at Clements Bridge near Westcottville. Letter, Lt. Col. Johann von Cochenhausen to Maj. General Friedrich Christian Arnold Jungkenn, October 26, 1777, Donald Londahlsmidt, ed., "German and British Accounts of the Assault on Fort Mercer at Redbank, NJ in October 1777," *Journal of the Johannes Schwalm Historical Association*, 26 vols. (Scotland, PA, 2013), vol. 16, 24.

42 Carl von Bultsingsloewen, "Journal of Second Lieutenant Carl Wilhelm von Bultsingsloewen," Donald Londahlsmidt, ed., "German and British Accounts of the Assault on Fort Mercer at Redbank, NJ in October 1777," *Journal of the Johannes Schwalm Historical Association*, 26 vols. (Scotland, PA, 2013), vol. 16, 8. Letter, von Wurmb to Jungkenn, October 25, 1777, 13. Turning to the northeast they followed modern Caulfield Avenue and skirted Woodbury along Deptford Avenue and then over what is now called Hessian Avenue before arriving in the woods in front of the fort. Smith, *Fight for Delaware*, 20.

Having received Fisler's message, Christopher Greene ordered Capt. Oliver Clark and Lt. Robert Rogers of the 1st Rhode Island and an ensign from the 2nd Rhode Island "to reconnoiter & gain Intelligence where they [the Hessians] were." The three officers ventured three miles from the fort to within thirty yards "of the Enemy before we discovered each other, upon their seeing us they discharg'd a whole volley of Musketry at us which thro' the goodness of kind Providence hurt neither of us." One of the rounds, however, wounded the ensign's horse "in the buttock as we all wheel'd to the right about which you must imagine we did very willingly." Hessian jaegers chased them and "took Capt Clarke, his horse being poor, the rest got Clear & arriv'd safe at the fort where we thought ourselves safe as a Mouse in a Cheese." Johann Ewald thought Clark a forager who "had been ordered to get fresh meat at a plantation and knew nothing of our approach." However, Hessian adjutant Friedrich Werner reported Clark "had been sent out of the fort to reconnoiter."[43]

Von Donop's column approached Fort Mercer after a grueling eight-hour march covering 17 miles. The time was now approaching 1:00 p.m. The Hessians could now assault the fort by land from three sides, with the Delaware River running along the entire western side of the works. On the north, east, and to a lesser degree, the southeast, the Americans had cleared the land (the orchards and fields of James Whittall) for a distance of 400 yards to permit a field of fire for their artillery. Thick woods lay beyond this clearing.[44]

The Hessians took up a position at the edge of those woods. Carl von Donop's moment of decision had arrived.

43 Letter, Robert Rogers to his brother, October 25, 1777, scanned copy in author's possession. This skirmish likely took place near the modern intersection of Route 45 and Hessian Avenue in Woodbury. Ewald, *Diary*, 97-98; "Report of Werner," 6.

44 Ironically, this is the same distance the flanking column marched at Brandywine prior to their attack at Birmingham Hill.

Chapter 5

The Assault on Fort Mercer

October 22-23, 1777

"They had already reached the abatis, and were endeavoring to pull up or cut away the
branches, when they were overwhelmed with a shower of musket shot,
which took them in front and flank."[1]

— Marquis de Chastellux, December 8, 1780

Decisions at Fort Mercer

Although warned that the enemy was approaching, Christopher Greene's Americans appeared unprepared when they actually made an appearance. The Hessians took note.

To get to the fort, recalled jaeger Lt. Heinrich von Feilitzsch, "the Jagers had to crawl out on their stomachs up to the abatis, half a cannon shot from the fort . . . many from the garrison were walking around outside the fort and were joking, and knew nothing about us." Johann Buettner agreed, observing that the Rhode Islanders were "hanging out their wash to dry." Whoever penned the journal kept by the Grenadier Battalion von Minnigerode recorded that "the door of the fort stood open and the sentinels at the gate and in the fort were pacing quietly up and

---

1 Chastellux, *Travels in North America*, vol. 1, 158.

down with their guns on their shoulders, probably unloaded." Appearances, however, were deceiving. Greene knew of their approach and had discussed it with Lt. Robert Rogers, including information about his recent scrape with the jaegers.[2]

Several officers accompanied Col. Carl von Donop to the edge of the woods to inspect Fort Mercer. One of just two British officers on the expedition was among them. Major Charles Stuart had fallen into disfavor with William Howe and remained without a command; going along with and helping the Hessians in the field was how he hoped to redeem his reputation. The officers did not tarry long along the ragged wood line. American gunners noticed the Hessians and "fired a Cannon or two at them on which they Retired, and kept Sculking in the woods," recorded Col. Israel Angell of the 2nd Rhode Island.[3]

What von Donop, Stuart, and others discovered was that "On examining the works they found them much stronger than what they were supposed to be." Stuart "agreed with von Donop on the impropriety of attacking them without cannon." The Hessian commander wanted permission to delay the attack and went so far as to seek that permission from Major Stuart. According to Maj. Gen. James Robertson, who likely learned the information from Stuart himself, "The Major said that he was too young, and had not sufficient authority to have a delay of the Commander in Chief's orders rest upon his shoulders."[4]

Von Donop's request was odd. Howe's order was not to make "the attack at all hazards." Rather, von Donop "was to be guided by his own judgement on the spot, but the attack was to be made, unless he saw good reason to the contrary." He could wait until October 23 to attack, which would provide time for Admiral Howe to move ships into position to support his effort.[5]

Staff Captain Christian von Urff heard von Donop's comments after scouting the fort. "We are in a difficult position, if I get it, we will lose many men," he wrote in a letter soon thereafter. "I am almost of the opinion to report to Howe that it is impossible, then he will not believe me and say the Hessians are not up to it. So, we

---

2 von Feilitzsch, *Journal*, 112; Johann Carl Buettner, *Narrative of Johann Carl Buettner in the American Revolution* (New York, 1915), 51; Journal of the Grenadier Battalion von Minnigerode, Donald Londahlsmidt, ed., "German and British Accounts of the Assault on Fort Mercer at Redbank, NJ in October 1777," *Journal of the Johannes Schwalm Historical Association*, 26 vols. (Scotland, PA, 2013), vol. 16, 10.

3 Angell, *Diary*, n.p.

4 Mrs. E, Stuart Wortley, ed. *A Prime Minister and His Son: From the Correspondence of the Third Earl of Bute and Lt. General The Honourable Sir Charles Stuart, K.B.* (London, 1925), 117.

5 *Narrative*, 28-29; Journal of von Minnigerode, 10.

will try our luck." Von Donop's hell-bent desire to attack a day earlier than need be is unclear. Either he misunderstood Howe's orders or was so focused on restoring Hessian honor without British assistance that he was willing to risk a bloody defeat.[6]

As the officers conversed about what to do, von Donop asked jaeger Capt. Johann Ewald to "inspect the fort and to give him my opinion." The veteran foot soldier "approached the fort up to rifle-shot range and found that it was provided with a breastwork twelve feet high, palisaded and dressed with assault stakes." Sharpened stakes or pickets were placed on the top of the earthwork and abatis around the land sides of the redoubt. Branches of trees and bushes placed on the ramparts and partly covered with earth concealed the fort's 14 guns.[7]

The 33-year-old Ewald was returning to deliver his field report when he passed Major Stuart, together with a drummer and two of von Donop's staff officers, preparing to summon the fort. According to Ewald, the men were joking, and no one seemed to be taking the situation seriously. Perhaps they were thinking of past encounters. The previous year around New York City, the Americans had abandoned one fortified position after another. Fort Washington, the one fortification they did not abandon, was stormed by the Hessians a year earlier and resulted in the capture of some 2,000 men. Thus far around Philadelphia, the British had repeatedly defeated the Continentals. Fort Mercer was nothing to fear.

Colonel Greene's garrison consisted of his own 1st Rhode Island and Col. Israel Angell's 2nd Rhode Island. Capt.-Lt. David Cook's Continental artillery company provided the manpower to man the fort's cannons. Angell's regiment covered the northern face of the fort and Greene's watched the eastern and southern faces. The total garrison numbered about 550 men including the return of those Greene had sent to reinforce Fort Mifflin. Colonel von Donop likely had an idea of the strength in the fort and knew he held more than a four to one advantage. Hessian arrogance influenced decisions that day. If they offered Greene's garrison a show of force, the Americans would collapse as they always did.[8]

---

6 Letter, Staff Captain Christian Friedrich von Urff to Georg Ernst von und zu Gilsa, October 26, 1777, Donald Londahlsmidt, ed., "German and British Accounts of the Assault on Fort Mercer at Redbank, NJ in October 1777," *Journal of the Johannes Schwalm Historical Association*, 26 vols. (Scotland, PA, 2013), vol. 16, 28.

7 Ewald, *Diary*, 98.

8 Some accounts claim Lt. Col. John Green with the 6th Virginia Regiment supported the Rhode Islanders. However, Washington ordered the Virginians to report to Fort Mifflin and Christopher Greene did not detain the 150 men. Jackson, *Navy*, 182 & 442.

Hoping to induce surrender, von Donop was sending Major Stuart out with a drummer to parlay with the Americans—a logical choice since Stuart spoke English. Captain Stephen Olney of the 2nd Rhode Island confirmed Stuart "acted as linguist." The Marquis de Chastellux, who later visited the site and interviewed witnesses, described the arrogant and pompous exchange that followed. The accounts are uniformly consistent as to how the parlay played out.

Greene sent Lt. Col. Jeremiah Olney of the 2nd Rhode Island out to meet Stuart. Stuart demanded in as loud a voice as he could muster: "The King of England orders his rebellious subjects to lay down their arms, and they are warned that if they stand battle, no quarter will be given." Stuart's "harangue," recalled de Chastellux, "was so insolent that it only served to irritate the garrison and inspire them with more resolution." Chaplain Ebenezer David of the 2nd Rhode Island heard Olney's reply: "seeing Col Green was altogether needless . . . that He would defend the Fort as long as he had a Man, & as to Mercy it was neither sought nor expected at their hands." A Rhode Island sergeant named Jeremiah Greenman confirmed these secondhand accounts. Major Stuart, he recalled, threatened "to put the Garrison to death if he [Greene] did not surrender it immediately, Colo. Green answered with disdain, that he would defend it 'till the last drop of his blood." Colonel Angell of the 2nd Rhode Island provides the only known eyewitness account. "They sent in a flagg Demanding the fort but was answered that the fort was not to be Given up on any terms, in Reply to this, they answered that if we Still remain'd obstinate, our blood might be upon our own heads, for we Should have no Mercy Shone us. our Answer was we asked for none and Expect none."[9]

When Stuart returned with Greene's reply, von Donop could no longer back down without losing his honor. The Hessian had backed himself into a corner. Captain Johann Krug of von Donop's staff offered his thoughts to Captain Ewald: "He who has seen forts or fortified places captured with sword in hand will not regard this affair as a small matter, if the garrison puts up a fight and has a resolute commandant. We have let luck slip through our fingers," Krug continued. "We should not have summoned the fort, but immediately taken it by surprise, for no one knew of our arrival. But now they will make themselves ready, and if our preparations are not being made better than I hear, we will get a good beating." In

---

9 Mrs. Williams, *Revolutionary Heroes: Containing the Life of Brigadier Gen. William Barton, and also, of Captain Stephen Olney* (Providence, RI, 1839), 223; Chastellux, *Travels in North America*, vol. 1, 158; David, *A Rhode Island Chaplain*, 53; Greenman, *Diary*, 82; Angell, *Diary*, n.p.

fact, von Donop never truly held the element of surprise. As far as Johann Ewald was concerned, the entire expedition had been poorly planned. "Since this day was not bread or provisions day, very few had any bread to break or bite. The officers, especially, were not provided with anything. . . . Since we had flattered ourselves in advance with a successful surrender," recorded Ewald, "no retreat was then thought of, and no wagons brought to transport the wounded."[10]

Preparations for the Assault

The Hessians could not immediately storm the fort because von Donop's guns were not in position, so a delay ensued as the artillerymen rolled them into position along the edge of the tree line. Ewald recalled placing "sixteen good marksmen at the edge of the wood in the vicinity of the battery, who were to shoot at those men who showed themselves on the parapet." The Hessians also constructed fascines, thick bundles of sticks tied together to protect them from enemy bullets and shells. According to Ewald, "One hundred men from each battalion [300 total men] were to carry the fascines, and march in a line at a distance of two hundred paces in front of the battalion. With these the ditch was to be filled, crossed, and the fort scaled with sword in hand." In order to reach the ditch, however, the assaulting force would have to first negotiate the abatis fronting the fort. Somehow, "no one thought about axes or saws with which the obstructions and palisades could be cut down," recalled Ewald. The odds against the Hessians were mounting by the minute.[11]

Von Donop organized his force to attack from three directions. The von Minnigerode Battalion of grenadiers deployed on the right fronting the northern section of Fort Mercer, which the Americans had abandoned after reducing the fort's footprint. In the center, toward the eastern face of the redoubt, the von Mirbach Regiment prepared to go forward. On the left with orders to assault the southern face of the redoubt stood the von Linsing Grenadier Battalion. The jaegers and the von Lengerke Grenadier Battalion remained in reserve.

While the Hessians were bringing up their artillery and aligning their infantry and grenadiers for the assault, Chrisopher Greene calmly paced along the top of the ramparts observing the enemy preparations. On his order, signal flags rose above Mercer alerting the naval elements in the river to come to his assistance. According

10 Ewald, *Diary*, 98-99.

11 Ibid.

to one Hessian account, Greene communicated with the naval elements "by means of speaking tubes."[12]

After one final attempt to end the matters under a surrender flag was rebuffed, von Donop ordered the artillery to open on the fort. According to von Donop's adjutant, Lt. Levin von Heister, "the colonel had given a short but powerful speech, all of the horses were sent back, and each placed himself at the head of his detachment." The Hessian guns bucked and flamed with a "tremendous discharge of grape shot and ball." The enemy iron, recalled Capt. Stephen Olney, "made the gravel and dust fly from the top of our fort, and took off all the heads that happened to be in the way." Lieutenant Robert Rogers of the 1st Rhode Island confirmed "they began with a most severe Cannonade from several field pieces." British artillery officer Francis Downman described the barrage as a "brisk and close fire . . . which continued some little time. . . . Colonel von Donop then ordered the whole to cease, and called to his troops to advance."[13]

The artillery fired for just ten minutes, which was not long enough to seriously damage the fort. The booming Hessian artillery, however, did alert American naval elements that the attack on Mercer was underway. In reply, American gallies unleashed their fire into the woods sheltering the Hessians. "The rebels' ships started a hellish fire and swept the whole place where the attack was being made," recalled one eyewitness. "They fired with the so-called cross-bar shot up through the trees so that the falling branches and pieces of timber did us the greatest injury." The sun was just beginning to set about 4:45 p.m. when the Hessians emerged from the woods.[14]

12 Buettner, *Narrative*, 52; McGuire, *Campaign*, vol. 2, 161. Early speaking tubes consisted of two cones of wood or metal, one end shaped to fit the speaker's mouth, connected to the other flared to amplify the sound. Essentially, these were an early form of a bull horn.

13 The Hessian artillery position was located about where Monument Road and Fourth Street intersect in National Park, NJ. Levin Carl von Heister, "Diary of Lieutenant Levin Carl von Heister," Donald Londahlsmidt, ed., "German and British Accounts of the Assault on Fort Mercer at Redbank, NJ in October 1777," *Journal of the Johannes Schwalm Historical Association*, 26 vols. (Scotland, PA, 2013), vol. 16, 14; Williams, *Revolutionary Heroes*, 223; Letter, Robert Rogers to his brother, October 25, 1777; Whinyates, *Services*, 43.

14 Journal of von Minnigerode, 10.

The Assault on Fort Mercer

Sergeant Jeremiah Greenman of the 2nd Rhode Island was unimpressed with the Hessian assault, which "rushed on very Rash that even Success could not justify its temerity." The 430 men of the von Minnigerode Grenadier Battalion confidently assaulted on the Hessian right. "They advanced and marched to the first entrenchment," recalled French engineer du Plessis-Mauduit, and "finding it abandoned but not destroyed, they thought they had driven the Americans from it." The confident Hessians threw their fascines into the ditch, climbed over the parapet, and entered the abandoned northern section of the fort. Once there, they wheeled left and advanced 200 yards south to strike the northern face of the American redoubt. Although raked by naval grapeshot fired through the low ground around the ravine north of the fort, they had yet to encounter musket fire. Thus far, "supposing they were masters of the fort [the Hessians] huzzaed! and came on, perhaps, to cut up their prisoners," thought Captain Olney. Greene's French engineer agreed: "They then shouted 'victoria,' waved their hats in the air, and advanced toward the redoubt." An anonymous letter printed in the *New Jersey Gazette* confirmed their thinking by reporting the Hessians "got into the old part of the works, they thought it was their own, and gave three cheers."[15]

Ten yards from the redoubt, the grenadiers needed to pass through abatis and then another ditch in order to get up and over another parapet. One of the attackers, Johann Carl Buettner, remembered reaching abatis "made of fruit trees, the branches of which had been sharpened." Von Donop, who did not believe he should command in the rear, personally led the advancing grenadiers south through the abandoned section of Mercer. While slashing their way through the abatis, the Rhode Island defenders rose, leveled their muskets on the top of the parapet, and fired a devastating volley that blew back Hessians trapped in the tangled brush. Buettner recalled how "a hail of rifle bullets and cannon balls fell around us; warriors dropped on every side." Raking musket fire slashed them in front, while grape shot tore into their right flank from the river. "The enemy . . . began a terrible bombardment from the fort and also from the ships. It was so heavy, that individual shots could not be distinguished," recorded one jaeger

---

15 Greenman, *Diary*, 82; Chastellux, *Travels in North America*, vol. 1, 158; Williams, *Revolutionary Heroes*, 224; Frank Moore, *Diary of the American Revolution from Newspapers and Original Documents*, 2 vols. (New York, 1860), vol. 1, 514.

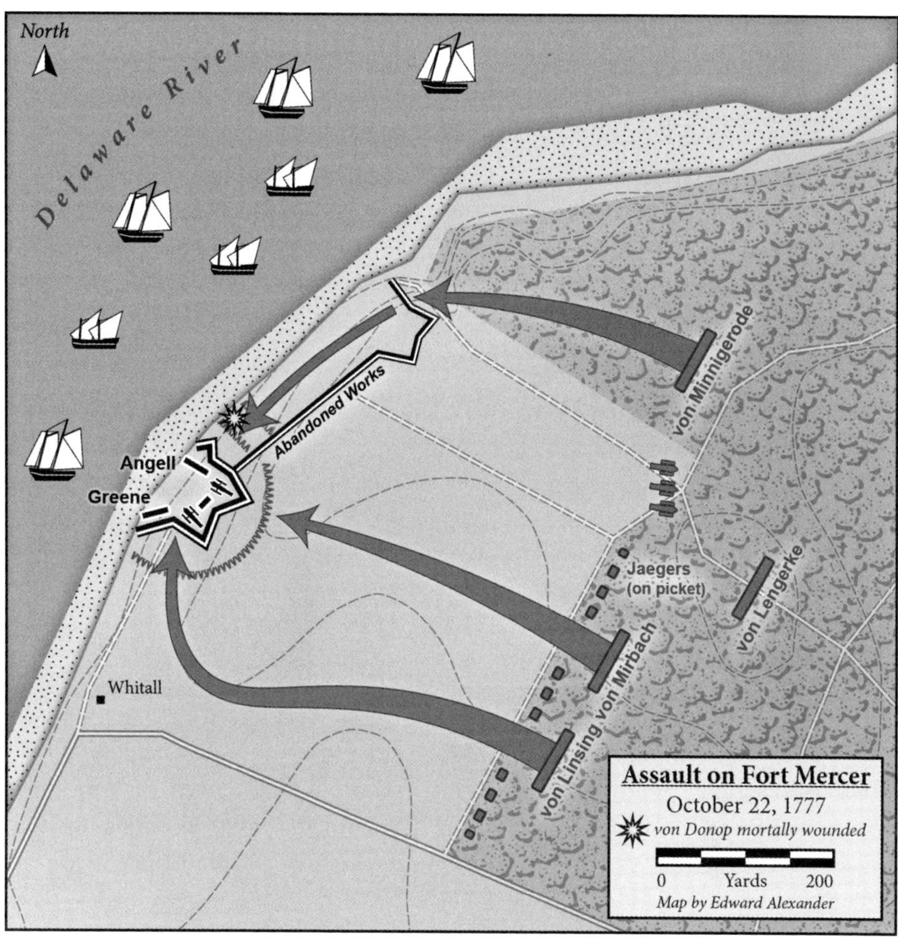

officer. "[T]he rockets, shot by the ships, toppled the tops and limbs of trees, and so frequently, that we Jagers had to move out into the open."[16]

Hessians fell thick and fast, especially the officers. The capable veteran Colonel von Minnigerode was shot through both legs, while Capt. Henrich Wachs collapsed with a right arm wound and Lts. Georg Hille and Karl von Offenbach were both killed. Captain Johannes von Groning was killed and Lt. Hermann Hendorff collapsed with a right thigh wound. Command and control dissolved

---

16 Buettner, *Narrative*, 52; von Feilitzsch, *Journal*, 113. According to surgeon Peter Turner of the 1st Rhode Island, Christopher Greene jumped off the rampart and told the men "Fire low, men, they have a broad belt just above their hips,—aim at that." George Washington Greene, *Life of Nathanael Greene, Major-General in the Army of the Revolution*, (New York, 1867), vol. 1, 489-490.

amongst the grenadiers. The young drummer who had summoned the surrender a few hours earlier went down in the first volley. Wilhelm von Knyphausen's adjutant reported that Capt. Johann Wagner of von Donop's staff fell mortally wounded when "both of his legs were shot to pieces and another bullet entered his mouth and came out through his cheek." Maj. Charles Stuart, who had arrogantly demanded surrender prior to the assault, had a bullet come so near his "ear that for a while he lost his hearing." No one was immune from the flying lead and iron, including Colonel von Donop, who suffered a mortal wound when a musket round passed through his upper left femur just below the hip, shattering the bone. He fell in the bloody tangled abatis.[17]

"They had already reached the abatis, and were endeavoring to pull up or cut away the branches, when they were overwhelmed with a shower of musket shot, which took them in front and flank," recalled du Plessis in his description of the repulse of the grenadiers. Captain Olney's men had helped stop the assault of von Minnegerode's grenadiers. "My company was stationed in a salient angle, connected with the curtain of the breast work, to rake the ditches on each side. When fighting, I thought my company quite secure, as the enemy looked to the bastions on each side," recalled Olney, "therefore my men were deliberate, except one little Irishman, who was frightened out of his senses, but a few strokes with the but-end of my gun brought him to his duty." Olney went on to describe the actions of one of his men. "While the enemy were in confusion, not more than 20 paces off, a man by the name of Sweetzer insisted that I should see him kill when he fired. I indulged him four or five times, and his object fell. I then directed him to fire at an officer, and he only made him stagger a little."[18]

Jeremiah Greenman called the repulse a "Great Slawter." The Hessians "advanced as far as the abbatis, but they could not remove it (tho sum few got over)

---

17 "List of the Killed and Wounded, Prisoners, and Missing of the Officers, Non-Commissioned Officers, and Privates at the storming of the Fort Redbank the 22 October 1777," Donald Londahlsmidt, ed., "German and British Accounts of the Assault on Fort Mercer at Redbank, NJ in October 1777," *Journal of the Johannes Schwalm Historical Association*, 26 vols. (Scotland, PA, 2013), vol. 16, 4; McGuire, *Campaign*, vol. 2, 164-165; Carl von Baurmeister, *Revolution in America: Confidential Letters and Journals 1776-1784 of Adjutant General Major Baurmeister of the Hessian Forces*, Bernhard A. Uhlendorf, trans. & ed. (New Brunswick, NJ, 1957), 127. Von Knyphausen reported "they will try to amputate his [Wagner's] legs" but "his present state of health is hopeless." Wagner died soon thereafter. Letter, Lieutenant General Wilhelm von Knyphausen to Landgraf Friedrich II, October 25, 1777, Donald Londahlsmidt, ed., "German and British Accounts of the Assault on Fort Mercer at Redbank, NJ in October 1777," *Journal of the Johannes Schwalm Historical Association*, 26 vols. (Scotland, PA, 2013), vol. 16, 3; Wortley, ed. *A Prime Minister and His Son*, 117.

18 Chastellux, *Travels in North America*, vol. 1, 158; Williams, *Revolutionary Heroes*, 224.

being repulsed with great loss." Engineer du Plessis agreed: "The officers were seen continually rallying their men, marching back to the abatis, and falling amidst the branches they were endeavoring to cut." Some of the Hessians tried to escape the devastation by hiding along the river embankment on their right flank but "the fire from the galleys sent them back with great loss of men." The American galleys fired chain shot into the Hessian flank which "knocked down whole rows of men."[19]

As he turned to retreat, Hessian Johann Buettner tried to "pass between the stakes of the palisade," but "was struck by a rifle bullet that entered under one of my shoulder blades, passed over my spinal column and out through the other shoulder blade." Buettner "dropped to the ground. . . . Racked with agony, listening to the screams of pain from my comrades, I lay there unattended, through the chill October night. Not being able to see my wound I did not know myself how seriously I had been hurt." The Americans recovered Buettner the next day. According to the *Journal of the von Minnigerode Battalion*, "However bravely and well the grenadiers and the regiment stood their ground, hewed down the barriers before the fort, forced their way through, tore up the first line of palisades and scaled the first outer wall, no man could remain under the fire from the fort and particularly from the ships." The von Minnigerode Battalion lost a staggering 147 killed, wounded, and captured out of 430.[20]

As the fighting died down on the northern face of the redoubt, things heated up to the east and south. The 550 men of the von Mirbach Regiment headed for the fort's gate from the east. The steady Rhode Islanders easily repulsed this attack as well. According to Johann Ewald, "the gallant Colonel [Justus von] Schieck, who commanded the Regiment von Mirbach, was shot dead at the barred gate." As one Hessian lieutenant put it, "There was nothing to do but die or retire. We could not become master of the fort since we did not have any heavy artillery to breach the walls. We also lacked scaling ladders to climb the walls. Our bravery was for nothing. In the entire American war no attack was more furious than this one." Lieutenant Carl Rueffer also described the regiment's repulse: "Because of the extensive losses and the indescribable cannonade and small arms fire from the fort and the almost impassable abates before the main fort, plus the fascines being of little value at the eighteen-foot high parapet, necessitated a withdrawal without accomplishing our purpose." In addition to von Schieck's fall, several subordinates went down with him. Captain Wilhelm von Bojatzky and Lieutenants Conrad

---

19 Greenman, *Diary*, 82; Chastellux, *Travels in North America*, vol. 1, 158; von Heister, "Diary," 14.

20 Buettner, *Narrative*, 52; Journal of von Minnigerode, 10.

Riemann and Carl von Wurmb were killed. Capt. Friedrich Schotten's right arm was shot off, Lt. Rueffer's left foot was smashed, and Lt. Hieronymus Berner's right leg was shot to pieces. Out of the 550 men, 40 were killed, 59 wounded, and 15 captured.[21]

The 430-man von Linsing Grenadier Battalion got through the abatis and ditch on the south side and climbed the parapet. "They were stopped by the pointed stakes [fraise]," noted du Plessis. Stymied by the fort's fraise, the Rhode Island defenders again leveled their muskets and fired off a volley into these fresh Hessian grenadiers. Stephen Olney recorded "one or two officers were killed or wounded on the brim of the breastwork." The Americans shot Captain Ludwig von Stamford through the chest, right shoulder, and left shin. Lieutenant Konrad du Puy was killed. Four others were wounded: Captain Ernst von Eschwege (in the neck), and Lieutenants Johann Rodemann (hit in right leg), Wilhelm von Eschen (shot through the neck, right arm and right side), and Dietrich von Gottschall (had his right knee shattered). Lieutenant Ernst Heymell was wounded in the leg and left behind. The battalion that began with 430 men also lost heavily with 29 killed, 84 wounded, and two captured.[22]

The Americans in the fort also took casualties. Jaeger sharpshooters 200 yards away shot at anything they could see outlined above the parapet. Jeremiah Greenman's company commander, Capt. Sylvanus Shaw, took a shot through the neck that killed him. "The first line of the enemy's artillery," admitted Captain Olney, "intimidated some of the men so much they were afraid to show their heads above the breastworks." Some "raised their guns and fired by guess work."[23]

It did not take long for the Hessians to realize their efforts were fruitless. The American defense, admitted Lieutenant Werner, was "astonishingly vigorous," as

21 von Bultsingsloewen, "Journal," 8; "Diary of Rueffer," 9; Ewald, *Diary*, 99-102. The remnants of Schotten's arm were amputated. Berner's left leg was also hit. "List of the Killed and Wounded," 4; Journal of the Regiment von Mirbach, Donald Londahlsmidt, ed., "German and British Accounts of the Assault on Fort Mercer at Redbank, NJ in October 1777," *Journal of the Johannes Schwalm Historical Association*, 26 vols. (Scotland, PA, 2013), vol. 16, 8.

22 Williams, *Revolutionary Heroes*, 224. Von Stanford commanded the battalion's assault. Lt. Col. von Linsing was incapacitated with a stomachache. Von Knyphausen hoped von Stamford could recover "as the ball has been cut out of his shoulder, I trust he is out of danger." Letter, von Knyphausen to Landraf, October 25, 1777, 3; Ewald, *Diary*, 102. The wounded Gottschall was left behind and captured. Von Knyphausen reported the lieutenant was "in danger of losing his leg, or else of dying of his wound." He died on October 26. Von Groening was carried back to Philadelphia but died six days later. "List of the Killed and Wounded," 4.

23 McGuire, *Campaign*, vol. 2, 165; Williams, *Revolutionary Heroes*, 225.

was "the fire from the galleys," which combined to "make the taking of the fort impossible." It was all over in about 40 minutes. Unable to scale the works, and taking heavy losses in all three columns, the Hessians began pulling away from the abatis and ditches of Fort Mercer. Many of their dead and wounded, including the dying Colonel von Donop, were left behind.[24]

Aftermath

Many wounded Hessians found themselves incapable of dragging themselves away. Heinrich von Feilitsch described the horror: "I could still hear the wounded call out, 'Officer, by the grace of God, take us along, we have done our duty; crawled after the others, but now our strength is leaving us,' and so on, and when all that did not help . . . they screamed: 'Comrad, you know I have done my duty, and now no one is helping me in my misery, remember that, be smarter, a soldier gets no thanks.'" During the chaotic withdrawal, Lt. Col. Ludwig von Wurmb realized Colonel von Donop was missing. "Lt. Col. von Wurmb addressed the Hessian Jagers, and told them that he had found out that Col. von Donop still lay wounded on the battlefield," recalled Von Feilitsch, "and since he knew the loyalty and

---

24 "Report of Werner," 6. Local legend has Anne Whiteall at her spinning wheel during the fighting until driven to the cellar when a cannonball passed through the house. Benson Lossing claimed to hear the story from her grandson in 1848: "his grandmother was urged to flee from the house, she refused, saying, 'God's arm is strong, and will protect *me*; I may do good by staying.' She was left alone in the house; and while the battle was raging, and cannon-balls were driving like sleet against and around her dwelling, she calmly plied her spinning-wheel in a room in the second story. At length a twelve-pound ball, from a British vessel in the river, grazing the American flag-staff (the walnut tree) at the fort, passed through the heavy brick wall on the north gable, and with a terrible crash perforated a partition at the head of the stairs, crossed a recess, and lodged in another partition, near where the old lady was sitting. Conceiving Devine protection a little more certain elsewhere after this manifestation of the power of gun-powder, the industrious dame gathered up her implements, and with a step as agile as a youth, she retreated to the cellar, where she continued spinning until called to attend the wounded and dying who were brought into her house at the close of the battle. She did indeed, 'do good' by remaining; for, like an angel of mercy, she went among the maimed, unmindful whether they were friend or foe, and administered every relief to their sufferings, in her power. She scolded the Hessians for coming to America to butcher the people. At the same time, she bound up their wounds tenderly, and gave them food and water. The scar made by the passage of that iron ball is quite prominent in the gable; it is denoted in the engraving by the dark spot. I saw within the house where the missile cut off the wood-work in its passage, and where it lodged." The story could well be true, but it would have been impossible for a British round to enter the north end of the house because the British ships were positioned south of the dwelling. If the house was hit by artillery, the round(s) likely came from American guns in the fort. Benson J. Lossing, *The Pictorial Field-Book of the Revolution; or, Illustrations, by Pen and Pencil, of the History, Biography, Scenery, Relics, and Traditions of the War for Independence* (New York, 1852), vol. 2, 290-291. The current park staff, however, claims there is no known artillery damage to the existing house.

courage of the Jagers, he hoped that several would step forward, and go and pick him up with their usual fearless courage; after a pause, a non-com stepped forward." After the sergeant went out looking for the colonel, he "brought back the answer that the Col. wished to be left there because his wounds were too severe." Von Donop "gave this sergeant his watch as a token of his gratitude that he had found him and spoken with him."[25]

By the time von Wurmb took command of the survivors in the immediate aftermath and ordered a retreat, darkness was upon them. Ewald recalled "the seriously wounded officers were carried on the guns and horses, and all the privates who could not drag themselves away on their wounded limbs fell into enemy hands."[26] Royal Artillerymen Francis Downman left a detailed description of the night's misery that is worth reproducing at length:

> We were obliged to retire, and that in much confusion, for by this time it was quite dark. We retired about a mile all in bustle and disorder, then stopped about an hour or so to get the troops disposed into some order, and to collect the wounded and carry them in the best way we could, for not a waggon was thought of, and had it not been for the ammunition waggons a number must have been left behind. This night's march was as melancholy and as disagreeable a one as ever I experienced; it was dark and excessively cold; the roads were deep and narrow and enclosed with wood; we lost our way twice and had to turn about the guns and waggons in the narrow road; the very worst of maneuvers. The horses were very bad and almost tired out, the drivers were a set of scoundrels. Add to this the groans of the wounded; the idea of being attacked in the rear by a sally from the fort while pent up in a road where we could not possibly make use of our cannon, and the probability of an encounter in front or flanks, for until day appeared we had no flanking parties out. We were lucky in meeting with no molestation except a few shot that did no harm.[27]

Many of the wounded were left behind to avoid slowing down the column as it retreated through Woodbury. There were few wagons available to carry the wounded, so many injured officers were strapped to guns and gun carriages. The Hessians confiscated wheeled vehicles from civilians along the route to help alleviate the suffering. Somewhere along the march, Colonel von Linsing took command from von Wurmb. When the column reached Clements Bridge at Big

---

25 von Feilitzsch, *Journal,* 114-115.

26 Ewald, *Diary,* 99.

27 Whinyates, *Services,* 44. Lieutenant Carl von Bultsingsloewen commanded the von Mirbach Regiment during the retreat. von Bultsingsloewen, "Journal," 8.

Timber Creek, the unbloodied von Lengerke Battalion, which had been held in reserve during the attack, deployed to cover the crossing. The fitfully moving column crossed by midnight and "pulled down part of" the bridge to prevent a pursuit that was not underway.[28]

The New Jersey militia hovering in the area under Silas Newcomb's command made little effort to assist the fort or slow the withdrawal of the Hessians. Chaplain Ebenezer David of the Rhode Island Continentals, who had left the fort a few days before the Hessians struck and was with the New Jersey militia during the attack, would recall a conversation he had with Newcomb "urging the importance of a few men if more was not attainable falling on the Enemies rear in time of the attack—But such stupidity such infamous Conduct I never saw—if the Salvation of the Brave Men in the Fort if the Salvation of America had ought depended upon them all had been lost—for they appeared lost to all sensibility."[29]

Once darkness settled over the battlefield and the enemy had withdrawn, French engineer du Plessis wanted to repair the abatis and fraise. Marquis de Chastellux later visited the site and interviewed the participants "He sallied forth with a few men, and was surprised to find about twenty Hessians standing on the berm and glued against the face of the parapet," recalled de Chastellux. "These soldiers, who had been bold enough to advance thus far, realized that there was still more danger in turning back, and decided not to risk it; they were captured and brought into the fort." A short time later a voice called out in English from the tangled carnage north of the redoubt. "Whoever you are, take me out of here." It was the badly wounded Colonel von Donop. The Americans carried the officer into the fort a prisoner. Rather than exact revenge for his threat of no quarter prior to the assault, the Americans spared him and provided medical attention.[30]

An exhausted Captain Olney commanded the fort's guards that night and stood his duty while enduring the pitiful cries of the wounded. "The part [of the

---

28 Reed, *Campaign*, 297-298. Many wounded were left at Woodbury Friends Meetinghouse and other buildings. Those who died were buried in the Strangers' Burying Ground. Jackson, *British Army*, 66; Letter, von Wurmb to Jungkenn, October 25, 1777, 13; "Report of Werner," 6. Many others were buried at the Ashbrook Burial Ground in Glendora near Clement's Bridge.

29 David, *A Rhode Island Chaplain*, 53-54.

30 Chastellux, *Travels in North America*, vol. 1, 159-160. Some accounts claim Maj. Simeon Thayer found and recovered von Donop. The original source is an 1867 account of Thayer participating in the Canadian invasion but includes no primary source for Thayer's supposed role at Fort Mercer. Edwin Martin Stone, *The Invasion of Canada in 1775: Including the Journal of Captain Simeon Thayer, Describing the Perils and Sufferings of the Army Under Colonel Benedict Arnold, in its March Through the Wilderness to Quebec: With Notes and Appendix* (Providence, RI, 1867), 75.

fort] we had evacuated on the preceding day, was covered with dead, wounded and dying Hessians. The groans and cries of the wounded and dying, were dreadful music to my ears; and but for the reflection of what would have been our fate had they been victorious, our sympathy would have been truly distressing." Several of the wounded, continued Olney "appeared to suffer with the cold. I had them removed into a little hut without any floor, where [there] was a little fire, which rendered them more comfortable than in the open air."[31]

Two men with the Hessian column proved especially unlucky. American patrols grabbed John McIlvaine and Dick Ellis, the two guides helping the withdrawing Hessians. Ellis, an African American slave, belonged to Maj. William Ellis of the New Jersey militia. The pickets took them to the fort and put them on trial. Capt. Samuel Massey summed up their fate. "The Master of the Negroe [Major Ellis] not in the least interceeding for the conduct of his Servant, (and) the persons who were insulted by McIlvaine anxious he should meet with his just demerits. . . . The Court resolved (the prisoners) should be made an Example (of) to deter any others from a future Conduct of the same Nature." Thus decided, the court ordered them hanged, "which sentence was put into Execution & the persons hung in Sight of (the American) Garrison & Fleet Soon after the Return of the retreating (Hessian) Troops to Philadelphia." The Americans nearly hung Reverend Nicholas Collin, as well. Collin, a German-speaker, arrived at Fort Mercer around the same time hoping to help the wounded. Greene, however, believed he was a spy, arrested him, and threatened to hang him on the gallows "to which two miserable fellows [the two guides] were just then being led." The clergyman was eventually released.[32]

The Overall Human Cost

The roughly 500 Rhode Island defenders repulsed 2,200 Hessian veterans at a cost of just 14 killed, 23 wounded, and one captured, or about 7% of the garrison. Several of these casualties were not from Hessian fire but the flying fragments from a cannon inside the fort that exploded during the fighting. The Battle for Fort

---

31 Williams, *Revolutionary Heroes*, 225. Many wounded ended up in the Whitehall House the next day. Job Whitall jotted into his diary that the wounded "had filled the kitchen, shop, big room, the long room upstairs and two others down stairs which forced us to move out." Whittall, "Diary," 259.

32 Massey, "Journal," 234-235; Nicholas Collin, *The Journal and Biography of Nicholas Collin 1746-1831*, Amandus Johnson, trans. (Philadelphia, 1936), 240.

Mercer (also known as the Battle of Red Bank) was one of the most lopsided victories of the entire war, and the only American triumph of the entire Philadelphia campaign. The Hessians suffered 370 casualties, or 17% of their attacking force. The three assaulting regiments were unfit for some time due to their casualties and officer losses. The Americans spent the next couple days tossing the dead in the ditches of the fort and covering them with dirt. Isaac Armstrong of the New Jersey militia remembered several decades later arriving at the fort "a day or two afterwards [and] helped to haul dirt to cover the dead, many of whom were then lying exposed." Charles Simpkins, also of the militia, returned to the fort after the battle and "saw the ground stained with blood."[33]

Many wounded were treated in the Whitehall House. Colonel von Donop was carried to the home of Joseph Low across Woodbury Creek. Civilian clergyman Nicholas Collin described the Whitehall House as "a pitiable sight. About 200 were lying on straw in two large rooms, some without arms or legs and others again with their limbs crushed like mush by langrel, some floated in blood, and told me that some had died for lack of something to bandage their wounds with." According to Hessian Johann Buettner, "Messengers were then dispatched to the Hessian army division for surgeons to take care of us. A few of these arrived that same day, and were able to help at least a few of us. Some of us were promptly bandaged, and on others amputations of legs or of arms were performed."[34]

33 The exploded cannon remains on display at the fort (see photo on the next page). Stewart, *Battle of Red Bank*, 13. Hessian casualties included eight officers, seven NCOs, and 67 privates killed; 11 officers, 24 NCOs, and 193 privates wounded; three officers, two NCOs and 55 privates captured. "List of the Killed and Wounded," 4. The dead, including von Donop, were later buried along the riverbank about 100 yards north of the Whitehall House, which since that time has suffered from heavy erosion. According to New Jersey historian Frank Stewart in 1929, "Years ago his [von Donop's] bones together with those of a large number of his men were washed down the bluff by erosion of ice and water. The upper part of his skull is said to be in the hands of a well-known physician, who got it from his father, who had it a long time." Moffett, ed., Year Book for 1928, 44. Major Samuel Ward of the 1st Rhode Island, on behalf of Christopher Greene, penned a report on the battle for Washington. Ward detailed "Colo. Greens Regt has 2 Serjts—1 fife & 4 Privates Killd—1 Serjt & 3 Privates wounded and one Captain (who was reconnoitering) taken prisoner—Colo. Angel has 1 Capt. killed—3 Serjts 3 Rank & file—& one Ensign 1 Serjt & 15 R. & file wounded. 2 of Capt. Duplessis Company were slightly wounded." Chase and Lengel, eds., Papers, vol. 11, 591; Revolutionary War Pension and Bounty-Land-Warrant Application Files (M804) [RWPF], files S2038 & R9588.

34 Jackson, *Navy*, 187; Chastellux, *Travels in North America*, vol. 1, 159-160; Collin, *Journal*, 241; Buettner, *Narrative*, 53. The Low house was located south of the dam on Woodbury Creek (near the present Woodbury High School) more than two miles from the battlefield. Other Hessians were taken to a house no longer standing opposite the courthouse in Woodbury. Stryker, *Forts on the Delaware*, 22 & 26.

An artillery piece damaged during the fighting at Fort Mercer. *Author*

William Howe sent Hessian surgeons Wilhelm Bausch and Johann Conrad Gachter and British surgeon Alexander Grant, taking with them "needed medicines and bandages as well as other necessaries." Bausch treated von Donop. Both he and Dr. Grant believed von Donop's wound "to be incurable." They were right. He lingered in agony for three days before dying. According to French engineer du Plessis, von Donop's final words were, "I die a victim of my own ambition and the avarice of my sovereign." Following his death, von Donop's silver watch and spurs were taken by Surgeon Peter Turner of the 1st Rhode Island—whose descendants retained them as late as 1901. American surgeons also pitched in to help the wounded. Dr. John Keemle from the 3rd Virginia received orders to leave a hospital in Burlington, New Jersey, to help those at Fort Mercer. "Two or three days after the wounded were dressed, I was ordered on to Princeton with several wagon loads of wounded."[35]

35 Colonel von Loos, commander of the Combined Hessian Battalion, claimed von Donop's last words included, "I did my duty as a soldier. But as a brigadier, I behaved like an ensign. What will the Landgraf say when he hears that I lost so many men? I fear that." Von Loos may have heard this

Once he heard that his men were robbing the Hessian dead, Greene issued strict orders on October 25 against it:

> The Colo. positively orders yt [that] all persons belonging to ye Garrison immediately turn into Qr. Master Angell all ye articles of every Kind, as well as cash and other things taken from ye Dead & Wounded Hessian Troops in ye late Action. Whoever is possess'd of any thing whatever, altho of ye smallest value, & secrets ye same, or neglects to turn them in as mentioned above, by sun rising tomorrow Morning, shall undergo ye severest Sentence of a Court Martial.[36]

The 1st British Light Infantry Battalion and 27th Regiment of Foot were sent across the Delaware to protect the returning Hessians. The survivors arrived at Cooper's Ferry by noon, putting an official end to "this fruitless expedition," noted Lt. Friedrich Werner of the Hessian Artillery. By late afternoon of the 23rd, von Donop's exhausted Hessians made it back to Philadelphia. Civilian J. P. Norris was on his way to the riverfront to watch the naval fight when he "met several wagons with wounded soldiers—many of them in great pain—their moans and cries were very distressing."[37]

Contemporary Analysis

Rumors of the defeat quickly spread through Philadelphia. Loyalist Robert Morton believed the American army required respect. "The great Count, who petitioned for the command in order to signalize himself and his famous Hessians, rec'd a fatal blow of which he shortly died. . . . From this instance we see the important effects of despising the American army, and of Red Bank not being possessed by the British at the time they took Billingsport." The survivors returned exhausted and thoroughly disgusted. British artilleryman Francis Downman

from others but was not personally present. Letter, von Loos to von Jungkenn, October 30, 1777, 21; Letter, von Knyphausen to Landraf, October 25, 1777, 3; Carl von Baurmeister, Journal of Major Carl Leopold Baurmeister, Donald Londahlsmidt, ed., "German and British Accounts of the Assault on Fort Mercer at Redbank, NJ in October 1777," *Journal of the Johannes Schwalm Historical Association* Vol. 16 (Scotland, PA, 2013), 27; Revolutionary War Pension and Bounty-Land-Warrant Application Files (M804) [RWPF], file S5652.

36 Orderly Book of Colonel Christopher Greene in Moffett, ed., *Year Book for 1928*, 46.

37 Reed, *Campaign*, 298; "Report of Werner," 6; John F. Watson, *Annals of Philadelphia and Pennsylvania, in the Olden Time; Being a Collection of Memoirs, Anecdotes, and Incidents of the City and its Inhabitants*, 2 vols. (Philadelphia, PA, 1855), vol. 2, 287.

recorded "between 4 o'clock in the morning of the 22nd and 11 o'clock in the morning on the 23rd, we had marched about 42 miles, and been well thrashed into the bargain. . . . I crossed the river and went home most heartily tired and very low spirited." Hessian jaeger commander Lt. Col. Ludwig von Wurmb emoted four days later, "It is painful to me to lose so many good people, I can't describe it. . . . The tragedy of our poor wounded here in America is not describable without shedding tears and those left behind with the enemy have no aid."[38]

Two Hessian officers in Philadelphia who did not participate in the expedition against Fort Mercer left their own views of the debacle. Colonel Johann von Loos of the Combined Hessian Regiment despaired over the loss of his friend von Donop. "Now that he is dead, he gets blamed. That's the way it is when the fortunes of war turn. The mistakes of the big [Howe] are atoned for by the small [von Donop]." Captain Friedrich von Muenchhausen, a member of William Howe's staff, crossed the river with wagons the day after the battle to help recover the wounded. "I cannot describe my feeling, especially when I saw the company to which I had just been assigned and which is very dear to me. It came back with loss of 37 men. . . . The three battalions, which had lost almost all their officers and nearly 400 men, were lodged in the barracks, for they could not possibly do service very soon." Hessian Brigade Major Johann Du Buy felt much the same. "Should this terrible war still continue for some time, many other brave men will lay down their lives here," he wrote to Lt. Gen. Wilhelm von Ditfurth four days later. "The rebels become better soldiers every day, and fight desperately." Another staff officer, Capt. Christian von Urff, penned that "Donop is widely blamed, but if it had succeeded he would have received the greatest fame. Now someone is at fault. This much is certain, if he was not so fiery, as he always is, there would have been less bad luck. He should have awaited our ships which would have countered the fire of the row galleys and allowed him to take the fort . . . before everything is over, many more of us will bite the dust."[39]

Perhaps Captain Ewald summed up the fruitless attack best when he observed, "On the whole, this attack belongs to the quixotic variety, which occurs in war at

---

38 Morton, "Diary," 22; Whinyates, *Services*, 44; Letter, von Wurmb to Jungkenn, October 25, 1777, 13.

39 Letter, von Loos to von Jungkenn, October 30, 1777, 21; Von Muenchhausen, *At Howe's Side*, 41; Letter, Major Johann Christian Du Buy to Lieutenant General Wilhelm Maximilian August von Ditfurth, October 26, 1777, Donald Londahlsmidt, ed., "German and British Accounts of the Assault on Fort Mercer at Redbank, NJ in October 1777," *Journal of the Johannes Schwalm Historical Association*, 26 vols. (Scotland, PA, 2013), vol. 16, 21; Letter, von Urff to Gilsa, October 26, 1777, 28.

times. For it was impossible to capture this work without the aid of armed ships, which had to be assigned to drive away the enemy vessels. In a word, Colonel Donop was a man of action," Ewald continued. "He had compared the siege of Mud Island with those of Bergen op Zoom and Olmutz, and had offered to capture Fort Red Bank with one grenadier battalion, which offended the pride of the English. They led him into danger and he fell, wherby so many men—indeed, so many really brave men—had to bite the dust." The carnage moved Ewald deeply. "This day was especially sad for me. I lost five of my oldest friends, among whom was a relative, and four of my best friends were severely wounded." The veteran of many fights in Europe and North America was especially moved by the Fort Mercer debacle: "As long as I have served, I have not yet left a battlefield in such deep sorrow."[40]

Artillerist Francis Downman blamed the initial indecision upon reaching the fort for the loss. "We arrived before the place about one o'clock; at noon we [had] examined it, and saw the rebels at work which showed that the fort was not finished, or that they were adding something to it on hearing we were near them. I think, therefore, we should have stormed it directly without the least loss of time as it was to be done in daylight, but instead of an immediate attack, we did not begin till 5 o'clock in the afternoon."[41]

Lieutenant Colonel William Harcourt of the 16th Light Dragoons assigned the loss another cause in a letter to his father on October 26: poor intelligence. Twenty days before during the Billingsport operation, the British had learned that Fort Mercer lacked a garrison. Much changed over those three weeks with the addition of the Rhode Island Continentals and the reconfiguration of the fortification. William Howe had no reason to believe the Hessians would encounter trouble. "Unfortunately our intelligence was bad, and what was represented as a Battery erected entirely against the ships and open behind, proved a very strong Fort with a deep ditch." Harcourt expressed his concern about the war's progress in a prescient opinion that the coming weeks and months would bear out. "All these checks following so close upon the back of each other, together with the account . . . of General Burgoyne's Army having been obliged to lay down their Arms . . . must necessarily reduce us to the defensive for the rest of the Campaign; and will probably oblige us to evacuate a conquest which I have ever been of opinion

40 Ewald, *Diary*, 102-104.

41 Whinyates, *Services*, 43.

should not have been thought of till a junction with the Northern Army was effected, but which, circumstanced as we are at present, cannot be maintained."[42]

The news reached York, Pennsylvania, where the Continental Congress continued to hold sessions in exile, by October 25. War conditions appeared to be on the upturn. "I have a seized a Moment, to congratulate you on the great and glorious Success of our Arms at the Northward [Burgoyne's surrender], and in Delaware River," wrote an elated John Adams to his wife. "The Forts at Province Island and Red Bank have been defended, with a Magnanimity, which will give our Country a Reputation in Europe." Major Benjamin Tallmadge of the Continental Dragoons wrote a letter to Col. Samuel Webb (a prisoner on parole) three weeks later. "By a gentleman from Philadelphia I am told that nothing could equal the mortification and disappointment of the enemy on that repulse [at Fort Mercer], as they expected but little resistance would have been made."[43]

Resignations

George Washington, meanwhile, responded to Samuel Smith's requested resignation. After explaining the importance of Fort Mifflin to the disgruntled temporary commander, Washington informed him, "I now leave it to your own Option whether to rejoin your Corps [his Maryland regiment] or continue where you are [Fort Mifflin], & have no doubt but you will determine upon that which in your opinion is most serviceable & consistent with the Character of an Officer." After giving him that choice, how could Smith do otherwise? He remained at Fort Mifflin.[44]

Sometime during the day of the fighting at Red Bank, and almost certainly before he learned the results of the Fort Mercer operation, William Howe submitted his resignation to Lord George Germain. "From the little attention, my Lord, given to my recommendations since the commencement of my command,"

---

42 Edward William Harcourt, ed., *The Harcourt Papers*, 14 vols. (Oxford, n.d.), vol. 11, 222-223. Harcourt entered the army in 1759 and bought a captaincy in the 16th Light Dragoons. He helped his father escort the future Queen Charlotte to England and in doing so, became her friend. After service in the siege of Havana in 1762, Harcourt essentially became commander of the 16th with the regiment's colonel—John Burgoyne—serving as a general officer.

43 L. H. Butterfield, ed., *The Adams Papers: Adams Family Correspondence*, 2 vols. (Cambridge, MA, 1963), vol. 2, 360-361; J. Watson Webb, *Reminiscences of Gen'l Samuel B. Webb, of the Revolutionary Army* (New York, 1882), 292.

44 Chase and Lengel, eds., *Papers*, vol. 11, 580.

asserted the frustrated commander, "I am led to hope I may be relieved from this very painful service, wherein I have not had the good fortune to enjoy the necessary confidence of my superiors. . . . I humbly request I may receive his Majesty's permission to resign the command." The letter would take at least five weeks to reach King George III and even longer to get a response. There would be much to do in the interim. General Howe could not escape his problems that easily—or quickly.[45]

The River War Continues

While the Hessians spent a night in Haddonfield and another night retreating from Fort Mercer, the Americans on Mud Island spent them improving Mifflin's defenses. The improvements included the installation of a double chain of floating timbers and iron chains along the southwest flank of the island to prevent a British party from landing and storming the fort. It was difficult work. The men spent both miserable nights standing in cold water twenty feet from the island's bank driving large stakes fifteen feet apart into the bed of the channel. before attaching the chains to the stakes.[46]

Unaware of the day's outcome, George Washington wrote to New Jersey militia commander Silas Newcomb to stress the importance of holding both forts. "I cannot forbear observing to you, & the Inhabitants of jersey the dreadful consequences that must follow should the Enemy keep possession of Phil[l]a., & that if they get Red Bank into their hands, a considerable force must consequently be kept there by them, to the distress & terror of those within their reach, this I hope will stimulate the Militia to a speedy & Vigorous opposition." Washington concluded, "I must request that you do ev[er]y thing in yr Power to throw in supplies of Provision to Fort Mifflin & Red Bank, this I conceive to be a matter of the utmost importance, as the Enemy may intend to starve them out."[47]

---

45 *Report on the Manuscripts of Mrs. Stopford-Sackville, of Drayton House, Northhampshire*, 2 vols. (London, 1910), vol. 2, 80. The king accepted Howe's resignation on February 4, 1778.

46 Jackson, *Fort Mifflin*, 40.

47 Chase and Lengel, eds., *Papers*, vol. 11, 578-579 & 583. Unhappy with the results of a court of inquiry into his actions at Paoli, Gen. Anthony Wayne begged Washington for a full court martial proceeding on October 22. Wayne's wish was granted the next day.

The *Augusta* and the *Merlin*

While the fighting swirled around Fort Mercer, several larger British vessels eased into position just below the *chevaux-de-frise* and engaged the American fleet in an attempt to divert their fire from the attacking Hessians. Admiral Richard Howe ordered the ships upriver "to second the Attempt of the Troops which were seen to be very warmly engaged." Around 5:00 p.m., as the Hessian assault was beginning to fizzle out, Capt. Francis Reynolds of the HMS *Augusta* sent an officer "to each of the other ships acquainting the Captains that my intention was to go as near the upper Cheveaux defrize as possible, in order to draw the fire of the [American] Galleys from the Hessians, and I desired they would do the same." Reynolds wanted "to comply with Lord Howe's Instructions in giving every Assistance to the Hessians." The vessels included the *Augusta, Roebuck, Pearl, Liverpool, Merlin,* and *Cornwallis.* The warships struggled to tack into position as "a completely contrary [north] wind prevented the warships that had received orders, from coming up the river," noted Hessian aide Capt. Friedrich von Muenchhausen. "The diversion was endeavoured to be continued by the frigates, at which the fire from the enemy's gallies were chiefly pointed for some time," penned Admiral Howe a month later, "but as the night advanced, the Hessian detachment having been repulsed, the firing ceased."[48]

Howe's ships were now tightly bunched in the channel just north of Billingsport. Captain Samuel Reeve with the *Merlin* had no choice but to run aground to prevent colliding with the *Roebuck.* Simultaneously, Reynolds testified "about coming to anchor" and engaging Fort Mercer, but the *Augusta* also grounded. As the tide fell, the 64-gun *Augusta* and 18-gun frigate *Merlin* sat motionless. Commodore Hazelwood took in the obvious confusion and sent four fire ships downriver, all of which were deflected by the British. Freeing the two grounded ships consumed every hour of the darkness. Captain Andrew Hamond's HMS *Roebuck* spent its efforts attempting to free the *Augusta* by cable. However, the wind continued from the north all night which "chequed the Flood [tide]." Reynolds's sailors "hove without any Effect." Matters did not improve when the next tide came in about one foot lower than usual. According to the Journal of the

---

48 Letter, Vice Admiral Richard Viscount Howe to Philip Stephens, Secretary of the Admiralty, October 25, 1777, Donald Londahlsmidt, ed., "German and British Accounts of the Assault on Fort Mercer at Redbank, NJ in October 1777," *Journal of the Johannes Schwalm Historical Association,* 26 vols. (Scotland, PA, 2013), vol. 16, 2; HMS *Augusta* court martial documents, British Archives, London, United Kingdom, ADM 1/5308; Jackson, *British Army,* 68; Von Muenchhausen, *At Howe's Side,* 41.

Vigilant, Cmdr. John Henry sent "Boats to Assist them but could not get them Off."[49]

October 23 dawned with the two ships still fixed to a sand bar. About 9:00 a.m., several warships tacked into position south of the *chevaux-de-frise*, including the *Liverpool*, *Isis*, *Pearl*, and *Cornwallis*. Heads turned when a thunderous roar erupted across the waters of the Delaware: the guns in Forts Mifflin and Mercer were launching artillery rounds into the British fleet. At the same time, American ships moved downriver to engage them. British batteries on Carpenter's and Province islands, in turn, engaged Fort Mifflin. And thus, the first large-scale action on the Delaware River in the campaign began.

In the midst of the chaos on the river, the Pennsylvania Navy launched fire ships that drifted into the stationary British vessels. According to Pennsylvania militia officer William Bradford, the fire ships proved ineffective when their crews panicked. The British shot "flew so thick around them and indeed cut their rigging so much that the crews got frightened and set them on Fire [too] soon," declared Bradford.[50] A Rhode Island sergeant named Jeremiah Greenman watched the action from Mercer. It was, he observed:

> One of the Most Solumest Actions commenced, that may be seen by a soldiers eye, the Spectacle was magnificent, to see at once, the river covered with Ships, four great fire ships, in a blasé, floating on the Water / the Island & Main covered with Smoak & fire / part of the English Army drew up in battle array on Province Island ready to thro them selves into boats, to storm the Fort [Mifflin], which appeared involved with fire & was the prise of the day, the firing lasted 'till 2 o'clock PM. with relentless fury.[51]

Incoming British fire destroyed the northeast blockhouse and set ablaze a section of the palisades at Mifflin. "All inside of the Fort torn up as if ploughed, or rather as if dug in Holes," recalled an anonymous writer. During the fighting, the unknown writer "made two lucky Escapes, one Ball struck within 4 Inches of my Foot, just as I was lifting my other; and a Shell, in our Platform, within a Foot of

---

49 The *Augusta* and the *Merlin* were aground near the mouth of Mantua Creek. McGeorge, *Battle of Red Bank*, 9; Smith, *Fight for Delaware*, 25; HMS *Augusta* court martial documents, ADM 1/5308; Crawford, ed., *Naval Documents*, vol. 10, 240.

50 Jackson, *British Army*, 69-70. The fire ships sent down toward the *Augusta* included the fire brigs *Comet*, *Hellcat*, and *Volcano* and the fire sloop *Aetna*. Jackson, *Navy*, 197; Hazard, et al, eds., *Archives*, Series 1, vol. 5, 708.

51 Greenman, *Diary*, 82-83.

me. They set Fire to our BlockHouse, full of Men, without hurting a Man, which we soon extinguished." The incoming rounds eliminated one American problem when an iron ball smashed into the wall against which Col. Henry d'Arendt was leaning. A ragged brick fragment flew into his groin and forced his evacuation. D'Arendt, who had earlier shown his cowardice, never returned to Mifflin.[52]

Hoping for Fort Mifflin's demise, 200 British grenadiers on Province Island "were in readiness to make the assault if the attack of the ships" found success, explained Capt.-Lt. John Peebles of the 42nd Highlanders's grenadier company. From the hills near the Blue Bell Tavern, Col. Elias Dayton of the 3rd New Jersey (part of McDougall's Darby expedition) viewed the fort through the swirling battle smoke about five miles away. "At this place I had a full view of Fort Mifflin . . . three large ships of the enemy lay before it; two appeared to be at anchor, the third frequently put about and fired her broadsides by turns. I took particular notice of the number of shots fired at this attack," continued Dayton, "and found they fired six a minute for six hours. During the time I was looking on, our people in the fort seemed quite easy, and very seldom fired a single shot." If Dayton's account is accurate, McDougall made no effort to move closer to Province Island to prevent a British grenadier assault on the fort.[53]

The *Augusta* caught fire around 11:00 a.m., though the accounts differ on the cause. Ship captain Reynolds testified at his trial, "I was on the Quarter deck with the Master . . . I thought I heard an odd Crackling kind of noise, I sent [the ship's master, Robert Reed] into the Cabin to see what it was, he returned and told me, the Ship was on fire, I found the Sides, afterpart of the Ship, and above the Cabin all in flames." Reynolds declared that "every means were then used to put it out but without any Effect." Other British sources claim the crew deliberately set the ship ablaze or that wadding from the guns accidently set the rigging on fire. Admiral Howe reported "it was probably caused by the Wads from her Guns." During the court martial proceedings, none of those interviewed by the court knew the reason. Midshipman John Reid testified, "I suppose by her Wads." Some American accounts credit the fireships or "hot shot" heated in furnaces at Fort Mifflin. One of the most likely reasons is found in Ambrose Serle's journal. Serle, who served as Admiral Howe's secretary, noted that the *Augusta* "caught Fire upon the Poop by a

---

52 Jackson, *Fort Mifflin*, 50-51; Pancake, *1777*, 201; Crawford, ed., *Naval Documents*, vol. 10, 264.

53 John Peebles, *John Peebles' American War: The Diary of a Scottish Grenadier, 1776-1782*, ed. Ira D. Gruber (Mechanicsburg, PA, 1998), 145; Dayton, "Papers," 187. Dayton was likely on one of the hills that now contain Mt. Moriah Cemetery.

Modern view of the HMS *Augusta* sinking site, looking southwest
from the New Jersey shoreline. *Author*

marine firing into a Hammock, wch, being unperceived, communicated to the
Shrouds, & from thence to other Parts past all Prevention." The flames spread as
the British evacuated. Bradford, assisting the Pennsylvania Navy, wrote the
distressed *Augusta* was "laying Broadside too aground, and Flames issuing thro
every Port she had." According to Jeremiah Greenman, the ship "suddenly took
fire at the stern, and in a moment She wass in a blasé, & soon after blew up, with a
thundering noise, before the Enemy could take out all their hands."[54]

Captain John Barclay, commander of the Royal Marine detachment on the
Augusta, testified during the court martial that Captain Reynolds ordered him "to
go on board the different Ships for Boats and Assist once to save the people."
According to British engineer John Montresor, "Before the Explosion of the
Augusta's Powder Magazine . . . many of the seamen jumped overboard
apprehending it, some were taken up by our ships boats, but the Chaplain, one
Lieutenant and 60 men perished in the water." Some of these casualties may have
occurred prior to the blast.[55]

---

54 HMS *Augusta* court martial documents, ADM 1/5308; McGuire, *Campaign*, vol. 2, 173;
Crawford, ed., *Naval Documents*, vol. 10, 292; Ambrose Serle, *The American Journal of Ambrose Serle,
Secretary to Lord Howe, 1776-1778*, Edward H. Tatum, Jr., ed. (San Marino, CA, 1940), 261;
Greenman, *Diary*, 83; Hazard, et al, eds., *Archives*, Series 1, vol. 5, 708.

55 HMS *Augusta* court martial documents, ADM 1/5308; Montresor, "Journals," 470. The
remnants of the *Augusta* were raised and towed to Gloucester, New Jersey, in 1876. The American

The explosion was so loud that William Smith of the Delaware Regiment, serving with the Fort Mifflin garrison, lost his hearing. The detonation shattered windows in Philadelphia and sent a mushroom cloud hundreds of feet into the air. By this time Alexander McDougall's column was marching back to the main Continental camp. Colonel Dayton of the New Jersey Line heard the explosion while resting 11 miles away at Merion Meetinghouse. "The explosion was almost equal to an earthquake," he exclaimed, "and from the prodigious cloud of smoke seen immediately to ascend into the air, every one concluded a ship was destroyed." Hugh Smyth, a postmaster at Washington's camp in Whitpain felt the shock and "several Windows being broke close by us." Nathanael Greene's column, north of the Schuylkill River moving as a diversion toward the British defenses above Philadelphia, did not hear the sounds of McDougall's attack because the British protecting the supply line had already left. When enough time passed, Greene led his command back to Whitpain. Thomas Paine, riding with the column on its march back to the main camp, heard the explosion, and described the blast in a letter to Benjamin Franklin. The column was moving through Chestnut Hill about 18 miles away when "we were stunned with a report as loud as a peal from a hundred cannon at once, and turning round I saw a thick smoke rising like a pillar and spreading from the top like a tree."[56]

Civilians throughout eastern Pennsylvania heard the battle itself, and the mighty roar that followed. "Many," recalled Quaker Elizabeth Drinker in occupied Philadelphia, "were not sensible of any Shock, others were . . . and appear'd to some like an Earth Quake." Later in life, civilian J. P. Norris used the same description: "the blowing up of the *Augusta* was attended with a shock similar to that of an earthquake." Thirty miles away in the village of Trappe, Rev. Henry Muhlenberg recalled "a blast or roar which shook our house, and after this no more cannonading was heard." Some 65 miles west in Reading, Jacob Hiltzheimer noted "Great Fireing . . . this forenoon." Even further west in Lancaster Christopher

---

Dredging Company removed the sand and silt from the wreck before she was raised on pontoons and the water pumped out. Her remaining ribs and keel could still be seen at low water off Proprietors Park, just south of the Walt Whitman Bridge in Gloucester, as late as 1965. Reed, *Campaign*, 414. The effort to raise the ship stemmed from a moneymaking venture for the Centennial Exposition in Philadelphia. The effort failed but many pieces of her wood were sold as souvenirs—enough to reconstruct a William & Mary-era English dining room at the DAR headquarters in Washington, D.C. McGeorge, *The Battle of Red Bank,* 11.

56 McGuire, *Campaign,* vol. 2, 173; Dayton, "Papers," 187; Revolutionary War Pension and Bounty-Land-Warrant Application Files (M804) [RWPF], file S40460; Hazard, et al, eds., *Archives,* Series 1, vol. 5, 703; "Military Operations," 291-292.

Marshall's neighbors heard "a constant heavy firing." After listening carefully, Marshall "heard a heavy firing. . . . I apprehended it, to be platoon or broadside firing."[57]

British woes on the water were not soon to end. Soon after the *Augusta* exploded, the crew of the grounded *Merlin* set her on fire as well. A lieutenant named Applin from the *Roebuck* came aboard the *Merlin* and ordered the men removed and the ship destroyed. She, too, soon exploded, though less dramatically than the earlier fireball. To prevent further destruction and loss, the remaining British ships retired downriver to Hog Island. They did not escape unscathed. American artillery hulled the *Roebuck* several times and inflicted 16 casualties doing so. Commodore Hazelwood claimed he damaged the ship "much & drove off, & had she laid fast we shou'd have had her in the same situation [as the *Augusta*]." As the fighting tapered off, Hazelwood ordered crews out to the wrecks of the *Augusta* and *Merlin* to salvage their guns and anything else the Americans could put to use.[58]

The Whiskey Scrape

After failing to find and attack the British protecting the supply route from the fleet to Philadelphia, Alexander McDougall's expedition slowly made its way back to Whitpain that night. Taking a slightly different route back, the column crossed the Schuylkill at Matson's Ford at sunset. "The river was not so wide here" as where they previously crossed the river, "but the water was deeper, it was to the breast," remembered Joseph Plump Martin. Quartermaster wagons met the cold, hungry, and tired men in the gathering darkness on the other side of the river.[59]

The wagons lacked food but did have the alcohol aboard to issue rum rations. Each man was entitled to one gill. The dark upset that plan. "[T]he actions of the men could not well be seen by those who served out the liquor," recalled Martin,

---

57 Elizabeth Drinker, *The Diary of Elizabeth Drinker*, Elaine Forman Crane, ed., 3 vols.(Boston, 1991), vol. 1, 248; Watson, *Annals*, vol. 2, 287; Muhlenberg, *Journals*, vol. 3, 91; Jacob Hiltzheimer, *Extracts from the Diary of Jacob Hiltzheimer, of Philadelphia. 1765-1798*, ed. Jacob Cox Parson (Philadelphia, 1893), 36; Christopher Marshall, *Extracts from the Diary of Christopher Marshall, Kept in Philadelphia and Lancaster, During the American Revolution, 1774-1781*, William Duane, ed. (Albany, NY, 1877), 138.

58 Smith, *Fight for Delaware*, 25; Jackson, *British Army*, 69; Chase and Lengel, eds., *Papers*, vol. 11, 587-588; Reed, *Campaign*, 303. Congress later awarded presentation swords to the three prominent officers involved on October 22 and 23: Samuel Smith, Christopher Greene, and John Hazelwood.

59 Matson's Ford is in modern Conshohocken. Martin, *Private Yankee Doodle*, 78.

"each one drank as much as he pleased; some, perhaps, half a gill, some a gill, and as many as chose it drained the pint." Alcohol on empty stomachs was a recipe for disaster.[60]

The column started moving again before the alcohol took full effect. "We had not proceeded far before we entered a lane fenced on either side with rails, in which was water plash, or puddle. The fence was taken down on one side of the road to enable us to pass round the water," wrote Martin. "It was what is called a five-rail fence,"

> only the two upper rails of which were taken out; here was fun. We had been on the march since we had drank the whiskey just long enough for the liquor to assume its height of operation; our stomachs being empty the whiskey took rank hold and the poor brain fared accordingly. When the men came to the fence, not being able, many or most of them, to keep a regular balance between head and heels, they would pile themselves up on each side of the fence, swearing and hallooing, some losing their arms, some their hats, some their shoes, and some themselves. Had the enemy come upon us at this time, there would have been an action worth recording. But they did not, and we, that is, such as could, arrived at camp about midnight.[61]

Martin added, "I had then been nearly thirty hours without a mouthful of anything to eat" except some walnuts and "having been the whole time on my feet (unless I happened to fall over the fence, which I do not remember having done) and wading in, and being wet with the water of the river." Once safely back in camp at Whitpain, Martin "rolled myself up in my innocency, lay down on the leaves and forgot my misery till morning."[62]

Analysis

The significant defeats at Brandywine, Paoli, and Germantown notwithstanding, George Washington's current strategy was working. American fortifications, obstructions, and naval elements continued blocking British naval access to Philadelphia. His battle-tested army remained full of confidence and ready to block the roads leading to the city from the north and west. If the

---

60 Ibid., 79. A "gill" was about a quarter of a pint.

61 Ibid.

62 Ibid., 79-80.

Continentals could maintain this strategy for another five weeks, the Delaware would freeze and eliminate any hope of resupply for William Howe. With continued good fortune, Washington could starve General Howe out of Philadelphia much as he did at Boston two years earlier. Soon-to-be president of Congress Henry Laurens, was confident Howe would be forced "toward a shameful retreat or a more shameful surrender . . . as now in all probability we shall, to be masters of the river, he will in a few days have nothing to eat."[63]

Washington's growing optimism crept into a letter to John Hancock on October 24. "The damage the Enemy have sustained in their Ships, I hope will prevent their future attempts to gain the passage of the river," he explained, "and the repulse of the Troops under Count Donop and his Captivity, I flatter myself will also be attended with the most happy consequence." Washington was far more restrained when writing to New Jersey militia brigade commander David Forman the next day (Silas Newcomb commanded one militia brigade in southern New Jersey, and Forman the other.) "I am far from conceiving that it will deter them [the British] from endeavouring by slower, and more effectual means, to possess themselves of it [Fort Mercer], to make themselves perfect Masters of the River and the defences of the *Chevaux-de-Frise*."[64]

Hoping to capitalize on the Delaware River successes at Fort Mercer and against the HMS *Augusta*, the delegates in Congress penned a letter summarizing these events to their commissioners negotiating an alliance in Paris, France. "We rely on your wisdom and care to make the best and most immediate use of this intelligence to depress our enemies and produce essential aid to our cause in Europe," they urged. "The public acknowledgement of the Independence of these United States would be attended with beneficial consequences, and whilst we proceed with diligence and care to profit from our advantage, we are sensible how essential European Aid must be to the final establishment and security of American Freedom and Independence." These recent successes followed closely on the heels of General Burgoyne's surrender at Saratoga and Washington's bold attempt at

---

63 Henry Laurens, *Correspondence of Henry Laurens, of South Carolina*, Frank Moore, ed. (New York, 1861), 58-59.

64 Chase and Lengel, eds., *Papers*, vol. 11, 596 & 613. Forman, a native of New Jersey, was born in 1745. He was authorized to raise Forman's Additional Continental Regiment and made a brigadier general of the New Jersey militia in the spring of 1777. He led that brigade at the Battle of Germantown prior to its return to New Jersey.

Germantown, and helped strengthen the American position for an alliance with France.[65]

Howe's hopes dipped to low ebb as darkness settled over the Delaware Valley that October 23. Despite defeating Washington in every land engagement, a small detachment of Continentals had somehow convincingly repulsed a veteran Hessian column at Fort Mercer and now his supporting naval force had lost two of its warships. Progress in the water and mud to construct the land batteries needed to besiege Fort Mifflin was moving at an agonizingly slow pace. The chevaux-de-frise remained in the Delaware between Red Bank and Fort Mifflin, blocking British shipping. If the situation did not improve soon, his men would begin starving. Howe decided there was nothing to do but double down on his river operations. "These disappointments however will not prevent the most vigorous measures being pursued for the reduction of the fort [Mifflin]," he penned Lord George Germain on October 25, "which will give us the passage up the river."[66]

Lieutenant Loftus Cliffe of the 46th Regiment of Foot wrote his brother the next day. "Our greatest difficulties, I mean exertion is to come, the Rebels have an Island difficult of approach being defended from our Shipping by Chevaux de fries within reach of their Guns," he explained, "which prevent us taking them up and by a work on the Jersys (Red Bank) on an Attempt of which the Hessians Yesterday sufferd severly, but had not the *Augusta* Man of War taken fire I believe both Mud Island & red Bank would have been ours. . . . I believe this necessary business will cost us some Men," he continued, "but I dare say it will be purchased as cheap as possible, it's the only Obstruction we have to our Shipping coming up, which we must have."[67]

The precarious conditions in Philadelphia included growing civilian bitterness, rising prices, black markets, and increasing depredations by both British and Hessian soldiers. "The ravages and wanton destruction of the soldiery will, I think, soon become irksome to the inhabitants," predicted Quaker civilian Robert Morton in his diary. Some people, he continued,

---

65 Smith, et al., eds., *Letters*, vol. 8, 215.

66 *The Parliamentary Register; or, History of the Proceedings and Debates of the House of Commons: Containing an Account of the most interesting Speeches and Motions; accurate Copies of the most remarkable Letters and Papers; of the most material Evidence, Petitions, &c laid before and offered to the House, During the Fifth Session of the Fourteenth Parliament of Great Britain*, 17 vols. (London, 1779), vol. 11, 439.

67 Letter, Loftus Cliffe to brother Jack, October 24, 1777, Loftus Cliffe Papers, William L. Clements Library, University of Michigan, Ann Arbor, MI.

are now entirely and effectually ruined by the soldiers being permitted under the command of their officers, to ravage and destroy their property. I presume the fatal effects of such conduct will shortly be very apparent by the discontent of the inhabitants, who are now almost satiated with British clemency, and numbers of whom, I believe, will shortly put themselves out of the British protection . . . had the necessities of the army justified the measures, and they had paid a sufficient price for what is taken, then [the British] would have the good wishes of the people, and perhaps all the assistance they could afford; but contrary conduct has produced contrary effects, and if they pursue their present system, their success will be precarious and uncertain.[68]

One British officer jotted down his own thoughts after digesting word of the disastrous land defeat, followed by the river debacle. "The desire of the Officers & Soldiers to distinguish themselves, not having an Opportunity of wiping off the Misfortune of Trenton, the Report of Sir Henry Clinton's having Storm'd the Forts of Montgomery & Clinton & the probability of the Army accusing him of want of Spirit if he [von Donop] return'd without attempting the Place, all conspired to induce him to give up his own Opinion & sacrifice his Life rather than his Honour."[69]

68 Morton, "Diary," 23-24.

69 Matthew Ankettle, *Journal of Officer B* located in the Sol Feinstone Collection of the American Philosophical Society, Philadelphia, PA, Item No. 409. In my previous two books on the Philadelphia campaign, I mistakenly listed the author as Frederick Augustus Wetherall. Recent research leads me to conclude Lt. Matthew Ankettle is the author. Historian Don Hagist assisted with this identification.

Chapter 6

Philadelphia Besieged

October 24-November 9, 1777

"How strange it is that Men, engaged in the same Important Service,
should be eternally bickering, instead of giving mutual aid."[1]

— Gen. George Washington, November 4, 1777

Continental Camp

Despite the recent American success at Fort Mercer and on the Delaware River the previous two days, Washington found no rest. He harbored hopes of attacking the British garrison in Philadelphia. However, his supply situation rendered his army unfit for field duty, and he complained about it to Congress on October 24. "It gives me great concern to inform Congress, that after all my exertions we are still in a distressed situation for want of Blankets and Shoes," he explained. "At this time no inconsiderable part of our force are incapable of acting, thro' the deficiency of the latter, and I fear

---

1 Philander D. Chase & Frank E. Grizzard, eds., *The Papers of George Washington*, Revolutionary War Series, 30 vols. (Charlottesville & London, 2002), vol. 12, 128.

without we can be relieved, it will be the case with two thirds of the Army in the course of a few days."[2]

The River War

Fort Mifflin remained the key to the American river defense system. The man charged with directing its defense, Henry d'Arendt, lacked confidence in the Mud Island position. "Now a word respecting this Place and its Defense," he penned Washington on the same day the army commander was writing to Congress. "Fort [Mifflin] is the worst constructed that I have ever seen," He began. "It would require 800 men,"

> to defend it, and then there would not be sufficiency for a necessary Reserve, and the Line of Troops would for the most part be only a single Rank—besides this there is no Rampart, the inclosure for the most part being of Palisades—no works to flank—in a word there are too many Defects to be enumerated here. The Battery which seems to be the strongest part, is in effect the weakest—for there the Enemy could land most readily—it could be defended but feebly by small Arms, and the Enemy once landed would be out of danger from the Canon.[3]

D'Arendt continued with an ominous statement: "the Defence of this place consists principally in this point, to hinder the Enemy from closing in upon us, it will be necessary for the Fleet to give us the assistance to the utmost, in firing upon the Boats destined to make a Descent upon us." The Mifflin commander claimed he spoke to Commodore John Hazelwood and "desired him to station Boats here [in the back channel] every night, which has not been hitherto—but last night he sent some—this Succour is of the greatest importance."[4]

The Americans relied heavily on the naval arm to defend Mifflin. Hazelwood's 13 single-gun galleys were apparently the only vessels capable of operating near the fort or around the *chevaux-de-frise*. The navy needed more than its baker's dozen for defensive operations, let alone to operate offensively against the British batteries on Province and Carpenter's islands.

---

2 Chase and Lengel, eds., *Papers*, vol. 11, 596.

3 Crawford, ed., *Naval Documents*, vol. 10, 263

4 Ibid; Jackson, *Fort Mifflin*, 53; Jackson, *Fort Mifflin*, 53.

Rainfall began during the day and continued, heavy at times, over the next seven. "At night a severe Tempest," recorded British engineer John Montresor on October 27. "No working parties this day and indeed from the nature of this overflowed land and the heavy rains and great freshet in the Delaware retards our progress beyond description." Weather problems notwithstanding, Howe ordered Fort Mifflin bombarded day and night over the next two days.[5]

British Philadelphia

Following recent reverses on the Delaware River, William Howe's officers' spirits sunk. Sir George Osborn of the British Brigade of Guards wrote his brother on October 25. "We are waiting here to get our shipping up this town and it may be another week before we can be able to march again forward to Mr. Washington, who is laying with his army within seven miles of us . . . We have gloomy reports of Burgoyne's army, which I trust is not true, for if that army does not get down to Albany, all we do here will be to little purpose."[6]

The River War

Washington exuded confidence in an October 26 letter to Benjamin Lincoln, who was recovering from his Saratoga wound. "Ever since the Enemy got possession of Philadelphia, their whole attention has been paid to reducing the Forts upon Delaware and endeavoring to remove the Chevaux de frize . . . but they were . . . warmly opposed" and had not yet broken through the defenses.[7]

The week-long nor'easter slammed into the region flooding the camps of both armies and turning the Delaware and the Schuylkill into raging torrents. Two feet of water covered much of Mud Island and Fort Mifflin. Lieutenant Colonel Samuel Smith remembered Mud Island "was overflowed. There was no dry place, except

5 Montresor, "Journals," 471; Smith, *Fight for Delaware*, 27. The Americans returned fire. A mile across the back channel from Fort Mifflin stood the Bleakley House. An American artillery round passed through the home and forced the family's evacuation for the duration of the contest. The home was later moved by the Daughters of the American Revolution to where it sits today across the road from Fort Mifflin. John L. Cotter, Daniel G. Roberts, and Michael Parrington, *The Buried Past: An Archaeological History of Philadelphia* (Philadelphia,1993), 255.

6 George Osborn's papers are in a private family collection. This quote relies on McGuire, *Campaign*, vol. 2, 192.

7 Chase & Grizzard, eds., *Papers*, vol. 12, 19.

the barracks and platform. Two feet of water [flowed] over every other spot; and the enemy's battery being similarly situated, all firing ceased, on both sides." Determined to batter Fort Mifflin into submission, Howe needed to move tons of supplies onto Province Island. To facilitate that operation, British engineers completed a bridge at Webb's Ferry. New Jersey militia general David Forman arrived at Red Bank around noon, conversed with Hazelwood, and reported to Washington the naval guard boats "near The mouth of the Schoolkill Heard a Constant rumbling of Wagons Comeing from Philad[elphi]a . . . and Crossing over to Province Island from Ten oClock until Near Day Break."[8]

British forces took up a position at Billingsport, New Jersey. Three weeks previously, the 10th and 42nd Regiments of Foot held the position before returning to Pennsylvania. Since then, the assault on Fort Mercer had failed, the *Augusta* and *Merlin* were lost, and the British remained deadlocked at Fort Mifflin. Howe anticipated a more methodical second attack on Fort Mercer and wanted a secure land force on the New Jersey shore, so he sent a detachment to Billingsport. "This day the marines of the Fleet took possession again at Billingsport in New Jersey," wrote engineer John Montressor in his journal on October 26. Montressor was referring to 100 Royal Marines who took up the position in the midst of the ongoing rainstorm.

Howe had a manpower shortage. Major John Clark, who was on spy duty, confirmed when he informed Washington that the British general removed marines from British shipping for land duty. "They have taken several Companies of Marines from on board to do duty as Foot, they curse Fort Mifflin heartily, & say, it has given them more trouble, than any thing they ever met with." Militia general David Forman messaged Washington three days later the British "have been Imploy'd in Throwing up a five gun Battery on The water side below the Bank [of the old Billingsport fort] as we suppose to prevent our Galley men getting The Guns and provisions out of" the *Augusta* and *Merlin*.[9]

Regardless, the Americans ventured to the wrecks to salvage materials. William Bradford of the Pennsylvania militia boarded the remains of the *Augusta* and reported, "I had the Pleasure of being on board Part of a 64 Gun Ship—most of

---

8 Smith, "Papers of Smith," 89; Chase & Grizzard, eds., *Papers*, vol. 12, 14. Forman maintained his headquarters at a home known as Ladd's Castle in the Colonial Manor section of Woodbury, New Jersey. Stewart, *Battle of Red Bank*, 17.

9 Montresor, "Journals," 471; McIntyre, *A Most Gallant Resistance*, 194-195. The Marines were joined the next day by 200 men from the 71st Highlanders and two 18-pounders. Chase & Grizzard, eds., *Papers*, vol. 12, 27 & 50.

her Guns are in the wreck and we brought off two of her 24 Pounders, and are this Day preparing to get the rest, if the ships do not come too near us. The smaller ships Guns are easily to be got." As Bradford quickly discovered, "The people on board the *Augusta* must have got off with great Precipitation, as we have found among the rubbish great number of Cloaths, part of their Books, &c., &c., that they seem to have taken nothing with them but what they had on." Commodore Hazelwood accompanied Bradford and reported to Washington, "I went down to the Wrecks, & find the Guns of both Ships may be got out if the enemy's Ships can b[e] kept at a proper distance—We brought off two 24 pounders."[10]

Two letters to Washington on October 26 highlight the lack of cooperation between the army and navy. Samuel Smith at Fort Mifflin informed the Virginian, "I am clearly of Opinion if we had a Commodore who would do his Duty, it would be impossible for the Enemy ever to get Possession of this fort, without we are properly guarded the Enemy may be with us before we can form. The Channell which they are to Cross is So narrow, in the Night they may bring their Boats & Embark opposite to us without our Seeing them." Smith detailed the miserable condition of his men: The "poor ragged fellows, now chiefly without Breeches, who are oblig'd to turn out before day, & perhaps may Soon be oblig'd to be So all Night, the last reinforcement are equally unfurnish'd." The garrison, he continued, "ought to be well-Cloth'd or we destroy their Constitutions." Commodore Hazelwood dispatched the second letter. "The Fleet is now so poorly Mann'd, & the constant cry from Fort Mifflin is to guard that Post, that I know not how to act without more assistance." Hazelwood expressed further concerns in a separate letter directly to d'Arendt and Smith that day. "All our armed Boats we have left mand is only five & we cannot fully man but five Galleys & if there is Much wind & sea going that Cannot keep The river with them, but must make a Harber som ware, & while its Still weather They Can lay to gard you," explained the commodore, "but when it Blows If you Can not defind the Island with The Trupes, you Can not depend on us Nor Could we Row them over to your Assistance[.] you have now a State of Our Situation, that you may Act Accordingly."[11]

Unwilling to detach more Continental regulars to the river forts, Washington informed Colonel Greene at Fort Mercer of his decision to instead send Pennsylvania militia. "I have sent down Lt. Colo. [John] Rollston with three

---

10 Hazard, et al, eds., *Archives*, Series 1, vol. 5, 708; Chase & Grizzard, eds., *Papers*, vol. 12, 18. For a full accounting of what the Pennsylvania Navy salvaged from the ship see Jackson, *Navy*, 203.

11 Chase & Grizzard, eds., *Papers*, vol. 12, 23; Crawford, ed., *Naval Documents*, vol. 10, 308-309.

hundred pennsylvania Militia to reinforce Forts Mercer and Mifflin. I therefore desire that you and Baron [d']Aren[d]t will settle the proportion that each is to have upon the most equitable terms. If you should have been joined by such a Number of New Jersey Militia as will render your post quite secure, you are to permit the pennsylvania Militia to pass over to fort Mifflin." Ralston's men, however, never arrived, and no other record of their movements exists.[12]

With the British fleet controlling the river below Red Bank and Mud Island, the captured American warship *Delaware* created a nuisance for American operations between Philadelphia and Cooper's Ferry on the New Jersey shore. Washington urged Hazelwood on October 27 to send a party at night to burn the *Delaware* on the Philadelphia waterfront—a bold but wise suggestion if only Hazelwood had followed through on it. Baron d'Arendt, meanwhile, declared himself too sick to exercise on-site command in Mifflin and instead moved into the Whitehall House near Fort Mercer instead.[13]

Despite the militia failures that plagued Washington throughout the campaign, the commander-in-chief continued to place hope in them. "I wrote you last eveng with respect to reinforcing Red Bank, & Fort Mifflin," penned the Virginian to New Jersey militia general David Forman on October 28, "my anxiety from the importance of those places, is so great, that I cannot help urging you again to throw in without loss of time, what assistance The Commanding officers and your self may think necessary, and such as you may be able to afford them." Neither Forman nor Silas Newcomb proved helpful. Forman's men were committed to guarding a salt works in Monmouth County and Newcomb's were scattered across southern New Jersey guarding bridges or harvesting crops. Washington complained to his brother Samuel, "before a Second set of Militia could be got, the first were always gone by which means we could never collect a respectable body at once."[14]

Major Francois de Fleury, the French engineer assisting Fort Mifflin, wrote to Alexander Hamilton. He, too, had little good to say about the navy. "The Galleys

12 John Ralston was a member of the Chester County militia. Chase & Grizzard, eds., *Papers*, vol. 12, 17. October 26 was a busy day in the Continental army and witnessed the conclusion of yet another court martial. The court, which had earlier investigated charges of drunkenness leveled by Lt. Col. William Heth against Brig. Gen. William Maxwell, on this day found "he was once during said time disguised with liquor in such a manner, as to disqualify him in some measure, but not fully, from doing his duty; and that once or twice besides his spirits were a little elevated by spiritous liquor." Although found guilty, Maxwell remained commanding the New Jersey Brigade. Ibid., 1.

13 Ibid., 32-33; Dorwart, *Fort Mifflin*, 42.

14 Dorwart, *Fort Mifflin*, 42; Chase & Grizzard, eds., *Papers*, vol. 12, 36-37.

which ought to be a Security to us, are absolutely useless—they have withdrawn to the Jersey Shore, the Channel between us and Province Island is perfectly clear," he complained, "and if the Enemy choose to make a descent here as I have no doubt they do—we cannot hinder them." By October 29, engineer officer de Fleury informed Alexander Hamilton that the only way to defend the fort "consists on this single point, to prevent the Enemy from landing, this is the business of our Fleet especially at night—at which time the Cannon of the Fort would do but little good."[15]

Earlier in the month, John Montresor had suggested to General Howe that things would be better if he left Germantown to personally oversee operations. Considering the lack of cooperation between the various American elements operating along the river, perhaps George Washington should have considered a similar move, shifting his headquarters to southern New Jersey to better oversee and even force cooperation. Instead, he attempted to direct operations from afar, mostly via the written word. "It is my most earnest desire, that every mode may be adopted, by which your force may be brought to Co-operate against the designs & approaches of the Enemy," he wrote in yet another letter to Hazelwood on October 28. Thus, he added, "a mutual Confidence & perfect understanding may take place. . . . As there is a greater possibility that the reduction of the Forts might be effected by surprize than any other means you will see the necessity of giving them every Aid by your Gondolas and Guard Boats, as may effectually prevent any mischance of this kind."[16]

Washington was only now beginning to realize that Lt. Col. Samuel Smith was the source for most of his problems along the Delaware. In an effort to compel cooperation, Washington wrote to Smith the same day. "You seem to have mistaken the Commodore's meaning," he chastised the same day he wrote Hazelwood. "From his letter I understand he will always assist you whenever it is in his power. He tells you that in rough Weather his galleys and armed Boats cannot live and therefore guards you against expecting much assistance from them at such times," Washington continued. "I beg you of all things, not to suffer any Jealousies between the land and sea service to take place. Consider that your mutual security depends upon acting perfectly in concert."[17]

15 Crawford, ed., *Naval Documents*, vol. 10, 334 & 344.

16 Chase & Grizzard, eds., *Papers*, vol. 12, 39.

17 Ibid., 42-43.

The storms continued to rage across the Delaware Valley and the Schuylkill continued to rise. When the waters carried away "the floating Bridge at Middle Ferry," the Americans at Mifflin captured the bobbing span together with many boats on October 28. John Montresor, chief engineer of Howe's army, had had enough and wanted out. The captain had full responsibility for reducing Fort Mifflin and progress remained painfully slow. Montresor was ill, short of supplies, and now the weather hampered operations. The veteran requested "6 months leave or to be relieved, if not permitted to resign." We are at this stage, he admitted four days later "an army without provisions or Rum, artillery for Besieging, scarce any ammunition, no clothing, nor any money." It was while in the midst of this despair coursing through the British camps that Howe received confirmation of Burgoyne's surrender. John Andre of Charles Grey's staff recorded the depressing news in his journal: "An officer of the Quarter-master-General's Department came from General Burgoyne, informing Sir William Howe of the Convention made with the Rebels."[18]

The Conway Cabal Begins

Horatio Gates's aide Col. James Wilkinson, meanwhile, stopped in Reading, Pennsylvania, on his way to brief Congress about John Burgoyne's surrender. Lord Stirling, one of Washington's division commanders resting in Reading after a fall from his horse, invited Wilkinson to dinner on October 28. Two of Stirling's aides, Majors James Monroe and William McWilliams, joined the dinner party. Stirling and Wilkinson drank to inebriation while the younger staffers wisely moderated their intake. Wilkinson was so in his cups that he forgot many of the details of the night while writing his memoir. "The conversation was too copious and diffuse for me to have charged my memory with particulars, and from the circumstances of it, it was confidential." Major McWilliams, however, was sober enough to remember and later disclosed details with Lord Stirling. Six days later Stirling shared the news with Washington: Thomas Conway had written Horatio Gates, "Heaven has been determined to Save your Country; Or a Weak General [Washington] and bad Counsellors would have ruined it." Washington confronted Conway over the accusation.[19]

---

18 Montresor, "Journals," 471-472; Andre, *Journal*, 62.

19 James Wilkinson, *Memoirs of My Own Times* (Philadelphia, PA, 1816), vol. 1, 331-332; Chase & Grizzard, eds., *Papers*, vol. 12, 111. The true cabal came later in December when Congress placed

Continental Camp

During a council of war on October 29, the decision was made to shift the army's camp "a little to our left" to stronger ground on Whitemarsh hills that "has been reconnoitered and reported by the Engineers." The council also suggested as many reinforcements as possible be sent to the river forts.[20]

The River War

Because the often-unreliable militia never arrived to assist, on October 28 Washington ordered James Varnum to take the Connecticut regiments of his brigade to bolster the river defenses. "The design," read his orders, "is to aid and give greater security to the garrisons" and cooperate with General Forman of the New Jersey militia. However, Washington could not "delineate particularly the line of conduct you are to observe. I leave it to your own discretion to be adapted to circumstances." Varnum was now the highest-ranking officer overseeing the river defenses. Washington carefully outlined his role. The exhausted Mifflin garrison, "greatly harassed by labor and watching, and in need of rest and refreshment," needed men. Varnum was to "send detachments, from time to time to relieve and replace an equal number . . . you are also occasionally to reinforce [the forts] . . . as they may stand in need of it." He was not, however, to assume personal command of either fort. The Virginian ordered Varnum to make his headquarters in Woodbury, New Jersey, to better oversee operations. If the British approached from Billingsport toward Fort Mercer, Varnum needed to operate "upon the rear or flanks of the enemy; not to throw your troops into the Fort." If Varnum used his fresh troops to relieve exhausted troops in the forts, as Washington intended, it is unclear what troops would be available to harass the British force at Billingsport.[21]

Varnum's arrival did nothing to alleviate the manpower shortage plaguing the naval vessels. Commodore Hazelwood notified Thomas Wharton on October 29 that the fleet lost more than 250 men "thro' cowardice of disaffection," i.e., desertion. However, "the remaining few we have left we are determined to spend

---

Horatio Gates on the Board of War with the authority to undermine Washington. The badmouthing of the commander-in-chief by Conway and others helped encourage Gates to take the position.

20 Chase & Grizzard, eds., *Papers*, vol. 12, 47.

21 Chase & Grizzard, eds., *Papers*, vol. 12, 44. Varnum crossed the Delaware at Bristol and proceeded to Woodbury via Mount Holly and Haddonfield. Reed, *Campaign*, 313.

the last drop of our blood in defense of this pass." Silas Newcomb, meanwhile, remained unhelpful, and New Jersey militia officer David Forman made sure Washington knew Newcomb was doing little to assist in the defense of the river. "From The best information I can Collect," explained Forman, "he has at no time given any assistance to the Garrisons or the fleet—particularly in The late Attack on red Bank he neither harassed The Enemy in Their Advanc, During The Assault or in Their retreat."[22]

The next day, Samuel Smith shared news of the conditions on Province and Carpenter's Islands. The British howitzers "are now up to their hobs [hubs] in water, altho' they have themselves cut two large places near their works to let it run out; they are obliged to wade knee deep to mount their guards." His own guns, he added, were desperately short of ammunition. Henry Knox had sent seventeen wagonloads of artillery ammunition to Varnum to help stock the forts but had sent the wrong caliber of ammunition for Mifflin's guns. Despite the difficulties facing the British, the occasional incoming British rounds paid off for the men inside Mifflin, while simultaneously restocking its ammo. According to Joseph Plumb Martin of the Connecticut Line, "The artillery officers offered a gill of rum for each shot fired from that [32-pounder British] piece. . . . I have seen from twenty to fifty men standing on the parade waiting with impatience the coming of the shot, which would often be seized before its motion had fully ceased and conveyed off to our gun to be sent back to its former owners. When the lucky fellow who had caught it had swallowed his rum, he would return to wait for another."[23]

Problems raging along the river notwithstanding, the Americans efforts continued to limit the supply flow into British Philadelphia. On October 30, Hessian Lt. Heinrich von Feilitzsch scribbled into his journal, "We received fewer and fewer provisions, because the enemy on Mud Island was becoming more watchful every day, and therefore it was very unsafe for the boats which were bringing such supplies. There was little to be had from the inhabitants," he added, "and what they were willing to part with was so expensive, that the common soldier simply could not afford it."[24]

22 Chase & Grizzard, eds., *Papers*, vol. 12, 49. Engineer de Fleury complained in his journal about poor naval cooperation and how the "want of concert or deficiency of boats disappointed our Enterprise." Crawford, ed., *Naval Documents*, vol. 10, 343.

23 Chase & Grizzard, eds., *Papers*, vol. 12, 64; Crawford, ed., *Naval Documents*, vol. 10, 343; Martin, *Private Yankee Doodle*, 90; Dorwart, *Fort Mifflin*, 46.

24 Von Feilitzsch, *Journal*, 120.

Unaware that Carl von Donop had passed away the previous night from the wound suffered at Fort Mercer, General Howe sent Capt. Friedrich von Muenchhausen of his staff to New Jersey to inquire of his condition. He only learned of the Prussian's fate once he arrived. Colonel Greene invited von Muenchhausen to dinner, "which invitation I declined," wrote the staffer, "mainly because [Greene] although he was very polite, betrayed signs of arrogance, partly because he had repulsed our attack on his fort, and partly because of the news that Burgoyne had been captured with his entire corps."[25]

British Philadelphia

By the end of October, Howe could count fewer than 12,000 troops capable of field service. Several hundred were operating against the American fortifications, which left him with fewer who could take the field. Washington's army was larger than Howe's. Desperately needed reinforcements left New York bound for Philadelphia. Henry Clinton loaded onto transport ships 4,000 men, including the 17th Light Dragoons, the 7th, 26th, and 63rd Regiments of Foot, convalescents of those battalions with Howe, and recruits from Europe. Two Anspach-Bayreuth regiments joined them. Major General Thomas Wilson and Brig. Gens. Alexander Leslie and James Pattison shipped out with them.[26]

Continental Camp

Now that Horatio Gates no longer needed the large force under his command, Washington desperately wanted several of the brigades with the Northern army sent south to join his army for an attack on Philadelphia. "What you are chiefly to attend to, is to point out in the Clearest and fullest manner, to Genl Gates, the absolute necessity that there is for his detaching a very considerable part of the

---

25 Von Muenchhausen, *At Howe's Side*, 42. At his own request, the garrison at Mercer buried Col. Carl von Donop with full military honors in the same mass grave as his men. McGuire, *Campaign*, vol. 2, 169. Legend has it that vandals looted the bones from the grave as souvenirs. Reed, *Campaign*, 300. Yet another court martial concluded on October 30. Anthony Wayne, who had been marking time at the main army's camp at Whitpain, was fully vindicated for his actions at Paoli.

26 British Archives, CO 5/253; Michael C. Harris & Gary Ecelbarger, "The Numerical Strength of George Washington's Army During the 1777 Philadelphia Campaign," *Journal of the American Revolution,* October 5, 2021, accessed online Jan. 8, 2022, https://allthingsliberty.com/2021/10/the-numerical-strength-of-george-washingtons-army-during-the-1777-philadelphia-campaign/; Jackson, *British Army*, 61.

Army at present under his Command to the reinforcement of this." Washington instructed his aide, Alexander Hamilton, on October 30. "A measure that will in all probability reduce Genl Howe to the same situation in which Genl Burgoine now is, should he attempt to remain in Philadelphia without being able to remove the obstructions in Deleware, & opening a free communication with his Shipping." Washington tasked the young staff officer not only with imploring Gates to send the main army reinforcements, but also to visit Israel Putnam in the Hudson Highlands and pry troops away from him, too. Hamilton carried with him from Washington a note reprimanding Gates. "I cannot but regret, that a matter of such magnitude [news of Burgoyne's surrender] and so interesting to our General Operations, should have reached me by report only, or through the channel of Letters not bearing that authenticity, which the importance of it required, and which it would have received by a line under your signature, stating the simple fact."[27]

On October 31, a disgusted Benjamin Rush wrote to John Adams regarding army mismanagement and asked Congress for two resolutions: "If any major or Brigadier General shall drink more than One quart of Whisky, or get drunk more than Once in 24 hours he shall be publickly reprimanded at the head of his division or brigade," was Rush's first reasonable request. His next, however—"that in all battles and Skirmishes the major and Brigadier generals shall not be more than 500 yards in the rear of their respective divisions or brigades upon pain of being tried and punished at the discretion of a court martial"—was a bit more problematic. Rush's demands demonstrated that, in the aftermath of Germantown and the current investigation of Maj. Gen. Adam Stephen's conduct, cracking down on drunkenness made sense.[28]

Reports arrived that the British had begun constructing a supply depot at Grub's Landing below Marcus Hook. On the last day of the month, General Washington instructed James Potter, a Pennsylvania militia general operating in that region, to "endeavor to break up the Road by which the enemy have a communication with their shipping over the Islands if it is practicable." Washington also wanted Potter "to remove the running Stones [millstones] from the Mills in the neighborhood of Chester and Wilmington." This last task would

---

27 Lender, *Caball*, 77; Chase & Grizzard, eds., *Papers*, vol. 12, 60-61.

28 Taylor, ed., *Papers of Adams*, vol. 5, 324.

prevent the British from using the mills to grind grain stolen from the regional farms.[29]

The River War

On November 1, elements of General Potter's militia fulfilled Washington's orders by cutting a dam to flood parts of Carpenter's Island and destroying sections of the road to Bow Creek. Engineer Montresor was working on the flooded island. "Somewhat dejected by Burgoyne's capitulation," admitted the captain, "and not elated with our late maneuvers as Dunop's repulse and the *Augusta's* and *Merlin* being burnt and to compleat all, Blockaded."[30]

While all seemed bleak to the worn-out Montresor, Washington's grip on the river remained tenuous and his confidence in Silas Newcomb had reached its nadir. The Virginian informed Congress of the situation on November 1. "As to General Newcomb, who is in the Neighborhood of Red Bank," he began, "notwithstanding my most urgent and repeated solicitations, I have little to expect from him, if I may form an estimate of his future services from those he has already rendered. Under these circumstances," he added, "I have been obliged to detach a further reinforcement of Continental Troops under Genl Varnum to maintain the two Garrisons if possible."[31]

Whitemarsh

The next day, November 2, Washington moved the army forward to Whitemarsh in accordance with the council of war and camped on the high ground there. Early morning fog drifted lazily just off the ground and frost covered the grass. The army was now positioned on a series of hills 14 miles north of Philadelphia. Off to the northeast was Camp Hill, a large steep ridge rising above Sandy Run that commanded the Whitemarsh Valley with a clear view to Chestnut Hill three miles distant. In the center was the smaller Fort Hill rising above Bethlehem Pike. Across the Wissahickon Creek to the southwest was another long

29   Chase & Grizzard, eds., *Papers*, vol. 12, 68.

30   Jackson, *Navy*, 221; Montresor, "Journals," 472.

31   Chase & Grizzard, eds., *Papers*, vol. 12, 79. Also on November 1, Henry Laurens replaced John Hancock as president of Congress.

The Camp Whitemarsh marker, erected in 1891. *Author*

ridge called Militia Hill, which ran toward Barren Hill about five miles away. The new American front now stretched five miles.[32]

32 To reach the new Whitemarsh position, Smallwood's militia, with Wayne's, Sullivan's and Stirling's divisions, moved down Skippack Pike while Irvine's militia, with McDougall's, Greene's, and Stephen's commands, marched down Morris Road to Pennsylvania Avenue. Reed, *Campaign*, 319; Jackson, *Whitemarsh*, 9-10. Washington established army headquarters in the two-and one-half story stone Emlen House built 30 years earlier in Upper Dublin Township. George Emlen, a Philadelphia wine merchant, bought the 236-acre property in 1745 as a summer estate. He died in

A modern view from Fort Hill looking toward Edge Hill. *Author*

Three years later, the Marquis de Chastellux visited the position and described its natural strength in his journal. "The position is excellent and does great honor to General Washington, who managed to discover it, as if by instinct, through the woods with which the country was then covered. Descending from the heights of Germantown," he continued, detailing the position's qualities,

you find very thick woods; on coming out of these woods, to the west, you see a fairly high hill, at the foot of which flows a brook [Wissahickon Creek], with steep banks, which turns towards the north and protects the right [west] of the camp. Six pieces of cannon were

1776, and the home was occupied by his widow, son, and daughter-in-law in 1777. Several officers found quarters in Flourtown, including Elias Boudinot, the Commissary General of Prisoners. The army medical department under Dr. John Cochran took over the home now known as Hope Lodge, the residence of William West. Hope Lodge was named for Henry Hope of the Hope Diamond fame (though Henry never lived on the property). West purchased it in 1776. Nathanael Greene established quarters across the road from Hope Lodge. Commissary General Clement Biddle began operating on Skippack Road above Wissahickon Creek. Post office operations took place near Mather Mill and the bridge over the Wissahickon Creek. Stephen Moylan of the 4th Continental Light Dragoons found quarters at Sandy Run Tavern on Bethlehem Pike adjacent to the present Clifton House. Christopher Ludwick, the baker general, set up his ovens on the grounds of Cliveden in Germantown in front of the American lines, which indicated that Washington did not fear an attack from Howe at that time. Jackson, *Whitemarsh*, 13-14; Thompson, *Whitemarsh*, 11-12; Cotter, Roberts, & Parrington, *The Buried Past*, 389-390.

A modern view from Militia Hill looking toward Edge Hill. *Author*

placed on this height, with four hundred men who formed an advanced post. A little church [St. Thomas's] which is on the summit of the hill has given it the name of Chestnut Church ["Church Hill"]: behind this height and behind the woods which stretch from east to west, the ground rises considerably, and forms two hills ["Fort Hill" and "Camp Hill"] with gentle slopes which command Chestnut Church ["Church Hill"]; here the army was encamped. These hills are separated only by a small hollow; the summit of each was fortified with a redoubt and the slope defended by an abatis. The hill on the left [east, i.e., "Camp Hill"] was still further protected by a brook [Sandy Run], which could be increased at pleasure, as it ran behind the camp and it was easy to make the dams necessary for raising the waters. To be sure, the front of this position is covered with woods, but these woods terminate at three hundred paces from the front lines; an enemy therefore would have had to come out of them uncovered, and how, furthermore, could they come through a wood where there is no road and which had been filled with militia and 'riflemen'?

Washington, concluded Chastellux, "was verily an eagle's eye, for it seems as if he must have soared above the treetops in order to see the ground beneath them."[33]

William Smallwood's Maryland militia formed on the left flank of the new position near the modern intersection of Susquehanna and Twining Roads. Extending down Camp Hill from Smallwood were Greene's and then Sullivan's commands. James Irvine's Pennsylvania militia formed on Militia Hill on the American right flank. A forward post with 400 men and six guns guarded the hill at

---

33 Chastellux, *Travels in North America*, vol. 1, 168-169. See map on page 280 in Chapter 9.

the intersection of Church Road and Bethlehem Pike where Whitemarsh Church sits. This same intersection had hosted a rearguard action during the retreat from the Battle of Germantown. American patrols roamed closer to Philadelphia on Edge Hill to the left, Chestnut Hill in the center, and Barren Hill to the right. As the weeks passed, the army built a redoubt on Fort Hill and another on Camp Hill. The entire line was soon fronted with abatis along the base of the hill along Sandy Run (which at that time was deeper and wider). The Americans would also dam the creek so the valley could be flooded during an attack.[34]

The opposing armies spent the next several weeks strengthening their respective positions while nipping at one another in a string of guerilla actions in the no-man's land between Whitemarsh and the Northern Liberties of Philadelphia. Partisan warfare that had marked the early days of the campaign in northern New Jersey resumed while the fighting along the Delaware played out. The partisan actions were "carried on constantly in full force," Johann Ewald recorded in his diary. "Not a day passed in which the Jager Corps, the light infantry, and the Queen's Rangers were not alarmed, and several people of the parties killed, wounded, or captured."[35]

British Philadelphia

Howe, meanwhile, desperately searching for a viable path to victory, requested and received a conference with Thomas Willing, a business partner of Congressman Robert Morris. Most patriots had fled Philadelphia prior to British occupation, but Willing remained to attend to his business affairs. He soon learned Howe's utterly unrealistic idea was that the Americans need only rescind the Declaration of Independence and return to the Crown's rule for peace to once more settle over the colonies. Coming as it did when the Americans were increasingly optimistic of starving the British out of Philadelphia, Howe's pleadings were bold and arrogant, and they were naïve and unworkable. As one historian

---

34 Jackson, *Whitemarsh*, 10. The artillery park was located where the modern Fort Washington interchange for the Pennsylvania Turnpike sits today. Modern St. Thomas Church occupies the site of Whitemarsh Church. All remnants of the redoubts are gone. The WPA accidentally destroyed the one on Fort Hill in the 1930s and a reconstructed one now sits on the original site within Fort Washington State Park.

35 McGuire, *Campaign*, vol. 2, 232-233; Ewald, *Diary*, 104. When Washington moved the army to Whitemarsh, the seriously sick were moved to Gwynedd Meetinghouse at the intersection of North Wales Road and Swede's Ford Road, the modern intersection of Route 202 and Sumneytown Pike. Jackson, *Whitemarsh*, 9.

recently noted, "Such an offer might have been acceptable to Americans in 1775, but by late 1777, wartime destruction and deaths had poisoned relations."[36]

The River War

As Washington maneuvered the main army into the Whitemarsh hills, General James Varnum arrived at Woodbury, New Jersey, with the 4th and 8th Connecticut regiments. When the Nutmeg State troops reached Fort Mercer on November 3, Varnum sent portions of the two regiments across the river to reinforce Fort Mifflin and a situation report to Washington. "I have taken a view of the Forts and think them in a good State of Defense," explained Varnum. "The want of Confidence between the Commodore [Hazelwood] and Colo. Smith, is very great. I shall do every Thing in my power to cause mutual Support between the Land and Water Forces. . . . There are no Militia of Consequence in force here." While Varnum was reinforcing Mercer and Mifflin, the British were sneaking supplies at night up the 500-foot-wide back channel past the latter fort. The gunners in the fort, noted de Fleury in his journal, could not open on the supply boats because "the Shade of Trees prevents our being informed of their passage otherwise than by the noise of oars, and firing at Sounds would be wasting precious Amunition."[37]

On November 4, to help assist both forts, Varnum erected a fascine battery on a small hill on the north bank of Mantua Creek along the New Jersey shore. Captain

---

36 McBurney, *George Washington's Nemesis*, 88-89. Willing sent another associate, John Brown, to deliver Howe's offer verbally to Congress in York. Willing and Brown miscalculated how others would come to see their role. Congress viewed it tantamount to treason and the Pennsylvania Council of Safety jailed Brown. He languished until January 1778, when Washington and Morris lobbied for his release.

37 The other two regiments of Varnum's brigade (the 1st and 2nd Rhode Island) were already serving at Fort Mercer. Chase & Grizzard, eds., *Papers*, vol. 12, 111-112. This water route became available to the British after they breached the *chevaux-de-frise* at Billingsport. Flat-bottom boats came up the inner channel between Tinicum and Billings islands and the Pennsylvania shore to the lower end of Hog Island before turning into Bow Creek. Initially, supplies were off-loaded at the lower end of Carpenter's Island and transported overland to be ferried over the Schuylkill River. After James Potter and the Pennsylvania militia cut the road to Bow Creek, the British landed farther up Bow Creek, where supplies were shifted to smaller boats and transported up Eagle Creek, portaged around Guyer's dam to Mingo Creek, and then moved into the Schuylkill River. Bow, Eagle, and Mingo creeks were small tidal waters separating Carpenter's and Province Islands from the mainland. This exceptionally time-consuming and laborious process was abandoned in favor of sneaking boats at night up the back channel past Fort Mifflin. The present Fort Mifflin Road was once the back channel. Smith, *Fight for Delaware*, 27; Crawford, ed., *Naval Documents*, vol. 10, 385-386. November 3 also witnessed the beginning of the court martial of Adam Stephen.

James Lee of the Continental Artillery commanded the battery, an 18-pounder and a 12-pounder. Washington, in response to Varnum's discouraging letter regarding the state of command affairs along the river, dispatched a letter. "How strange it is that Men, engaged in the same Important Service, should be eternally bickering, instead of giving mutual aid," penned the exasperated Virginian. "Officers cannot act upon proper principles who suffer trifles to interpose to create distrust, & jealousy—All our actions should be regulated by one uniform Plan—& that Plan should have one object only in view, to wit, the good of the service."[38]

Whitemarsh

As Varnum settled into his new role on November 4, Washington sought to replace his absence in the main army. The Virginian urged Israel Putnam, the commander in the Hudson Highlands, to forward reinforcements from the Northern army and emphasized the need for food supplies from New England. "You must not forget to send as many Cattle forward as you possibly can," he insisted, "for not having any supplies from New England since August last we have exhausted the Beef in this quarter very considerably, and you know our Army will be much increased."[39]

The River War

The British were not about to ignore Varnum's new battery. On November 5, warships moved above the *chevaux-de-frise* at Billingsport and opened fire about 9:00 a.m. Varnum returned the fire and elements of the American fleet arrived to add their weight to the effort. When the British discovered they could not elevate their guns enough to fire over the bank into the American battery, they withdrew. It did not go well, and the HMS *Isis* almost immediately ran aground. Hoping she would meet the same fate as the *Augusta*, an ecstatic Varnum reported the affair to Washington the next day as his guns pounded the stricken ship. "The Flood Tide making, floated the [*Isis*] but, as there was no Wind, she could not get far from [the

---

38 Chase & Grizzard, eds., *Papers*, vol. 12, 128. This battery, on the property of Tench Francis just east of Mantua Creek where Route 44 crosses today, was somewhere between modern Paradise Road and Leonard Lane (west of Little Mantua Creek). Today, the heavily industrialized area is in private hands. No trace of the knoll has been found. Smith, *Fight for Delaware*, 33.

39 Chase & Grizzard, eds., *Papers*, vol. 12, 126-127.

fascine battery], by w'ch means, she suffered extremely from our Eighteen & twelve Pounders. [The *Isis*] hoisted Signals of Distress; the Commodore [Hazelwood] came down with a great naval Force, and began a tremendous Fire . . . he advanced firing 'till some [of] his Shot reached [the enemy] ships." Varnum was unimpressed with the overall effort, however: "Had The galleys behaved tolerably well, the [*Isis*] must, beyond a Doubt, have fallen into our Hands."[40]

British sources confirm the action. The Lieutenant's Journal of the *Isis* admitted its "Hull and rigging [was] much damaged," and the journal of the HMS *Pearl* recorded the American shot "cut some of our Rigging." Varnum, however, overvalued the Mantua Creek position and unfairly criticized the naval effort. The *Isis* was below the *chevaux-de-frise* and surrounded by the entire British river fleet. The weak American galleys had done all they could that day. Washington heard the naval bombardment, rode to Germantown, and climbed to the top of Cliveden in an effort to observe the fighting. It was for naught, admitted aide John Laurens in a letter to his father, for "we could discover nothing more than thick clouds of smoak, and the masts of two vessels, the weather being very hazy."[41]

As inconclusive fighting swirled near Mantua Creek, the British launched a floating battery near Fort Mifflin. Howe transferred the 27th and 28th Regiments of Foot onto the islands and arrived personally to inspect the batteries. The Americans soon zeroed in on his position, as described by the diary of his Hessian aide. "The rebels on Fort Island and several of the galleys, with 32-pounders, who must have seen the General on Province Island, directed some of their cannon on a spot from which we had just come and to which we would have to go on our way back," wrote von Muenchhausen. "When we passed this post . . . as we rode back, we got a whole salvo of cannon balls, but none of them fulfilled the hopes of the enemy in spite of the fact that the General stopped at this place for several minutes."[42]

---

40 Jackson, *Fort Mifflin*, 60; Smith, *Fight for Delaware*, 28; Reed, *Campaign*, 327; Chase & Grizzard, eds., *Papers*, vol. 12, 146.

41 Crawford, ed., *Naval Documents*, vol. 10, 405; William Gilmore Simms, *The Army Correspondence of Colonel John Laurens in the Years 1777-8* (New York, 1867), 63. Other British ships involved included the *Pearl* and *Cornwallis*. Jackson, *Fort Mifflin*, 59-60.

42 Reed, *Campaign*, 329; Von Muenchhausen, *At Howe's Side*, 42. Help was on the way for William Howe. Reinforcements under Brig. Gen. Thomas Wilson left New York Harbor on 40 ships on November 5. The HMS *Experiment* and HMS *Bristol* protected the transport ships. Johann Ernst Prechtel, *A Hessian Officer's Diary of the American Revolution*, Bruce E. Burgoyne, ed. & trans. (Westminster, MD, 1994), 12; Dohla, *A Hessian Diary*, 12.

James Varnum continued to have little good to say about the American navy. "The Commodore says he cannot prevent the Enemies Boats from passing up and down the River, as they are covered by their Batteries upon Province Island," he wrote in his November 6 report to Washington. "The Commodore appears to be a very good kind of a Man, but his extreme good Nature gives too great a License to those under his Command."[43]

British Philadelphia

The desperation over dwindling supplies in the city, meanwhile, increased. Not only were provisions increasingly scarce for Howe's soldiers, but the civilian population suffered likewise. "The Hessians go on plundering at a great rate, such things as, Wood, Potatoes, Turnips, &c—Provisions are scarce among us," Elizabeth Drinker recorded in her diary. Many attempted to flee to the Pennsylvania backcountry in search of better conditions. Two women arrived at Rev. Henry Muhlenberg's home in Trappe on the night of November 4 and reported on conditions in the city. "These weak vessels," wrote Muhlenberg "had fled from Philadelphia . . . and had covered the twenty-six miles on foot in three days."[44]

Price gouging was rampant in the city. "A pound of tea, which was worth as much as 3L, was sold for 5s, and sugar for 2s. 6d. in specie. Butter is no longer to be had. Ox-head, which even the poorest people used to avoid, is now worth 10s. The wives of Hessian soldiers," continued Muhlenberg, "are sitting in the marketplace and selling all sorts of vegetables which their husbands fetch from gardens taken over from poor people living on the outskirts of the city, and so they are harvesting what they have not planted." John Laurens of Washington's staff noted much the same in a letter to his father on November 7: "[T]here have been several women from Ph[iladelphi]a within the two days past, who have applied for leave to pass into the country—declaring that unless this indulgence be granted to them, they must inevitably starve."[45]

---

43   Chase & Grizzard, eds., *Papers*, vol. 12, 147.

44   Drinker, *Diary of Elizabeth Drinker*, 250; Muhlenberg, *Journals*, vol. 3, 97

45   Simms, *Correspondence of Laurens*, 71. James Potter of the Pennsylvania militia had reported to the Pennsylvania assembly on October 27: "From the Best Accounts I can Receve, provisions is very scarce and Deer in the City; they are Killing there Milk Cows and Selling the Beef at 2/6 per pound.

Conway Cabal

Lord Stirling's disturbing letter containing details of the October 28 dinner with James Wilkinson reached Washington on November 4. "[S]uch wicked duplicity of Conduct," Stirling asserted, "I shall always think it my duty to detect." After mulling its contents, the stoic Virginian confronted his brash brigade commander—Thomas Conway—the next day. "A Letter which I receivd last Night, contain the following, paragraph. In a Letter from Genl Conway to Genl Gates he says—'Heaven has been determined to save your Country; or a weak General [Washington] and bad Councellors would have ruind it." These two sentences represent Washington's entire communication to Conway. Brief and to the point, Conway could no longer hide his machinations.[46]

Conway responded to Washington the next day. "I spoke my mind freely, I found fault with several Measures pursued in this army," he admitted. "[M]y opinion of you sir without flattery and envy is as follows: you are a Brave man, an honest Man, a patriot, and a Man of great sense. Your modesty is such, that although your advice in council is commonly sound and proper, you have often been influenc'd by men who Were not equal to you in point of experience, Knowledge or judgment. . . . I believe I can attest that the expression *Weak General* has not slipped from my penn [emphasis in original]." In other words, Conway was denying he had written those words.[47]

On November 5, Congress resolved to give more power and authority to Horatio Gates. The commander in the north received authorization to call on eastern states for any necessary troops and materials to keep the Hudson clear of British forces. Israel Putnam in the Hudson Highlands could now take 2,500 of his troops to reinforce Washington's army, but the rest of his command now reported to Gates. The victor of Saratoga no longer needed to report to Washington on these matters and the commander-in-chief had to ask Gates's permission if he wanted any more of his own troops from the north.[48]

Alexander Hamilton, who Washington dispatched north to bring those brigades down to Philadelphia, penned a terse letter to Gates on November 5 after

---

The Torreys I am told Loock as Cain did of old, and the Whigs Begin to Rejoice." Hazard, et al, eds., *Archives*, Series 1, vol. 5, 719.

46 Chase & Grizzard, eds., *Papers*, vol. 12, 111 & 129.

47 Ibid., 130.

48 Lender, *Cabal!*, 78.

inspecting the troops he proposed to provide. "I have learned that General Patterson's brigade, which is the one you propose to send is, by far, the weakest of the three now here," began Hamilton,

> and does not consist of more than about 600 rank and file fit for duty. . . . I cannot consider it either as compatible with the good of the service or my instructions . . . to consent, that that brigade be selected from the three, to go to him; but I am under necessity of requiring, by virtue of my orders from him, that one of the others be substituted instead of this . . . Knowing that General Washington wished me to pay great deference to your judgement, I ventured so far to deviate, from the instructions he gave me as to consent, in compliance with your opinion that two brigades should remain here instead of one . . . my ideas coincide with those of Gentlemen, whom I have consulted . . . whose judgement I have more reliance upon than my own and who must be supposed to have a thorough knowledge of the circumstances . . . Their opinion is, that one brigade . . . would amply answer the purposes of this post.[49]

Rumblings of discontent with Washington's performance in the field after Horatio Gates's stunning success at Saratoga began filtering into Washington's headquarters. Some of these rumors emanated from Congress. Problems had been brewing for some time. Gates's decision to inform Congress directly of the Saratoga victory without informing Washington was a deliberate slight to the Virginian. Gates had also consistently failed to keep Washington informed of matters occurring in the north—which Washington took as a clear dereliction of duty. Finally, Washington wanted the Continental regiments in Gates's army returned to his army, but the subordinate continued stonewalling the effort. By mid-month Washington had had enough and fired off a letter to Congressional President Henry Laurens on November 17. "I am informed that it is a matter of amazement, and that reflections have been thrown against this Army, for not being more active and enterprising than, in the opinion of some, they ought to have been. If the charge is just," he continued, "the best way to account for it, will be to refer you to the returns of our Strength and those which I can produce of the Enemy, and to the inclosed Abstract of the Cloathing now actually wanting for the Army." Washington was not finished. "I think the wonder will be, how they keep the feild at all, in Tents, at this Season of the Year." "There are besides, most of those in the Hospitals more bare than those in the Feild. Many remain there for want of Cloaths

---

49 Letter, Alexander Hamilton to Horatio Gates, November 5, 1777, https://founders.archives. gov/documents/Hamilton/01-01-02-0335, accessed September 3, 2023.

only." Thomas Conway had spent weeks plotting to have Washington replaced with Gates as commander-in-chief, and several high ranking officers were involved in the effort. Washington found out about the full extent of the plot on November 8.[50]

Urged to action by the cabal and with a firm desire to strike at a weakened Howe, Washington held another council of war on November 8. "The following question was put," wrote the commanding general: "Whether, in Case the Enemy should make an attack upon the Forts upon Delaware, it would be proper with our present Force to fall down and attack the Enemy in their Lines near Philada? Ansr. In the Negative unanimously." This placed Washington squarely on the horns of a dilemma. If he did not act soon, Howe would use the lull in active field operations to marshal additional assets and perhaps capture Fort Mifflin.[51]

"The importance of the Post at Red-Bank," Washington urged Maj. Gen. Philemon Dickinson of the New Jersey militia, "makes it necessary for us to employ all possible resources in rendering it so respectable by the Strength of the Garrison, and the number of Troops stationed within distance to cooperate with it, as not to fear even a more formal Attack than was exhibited in the first successless effort of the Hessians—All the men in your State that can be spared should therefore be collected and march'd to join Genl Varnum."[52]

Whitemarsh

The clothing and supply situation for Washington's army had reached a critical point. He could not launch an attack against Howe in Philadelphia with most of his army improperly fed and clothed—and his generals said as much in their

50 Chase & Grizzard, eds., *Papers*, vol. 12, 295. As noted earlier, a month after submitting his resignation and disappearing from his quartermaster duties with Washington's army, Congress accepted Thomas Mifflin's resignation and appointed him to the Board of War—a position that gave him oversight of Washington's army. Lender, *Cabal!*, 76-77. On November 6, Alexander Hamilton wrote to Washington from Albany, New York, after meeting with Gates, who was reluctant to dispatch the requested troops. Hamilton explained his reluctance to push the issue: "On the whole it appeared to me dangerous to insist on sending more troops from hence while General Gates appeared so warmly opposed to it. Should any accident or inconvenience happen in consequence of it, there would be too fair a pretext for censure, and many people are too-well-disposed to lay hold of it." Chase & Grizzard, eds., *Papers*, vol. 12, 141.

51 Chase & Grizzard, eds., *Papers*, vol. 12, 163. Washington was not yet aware that the 40-ship fleet of reinforcements for Howe's army had entered the Delaware River during the day and anchored near Reedy Island off the coast of Delaware. Prechtel, *A Hessian Officer's Diary*, 12.

52 Chase & Grizzard, eds., *Papers*, vol. 12, 167.

unanimous negative opinion on the subject at the recent council of war. William Smallwood wrote the governor of Maryland on November 8 that his brigade's "ragged situation, the approaching season, & the improbability of procuring supplies of Cloathing, produced sensations that must affect any Person of Humanity." Similar appeals went to the governors of New Jersey, Delaware, and Virginia. The Pennsylvania Council of Safety decided the best course to rectify the situation was to simply take what was needed from part of the civilian population, and appointed commissioners on November 8 to confiscate "from such of the Inhabitants . . . as have not taken the Oath of Allegiance and Abjuration, or who have aided or assisted the enemy, arms, accoutrements, blankets, Woolen & Linsey Woolsey Cloth, Linnen, shoes, and stockings for the Army."[53]

The partisan war north and west of Philadelphia, meanwhile, intensified on November 9 when the British nearly captured dragoon commander Casimir Pulaski, a brigadier general from Poland tasked with leading Washington's mounted arm. Major Samuel Hay of the 7th Pennsylvania reported the incident to his colonel, William Irvine. "General Polaskey (the commander of all our Light Dragoons) with a body of his troops attacked a body of the Enemy's Light horse," reported the major. "Our people charged the Enemy, as it is our General's rule; he sets no score by carbines or pistols, but rushes on with their swords; they had severe cutting and slashing; the enemy had 5 killed and two taken prisoners, besides a number wounded. We lost one killed, and two taken prisoners; General Polaskey was taken prisoner, and retaken again."[54]

The River War

By November 9, the Mifflin garrison numbered only 115 men fit for active duty, all of who labored under very demoralizing conditions. Of his original 200, Lieutenant Colonel Smith reported to Washington, only 69 were fit for service. The 6th Virginia regiment added 120 reinforcements, but only 46 were still available.[55]

---

53 *Minutes of the Supreme Executive Council of Pennsylvania, From its Organization to the Termination of the Revolution* (Harrisburg, PA, 1852), vol. 11, 339; William H. Browne, ed., *Archives of Maryland: Journal and Correspondence of the State Council March 20, 1777-March 28, 1777* (Baltimore, MD, 1897), 413.

54 Letter, Samuel Hay to William Irvine, November 14, 1777, Lyman Draper manuscript collection, Wisconsin Hist. Soc., Madison, WI. At that time, William Irvine was a prisoner on parole.

55 Chase & Grizzard, eds., *Papers*, vol. 12, 184. The fort by November 9 had one 32-pounder, one 24-pounder, 31 8-pounders, one 12-pounder, and two 4-pounders. Jackson, *Fort Mifflin*, 64.

Francois de Fleury had engineered a number of improvements to the position over the previous few weeks. The main battery now included traverses and excavated ditches fronted with a fraised earthen rampart on the southeast salient to protect gunners from enfilade and ricochet shot. A double chain along the water's edge helped protect the right side of the battery. Fraises were added on the earthen ramparts of the north and west sides in front of the main battery which, along with the wolf pits, would make it much harder for a British storming party to get up and over the walls. A battery of two 18-pounders was added near the blockhouse and another of a pair of 4-pounders at the old ferry wharf. A banquette was raised along the stone wall allowing musket men a field of fire to the east. A redoubt shaped like a Greek cross was constructed in the middle of the parade as a last line of defense.[56]

A British prisoner from HMS *Camilla* informed James Varnum that the British ships had "Orders to move, some to New York . . . in a Fortnight, Should they not take the Forts . . . the Ships have not more than a Third of their Compliment" with many "very sickly." The informant also claimed the signal to begin the bombardment of Fort Mifflin was the hoisting of the "English Jack" on Province Island. Varnum passed along the information on to Washington on November 9.[57]

By this time the British had three batteries deployed on Carpenter's Island, just 600 yards from the fort. They also had a battery on Province Island and another at Webb's Ferry. A combined land and naval bombardment was set to begin on November 10, when a full moon and higher tides would aide the supporting naval vessels. The British plan called for prolonged bombardment of the fort's defenses for three or four days before a detachment of 300 British Guards crossed the river in "8 Flat Bottomed Boats, 35 soldiers each together with Engineers, a company of Carpenters, fascines, scaling ladders, flying bridge, etc." Sir George Osborne of the British Guards was tasked with leading the daring mission.[58]

---

56 Jackson, *Navy*, 227. A banquette was a raised firing step leading up to the rampart.

57 Chase & Grizzard, eds., *Papers*, vol. 12, 186.

58 The northernmost battery on Carpenter's Island had six 24-pounders from HMS *Eagle*, one 8-in Howitzer, and an 8-in mortar. A battery to the south held one 8-in mortar and one 8-in Howitzer. Farther south was a 13-in mortar. A battery near the Pest House on Province Island had two 32-pounders from HMS *Somerset* and another emplacement with an 18-pounder at the old Ferry Wharf opposite Fort Mifflin. Two more 32-pounders from the *Somerset* were used on floating batteries. The battery at Webb's Ferry had a pair of 12-pounders and one 18-pounder. Jackson, *Fort Mifflin*, 64; Martin, *Philadelphia*, 138; Montresor, "Journals," 477. The southernmost batteries were at the northern end of the runways for the Philadelphia International Airport.

On November 9, the HMS *Somerset* passed the *chevaux-de-frise* at Billingsport to add her broadsides to the impending bombardment. The fleet of reinforcements from New York anchored in New Castle harbor late in the day. Howe had confidence in the plan but worried that Washington might launch his own attack against the rear of the batteries on Province and Carpenter's islands. This was possible because Potter's Pennsylvania militia had been making "a practice of firing at each other [British pickets on Carpenter's Island] without comg to any action," reported John Laurens in a letter to his father on November 7. To protect against that, Howe positioned the 27th and 28th Regiments of Foot on the island facing west. He was right to be concerned because Washington was thinking about doing exactly that. He ordered Potter two days later to "disturb . . . the Enemy upon Carpenter's Island; especially while they are in the height of their operation against Fort Mifflin," but his council of war had denied Washington's wish.[59]

On the eve of the British bombardment, the combined American command lacked cohesion. Samuel Smith, the commanding officer at Fort Mifflin, despised Commodore John Hazelwood. Fort Mifflin's engineering officer, Maj. Francois de Fluery, bickered with Smith over responsibility for engineering the fort's defense. James Potter's Pennsylvania militia refused to destroy the meadow banks and flood Province and Carpenter's islands. The New Jersey militia had consistently failed to reinforce Fort Mercer. Colonel Christopher Greene seemed to be the only officer uninvolved in the internal bickering. Brigadier General James Varnum, who Washington had dispatched to soothe poor feelings and exercise overall command of the river operations, failed to unify the various elements.[60]

How the fractured command system would hold up in the face of a concerted British attack remained to be seen.

59 McIntyre, *A Most Gallant Resistance*, 224; Prechtel, *A Hessian Officer's Diary*, 12; Von Muenchhausen, *At Howe's Side*, 42; Simms, *Correspondence of Laurens*, 70; Chase & Grizzard, eds., *Papers*, vol. 12, 213.

60 Dorwart, *Fort Mifflin*, 45-46.

Chapter 7

The Battle for Fort Mifflin

November 10-16, 1777

"The Americans "defended it [Fort Mifflin] with a Spirit, they have shewn no where else to an equal Degree during the War."[1]

— Adm. Richard Howe's secretary, Ambrose Serle, November 22, 1777

November 10

William Howe could seize the American position on Mud Island, he could begin removing the upper rows of *chevaux-de-frise* and open the way for supply ships to dock at Philadelphia's wharves. One month earlier, the British completed their first land battery in their effort to prepare for the operation. Since that time, engineer John Montresor had completed several others and added heavy ordnance brought up from the fleet. This impressive array opened on Fort Mifflin at 7:30 a.m. on November 10 with a bombardment seldom witnessed in North America. Orders to the battery commanders directed them to fire 80 rounds per gun, followed by sporadic firing until otherwise ordered. The two sides pounded away at each other at just 500 yards. Fort Mifflin took a beating.[2]

1 Serle, *Journal*, 264.

2 Jackson, *Fort Mifflin*, 66.

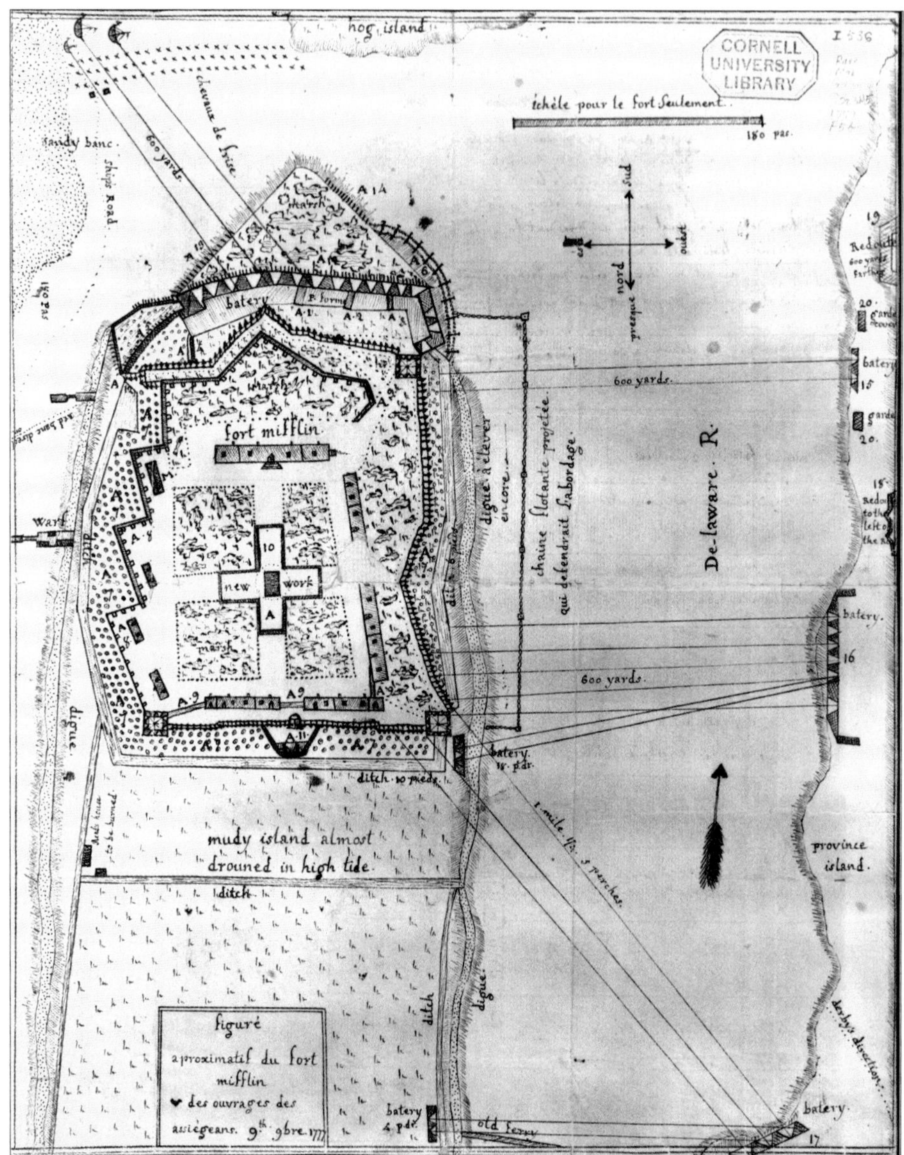

Map of Fort Mifflin on the Delaware River (south is at top of image). *Cornell University Library*

According to Mifflin's commander, Lt. Col. Samuel Smith, "a continued discharge on the Fort was maintained, the whole day, from the [Pest] Hospital and battery, of shot, shells, and carcasses." The latter, he continued, "are made, about two feet square, filled [with] combustibles, and having sharp hooks, which keep them fast to the shingles. They were extinguished by raw hides, which had been soaked in water for the purpose. They gave much trouble and no little fatigue." One of the iron enemy rounds, Smith reported to Washington, "were so fortunate to strike one of our 18 pounders in the two Gun Battery on the Muzzle, by which, she is rendered useless." The enemy fire was effective, raking "the Pallisades fronting the Meadow . . . they have laid open a great part of that side, and chiefly destroyed that range of Barrocks . . . they have dismounted 3 of our Blockhouse Guns, and much injured the Block houses and the other Range of Barrocks." The incoming rounds knocked out two 18-pounders moved into a new battery facing Carpenter's Island early in the day, knocking off the muzzle and trunnions of one. By noon, the British batteries had expended 1,020 rounds onto the Mud Island position, pummeling the American batteries and breaching the palisade wall in numerous places.[3]

"This day the Enemy Opened five new Batteries on fort Mifflin," wrote Israel Angell, who was stationed at Fort Mercer with his Rhode Island regiment, "which played briskly During the whole day, and the Evening until nine oClock." From what he could witness, the bombardment "did no great Dammage." In a letter three months later on February 17, 1778, Angell expounded on the gunnery, noting "there was no place of safety in any part of the fort. Such was the situation of the batteries, that they kept up a cross fire in almost every direction. The only covering the troops had was without the fort, under the wall, and this afforded a shelter from nothing but the enormous balls." Somehow, the Americans passed through the prolonged shelling without suffering a single recorded casualty.[4]

John Miller, a magistrate in Germantown 15 miles away, listened to the gunfire as he scribbled in his diary: "[T]he cannonade at the fort is still very heavy, and still shaking the very earth." Virginia loyalist James Parker rode down to Province Island from Philadelphia to observe the action. "A brick Chimney on the Rebel fort was broke down, and a good [deal] of damage done to the front of their battery parallel to our middle one," the British supporter jotted into his journal. "We lost one man this day in the Works & two others by random shot . . . Lord C. Wallace Genl. Grant & some other Genl. officers were there." Howe's Hessian aide, Capt. Friedrich von Muenchhausen, recorded that the Americans got lucky—as he put it,

3 Smith, "Papers of Smith," 89; Chase & Grizzard, eds., *Papers*, vol. 12, 203-204; Smith, *Fight for Delaware*, 29; Jackson, *Fort Mifflin*, 66. A "carcass" was a type of incendiary shell designed to set targets on fire.

4 Angell, *Diary*, n.p; Benjamin Cowell, *Spirit of '76 in Rhode Island: or, Sketches of the Efforts of the Government and People in the War of the Revolution* (Boston, 1850), 296-7.

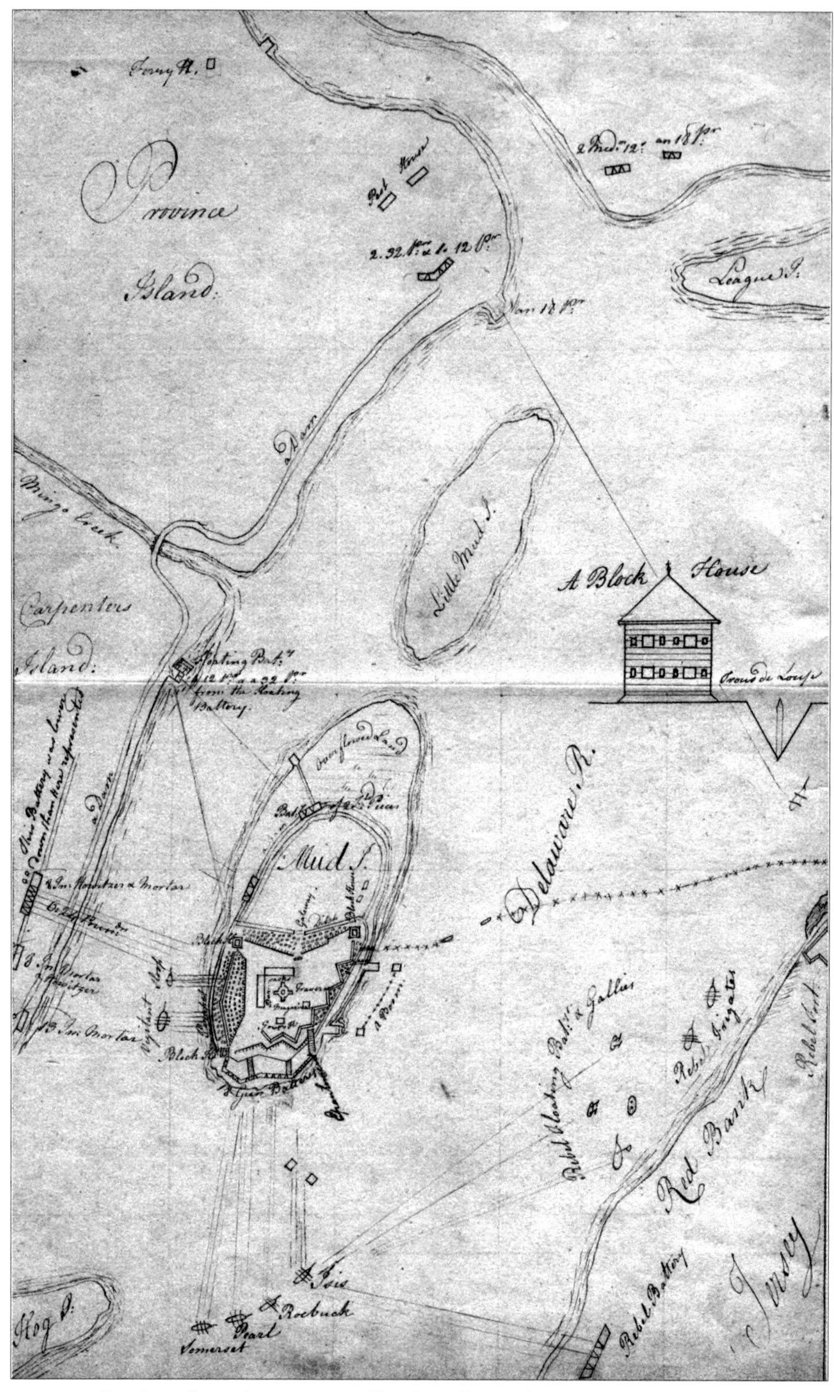

The plan of attack on Fort Mifflin, by John Andre. *William Clements Library*

"something that happens very rarely," when a 12-pound ball landed "directly into the barrel of one of our 24-pounders, without damaging our cannon because it went in so accurately."[5]

British artillery fire tapered off around 2:00 p.m. when a heavy downpour started and strong wind gusts swept the area. Temperatures dropped as the hours passed and the ground froze solidly. The strong gusts out of the southwest forced the American galleys and guard boats to seek shelter away from Fort Mifflin.[6]

Smith sent a situation report to Washington that evening. After listing the fort's damage, the beleaguered garrison sheltered on the east side of the stone wall, "and have the good fortune as yet to escape unhurt." Smith warned the Virginian, however, that "In 5 or 6 days (unless the Seige can be rais'd) the fort will be laid open, and everything destroyed, if they continue to Cannonade and Bombard us as they have done, of which I haven't the smallest doubt. Our men already half Jaded to Death with constant fatigue, will be unfit for service." Mifflin's commander urged Washington to evacuate the fort and take the weaponry to Fort Mercer. The only way to keep it, he continued, was for Washington to assault the British batteries from the west. The Marylander acknowledged the galleys could not withstand the fire of the British batteries in the back channel. The river defense commander, James Varnum, informed Washington that he ordered Smith to move the men into the shattered barracks, "thinking that it is better to have a few killed or wounded, then to have the whole suffer, expos'd to the Inclemency of the Weather, upon mear Mud."[7]

Indefatigable chronicler Joseph Plumb Martin of the 4th Connecticut Regiment wrote about his experiences later in life. At Mifflin, he began, "I endured hardships sufficient to kill half a dozen horses. . . . In the cold month of November, without provisions, without clothing, not a scrap of either shoes or stockings to my feet or legs, and in this condition to endure a siege in such a place as that was appalling in the highest degree. It was utterly impossible to lie down to get any rest or sleep on account of the mud, if the enemy's shot would have suffered us to do so." He continued, "Sometimes some of the men, when overcome with fatigue and

---

5 Watson, *Annals*, vol. 2, 7; James Parker Journal, November 10, 1777, entry, Parker Family Papers, originals in Liverpool, England, microfilm copies at the American Philosophical Society, Philadelphia, PA, film 45, reel 2. Scotland native James Parker was born in 1729, emigrated to America in 1750, became a wealthy merchant in Norfolk, Virginia, and linked up with Howe's army in Maryland and accompanied the British into Philadelphia. Von Muenchhausen, *At Howe's Side*, 43.

6 Jackson, *Navy*, 231 & 235; McGuire, *Campaign*, vol. 2, 197.

7 Chase & Grizzard, eds., *Papers*, vol. 12, 204-205.

want of sleep, would slip away into the barracks to catch a nap of sleep, but it seldom happened that they came out again alive. I was in this place a fortnight and can say in sincerity that I never lay down to sleep a minute in all that time." Each night the Americans ferried supplies over from New Jersey. "What little provisions we had was cooked by the invalids in our camp and brought to the island in old flour barrels," Martin recalled. "[I]t was mostly corned beef and hard bread, but it was not much trouble to cook or fetch what we had." Every half hour that night, the British sent a round of shells into the fort to prevent repairs and keep the garrison awake.[8]

November 11

The cold rain stopped during the night, and November 11 dawned with frigid winds and heavy frost. To the distress and anxiety of the Americans, the British bombardment continued. Germantown resident John Miller remembered "a hard frost" on the ground and "snow having fallen all the preceding night." Commander Smith and Capt. Samuel Treat of the artillery "were conversing, near the thirty-two pounder, when a ball from the enemy came," recalled Smith. "It lodged in the traverse. Captain Treat tottered." Smith held him upright and with "a slight squeeze of the hand . . . he expired." To Smith's surprise, "no wound was apparent." The shell's concussion had killed him. French engineer Francois de Fleury recorded changes the British had made to their gun positions during the night. "They have changed the direction of their Embrasures—and instead of battering our Palisades in front," he noted in his journal, "they take them obliquely and do great injury to our north side."[9]

Captain Cord Hazzard of the Delaware Line was nearly killed by another round. The captain was looking out the window of the blockhouse near the 32-pounder when Commander Smith asked him to come down and not recklessly expose himself. There was "no risk," shot back the officer. Within moments a British round struck the wood a foot above Hazzard's head. Smith believed he had

---

8 Martin, *Private Yankee Doodle*, 85, 89 -90; Jackson, *Navy*, 235. While the bombardment was underway on November 10, Horatio Gates finally acquiesced to Washington's pleas and ordered the brigades of John Glover and John Paterson to start marching south.

9 Watson, *Annals*, vol. 2, 70; Smith, "Papers of Smith," 89-90. Pvt. Alvin Ames, 4th Connecticut, was also killed that morning. Lt. John George of the artillery was wounded and evacuated. The British did not escape unscathed. Two men were killed and another two wounded in their batteries. Jackson, *Navy*, 239 & 242; De Fleury Fort Mifflin journal; Stryker, *Forts on the Delaware*, 38.

been killed outright. He was wrong. The men carried the wounded officer down and the surgeon bled him. Hazzard recovered, but was completely deaf.[10]

Later that morning, James Varnum's brigade major arrived for a report. Smith went into the shell-pocked barracks to pen the document. As he recalled, he handed "the report with his right hand—his left being behind him, and his back to the chimney [when] a ball came through the stockade, the barracks, and two stacks of chimneys: and nearly spent, it struck him on the left hip and dislocated his wrist." Smith collapsed as dust, masonry, and splinters filled the room and the chimney caved in on him, covering him with bricks that severely bruised him, "every joint in his body appeared to be loosened." Smith's staff were similarly "covered with bricks and mortar, and so astonished as to give no assistance." Unable to stand, the wounded officer "rolled over and over, until got to the front door." After bleeding Smith and resetting the wrist, Dr. Thomas Skinner evacuated the incapacitated commander across the river to Varnum's headquarters in Woodbury. "I imprudently went into my Barracks to answer a Letter from Gen. Varnum," Smith related to Washington the following day, "& a Ball came through the Chimney & Struck me on the Hip so forcibly that I remain'd senseless for Some time. However I am happy to find myself less hurted than I at first imagin'd & Hope in 5 or 6 days to be again fit for duty." Lt. Col. Charles Simms of the Virginia Line assumed garrison command. Unfortunately for Smith, he would never command in the field again.[11]

Fort Mifflin's commander and its artillery chief both went down within a few hours and the fort was in disarray. "The Enemy," Varnum reported to Washington that night, "have battered down a great Part of the Stone Wall: The Pallisades and Barracks are prodigiously shattered . . . I expect we shall cause an evacuation this Night."[12]

During the fighting on November 11, Fort Mercer's artillerists tried to engage British shipping, but the vessels were too far for the guns to be effective. Sometime during the day there, an 18-pounder that may have come from the *Augusta* burst, killing one and wounding several others. Two British ships moved into position

---

10 Hazzard resigned on January 27, 1778, believing "no man ought to hold a Commission who could not perform its duties." Smith, "Papers of Smith," 90.

11 Smith, "Papers of Smith," 90; Jackson, *Fort Mifflin*, 69; Dorwart, *Fort Mifflin*, 48; Chase & Grizzard, eds., *Papers*, vol. 12, 231. Smith returned to Baltimore to recover from his wounds. Patrick K. O'Donnell, *Washington's Immortals: The Untold Story of an Elite Regiment Who Changed the Course of the Revolution* (New York, 2016), 168.

12 Chase & Grizzard, eds., *Papers*, vol. 12, 217.

The damaged gun from the sunken HMS *Augusta* at Fort Mercer. *Author*

near the mouth of Mantua Creek and opened fire on Americans trying to build a new battery north of the creek. According to Capt. John Linzee of the HMS *Pearl*, "*Cornwallis* Galley & a Tender belonging to the *Eagle* firing on a battery on the Jersey shore, the Rebels being at work there." The effort made sense. Varnum had noted in a letter November 6 letter to Washington that this new battery would "oblige the [British] Shipping to keep down the River as low as Billingsport." Howe could not allow the noose around his supplies to get any tighter.[13]

As evening descended on the day's action and the rain started to fall once more, James Varnum held a council of war with Colonel Greene and d'Arendt (who was still technically in command at Fort Mifflin). The naval arm's critical role in the defense of Fort Mifflin was obvious, but Commodore Hazelwood was not present for the meeting. Varnum noted in a dispatch to Washington that evening that the evacuation of Fort Mifflin "may enable us to take Billingsport," an idea Varnum repeatedly found interesting. The three officers concluded that Mifflin's garrison could hold out longer and directed the men to defend "at all Events" until otherwise instructed by Washington. Lieutenant Colonel Giles Russell of the 4th Connecticut was ordered to take command of the garrison. The French and Indian

13 McIntyre, *A Most Gallant Resistance*, 231; Jackson, *Navy*, 238. Smith, *Fight for Delaware*, 33; Crawford, ed., *Naval Documents*, vol. 10, 467; Chase & Grizzard, eds., *Papers*, vol. 12, 146.

Modern-day Fort Mifflin, as viewed from New Jersey. *Author*

War veteran was already physically and mentally exhausted from service on Mud Island. The Mifflin infantry and artillerists huddled in frigid conditions that night as thick ice formed on water pools. They had no firewood, and the constant shelling prevented gathering fragments of the fort to start fires. Rations were eaten cold.[14]

Despite the success of the British land batteries, army leadership wanted the navy to add its weight to the effort. Admiral Howe agreed and decided Maj. John Henry's *Vigilant* could be moved close enough to the southern end of Mifflin to blast anything that moved. To do so, the *Vigilant* had to be lightened and her decks and bulkheads reinforced with barricades so she could move up the back channel. She carried one 24-pounder, nine 2-pounders, and six 4-pounders (all on one side with ballast on the other). At midday, Captain Henry attempted to move into the back channel but "being in a very narrow part of the Channel we got aground."[15]

14 Chase & Grizzard, eds., *Papers*, vol. 12, 217-218; McIntyre, *A Most Gallant Resistance*, 232; Reed, *Campaign*, 336-337.

15 Smith, *Fight for Delaware*, 34; Crawford, ed., *Naval Documents*, vol. 10, 467; McGuire, *Campaign*, vol. 2, 203. One reason Washington lacked the ability to do more for Fort Mifflin was a lack of provisions for the main army. Washington wrote to Congress on November 11 with his concerns. "The mode of seizing and forcing supplies from the Inhabitants, I fear, would prove very inadequate to the demands, while it would certainly imbitter the minds of the People, and excite perhaps a hurtful jealously against the Army. I have had officers out for the purpose of purchasing and making voluntary collections of necessaries, and in a few instances more coercive measures have been exercised—But all these have proved of little avail—Our distresses still continue, and are becoming greater." Chase & Grizzard, eds., *Papers*, vol. 12, 208.

November 12

After Smith fell, effective command inside Fort Mifflin fell to Capt. Francois de Fleury. The French engineer informed Washington that "the fire of the enemy has been successful enough to spoile our three Block houses, and dismount the canon of all, except two . . . some of our palisade at the nordside are broken, but we can mend them every night. In all the fort is certainly Yet in state to be defended," he continued, "but the garrison is so dispirited that if the enemy, will attempt to storm us, I am afraid that they will succeed." Joseph Plumb Martin confirmed de Fleury's efforts many years later. The engineer, he wrote, "was a very austere man and kept us constantly employed day and night; there was no chance of escaping from his vigilance." Martin and his comrades watched for a chance "to escape from the vigilance of Colonel Fleury" and, when the opportunity offered, would run inside "for a minute or two's respite from fatigue and cold. When the engineer found that the workmen began to grow scarce, he would come to the entrance and call us out. He had always his cane in his hand, and woe betided him he could get a stroke at." When the Frenchman began swinging his cane, Martin "always jumped over the ditch and run down the far side, so that he could not reach me, but he often noticed me and as often threatened me, but threatening was all, he could never get a stroke at me, and I cared but little for his threats."[16]

De Fleury was right. The garrison was demoralized, and it could not hold on indefinitely. The men, he reported "are so exhausted, by watch, cold, Rain & fatigue, that their Courage is very Low, and in the Last allarme one half was unfit for duty . . . I think necessary for my honour to put under your eyes the same observation, to not be thought guilty in case of the event" of evacuation. Thankfully for the Americans, strong gales prevented British naval participation in the bombardment that day. Civilians like Elizabeth Drinker, meanwhile, heard the British fire: "great part of last Night and most of this day at times, we have heard the Cannon below."[17]

After holding his own council of war that morning, Washington wrote to Varnum at 1:00 p.m.: "the Fort be held to the last extremity." Varnum agreed. "The Garrison hold out; tho' the Enemy continue to batter with great Success upon the Works, but few Men are killed and wounded. Should the Enemy continue their Cannonade the Island will be lost," he continued, "however, the Garrison will

---

16   Chase & Grizzard, eds., *Papers*, vol. 12, 224-225; Martin, *Private Yankee Doodle*, 88-89.

17   Chase & Grizzard, eds., *Papers*, vol. 12, 225; Drinker, *Diary of Elizabeth Drinker*, 252.

continue 'till your Excellency should order otherwise." Washington understood Varnum's difficult situation but wanted him to hold out until all other possibilities were considered. "I am sorry . . . that the fire of the Enemy made so great an impression on the Works of Fort Mifflin that you thought an evacuation would be necessary. I hope it is not carried into execution. We are now thinking if there is any possibility of attacking the enemy in reverse and thereby raising the Seige," he continued, "if it can be done with any probability of Success. Therefore endeavor to hold the Island till the practicability of that measure at least is determined upon." Washington urged him to use the cover of darkness to remove "all the invalids and fatigued Men, and fill up their places with the most fresh and robust, and that the Troops in the garrison be often exchanged, that they may by that means obtain rest." The Virginia commander was confident the British would not storm the fort so long as the palisades and entrenchments were "kept in tolerable repair and there is an appearance of Force upon the Island, and I therefore would have you to endeavor to prevail upon the Militia to go over at Night, when there is a cessation of firing, and work till day light . . . This will greatly relieve the Continental Troops."[18]

Still, Washington was a realist and knew the defense was nearly played out. Later that night he issued a second set of orders to Varnum: "The Cannon and Stores ought immediately to be removed, and every thing put in a disposition to remove totally at a minutes warning; but as every day that we can hold even the Island is so much time gained, I would recommend that a party be left, who might find good Shelter behind the ruined works, and when they abandon, they should set fire to the Barracks and all remaining Buildings."[19]

For reasons that remain unclear, Washington was unwilling to detach any Continentals to attack the British lines. Instead, on November 11, he had written to James Potter of the Pennsylvania militia that "It would be a great, and glorious thing, if you could disturb the Enemy upon Carpenter's Island; especially while they are in the height of their operation against Fort Mifflin." Potter, however, reported back that the enemy "have strengthened that place [Carpenter's Island] with men and works and cannon," and he could not attack it. "[It] will be mutch more dificqualty in Redusing it then would have been eight days ago."[20]

18   Chase & Grizzard, eds., *Papers*, vol. 12, 225, 232-234.

19   Ibid., 232-234.

20   Ibid., 213, 229-230.

As the hours ticked past without the evacuation of Mifflin, British frustration mounted. "I wish we would finally capture this cursed fort," penned Howe's exasperated Hessian aide Captain von Muenchhausen. "[I]t makes us aides ride around so much. It is especially inconvenient to ride during the night because everything is swampy, and besides, one is very exposed to enemy shells if one does not happen to be standing in a battery." Robert Morton, a civilian in Philadelphia, told his diary on November 12, "This day severe firing by which the American Barracks was several times set on fire, but soon extinguished."[21]

British engineer John Montresor had his men begin constructing more batteries in awful conditions—"such cold weather never set in so soon. Some trifling snow fell this morning, mixed with rain." Montresor also needed to spend time repairing his batteries because American fire had breached several embrasures, upset guns, and disabled a pair of 8-inch howitzers.[22]

Howe, meanwhile, decided enough was enough and set about planning to storm the island to finish off the tenacious garrison. Ensign Carl Rueffer of the Hessian Regiment von Mirbach noted in his diary that "ten privates from each company of the Light Infantry, as well as the Grenadier Company of the English Guards . . . marched to Province Island in order to attack the batteries on Mud Island." Lieutenant Colonel George Osborne of the British Guards was put in command of this force, with the 27th and 28th Regiments of Foot in support. Artilleryman Francis Downman confirmed in his journal a Guard's detachment was "in readiness to storm." After a careful observation of the fort's condition, John Montresor believed that entering Mifflin on the northeast front of the palisades was "practicable in 20 places."[23]

Strong winds throughout the day limited the operations of both fleets. The heavy rain and winds, wrote Monstresor, made the water "very tempestuous." Still, Admiral Howe was determined to silence the American battery above Mantua Creek in New Jersey before bringing his ships into the attack against Mifflin. According to Capt. Andrew Hamond of the HMS *Roebuck*, the *Isis* and *Cornwallis* moved into position in an unsuccessful attempt to silence the battery. Simultaneously, British engineer Archibald Robertson left with a 50-man

---

21 Von Muenchhausen, *At Howe's Side*, 43; Morton, "Diary," 27.

22 Montresor, "Journals," 475; Jackson, *Fort Mifflin*, 71.

23 Bruce E. Burgoyne, ed., *Enemy Views: The American Revolutionary War as Recorded by the Hessian Participants* (Bowie, MD, 1996), 235; Whinyates, *Services*, 50; Montresor, "Journals," 475.

detachment from Billingsport to reconnoiter "Manto [Mantua] Creek and a Battery the Rebels were Erecting about 800 Yds from the mouth of it."[24]

Despite rough waters, the British were determined to move desperately needed supplies up the back channel to Carpenter's Island, including ammunition for the land batteries. That night, two brigs and two sloops jammed with supplies made the attempt. American batteries shot away the rigging of one of the sloops, forcing it aground. According to Capt. John Andre, the boats "passed between Province Island and the fort. They received very little damage either from the fort or the gallies, one only (a small sloop) having had part of her rigging shot away." The supplies helped, but the lack of fodder for the animals forced the British to kill a number of horses they needed for fatigue work.[25]

November 13

Preparation to attack Fort Mifflin continued, By November 13, Lt. Col. George Osborne's detachment was on Province Island. According to Hessian quartermaster Lt. Col. von Conchenhausen, Osborne had "all necessary assault equipment." The British continued pounding the fort to soften it for the storming party. "[T]hese Rascals on Mudd Island hold out well, & fire a shot now & then," Captain-Lieutenant John Peebles of the 42nd Highlanders noted in his diary. Ensign Carl Rueffer of the Hessian von Mirbach Regiment recalled "Direct bomb hits on the Mud Island fort had started several fires, which were extinguished each time however. Since yesterday evening and throughout the entire day, the fort has been exceedingly heavily bombarded, but the enemy has not answered in a like manner."[26]

Artillery captain Francis Downman was a keen observer, though not overly optimistic. "The wind blows exceedingly hardly," he scribbled in his diary. "The *Vigilant* cannot come up, nor the floating battery get down." Nevertheless, the British batteries "keep up a constant fire with cannon and mortars." To Downman,

---

24 Jackson, *Navy*, 242; Montresor, "Journals," 475; Crawford, ed., *Naval Documents*, vol. 10, 473; Robertson, *Diaries*, 154.

25 Andre, *Journal*, 63; Jackson, *Fort Mifflin*, 70-71.

26 Letter, Johann Ludwig von Cochenhausen to Friedrich von Jungkenn, November 28, 1777"; Henry Retzer and Donald Londahlsmidt, eds. "The Philadelphia Campaign, 1777-1778: Letters and Reports from the von Jungkenn Papers. Part 1—1777," *Journal of the Johannes Schwalm Historical Association*, 26 vols. (Pennsauken, NJ, 1998), vol. 6, no. 2, 18; Peebles, *Diary*, 148; Burgoyne, ed., *Enemy Views*, 236.

Fort Mifflin appeared "a perfect wreck; they return our fire but very faintly." Admiral Howe's effort to position ships to shell the Mantua Creek battery was unsuccessful. Amidst high winds, the *Liverpool, Isis,* and *Cornwallis* managed to harass American efforts north of Mantua Creek. Around 9:00 a.m., Capt. Henry Bellew of the HMS *Liverpool* placed "a Small Anchor, out to Steady the Ship & begun to fire on the Rebels." Captain Andrew Hamond added additional detail in the Master's Journal of his HMS *Roebuck* when he noted "the *Liverpool* dropt up and with the *Isis* &ca Fired on the Enemys Works."[27]

After serving as commander of Fort Mifflin for just one day, Lt. Col. Giles Russell asked to be relieved; Varnum replaced him with Col. John Durkee of the 4th Connecticut. According to de Fleury, the men are "exhausted with Fatigue and ill-health [and are] extremely discouraged and I fear would make but an indifferent Defence in case of storm—at the last Alarm, one half were incapable of Duty." The Frenchman continued overseeing repairs each night, but "it is impossible however with watry mud alone to make works capable of resisting the Enemys 32 Pounders." Additional elements of the 4th and 8th Connecticut regiments came over from New Jersey to reinforce the garrison.[28]

Sensing the inevitable, Washington asked Commodore Hazelwood two questions: "whether it will be possible for you to remain at or near your present station with the fleet, after our people have totally evacuated the Island, and the Enemy have taken possession?" and "whether it will be in your power to hinder them from erecting new Works upon the Island by the Fire of your Ships, Floating Batteries and Gallies?" If the Americans can keep possession of the Jersey side of the river "three Weeks longer," he added, "we may possibly hinder them from getting a clear passage thro' the Chevaux de frize this winter."[29]

27 Whinyates, *Services,* 50; Jackson, *British Army,* 76; Jackson, *Navy,* 244; Crawford, ed., *Naval Documents,* vol. 10, 478.

28 De Fleury Fort Mifflin journal.; Dorwart, *Fort Mifflin,* 50 & 70. The 4th Connecticut was commanded by Col. John Durkee and the 8th Connecticut by Col. John Chandler. Twenty artillerymen under Capt. James Lee also reinforced the garrison. Lee was transferred from the Mantua Creek battery to Fort Mifflin. The Americans lost three killed and seven wounded during the day. Jackson, *Navy,* 248; Smith, *Fight for Delaware,* 29.

29 Chase & Grizzard, eds., *Papers,* vol. 12, 238.

November 14

The British completed two more land batteries by November 14. One contained six 24-pounders and the other four 32-pounders. "Although we see that the enemy works are seriously damaged," recorded Hessian staff officer Maj. Carl von Baurmeister, "the enemy garrison shows the greatest steadfastness in their defense." The steady bombardment from the land batteries continued, but the British men-of-war had yet to significantly add their weight to the contest. They struggled to maneuver the grounded *Vigilant* back into the channel between Mud Island and Province Island. According to Commander John Odre of the sloop *Zebra*, "the Ships warpt higher up & began a heavy fire on the rebel floating batteries & at mud Isl."[30]

The British moved a floating battery down the Schuylkill River to a position across the back channel from Mifflin's northwest blockhouse. The American defenders achieved some success when they silenced the floating gun platform by killing one of its crewmen. According to Captain Andre, the incoming fire "was so hot that the crew jumped overboard and waded ashore after firing a very few shots."[31]

Samuel Smith, recovering from his wounds in Woodbury, New Jersey, attempted to exercise command over Fort Mifflin from afar, an attempt that frustrated engineer de Fleury. "Our Commanding Officer issues orders from Woodberry—if he were nearer, he would be a better judge of our Situation," Fleury recorded in his journal. Colonel Durkee had taken command of Fort Mifflin the previous night, which raises the question of just who was in command of the place? Henry d'Arendt, Samuel Smith, and Simeon Thayer each gave orders at various times during the siege. One historian concluded, "in the end, overall responsibility for this conundrum resides with Varnum, as Washington had vested him with the power to make decisions on the scene as he saw fit." Despite all the problems, de Fleury remained fairly confident: "I repeat it—their fire will kill us men, because we have no cover, but it will never take the Fort, if we have sufficient courage to keep

---

30 Carl von Baurmeister, "Journal Installment from Major Carl Leopold Baurmeister," Henry Retzer and Donald Londahlsmidt, eds. "The Philadelphia Campaign, 1777-1778: Letter and Reports from the von Jungkenn Papers. Part 1-1777," *Journal of the Johannes Schwalm Historical Association*, 26 vols. (Pennsauken, NJ, 1998), vol. 6, no. 2, 12; Crawford, ed., *Naval Documents*, vol. 10, 493.

31 Jackson, *Fort Mifflin*, 71; Andre, *Journal*, 63.

our ground—but a Stronger Garrison is indispensably necessary we are not secured against Storm, if the Enemy attempt it."[32]

Apparently unhappy with Durkee commanding Fort Mifflin, Varnum sent his Brigade Major through the ranks seeking a suitable volunteer to replace him. The man who stepped into the power vacuum caused by Samuel Smith's wounding was Maj. Simeon Thayer of Rhode Island, who assumed command by November 14. Thayer exuded confidence that day in his report to Varnum. "I would give you to understand that the cannonade we have here we value not, nor can [I] conceive how any one can dream of delivering up so important a post as this at present; from Cannon we have nothing to fear, if there should be no sudden storm." The American defenders seemed to look past the fact that, eventually, the British navy would get involved.[33]

British artillery fire continued pounding Mud Island. Joseph Plumb Martin recalled changing British tactics. "The British knew the situation of the place as well as we did. And as their point-blank shot would not reach us behind the wall, they would throw elevated grapeshot from their mortar, and when the sentries had cried, 'a shot,' and the soldiers, seeing no shot arrive, had become careless, the grapeshot would come down like a shower of hail about our ears." Despite the chaos and destruction all around him, de Fleury remained optimistic in his daily journal entry: The British "may kill us men but this is the fortune of War, And all their bullets will never render them masters of the Island, if we have courage enough to remain on it." "[O]ur Ruins," he added, "will serve us as breast-works, we will defend the Ground inch by inch, and the Enemy shall pay dearly for every Step."[34]

---

32 Crawford, ed., *Naval Documents*, vol. 10, 490 & 492.

33 The level of command confusion Varnum created cannot be explained. Christopher Greene and Israel Angell, the two senior colonels at Fort Mercer, refused the command, while the wounded Smith still considered himself the commander. Technically, the sick d'Arendt also remained in command above Smith. Russell quit, Durkee was found wanting, and Thayer took the command. It was a real mess. Jackson, *Fort Mifflin*, 74. Thayer joined the army in May 1775, was captured at Quebec that December, and exchanged in July 1777. Smith, *Fight for Delaware*, 32; Letter, Simeon Thayer to James Varnum, November 14, 1777, *The Pennsylvania Magazine of History and Biography*, 148 vols. (Philadelphia, 1895), vol. 19, 248.

34 Martin, *Private Yankee Doodle*, 89. Lieutenant Aaron Steele of the 7th Massachusetts was severely wounded in Fort Mifflin on November 14. He was evacuated and died of his wounds on November 24. McIntyre, *A Most Gallant Resistance*, 246. Other casualties included Pvts. Constant Matthewson and Luther Waterman of the Connecticut Line. Stryker, *Forts on the Delaware*, 38; Crawford, ed., *Naval Documents*, vol. 10, 490.

Despite a serious injury eight days earlier after his horse bucked him off, Nathanael Greene rode from the Continental Army's camp at Whitemarsh to the heights of Darby overlooking Fort Mifflin. He reported his observations to Washington that night. "It is the opinion of several of the gentlemen that the enemy may be best dislodged from the Islands by detachment, others are of opinion that it would be dangerous unless the party was coverd, by the Army," explained Greene, "but all are of opinion, it is practicable either the one way or the other and considering the good consequences that will result from it, it ought to be attempted—Darby is not the most eligible post I ever saw, but it is not so dangerous as to discourage the attempt to relieve fort Mifflin."[35]

Greene also reported "there has been a very severe cannonade today." The British, he continued, "were attempting to get up a thirty-gun frigate [*Vigilant*]." Thanks to the winds and tide, they could not get the vessel into position. "The enimy are greatly discouraged by the forts holding out so long and it is the general opinion of the best of the citizens that the enemy will evacuate the city if the fort holds out until the middle of next week. The flag was flying at Fort Mifflin at sunset this evening."[36]

British accounts confirm the continued frustration. John Montresor forced a working party of 100 to labor all night repairing the damage to the land batteries. Suffering was widespread among the British troops with provisions, clothing, and firewood in short supply. Many horses succumbed to the hard work in the heavy mud, the unseasonably cold weather, no dry pasture land, and no grain.[37]

To help with the supply problem, Lt. Loftus Cliffe of the 46th Regiment of Foot received orders to escort supplies up from the fleet that night. He left a detailed account of his experience:

> I got into the Officers Man of War Boat, that lead 15 or 16 Ammunition & Provision Boats: it was a full Moon, and I thought gave greater Light than ordinary that Night. We were stealing down in the profoundest Silence, with muffled Oars, when unluckily I coughed, tho' very softly, the Naval Officer told me the Consequence, Bang comes a twelve pounder close to our Stern and then another, they fired the fourth and some small Arms, providentially without hurting our Boat & only grazing one, when a few shells

---

35 Gary Ecelbarger, *George Washington's Momentous Year: Twelve Months that Transformed the Revolution*, vol. 1 (Yardley, PA, 2024), 191; Chase & Grizzard, eds., *Papers*, vol. 12, 252.

36 Chase & Grizzard, eds., *Papers*, vol. 12, 252-253.

37 Jackson, *Navy*, 247.

thrown in from Province Island amongst them made them quiet. I was amply rewarded for the fright they put me into, both in the Supplies I got, and in having the Satisfaction of the full view of the Naval Attack at once upon Mud Island.[38]

During the day, Admiral Howe assigned the 70-gun *Somerset*, 50-gun *Isis*, *Liverpool*, *Roebuck*, *Camilla*, and *Cornwallis* to add their weight to the Mifflin bombardment the next day. The *Augusta's* loss left Capt. George Oury of the *Somerset* as senior officer. The commanders scouted the area around the *chevaux-de-frise* to mark the positions for the following day. Captain Oury was not among them.[39]

Washington's long and trying day included finding time to write William Howe to complain of the treatment of American prisoners. It is a letter worth reprinting nearly in full. "I am constrained to observe," he began,

that I have a variety of Accounts, not only from prisoners who have made their escape, but from persons who have left philadelphia, that our private Soldiers in your hands are treated in a manner shocking to humanity; and that many of them must have perished through hunger had it not been for the charitable contributions of the Inhabitants. It is added in aggravation, that this treatment is to oblige them to inlist in the Corps [Loyal Americans] you are raising. The Friends of these unhappy men call daily upon me for their relief, and the people at large insist on retaliating upon those in our possession. Justice demands it . . . I must also remonstrate against the cruel treatment & confinement of Our Officers. This I am informed is not only the case of those in philadelphia, but of many in New York. Whatever plausible pretences may be urged to authorize the condition of the Former, It is certain, but few circumstances can arise to justify that of the latter.[40]

---

38 Letter, Loftus Cliffe to brother Jack, November 12, 1777, Loftus Cliffe Papers, William L. Clements Library, University of Michigan, Ann Arbor, MI.

39 Jackson, *British Army*, 76. At some point during this phase of the campaign, Lt. Samuel Lyon and seven men from the galley *Dickinson* and Lt. Samuel Ford of the galley *Effingham* deserted to the British. The two officers were later retaken, tried for desertion, found guilty, and shot in September 1778. Jackson, *Navy*, 250. Also during November 14, the Thomas Conway problem reared its ugly head once more. The army's junior brigadier general wrote to Congressman Charles Carroll from the army's camp at Whitemarsh outlining why he deserved a promotion to major general over all the other brigadiers. "I will undertake to show that my request of being made a major general had nothing in it so unreasonable as to cause your astonishment, and the most disobliging reflections, thrown by you Sir, and other members of Congress." In anger, Conway submitted his resignation. Kate Mason Rowland, *The Life of Charles Carroll of Carrollton, 1732-1832, with His Correspondence and Public Papers*, 2 vols. (New York, 1898), vol. 1, 226.

40 Chase & Grizzard, eds., *Papers*, vol. 12, 256.

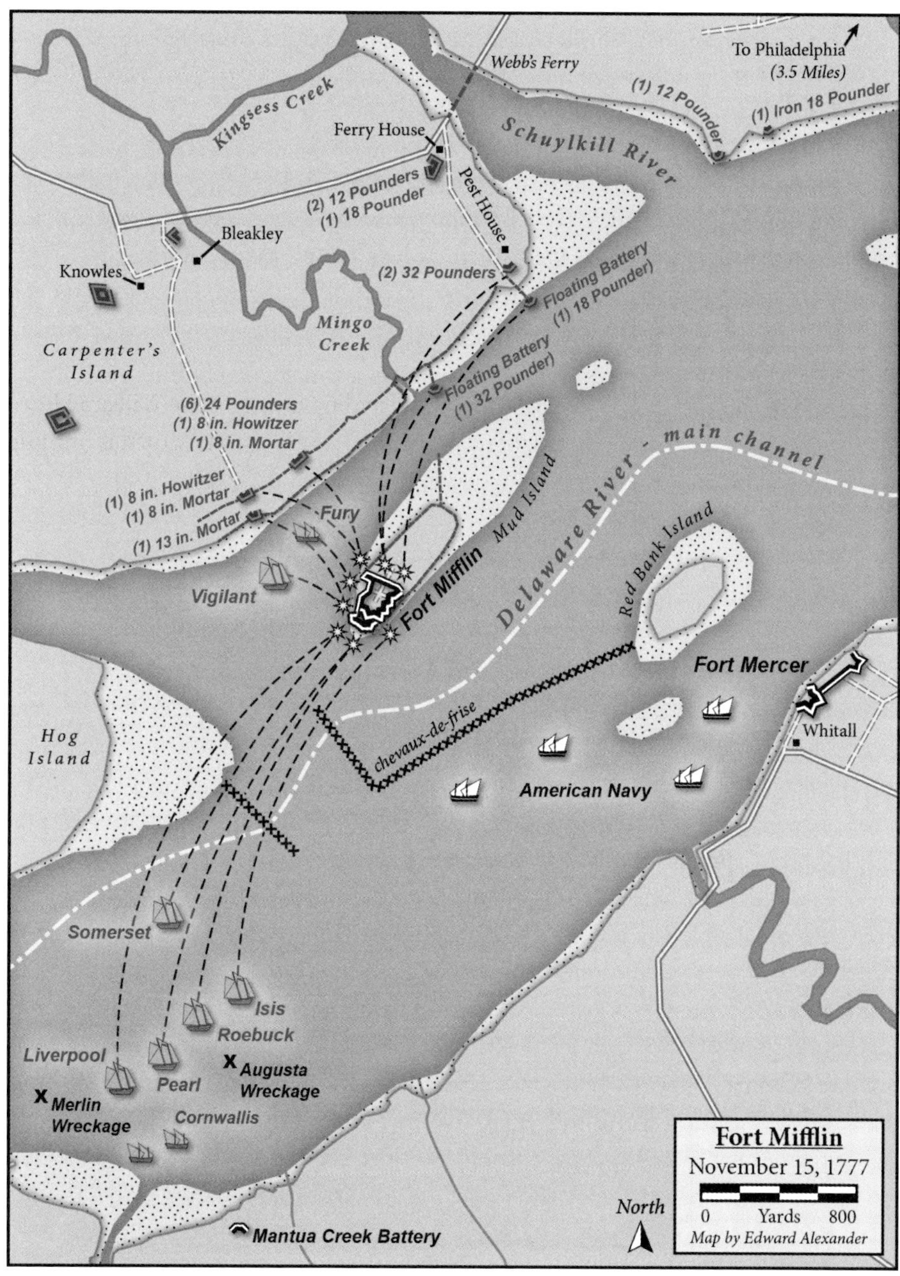

November 15

The American garrison was barely hanging on in Fort Mifflin when the British navy joined the fight around 8:00 a.m. on November 15. The *Somerset* and *Isis* tacked into position below the *chevaux-de-frise* and opened fire while the *Roebuck*, *Cornwallis*, *Pearl*, and *Liverpool* engaged the Mantua Creek battery. The *Vigilant*, recorded Captain von Muenchhausen, "luckily worked herself through and anchored about 200 paces from the fort. With her, a small sloop [*Fury*] arrived. At the same time five large warships moved as close as possible to the chevaux de frise and covered the battery ship with continuous strong fire, for the rebel ships that were near Red Bank tried to come around [Mud Island] to ruin the *Vigilant* and the sloop with their much heavier fire." The largest concentration of firepower in the American Revolution unleashed on Fort Mifflin. According to historian Jeffrey Dorwart, "the British fired an estimated one thousand rounds in the first hour of attack." Hessian officer Johann Prechtel was waiting downriver on a transport ship with other reinforcements from New York when he wrote in his diary, "the terrible bombardment by the English warships continued without let-up."[41]

Captain James Wallace recorded his views of the naval attack in the Journal of the HMS *Experiment*: "the *Isis*, *Roebuck*, & *Somerset*, Unmoored and got higher up, the *Roebuck*, *Pearl*, & *Liverpool* fired Briskly on the Rebles on the South Shore, and had Several Shot returned, the *Isis* got into her Birth & Kept a Constant fire on Mud Island Batteries, and had Several Shot thrown at her from them." Captain William Cornwallis confirmed receiving "several Shott" from Fort Mifflin in the Lieutenant's Journal of the HMS *Isis*. Eventually, the fire from Mifflin "Slack'd by the *Vigilant* & *Fury* Sloop," noted Capt. George Ourry in the Master's Log of the HMS *Somerset*. Civilian Elizabeth Drinker, a keen observer of the fighting, noted that the day's bombardment "has been like thunder."[42]

The Americans wheeled a 32-pounder and an 18-pounder into position and fired into the *Vigilant* as many as 14 times before the warship's guns silenced the effort. According to Commodore Hazelwood, he attempted to move into the back channel with some of his galleys and drive away the *Vigilant*, but "Six Battery's playing on us from the shore to Westward besides two nine inch mortars, & two floating Batterys, & Seven Ships that with their shot from their Batterys & ships, the River was cover'd with shot on all sides of us and cross Fire in such manner I was surprised the Fleet never gave way." His fleet lost 38 men killed and wounded

---

41 Reed, *Campaign*, 342. The *Isis* and *Roebuck* were just 600 yards southeast of Fort Mifflin. Jackson, *British Army*, 77. The American battery north of Mantua Creek engaged the British shipping to little effect. Jackson, *Navy*, 254; Von Muenchhausen, *At Howe's Side*, 43. The *Fury* was commanded by Lt. John Botham. McGuire, *Campaign*, vol. 2, 203; Dorwart, *Fort Mifflin*, 53; Prechtel, *A Hessian Officer's Diary*, 125.

42 Crawford, ed., *Naval Documents*, vol. 10, 505-506; Drinker, *Diary of Elizabeth Drinker*, 253.

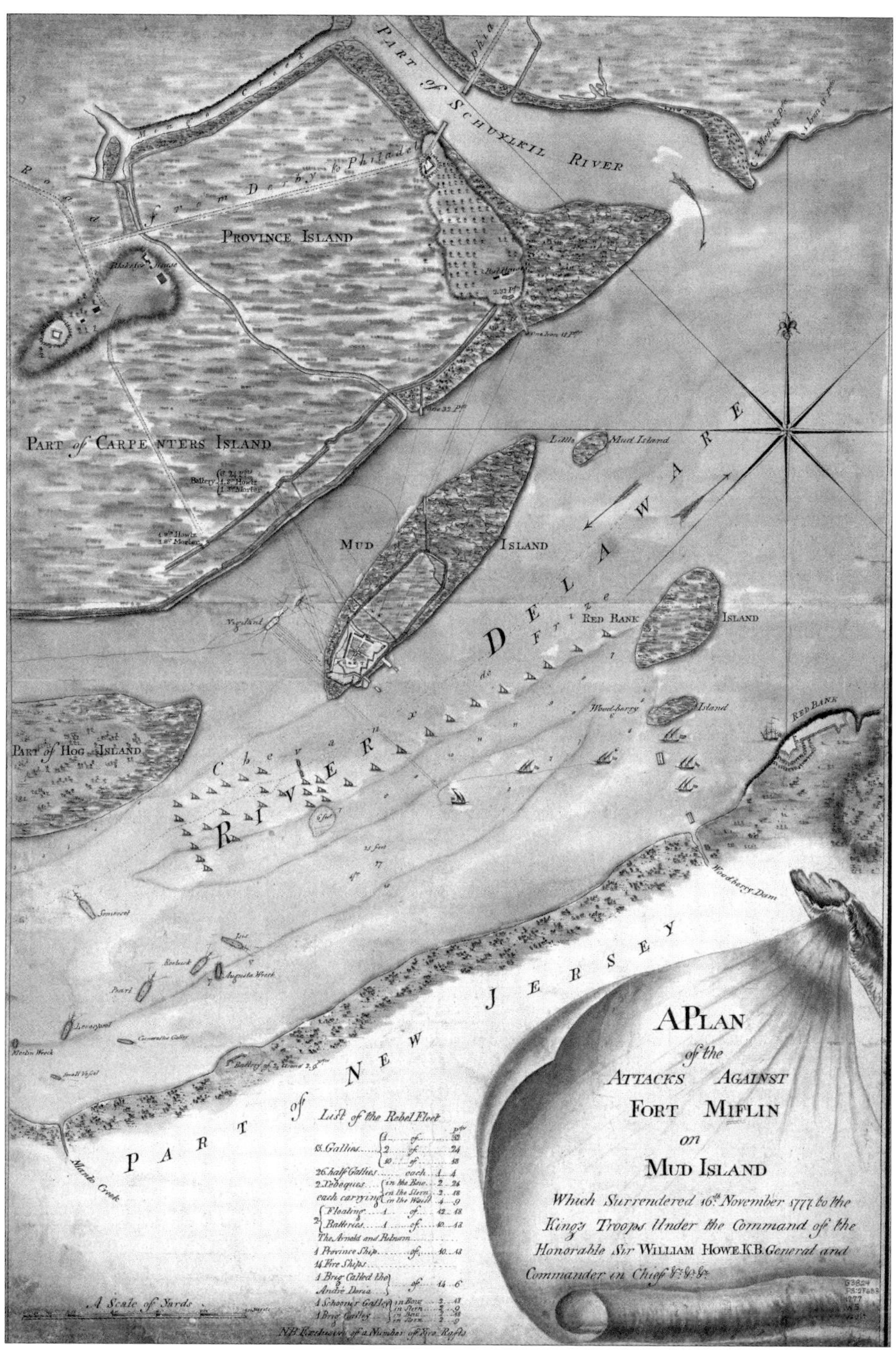

Plan of attacks against Fort Mifflin. LOC

in the action, and "all the Galleys Except one much shatter'd with shot." Loyalist James Parker echoed Commodore Hazelwood's report, noting the American galleys "moved down . . . below the End of the Island to annoy the *Vigilant* & Sloop, but the big ships soon drove them up again." The withdrawal of the vessels left Mud Island's defenders alone. Varnum complained the next day to Washington that the galleys "warp'd over to the [Mud] Island, & there held a Council, lost a few of their Men, & then returned, without attempting any Thing."[43]

British Lieutenant Loftus Cliffe left a good description in a letter to his brother:

> The *Isis* & *Somerset* engaged Red Bank, the most distant Object: the *Isis* did her duty, moving as close as possible to the Chevaux de fries, the other by some Error, in heaving her Anchor lost near half a Mile of her Station, a great loss, as her lower Tier were 32 Pounders, the only Ship with that Mettle, but however their Shiping & Mud Island felt her: the Frigates & Sloops attacked the two Gun Battery, and the *Vigilant* an old India Man cut down to draw but 10 Foot Water with 18 or 20 Guns got into the Boat Channel between Mud & Province Islands, withen 200 Yards of her Object, Mud Island; which by her & Province Island Batteries was soon silenced; the fire was furious & incessant.[44]

According to Col. Johann von Loos, commander of the Combined Hessian Battalion, "Mud Island was shot to pieces by the British ships." He went on to describe the cannonade as "ferocious," and in a bit of hyperbole, that all the American "mounted batteries, cannons of the largest caliber, were not only dismounted, but buried in the rubble. Blood, brains, arms, legs, everything lay about."[45]

The bombardment may have been loud and often effective, but Admiral Howe was angry: most of his ships were out of position. Captain Andrew Hamond of the *Roebuck* witnessed Howe take out his frustration against the commander of the *Somerset.* The admiral, reported Hamond, was in "a great Rage, and in the act of superseding our Officer, who could have lain near a week within 2 miles of the Fort he was going to attack, and not having informed himself and the Captains of the other Ships, of the anchorage each should take up." Captain Oury failed to sound

---

43 Jackson, *Navy*, 254, 267; Samuel Hazard, ed., *Pennsylvania Archives: Selected and Arranged from Original Documents in the Office of the Secretary of the Commonwealth*, 12 vols. (Philadelphia, 1853), Series 1, vol. 6, 48; Parker Journal, November 15, 1777 entry, Parker Family Papers; Jackson, *Delaware Bay*, 21; Chase & Grizzard, eds., *Papers*, vol. 12, 283.

44 Letter, Loftus Cliffe to brother Jack, Nov. 12, 1777.

45 Letter, von Loos to von Jungkenn, Oct. 30, 1777, 21.

the river, the captain was left unsure where to position his ship for the greatest effect for the attack on Mud Island, as others had done the previous day. These and other missteps notwithstanding, several other ships participated and took fire from American artillery. According to Howe, "the [*Isis*] and *Roebuck* . . . were struck many times from the Gallies and Works."[46]

The dawn brought with it a fearsome sight, recalled Private Martin of the Connecticut Line: "[W]e discovered six ships of the line, all sixty-fours, a frigate of thirty-six guns, and a galley in a line just below the *chevaux-de-frise*; a twenty-four-gun ship (being an old ship cut down,) her guns said to be all brass twenty-four-pounders, and a sloop of six guns in company with her, both within pistol shot of the fort, on the western side." The fort did its best to reply. "The enemy soon began firing upon us and there was music indeed," continued Martin. "The soldiers were all ordered to take their posts at the palisadoes, which they were ordered to defend to the last extremity, as it was expected the British would land under the fire of their cannon and attempt to storm the fort." About 250 heavy guns "all playing at once upon our poor little fort, if fort it might be called."[47]

The 2nd Rhode Island's Sgt. Jeremiah Greenman provided his own vivid description of conditions on Mud Island. The *Vigilant* "came up under the protection of the Land Batteries, behind Hog Island & anchored four yards from the Angle of the SW Battery, the Fort had been very much exposed on this side—then on it, did not remain one Single Gun excep those that was dismounted." As soon as the *Vigilant* was ready, "she began to play, all resistance became imposable, in 3 or 4 Broad Sides and from the tops with Cowhorn filled with Grape Shot so that it was impossible for a man to move without being killed." The enemy iron tore apart the parapet, gun carriages, and "even the Iron of the guns were broken the platforms destroyed an[d] in half an hour, not a Gun in the fort was able to fire." The defenders found themselves "buried in ruins unable to retreat during the day & unwilling to do it, as long as they could expect a

---

46 Moomaw, "Career of Hamond," 370; Crawford, ed., *Naval Documents*, vol. 10, 584-588. The *Somerset* had five seamen wounded, the *Isis* three seamen wounded, the *Roebuck* three seamen killed and seven wounded, the *Pearl* one master killed and three seamen wounded, the *Vigilant* one midshipman killed and one seamen killed, and the *Cornwallis* suffered one pilot wounded. Captain John Linzee noted in the Journal of the *Pearl*": "Mr. Lamb [the] Master one who died shortly after." He was buried the next afternoon on the New Jersey shore. Crawford, ed., *Naval Documents*, vol. 10, 507. Howe's Hessian aide von Muenchhausen noted the *Isis* took "34 shells that went right through her." Von Muenchhausen, *At Howe's Side*, 43.

47 Martin, *Private Yankee Doodle*, 90-91.

reinforcement, had not much expectation but to sell their selvs as dear as they could."[48]

Commander John Henry, who was aboard the *Vigilant*, wrote from the opposing perspective. "At 7 AM . . . we warped over to the Weather Shore ready to come to sail, at ½ past 7 the *Isis, Roebuck, Liverpool* & *Pearl* ran up the Eastern Channell close to the Cheveaux de frize, and soon after the *Somersett* following them," he penned in the ship's journal, "and began firing on the enemy's Works on Mud Island, and their Battery on the Jersey's, at 10 we weighed and ran close up to the Fort on Mud Island having a Sloop with 3 Eighteen pounders on Board to Assist us, moored Head and Stern and began firing on the Fort." Royal Marines had climbed into the rigging and positioned themselves to shoot at the fort's defenders from "the Tops, doing good execution, the enemy firing at us from the Fort, the Gallys and floating Battery."[49]

Reuben Cave of the 5th Virginia recalled the horrors of that day when applying for a pension many years later. "I was wounded there a cannon ball struck the forte near whar I sttod." A large chunk of the stone wall struck him in the cheek just below one eye, smashing the bone and nearly blinding him. "I was relieved from duty for some time and since I frequently have been afflicted with fits and do believe that to be the cause."[50]

The carnage inside Mifflin mounted. "The enemy's shot cut us up," admitted Private Martin. "I saw five artillerists belonging to one gun cut down by a single shot, and I saw men who were stooping to be protected by the works, but not stooping low enough, split like fish to be broiled. Our men were cut up like cornstalks." By this time the bastion had been pulverized beyond recognition. "The fort exhibited a picture of desolation," continued Martin. "The whole area of the fort was as completely ploughed as a field. The buildings of every kind [were] hanging in broken fragments, and the guns all dismounted, and how many of the

---

48 Greenman, *Diary*, 85. It is unclear whether Sergeant Greenman was present during the bombardment or relating stories from others.

49 Crawford, ed., *Naval Documents*, vol. 10, 508.

50 Revolutionary War Pension and Bounty-Land-Warrant Application Files (M804) [RWPF], file S8140. Among the wounded was artillery lieutenant John George. Captain Stephen Brown of the 4th Connecticut and Capt. Nathan Stoddard of the 8th Connecticut were killed. Francis B. Heitman, *Historical Register of Officers of the Continental Army During the War of the Revolution April, 1775, to December, 1783* (Washington, D.C., 1914), 127, 245, & 522. The 8th Connecticut lost Pvts. Modecai Bedeant, Nathan Brown, Nathaniel Harris, William Jenkins, and Samuel Patten. The dead in the 4th Connecticut included Pvts. Beriah Halbard, Uriah Pease, and Richard Sowas. Stryker, *Forts on the Delaware*, 38.

garrison sent to the world of spirits, I knew not. If ever destruction was complete, it was here." Varnum reported to Washington the next day that the *Vigilant's* "incessant Fire, Hand Grenades & Musketry from the Round Top" tore into the fort's garrison. According to Silas Talbot, the Royal Marines were "within the toss of a biscuit" of the fort and the dead lay where they fell unless blocking the gun crews, when they were "rolled out of the way."[51]

Around mid-morning, the officers wanted to hoist a flag to signal Commodore Hazelwood to bring his galleys to their aid. Private Martin watched with anxious anticipation as an artillery sergeant volunteered for the dangerous duty of hauling down the striped garrison flag and hoisting the signal flag in its place. When the garrison flag began its fitful journey toward the ground, the British slackened their fire and cheered, thinking the fort was finally surrendering. In reply, the resilient American officers shouted, "Up with the flag!" The sergeant did as instructed. The artilleryman had just come down "and had not gone half a rod from the foot of the staff when he was cut in two by a cannon shot." A philosophical Martin later reflected, "had I been at the same business I might have been killed, but it might have been otherwise ordered by Divine Providence, we might have both lived. I am not a predestinarian enough to determine it."[52]

"We have lost a great many Men to day, a great many of the Officers are killed and wounded," reported Varnum to Washington that night. "My fine Company of Artillery is almost destroy'd." Major de Fleury described, in the third person, how "The Blockhouses flew about in splinters—a Piece of Timber torn from the Blockhouse on the right, struck down Capt. [James] Lee [of the artillery] and Major Fleury." Lee "was kill'd and the latter remain'd senseless." Major Silas Talbot ran to help them and "was wounded with two Grape Shot in the thigh and Arm."[53]

Fort Mercer's commander, Christopher Greene, wrote to Pennsylvania militia general James Potter about what he witnessed from across the main channel at Red Bank on November 15. "Since my last the Cannonade has been very severe upon Fort Mifflin—this Day the Ships have come as near as the Chevaux de Frize would allow them. A floating Battery with 18-24 prs came up between Fort Mifflin & Province Island, and the Fire from Them together with that of their Batteries has

---

51 Martin, *Private Yankee Doodle*, 92; Chase & Grizzard, eds., *Papers*, vol. 12, 283; Talbot, *Life of Talbot*, 29.

52 Martin, *Private Yankee Doodle*, 91-92.

53 Chase & Grizzard, eds., *Papers*, vol. 12, 274; Crawford, ed., *Naval Documents*, vol. 10, 504. Talbot was later Commodore Silas Talbot of the U.S. Navy. Jackson, *Navy*, 255.

dismounted all the Guns but two." The bombardment, he continued, "Almost destroyed the works—and have killed and wounded a very considerable Number."[54]

Hessian aide von Muenchhuasen observed the Howe brothers watching the attack together. "General Howe as well as Lord Howe, who had come up by boat early this morning, were in the mortar battery till seven o'clock in the evening." During the ride back to Philadelphia, "he ordered the cannonading and bombing to continue throughout the night." The Hessian officer was ill, but did not want to miss what promised to be the climactic moment of the entire operation. "In spite of not being well, I was there all the same; the intense fire was too beautiful a spectacle to miss by staying home. In the army it is forbidden to anyone to leave his post or regiment to watch something," he continued, "[yet] everyone believed and wished that the General would give the command to storm any moment. But he did not do so, for he maintained that the enemy could not stand our dreadful fire much longer." The British batteries and warships did not stop pounding Mud Island until about 5:00 p.m.[55]

The American garrison's command structure was shattered, little was left of the fort, and few men were able to perform their duties by the night of November 15. The wounded Samuel Smith found himself well enough to write to Washington. "My Arm will this Night or tomorrow Night permit me to take the Command at fort Mifflin," he optimistically, if incorrectly, reported. "I was there last Night, it is now one Heap of Ruin & must be defended with Musquetry in Case of Storm."[56]

Simeon Thayer, the fort's newest commander, issued orders after dark to evacuate and destroy anything left behind. Joseph Plumb Martin "happened to be left with a party of seventy or eighty men to destroy and burn all that was left in the place." The private was moving about the shattered remnants when he heard British voices on the *Vigilant*: "We will give it to the d——d rebels in the morning." Martin thought otherwise. "The d——d rebels will show you a trick which the devil never will," he thought. "[T]hey will go off and leave you." The rearguard was ordered to dump several hogsheads of rum, though Martin admitted being "desirous to save a trifle of their contents." He lent his canteen to a friend that

---

54 Letter, Christopher Greene to James Potter, November 15, 1777, *The Pennsylvania Magazine of History and Biography*, 148 vols. (Philadelphia, 1895), vol. 19, 369.

55 Von Muenchhausen, *At Howe's Side*, 43; Jackson, *Navy*, 258.

56 Chase & Grizzard, eds., *Papers*, vol. 12, 271.

morning, and when he searched for him to retrieve it, "found him, indeed, but lying in a long line of dead men who had been brought out of the fort to be conveyed to the main . . . Poor young man! He was the most intimate associate I had in the army, but he was gone, with many more as deserving of regard as himself."[57]

Around midnight, the last of the garrison ignited what they could of the materials left in the fort, boarded boats, and rowed across the river to Red Bank. "Before we could embark the buildings in the fort were completely in flames, and threw such a light upon the water that we were plainly seen by the British as though it had been broad day. Almost their whole fire was directed at us," recalled Martin. "Sometimes our boat seemed to be almost thrown out of the water, and at length a shot took the sternpost out of the rear boat. We had then to stop and take the men from the crippled boat into the other two, and now the shot and water flew merrily, but by the assistance of a kind Providence we escaped without further injury." Some 450 men had served on Mud Island during the prior five days, but fewer than 200 left the island unharmed. British casualties totaled fewer than a dozen killed, though many more were wounded.[58]

Washington had been kept up to date regarding the disastrous conditions inside Fort Mifflin but was awaiting reinforcements from Horatio Gates's army before moving heavily against Howe's threat. Once Daniel Morgan's riflemen arrived from Gates's command, he prepared two columns to march the next day, one to attempt to cut off Howe's supply line along the road from Chester, and the other to disrupt the threat against the fort. "[W]e are in High spirits and full of hope of Bringing This most Horrid War to a Conclusion by Defeating Genl. Howe in a few days," wrote brigade commander Charles Scott to his wife on November 15. "I am to march tomorrow morning with my Brigade to Cut off the Enemys Supplies of provisions from the Shipping. Colo. [Daniel] Morgan with his lite Coar [riflemen] and Genl. [William] Woodfords Brigd. marches at the same time." The

---

57 Martin, *Private Yankee Doodle*, 93. Among the wounded was QM Sgt. Thomas Hubbard of the 1st Virginia, taken out by fragments of an exploding shell. Revolutionary War Pension and Bounty-Land-Warrant Application Files (M804) [RWPF], file S17277. Thomas Bailey of the 4th Virginia was wounded in the upper part of the left arm by a musket ball. Ibid., file S10334. John Smith was wounded in the thigh. Ibid., file S38389. George Ashby, 8th Virginia, received a leg wound. Bounty-land Records in the Library of Virginia, C. Leon Harris, ed. & trans., revwarapps.org/VAS2300.pdf. Accessed online April 11, 2022.

58 Martin, *Private Yankee Doodle*, 93-94; Thompson, *Whitemarsh*, 37.

confident brigadier had "no doubt of Success and indeed doing something very Cleaver."[59]

Scott's orders were the result of a council of war held earlier that day. Two columns from Washington's army would strike the enemy five miles apart from one another. A sizable bulk of the army would march across Matson's Ford and then south to Darby. Anthony Wayne's division with Daniel Morgan's riflemen would march directly on Fort Mifflin via Province Island. The plan was for Washington's column to assault British positions at the Middle Ferry while Wayne and Morgan attacked the British siege lines pounding Mifflin. Alas, Washington's effort was too late: Mifflin was empty. The operation was canceled.[60]

Two days later, Anthony Wayne expressed frustration over war councils when he wrote to Secretary of War Richard Peters. "Six weeks envestiture and no attempt to raise the siege of that fort, will scarcely be credited at any other day," complained Wayne, who fully believed the army had failed the garrison. "The army was to have passed the Schulkill and taken post near the middle ferry (Market street), whilst my Division with Morgan's corps, were to proceed to Province Island, and there storm the enemy's lines, spike their cannon, and ruin their works." Wayne continued, "the Evacuation of that important fortress the evening preceding the day on which the storm was to have taken place frustrated an expedition which afforded the most flattering prospect." The frustrated Wayne concluded, "the surest way to do nothing" is to call a council and "there has been more than one instance of the truth of this observation during this campaign." Washington had waited too long, and by the time he issued his orders (as demonstrated by Scott's letter), it no longer mattered.[61]

November 16

Dawn broke on November 16 to reveal the torn and tattered garrison flag flying above an empty and mostly ruined Fort Mifflin. "[T]he Colours was left flying which we saw in the morning halled down by the Enemy," wrote a proud Sgt.

---

59 Daniel Morgan had just returned after serving with Gates at Saratoga. Letter, Charles Scott to wife, November 15, 1777, John Reed Manuscript Collection, Valley Forge National Park, Valley Forge, PA. Charles Scott began the war as lieutenant colonel of the 2nd Virginia before being put in command of the 5th Virginia in May 1776. He rose to brigade command in April 1777.

60 Ecelbarger, *Momentous Year*, 193.

61 John R. Spears, *Anthony Wayne, Sometimes Called "Mad Anthony"* (New York, 1903), 98-99.

Jeremiah Greenman of the Rhode Island Line. Captain von Muenchhausen of William Howe's staff thought the Americans "did not strike the rebel colors, because they believed this to be more respectable than to let them fall into our hands." Joseph Plumb Martin agreed: "We left our flag flying when we left the island, and the enemy did not take possession of the fort till late in the morning after we left it." Martin recalled that when he arrived in New Jersey, "I wrapped myself up in my blanket and lay down upon the leaves and soon fell asleep and continued so till past noon, when I awoke from the first sound sleep I had had for a fortnight." The Americans had been driven out of Mifflin, but they had never surrendered it.[62]

Later that morning, James Varnum penned a report to Washington. "Agreeable to what I wrote you last Evening, we were obliged to evacuate Fort Mifflin," he began. "Every Thing was got off, that possibly could be. The Cannon could not be removed without making too great a Sacrifice of Men . . . we could have held the Island, had the Ship [*Vigilant*] been destroy'd.[63]

For the first time in more than a month, the river line was silent. "At break of day we discovered the rebel colours still flying and the fort almost totally destroyed but no appearance of any person," wrote British artillery Captain Downman in his diary. "In a little time the *Vigiliant* sent her boat well manned ashore; one of the jacks mounted the flagstaff, tore down the rebel and hoisted in their stead English colours." The journal of the *Vigilant* confirmed the event: "at 6 AM sent the Marines on shore to take Possession of the Fort, hauled down the Rebel Flag and hoisted an English Jack." Around 8:00 a.m., a "Party of the Guards came & took charge of the Fort, & our Marines returned on board."[64]

Reprieved from having to take the fort by storm, George Osborne's small detachment moved in quietly and occupied the position. Engineer John Montresor went with them and "embarked from Carpenter's Island in 8 Flat Bottomed Boats, 35 soldiers each together with Engineers, a company of Carpenters, fascines, scaling ladders, flying bridge, etc., and took possession of the Fort & immediately began on a Battery for four 32 pounders, partly for the Defence of that post and partly to prevent their vessels annoying us in removing the Cheveaux de frise." Captain Downman, who also made his way to Mifflin, remained delighted that the

---

62 Greenman, *Diary*, 86; Von Muenchhausen, *At Howe's Side*, 43; Martin, *Private Yankee Doodle*, 94; Reed, *Campaign*, 346.

63 Chase & Grizzard, eds., *Papers*, vol. 12, 283.

64 Whinyates, *Services*, 51; Crawford, ed., *Naval Documents*, vol. 10, 513.

British did not storm the works. Somehow, despite the intensity and size of the barrage, the bones of the fort remained intact. "The fort is strong and had it been stormed a very considerable loss would have been the consequence. Nothing that could add to its strength was left undone."[65]

The British artillery fire had heavily damaged the American gun positions. "The blockhouses were knocked entirely to pieces, a great number of their guns and carriages were rendered useless by the shot they have received, in short," recorded Downman, "it is in such a battered situation that it is past describing. In almost every place you see blood and brains dashed about, and hardly a spot in the whole place that has not a shot." After inspecting the fort, Gen. Samuel Cleaveland, the British artillery commander, found more than 4,100 round, bar, and grape shot lying about the fort. Where all these rounds were when the Americans were scrambling about for ammunition during the heroic defense remains a mystery.[66]

Several officers went over to see the damage themselves. Hessian quartermaster Col. von Cochenhausen reported in a November 28 letter that Mud Island was "nothing but a charred camp and bloodstains . . . the entire place is a rock pile." "The house of the commandant has so many holes that more than 1,000 can be counted and the floors are as blown up as when a herd of swine had been there," recorded Hessian officer Ens. Carl Rueffer in his journal. "Noteworthy is the fact that, one year ago today [Fort Washington] fell into our hands." After a visit to Fort Mifflin on November 22, British grenadier John Peebles observed that the fort was "prodigiously shatter'd & torn to pieces & leaves a spectacle very much to the honor of those that defended it."[67]

The human toll was as immense as it was grisly. Lieutenant Loftus Cliffe of the 46th Regiment of Foot informed his brother on November 23, "I am told that when our People came on it, it was one clot of Blood; every Corner contained Limbs Skin & Gutts." Captain Downman observed the cleanup effort by Osborne's men: "digging up or pulling out of the ditches the poor wretches that had been killed, most dismally torn and mangled by cannon shot, and stripping them of their shoes or whatever they had on them, and then dashing them into the holes again with as little concern or feeling as a butcher shows in killing or cutting

---

65 Montresor, "Journals," 477; Whinyates, Services, 50-51.

66 Whinyates, *Services*, 50-51. What Cleaveland did not find was any powder or cartridges. Jackson, *British Army*, 78; Jackson, *Fort Mifflin*, 79.

67 Letter, von Cochenhausen to von Jungkenn, November 28, 1777," 18; Burgoyne, ed., *Enemy Views*, 236; Peebles, *Diary*, 150.

up an ox." The British remained short on supplies and salvaging useable items from the dead Americans was an imperative.[68]

Captain Andrew Hamond of the HMS *Roebuck* described the American evacuation as a "most fortunate Circumstance for the [British] Army." Hamond learned the Americans had placed an underwater chain to prevent British boats from approaching any closer than 50 yards to Mud Island. In water just seven or eight feet deep, "every Man in the Boats would have been destroyed." Others inspected the damage on their ships. Captain William Cornwallis of the *Isis* admitted, "our Masts, Hull & rigging much shatter'd."[69]

Despite the loss of Mud Island, James Varnum felt confident he could keep the British shipping downriver. "I dont think the Shipping can pass the Chevau de Frize while we keep this [New Jersey] Shore," he reported to the commanding general. "The two Gun Battery, near Manto Creek, annoy'd them very Much Yesterday. It is still firing slowly; but, the Shipping having remov'd out of direct Distance too much firing would be Profusion. We are erecting a Battery between Red Bank and Manto Creek Battery, directly opposite the Frizes," he continued, "w'ch I believe will be finished to day." Varnum was thinking ahead. "Our troops are so extremely fatigued," he offered,

> that no time will be lost in knowing your Excellency's Orders, whether the Troops commanded by Colo. Smith shall remain here, or return to Camp. The Officers seem anxious to join the Army as their Men are much harass'd. However, they have had two Nights Rest, & are necessary here, should we attack Billings port. As a great part of my own Brigade have been lost at Fort Mifflin I shall not be able to make any hostile attempt this Night; but am of the Opinion that the Enemy should at all Hazards, be dispossessed of this Shore.

Varnum added an ominous statement: "While we keep the Shipping down, our Navy will be safe; but, should our Defenses prove ineffectual, we shall take out a part of their Guns & let the others attempt passing the City.[70]

68 Letter, Loftus Cliffe to brother Jack, November 12, 1777; Whinyates, *Services*, 51.

69 Moomaw, "Career of Hamond," 372; Crawford, ed., *Naval Documents*, vol. 10, 512.

70 Chase & Grizzard, eds., *Papers*, vol. 12, 283-284.

Contemporary Analysis

The garrison at Mifflin withstood a remarkable onslaught for several weeks, one that culminated in the largest cannonade in North America until Gettysburg in 1863. Private Martin looked back on the siege many years later with the advantage of hindsight, "I was at the siege and capture of Lord Cornwallis [Yorktown], and the hardships of that were no more to be compared with this than the sting of a bee is to the bite of a rattlesnake. But there has been but little notice taken of it," he lamented, "the reason of which is, there was no Washington, Putnam, or Wayne there. Had there been, the affair would have been extolled to the skies. No, it was only a few officers and soldiers who accomplished it in a remote quarter of the army. Such circumstances and such troops generally get but little notice taken of them, do what they will. Great men get great praise; little men, nothing."[71]

Admiral Richard Howe's private secretary, Ambrose Serle, thought the Americans "defended it [Fort Mifflin] with a Spirit, they have shewn no where else to an equal Degree during the War. I went on shore to survey this celebrated Place. Nothing surely was ever so torn & riven by Cannon-Balls. A more dismal Picture of Ruin," he concluded, "can scarce be conceived." Captain James Murray of the 57th of Foot believed "Mud Island was a most unfortunate obstacle, and cost us two of the most precious months of the war. If the Rebels had taken every advantage of their situation, it is not certain that we should have been able to have cleared the passage at least this campaign."[72]

"It is impossible to do justice to the officers and soldiers who defended it," wrote Benjamin Rush to James Searle four days after the November 15 evacuation. "I was a witness for one day . . . of their patience and fortitude under the most complicated dangers and sufferings."[73] Four months later, Thomas Paine, author of *Common Sense*, addressed an essay to William Howe on March 21, 1778:

> For several weeks did that little unfinished fortress stand out against all attempts of Admiral and General Howe. It was the fable of Bender realized on the Delaware. Scheme after scheme, and force upon force were tried and defeated. The garrison, with scarce anything to cover them but their bravery, survived in the midst of mud, shot, and shells,

---

71 Martin, *Private Yankee Doodle*, 95.

72 Serle, *Journal*, 264; James Murray, *Letters from America, 1773-1780: Being the letters of a Scots officer, Sir James Murray, to his home during the War of American Independence*, E. Robson, ed. (New York, 1950), 50.

73 L. H. Butterfield, ed., *Letters of Benjamin Rush* (Princeton, NJ, 1951), vol. 1, 166.

and were at last obliged to give it up more to the powers of time and gunpowder than to the military superiority of the besiegers.

Paine encouraged Howe to give up the ghost. "Go home, sir, and endeavor to save the remains of your ruined country, by a just representation of the madness of her measures. . . . You are fighting for what you can never obtain, and we are defending what we never mean to part with. . . . Let England mind her own business and we will mind ours."[74]

George Washington reported to Continental Congress president Henry Laurens on November 17 to ward off any criticism about how he had handled the Mifflin affair. "I am sorry to inform you that Fort Mifflin was evacuated . . . after a defence that does credit to the American arms, and will ever reflect the highest honor upon the Officers and Men of the Garrison," he began. "Nothing in the Course of this Campaign," he continued, "has taken up so much of the attention and consideration of myself and all the General Officers, as the possibility of giving further relief to Fort Mifflin, than what we had already afforded."

In light of Conway's political machinations, Washington sought to defuse any claims that he had not given enough support to the garrison, or that more men could have held the fort. "Such a Garrison was thrown into it, as has been found by experience, capable of defending it to the last extremity," he explained, "and Red Bank, which was deemed essentially necessary not only for the purpose of keeping open the communication, but of annoying the Enemy's Ships and covering our own Fleet, has been possessed by a considerable detachment from the Army."[75]

Washington could have assaulted Province Island from the west earlier, which may have relieved Fort Mifflin. Three weeks earlier, an army detachment proved that an early morning assault was possible from the direction of Darby. For reasons that remain unclear, Washington insisted this was no longer possible. As he explained it, "The only remaining and practicable mode, of giving relief to the Fort, was by dislodging the Enemy from province Island, from whence they kept up incessant fire. But this, from the Situation of the Ground, was not to be attempted with any degree of safety to the attacking party, without the whole or a considerable part of the Army should be removed to the West side of the Schuylkill, to support and cover it." After laying out the difficulties, he decided no more could be done until reinforcements from Gates's army arrived. "It was therefore determined, a

---

74 Thomas Paine, Crisis #4, available at www.ushistory.org/Paine/crisis/c-05.htm.

75 Chase & Grizzard, eds., *Papers*, vol. 12, 292-295.

few days ago, to wait the arrival of the Reinforcement from the Northward, before any alteration could safely be made in the disposition of the Army, and I was not without hopes, that the Fort would have held out till that time."[76]

John Laurens of Washington's staff put the blame for the evacuation squarely on the shoulders of Commodore Hazelwood and the American navy. "I hate to blame without sure grounds," he wrote in a letter to his father on November 18, "but as far as I can judge at this distance, the naval department has been deficient in its duty. The Commodore is brave, but has no command." Hazelwood eventually heard the rumors against his character and leadership and wrote a remarkable letter to the Pennsylvania authorities on February 8, 1778: "I have been informed . . . That a Colo Smith [Lt. Col. Samuel Smith] . . . has made free with my character, which surprizes me much." One day during the siege, Smith made some damning accusations about the naval elements. Hazelwood, in turn, called him "a lying scoundrel, [and] with that he made a stroke at me, & nothing prevented me for treating him as he deserved but Genl Vernom [Varnum] & a number of other officers who interfered, & I was deteremined to take an opportunity to call him to account for it," continued the commodore, "but Gen'l Vernom constantly begging me to make the matter up . . . After a great deal of persuasions of both sides, the matter was settled; we drank together & parted friends."[77]

In the end, the Pennsylvania Supreme Executive Council concluded Hazelwood was not to blame. "[B]oth Officers and Men, in Many of the Boats, merit praise, rather than deserve Censure," it reported on December 20, "the reproaches of some has proceeded, I dare say, from Ignorance of the Orders given, or want of knowledge of their circumstances; and of Others from a desire to throw the blames from off their own shoulders on to those of others."[78]

The deadly defense of Fort Mifflin by its brave garrison became the stuff of legend in the eyes of many Americans, including members of Congress. "The Garrison have already immortalized themselves by uncommon Valour and Perseverance," wrote New York delegate James Duane in a letter to Philip Schuyler

---

76 Ibid. Daniel Morgan's men were among the first to arrive from Gates's army.

77 Simms, *Correspondence of Laurens*, 79; Hazard, ed., Pennsylvania *Archives*, Series 1, vol. 6, 246.

78 According to Smith's son, his father never forgave Hazelwood: "Colonel Smith always held the Commodore in great contempt thinking that he did not discharge his duty with becoming zeal. They had several animated altercations, during the siege; and after the evacuation of the Fort, the Colonel refused to return his salutation in the streets of Philadelphia . . . so gross was the insult [it was expected] that Colonel Smith would be challenged the next day." Smith, "Papers of Smith," 88; Hazard, ed., Pennsylvania *Archives*, Series 1, vol. 6, 121.

on November 19. Cornelius Hartnett of North Carolina wrote to William Wilkinson the same day: "Our Little fleet & forts on the Delaware have behaved nobly." Richard Henry Lee informed Samuel Adams on November 23, "we have lost fort Mifflin, which our brave garrison was obliged to abandon after a most gallant defence, in which all their guns were dismounted but two, and all the works beaten away about a rod and a half."[79]

Fort Mifflin was a grave loss for Washington and a much-needed win for Howe. Now the embattled general had to explain it to interested parties back home. "From a variety of difficulties attending the construction of additional batteries in a morass, against the fort upon Mud Island, and in transportation of the guns and stores, they were not opened against the enemys defences until the 10th instant," explained Howe to Lord Germain on November 28. The Americans, he continued "dreading an impending assault, evacuated the island in the night between the 15th and 16th, and it was possessed the 16th at day-break by the grenadiers of the guards. Much commendation is due to Brigadier General Cleaveland, to the officers and men of the corps of artillery, and to the troops in general employed upon this service, attended with great fatigue." Howe continued:

> The enemy's fire upon the ships of war, the *Vigilant* and hulk, from two floating batteries, 17 galleys and armed vessels, and from a battery on the Jersey Shore, was exceedingly heavy; but the gallantry displayed by the naval commanders, their officers and seamen , on this occasion, frustrated all their efforts, and contributed principally to the reduction of the enemys works. Permit me at the same time to report to your Lord that the perseverance of the officers and seamen employed in bringing up stores from the fleet, under the conduct of Captain Duncan of the *Eagle*, demand my highest acknowledgments; and that the services they rendered were most esential, and borne with the utmost cheerfulness.[80]

With the fort finally in British hands, Howe and his men needed to clear the remaining American obstacles along the Delaware to open up the river and keep Philadelphia.

79 Elbridge Gerry wrote to Joseph Trumbull on November 27 "The Enemy have obtained possession of Delaware River, from the Delay of the Army to support Fort Mifflin & Red Bank; I think that an Enquiry into this affair . . . will necessarily take place." Smith, et al., eds., *Letters*, vol. 8, 282, 284, 310-311 & 327.

80 *The Parliamentary Register; or, History of the Proceedings and Debates of the House of Commons: Containing an Account of the most interesting Speeches and Motions; accurate Copies of the most remarkable Letters and Papers; of the most material Evidence, Petitions, &c laid before and offered to the House, During the Fifth Session of the Fourteenth Parliament of Great Britain*, 17 vols. (London, 1779), vol. 10, 439-440.

Chapter 8

The River War Concludes

November 16-December 3, 1777

"Fort Mifflin and that at Red Bank mutually depended on each Other for support,
& the reduction of the former made the tenure of the latter
extremely precarious, if not impracticable."[1]

— Gen. George Washington, November 23, 1777

The British capture of Fort Mifflin was a boost for British morale and was potentially a major turning point in the river war and ongoing campaign, but there was still much to be done to open the river to English shipping. And William Howe was running out of time.

The supply situation plagued both armies. Washington's command was in a desperate condition. The long campaign and hard marching (some 400 miles, all told) had worn down men and animals alike. With the British occupying New York and Philadelphia, supplies for the Continental army trickled in from New England and Virginia. Inflation exacerbated the situation. Congress responded by issuing millions of dollars of nearly worthless paper currency. Locals were barely scraping by and unable to provide forage to either army. In many ways, the two opposing

---

1 Chase & Grizzard, eds., *Papers*, vol. 12, 364.

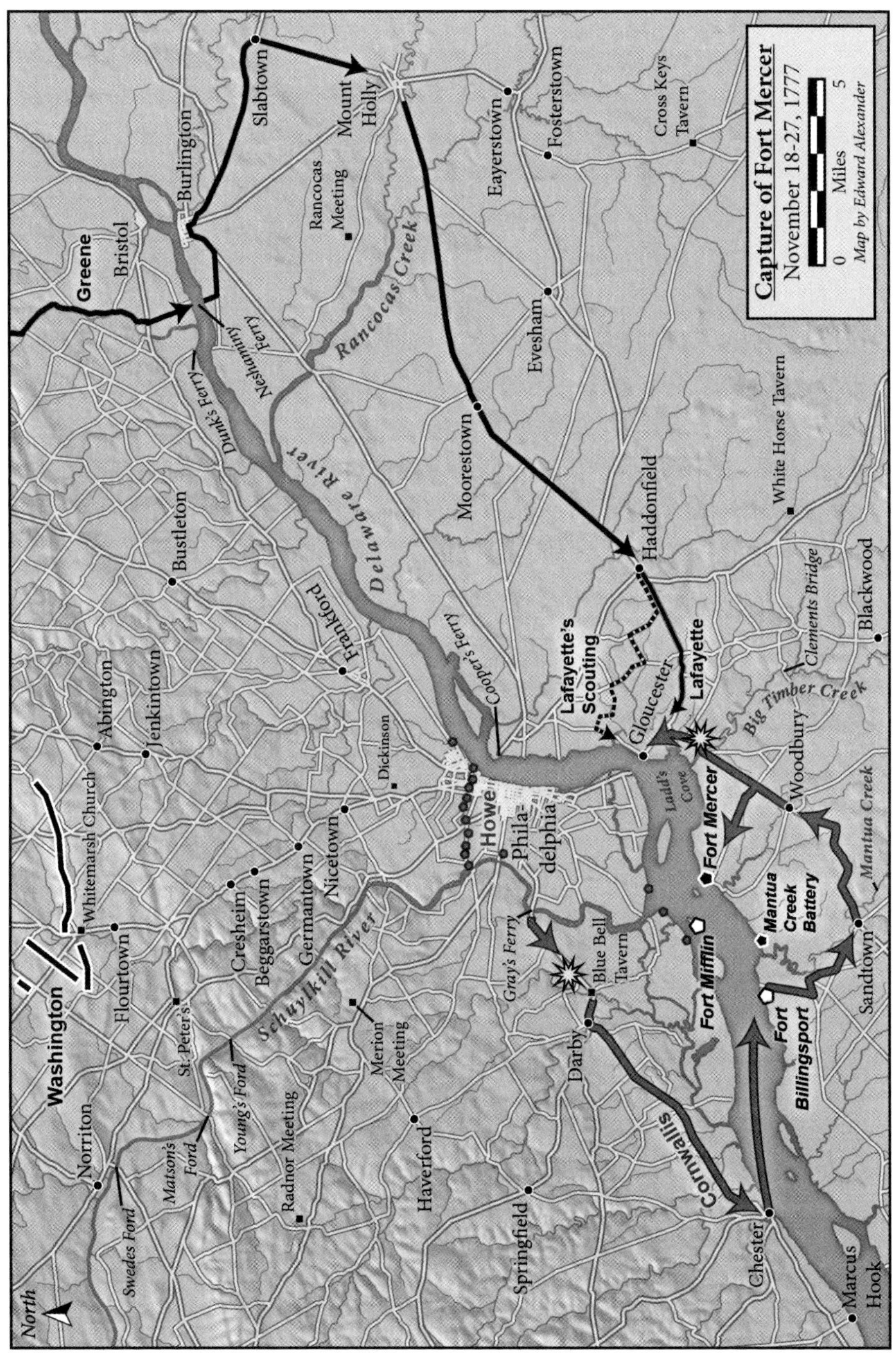
North
Washington
Norriton
Whitemarsh Church
Abington
Jenkintown
Bustleton
Flourtown
St. Peter's
Swedes Ford
Matson's Ford
Young's Ford
Radnor Meeting
Cresheim
Beggarstown
Germantown
Nicetown
Merion Meeting
Haverford
Springfield
Schuylkill River
Frankford
Dickinson
Howe
Phila-
delphia
Gray's Ferry
Blue Bell Tavern
Darby
Cooper's Ferry
Delaware River
Dunk's Ferry
Neshaminy Ferry
Greene
Bristol
Burlington
Slabtown
Mount Holly
Rancocas Meeting
Rancocas Creek
Eayerstown
Fosterstown
Cross Keys Tavern
Evesham
Moorestown
Haddonfield
White Horse Tavern
Lafayette's Scouting
Gloucester
Lafayette
Blackwood
Big Timber Creek
Clements Bridge
Woodbury
Ladd's Cove
Fort Mercer
Mantua Creek
Mantua Creek Battery
Fort Mifflin
Fort Billingsport
Sandtown
Chester
Cornwallis
Marcus Hook
Capture of Fort Mercer
November 18-27, 1777
0   Miles   5
Map by Edward Alexander

armies faced the same problem. Now, Mifflin was gone, and Washington's army was ill-shod and hungry. He needed a new strategy.[2]

The River War

Washington's letter to Congress on November 17 explained that "keeping possession of Red Bank, and thereby still preventing the Enemy from weighing the Chevaux de frize before the Frost obliges their Ships to quit the River, has become a matter of the greatest importance." He ordered Arthur St. Clair, Henry Knox, and Johann de Kalb "to take a view of the Ground, and to endeavor to form a Judgement of the most probable means of securing it. They will, at the same time, see how far it is possible for our fleet to keep their Station since the loss of Fort Mifflin." The orders to the three generals included reporting "the Practicability of hindering the Enemy from clearing the main Channel of the Chevaux de fries" and "what farther Aid would be required from this Army to effect the purpose" and "whether our Fleet will be able to keep the River in case the Enemy make a Lodgement and establish Batteries on Mud Island." Lastly, the three needed to consult with Varnum, Hazelwood, and Christopher Greene before reporting back to Washington.[3]

Colonel Greene, commanding Fort Mercer, wrote to Washington on November 17 to express concerns about holding the post now that Mifflin had fallen. "Fort Mercer is tolerable secure against a Storm only," he began. "The communication to Red Bank by Water is nearly interrupted, and should a part of the Enemy invest this Fort by Land our whole supply, would be cut off, and should they erect Bombattere on the Land side would be able to throw shells to us on all sides." He concluded by noting "that an Army investing us sufficient to keep the Field will reduce the Garrison, and make the survivors Prisoners as we could have no retreat." Greene counted some 565 men in the garrison. There were 211 from his own regiment, another 215 from Angell's and perhaps 65 from Forman's New

---

2 McGuire, *Campaign*, vol. 2, 218. To eliminate one of his headaches, Washington allowed Thomas Conway to leave the army on November 16 pending Congress's acceptance of his resignation.

3 Chase & Grizzard, eds., *Papers*, vol. 12, 295 & 298. Fort Mifflin's loss sparked more criticism in Congress. Richard Henry Lee of Virginia wrote to Samuel Adams on November 23 that they needed "indispensable changes in our Army" and that placing Horatio Gates at the head of a new Board of War was that "indispensable change." Smith, et al., eds., *Letters*, vol. 8, 313. Congress's elevation of Gates to lead the Board initiated what is known today as the Conway Cabal. Conway's earlier machinations were merely a precursor to the true cabal: Gates's elevation.

Jersey militia brigade. Another 74 officers and men served the artillery. Fort Mifflin's survivors, recovering in Woodbury, were incapable of aiding Greene.[4]

Howe controlled Mud Island, but the *chevaux-de-frise* river obstructions remained in place and the guns at Fort Mercer continued to protect them. Seizing Mifflin was a necessary step toward full control of the Delaware River, but the threat at Red Bank had to be eliminated to do so. The pesky American navy would be no match for its counterpart if Mercer fell.[5]

On November 18, Howe ordered Lord Charles Cornwallis to march to Chester with 2,000 men, cross the river, and seize Fort Mercer. The force included the 1st Battalion of British Grenadiers, the 1st Battalion of British Light Infantry, the 27th and 33rd Regiments of Foot, the Hessian Grenadier Battalion von Lengerke, and 50 Hessian jaegers. An American picket post (likely Pennsylvania militia) fired on the column near the Blue Bell Tavern. The marching men were "fired at by 14 rebels from a house near Derby," Loyalist James Parker detailed in his journal. "A Seargeant Majr. [of the 33rd Regiment] & a private were killed." The Americans "then surrendered, fully relying on that lenity which has so long encouraged them in Acts of insolence & Cruilty." Instead of leniency, the British retaliated by putting "the bayonet into five of them & took the Others." Cornwallis crossed over the river and landed at the same spot Col. Thomas Stirling had used six weeks earlier for his attack on Billingsport.[6]

Wanting to avoid another disaster like the Hessian fiasco on October 22, Howe bolstered Cornwallis with reinforcements from New York. Major General Thomas Wilson's 4,300 men had seen and heard the assault on Fort Mifflin while waiting on transport ships. They landed in New Jersey with Cornwallis. Wilson's command included the 7th Royal Fusiliers, the 26th and 63rd Regiments of Foot, the 17th Light Dragoons, and two battalions of Anspach Grenadiers from the garrison in New York. Another 300 jaegers, more than 400 convalescents, and 70 men for the Brigade of Guards also arrived with Wilson. The jaeger contingent included two new companies and recruits to replace losses from the campaign in

---

4 Chase & Grizzard, eds., *Papers*, vol. 12, 288; McIntyre, *A Most Gallant Resistance*, 274.

5 Reed, *Campaign*, 352.

6 The von Lengerke Battalion remained in reserve during the assault on Fort Mercer and was the freshest of the Hessian battalions Howe could have selected for this operation. Cornwallis also took 12 cannon and several howitzers. Letter, Thomas Stanley to "dearest friend," November 28, 1777, American Revolutionary War Manuscripts Collection, Boston Public Library, Boston, MA; Robertson, *Diaries*, 155. Blue Bell Tavern stands at the present intersection of Cobbs Creek Parkway and Woodland Avenue. Parker Journal, November 19, 1777 entry, Parker Family Papers.

the existing battalion. They could not, however, replace the highly trained veteran troops who had seen action earlier in the campaign. Captain Ewald was unimpressed with the new arrivals, who he described as "deserters from all nations, partly ruined officers and noblemen, students from all the universities, bankrupts, merchants, and all kinds of adventurers." Artilleryman Francis Downman felt confident about Cornwallis's chances: "The junction of the parties will be the decisive stroke against that place [Fort Mercer], for the very idea of being surrounded is what they [the Americans] cannot bear."[7]

Late that night, Washington's three emissaries sent to New Jersey (St. Clair, Knox, and de Kalb) dispatched a situation report. If the British fortified Mud Island (which they had already begun to do), the American navy could not stay in the river below Philadelphia. The three generals recommended Commodore Hazelwood attempt to move his ships upriver past Philadelphia. Early reports of Cornwallis's landing had reached Woodbury, and the generals knew he would get there before Fort Mercer could be reinforced. Hazelwood knew his position was untenable unless Washington reinforced Mercer. With Red Bank's abandonment likely, the generals informed Washington that General Varnum should move his troops north of Big Timber Creek. If and when Colonel Greene evacuated Fort Mercer, they recommended blowing up the works. Although Varnum's weak leadership had contributed to the current tactical situation, Varnum wrote Washington the previous day disagreeing with the naval proposal to escape north: "Was our Fleet to continue under the Cover of this Place [Fort Mercer], the Enemy's Shipping would be in a worse Situation; but as they seem to be upon the Wing, the Enemy will soon be able to open Bomb Batteries from Fort Mifflin."[8]

November 19 dawned with Cornwallis probing the American lines along Mantua Creek. Pushing north from Billingsport, he forced the Americans to abandon the gun position north of the creek. British engineer Archibald Robertson recorded the events in his diary: "2 Companies Light Infantry were landed on the other side of the mouth of Manto Creek to see if the Battery was evacuated but it was so Dark that they could not find their way. They were fired on by a Sentry from

---

7 Letter, Thomas Stanley to "dearest friend," Nov. 28, 1777; Robertson, *Diaries*, 154-155. Brigadier Generals Alexander Leslie and James Pattison accompanied Wilson. The 42nd Highlanders were also sent across the river at Philadelphia to Cooper's Ferry to create a beachhead for Cornwallis's eventual return from New Jersey. Smith, *Fight for Delaware*, 38; Stone & Schopp, *Gloucester*, 58; Ewald, *Diary*, 105; Whinyates, *Services*, 52.

8 Jackson, *Navy*, 271; Smith, *Fight for Delaware*, 38; Chase & Grizzard, eds., *Papers*, vol. 12, 300.

a Small Guard and return'd." The next morning, two other companies were sent over "and found the Battery evacuated and a 24-Pounder unspiked."[9]

The pace and direction of events convinced Hazelwood that his navy must attempt to move past Philadelphia early the next morning. During the day, he shifted his ships into Ladd's Cove at the mouth of Big Timber Creek, just above Fort Mercer. Knox, de Kalb, and St. Clair were right: Cornwallis held all the advantages. Varnum could only gather perhaps 2,000 men (including 200 New Jersey militia) in Gloucester County to oppose Cornwallis's 6,800 troops. The balance of the reinforcements from Gates's northern army were still several days away. John Paterson's brigade lingered in the Hudson Highlands and John Glover's troops remained enroute to Morristown, New Jersey. A desperate Washington ordered Jedediah Huntington's brigade from where the army camped at Whitemarsh across the Delaware to reinforce Varnum. He was unwilling to further reduce his main army. "It is my desire & you are herby order'd," wrote Washington to Glover that night, "to March by the most convenient Route after receipt of this to Join the Continental Army which may be in the Neighborhood of Red Bank."[10]

Commodore Hazelwood, meanwhile, split his fleet in half for the move north past Philadelphia. The Continental and large Pennsylvania State naval ships would use the main channel. The smaller vessels would move up the eastern channel. Hazelwood prepared every ship with combustible materials. If any vessel was caught in an unfavorable wind, damaged by enemy fire, or grounded and risked being captured, it was to be burned and abandoned. At 3:00 a.m. on November 20, Hazelwood sent 13 galleys and nine guard boats upriver. They arrived at Bristol, Pennsylvania, seven hours later. Hazelwood delayed sending the larger ships because of the risk of losing the large amounts of supplies stockpiled at Ladd's Cove.[11]

---

9 Robertson, *Diaries*, 156.

10 Jackson, *Navy*, 272; Smith, *Fight for Delaware*, 38; Chase & Grizzard, eds., *Papers*, vol. 12, 317. Washington did not know that Glover was not with his brigade because he was marching the Saratoga prisoners to Boston. Glover's absence and possible miscommunication could explain the brigade's delay in arriving at the Delaware River front. Colonel William Shepard, temporarily commanding the brigade, informed Washington of the command change on November 18: "I am now on my way to Delaware River with Genl Glovers Brigade now under My Command." Chase & Grizzard, eds., *Papers*, vol. 12, 312.

11 Jackson, *Navy*, 272-273.

Cornwallis continued probing American positions south of Woodbury on November 20. He also sent the 1st Light Infantry Battalion to repair "the bridge at Sand Town [modern Mount Royal] over Manto [Mantua] Creek about 4 ½ miles in Front" of Billingsport. Varnum, meanwhile, withdrew from Woodbury to Haddonfield, leaving Colonel Greene without support at Fort Mercer. The move to Haddonfield placed Varnum in position to monitor Cornwallis's force and Cooper's Ferry, where Howe had positioned the 42nd Highlanders to protect the area for Cornwallis. When he learned of Varnum's retreat, Greene decided to abandon Fort Mercer and set out for Woodbury. A 55-man detachment was sent back to complete the destruction of the works. Varnum's decision directly led to the abandonment of Red Bank. "It is astonishing to think of the Precipitate retreat from Fort Mercer," wrote William Bradford to Thomas Wharton (president of Pennsylvania) on November 22, "they seemed determined not to see the Enemy. How General Varnum will account for his Conduct, others must judge."[12]

While Varnum was exposing Mercer and Greene was evacuating the bastion, Washington was desperately searching about for ways to bolster his army with men and supplies. The brigades from Gates's northern army were taking much too long to arrive. On November 20, he ordered John Paterson and Enoch Poor to hurry their brigades south. He next appealed to the unreliable New Jersey militia, begging them to turn out: "The Enemy have thrown a considerable Force into your State, with intent to possess themselves of the post at Red Bank, and after clearing the obstructions in Delaware, make incursions into your Country . . . I therefore call upon you, by all that you hold dear," he insisted, "to rise up as one man, and rid your Country of its unjust invaders." Needing a more reliable source of manpower to stay Cornwallis's threat, Washington ordered Nathanael Greene to New Jersey with his division. The Marquise de Lafayette, having recovered enough from his Brandywine wound to return to the saddle, rode with Greene. The next day, Washington ordered Ephraim Blaine "to repair immediately to the State of Jersey and use every prudent possible exertion to procure such quantities [of wheat and flour] as may be Necessary [for the army]."[13]

---

12 Robertson, *Diaries*, 156; Reed, *Campaign*, 354; Jackson, *Navy*, 270-276; Hazard, ed., *Pennsylvania Archives*, Series 1, vol. 6, 27-28.

13 Chase & Grizzard, eds., *Papers*, vol. 12, 334 & 339; Smith, *Fight for Delaware*, 38.

Conway Cabal

Letters from Congressional delegates continued to question Washington's ability. "We want a General," penned Jonathan Dickinson Sergeant to James Lovell on November 20. He continued:

> [T]housands of Lives & Millions of Property are yearly sacrificed to the Insufficiency of our Commander in Chief. Two Battles he has lost for us by two such Blunders as might have disgraced a Soldier of three Months Standing: and yet we are so attached to this Man that I fear we shall rather sink with him than throw him off our Shoulders. And sink we must under his Management. Such Feebleness & Want of Authority, such Confusion & Want of Discipline, such Waste, such Destruction will exhaust the Wealth of both the Indies & annihilate the Armies of all Europe & Asia.[14]

Fleet Destroyed

Late that night, before Commodore Hazelwood could return from Bristol, his larger ships attempted to move north without orders. Unlike the smaller vessels, the British spotted them this time and opened fire. "Last night the rebels set fire to four of their ships, and at the same time five of their best galleys crept up with the high tide and a good wind, and got past our frigate [*Delaware*] before they were noticed," wrote Howe's Hessian aide von Muenchhausen. "Nevertheless, they were subjected to the intense fire from our frigate and from our shore batteries near the city." The visual spectacle mesmerized the Hessian. "There was never a more beautiful fireworks than the one caused by 15 burning ships during the dark night. They moved up and down with the tide, and as soon as the fire reached the powder magazines they blew up with loud explosions. It was the most spectacular sight I have ever seen."[15]

The Americans, concluded ubiquitous loyalist James Parker, knew that "when redbank fell into our hands that the Ships must move. Certain distruction was their

---

14 Smith, et al., eds., *Letters*, vol. 8, 296. This same day, a court martial found Adams Stephens guilty; Washington approved the sentence and dismissed him from the service. On November 28, Congressman James Lovell wrote to Joseph Trumbull: "Genl. Stevens is dismissed with several inferior Officers by sentence of Court martial *approved* by Genl. Washington, which looks a little like firmness and rising Discipline. Cowardice, Theft & Drunkeness must take warning." Ibid., 339. For more on Stephen's court martial, see Harris, *Germantown*, 443-449.

15 Jackson, *Navy*, 272-273; Von Muenchhausen, *At Howe's Side*, 44.

fate, either from Lord [Richard] Howe below or from our batterys & *Delaware* above." The spectacle awakened the entire city. "The Wharfs of the City were crouded with Men, Women, & Children. the thundering of the Cannon, enrich'd by the alternate blowing up of the ships, & buzzing noise of the People more Visible by the flashes of fire, All together exhibited materials unparalleled for a fine discriptive fancy."[16]

Civilian Elizabeth Drinker confirmed details in her journal. "I was awaken'd this Morning befor 5 o'clock by the loud fireing of Cannon, my Head Aching very badly . . . all our Neighbours were also up, and I believe most in Town," she recorded. "[W]e heard the explosion of 4 of 'em when they blew up, which shook our Windows greatly—We had a fair sight of the blazeing Fleet, from our upper Windows." Another civilian, Robert Morton, noted "the American Navy on fire coming up with the flood tide, and burning with the greatest fury. Some of them drifted within 2 miles of the town and were carried back by the ebb tide. They burnt nearly 5 hours; four of them blew up." As the ships passed Philadelphia, wrote Bradford in his letter to Wharton, the captured *Delaware* joined a "very hot fire of shot and shells from the Town," damaging several vessels.[17]

One schooner, three guard boats, four sloops, and the brig *Convention* managed to run the gauntlet and escape to Bristol. A few smaller boats remained at Ladd's Cove. Hazelwood lost all of his other vessels—the Continental ships, the State armed ship *Montgomery*, and two floating batteries. Congress would order an investigation into Hazelwood's actions, but it fizzled out by leveling nothing more than strongly worded criticism against the inept commodore. "The burning of part of the Delaware fleet, the precipitate retreat of the rest, the little service rendered by them, and the great expense they were at," concluded Thomas Paine to Benjamin Franklin in May 1778, "make the only material blot in the proceedings."[18]

New Jersey Operations

As the sun rose the next morning, Nathanael Greene's division arrived in Burlington, New Jersey, after crossing at Neshaminy Ferry—but moved no farther. A lack of scows kept the division's supply wagons across the river. Greene's new

16 Parker Journal, November 21, 1777 entry, Parker Family Papers.

17 Drinker, *Diary of Elizabeth Drinker*, 255-256; Morton, "Diary," 29-30; Hazard, ed., *Pennsylvania Archives*, Series 1, vol. 6, 28. The fleet was set afire near League Island. Smith, *Fight for Delaware*, 40.

18 Jackson, *Navy*, 273-274.; "Military Operations," 294.

area of operations included rich soil where farmers tilled and raised livestock. During better times, they sold their surplus wheat, corn, and meat across the river in Philadelphia. Numerous watercourses intersected the gently rolling picturesque landscape dotted by forests. The three counties along the Delaware (Burlington, Gloucester, and Salem) were overwhelmingly inhabited by Quakers, with a smattering of English, Dutch, and Swedes. Most of these 30,000 residents lived close to the river.[19]

Unaware of Red Bank's abandonment, Washington hoped Greene's force could attack the British rear besieging Fort Mercer. Greene was also working in the dark, though rumors of Mercer's fate were beginning to reach him. He wrote to James Varnum on November 21 seeking information. "I make no doubt you are acquainted with the marching of my troops to join you. I am at a loss respecting your situation, the condition of Fort Mercer, or the operations of the Enemy in the Jerseys," explained the general. "A report prevails here this morning that Fort Mercer is evacuated and the fleet below burnt. Youl please to inform me as to the truth of the reports, where you are, where the enemy is, and where you think a junction of our forces can be easily form'd, and also if you think an attack can be made upon the enemy with a prospect of success." The Rhode Islander also informed Varnum that he was "a stranger to all the lower part of the Jerseys."[20]

After meeting with Hazelwood and Col. Israel Shreve of the New Jersey Line on November 21, Greene reported to Washington. "Col. Shrieve was with me this afternoon about turning out the Militia—I wish he may succeed, but from the temper of the People there appears no great prospect," admitted the newly arrived officer. "I have heard nothing from General Glovers brigde—I hope Col. [Daniel] Morgans Corps of light troops will be on in the morning . . . The fleet are greatly disgusted at the reflections thrown out against the officers; the Commodore thinks the Officers are greatly injurd, he asserts they did their duty faithfully." The lethargy of the brigades marching to join Washington frustrated Greene as well.[21]

In addition to superseding Varnum's authority, Greene needed to create a gathering point for troops coming down from the north. John Glover's and

19 Reed, *Campaign*, 354 & 357. The ships that escaped helped ferry Greene's troops across the river to Burlington. Neshaminy Ferry was located above modern Neshaminy State Park but below modern Burlington Bristol Bridge. Jackson, *Navy*, 274; Herrera, *Feeding Washington's Army*, 55.

20 Richard K. Showman, Robert M. McCarthy, and Margaret Cobb, eds., *The Papers of General Nathanael Greene*, vol. 2, *1 January 1777-16 October 1778*, 13 vols. (Chapel Hill, NC, 1980), 201-202.

21 Chase & Grizzard, eds., *Papers*, vol. 12, 340. Shreve was staying in New Jersey recovering from his Brandywine wound.

Ebenezer Learned's Massachusetts brigades were still tramping in his general direction. Daniel Morgan's reduced command reinforced Greene from Whitemarsh, though only "one hundred and Seventy of Morgan's Corps [were] fit to march." Lieutenant Colonel Richard Butler was in command of the detachment from Morgan's corps. Huntington's Connecticut brigade, which arrived from Whitemarsh before Greene's division, linked with Varnum's men and retired to Mount Holly, New Jersey. By the end of the day the commands of Varnum, Huntingdon, Greene (Muhlenberg's and Weedon's brigades), and Morgan totaled some 4,400 troops, a sizable force intent on stopping Cornwallis.[22]

With the bridge across Mantua Creek now repaired, Cornwallis marched north from Billingsport on November 21. The 7th and 63rd Regiments of Foot were left at the bridge to "keep up the Communication with Billingsport and to Collect Cattle," according to Archibald Robertson's diary. Once in Woodbury, the British camped "on very advantageous ground round the Village." Cornwallis dispatched the 1st Light Infantry Battalion to the recently abandoned Fort Mercer and another detail to repair the bridge over Big Timber Creek. The light companies from the 4th, 5th, 10th, 15th, and 17th Regiments of Foot took boats across the creek to provide cover during the repair. That night, New Jersey militia hit the five companies north of the creek. "In the Evening small party's of the Rebels appear'd and began to be troublesome firing on us from a railing on the Other side of a small swamp, from which we soon drove them," recalled Lt. Henry Stirke of the 10th's

---

22 Chase & Grizzard, eds., *Papers*, vol. 12, 349; Smith, *Fight for Delaware*, 39. Butler was born in Ireland and emigrated to Pennsylvania. In 1764, he participated in the British military expedition to the Ohio country. When the Revolution broke out, Butler served as major of the 8th Pennsylvania and became colonel of the 9th Pennsylvania in June 1777. Almost immediately he was detached to serve with Morgan's Rifle Corps. Stone & Schopp, *Gloucester*, 54-55; Smith, *Fight for Delaware*, 39. John Peter Gabriel Muhlenberg, a native Pennsylvanian and son of Henry Melchior Muhlenberg, was an ordained minister serving a Lutheran congregation in Virginia when the war began. A former member of the House of Burgesses, Muhlenberg was commissioned colonel of the 8th Virginia before rising to brigade command. Aside from political problems, Washington had to deal with his careless supply officers. Orders issued on November 21 read: "Complaint is made that by the carelessness of the butchers, the hides are greatly damaged in taking them off—The issuing Commissaries are enjoined duly to inspect the butchers they employ, and see that they take off the hides with proper care." The army needed the hides for new shoes. The next day Washington ordered: "The Commander in Chief offers a reward of *Ten dollars*, to any person, who shall . . . produce the best substitute for shoes, made from raw hides." Chase & Grizzard, eds., *Papers*, vol. 12, 338 & 344.

light company, "with the loss of 2 men of the 5th light Company kill'd, and a man of ye 4th Company Wounded."[23]

Woodbury, recalled Hessian Johann Dohla on November 22, was "a large, long, and wide-spread, but beautifully laid-out village that is at the same time almost a city. It lies in a pleasant and fertile region and is populated for the most part by Quakers, who are very rich people. Here we built huts because the weather was exceptionally cold. We also caught pigs and cattle and slaughtered them. In this way we obtained meat, but seldom had bread."[24]

Around noon the British light infantry occupied the remnants of Mercer and raided the Whitall property. The English, complained Job Whitall, "took two mares from me, one sorrel horse out of the stable, the other out of the lot, a brown mare, both with foal, and while ye army was passing they came in and took our bread, pie, milk, cheese, meat dishes, cups, spoons, and then took shirts, sheets, blankets, coverleds, stockings, breeches and drove our cattle out of ye brick shed." Cornwallis's position included outposts extending from Mantua Creek to Little Timber Creek. Units garrisoned Billingsport and Fort Mercer, including Royal Marines assigned to complete the destruction of the later place. According to Hessian Dohla, "the fort was completely demolished and leveled. The cannon, which could not be taken because of their size and weight, were spiked and thrown into the Delaware."[25]

Many men were thankful they did not have to storm the fort. "They have thought proper to abandon Red Bank," penned Capt. Thomas Stanley of the 17th Light Dragoons to a friend on November 28, "for which I think we are much obliged to them, as it would have been pretty tuff to have stormed."[26]

---

23 Robertson, *Diaries*, 156; Stone & Schopp, *Gloucester*, 51; Henry Stirke, "A British Officer's Revolutionary War Journal, 1776-1778," S. Sydney Bradford, ed., *Maryland Historical Magazine*, 119 vols. (1961), vol. 56, 175. The two men killed were Pvts. Stephen Sutton and John Key. This action took place just east of the present Brooklawn Circle. Don Hagist, *These Distinguished Corps: British Grenadier and Light Infantry Battalions in the American Revolution* (Warwick, England, 2021), 128.

24 Dohla, *A Hessian Diary*, 60.

25 James Pattison of the Royal Artillery reported the stores found in the fort on November 23: six 8-pounders (one unserviceable), three 18-pounders (two unserviceable), two spiked 6-pounders, three spiked 4-pounders, one spiked 3-pounder, 15 swivel howitzers, and nearly 3,350 artillery rounds. *New York Gazette & Weekly Mercury*, March 16, 1778; Whittall, "Diary," 260. Cornwallis made his headquarters at the home of John Cooper. Jackson, *Navy*, 277; Dohla, *A Hessian Diary*, 59-60.

26 Letter, Thomas Stanley to "dearest friend," November 28, 1777.

British Philadelphia

The ambushing and sniping between the American camp in Whitemarsh and William Howe's defensive redoubts north of Philadelphia continued. Howe issued orders on November 22 to burn all the homes and structures outside his line of redoubts so the rebels could not use them as outposts. One of those torched was Fair Hill, the former country estate of Declaration signer John Dickinson. "The Rebels have occupied Mr. Dickinson's house for a lookout post where a Videt was kept, from the top of the house our movements along the front of the line were seen & Signals made by blowing a horn," recorded Loyalist James Parker. "The house with Several others about it were burnt & the Videt taken."[27]

The burnings horrified civilian Robert Morton. "The reason they assign for this destruction of their friends' property is on acco[unt] of the Americans firing from these houses and harassing their Picquets," he explained. "But what is most astonishing is their burning the furniture in some of those houses that belonged to friends of government, when it was in their power to burn them at their leisure. Here is an instance that Gen'l Washington's Army cannot be accused of," he continued. "There is not one instance to be produced where they have wantonly destroyed and burned their friends' property." As they had done the previous morning to better witness the fleet's destruction, Philadelphians climbed onto their roofs to view the fires. Morton scurried into the Christ Church steeple "and had a prospect of the fires." According to Elizabeth Drinker's diary, "the burning [of] those Houses tis said is a premeditated thing, as they serve for skulking places; and much anoy the Guards. They talk of burning all the Houses &c within four miles of the City, without the lines."

West of the city in the village of Trappe, Henry Muhlenberg saw the flames, too. "Between six and seven o'clock in the evening we saw high flames in the direction of Philadelphia which lasted about three hours." Later on November 30, Washington's former military secretary and now confidant without portfolio, Joseph Reed, wrote to Thomas Wharton: "The enemy have made great destruction of the little villas in the neighbourhood of their lines. The bare walls are left; the doors, windows, roofs and floors are all gone to make huts. Not the least trace of a fence or fruit tree is to be seen. About fifteen houses are totally demolished, some

---

27 Fair Hill stood on the Germantown Road just below Stenton. Parker Journal, November 22, 1777 entry, Parker Family Papers.

in that way I have mentioned, others burnt." Howe was not winning the hearts and minds of the populace.[28]

While structures were burning outside the redoubts, light draft supply boats were moving over the floating chain or, one at a time, through the opening in the *chevaux-de-frise* the Americans had cut for their own vessels and docking at Philadelphia. Richard Howe's navy finally controlled the river. William Howe ordered the batteries on Province and Carpenter's islands, Fort Mifflin, and Fort Mercer, destroyed.[29]

New Jersey Operations

While fires burned outside Philadelphia, Nathanael Greene rode with the Marquis de Lafayette down to Mount Holly to meet with Varnum on November 22 and investigate conditions for themselves. Greene sent Daniel Morgan's riflemen forward to Haddonfield to scout the British position and sought Washington's permission to attack Cornwallis. The next day Washington informed Congress, "if an Attack can be made on Lord Cornwallis with a prospect of success, I am persuaded it will be done." Greene remained unaware that Howe had ordered Cornwallis to destroy Fort Mercer, disperse the American fleet, and return to Philadelphia. Greene, who fully expected Cornwallis to advance toward him and not remain idle in Woodbury, set up a defensive line along Rancocas Creek. He was anxious to attack Cornwallis but wanted to await the arrival of more troops from Gates's army and Light Horse Harry Lee's dragoons. Until Lee arrived, Greene used Morgan's riflemen to screen the American position.[30]

Washington, meanwhile, learned of Fort Mercer's loss and reported it to Congress on November 23. "I am sorry to inform Congress, that the Enemy are now in possession of All the Water defences," he admitted. "Fort Mifflin and that at Red Bank mutually depended on each other for support, & the reduction of the

---

28 Morton, "Diary," 30-31; Drinker, *Diary of Elizabeth Drinker*, 256; Muhlenberg, *Journals*, vol. 3, 106; Reed, *Life of Reed*, 341. It is widely believed that the Philadelphia area suffered a minor earthquake that day. Von Muenchhausen noted, "at seven o'clock in the morning we felt some rather strong tremors of an earthquake." Von Muenchhausen, *At Howe's Side*, 44.

29 Reed, *Campaign*, 357-358.

30 Ibid., 357; Chase & Grizzard, eds., *Papers*, vol. 12, 365; Jackson, *Navy*, 278.

former made the tenure of the latter extremely precarious, if not impracticable." Washington went on to provide a summary of the events leading to their loss.[31]

By November 24, Glover's brigade from the northern army arrived at the Black Horse Tavern (modern Columbus, New Jersey) eight miles away from Greene's position. The strength return for Greene's command that day showed nearly 6,500 troops present—about 600 of whom were sick or detached. Washington's trusted subordinate sent out detachments to scout enemy positions. Burlington County militia moved to Moorestown. George Weedon rode forward to Haddonfield along with the Marquise de Lafayette. After reconnoitering, Weedon sent a situation report back to Greene. The British, he noted, "have this Day Advanced on this side Great Timber Creek with their main Body, and have [picket] on this side of Little Timber Creek also. Some of the prisoners were taken within two miles of" Haddonfield. "They have no Troops at Red Bank and but few at Billingsport."[32]

Washington left the decision to attack with Greene. The Rhode Islander pondered his options and wrote to Washington that evening. "Would you advise me to fight them with very unequal Numbers?" he asked. Greene seemed unaware that his force was nearly Cornwallis's equal. "For your Sake, for my own Sake & for my Country's Sake I wish to attempt every thing which will meet with your Excellency's Approbation—I will run any Risque or engage under any Disadvantages if I can only have your Countenance if unfortunate. With the Publick I know Success sanctifies every thing, and that only."[33]

The rumblings of the Conway matter filtered throughout the army "I have seen of late, the difficulty your Excellency seemed to labour under, to satisfy the Expecations of an ignorant Populace, with great Concern," continued Greene. "It is our Misfortune to have an Extent of Country to cover, that demands four times our Numbers—the Enemy so situated as to be very difficult to approach, and from pretty good Authority, superior to us in Numbers." Greene continued:

> Under these Disadvantages—Your Excellency has the choice of but two things, to fight the Enemy without the least Prospect of Success, upon the common Principles of War, or

31 Chase & Grizzard, eds., *Papers*, vol. 12, 364.

32 November 24, 1777, Nathanael Greene strength return, Revolutionary War Rolls, 1775-1783, Record Group 93, National Archives, Washington, D.C. Also available on Fold3.com. Stone & Schopp, *Gloucester*, 59; Showman, McCarthy, and Cobb, eds., *Papers of Greene*, vol. 2, 214.

33 Chase & Grizzard, eds., *Papers*, vol. 12, 377-378.

remain inactive, & be subject to the Censure of an ignorant & impatient populace. In doing one you may make a bad matter worse and take a Measure, that, if it proves unfortunate, you may stand condemned for, by all military Gentlemen of Experience; in pursuing the other you have the Approbation of your own mind, you give your Country an opportunity to exert itself to supply the present Deficiency, & also act upon such military Principles as will justify you to the best Judges in the present day, & to all future Generations . . . The Cause is too important to be trifled with to shew our Courage, & your Character too deeply interested, to sport away upon unmilitary Principles.[34]

Whitemarsh Camp

While Greene wrestled with options in New Jersey, Washington held a council of war with the senior generals remaining in camp. The Virginian continued to harbor thoughts of attacking Howe's lines protecting the city. But how? Militia general John Cadwalader put together a plan of attack against Philadelphia eerily reminiscent of the dawn Germantown assault, and Washington wanted the opinions of his top officers. Sometime on Sunday November 23, Cadwalader presented the attack plan. He suggested that eight Continental brigades attack the British lines at dawn, while three additional brigades crossed into New Jersey by ferry above Trenton. This second column would come down the east bank of the Delaware, recross the river, and attack down Philadelphia's streets to strike the British from the rear. Meanwhile, Pennsylvania and Maryland militia, the North Carolina Continental brigade and three other independent Continental battalions would threaten the right flank of the British lines along the western shore of the Delaware. Cadwalader also hoped Nathanael Greene would be positioned to detach 2,000 men to assist the attack from New Jersey. The militia general wanted to commence the main assault at dawn on November 27. The men debated the merits of the complex plan and, lacking a consensus from his generals, Washington rode off to personally inspect the British lines. He determined them too strong to assault.[35]

Anthony Wayne, one of the generals in attendance at the inconclusive council of war, responded to Washington's decision the next day. "The eyes of all America are fixed on you, the junction of the Northern Army—which—Obliged Genl

---

34   Chase & Grizzard, eds., *Papers*, vol. 12, 377-378.

35   Ecelbarger, *Momentous Year*, 202-206. Cadwalader led the Pennsylvania Associators earlier in the war but turned down a commission as a Continental brigadier in 1777. That fall, he was serving as a brigadier general of Pennsylvania militia.

Burgoyne to lay down his Arms—gives the Country & Congress some expectation—that a vigorous Effort will be made to Dislodge the Enemy," he insisted. "It's not in our power to Command success but it is in our Power to produce a Conviction to the World that we Deserve it."[36]

British Philadelphia

Although the British now occupied Mud Island and had eliminated the threat at Fort Mercer, provisions remained scarce in Philadelphia. Richard Howe's secretary, Ambrose Serle visited the main market in the city on November 24, but "did not see one Piece of meat or a Fowl, and but very few Vegetables, all necessaries of Life being extremely dear, owing to the very small Extent of Country at this time under our Command."[37]

Gloucester Engagement

With Fort Mercer empty and the American fleet destroyed or escaped upriver, Cornwallis was now free to follow his orders and return to Philadelphia. Rather than move toward Cooper's Ferry and exposing his right flank to the Americans, he swung left toward Gloucester on November 24. The small village sat on a neck of ground formed by King's Run to the north and Big Timber Creek to the south, its middle cleaved by Little Timber Creek. Unless an attacking force crossed the easily defended creek crossings, the only access to the community came along King's or Salem Road. With ravines and marshes bordering the road in many places, an attacking force would have but little room to maneuver and the woods provided cover for Cornwallis's defenders. The aforementioned road ran from Salem to Burlington. As King's Road curved south toward Woodbury, a branch route called High Street led to Gloucester. After passing through a quarter-mile of fields and woodland, it arrived in the hamlet only 300 yards from the Delaware River. The hamlet consisted of a courthouse, tavern, ferry landing, and a few other dwellings. The village, observed Hessian Johann Dohla in his diary, "lies on the bank of the

36 Chase & Grizzard, eds., *Papers*, vol. 12, 403.

37 Serle, *Journal*, 265.

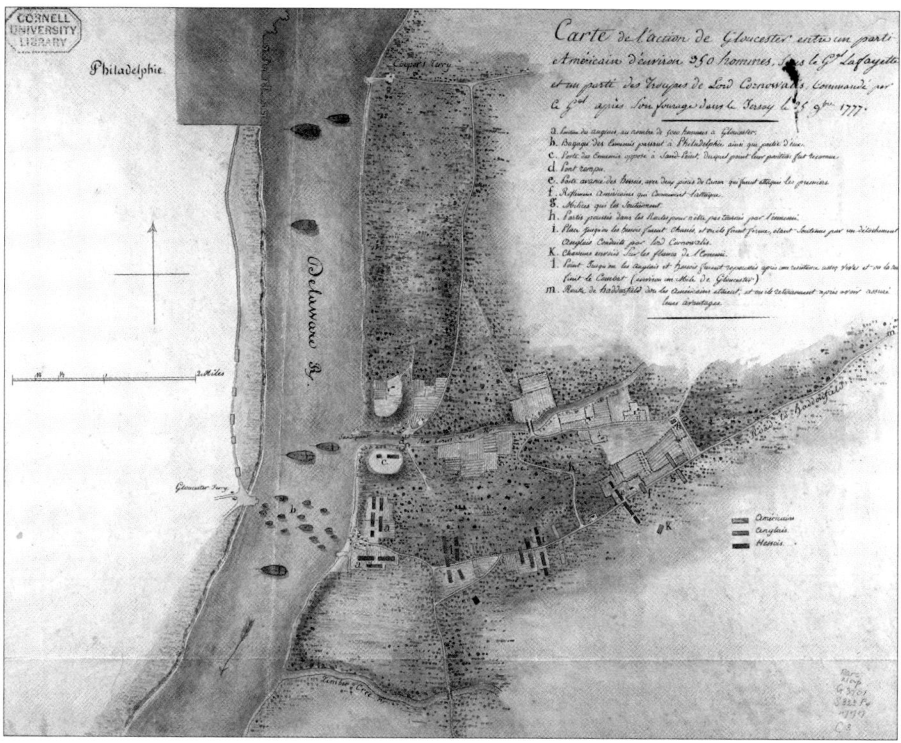

Map of the Battle of Gloucester. *Cornell University Library*

Delaware River, is not very big nor symmetrical, but it does have an imposing townhall."[38]

With only two wharves at Gloucester, Cornwallis required two days to get across to Philadelphia. Foraged cattle, army horses, baggage, and artillery needed to be ferried over, in addition to his troops. The 10-gun *Viper* and the *Vigilant* anchored offshore to cover the operation. Early the next day, the 17th Light Dragoons and Royal Artillerymen ferried across. Cornwallis placed strong outposts on his perimeter to protect the ongoing operation, including pairs of artillery pieces

---

38 Cornwallis established his headquarters in the one and one-half story 17th century home of Col. Joseph Ellis of the New Jersey militia. Ellis had served as a captain during the French and Indian War and participated in the attack on Fort Ticonderoga. When the Revolution erupted, he became colonel of the 2nd Gloucester Country Militia Regiment and led it in the skirmishing around Mount Holly in December 1776. Dohla, *A Hessian Diary*, 60; Stone & Schopp, *Gloucester*, 2-8 & 14. The population of Gloucester Township consisted largely of Quakers with a smattering of Irish and Dutch. Almost 20% of the population were slaves or former slaves.

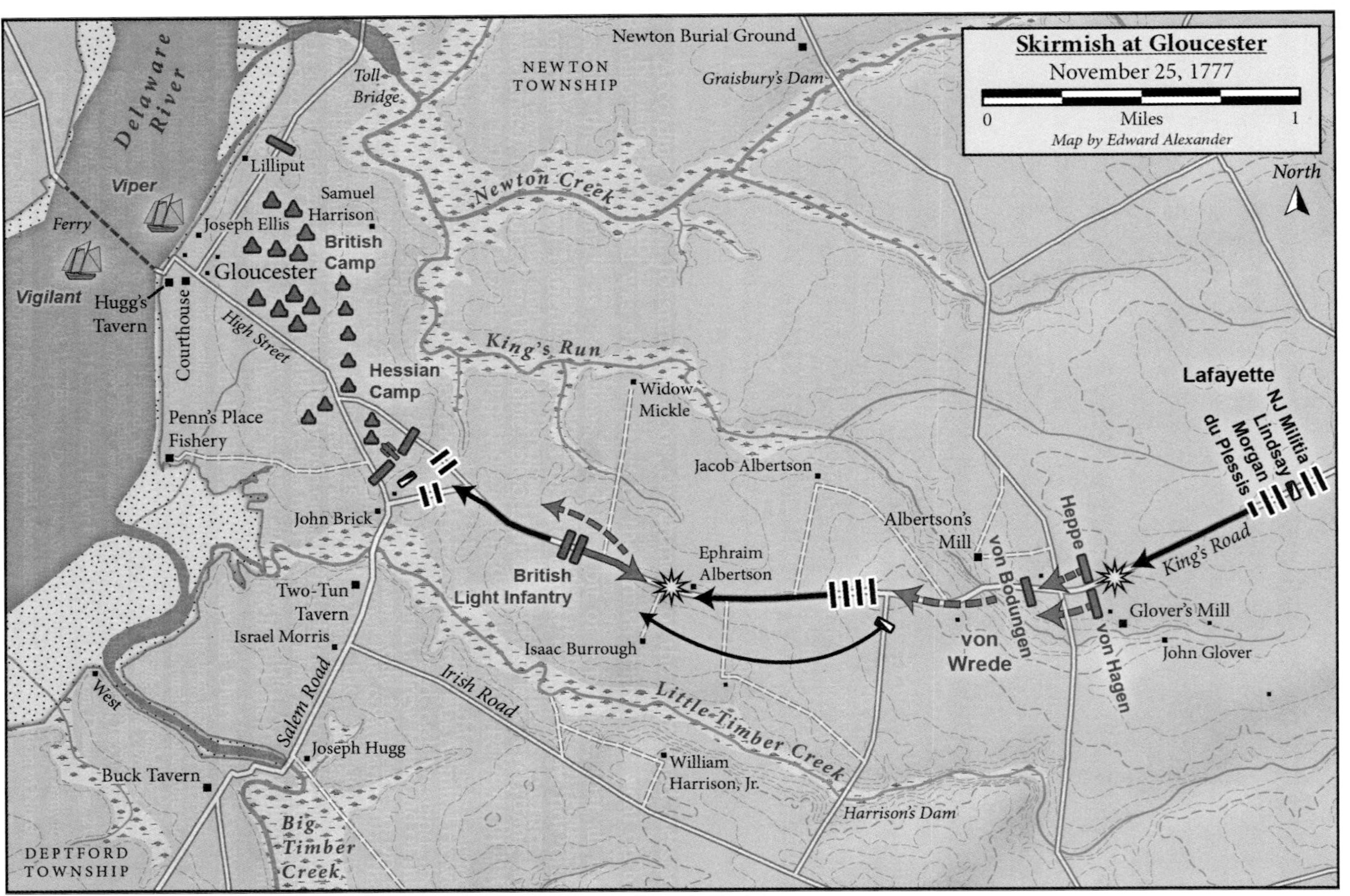

Skirmish at Gloucester
November 25, 1777
0   Miles   1
Map by Edward Alexander
North
Newton Burial Ground
NEWTON TOWNSHIP
Graisbury's Dam
Delaware River
Toll Bridge
Newton Creek
Viper
Lilliput
Ferry
Samuel Harrison
Joseph Ellis
British Camp
Vigilant
Gloucester
Hugg's Tavern
Courthouse
High Street
King's Run
Lafayette
NJ Militia
Lindsay
Morgan
du Plessis
Hessian Camp
Widow Mickle
Heppe
Penn's Place Fishery
Jacob Albertson
Albertson's Mill
King's Road
John Brick
Ephraim Albertson
von Bodungen
British Light Infantry
Glover's Mill
Two-Tun Tavern
Israel Morris
Isaac Burrough
von Wrede
John Glover
West
Salem Road
Irish Road
Little Timber Creek
Joseph Hugg
Buck Tavern
William Harrison, Jr.
Harrison's Dam
DEPTFORD TOWNSHIP
Big Timber Creek

east and south of the village. Lieutenant Colonel Adam Comstock, who Greene had sent to Haddonfield to keep him apprised of British movements, learned about the vulnerability of the British camp from prisoners—and passed it on to his superior. "I could wish your Army was here now for I think they may be supprisd very easy . . . O how I want to give em a Floging before they Leave the Gerseys."[39]

While all this was happening, Lafayette with his aides, a few New Jersey militia, and some of Morgan's riflemen swung north and west to scout Gloucester from the north. Working their way west, the party arrived just north of the mouth of Newton Creek and observed Cornwallis's crossing operation. When they had seen enough, they returned to Haddonfield.[40]

Like Comstock, Lafayette was also convinced of the vulnerability of the British operation and persuaded Col. Joseph Ellis of the New Jersey militia to help him attack the picket posts. About 150 militiamen joined about the same number of Morgan's riflemen and began marching from Haddonfield about 3:00 p.m. A scouting party led by French engineer Capt. Thomas-Antoine de Mauduit du Plessis, who had served so well at Fort Mercer, rode at the head of the column. Colonel Richard Butler with Morgan's riflemen followed du Plessis, with Lafayette escorted by ten Continental Light Dragoons under Lt. William Lindsay behind them. A mixed group of Jersey militiamen representing several counties brought up the rear. Ellis sent out militia parties to protect his flanks.[41]

After marching two miles, Butler's riflemen engaged a picket post around 4:00 p.m. Jaegers were covering the British crossing when the firing erupted. Lieutenant Colonel Haight of the militia ordered one-third of his men to stop as a rearguard and rushed forward with the remaining militiamen, perhaps 100 strong.[42]

Hessian jaeger Lt. Wilhelm Freyenhagen by far provides the best description of the ensuing fight. "The enemy came out of a woods on our front and attacked our pickets, which consisted of Lt. [Friedrich] Kellerhausen and 26 foot jaegers. Captain v. Wrede immediately collected the three newly arrived Jager companies, plus 30 Jagers from our command." Freyenhagen continued:

---

39 Jackson, *Navy*, 280; Stone & Schopp, *Gloucester*, 52 & 62; Showman, McCarthy, and Cobb, eds., *Papers of Greene*, vol. 2, 215.

40 Stone & Schopp, *Gloucester*, 62-65. Lafayette's party would have scouted from the area where N. Broadway crosses Newton Creek outside Gloucester City today.

41 Ibid., 65-67.

42 The fighting began near modern Haddon Lake in the present municipalities of Audubon and Haddon Heights. Ibid., 67 & 101.

We then received orders to reconnoiter the enemy with the entire Jager Corps. Capt. Wrede took the corps forward toward the woods; he detached Lt [George Hermann] Hep[p]e with a command to the left, Lt [Carl] v. Hagen to the right side, to protect our flanks. He left Lt [Franz] v. Bodungen in reserve with a company to await further orders not far from the pickets. We barely advanced 100 paces when the enemy advanced on us in the best order with overwhelming superior numbers. He attacked with the heaviest musket fire and he was able on the flanks to mortally wound both Lts. Heppe and v. Hagen and force their commands back. Then with force and bravery he stormed the remainder. As we were outflanked on all sides Capt. v. Wrede began a retreat to near the picket's position.[43]

Although the jaegers outnumbered the American riflemen, almost all of them were raw recruits. Ewald's description was precisely correct: they had no experience in North American conditions and little firearms training. Captain von Wrede later admitted to General von Knyphausen that the recruits "inexperience in maneuvers and lack of promptitude in loading" caused the embarrassment. The jaegers encountered by Lafayette's detachment comprised a pair of companies of reinforcements from Hesse that "consisted of very old men or young lads." Lieutenant Heinrich von Feilitzsch described the action (although he was not present himself). The young and old, "most of them journeymen who had never held a gun in their hands and knew even less about bullets; against these men the rebels sent a small patrol, which had to lure them into an ambush; Capt. Wreden . . . tried in vain to hold them back, no half moon [hunting horn], nor any other signal helped."[44]

The jaegers tried to rally but could not withstand the advancing New Jersey militia. They were, however, able to manage a ragged return fire that found American flesh. Lieutenant David Mulford took a round between the shoulders and died later that night. The lieutenant, Azariah More, wrote his brother later that night, "was mortally wounded as the action began." Another casualty, Lt. John Lucas, was killed by a rifle ball that entered just below his left nipple. Ensign John Tilton's left shoulder was smashed by a round. Enlisted men Thomas Harris and Hugh Jones were also hit, the former suffering a broken arm and the latter struck in

---

43 Wilhelm Freyenhagen, Journal of Ensign/Lt/ Wilhelm Johann Ernst Freyenhagen Jr—1776-78, Donald Londahlsmidt, ed. & Henry J. Retzer, trans, *Journal of the Johannes Schwalm Historical Association* Vol. 14 (Scotland, PA, 2011), 71.

44 Stone & Schopp, *Gloucester*, 68; Wilhelm von Knyphausen to the Landgrave, letter November 3, 1777, Hessian Documents of the American Revolution, American Philosophical Society, Philadelphia, PA, Letter G, Hessian documents, Fiche No. 56, 129; von Feilitzsch, *Journal*, 132-133.

the left side. The militiamen, however, redeemed their earlier failures in the campaign by standing to the work. Sergeant Richard Sayres recalled in his pension account that "most of the militiamen fired from behind trees, and while they continued in the woods had the advantage of the enemy & compelled them to withdraw." The jaegers were driven more than two miles.[45]

Hessian Johann Dohla was not present at the fight but promptly heard the details. "This evening the jaegers, which were the rear guard and were posted on a bridge one-half hour from Gloucester, were attacked and surrounded by the enemy," he scribbled in his diary. "However, two companies of light infantry hurried to their assistance and saved them from captivity." The arrival of veteran British light infantry and two 6-pounders stabilized the front. According to Lt. Wilhelm Freyenhagen, "The enemy pursued . . . but upon seeing we received a cannon and reinforcements, they stopped and then retreated. We pursued them about two Engl. miles in order to collect and rescue our wounded as they had been left behind before."[46]

With sunset at 4:41 p.m., the action was over by 5:00 and Lafayette ordered a withdrawal. Some British and Hessians attempted a weak pursuit but were quickly discouraged by some of Butler's riflemen. The jaegers lost nine men killed, 21 wounded, and two missing. No British light infantrymen reported serious wounds. American losses were light, with two officers killed and five privates wounded. For the Hessians, the Gloucester skirmish was the latest in a string of embarrassments beyond Trenton and Fort Mercer. Lafayette, meanwhile, returned to the main camp around Haddonfield where Greene's force suffered in the cold. Surgeon Albigence Waldo recorded that the men "lay in the Forest of Haddonfield, cold and uncomfortable."[47]

"I take the greatest pleasure to let you know that the conduct of our soldiers is above all praises—I never saw men so merry, so spirited, so desirous to go on to the enemy," Lafayette reported to Washington the next day. The French officer

---

45 Stone & Schopp, *Gloucester*, 69-72 & 76; Moffett, ed., *Year Book for 1928*, 60. The next morning, James Murphy and Patrick McCollum went looking for Lucas's body. They found him in "a ditch and covered with some rubbish and was pretty much stripped of his clothes." Revolutionary War Pension and Bounty-Land-Warrant Application Files (M804) [RWPF], files S2768& S4660.

46 Dohla, *A Hessian Diary*, 60; Freyenhagen, Journal, 71.

47 Stone & Schopp, *Gloucester*, 74 & 81. Jaeger dead included Friedrich Schoinanus, Niclaus Koch, Caspar Weyrauch, and Adam Schelhasse; Hugh F. Rankin, ed., *Narratives of the American Revolution: As Told by a Young Sailor, a Home-Sick Surgeon, a French Volunteers, and a German General's Wife* (Chicago, 1976), 175. While Lafayette fought at Gloucester, Nathanael Greene was joined by Glover's brigade.

found the riflemen "above even their reputation and the militia above all expectations I could have. I must tell too that the riflemen had been the whole day running before my horse without eating or taking any rest." Colonel Richard Butler of Morgan's Corps also bragged about the riflemen and his role while diminishing Lafayette's guiding hand in a letter penned January 22, 1778. "I there attacked Lord Cornwallis's army and killed about 30 and brought seven prisoners off the field . . . This you may see ascribed to the Marquis De la Fayette," he added, "because he came to me when the battle was nearly over."[48]

Washington expressed the need to reward Lafayette in a letter to Henry Laurens on November 27. "He is more & more solicitous to be in actual service & is pressing in his applications for a Command," he began. "I ventured before to submit my Sentiments upon the measure, and I still fear a refusal will not only induce him to return [to France] in disgust—but may involve some unfavorable consequences." He reminded the president of Congress of his shortage of major generals and recommended Lafayette be given a division. Congress agreed and resolved on December 1, "it is highly agreeable . . . that the Marquis de la Fayette be appointed to the command of a division in the continental army." The young major general would finally lead his own division.[49]

In the wake of Lafayette's success, Nathanael Greene lined up his command for a renewed attack the next morning (November 26). Varnum's and Huntington's brigades formed the right wing with Varnum exercising command, and Muhlenberg's and Weedon's brigades formed the left wing under Muhlenberg's command. New Jersey militia covered both flanks with Morgan's riflemen reinforcing the militia on the left. Glover's brigade formed the second line.[50]

---

48 Chase & Grizzard, eds., *Papers*, vol. 12, 418-419; Moffett, ed., *Year Book for 1928*, 58-59. The fighting took place between Newton and Little Timber Creeks in modern Gloucester, New Jersey, along today's Market Street. The first shots were fired near the modern intersection of Market St. and Route 551 in Mt. Ephraim. The Americans pushed back the Hessian outposts to where Gloucester City High School sits today.

49 Chase & Grizzard, eds., *Papers*, vol. 12, 420; Worthington Chauncey Ford, ed., *Journals of the Continental Congress 1774-1789*, 34 vols. (Washington, D.C., 1907), vol. 9, 982-983.

50 Reed, *Campaign*, 359. Garry Wheeler Stone and Paul W. Schopp estimate 1,185 New Jersey militia present in the Haddonfield camp in late November. However, it is highly unlikely they accompanied Greene's push toward Gloucester. Many of these militiamen would have been watching various roads and byways. Also, several were likely unfit for combat conditions. Stone & Schopp, *Gloucester*, 54. More importantly, militia colonel Joseph Ellis reported to Greene on

The 1958 Battle of Gloucester marker. *Author*

Greene scouted Cornwallis's position but held back from pulling the trigger. After holding a council of war, he learned that his subordinates opposed the attack despite Lafayette's success. "We have a fine body of troops and in fine spirits, and every one appears to wish to come to action," explained Greene. "I proposed to the Gentlemen [his brigade commanders] drawing up in front of the enemy and to

November 24 just 400 militia at Haddonfield and another 100 along Mantua Creek, far short of Stone and Schopp's estimate. Showman, McCarthy, and Cobb, eds., *Papers of Greene*, vol. 2, 207.

attack their Picquet and endeavour to draw them out but they were all against it, from the improbability of the enemies coming out." As Greene later reported to Washington, "I am sorry our march will prove a fruitless one—the enemy have drawn themselves down upon the peninsula at Gloucester—the ships are drawn up to cover the Troops—there is but one road that leads down to the point, on each side the ground is swampy & full of thick under brush, that it makes the approaches impracticable almost." Greene also took note of the enemy warships, "being so posted as to cover the Troops and this country is so intersected with creeks, that approaches are rendered extremely difficult, and retreats very dangerous."[51]

Whitemarsh Camp

"Our Situation," replied Washington to Greene's recent letter, "as you justly observe is distressing, from a variety or irremediable causes; but more especially from the impracticability of answering the expectations of the world without running hazards which no military principles can justify, and which, in case of failure, might prove the ruin of our cause." Greene's failed efforts angered Washington, who blamed his inability to come to grips with Cornwallis and save the river fort on Gates's dilatory effort to reinforce his army. Washington admitted as much in a letter to his brother the same day: "had the reinforcement from the Northward arrived but Ten days sooner it would, I think, have put in my power to have saved Fort Mifflin . . . and consequently have rendered Phila. a very ineligible Situation for them this Winter."[52]

As earlier noted, Washington personally crossed to the south side of the Schuylkill River to reconnoiter the line of British redoubts north of Philadelphia to determine the feasibility of an attack proposed by General Cadwalader. He did so with John Laurens, who penned a letter to his father Henry, the president of Congress, on November 26: "Our Commander in chief wishing ardently to gratify the public expectation by making an attack upon the enemy—yet preferring at the same time a loss of popularity to engaging in an enterprise which he could not justify to his own conscience and the more respectable part of his constituents, went yesterday to view the works." After describing the formidable British defensive line, Laurens continued: "General du Portail declared that in such works

---

51 Showman, McCarthy, and Cobb, eds., *Papers of Greene*, vol. 2, 219; Chase & Grizzard, eds., *Papers*, vol. 12, 408.

52 Chase & Grizzard, eds., *Papers*, vol. 12, 407 & 426.

with five thousand men he [William Howe] would bid defiance to any force that should be brought against him." Despite 2,400 additional troops in the newly arrived brigades of Ebenezer Learned, Enoch Poor, and John Patterson, Washington decided against launching the attack. As Washington scouted British positions and Greene gave up thoughts of attacking Cornwallis, the British cut through the floating chain in the Delaware to open a narrow lane for shipping.[53]

British Philadelphia

On the land front in New Jersey, Cornwallis's men "burnt about one-half of a house near Gloucester belonging to one Hogg [William Hugg], a person that is reported to be an American Patriot," noted Philadelphia resident Robert Morton. The British commander pulled the last of his troops out of the state about 2:00 p.m. on November 27. About 200 men composed of New Jersey militia and Morgan's riflemen opened fire as the last boats pulled away. One of Morgan's men, Richard Butler, recorded what he witnessed in a letter dated January 22, 1778. "I then went to Gloucestertown and fell on the rear of the British Army where Cornwallis was in person with 2000 men, and beat them on board under the fire of three ships of war. This I sustained three-quarters of an hour," he explained, "with no support but Captain Lee [Light Horse Harry] and his troops of horse to cover my retreat in case we were beat."[54]

Captain John Andre, aide to British Gen. Charles Grey, added a few details to the American efforts to disrupt the operation. Morgan and some New Jersey militia, recorded Andre, "assembled in his [Cornwallis's] rear and began firing on the last Troops who embarked, but the *Vigilant*, a galley and an armed Schooner having brought their guns to bear and cross their fire upon the places where they [the Americans] were collecting, dispersed them." The British cost was "a seaman and a soldier wounded." Light infantryman Lt. Henry Stirke added to the event and the casualty list by observing "a large body of the Rebels threw themselves into a Wood, near the beech, and were very troublesome. . . . We had one officer and several men slightly wounded." A Hessian officer also described the scene, recalling how the Americans "followed us to the water where they had to withstand

---

53 Simms, *Correspondence of Laurens*, 81-82; Jackson, *Whitemarsh*, 27. Brigadier General Learned's brigade was commanded by Col. John Bailey with Learned home on sick leave. Thompson, *Whitemarsh*, 46.

54 Reed, *Campaign*, 352 & 361; Morton, "Diary," 31; Moffett, ed., *Year Book for 1928*, 59.

musket fire from the boats and a strong cannonade from HMS *Vigilant* plus a frigate [*Zebra*] and row-galley [*Cornwallis*]. The enemy withstood this with the greatest courage and resistance," he admitted, "which the troops already ferried over could see clearly from the other side." The naval commanders also recorded the affair. John Odre of the HMS *Zebra* noted "the Rebels began to fire musquetry from the Woods on which we began to fire upon them," and Lt. Edward Pakenham of the HMS *Viper* wrote the same, noting the firing began "At 2 PM." when the enemy attacked "our Rear Guard." With Cornwallis out of New Jersey, Nathanael Greene withdrew his command to Mount Holly, marched to Burlington, crossed the Delaware River, and camped at Bristol, Pennsylvania.[55]

With the river finally open, British supplies and luxury goods began flowing into the city for the first time in years (the Non-Importation Act had prevented earlier access). Elizabeth Drinker thought it was "an agreeable sight to see the Warfes lin'd with Shippin." Admiral Richard Howe docked his flagship HMS *Eagle* at a Philadelphia wharf, signifying the end of the fighting for the Delaware River. Perhaps historian William Stryker summarized the British situation best when he observed, "The expeditions and the fightings had . . . secured to the British a pleasant city for the winter of 1777-8, giving them a chance to get food from the storehouses in New York, but they had accomplished really nothing in the way of subduing the rebellion in what they considered the colonies of the British empire."[56]

---

55 Andre, *Journal*, 66; Stirke, "Journal," 175; Freyenhagen, Journal, 71; Crawford, ed., *Naval Documents*, vol. 10, 617. Cornwallis carried off 400 head of New Jersey cattle. Reed, *Campaign*, 362.

56 McGuire, *Campaign*, vol. 2, 236; Drinker, *Diary of Elizabeth Drinker*, 257; Reed, *Campaign*, 361; Stryker, *Forts on the Delaware*, 45. General Howe knew there were no reinforcements coming from Great Britain and wanted to exchange prisoners to get men back into the ranks. He proposed a mutual parole of officers, and Washington agreed. Washington reported to Congress on November 27 that he sent Elias Boudinot, Commissary of Prisoners, to "immediately take measures for releasing the [British] Officers on Parole, that we may relieve an equal number of ours." Chase & Grizzard, eds., *Papers*, vol. 12, 422. Boudinot wrote on November 24 to Joshua Loring (the British Commissary of Prisoners) "desirous t[hat] those of our Officers longest in Captivity may have their Exchange perfected . . . I am of opinion that could we meet on this Business, the whole might be easily settled on rational Terms, but at all events, I could wish all the Prisoners might be released before Winter, either on Parole or Exchanged Man for Man & Officer for Officer." Elias Boudinot, *"Their Distress is almost intolerable:" The Elias Boudinot Letterbook, 1777-1778*, Joseph Lee Boyle, ed. (Westminster, MD, 2008), 50-51. Elias Boudinot was born in 1740 and was a prominent New Jersey attorney and member of that colony's Assembly when the war began. He was appointed to his position in April 1777 by Washington. Boudinot's role was supervising prisoner of war compounds and ensuring that American prisoners of war were receiving proper treatment.

The fighting at Gloucester effectively ended the battle for control of the Delaware River. Benjamin Franklin in Paris was busy negotiating a treaty of alliance with the French when he heard the news. The shrewd diplomat downplayed the significance to the Duke of La Rochefoucauld by referring to them as "petty Forts" and "Tis a wonder they held out so long"[57]

Whitemarsh Camp

Greene was on his way back to the main army when Washington received another letter of support—this time from Henry Knox on November 26. "I believe perfectly that there are some people who speak disrespectfully of your Excellency," admitted Knox. "The Gentlemen who urge the desperate measure of attacking the enemies Line, Redoubts and city of Philadelphia Seem to Forget the many principles laid down by people experience'd in the art of war against our engaging in General actions upon equal terms—against our risquing our all on the event of single Battles."[58]

Following the end of the river operations, a natural phenomenon occurred on November 27—an Aurora Borealis. Up in Allentown, "Friday evening was the most singular Aurora Borealis I ever saw," wrote attorney James Allen. "The sky red as blood interspersed with white streaks & when the Redness grew less, it was as light as when the moon is just risen." Joseph Plumb Martin of the Connecticut Line (and everyone else who had served in the river forts) who was on his way back to Washington's army with General Greene's column remembered seeing the atmospheric light show: "At one time the whole visible heavens appeared for some time as if covered with crimson velvet. Some of the solders prognosticated a bloody battle about to be fought."[59]

---

57 William B. Willcox, ed., *The Papers of Benjamin Franklin*, 37 vols. (New Haven, CT, 1986), vol. 25 475.

58 Chase & Grizzard, eds., *Papers*, vol. 12, 415.

59 James Allen, "Diary of James Allen, Esq., of Philadelphia, Counsellor-at-Law, 1770-1778," *The Pennsylvania Magazine of History and Biography*, 148 vols. (Philadelphia, 1896), vol. 9, 428; Martin, *Private Yankee Doodle*, 99.

Conway Cabal

The fighting along the Delaware had petered out, but a new battle was brewing off the Philadelphia-area battlefield: Congress attempted to undercut Washington's authority. Earlier on November 27, the legislators once again changed the structure of the Board of War. Because of the overwhelming work, Thomas Mifflin received Congress's permission to add two members to the Board. Richard Peters and Horatio Gates got the nod. General Gates was also named president of the Board—with the power to reorganize the Continental Army. Congress reconstructed the Board without ever directly consulting Washington and tasked the new configuration with overseeing critical aspects of the commander-in-chief's war effort. "This was too large an omission to attribute to some innocent oversight," concluded historian Mark Lender, "and we can reasonably conclude Congress thought it was time for some fresh thinking on how to fight the war."[60]

The ripples from the loss of Mud Island turned into political waves that washed over Washington. Massachusetts Congressman James Lovell dashed off a letter to Horatio Gates on November 27. The New Englander desperately wanted Gates to take control of affairs. "Good God! What a Situation are we in! how different from what might have been expected!" he declared. "You will be astonished when you come to know accurately what numbers have at one time and another been collected near Philada. to wear out stockings, shoes and breeches. Depend upon it for every ten Soldiers placed under the Command of our Fabius [Washington], 5 Recruits will be wanted annually during the war." Lovell blamed the recent defeat on Washington's lack of support. "The brave fellows at Fort Mifflin & Red Bank have despaired of Succour, and been obliged to quit. The naval departments have fallen into Circumstances of seeming disgrace." Lovell was far from alone. The next day, Connecticut Congressman Eliphalet Dyer wrote to former commissary general Jonathan Trumbull and described Washington's Continentals as a "Naked Undisciplined Army."[61]

Congress went a step further by creating a Committee at Headquarters, which included Elbridge Gerry, Robert Morris, and Joseph Jones, to inquire about Washington's inactivity and Pennsylvania's concerns over location of the pending winter encampment. Congress also laid the groundwork to make it easier to hold Washington accountable for future actions by passing the following resolution:

---

60 McBurney, *George Washington's Nemesis*, 108; Lender, *Cabal!*, 116 & 118.

61 Smith, et al., eds., *Letters*, vol. 8, 329 & 334.

"That whenever any expedition which may be undertaken . . . shall fail in the execution; or whenever any important post, fort, or fortress, garrisoned and defended at the expence of the United States, shall be evacuated, or taken by the enemy, it be an established rule in Congress to institute an enquiry into the causes of the failure . . . and into the conduct of the principal officer or officers conducting the expedition so failing."[62]

When Thomas Mifflin, one of the plotters against Washington, learned that the Virginian had confronted Thomas Conway, he scribbled out a letter of warning to Gates on November 28, "An extract from General Conway's letter to you has been procured. And sent to head-quarters," cautioned Mifflin, and "General Washington enclosed it to General Conway without remarks. . . . My dear General, take care of your sincerity and frank disposition; they cannot injure yourself, but may injure some of your best friends."[63]

Whitemarsh Camp

With rumors circulating of a possible British move, Washington urged Nathanael Greene to hasten his return. Greene marched across Neshaminy Creek, through Abington, and rejoined the main army at Whitemarsh at 8:00 p.m. on November 28. "We again turned into a wood for the night," wrote Joseph Plumb Martin about the miserable night of their arrival. "The leaves and ground were as wet as water could make them. It was then foggy and the water dripping from the trees like a shower. We endeavored to get a fire by flashing powder on the leaves," he continued, "but this and every other expedient that we could employ failing, we were forced by our old master, Necessity, to lay down and sleep if we could, with three others of our constant companions, Fatigue, Hunger, and Cold."[64]

Concerns that Howe would move against the Americans persisted. "[E]very intelligence agrees that Gen. Howe now no doubt wth his whole force is immediately to take the field in quest of this army," wrote Pennsylvania militia commander John Armstrong on November 29 to Thomas Wharton (the president of Pennsylvania). Washington still harbored dreams of attacking the British in

---

62 Lender, *Caball*, 36; Ford, ed., *Journals of Congress*, vol. 9, 976.

63 Chase & Grizzard, eds., *Papers*, vol. 12, 131.

64 Reed, *Campaign*, 361; Martin, *Private Yankee Doodle*, 98. Washington used the slight lull in the fighting to reorganize part of his army. On November 28, the Pennsylvania State Regiment became the 13th Pennsylvania Regiment.

Philadelphia and continued to send patrols out to probe the enemy front.[65] Washington confidant Joseph Reed wrote to Thomas Wharton on November 30 with one of the best descriptions of Howe's defensive network in front of Philadelphia:

> upon reconnoitering their works from the west side of the Schuylkill, they appeared so exceedingly strong as to damp the ardour of the most enterprising. They have constructed a chain of redoubts on the most commanding ground, extending from the Schuylkill to the Delaware . . . they are framed, planked, and of great thickness, surrounded with a deep ditch and freized. The intervals are filled with an abattis composed of all the apple trees in the neighbourhood, and many large trees . . . though I for one was very much for some vigorous measure, it appeared on view too hazardous. If there was an opportunity of forcing them out of the city, I fear it is gone, and that we must lay our account with their wintering there.[66]

British Philadelphia

Even with the control of the river, the British supply situation remained acute. Howe's Commissary General of Stores & Provisions, Daniel Wier, penned a summary of the situation for officials in London. "The whole Country around us is possessed by the Enemy," he began, and Howe's command in the city "can expect no supplies or Assistance from this Country but must place our whole Dependence on what we receive from the other side of the Water. It is with the greatest Difficulty & at the Hazard of Mens Lives that we are even able to obtain fresh provisions sufficient for our Hospitals as we cannot with Safety go an hundred Yards beyond our Lines without a large Escort." Captain Thomas Stanley of the 17th Light Dragoons hinted at Howe's motives for the approaching Whitemarsh operations when he penned a friend on November 28, "we are now surrounded but [hope] in a few Days we shall clear the country about us, so as to be [able to enter] our Winter quarters."[67]

---

65   Hazard, ed., *Pennsylvania Archives*, Series 1, vol. 6, 43.

66   Reed, *Life of Reed*, 341.

67   Daniel Wier to John Robinson, November 29, 1777, "Copies of Letters from Danl. Wier, Esq., Commissary to the Army in America, to J. Robinson, Esq., Secretary to the Lords Commissioners of the Treasury; and from John Robinson, Esq., in Answer thereto in the Year 1777," Ferdinand J. Dreer Collection, Historical Society of Pennsylvania, Philadelphia, PA, Vol. 60; Letter, Thomas Stanley to "dearest friend," Nov. 28, 1777.

While Howe consolidated his gains and took stock of his perilous situation, he penned a letter to Lord George Germain, Secretary of State for the Colonies, on November 30. Howe had already submitted his resignation and had received confirmation of Burgoyne's surrender. "I candidly declare my opinion, that in the apparent temper of the Americans a considerable addition to the present force will be requisite for effecting any essential change in their disposition, and the re-establishment of the King's authority," he bluntly asserted, before offering the more shocking statement, "and that this army, acting on the defensive, will be fully employed to maintain its present position." Any uncertainty in England about Howe's true situation vanished upon receipt of his letter. At least one officer believed Howe could blame no one but himself. Lieutenant Colonel William Harcourt of the 16th Light Dragoons wrote his brother on November 29 that Burgoyne's surrender "was unavoidable from the moment we sailed from New York." In other words, the decision to do so was Howe's, and Burgoyne's ultimate defeat rested on Howe's shoulders.[68]

Rumors of Washington's potential political demise filtered into the British camp. On December 1, Hessian staff officer Carl von Baurmeister noted in a letter, "All the deserters tell us that he [Washington] has fallen out with Congress and that General Gates is now esteemed much more." That same day, General Howe appointed prominent loyalist Joseph Galloway as superintendent general of Philadelphia. Galloway had helped supply Howe with guides throughout the campaign, especially at Brandywine. The general wanted to present the appearance of civilian authority in the city, but Galloway was nothing more than a figurehead. Since moving the army from Germantown into Philadelphia, Howe authorized the recruitment of loyalist regiments to patrol the area between the British defensive lines and the American positions at Whitemarsh. Alfred Clifton recruited for a regiment of Roman Catholics. William Allen did so for a battalion of Pennsylvania Loyalists, and James Chalmers did likewise for Maryland loyalists. Richard Hovenden raised a troop of Philadelphia Light Dragoons. Efforts to fill the ranks of these units, however, proved less than successful.[69]

---

68 *Report on Stopford*, 81; Harcourt, ed., *Papers*, 225.

69 Von Baurmeister, *Revolution in America*, 129; Jackson, *British Army*, 98-101. Howe appeared to be settling in for the winter. Admiral Richard Howe assigned Capt. Andrew Hamond command of the flotilla that would remain in the Delaware to support his brother's army when the admiral returned to New York. Hamond was in command of *Roebuck* and the *Experiment* and given others that had been at one point under his command, including the frigates *Liverpool, Pearl, Camilla, Vigilant*, and sloop *Zebra*. The galley *Cornwallis*, ex-Continental frigate *Delaware*, armed schooner *Viper*, store ship

Whitemarsh Camp

Rumors of a British advance continued to trickle into Washington's camp on December 2. Captain Charles Craig of the 4th Continental Light Dragoons reported to Washington that "the enemy intend to make a push out—and endeavor to drive your Excellency from the present encampment." One of Washington's spies, Maj. John Clark, reported the British "hold themselves in readiness when call'd for . . . and 'twas the current language in the City among the Troops, & Citizens that they were going to make a move." Pennsylvania militia commander John Armstrong had reported on November 29 to Thomas Wharton that "every intelligence agrees that Gen. Howe now no doubt with his whole force is immediately to take the field in quest of this army." Rumors were also circulating in the streets of Philadelphia. "There is talk to day, as if a great part of the English army, were making ready to depart, on some secret expedition," jotted Elizabeth Drinker in her diary on December 1.[70]

On December 3, a delegation from Congress arrived to observe the army. Rumblings continued about Washington's fitness for command, but bigger issues loomed for the Virginia general. He wanted nothing more than for Howe to launch his men against his strong position at Whitemarsh. A stout defensive win might quell the rumblings against him. His army had to be prepared for every contingency, so general orders were issued on December 2 that read: "Whether the alarm is given or not, the whole army is to be under arms at their respective alarm posts at day light to morrow morning, and the lines properly formed by the Major General[s]."[71]

Pressure from the Congressional delegation mounted, forcing Washington to poll his generals about undertaking a winter offensive. Nathanael Greene scoffed at the idea. "However desirable the destruction of General Howe's army may be and however impatient the public may be for this desirable event," he wisely replied on

---

Adventure, and various armed tenders brought the number of pendants (or commissioned vessels) to 25. There were also three divisions of transports and all the flatboats, the repair of which Hamond was to make an object of his 'particular care.' Moomaw, "Career of Hamond," 374.

70 Chase & Grizzard, eds., *Papers*, vol. 12, 495 & 512; Hazard, ed., *Pennsylvania Archives*, Series 1, vol. 6, 43; Drinker, *Diary of Elizabeth Drinker*, 260.

71 Chase & Grizzard, eds., *Papers*, vol. 12, 494.

December 3, "I cannot recommend the measure. . . . We must not be governed in our measures by our Wishes."[72]

With Greene's return from New Jersey and the addition of several brigades from the northern army, Washington had no choice but to reorganize his ranks. Greene was put in command of the left wing of the army running along Camp Hill. John Sullivan commanded the right wing stretching across Fort and Militia Hills. Off the left flank stood the Maryland militia and Daniel Morgan's riflemen, and on the right flank the Pennsylvania militia. Lord Stirling commanded the reserve in a second line.

The army went to sleep on the night of December 3 knowing that the morrow would prove whether the rumors of a British movement were true, and if the newly reinforced Continental Army was ready to meet them.

72 Showman, McCarthy, and Cobb, eds., *Papers of Greene*, vol. 2, 231.

Chapter 9

The Whitemarsh Operation: Chestnut Hill

December 4-6, 1777

"Before our arrival they had increased their fires, lighting many large ones in straight and deep lines, so that it looked as if fifty thousand men were encamped there."[1]

— Maj. Carl von Baurmeister, December 16, 1777

State of the Armies

Even without a major engagement, the two months following the battle of Germantown on October 4, 1777, were momentous. Portions of the Continental and British armies engaged in a deadly minuet of maneuver, parry, and thrust at Fort Mercer, Fort Mifflin, Gloucester, and up and down the Delaware River. Everything was at stake. Both armies received new troops and instituted leadership and organizational realignments.

In early October, Washington led more than 17,000 troops at Germantown arranged in a dozen Continental infantry brigades, light dragoons, and artillery supported by four militia brigades. He had arranged his army in two attack wings, each containing five Continental brigades. The militia formed on either flank of the

---

1 Von Baurmeister, *Revolution in America*, 135-136.

Continental Line, and a general reserve of two Continental brigades supported the army.[2]

Much had changed since then. Four of Washington's generals had faced court martials; one of them, Adam Stephen, was removed from the army. An influx of generals arrived from the north after Horatio Gates's victory at Saratoga, bringing with them five Continental brigades, several independent regiments, and Col. Daniel Morgan's rifle corps. A brigade of New Jersey militia under David Forman had fought at Germantown but returned to serve in their home state during the Delaware River fighting. They never returned to Pennsylvania and the main army. Other militia, Col. William Rumney's command from Virginia, joined the main army after Germantown, essentially replacing the Jersey men. By December 3, Washington had assembled more than 24,000 troops on the Whitemarsh hills.[3]

Just three months earlier, Washington had led his inexperienced army into battle at Brandywine, Paoli, and Germantown. Each action provided the experience needed to hone the men into veterans. Four of the five brigades arriving from the northern army gained similar experience during the Saratoga campaign. Only Brig. Gen. Jedidiah Huntington's Connecticut brigade lacked combat experience. Although militia was typically unreliable, Pennsylvanians and Marylanders of that variety had served with Washington at all three of the prior battles. Only the Virginia militia lacked experience.

The new brigades from Gates's army needed to be incorporated into the main army. Washington essentially maintained divisions comprised of two or three brigades, which he had used since the spring, and organized them into two wings (each of two or three divisions) plus a general reserve—much as he had for the attack at Germantown. He established his front line, divided into wings, on a long and formidable ridge running east from Bethlehem Pike to Susquehanna Road.[4]

The left wing of the army was given to Nathanael Greene. The 35-year-old Rhode Islander provided effective service at Trenton, Brandywine, Germantown, and southern New Jersey, and had become one of Washington's close confidants.

Greene directed nearly 8,000 troops divided into two divisions and miscellaneous units. His own division, under Brig. Gen. Peter Muhlenberg,

---

2 Michael C. Harris & Gary Ecelbarger, "The Numerical Strength of George Washington's Army During the 1777 Philadelphia Campaign," *Journal of the American Revolution,* (Westholme Publishing LLC, 2022), 110-111.

3 Harris & Ecelbarger, "Numerical Strength," 111.

4 This ridge runs roughly parallel to the Pennsylvania Turnpike today.

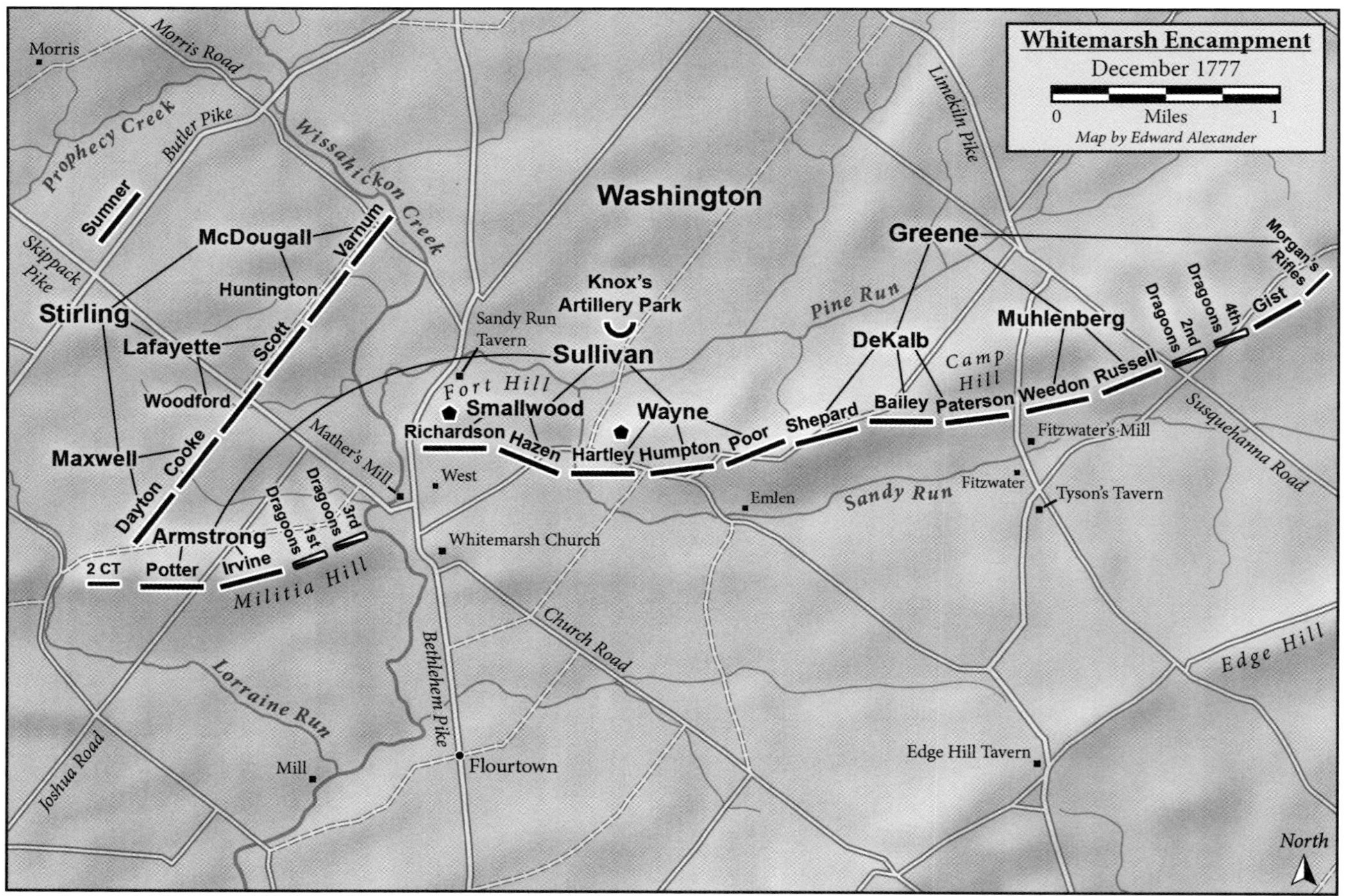

Whitemarsh Encampment
December 1777
0   Miles   1
Map by Edward Alexander
Morris
Morris Road
Prophecy Creek
Butler Pike
Wissahickon Creek
Limekiln Pike
Washington
Greene
Morgan's Rifles
Sumner
Skippack Pike
McDougall
Varnum
Knox's Artillery Park
Pine Run
Gist
Dragoons
4th
2nd
Dragoons
Stirling
Huntington
Scott
Sandy Run Tavern
Sullivan
DeKalb
Muhlenberg
Lafayette
Camp Hill
Woodford
Fort Hill
Smallwood
Wayne
Shepard
Bailey Paterson Weedon Russell
Maxwell
Dayton Cooke
Richardson Hazen
Hartley Humpton Poor
Fitzwater's Mill
Susquehanna Road
Mather's Mill
West
Emlen
Sandy Run
Fitzwater
Tyson's Tavern
Armstrong
Dragoons
3rd
1st
Dragoons
2 CT
Potter
Irvine
Militia Hill
Whitemarsh Church
Lorraine Run
Bethlehem Pike
Church Road
Edge Hill
Joshua Road
Mill
Flourtown
Edge Hill Tavern
North

consisted of two brigades, Muhlenberg's 1st Virginia Brigade under Col. William Russell and the 2nd Virginia Brigade under Brig. Gen. George Weedon. Greene's second division, under Maj. Gen. Johann DeKalb, boasted three Massachusetts brigades—the 2nd, 3rd, and 4th. Two of them (the 2nd and 4th) lacked their veteran commanders (John Glover remained in the northern theater overseeing the Saratoga prisoners, and Ebenezer Learned went home on sick leave following the fighting there). The three brigades were now led by Brig. Gen. John Paterson, Col William Shepard, and Col. John Bailey. His troops unattached to a specific division included Daniel Morgan's Rifle Corps and the Maryland Militia under Col. Mordecai Gist. Washington positioned Greene's wing on the army's left, his brigades aligned (left to right): Russell, Weedon, Paterson, Bailey, and Shepard. Two regiments of Continental light dragoons (the 2nd and the 4th led by, respectively, Cols. Elisha Sheldon and Stephen Moylan) and the Maryland militia extended the line leftward, with Morgan's Rifle Corps holding the far left flank of the army, all likely north of Susquehanna Road.[5]

John Sullivan commanded the other wing of the army. Despite criticism after Brandywine and a court martial hearing, Sullivan retained Washington's confidence. His nearly 7,000 men comprised two divisions totaling five brigades deployed to the right of Greene's command on the same ridge line. Brig. Gen William Smallwood served with the Maryland militia through the Battle of Germantown, and his return to Sullivan's division made him the senior officer and commander in charge of the division once Sullivan was elevated to exercise wing command. With Smallwood's return, Col. Moses Hazen returned to brigade command and Col. William Richardson commanded Smallwood's own brigade. The brigades consisted of the army's Maryland Continentals as well as the Delaware Regiment and the 2nd Canadian Regiment. Despite the cloud of Paoli, Sullivan's other three-brigade division was led by Brig. Gen. Anthony Wayne. Wayne's two Pennsylvania brigades continued to be led by colonels Thomas Hartley and Richard Humpton. Wayne's third brigade of New Hampshire and

---

5 Russell became colonel of the 13th Virginia Regiment in December 1776. Weedon was a native Virginian, a veteran of the French and Indian War, and an innkeeper in Fredericksburg before the war. The German Regiment (with men from Maryland and Pennsylvania) served with the 1st Virginia brigade, and the 13th Pennsylvania Regiment with the 2nd Virginia Brigade. Col. Mordecai Gist was put in command of the Maryland militia when William Smallwood returned to the Maryland Continentals. Born in 1743, Gist was a tradesman when the war erupted. After organizing an independent company, he became major of Smallwood's regiment in 1776. After service on Long Island and White Plains, Gist was made colonel of the 3rd Maryland and was detached with Smallwood to help raise the Maryland militia. He had minor roles at Paoli and Germantown.

New York Continentals was under Brig. Gen. Enoch Poor, who arrived from Gates's army prior to being attached to Wayne's command. Sullivan's wing was on the right side of the army line, his brigades aligned (left to right): Poor, Humpton, Hartley, Hazen, and Richardson.[6]

The Pennsylvania militia, the 2nd Connecticut Regiment and the army's other two light dragoon regiments (the 1st and the 3rd under Cols. Theodorick Bland and George Baylor) were positioned on their own hill manning the army's right flank south of Bethlehem Pike. Major General John Armstrong's Pennsylvania militia remained divided into two brigades commanded by Brig. Gens. James Potter and James Irvine. Washington detached Col. Charles Webb's Connecticut regiment from its brigade to help bolster his often-unreliable militia.

Lord Stirling commanded Washington's general reserve at Germantown and remained in that role at Whitemarsh. Stirling's nearly 9,000 men consisted of six brigades in three divisions positioned in the low ground behind the hills on the right side of the line. With Stirling commanding the reserve, Brig. Gen. William Maxwell was elevated to lead Stirling's former division. Despite losing an independent command earlier in the campaign and facing a court martial for his actions, Maxwell remained a senior brigadier general in the army. Colonel Elias Dayton commanded Maxwell's New Jersey brigade as he had at Brandywine. When Congress appointed Thomas Conway major general and inspector general of the army, his Pennsylvania brigade fell to its senior colonel, William Cooke. Adam Stephen's court martial and removal from the army left a vacancy for the Marquis de Lafayette to command the two Virginia brigades. Lafayette was officially elevated to the position on December 4 after Washington wrote to Congress about army vacancies about a week earlier. "There are now some vacant Divisions in the Army, to one of which he may be appointed, if it should be the pleasure of Congress," he suggested on November 26. "I am convinced he [Lafayette] possesses a large share of that Military ardor which generally characterizes the Nobility of his Country." Lafayette's two brigades were led by Brig. Gens. William Woodford and Charles Scott. The Virginia militia was attached to Scott's brigade.

---

6 Massachusetts native Mose Hazen was a seasoned combat veteran by the time his regiment deployed outside Philadelphia. He fought in the French and Indian War as the commander of a company in Roger's Rangers before settling in Canada. From 1761 to 1763, Hazen served as a lieutenant in the British 44th Regiment of Foot. He was a prominent Canadian landowner when the Revolution began. Hazen joined Richard Montgomery's advance into Canada in 1775, and was commissioned a colonel in January 1776, to raise a regiment of Canadians. A lack of qualified generals elevated Hazen to command Sullivan's division at Germantown. The 44 year-old Humpton was a native of Yorkshire, England, and had served as a captain in the British Army.

Stirling's third division under Maj. Gen. Alexander McDougall was comprised of Brig. Gen. James Varnum's Rhode Island and Connecticut brigade and Brig. Gen. Jedidiah Huntington's inexperienced Connecticut brigade. Stirling's brigades were aligned left to right as follows: Varnum, Huntington, Scott, Woodford, Cooke, Dayton.[7]

Washington placed a third line behind Stirling under Col. Jethro Sumner consisting of Sumner's own brigade of North Carolina Continentals and five unattached Continental regiments, about 2,200 all told. Henry Knox oversaw the emplacement of Continental artillery along the entire line. A December 22 strength return for the artillery lists 47 guns, but does not include two companies detached from the army after the Whitemarsh operations. Washington's army likely included around 50 artillery pieces as follows: eight 3-pounders, seven 4-pounders, 24 6-pounders, two 12-pounders, five 5 ½-inch howitzers, and one 8-inch howitzer.[8]

The army gathered on the Whitemarsh ridges and hills in early December 1777 was the most seasoned Washington had led to date, and the largest he would command during the war. The experience gained thus far in the Philadelphia campaign and in New York at Saratoga provided all the hard lessons of war these men required to stay in the field and confront Howe's veteran command. Whether they could withstand a bayonet attack remained an open question.

*   *   *

William Howe's army experienced little in the way of change during this same period. The casualties suffered at Germantown, Fort Mercer, and other minor engagements were more than made up by reinforcements from New York. By early December, Howe fielded approximately 19,000 troops, ably supported by veteran Lt. Gens. Charles Cornwallis and Wilhelm von Knyphausen.[9]

---

7 Stirling's command was positioned about where Sheaff Lane is today. Chase & Grizzard, eds., *Papers*, vol. 12, 420-421, 534. For all these alignments of Washington's brigades, see Chase & Grizzard, eds., *Papers*, vol. 12, 535.

8 Sumner's command was located where Butler Pike is today. December 2, 1777, artillery strength report, Timothy Pickering Papers, Massachusetts Historical Society, Boston, Massachusetts.

9 December 13, 1777, provision return, "Copies of Letters from Danl. Wier, Esq., Commissary to the Army in America, to J. Robinson, Esq., Secretary to the Lords Commissioners of the Treasury; and from John Robinson, Esq., in Answer thereto in the Year 1777," Ferdinand J. Dreer Collection, Historical Society of Pennsylvania, Philadelphia, PA, Vol. 60.

The backbone of Howe's army remained its five brigades of British and two brigades of German infantry. Major General James Grant still commanded the First and Second British Brigades and Maj. Gen. Charles Grey the Third Brigade. With James Agnew's death at Germantown, Grey found himself overseeing the Fourth Brigade as well as his own. Brigadier General Alexander Leslie arrived from New York in mid-November with his Fifth Brigade. Major General Johann von Stirn remained at the head of the Hessian Brigade, and Col. Friedrich von Salzburg led the newly arrived Ansbach-Beyreuth Brigade from New York.[10]

Several elite British units remained to spearhead Howe's operations, including The British Brigade of Guards (Brig. Gen. Edward Mathew), the British Grenadier Brigade (Lt. Col. Henry Monckton), the British Light Infantry Brigade (Lt. Col Robert Abercrombie), and the Hessian Grenadier Brigade. Who was in command of the Hessian grenadiers after Carl von Donop's death at Fort Mercer remains unclear. Lieutenant Colonel Ludwig von Wurmb's elite Hessian jaegers also supported Howe's operations.[11]

Howe's Philadelphia-based command included other unattached units, including the large 71st Highlanders. The 16th Light Dragoons remained and were joined by the 17th Light Dragoons from New York. Several Loyalist units assisted Howe including the Queen's Rangers, 2nd Battalion of New Jersey Volunteers, Guides and Pioneers, Roman Catholic Volunteers, Maryland Loyalists, and Pennsylvania Loyalists. Finally, several batteries of Royal Artillery bolstered the army.[12]

---

10 Johann von Stirn was born in Borken in October 1712 and entered Hessian service in 1728. He rose through the ranks of the Regiment Prinz Friedrich and was a major by 1757. By the time the Revolution began he was colonel of the Leib Regiment Infanterie and led a brigade in the Hessian army.

11 Edward Mathew was born in 1729 and became an ensign in the Coldstream Guards in 1746. By 1775 he was a colonel and aide-de-camp to King George III. He was made commander of the Brigade of Guards when the Revolution erupted and fought throughout the 1776 campaign in New York.

12 The 16th and 17th Light Dragoons were designed to be highly mobile and heavily armed, with every trooper carrying two pistols, a short-barreled carbine, and a long cavalry sword. Fischer, *Crossing*, 36. Howe's army included: ten 3-pounders, 24 6-pounders, two medium 12-pounders, four light 12-pounders, and two 5 ½" Howitzers. British Artillery Return, December 1, 1777, James Pattison Papers, microfilm 47, reel 1, American Philosophical Society, Philadelphia, PA. The number and type of Hessian artillery pieces attached to the army remains unclear.

A Warning by Lydia Darragh?

Howe was itching for a fight. Washington wanted him to attack. It was at this point in the colonial drama that a woman named Lydia Darragh enters the story. Nearly every source covering the Whitemarsh operation includes the story of how she warned Washington that the British army soon would advance against him.

The tale originates from an 1827 article by Robert Welsh in *American Quarterly Review*. As the story goes, Howe located his headquarters in the home of American militia officer John Cadwalader's home on Second Street in Philadelphia. Lydia Darragh and her family lived across the street. According to Welsh, a "superior officer of the British army, believed to be the Adjutant General, fixed upon one of their [the Darragh's] chambers, a back room, for private conference; and . . . frequently met there . . . in close consultation." On December 2, 1777, the adjutant general informed Lydia that he needed to hold a meeting in the back room at 7:00 p.m. He "wished the family to retire early to bed." Lydia did as instructed but her curiosity got the better of her and she "put her ear to the key-hole of the conclave. She overheard an order read for all the British troops to march out, late in the evening of the fourth, and attack General Washington's army, then encamped at White Marsh." She scrambled back to bed and soon thereafter the British officers soon knocked on her door, "but she rose only at the third summons, having feigned to be asleep." After asking her to lock up, the officers left.[13]

"Supposing it to be in her power to save the lives of thousands of her countrymen," Lydia decided to get the news to Washington. When she told General Howe she needed to find flour, he "readily granted" a pass through the lines. She left her empty flour bag at a mill in Frankford and hastened west toward the Americans. Along the way, Welsh claims she ran into Lt. Col. Thomas Craig, who recognized Lydia. When she announced she sought her son, an officer in the army, he began walking with her. "To him she disclosed her momentous secret, after having obtained from him the most solemn promise never to betray her individually, since her life might be at stake." Unable to go further, Craig left Lydia in a nearby house and sped off for Washington's headquarters to share the news.[14]

"Washington made, of course, all preparation for baffling the meditated surprise," continued the story. Lydia, meanwhile, picked up her flour in Frankford and returned home. She listened as the British marched out of Philadelphia on

13 *American Quarterly Review* (No. 1), March 1827, 32-33.

14 Ibid., 33.

December 4 and witnessed their return a few days later. "The next evening, the Adjutant General came in, and requested her to walk up to his room, as he wished to put some questions." Lydia was sure that "she was either suspected, or had been betrayed." The British officer informed Lydia, "I know you were asleep, for I knocked at your chamber door three times before you heard me—I am entirely at a loss to imagine who gave General Washington information of our intended attack, unless the walls of the house could speak." This, then, insisted Welsh, "is the substance of Lydia's narrative, heard from her mouth by several most respectable persons of our acquaintance, and implicitly believed by all of them, who knew her character and situation." The loss of many Americans and "even more disastrous consequences, were, in all likelihood, averted by her courageous stratagem."[15]

Many reputable historians over the ensuing decades questioned the accuracy of Lydia's incredible account, for all the obvious reasons. And then, in 1890, came the publication of Elias Boudinot's memoir. Boudinot was Washington's commissary general of prisoners and as such, may have had direct access to Army headquarters. According to his account, Boudinot managed Washington's intelligence operation and scouted between the lines in early December. He recalled dining at the Rising Sun Tavern three miles from the city when "a little poor looking insignificant Old Woman came in." According to him, she begged for permission to go into the country to buy flour, "curiously" obtained from General Howe, and had purportedly left her empty bag in Frankford prior to seeking access to Washington. In the original 1827 account, Lydia contacts Craig, and never makes contact with anyone at Washington's headquarters. Boudinot, however, adds tantalizing details. "She walked up to me and put into my hands a dirty old needlebook, with various small pockets in it." After the woman left, Boudinot dug through the needlebook and "found a piece of Paper rolled up into the form of a Pipe Shank.—on unrolling it I found information that Genl Howe was coming out the next morning with 5000 Men—13 pieces of Cannon—Baggage Waggons, and 11 Boats on Waggon Wheels." Boudinot dashed off to headquarters to warn Washington.[16]

Versions of the 1827 Darragh story mixed with statements from Boudinot's 1890 memoir have been repeated ever since. Most modern sources make the natural leap that the "Old Woman" Boudinot met was Lydia Darragh. More careful narratives acknowledge the 1827 version that the woman Boudinot met was more

---

15 *American Quarterly Review*, 33-34.

16 Elias Boudinot, *Journal or Historical Recollections of American Events During the Revolutionary War* (Trenton, NJ, 1890), 50.

likely someone Lydia sent from the house where she stopped after meeting Craig. Other sources add that Lt. William Barrington, supposedly one of Lydia's cousins and member of the 7th Royal Fusiliers, approached Lydia to use her home for the meetings she overheard. Sources demonstrate this was impossible.[17]

Lieutenant William Barrington was captured in Rhode Island on July 14, 1777, along with Maj. Gen. Richard Prescott. Just before his capture or during captivity, he obtained a captaincy with the 70th Regiment of Foot. He was either released or paroled in December 1777 and returned to Rhode Island on the 21st. It was impossible for Barrington to have been in Philadelphia in early December 1777.[18]

Lydia was born in Ireland in 1728, married in 1753, and emigrated to America. According to historian Melissa Bohrer, "Lydia had broken with her Quaker mandate to stand apart from the war. She had divorced herself from the Quaker ethos of neutrality, actively deciding to become a participant." Her son Charles ignored his Quaker faith and was serving as a lieutenant with the 2nd Pennsylvania Regiment with Washington's army. Lydia died in 1789, 38 years before Robert Welsh's article on her was published. Edward Lengel concluded, "Lydia herself never left a scrap of writing in support of the claim, which seemed to rest upon nothing more than family tradition—the same anonymous 'experts' and distant relations who certified most other legends of this sort."[19]

A deeper look into Elias Boudinot's history also sheds light on the veracity of the story. As it turns out, Boudinot did not play any role in Washington's intelligence operations in 1777, though he did busily negotiate with William Howe

17 Nagy, *Spies in the Capital*, 48. "The story of Lydia Darragh was recounted later by her daughter Ann," wrote historian John Reed in 1965. "Since Lydia Darragh, herself, never publicly related the tale, Ann Darragh may have consciously or unconsciously embellished it; there are some unexplained discrepancies in the narrative that have caused certain historians to doubt its veracity. It would appear, however, that the main facts are essentially true, since Elias Boudinot corroborated several of them." Reed left his measured approach by spinning the entire tale into his campaign narrative. Reed, *Campaign*, 373. David Martin repeated Reed's statements in his 1993 campaign study. Martin, *Campaign*, 158-159. Thomas McGuire handled the account thusly: "It seems that through the eavesdropping of a seamstress, Mrs. Lydia Darragh, word got out of the city to give Washington notice." McGuire, *Campaign*, vol. 2, 240.

18 Barrington's background is unclear, so connectiing his Irish lineage to Lydia Darragh is difficult. Steven M. Baule & Stephen Gilbert, *British Army Officers Who Served in the American Revolution, 1775-1783* (Heritage Books, 2004), 10; Christian M. McBurney, *Kidnapping the Enemy: The Special Operations to Capture Generals Charles Lee & Richard Prescott* (Yardley, PA, 2014), 162. Historian Don Hagist provided many of the Barrington details.

19 Melissa Lukeman Bohrer, *Glory, Passion, and Principle: The Story of Eight Remarkable Women at the Core of the American Revolution* (New York, 2003), 129. Edward G. Lengel, *Inventing George Washington: America's Founder, in Myth & Memory* (New York, 2011), 126-127.

for better conditions for American prisoners. Boudinot was briefly involved in intelligence gathering—but in 1779, not 1777. Three letters written by Boudinot have been found dating from early December, one on the 1st and two on the 4th from "camp," implying he wrote them at the army's camp at Whitemarsh and not while scouting between the lines. Additionally, he penned two accounts of the fighting at Whitemarsh in letters dated December 9 and 14. Neither mentions any intelligence gathering or supposed role in warning Washington, which would have been something worthy of bragging about in a letter.[20]

Welsh's 1827 tale about Lydia Darragh, passed down through generations, appeared in the aftermath of the Marquis de Lafayette's famous visit to Philadelphia in 1824. An untold number of stories emerged in the 1820s of people claiming roles for themselves or relatives in pivotal moments of the Revolution. Later writers claimed knowledge of Lydia's tale from her or from her great-granddaughter. Writers spanning two centuries have claimed Boudinot's memoir verifies the Darragh story, but historian Lengel disagrees: "Boudinot, whose rambling and self-serving account of the war always placed him in the heat of the action, with critical responsibilities, gave a very different version of the period."[21]

In the end, it was irrelevant whether Lydia's story was true. Contemporary accounts from different members of Washington's army who were involved in scouting operations or intelligence gathering confirm the American commander was alerted to a potential British move prior to December 3.[22]

December 4

For most of Washington's men on the Whitemarsh line, December 4 passed quietly. That was not true for Virginian Andrew Harwell and his direct comrades, who recalled later in life, "[W]hilst there the scouts had frequent skirmishes with the enemy and provisions were uncommonly scarce, and we had very hard times." But for most in the Continental camp, that Thursday passed uneventfully. "We have Remained in peas and quietness and nothing Extraorny has happened," Fort Mercer veteran Col. Israel Angell of the 2nd Rhode Island jotted in his diary.

---

20 Lengel, *Inventing Washington*, 127; Boudinot, *Letterbook*, 52-57; Reed, *Correspondence of Reed*, 351.

21 Lengel, *Inventing Washington*, 127.

22 John Laurens wrote his father on December 3: "We have received several accounts from outposts within a few days intimating that an attack upon us was meditated." Simms, *Correspondence of Laurens*, 90.

Washington harbored hopes he could find a way to successfully attack the British, but Brig. Gen. Anthony Wayne did his best to dissuade him. "I am not for a Winter's Campaign in the Open field," insisted the veteran general, "the Distressed and Naked Situation of your Troops will not admit of it."[23]

American patrols continued to operate along the roads between Whitemarsh and the British redoubts north of Philadelphia. Washington had established picket posts in the valley below the Whitemarsh hills and several closer to the British lines. Captain Charles Craig and a dragoon detachment watched the Frankford Road running north from Philadelphia where it crossed Frankford Creek. Another commanded by Capt. Allen McLane kept an eye on the intersection of Old York Road and the Germantown Road where the Rising Sun Tavern stood.[24]

These posts contributed to the flood of intelligence pouring into headquarters for days. Washington provided Maj. John Clark with "an unlimited command and power to act as I pleased." With that authority, Clark "soon discovered the whole of the enemies design and communicated it to Gen. Washington with so much exactness that he made the formidable disposition at White Marsh." Writing from Frankford north of Philadelphia, William Dewees informed Washington, "I Have Just Recd Information which I Believe to be the Best Can be Obtaind that the British Army has Last Night Packd up all their Baggage & each Man four Days Provision Coock'd; their Horses hitchd to their Artillery & every Appearance of marching out Immediately." Dewees confidently informed the Virginian, "it is Expected they are Determined to Attack you where you Now Are . . . for Beyound all Doubt they are Determind to Attack at all Events."[25]

Washington, in turn, informed Congress on December 10 that "from a variety of intelligence I had reason to expect that Genl Howe was preparing to give us a general Action." Word soon spread through the army. "His excellency had previous Intelligence of his move & designs," wrote Brig. Gen. George Weedon on

23 Revolutionary War Pension and Bounty-Land-Warrant Application Files (M804) [RWPF], file S31104; Angell, *Diary*, n.p.; Anthony Wayne to George Washington, December 4, 1777, Anthony Wayne Papers, Historical Society of Pennsylvania, Philadelphia, PA, vol. 4.

24 Today, this is Frankfort Avenue. Craig's picket post was about five miles from the British redoubts. Craig was wounded at Brandywine but rejoined the army as part of Washington's intelligence operation. McLane's picket post was more than three miles west of the Frankford Road picket post and three miles from the British redoubts.

25 John Clark, "Memoir of Major John Clark, of York County, Pennsylvania," *The Pennsylvania Magazine of History and Biography*, 148 vols. (Philadelphia, 1896), vol. 20, 78; Chase & Grizzard, eds., *Papers*, vol. 12, 538. Dewees was an ironmaster and part owner of the Valley Forge. He was operating with either the militia or as part of Washington's intelligence operation.

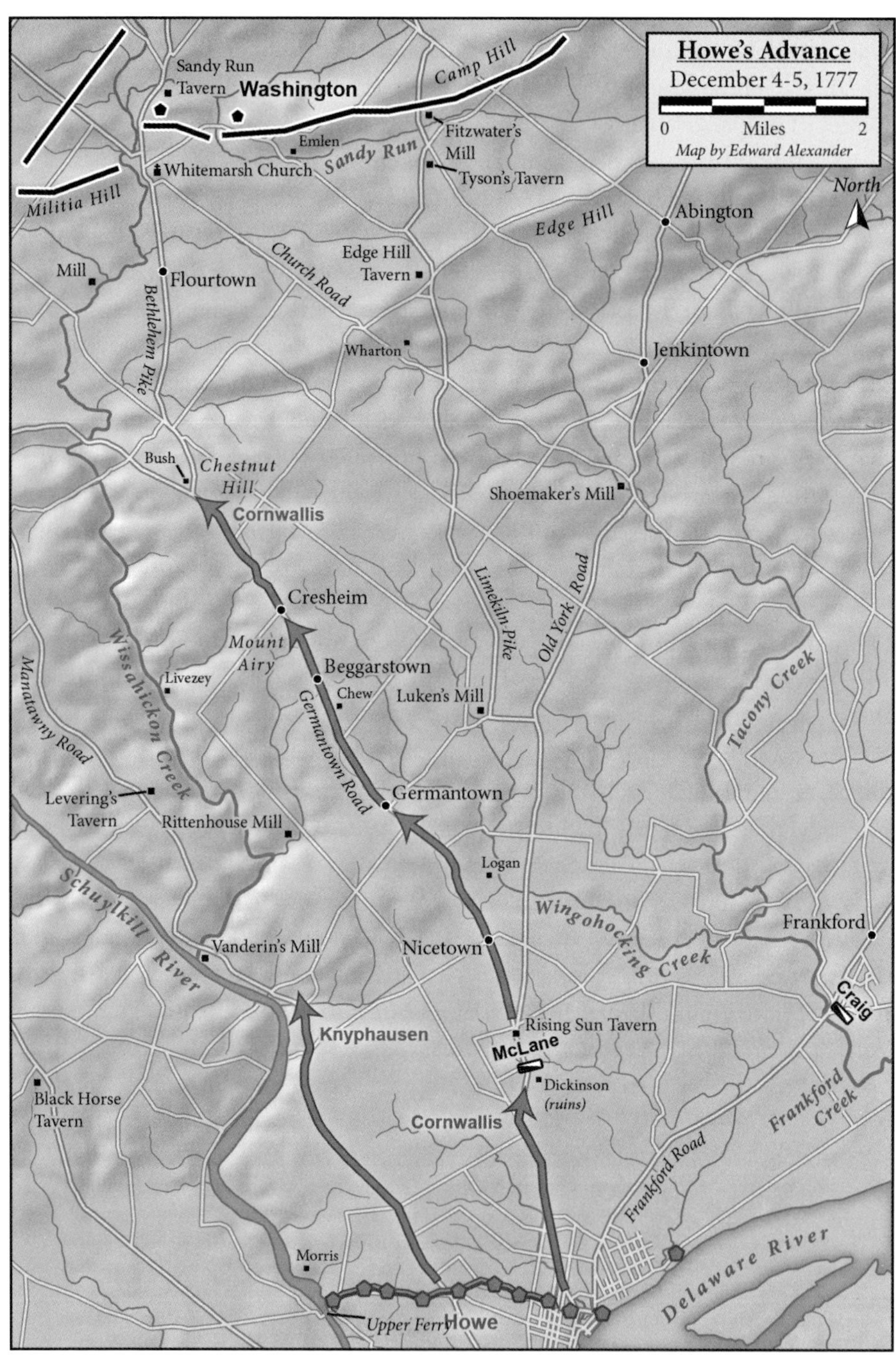

Howe's Advance
December 4-5, 1777
0   Miles   2
Map by Edward Alexander
North

Sandy Run Tavern
Washington
Camp Hill
Emlen
Sandy Run
Fitzwater's Mill
Whitemarsh Church
Tyson's Tavern
Militia Hill
Edge Hill
Abington
Mill
Flourtown
Church Road
Edge Hill Tavern
Bethlehem Pike
Wharton
Jenkintown
Bush
Chestnut Hill
Cornwallis
Shoemaker's Mill
Cresheim
Mount Airy
Limekiln Pike
Old York Road
Livezey
Wissahickon Creek
Beggarstown
Chew
Luken's Mill
Manatawny Road
Germantown Road
Tacony Creek
Levering's Tavern
Rittenhouse Mill
Germantown
Schuylkill River
Vanderin's Mill
Logan
Frankford
Nicetown
Wingohocking Creek
Knyphausen
Rising Sun Tavern
Craig
McLane
Black Horse Tavern
Dickinson (ruins)
Cornwallis
Frankford Road
Frankford Creek
Morris
Delaware River
Upper Ferry   Howe

December 17, "and made the proper disposition for his reception." Washington's commissary general of prisoners returned to his quarters and "Proposed it as a matter of prudence to have our Horses saddled & the Serv[ant]s ordered to have them at the door on the first alarm gun being fired."[26]

Washington's adjutant general, Timothy Pickering, wrote about Whitemarsh in 1811. William Howe, he recalled, was determined upon a "'forward movement' (as he called it)" to lead much of his army out Philadelphia and offer Washington battle. Although Howe had submitted his resignation letter after Germantown, the general decided to chance one more battle before going home. When he learned that elements of Horatio Gates's army had reinforced Washington, Howe informed Lord George Germain in a December 13 letter, "Upon a presumption that a forward move might tempt the enemy, after receiving such reinforcement, to give battle for the recovery of this place, or that a vulnerable part might be found to admit of an attack upon their camp," he issued orders for the army to march.[27]

Several sources confirm Howe wanted to begin the operation early. "This morning at seven o'clock the army is to advance in two columns," reads the diary of Hessian Ensign Carl Rueffer of the von Mirbach Regiment. After the desertion of five British soldiers, Howe worried the impending operation was compromised. "[T]he army's order to march was countermanded," added Rueffer. Howe had concern for worry. According to loyalist James Parker, an "artillery corporal deserted, & carried with him an orderly book, in which was the line of march, deserted also one of the guards one 17th Dragoon & two Battalion Men."[28]

This time Washington's intelligence network, which was not always reliable, operated efficiently. William Dewees's dispatch to Washington reported Howe's delay. "Something happening which is Not accounted for the orders were Countermanded; the Reason Assignd to me is they Expect our army to move their Camp very soon as they Have Recievd such Information and they think they will do Better to attack when your army moves as they have heard you are advantageously Posted."[29]

26 Chase & Grizzard, eds., *Papers*, vol. 12, 591; Letter, George Weedon to John Page, December 17, 1777, Original in Weedon Letters, Chicago Historical Society, Chicago, IL; Boudinot, *Journal*, 52.

27 Octavius Pickering, *The Life of Timothy Pickering*, 4, vols. (Boston, 1867), vol. 2, 84; *London Gazette*, January 18, 1778.

28 Burgoyne, ed., *Enemy Views*, 244; Royal Artillerymen Downman thought it was earlier than 7:00 a.m. Whinyates, *Services*, 54; Parker Journal, December 4, 1777 entry, Parker Family Papers.

29 Chase & Grizzard, eds., *Papers*, vol. 12, 538.

Howe sent out additional patrols to determine the level of American activity. "Our Jaegers made a patrol six miles ahead and discovered that the enemy no longer occupied his previous outposts and made contact with them initially at two o'clock in the afternoon, when a brief engagement occurred," Ensign Rueffer scribbled into his diary. Fifty members of the 17th Light Dragoons patrolled across the Schuylkill River as far as Darby and Chester. John Miller, a magistrate living in Germantown, recorded the British "were much in motion—had pressed yesterday numerous horses, wagons, &c."[30]

Howe planned which units would participate in the operation while awaiting reports from his patrols. The column, which comprised the large majority of his army, included two divisions, the vanguard headed by Lt. Gen. Charles Cornwallis, and Lt. Gen. Wilhelm von Knyphausen command. Cornwallis's 6,500 men included Lt. Col. Robert Abercrombie's British Light Infantry Brigade, Lt. Col. Henry Monckton's British Grenadier Brigade, the Hessian Grenadier Brigade, the 4th British Brigade, Lt. Col. Ludwig von Wurmb's dismounted Hessian jaegers, two squadrons of the 16th Light Dragoons, two medium 12-pounders and two Howitzers. Knyphausen's 8,300-man division included Maj. Gen. James Grant's 1st British Brigade, Brig. Gen. Edward Mathew's British Brigade of Guards, Maj. Gen. Charles Grey's 3rd British Brigade, the Hessian regiments Leib and von Donop, the 5th, 7th, 26th, and 27th Regiments of Foot, a battalion of the 71st Highlanders, Lt. Col. John Simcoe's Queen's Rangers, Lt. Col. Samuel Birch's 17th Light Dragoons, a squadron of the 16th Light Dragoons, the mounted Hessian jaegers, and four light 12-pounders. Hospital, rum, and empty wagons accompanied Knyphausen, protected by two squadrons of the 17th Light Dragoons and flanked by the Queen's Rangers.[31]

With nearly 14,800 troops slated for the operation, only some 4,200 were left to hold Philadelphia—10 battalions and other detachments commanded by Brig. Gen. Alexander Leslie, as follows: two regiments of Maj. Gen. Johann von Stirn's Hessian Brigade, three regiments of the 2nd British Brigade, Col. Friedrich von

---

30 Burgoyne, ed., *Enemy Views*, 244; von Baurmeister, *Revolution in America*, 135; Watson, *Annals*, vol. 2, 70.

31 December 13, 1777, provision return, "Copies of Letters from Danl. Wier, Esq."; Robertson, *Diaries*, 158-159; von Baurmeister, *Revolution in America*, 134-135. Historian Matthew Spring claimed it "was possible in winter to take troops into the field for brief periods by divorcing them from almost all their horses, which Howe did when he prevented the force with which he probed Washington's position at Whitemarsh in December 1777 from taking along its wagons." In fact, contemporary sources evidence that Howe used more than 100 wagons. Spring, *With Zeal*, 32.

Salzburg's Ansbach-Beyreuth Brigade, the 63rd Regiment of Foot, a battalion of the 71st Highlanders, a squadron of the 17th Light Dragoons, the 2nd Battalion of New Jersey Volunteers, the Pennsylvania Loyalists, the Maryland Loyalists, the Roman Catholic Volunteers, and the Guides and Pioneers.[32]

Howe issued the marching orders by 8:00 p.m. According to an anonymous American writing on December 10, Howe's army was "distressed for want of 'elbow room.'" The columns moved out of Philadelphia in a heavy frost toward Washington's waiting army at 10:00 p.m. Cornwallis moved out the Germantown Road toward the ground they had fought over two months earlier. Knyphausen led his men down the Manatawny Road along the Schuylkill River heading toward the mouth of the Wissahickon Creek, where the Hessian jaegers had camped and fought at Germantown. With Americans probing south of Frankford Creek, the army's wagons were vulnerable to attack, so Howe wisely sent Knyphausen and the wagons on the inside track.[33]

December 5

As the various British and Hessian regiments took their place in the column and departed Philadelphia, the units left behind replaced them along the line of redoubts. According to Lt. Carl von Bueltzingsloewen of the Hessian von Mirbach Regiment, "The Anspach regiments had to move into the line and Mirbach remained standing and had to occupy Redouts No. 9 and 10." Johann Dohla of the Anspach-Beyreuth Brigade confirms "Bayreuth and Anspach troops had to provide a two-hundred-man force which occupied some fortifications and redoubts outside the city." While Dohla went on watch in the fortifications, "Our regiments moved out of the barracks into Howe's field camp and camped in the huts of the English soldiers." Disappointed artilleryman Francis Downman could not tag along because of what he described as a "severe illness."[34]

32 Von Baurmeister, *Revolution in America*, 135.

33 Moore, *Diary of Revolution*, 526; von Muenchhausen, *At Howe's Side*, 45; Montresor, "Journals," 480.

34 Carl Wilhelm von Bueltzingsloewen, "My Journal of the Mirbach Regiment from the Day of Departure in 1776 to the End of 1777," Henry J. Retzer, trans. *Journal of the Johannes Schwalm Historical Association* Vol. 16 (Scotland, PA, 2013), 72; Dohla, *A Hessian Diary*, 61; Whinyates, *Services*, 54. Other Hessian accounts confirm the shifting of troops. Lieutenant Johann Prechtel of the Ansbach-Beyreuth Brigade wrote: "The Commanding General Howe moved forward with the main army and both Ansbach regiments moved into the army camp at Spring Gardens near Philadelphia." Prechtel,

Fully alerted to Howe's operation, Washington's light troops and militia harassed Cornwallis's advance up the Germantown Road. Much like William Maxwell's light infantry in the opening moments of the Battle of Brandywine, Washington's advance posts conducted a running fight along the route through the wee hours of Friday morning. According to jaeger Lt. Heinrich von Feilitzsch, Cornwallis assigned the British light infantry the lead "because it was night." Lieutenant Colonel von Wurmb's dismounted jaegers followed the light infantry within supporting distance. The Americans "as usual, already had news of our march," complained von Feilitzsch, "and therefore had placed pickets along the whole road, one after the other; they were hiding behind rock piles and hedges." As the light infantry approached, the Americans "fired and ran off to reinforce the next post." The *Jaeger Corps Journal* confirmed the action: "the enemy outposts skirmished continuously during the advance."[35]

One of the first ambushes took place near the burned ruins of Fair Hill Mansion. The light infantry next encountered a picket post at the Rising Sun Tavern. Just a dozen dragoons manned the post. Other than slowing the British pace, the fitful skirmishing posed no real threat to Howe's advance. Captain Johann Ewald of the Hessian jaegers recorded in his diary that the British light infantry ran into the outpost, "which was attacked with the bayonet and beaten back to the first houses of Germantown; some twenty Americans were captured." The British drove back patrols of American horse and advanced infantry detachments that fell back toward Germantown. According to Cpl. Thomas Sullivan of the 49th Regiment of Foot, some Hessian jaegers and a few 16th Light Dragoons "were challenged by two dragoons" of an American picket post at the lower end of Germantown "who fired their Carabines and retired to their body, which also fired a volley and ran to the next party; but being still forced, the whole retired."[36]

A Hessian Officer's Diary, 129. Corporal Stephen Popp of the same brigade recalled moving "into the Camp of the English troops." Stephen Popp, "Popp's Journal, 1777-1783," Joseph G. Rosengarten, ed., *The Pennsylvania Magazine of History and Biography*, (Philadelphia, 1902), vol. 26, 30.

35 Von Feilitzsch, *Journal*, 136-137; Marie E. Burgoyne & Bruce E. Burgoyne, eds., *Journal of the Hesse-Cassel Jaeger Corps and Hans Konze's List of Jaeger Officers* (Westminster, MD, 2008), 31.

36 Fair Hill was among the homes ordered burned by Howe earlier in the campaign in the no man's land between Whitemarsh and Philadelphia. Fair Hill was located near the present intersection of Germantown and West Indiana Avenue in Philadelphia. von Baurmeister, *Revolution in America*, 135; Ewald, *Diary*, 108; Thomas Sullivan, *From Redcoat to Rebel: The Thomas Sullivan Journal*, Joseph Lee Boyle, ed. (Bowie, MD, 1997), 157.

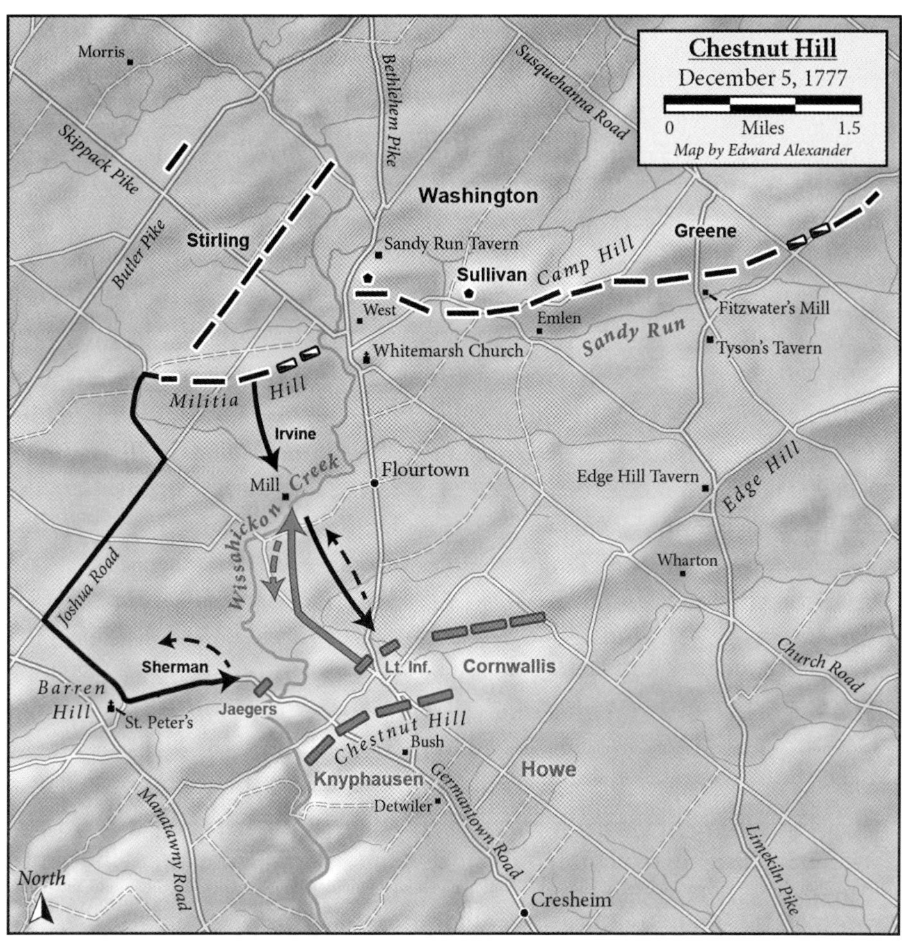

On December 10, John Laurens told his father Henry, president of Congress, the British "advanced through the village, forced the doors of the inhabitants with the butts of their muskets, uttering execrations against the rebels and all their abettors." Later that day, smoke rose from two "barns, and a square tower, which had been built as a look-out," he continued. These "were the only sacrifices they offered to tyranny in this neighbourhood." It was worse than Laurens knew. British aide John Andre added details: "On the Road a House was burnt, from which the Light Infantry had been fired upon." Civilian resident John Miller recalled the British "wantonly burning and destroying houses and property in the night time."[37]

37 *The Virginia Gazette,* December 26, 1777; Andre, *Journal,* 67; Watson, *Annals,* vol. 2, 70.

Having dislodged the Americans from Germantown, Cornwallis's column ascended Chestnut Hill around daylight "with some popping," recalled grenadier Lt. John Peebles. The outnumbered Americans grudgingly gave ground. Casualty estimates vary for Cornwallis's sluggish advance. Lieutenant Heinrich von Feilitzsch thought the light infantry "lost 30 men." A light infantry officer remembered the pesky Americans firing on them the whole way, but "lost only three Men wounded." Losses were insignificant, and the British professional machine marched on.[38]

As Cornwallis slowly made his way past Germantown, American patrols operated below Frankford Creek seemingly unopposed in the British rear. Robert Morton, a civilian in Philadelphia, observed that the Continentals at Frankford "moved off to Germantown." According to John Laurens, "These parties of ours had been posted at Frankford, and as the enemy did not extend themselves to the right of Germantown, they fell in upon the enemy's rear, and collected stragglers with impunity." Many of these prisoners "were for the most part drunk."[39]

Well before the British ascended Chestnut Hill to step within view of Washington's position on the Whitemarsh hills, picket posts driven in by Cornwallis sent word back to Washington. According to most accounts, the alarm guns were fired at 3:00 a.m. Within minutes the army "paraded, marched to and man'd the lines [on a]n excessive cold morning," recalled Lt. James McMichael of the 13th Pennsylvania. "We turned out and were counted off in platoons, and marched to our alarm post and lay there for a reinforcement," remembered Sgt. Ebenezer Wild of the Massachusetts Line. Howe's Hessian aide Friedrich von Muenchhausen heard the American signal guns as the British tramped across Mount Airy. The Americans were ready, manning a formidable line five miles in length. "We were previously prepared for them on a ridge of Hills extending Eastwardly & westwardly," wrote Elias Boudinot in a letter just nine days later. "Our Position was the best chosen possible, and our Troops sufficiently numerous & in high Spirits."[40]

---

38 Peebles, *Diary*, 152; von Feilitzsch, *Journal*, 137; Ankettle, *Journal of Officer B.*

39 Morton, "Diary," 34; *The Virginia Gazette*, 26 December 1777.

40 Rankin, ed., *Narratives of the American Revolution*, 176; Ebenezer Wild, *The Journal of Ebenezer Wild (1776-1781), Who Served as Corporal, Sergeant, Ensign, and Lieutenant in the War of the Revolution*, James M. Bugbee, ed. (Cambridge, MA, 1891), 28; Boudinot, *Journal*, 52; Boudinot, *Letterbook*, 56; Angell, *Diary*, n.p. Lieutenant James McMichael thought the signal guns were fired at 2:00 a.m. McMichael, "Diary," 156. Lieutenant Colonel Henry Dearborn thought it was 4:00 a.m. Lloyd A. Brown & Howard H. Peckham, eds., *Revolutionary War Journals of Henry Dearborn 1775-1783* (New York, 1971),

Washington ordered all excess baggage sent away in case the fighting went against him. The "Baggage was all imeadetly loaded into the waggons and drove off," wrote Rhode Island's Israel Angell. Staff officer Joseph Clark noted in his diary that "the tents were all struck and sent off with all the baggage 10 miles from the camp." After arriving on Chestnut Hill, Maj. Carl von Baurmeister commanding a Hessian grenadier battalion watched as Washington's "ammunition wagons, which had been in the center, scattered to all parts of the camp." writing about it eleven days later. The men would be at least a week without the army's baggage and tents as temperatures plummeted.[41]

It took three hours for Howe's legions to fan out in full view three miles from Washington's main line twelve miles from where they started the night before. It was now about 8:00 a.m. The light troops scoured the area between the Whitemarsh hills and Chestnut Hill with Hessian jaegers covering the left flank and the British light infantry the right. Jaegers moved forward into the Wissahickon Creek valley. As one German officer remembered, "We had barely placed our pickets and outposts, when the rebels positioned a picket close in front of us. Right away an officer and 50 men were ordered to dislodge said picket." Howe put an immediate stop to the action and "and bade the Jagers not to take the offensive for the time being."[42]

The columns under Cornwallis and Knyphausen formed a three-mile front on Chestnut Hill's rugged and heavily wooded terrain. Howe's left wing bordered Wissahickon Creek, and the right extended the line along the crest of Chestnut Hill stretching north. "We did not have a second line, but only a few reserve regiments posted here and there behind the first line," noted one of Howe's staff officers.

---

115. Staff officer Joseph Clark recalled hearing them at 8:00 a.m. Joseph Clark, "Diary of Joseph Clark," in *Proceedings of the New Jersey Historical Society* (Newark, 1855), 107; McMichael, "Diary," 156; von Muenchhausen, *At Howe's Side*, 45; Boudinot, *Letterbook*, 56.

41 Angell, *Diary*, n.p.; Clark, "Diary," 107; von Baurmeister, *Revolution in America*, 136. The army's baggage moved to Trappe.

42 The consensus of contemporary accounts put Cornwallis on Chestnut Hill at 6:00 a.m. von Feilitzsch, *Journal*, 137; von Muenchhausen, *At Howe's Side*, 45. Some offer a more vague "before daylight" or as late as 8:00 a.m. Burgoyne & Burgoyne, eds., *Journal of Jaeger Corps*, 31; Letter, Johann Ludwig von Cochenhausen to Friedrich von Jungkenn, January 19, 1778; Henry Retzer and Donald Londahlsmidt, eds. "The Philadelphia Campaign, 1777-1778: Letters and Reports from the von Jungkenn Papers. Part 2—1778," *Journal of the Johannes Schwalm Historical Association* Vol. 6, no. 3 (Pennsauken, NJ, 1999), 36; Freyenhagen, Journal, 71; von Baurmeister, *Revolution in America*, 135. It took time to deploy 12,000 troops, watches were not synchronized, and so times are always approximate. Ewald, *Diary*, 109. The jaegers were near modern Chestnut Hill College and the light infantry near James A Cisco Park. von Feilitzsch, *Journal*, 137.

Howe scouted the American position as his men deployed. Captain John Andre noted "the smoke and huts of the Rebel Camp were discernible." Ensign Wilhelm Feyenhagen of the von Donop Regiment recalled being able to see "the enemy camp between Whitemarsh and Ober Doppeln [Upper Dublin Township]."[43]

It did not take Howe long to fully realize that Washington's position was formidable. "Both their wings were fortified by strong abatis; the center approaches were completely covered by several batteries; the whole position was strongly fortified by fifty-two heavy pieces, and the slopes were patrolled by many pickets," observed Maj. Carl von Baurmeister in a December 16 letter. "Before our arrival they had increased their fires, lighting many large ones in straight and deep lines, so that it looked as if fifty thousand men were encamped there. By day we could see that this was merely a trick to deceive us. However, we could obtain no information, for we saw no deserters, or any people living in the neighborhood." "On Viewing their Camp when Day appeared," began Howe's Hessian aide von Muenchhausen, "we found great part of it Abbattisd and a strong Post at White Marsh Church with several Pieces of Cannon that Commanded the Road leading to their Camp across the Plain. The enemy, who was in position on the very high and wooded hills behind." They had, he continued, "extended their front considerably. In front of him, Washington had swampy water spanned by two bridges by which he maintained communication with some light troops on this side of Whitemarsh. Between him and us was a deep valley, which was also wooded, except that there was some rather level ground before our right flank, as well as some close to our left flank."[44]

Between Chestnut Hill and Washington's position was a heavily wooded and rugged valley bisected by Wissahickon Creek and Sandy Run that would disrupt advancing formations. Manatawny Road (modern Ridge Pike) followed the Schuylkill River toward Washington's right flank. Germantown Road paralleled the Manatawny. Washington could easily shift troops to block those avenues of attack. Bethlehem Pike headed toward Washington's left flank, but from Chestnut Hill it

---

43 Letter, von Cochenhausen to von Jungkenn, January 19, 1778, 36. The path Knyphausen took from the Manatawny or Ridge Road over to Chestnut Hill is not clear. Perhaps he utilized the Wissahickon Creek valley, though no road paralleled the creek in 1777. von Baurmeister, *Revolution in America*, 135. Howe established headquarters on the Mathias Bush property which was located near the modern Chestnut Hill East SEPTA station. Jackson, *Whitemarsh*, 39; von Muenchhausen, *At Howe's Side*, 45; Andre, *Journal*, 67; Freyenhagen, Journal, 71. The left of Washington's line extended through Upper Dublin Township.

44 Von Baurmeister, *Revolution in America*, 135-136; von Muenchhausen, *At Howe's Side*, 45.

seemed to present no clear advantage. Neither did a country byway closely following modern Stenton Avenue headed toward Militia Hill between Germantown Road and Bethlehem Pike. Howe had seen enough. Having led troops in the Bunker Hill disaster, he demurred attacking Washington in this position.[45]

Could he lure the Virginia commander into an open field fight? Washington would have to give up an exceedingly strong position, descend those hills, and attack him—an unlikely possibility. Howe's other option was to revert to his favorite tactic: a flanking maneuver. That would take time to plan and execute. Howe had moved out to Whitemarsh believing this would be a quick operation and had thus done so with limited provisions. Extending the operation meant he would need to bring more to the front. Orders went out and "the 71st [one battalion], 5th and 27th Regiments marched immediately Back to Philadelphia" to escort additional supplies from the fleet to the expeditionary force, recalled von Muenchhausen. The detachment reduced Howe's operational force by 950 men.[46]

Just as Howe was surveying the American front in search of an advantage, so too was Washington riding along his front studying British movements. John Donaldson of the Pennsylvania militia confirmed that "troopers were constantly employed in reconnoitering & watching the motions of the Enemy." A reconnaissance of the enemy line found that it extended "along the ridge of hills parallel to ours," noted Elias Boudinot. The redcoats were making "great Boasts of driving us beyond the blue Mountains," he continued, "and every Preparation & Movement, such as General Howe & other Principal Officers coming out, all the Troops drawn out of the City [Philadelphia], that could possibly be spared, & the great number of field Pieces, all bespoke their fixed determination to fight us." Howe and his officers were right: assaulting the British line on their own hill never crossed Washington's mind. "This led our Generals to keep their Posts on the Hills, where in Case of an Attack, in all human probability the common blessings of Heavn a Compleat Victory must have attended us," concluded Boudinot.[47]

---

45 Jackson, *Whitemarsh*, 36.

46 Von Muenchhausen, *At Howe's Side*, 45; December 13, 1777 provision return, "Copies of Letters from Danl. Wier, Esq." The choice of the 5th and 27th Regiments of Foot makes sense. They accompanied the expedition detached from their parent brigade. Likewise, the 71st Highlanders was not brigaded.

47 Reed, *Correspondence of Reed*, 351; Capt. J. H. C. Smith, "History of the 1st City Troop," based largely on the recollections of Trooper John Donaldson, First City Troop Archives, Philadelphia, PA; Boudinot, *Letterbook*, 56-57.

The morning dragged on as the two armies stared down one another. No fighting seemed imminent. "The Sun was near two hours high, then dismist the troops to git their breakfast," recorded Israel Angell. Joseph Clark added that the "troops paraded on the lines and waited some time, but as the enemy did not come on the attack, they grounded their arms at the lines, and went to their huts." From all appearances, the British appeared content with seizing Chestnut Hill. "The enemy came up within a mile and a half of our encampment, and appeared to be cutting a great store of wood," wrote Joseph Clark in his diary. Brigade commander George Weedon put a Biblical twist on the situation twelve days later: "the two Armies lay like Saul & the Philistines with only a small Vally between, and a General Action every moment expected."[48]

Howe certainly came out of Philadelphia looking for an advantageous fight, but he also took with him some 100 empty wagons to forage for supplies well outside the city limits. He would need to fill them, whether he fought or not. Many hoped Howe sought more than foraging. With nearly 24,000 men at Whitemarsh, and the northern brigades that had joined the army "being flushed with recent victory [Saratoga] and hoping that the other troops would vie with them in the contest, a battle was rather desired than avoided," wrote Maj. Benjamin Tallmadge of the 2nd Continental Light Dragoons.[49]

The stalemate of inaction ended when Washington decided to scout the British lines around mid-morning. He had learned hard lessons at Long Island, Brandywine, and along the Schuylkill and wanted to make sure that Howe was not using the road network to gain his right flank. An order passed down the ranks and reached Brig. Gen. James Potter about 8:00 a.m. to organize a force accordingly. Potter, in turn, directed Lt. Col. Isaac Sherman's 2nd Connecticut to join him. The directive surprised Sherman, who responded that his "Orders were to act independent of any Brigade." When he learned it was General Sullivan himself who had ordered the combination, Sherman "accordingly join'd him." Potter's three militia battalions of some 1,000 men, along with the 300 Connecticut troops, formed a 1,300-man force ready for the reconnaissance-in-strength. Sherman was put in command of the operation. Just over an hour later he advanced from Militia Hill into the Wissahickon Creek valley, closing the distance on more than 700 Hessian jaegers. Sherman reconnoitered "within eighty Rods of them," concealing

---

48 Angell, *Diary*, n.p; Clark, "Diary," 107; Letter, Geo. Weedon to John Page, December 17, 1777.

49 Benjamin Tallmadge, *Memoir of Col. Benjamin Tallmadge* (New York, 1858), 25.

his command under cover of a hill before detaching 60 men to determine the size of the enemy hidden in the woods opposite Wissachickon Creek.[50]

The heavily wooded creek valley concealed the approaching militiamen until "the picket signaled us," recalled Jaeger Lt. Heinrich von Feilitzsch. Eighty jaegers of Maj. Ernst von Prueschenck's company sprinted to the support of the pickets, opened fire, and drove back the handful of Americans.[51]

After a short pause, "the enemy attacked the picket furiously and almost came storming into camp with them," wrote von Feilitzsch. Sherman advanced to the creek with a larger force, but "found their numbers much larger than was apprehended, The Wood being full." The jaegers, meanwhile, jumped behind mounds of dirt for protection. "We planned to let the rebels come very close, but when their tirailleurs [sharpshooters] had come up to 40 feet from us, they stopped. Hereupon we maintained a very lively fire for a while." The two sides took position on opposing rises separated by the narrow creek. After less than 30 minutes of fitful firing Sherman withdrew, having identified Howe's left flank. As he later reported, "I therefore tho't prudent to retreat, and ordered one." He left behind one officer and 18 men to observe the jaegers, "formed with a determination to dispute with them had they attempted to." Howe denied a request by the jaegers to pursue. Sherman returned to Militia Hill.[52]

The fight cost Sherman five dead and seven wounded, and the jaegers one dead and seven wounded. "I escaped a spent bullet," recalled von Feilitzsch, "which I heard whistling toward me through the air, behind the corner of the mound, it hit the ground in front of me and then penetrated the thigh of Jager Kopp junior, the man next to me; a spent bullet is not gone, when one hears it whistling."[53]

About the same time Sherman was engaging the jaegers, a detachment of British light infantry seized a mill along the Wissahickon Creek holding an

---

50 Jackson, *Whitemarsh*, 36; McMichael, "Diary," 156; Letter, Isaac Sherman to George Washington, March 11, 1778, www.founders.archives.gov/documents/Washington/03-14-02-116. The column moved down Joshua Road, turned left on Germantown Pike, passed St. Peter's Lutheran Church [Barren Hill Church], deployed, and advanced into the Wissahickon Creek valley. December 13, 1777 provision return, "Copies of Letters from Danl. Wier, Esq."

51 Von Feilitzsch, *Journal*, 137-138.

52 Ibid., 138; Letter, Isaac Sherman to George Washington, dated March 11, 1778; Burgoyne & Burgoyne, eds., *Journal of Jaeger Corps*, 31. This action likely took place on the grounds of today's Chestnut Hill College.

53 Von Feilitzsch, *Journal*, 138-139.

American picket post. The Americans "retreated to the other side of the water and destroyed the bridges behind them," wrote Capt. Friedrich von Muenchhausen. By 10:00 a.m. an uneasy calm had once again settled over the two armies. "Our troops stacked their rifles and made campfires, but they were not permitted to move around," recorded Howe's Hessian aide.[54]

By 11:00 a.m. Washington had sent orders to the other Pennsylvania militia brigade under Brig. Gen. James Irvine to investigate Howe's center on the northeast side of Chestnut Hill. "As soon as their position was discovered, the pensylvania Militia were ordered from our Right to skirmish with their light advanced parties," wrote Washington. Irvine left with four of his battalions, about 600 men, descending Militia Hill and heading toward the Wissahickon Creek. After driving back the British from the mill they had just overrun, he halted his men in the hope of receiving additional reinforcements. When none were forthcoming, Irvine crossed the creek and approached Chestnut Hill around noon. Rather than disperse his command, Irvine kept his men in a compact formation.[55]

As they emerged from the tree cover of the valley, Irvine's troops stumbled right into the 750 men of Lt. Col. John Maitland's elite 2nd British Light Infantry Battalion. Though heavily bloodied at Brandywine and Germantown, Maitland's command remained combat ready. Robert Abercrombie's 1st British Light Infantry Battalion (740 men) supported him, and Howe deployed British grenadier battalions (1,100 men) within supporting distance. Irvine never stood a chance.[56]

At first, the militia nearly surrounded Lt. Thomas Armstrong's picket post. As they surged forward, Armstrong "gave the alarm," remembered Cpl. Thomas Sullivan. Maitland brought forward his entire battalion to the post's support. Militiaman Joseph Long remembered in his pension application he and his comrades "were going up a small hill [and] the Enemy fired down on them." With part of the 1st British Light Infantry Battalion on its left, Maitland's battalion advanced and fired two or three volleys. Irvine, recalled Long, leaped over a fence just as his "horse [was] shot under him." The same volley that took out Irvine's mount shot off three of his fingers, knocked him out of the saddle, and concussed

54 This was located at the modern intersection of Cricket Road & Valley Green Road on the Wissachickon Creek in Flourtown. von Muenchhausen, *At Howe's Side*, 45.

55 Chase & Grizzard, eds., *Papers*, vol. 12, 591. The militia advanced on Stenton Ave to approach the British center. Revolutionary War Pension and Bounty-Land-Warrant Application Files (M804) [RWPF], file W2137.

56 December 13, 1777 provision return, "Copies of Letters from Danl. Wier, Esq."

him. His leaderless men scattered. "[N]one of his men gave him the least assistance," wrote disgusted Pennsylvania militia commander John Armstrong two days later, "being at that time broke and running, as did the greater part of them very early."[57]

Hoping to redeem themselves after their disgraceful performance at Germantown, the British light infantry swept forward and drove the scattered Pennsylvania militia before them. British engineer Archibald Robertson noted Maitland's battalion "drove them back a mile and a half" and began approaching Washington's main positions on the Whitemarsh hills. "Everyone believed that this was the beginning of a general attack," recalled Maj. Carl von Baurmeister. The entire right side of the British line stirred to support the light infantry's advance, "and undoubtedly a total engagement would have ensued if the General [Howe] had not given repeated orders for the light infantry to retreat, since he believed that the enemy was intent on engaging us here, where they had the abatis and many cannon," reported Friedrich von Muenchhausen.[58]

Off to the south, the jaegers heard small arms fire for half an hour and learned "the rebels were overthrown with bayonet and were obliged to flee in disorder," recalled Lt. Heinrich von Feilitzsch. The Americans were "soon repelled," confirmed Capt. Friedrich von Muenchhausen. Captain John Andre reported that the "Rebels were driven back with some loss," a repulse Lieutenant Matthew Ankettle confirmed as "Routed." The performance did not surprise John Laurens, who informed his father that "the militia behaved as usual." Future Supreme Court justice John Marshall, who served with the 11th Virginia in Brig. Gen. William Woodford's brigade, also thought little of the militia who, he wrote later in life, "with very little other loss, were dispersed." An anonymous American writer offered a kinder observation five days after the fighting when he noted, "The skirmish was pretty warm, and the enemy being reinforced, our militia were obliged to retreat in some confusion." Lieutenant Colonel Henry Dearborn of the 3rd New Hampshire, watching the action from the main American line, confirmed "the

---

57 Sullivan, *Journal*, 158; Revolutionary War Pension and Bounty-Land-Warrant Application Files (M804) [RWPF], file W2137; Hazard, ed., *Pennsylvania Archives*, Series 1, vol. 6, 70.

58 Robertson, *Diaries*, 159-160; von Baurmeister, *Revolution in America*, 136; von Muenchhausen, *At Howe's Side*, 45.

Enimy advanc'd no further." By 12:30 p.m. both armies returned to their respective hills.[59]

Brigadier General Irvine was the most significant casualty of the morning's action. The advancing British light infantry captured him after he was left behind by his men. The capture, related John Laurens, took place while "he was making fruitless attempts to rally them." Numerous British and American accounts refer to the incident. One jaeger officer mocked his prewar profession: "a hatmaker from Philadelphia." One pensioner observed the fighting from Militia Hill. During Irvine's retreat, reserve units moved forward to cover the retreat to "a farmer's mill also on the Germantown road where we met four horse men leading Genl. Irwin's [wounded] horse." Apparently, saving the horse was more important than bringing off the general.[60]

American casualties were about 40 killed and wounded and 24 prisoners (including Irvine). Charles Willson Peale, who would soon be known as one of the finest portrait painters in American history, lamented the mortal wounding and capture of Michael Whitley, an officer he described as "a brave Captain." Whitley died a short time later. Loyalist James Parker recorded in his journal that Irvine and 23 others "were brought in this evening." Charles Grey's aide John Andre claimed, "five or six of the Rebel dead were found on the field," which seems too low. According to Heinrich von Feilitzsch, "From the prisoners we found out, that the corps, which had been staging these attacks, came from New England, they had already distinguished themselves at Saratoga or Stillwater, where they had taken the Englishmen and Braunschweigers under General Burgoyne prisoner. Now," he continued, "they had wanted to distinguish themselves here also and show this army how it was done, but had found a great difference between us and the

---

59 Von Feilitzsch, *Journal*, 139; Andre, *Journal*, 67; Ankettle, *Journal of Officer B*; *The Virginia Gazette*, December 26, 1777; John Marshall, *The Life of George Washington, Commander in Chief of the American Forces, During the War Which Established the Independence of His Country, and First President of the United States*, 5vols (Philadelphia, 1804), vol. 3, 318; Moore, *Diary of Revolution*, 526; Brown & Peckham, eds., *Journals of Dearborn 1775-1783*, 116; Civilian John Miller in Germantown "heard a heavy firing begun on Chestnut hill, and lasting for two or three hours." He likely heard both fights (the jaegers and the light infantry). Watson, *Annals*, vol. 2, 70.

60 *The Virginia Gazette*, December 26, 1777. Pennsylvania militiamen Abraham Ellis mistakenly claimed in his pension application that Irvine "was thrown from his horse and taken prisoner, but was exchanged in a few days and restored to his command." The unfortunate Irvine spent nearly four years as a prisoner. Revolutionary War Pension and Bounty-Land-Warrant Application Files (M804) [RWPF], file S16109; von Feilitzsch, *Journal*, 139; Revolutionary War Pension and Bounty-Land-Warrant Application Files (M804) [RWPF], file W2137.

Canadian army." Von Feilitzsch was wrong: no northern troops participated in the attack.[61]

British casualties totaled about a dozen killed and wounded. Loyalist James Parker listed "Three privates were killed & eleven Wounded," while John Andre recorded "three or four men" wounded and one killed. According to Lord Cantelupe of the British Brigade of Guards, the light infantry took "some prisoners without the loss of Man 5 or 6 wounded."[62]

The most significant British casualty was Capt. Sir James Murray, a 22-year-old with the 57th Regiment of Foot's light company. Murray had only recently returned to duty following a wounded ankle at Brandywine. This time he went down with a painful lead ball to his shin. American sources claim some of Howe's men were captured, but it remains unclear whether those occurred in Irvine's fight or elsewhere throughout the day. "There has ben Several prisoners taken to the Number of 13 among whom there is one Hessian Capt.," claimed Col. Israel Angell of the 2nd Rhode Island. Militia commander John Armstrong reported killing one and bringing "off his Sword."[63]

The remainder of December 5 played out with scouting and light skirmishing but no further fighting. "Nothing further remarkable ensued this Day," was how American surgeon Albigence Waldo put it in his journal. Washington, noted Hessian jaeger Johann Ewald, "pushed his outposts in front of ours." Each side "sent out pickets," reported Carl von Baurmeister. John Peebles, a veteran British grenadier, reduced the massive confrontation to four words: "the Great folks [generals] recnoitered." Virginia brigade commander George Weedon found the entire affair annoying. General Howe, he insisted, "is a very troublesome man and will not at all times afford leisure to write or indeed to sleep."[64]

---

61 Charles Coleman Sellers, *Charles Willson Peale: Early Life: 1741-1790*, 2 vols. (Philadelphia, 1947), vol. 1, 176; Parker Journal, December 5, 1777 entry, Parker Family Papers; Andre, *Journal*, 67; von Feilitzsch, *Journal*, 139; Revolutionary War Pension and Bounty-Land-Warrant Application Files (M804) [RWPF], file S2701. Peale misspelled the name as "Michard Whiteley." See https://tinyurl.com/3hsk3z5p.

62 Parker Journal, December 5, 1777 entry, Parker Family Papers; Andre, *Journal*, 67; Entry for December 4, Lord Cantelupe Diary, the Grey Papers, Durham University, England.

63 Parker Journal, December 5, 1777 entry, Parker Family Papers; England; Angell, *Diary*, n.p.; Hazard, ed., *Pennsylvania Archives*, Series 1, vol. 6, 70.

64 Rankin, ed., *Narratives of the American Revolution*, 176; Ewald, *Diary*, 109; von Baurmeister, *Revolution in America*, 136; Peebles, *Diary*, 152; Letter, George Weedon to John Page, December 17, 1777.

With the sun setting, both armies settled in for the night. Those lucky enough to have huts returned to them. Most of the Americans "lay on their Arms, the Baggage being all sent away except what a man might run or fight with," observed Dr. Waldo. When Washington sent away his baggage train, "some hundred of the troops have followed it under the pretext of getting necessarys," complained John Armstrong on December 7.[65]

General Howe, meanwhile, assigned Maj. John Simcoe's Queen's Rangers to protect the wagon train stretched out along the road to Philadelphia. Simcoe's men "made fires on the road that led to it [the army's camp], so that the approach of any parties of the enemy could easily be seen." Like the Americans, Howe's regiments "formed Line and lay upon their arms that night," wrote Ensign William Lord Cantelupe of the British Brigade of Guards. Some of the men were more than irritated with the discomforts. Someone recording in the *Journal of the von Minnigerode Battalion* complained "we bivouacked, for neither tents nor baggage had been brought with us." Fires sprang up along the line. Friedrich von Muenchhausen looked across at Washington's army and saw "a beautiful spectacle . . . the great number of our and Washington's fires." The peaceful view, however, was broken up at regular intervals: "alarms continued throughout the night," noted Capt. Johann Ewald.[66]

The 5th and 27th Regiments of Foot and battalion of the 71st Highlanders, meanwhile, made it to Philadelphia sometime that evening to begin loading provisions in wagons. The task of loading and hauling food to Howe's expeditionary force the next day meant they saw little or no rest that night. Once back, Lt. James Chrystie of the 71st Highlanders passed along information to the city that Washington's baggage was seen leaving Whitemarsh—a move any commander would make when "he expects an Attack." Loyalist James Parker was certain Washington did this to enable "a quick retreat."[67]

---

65 Angell, *Diary*, n.p.; Rankin, ed., *Narratives of the American Revolution*, 176; Hazard, ed., *Pennsylvania Archives*, Series 1, vol. 6, 70.

66 John Simcoe, *Simcoe's Military Journal: A History of the Operations of a Partisan Corps, Called the Queen's Rangers, Commanded by Lieut. Col. J.G. Simcoe, During the War of the American Revolution* (New York, 1844), 30-31; Entry for December 4, Lord Cantelupe Diary; von Baurmeister, *Revolution in America*, 136; Journal of the Hessian Grenadier Battalion von Minnigerode, Hessian Documents of the American Revolution, Microfiche No. 232, American Philosophical Society, Philadelphia, PA; von Muenchhausen, *At Howe's Side*, 45; Ewald, *Diary*, 109.

67 Andre, *Journal*, 67; Parker Journal, December 5, 1777 entry, Parker Family Papers.

The news that another major battle was in the offing set off some panic among the already-anxious civilians. "What will become of us?" wondered teenage Sally Wister. "Heaven defend us from so dreadful a sight. The battle of Germantown, and the horrors of that day, are recent in my mind. It will be sufficiently dreadful if we are only in hearing of the firing," she continued, "to think how many of our fellow-creatures are plung'd into the boundless ocean of eternity, few of them prepar'd to meet their fate."[68]

December 6

As morning dawned, Washington's regiments "soon paraded our selves & formed on top of ye hill & sent out guards," noted Sgt. Jeremiah Greenman of the 2nd Rhode Island. Having survived the ordeals at Forts Mercer and Mifflin, Greenman found himself in the reserve line at Whitemarsh. Lieutenant Samuel Armstrong of Massachusetts greeted that Saturday morning with a bout of rheumatism and an earache. He attributed his maladies to "standing in the Cold all ye Day before but turned out with the Rest by five in the Morning, where we tarried 'till Sun-sit and then Encamp'd." Both sides scouted the other, with "pickets of the two Armies Skirmishing alternately," reported General Weedon. Lieutenant Colonel John Lacey's Pennsylvania militia "was in several of those combats—in attacking and driving in the Enemies Picquets, who being reinforced, we were driven in turn, thus alternately advancing and retreating schrimminsing."[69]

Later in life, Connecticut Continental Joseph Plumb Martin claimed that he hoped the British attacked. "We had a commanding position and were very sensible of it. We were kept constantly on the alert, and wished nothing more than to have them engage us," he explained, "for we were sure of giving them a drubbing, being in excellent fighting trim, as we were starved and as cross and ill-natured as curs." Henry Dearborn of New Hampshire remembered how he and his comrades spent the day "Loocking at one or the other." Dr. Waldo was thankful there was little bloody work to attend to, "as our Wise General was determined not to be attack'd Napping." It was hard enough without the fighting.

---

68 Wister, *Journal*, 108.

69 Greenman, *Diary*, 87; Samuel Armstrong, "From Saratoga to Valley Forge: The Diary of Lt. Samuel Armstrong," *The Pennsylvania Magazine of History and Biography*, 148 vols. (Philadelphia, PA, 1997), vol. 121, 255; Letter, George Weedon to John Page, December 17, 1777; "Memoirs of Brigadier-General John Lacey, of Pennsylvania," in *The Pennsylvania Magazine of History and Biography*, 148 vols. (Philadelphia, 1902), vol. 26, 107.

Private Donald Sellers of the North Carolina Line complained about having to remain in line for two days "without anything to eat."[70]

Expiring enlistments and desertion weakened Washington's army by the day, the lack of bloodshed notwithstanding. Reverend Henry Melchior Muhlenberg experienced the effects 15 miles away when "several soldiers from the American camp passed through here on the way to Virginia, their home, because, as they said, the term of their service has expired." Several hours later Pennsylvania militia visited Muhlenberg. The men "wanted to go home to Lancaster County. They had a freight wagon with them. Since they would not be put off, we took them in; the neighboring houses were already full."[71]

Howe's soldiers echoed American accounts. Lieutenant von Feilitzsch remembered a quiet day. "There were some enemy patrols, but they stayed at a distance." Grenadier John Peebles agreed: "all quiet today, The Enemy seen making some movements, some think going off, but I believe its only altering position of some of their troops, much reconnoitering & speculation, but nothing done today." There was no way to get at the Americans, as the *Jaeger Corps Journal* made clear: "The two armies stood face to face, the enemy on a height protected by an abatis and a redoubt. Washington appeared to be awaiting an attack and stood his ground." To the veterans of Brandywine and Germantown, the day was quiet indeed. Civilians had a different reaction. As far as John Miller of Germantown was concerned, "the enemy and our light horse place us in much danger, as they patrolled our streets alternately."[72]

The fitful Whitemarsh skirmish fire heard in Philadelphia didn't surprise or cause any alarm amongst the soldiers there. Ensign Carl Rueffer of the von Mirbach Regiment simply noted that "the firing did not last very long, it is to be imagined that it was with their outposts." The 5th and 27th Regiments of Foot and the 71st Highlander battalion departed Philadelphia escorting the provision wagons to Howe's troops.[73]

---

70 Martin, *Private Yankee Doodle*, 98; Brown & Peckham, eds., *Journals of Dearborn 1775-1783*, 116; Rankin, ed., *Narratives of the American Revolution*, 176; Revolutionary War Pension and Bounty-Land-Warrant Application Files (M804) [RWPF], file R9376.

71 Muhlenberg, *Journals*, vol. 3, 110.

72 Von Feilitzsch, *Journal*, 139; Burgoyne & Burgoyne, eds., *Journal of Jaeger Corps*, 32; Peebles, *Diary*, 153; Watson, *Annals*, vol. 2, 71.

73 Burgoyne, ed., *Enemy Views*, 245; Parker Journal, December 6, 1777 entry, Parker Family Papers.

William Howe knew he needed a new plan. He could not sit indefinitely out in the countryside, and he could not attack with a decent prospect of success. As one jaeger officer noted, Howe "scouted the enemy camp, had found it, and established that it was well fortified and could not be attacked without great losses." General Grey's aide John Andre agreed: "The Rebels still remained on the hills, but appeared to be drawing their force towards their right, on which side we appeared to threaten them. Veteran Wilhelm von Knyphausen was of like mind: Washingtons position was "rendered inaccessible by thickets, bogs, barriers of felled trees and every possible obstacle." Engineer officer Archibald Robertson verified the various reports. "The Right of the Rebel Camp seem'd rather Difficult of Access and as we saw the Rebels all the 6th moving their Troops from their left to their Right." Howe's Hessian aide, probably repeating Howe's supposition, confirmed, "All information leads to the conclusion that Washington wants us to attack." As Howe would eventually inform Lord George Germain: "Not judging it advisable to attack the enemy's right."[74]

Howe had spent his entire tenure as commander-in-chief avoiding frontal assaults. The cost was often not worth the price because at that distance, it was exceedingly difficult to replace casualties. If Washington's formidable position made a direct attack impossible, he would revert to his favorite tactic against Washington: a flanking movement. Aide John Andre mentioned as much in his journal, when he recorded that, unable to attack, "The Commander-in-Chief . . . determined upon a movement towards their left."[75]

British accounts disagree on the time, but sometime before midnight Howe's force unfolded itself from its front position and began marching back down the Germantown Road in the direction of Philadelphia. "Contrary to expectations we set out to march back to Germantown," wrote a disappointed Friedrich von Muenchhausen. Howe reorganized his column for the move. The vanguard under Charles Cornwallis included the British light infantry and grenadiers, the Hessian grenadiers, and the Fourth British Brigade. The main body under Wilhelm von

---

74 Some of the men took to the roofs of country estates to scout the area. "The view from this building was excellent—overlooked the Dellaware and a large Part of Pennsylvania," reported Capt. August von Dincklage of the Hessian corps. August von Dincklage manuscript diary, December 6, 1777 entry: https://orka.bibliothek.uni-kassel.de/viewer/fullscreen/1366290520646/1/, accessed July 27, 2024; Feilitzsch, *Journal*, 139; Andre, *Journal*, 68; Wilhelm von Knyphausen Whitemarsh Report, translated copy located in Hessian Documents of the American Revolution, Letter, G, microfiche no. 56, American Philosophical Society, Philadelphia, PA; Robertson, *Diaries*, 160; von Muenchhausen, *At Howe's Side*, 45; *London Gazette*, January 18, 1778.

75 Andre, *Journal*, 68.

Knyphausen included the British Brigade of Guards, the First British Brigade, the 7th and 26th Regiments of Foot, the Hessian regiments Leib and von Donop, twenty-one mounted 17th Light Dragoons, four light 12-pounders and two howitzers, and the army's wagons protected by the dismounted dragoons. The rear guard was comprised of Charles Grey's command and included the Third British Brigade, the Hessian Jaegers, and John Simcoe's Queen's Rangers and a detachment of the 17th Light Dragoons under Lt. William Cathcart. Simcoe recalled quitting "this post . . . in great silence" and joining "the column that was marching under General Gray."[76]

Several structures in Cresheim, Bebberstown, and Germantown met the torch on the way back from the Whitemarsh front. Von Feilitzsch justified the wanton destruction. "Many houses on this route were burned, because so close to us, they could provide the enemy with very advantageous positions, and besides, the enemy had used them on our march over here, and had done great harm to the English." The sights and sounds appalled even a veteran like Capt. Johann Ewald. "[T]he conflagration was so great that the jagers and rangers could scarcely get through. The sight was horrible. The night was very dark. The blazing flames spread about with all swiftness and the wind blew violently," he recorded. "The cries of human voices of the young and old, who had seen their belongings consumed by the flames without saving anything, put everyone in a melancholy mood."[77]

The exhausted and cold soldiers passed the pock-marked Cliveden and turned left on Abington Lane onto a route leading through Cheltenham Township and Jenkintown. What none of them yet knew was that Howe was in search of Washington's left flank.[78]

---

76 Lieutenant Heinrich von Feilitzsch says midnight. von Feilitzsch, *Journal*, 140. Captain John Andre says 10 p.m. Andre, *Journal*, 68. Captain Friedrich von Muenchhausen says 9:00 p.m. von Muenchhausen, *At Howe's Side*, 45; von Baurmeister, *Revolution in America*, 136; Simcoe, *Journal*, 31.

77 Von Feilitzsch, Journal, 140; Ewald, *Diary*, 109.

78 Abington Lane is modern Washington Lane.

Chapter 10

The Whitemarsh Operation: Edge Hill

December 7-8, 1777

"This will probably give them fresh Spirits, and encourage them to annoy
the Environs of the Town through the winter."[1]

— Ambrose Serle, secretary to Lord Richard Howe, December 8, 1777

December 7

Howe's rearguard reached Germantown with the first rays of the sun peaking over the horizon. He briefly halted his column on Abington Lane before reorganizing his forces for a flanking maneuver. Two parallel columns would advance north toward Washington's left flank. Charles Cornwallis led the right column on Old York Road, and Wilhelm von Knyphausen commanded the left on Abington Road. The British light infantry spearheaded Cornwallis's advance, while the Hessian jaegers led Knyphausen's. John Simcoe's Queen's Rangers protected Knyphausen's left flank. Expecting a prolonged operation, Howe ordered more provisions from Philadelphia. Engineer John Montresor noted that a provision train left

---

1 Serle, *Journal*, 267.

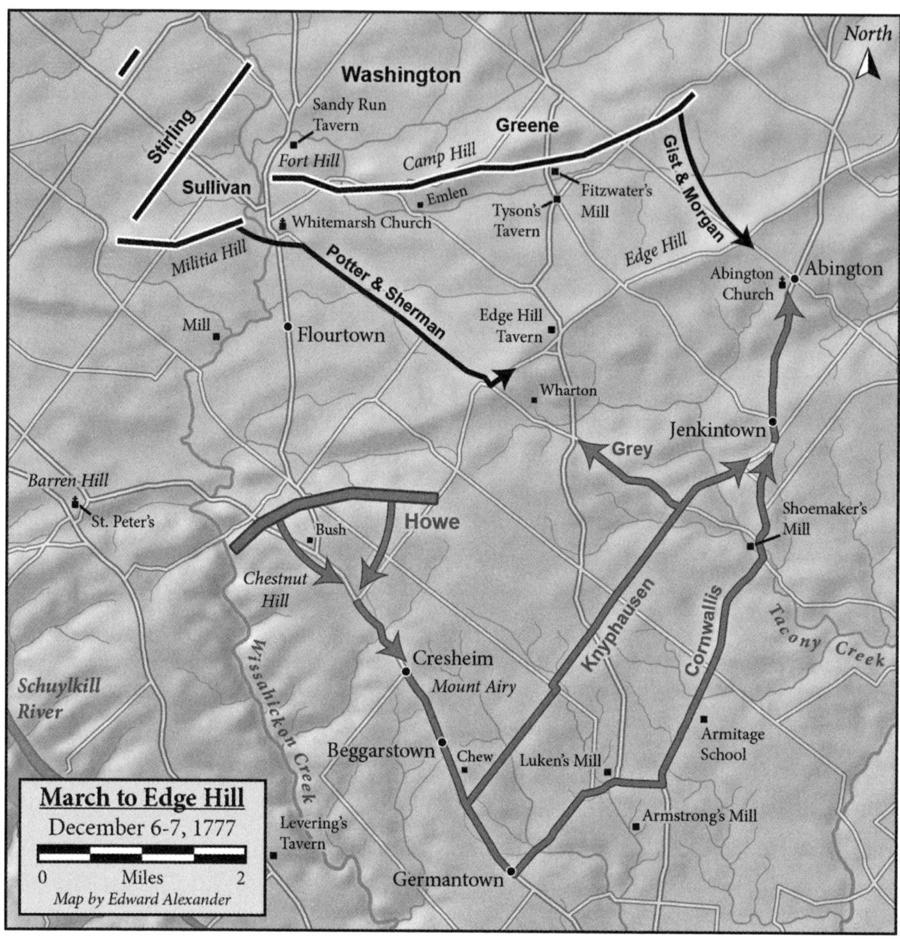

Philadelphia at 2:00 a.m., escorted by the 40th and 55th Regiments of Foot, along with the 71st Highlanders.[2]

As the sun rose that Sunday morning, American patrols soon reported the enemy's disappearance from Chestnut Hill. By 8:00 a.m., Lt. Col. Henry Dearborn recorded, "Several deserters came in who inform'd us that the Enimy ware Retreeting towards Germantown." Washington assumed Howe was returning to Philadelphia and around 10:00 a.m., he deployed Lt. Col. Isaac Sherman's 2nd

---

2 Ewald, *Diary*, 109; Montresor, "Journals," 480. Engineer Archibald Robertson confirmed that "2 Day's Provisions arrived from Philadelphia under Convoy of the 71st, 55th and 40th Regiments." Robertson, *Diaries*, 160. The 5th and 27th Regiments of Foot escorted the empty wagons into the city, but were too exhausted to return immediately to Howe. The 40th and 55th were pulled from the Philadelphia garrison.

Connecticut to "harass the Enemy on their Retreat." When Sherman reached Chestnut Hill, near the site of his engagement two days earlier, he discovered Howe's men had already passed through Germantown. He then returned to Militia Hill.[3]

After marching about a dozen miles, Howe's parallel columns converged at the village of Jenkintown. "This after noon we found that the Retreet which we heard the Enimy ware making this morning was in fact Shifting their ground from our Right wing to our Left," was how Lt. Col. Henry Dearborn of the 3rd New Hampshire recorded the event. The enemy, reported John Laurens to his father, were "endeavouring to turn our left; we changed our disposition in consequence." Washington moved quickly against the threat and dispatched several units to slow his advance including Daniel Morgan's riflemen, Mordecai Gist's Maryland militia, the 2nd Connecticut, and James Potter with his brigade of Pennsylvania militia. Sherman was just returning from his Chestnut Hill mission when Maj. Gen. John Sullivan ordered him to take his Connecticut regiment and "Attack the rear of their Left Flank."[4]

While Washington was responding, Howe was reorganizing his command for the fourth time during the operation. The British commander reached Jenkintown about the same time as the provision train dispatched from Philadelphia, which arrived to distribute "rum and biscuits," reported an elated Maj. Carl von Baurmeister. While the men drank and ate, Howe formed a new advance guard to keeep an eye on his left flank as the combined forces of Cornwallis and Knyphausen moved farther up Old York Road. The Queen's Rangers, Third British Brigade, and light infantry and grenadiers of the British Brigade of Guards joined the Hessian jaegers to form a powerful advance guard under the command of Charles Grey. Jaeger Lt. Heinrich von Feilitzsch believed Grey "was a man of great ability and reputation, and was very well liked in the army, it could be expected, that we were to have something to do with the enemy." General Grey moved his force up Church Road about a mile from Abington Road and halted at

---

3 Brown & Peckham, eds., *Journals of Dearborn 1775-1783*, 116; Letter, Isaac Sherman to George Washington, March 11, 1778.

4 Brown & Peckham, eds., *Journals of Dearborn 1775-1783*, 116; *The Virginia Gazette,* December 26, 1777; Hazard, ed., *Pennsylvania Archives*, Series 1, vol. 6, 71; Letter, Isaac Sherman to George Washington, March 11, 1778.

the intersection of the Limekiln Pike. The southern end of Edge Hill loomed before him.[5]

The general plan, explained Howe's Hessian aide Capt. Friedrich von Muenchhausen, was for Howe's main column to attack first, after which General Grey "could fall upon the enemy's left flank, and then align himself with the main corps." Grey's capable aide, John Andre, confirmed the Hessian's interpretation of Howe's battleplan: "a note came from the Commander-in-Chief to Major General Grey, desiring him not to move until he heard or saw signs of the main Column in motion." Grey's route carried him up Limekiln Pike to Edge Hill and drove in an American outpost in the process. Howe hoped Grey's move would draw American attention, allowing Howe to launch the main attack on the Susquehanna Road corridor.[6]

The long steep ridge known as Edge Hill ran parallel to and about a mile in front of the main American position. Hessian quartermaster Lt. Col. Johann von Cochenhausen considered it a formidable position, one laced with "obstacles, such as rocky hills and thick woods, to make our attack more difficult." The advance triggered a response in the form of Daniel Morgan, Isaac Sherman, and the militia rushing their troops toward the ridge to protect Washington's left flank. While Grey marked time at the Limekiln Pike intersection, Howe with the rest of the army continued moving up Old York Road. Howe's advance encountered American light horsemen and elements of Morgan's command about a mile into the march, which triggered a skirmish around the Old Abington Church and graveyard at the intersection of Susquehanna Road. According to Maryland militia commander Mordecai Gist, the British "drove our Picketts in and advanced with their Right Wing." Benjamin Tallmadge, who noted in his memoir that he was posted on the left "with a body of horse," may have commanded the detachment. Sergeant Thomas Sullivan of the 49th Regiment of Foot helped overrun the American pickets, "where a troop of the Dragoons surprised a party of their Light-horse." Enoch Edwards, who witnessed the skirmish, let Washington know the position had been overrun. The "Men is gone off & there is no reconnoitering Party here at

---

5 Von Baurmeister, *Revolution in America*, 137; von Feilitzsch, *Journal*, 140; Andre, *Journal*, 68. Church Road is modern Route 73 and Limekiln Pike is modern Route 152.

6 Von Muenchhausen, *At Howe's Side*, 45; Andre, *Journal*, 68. Edge Hill was at the intersection of Limekiln Pike and Edge Hill Road.

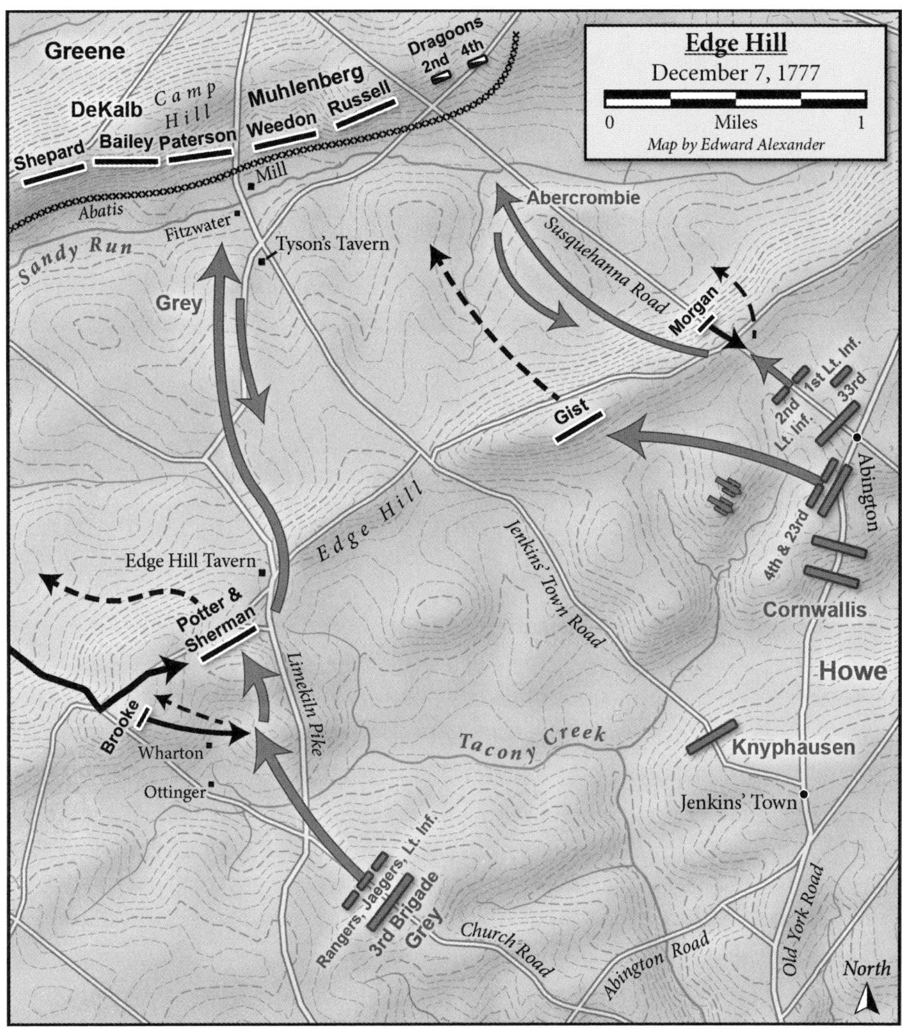

present," he messaged. "I shall tarry here [near the intersection] if you have any Commands."[7]

With Grey in position and his own column in control of the Susquehanna Road intersection, Howe sent out patrols to scout the formidable ridge looming

7 Letter, von Cochenhausen to von Jungkenn, January 19, 1778, 36; Letter, Mordecai Gist to unknown recipient, December 16, 1777, Mordecai Gist Letterbook, New York Public Library, New York, NY; Tallmadge, *Memoir*, 25; Sullivan, *Journal*, 158; Chase & Grizzard, eds., *Papers*, vol. 12, 568. Edwards had been a surgeon with the army and captured at Fort Washington. After exchange, he served as an aide to Lord Stirling at Brandywine.

The point of view of Gist's Maryland militia on Edge Hill (looking southeast). *Author*

before him. "During this time enemy [American] patrols showed up, but they kept at a distance," noted Lieutenant von Feilitzsch of the jaegers. "[S]everal volunteers went out beyond the outposts and shot 2 [American] officers dead." Howe's main column on the Susquehanna Road, meanwhile, "formed a line across the Road, keeping a strong detachment in our front," recorded Thomas Sullivan of the 49th Regiment of Foot. Howe personally rode out to reconnoiter. To his dismay, he found "the enemy's position here was even stronger than on the other side of Chestnut Hill," wrote his aide von Muenchhausen. "A range of heights called Edge Hill, in which the enemy had some 1,000 light troops, riflemen, etc., was between us and Washington's encampment." Fortunately for the Americans, Morgan's 300 riflemen and Gist's 900 Maryland militia had reached the position ahead of Howe's scouts. The British commander would later describe the enemy as "A corps of one thousand men, composed of riflemen, and other troops, from the enemy's Northern army, were found by the van-guard posted on this hill with cannon."[8]

While Howe was taking in the strong American position at Edge Hill and General Grey marked time off his left, Pennsylvania militia and the 2nd Connecticut approached Edge Hill to support Morgan's and Gist's right flank. Potter's nearly 1,000 militiamen arrived with roughly 300 Connecticut

---

8 Von Feilitzsch, *Journal*, 140-141; Sullivan, *Journal*, 158; von Muenchhausen, *At Howe's Side*, 45. Howe reviewed the position from the present location of Abington High School; *London Gazette*, January 18, 1778.

Continentals. The militia had demonstrated their inability to stand before the enemy just two days earlier when pressed into battle. Once again, they found themselves in front of the army.

The Americans lacked intelligence about what Howe was up to, and it fell to Potter to discern the positions of the enemy. According to 24-year-old Sherman, Potter was "perfectly unacquainted with [the terrain], and the Inhabitants pretending they were Ignorant of the Country, could not possible procure a Guide, which made reconnoitering highly necessary." Sherman "requested Genl Potter repeatedly, to reconnoiter the Enemy well before he attacked them." It was, he cautioned Potter "of the utmost importance, and perfectly consistent with every military Principle, to act with the greatest precaution." Sherman suggested they send out small parties "under faithfull and prudent Officers, and to march on slowly, that they might have time to reconnoitre the Country, examin the situation of the Enemy, and report to him." As the column approached the ridge, Maj. John Brooke of the Cumberland County militia "was detached with a party to reconnoiter the Enemy."[9]

Charles Grey was not a patient man, and waiting for Howe to begin his offensive proved more than frustrating. The lack of information from Howe only made matters worse. According to his own patrols, the American forces were approaching. "General Grey having waited far beyond the hour at which he had expected Orders to advance," recorded John Andre, "or to have information of Sir William Howe being in motion, determined to move forward." As the *Jaeger Corps Journal* reported, "It was necessary to dislodge an enemy advance corps before our army could make camp." Grey may have believed that no offensive operations were going to be attempted that day and wanted to secure his own position.[10]

Grey arranged his 3,100 men astride Limekiln Pike for a move toward Edge Hill and Brooke and his unsuspecting Pennsylvanians. The Hessian jaegers tramped directly up the road through woods supported by their artillery. The light infantry company of the British Brigade of Guards commanded by Col. Thomas Twistleton covered the right flank, while John Simcoe's Queen's Rangers covered the left. Grey's own Third British Brigade remained in reserve. Grey's men had pushed up Limekiln Pike about a mile when small arms fire "from a woody ridge to

---

9 The Pennsylvanians and Connecticut men marched down Church Road (modern Route 73) and turned left on modern Willow Grove Avenue to approach Edge Hill. Letter, Isaac Sherman to George Washington, March 11, 1778.

10 Burgoyne & Burgoyne, eds., *Journal of Jaeger Corps*, 32; Andre, *Journal*, 68.

the left" opened on them. The enemy, reported the *Jaeger Corps Journal*, were ensconced "on a steep height, very advantageously posted." According to one jaeger officer, the Americans (Brooke's detachment) "jumped from their ambush to attack us with bayonets, but their commanding officer was killed right away by a shot." Thereafter, recalled Jaeger Captain Johann Ewald, they "withdrew toward a wooded height." Sherman and Potter approached Edge Hill on horseback, "where we saw a considerable Body of the Enemy come out of a Wood, moving to our left." The mismanaged affair infuriated Isaac Sherman. "Genl Potter did not comply with my request, and I am very possitive that Majr Brooks made no report prior to our being fired upon, and that the situation of the Ground and Enemy were not properly examined," he seethed in his report to Washington.[11]

As Brooke's detachment rapidly fell back, Potter and Sherman advanced quickly in column in an effort to reach the high ground and form a line there to stop Grey's advance. "Such was the situation of the Regiment, that to have form'd the Line with the proper Front to the Enemy, it would have been necessary to have changed it to the right about," reported Sherman. The men ascended Edge Hill and "by Order fil'd off to the Left into a Wood, which was very full of under Brush, that we could see but a few Rods either way: which undoubtedly gave the Enemy a great advantage." The Continentals were attempting to fan out into a cohesive line when Joseph Reed arrived. Reed, who had previously served as Washington's adjutant general, was operating with the Pennsylvania militia during his visit to the army. He was on Edge Hill because Washington had asked Reed (and John Cadwalader) to scout British positions there. In a letter to Thomas Wharton, president of the Pennsylvania Assembly, Reed noted the enemy were first spotted "at Ottinger's, near your house [Wharton's country seat, Twickenham, in Cheltenham Township], but in a moment they moved, crossing your meadows in considerable numbers, but scattered."[12]

Reed's concern for protecting Wharton's property may have resulted in his decision to order troops around without the authority to do so. Reed held a general's commission from Congress, but was operating on this day as an intelligence agent and militia officer with no authority over regular Continental

---

11 Simcoe, *Journal*, 31; Andre, *Journal*, 69. This took place at the modern Waverly Road intersection; Burgoyne & Burgoyne, eds., *Journal of Jaeger Corps*, 32; von Feilitzsch, *Journal*, 141; Ewald, *Diary*, 109; Letter, Isaac Sherman to George Washington, March 11, 1778.

12 Letter, Isaac Sherman to George Washington, March 11, 1778; Reed, *Correspondence of Reed*, 350-351. The properties mentioned by Reed were approximately where today's Twickenham Road is in Cheltenham Township.

The British view of Edge Hill (looking northwest) from the
approximate position of their artillery. *Author*

troops. As Reed described it, "General Potter, Cadwalader, and myself endeavoured to draw up the troops in the woods, back of your house, in order to flank that wing." The actions outraged Isaac Sherman, who informed Washington that Reed rushed to the 2nd Connecticut Regiment "hurried it forward with such rapidity, altering its Disposition, ordering one Division this way, another that, puting Officers and Men into such confusion, that render'd it impracticable to keep that regularity so necessary when going into Action." Sherman told Reed "it was not in my power, or the Officers to keep the Men in order, if they went as he order'd," but the supernumerary "paid no attention to what I said—that, notwithstanding he took upon him the whole charge of the Regt." Sherman blamed Reed for the debacle that followed, charging him with "giving orders entirely counter to mine."[13]

Grey's men advanced during this confusion within the American ranks, pressing along in the wake of Brooke's retreating outpost. "The advanced guard followed them and the Corps deployed at once. We arrived in the flank and rear of the enemy corps," noted Johann Ewald. Andre concurred, writing that the jaegers and Queen's Rangers "formed and advanced upon them and the Light Infantry of the Guards with great activity and ardor ran around the foot of the ridge and came upon their flank." As Grey's men gained the advantage, the 2nd Connecticut "advanced 60 or seventy Rods in the Wood when the Van Guard was fired upon,

---

13   Reed, *Correspondence of Reed*, 351; Letter, Isaac Sherman to George Washington, March 11, 1778.

they having gained our Left Flank—A Front was formed as expeditiously as possible," recalled Sherman. The new front, however, was "hardly effected, before the Enemy fired upon us in front and upon the right Flank. The Militia having halted, and the Enemy got between us [Sherman's Continentals] & them [the militia]."[14]

Now nearly surrounded, Sherman's men would have to execute a fighting withdrawal to get back to the Pennsylvania militia or worse, cut their way out. Sherman described the chaotic situation:

> There was hardly a succession of a minute from the first fire, to our being fired upon in Front and both Flanks—In this situation the Men stood till they fired some four or five, the greater part three and none less than two rounds pr Man—the Enemy having the advantage of the Ground, were at least eight times our number—advanced within 12 or 14 Yards and began to close upon the rear of the Regt before I gave Orders to retreat, or a single Man gave way.[15]

Lieutenant Heinrich von Feilitzsch recalls how the "Jager corps ran up to win the hill completely, heated combat ensued, also small arms fire at a distance of 30 steps, but that did not last longer than approximately 10 minutes. The rebels retreated quickly and in disorder." Major John Simcoe, commander of the Queen's Rangers, recalled outflanking the Americans "on each wing," who were "turned in attempting to escape by the unparalleled swiftness of the light infantry of the guards, and driven across the fire of the Yagers, and the Queen's Rangers."[16]

The lightening enemy advance and small arms fire rapidly cut down the Connecticut men "Joseph Stiles," the second man to the right of Sgt. Lewis Hurd, "was shot through . . . I assisted in bringing him from the battle-ground and was left with him alone to close his eyes and bury him." Major Ames Walbridge took a wound to the head and Lt. John Harris was killed. Late in life, Zachariah Greene remembered that the bullet that struck his left shoulder "fractured the scapula and clavicle weakening and injuring the use of the arm." With his "garments . . . saturated with blood" Greene was evacuated to a field hospital, where "the severe fatigue of the battle, the loss of blood, with the chill of the cold night air, subjected

---

14 Ewald, *Diary*, 109; Andre, *Journal*, 69; Letter, Isaac Sherman to George Washington, March 11, 1778.

15 Letter, Isaac Sherman to George Washington, March 11, 1778.

16 Von Feilitzsch, *Journal*, 141; Simcoe, *Journal*, 31.

me to distressing cramps in my breast and limbs." Miraculously, Greene's brother "had eleven ball holes in his outside garment."[17]

The defeated Connecticut men streamed rearward through the ranks of the waiting Pennsylvania militia, hotly pursued by enthusiastic British and Hessian troops. Joseph Reed attempted to take control of Potter's militia and lead them into a counterattack, which quickly turned into a fiasco. Within a short time, Reed's horse was shot in the head and the rider "lost one of his Pistols, Sadddle & Bridle, which he was obliged to leave with the dead Horse, himself having a narrow escape," reported Maj. Gen. John Armstrong. Captain Allen McLane saw Reed's horse go down. McLane "charged the enemy's flanker who were running to bayonet Read, who, was recovering from his fall. Read was carried off the field by a light horseman." Reed and the militia, Sherman informed Washington, left the "Field with precipitation."[18]

Reed's account of the bloody affair was disingenuous. According to him, after "a sharp conflict they [militia] gradually gave way to a great superiority of numbers; having killed and wounded a number of the enemy, and also sustaining a loss of near twenty killed and wounded themselves.We were not so happy as to succeed as we wished," Reed concluded, "the troops giving way too soon, the enemy pressing on gave them a fire which completed their disorder." Washington's commissary general of prisoners, Elias Boudinot, offered a version that was more accurate: "the Pennsylvania militia greatly disgraced their country, running away at the first fire from half their number. . . . Reed had liked to have fallen a sacrifice to their

17 Lewis Hurd, "Sergeant Lewis Hurd (Written by Himself)," in Dena A. Hurd, *A History and Genealogy of the Family of Hurd in the United States* (New York, 1910), 73. Hurd went on to state the regiment was in confusion "with great loss of life and all their packs, blankets and camp kettles." Zachariah Greene, "Record of my Life and of the Greene Family," *Genealogies of Long Island Families: A Collection of Genealogies Relating to the Following Long Island Families: Dickerson, Mitchill, Wickham, Carman, Raynor, Rushmore, Satterly, Hawkins, Arthur Smith, Mills, Howard, Lush, Greene,* Charles J. Werner, ed. (New York, 1919), 129. Greene's account continues: "At the end of three weeks, we were removed to Reading, for the benefit of the Hospital; though the Yellow fever was among its inmates. There we hired a room; and there chanced to be a Surgeon of a British Regiment, then on parole in the village, by the name of Robinson, whom we engaged to perform the operation of removing the dead flesh and sawing and taking away the fractured bones. It was very painful, but necessary to a cure." Rankin, ed., *Narratives of the American Revolution*, 177.

18 Hazard, ed., *Pennsylvania Archives*, Series 1, vol. 6, 71; Handwritten extract from Journal of Captain Allen McLane, December 6, 1777, Joseph Reed Papers, New York Historical Society, New York, NY; Letter, Isaac Sherman to George Washington, March 11, 1778.

cowardice, his horse having been shot under him, and he escaped with great difficulty."[19]

After out-maneuvering and driving back Sherman's regiment and routing the Pennsylvania militia, Grey's men surged over Edge Hill toward Washington's main line. "The Jagers were in such fervor, that they did not hear the half moon, which was blown to signal them to stop, nor did they pay attention to the command of the general and the colonel, and the officers had to run along with them," admitted one of the jaegers. The result, reported the *Jaeger Corps Journal*, was that they chased the Americans "back nearly into the abatis."[20]

Casualty reports for the action along Limekiln Pike vary. Despite the severity of the brief action, the jaegers officially reported only three killed and nine wounded. One of Simcoe's mounted Queen's Rangers "was killed by a Yager, through mistake: he wore a helmet that had been taken from a rebel patrole a few days before." No American account detailing casualties exists. According to Johann Ewald, the Americans were "shot up so severely that a colonel, ten officers, and large number of men were killed, wounded, or captured." Another jaeger officer recorded, "The enemy left 42 dead, the wounded and the prisoners were taken to the rear right away by the English, but I am not sure of the exact number." As Simcoe proudly put it, "General Grey was pleased to express himself highly satisfied with the order and rapidity with which the Rangers advanced."[21]

Blame for the poor performance fell on Isaac Sherman and his 2nd Connecticut. "It is true the Regiment retreated in disorder," Sherman informed Washington, "but it was not in my power to have prevented it and considering its situation, I don't think any Troops in the World would have stood with more firmness, or have behaved with more Intrepidity." Sherman continued: "A Man's Reputation is his Life in the Military Line, and when he has once lost that his service is at an end and the publick Good loudly demands him to retire. I am by no means desirous of being an useless member of the Army, or instrumental of bringing

---

19 Reed, *Correspondence of Reed*, 350-352.

20 Von Feilitzsch, *Journal*, 141; Burgoyne & Burgoyne, eds., *Journal of Jaeger Corps*, 32.

21 Burgoyne & Burgoyne, eds., *Journal of Jaeger Corps*, 33. Lieutenant Heinrich von Feilitzsch reported eight killed and nine wounded. von Feilitzsch, *Journal*, 141- 142. Captain Johann Ewald reported four killed and 11 wounded. Ewald, *Diary*, 109; Simcoe, *Journal*, 31. Major Simcoe claimed nearly 100 American casualties. The *Jaeger Corps Journal* noted with some apparent surprise that "we only took thirty prisoners . . . while the enemy lost about twenty killed." Captain John Andre recorded American losses at "Between twenty and thirty of them . . . killed or wounded and fifteen taken prisoners." Andre, *Journal*, 69.

disgrace, and reflecting dishonour on my Countrymen. I should have requested Your Excellys permission to have retir'd."[22]

Charles Grey's fight was dying down just as William Howe's front a mile and half to the northeast was heating up. Howe had placed artillery on a small hill to pound the Americans before driving Daniel Morgan and Mordecai Gist off Edge Hill. Gist was pleased with the terrain held by his men. "[O]ur post was truly advantageous," he reported, "and the whole line waited with anxious Expectation for them to begin the attack." According to Gist, both he and Morgan were "orderd to attack their right flank in order to bring them on." Charles Eads, a rifleman with Morgan, later claimed they "attacked them and greatly annoyed them driving them frequently from their Cannon." Henry Dearborn of New Hampshire wrote that Morgan's command "gave a Party of them a Severe Drubing." British grenadier John Peebles, stationed on the left side of Howe's line, recalled around noon "a great deal of firing to our right which proved to be the advanced Corps of the main body meeting with different parties of the Rebels."[23]

By 1:00 p.m., Howe determined a general attack was needed to drive the Americans off Edge Hill. Sgt. Thomas Sullivan recalled the British light infantry put "their Blankets and Necessaries in waggons, and scouring the woods about two miles, forcing the Enemy's out-scouts" onto Edge Hill. Howe formed his 9,200 men into three lines. The two battalions of British light infantry formed the front line. Behind them deployed the British and Hessian grenadiers, British Brigade of Guards, and 7th, 26th, and 33rd Regiments of Foot. The First British Brigade, Stirn's Hessian brigade, and the 16th and 17th Light Dragoons formed the third line.[24]

The British light infantry advanced along the axis of Susquehanna Road directly towards Morgan's waiting riflemen supported by Howe's second line. Almost immediately, the third British line veered left to deal with Gist's Maryland

---

22 Letter, Isaac Sherman to George Washington, March 11, 1778. Sherman requested a court of inquiry to clear his name and the reputation of his regiment. "I therefore solicit your Excellency to appoint a Court, to examin into the behaviour of the Regiment on sd Day—that Officers if they misbehaved may be justly exposed to publick Censure, if not, honourably Acquited." No evidence has been found that a court of inquiry was ever conducted. Sherman remained in the army till war's end.

23 The artillery was likely placed where Abington High School sits today. Letter, Mordecai Gist to unknown recipient, December 16, 1777; Revolutionary War Pension and Bounty-Land-Warrant Application Files (M804) [RWPF], file S30392; Brown & Peckham, eds., *Journals of Dearborn 1775-1783*, 116; Peebles, *Diary*, 153.

24 Sullivan, *Journal*, 158-159.

militia. Initially, Morgan's sharpshooters bested the British lights. John Laurens informed his father the British light infantry "having made an imprudent use of their extraordinary allowance of rum, suffered, and every man that appeared would have been killed or taken if the rifle-men had been armed with bayonets." Laurens went on to state "Col. Morgan, who has no need of boasting to establish the reputation of his corps, says the British light infantry lost a great many in their skirmish with him." One anonymous American reported Morgan "attacked them with spirit, and did great execution. Burgoyne's grasshoppers [artillery captured at Saratoga] galled them extremely." Seven miles away, civilian Sally Wister "distinctly heard platoon firing. Everybody was at the door; I in the horrors. The armies, as we judg'd, were engag'd."[25]

British light infantrymen, Lt. Matthew Ankettle, remembered Edge Hill covered with "a strong thick Cover." The British advanced with the 1st Light Infantry Battalion right of Susquehanna Road and the 2nd Light Infantry Battalion left of the road. Morgan's men attacked the British right flank where the 1st Light Infantry Battalion took post in a wooded area. Charles Cornwallis overseeing the advance of the light infantry, brought the 33rd Regiment of Foot forward from the second line to deploy on the light infantry's right. Unaware of the 33rd's arrival in the dense woods, Morgan's men plowed into the front of the 1st Light Infantry Battalion rather than the British flank. Morgan hit five light infantry companies (those of the 10th, 15th, 17th, 26th, and 35th Regiments of Foot) "with great Spirit." Ankettle proudly wrote that the five companies received Morgan's attack "with great Steadiness & charg'd with fix'd Bayonets the Rebels ran off with Loss." However, noted Ankettle begrudgingly, "their fire was more destructive for the time & numbers engag'd than had happen'd this War." William Howe reported the Americans repulsed "with a considerable loss of officers and men, their cannon narrowly escaped." George Eads of Morgan's command noted the British "opportunely received a reinforcement [the 33rd Regiment of Foot] and we were compeled to give back." Captain John Jordan of Morgan's Corps wrote after the war "The enemy proved too powerful for him [Morgan] this corps was entirely discomforted & dispersed."[26]

---

25 *The Virginia Gazette,* December 26, 1777; Moore, *Diary of Revolution,* 526-527; Wister, *Journal,* 115. The long rifles carried by Morgan's men could not mount bayonets.

26 Ankettle, *Journal of Officer B*; Revolutionary War Pension and Bounty-Land-Warrant Application Files (M804) [RWPF], files S30392 & S38098. George Hangar wrote after the war "When Morgan's riflemen came down . . . flushed with success gained over Burgoyne's army, they marched to attack

Morgan's 300 men suffered notable losses in the effort against the British light infantry. The highest ranking casualty was Maj. Joseph Morris, detached from the 1st New Jersey Regiment to serve with Morgan. A bullet struck him in the head and he succumbed a month later. "This officer's distinguished merit," Light Horse Harry Lee eulogized in his war memoir, "had pointed him out to the commander-in-chief as peculiarly calculated for the rifle regiment, made up with a view to the most perilous and severe service, and which had, under its celebrated colonel (Morgan), eminently maintained its renown in the late trying scenes of the memorable campaign in the North; in all of which Morris bore a conspicuous part. His loss was deeply felt and universally regretted," concluded Lee, "being admired for his exemplary courage, and beloved for his kindness and benevolence."[27]

Besides Morris, John Laurens informed his father that Morgan's command lost 26 men. Captain John Jordan "was carried off the field badly wounded . . . severely wounded in the knee," according to his pension application. Lieutenant John Lapsley would later recall that "a Ball has passed through the left elbow, which has produced a perfect anchylosis [stiffness]: that the arm is considerably withered & diminished." Lord Cantelupe of the British Brigade of Guards claimed they "drove the rebels with the Loss of 9 killed & 19 wounded." The brave performance by Morgan's riflemen took its own pound of flesh. "The thickness of the wood where the Rebels were posted, concealing them from the view of our Battalions," reported Howe to Lord Germain, "occasioned the loss of one Officer

---

our light infantry . . . the moment they appeared" the light infantry "charge with the bayonet; not one man of them, out of four, had time to fire, and those who did, had no time to load again: they did not stand three minutes; the light infantry not only dispersed them instantly, but drove them for miles over the country…They never attacked, or even *looked at*, our light infantry again, without a regular force to support them." George Hangar, *To All Sportsmen, Farmers, and Gamekeepers* (London, 1814), 199-200. No evidence exists that Hangar was present or witnessed the fight.

27   "Revolutionary Pension Records of Morris County," *Proceedings of the New Jersey Historical Society, A Magazine of History, Biography and Genealogy*, 12 vols., New Series (1916), vol. 1, 91. Isaac Anderson of Morgan's corps claimed in his pension application that he "was at the battle of Edge Hill where Major Morris of his Regiment was killed & himself shot through the head . . . & left on the field for dead. He was however after lying 24 hours in the snow taken off the field & carried a prisoner to Philadelphia where he remained until the English Army evacuated that place, being left in the hospital after the evacuation by the British." In fact, Morris died well before the British evacuation. Revolutionary War Pension and Bounty-Land-Warrant Application Files (M804) [RWPF], file W4628. Surgeon Lewis Dunham of the 3rd New Jersey attended Morris "until his death which was occasioned by the wound he received in the above engagement." Minister Timothy Hohnes noted that Morris survived till brought home to his wife. After his death, he was buried the next day "with the Honors of War." "Revolutionary Pension Records of Morris County," 91-92; Lee, *Memoirs*, 105.

killed; 3 wounded, and about 30 men killed and wounded on our part, from their first fire."[28]

As the British light infantry and 33rd Regiment of Foot drove Morgan back, Howe's third line, the 4th and 23rd Regiments of Foot, dispatched Gist's Maryland militia on its left. Unfortunately, few accounts exist regarding this phase of the fighting. "The 4 regiment & 23d were Engaged & Lost some Men," Lord Cantelupe recorded in his diary. Gist, for a brief moment, had an advantage, recorded Lt. Matthew Ankettle. "A smart fire coming again on the Flank with 4th Regt halted."[29]

According to Mordecai Gist, "the Militia behaved with a Spirit becoming freemen—which his Excellency acknowledged—with his thanks in General orders." He went on to note "a very inconsiderable loss." Virginian John Marshall, a captain in 15th Virginia, left the best account of the action. "A small loss was also sustained in the militia," began the future Supreme Court justice. "The parties first attacked were driven in, but the enemy re-enforcing in numbers, and general Washington being unwilling to move from the heights in order to come to an engagement on the ground which was the scene of the skirmish, declined re-enforcing Gist and Morgan; who, in their turn, were compelled to give way." General Washington reported that the militia lost "Sixteen or Seventeen wounded."[30]

Timothy Pickering's 1811 recollection supports John Marshall's general account. Pickering was riding alone with Washington listening to the fighting on Edge Hill. "I wonder now whether it will be best to re-enforce Morgan or not?" asked Washington. "If a small re-enforcement be sent, they must soon give way," replied Pickering, the general's chief staff officer. "[I]f a large force be detached, a

---

28 *The Virginia Gazette,* December 26, 1777; Revolutionary War Pension and Bounty-Land-Warrant Application Files (M804) [RWPF], file S46397; John Lapsley pension application downloaded online www.revwarapps.org/VAS837.pdf, accessed August 5, 2023. Entry for December 4, Lord Cantelupe Diary; *London Gazette*, January, 18 1778.

29 Entry for December 4, Lord Cantelupe Diary; Ankettle, *Journal of Officer B.* This action took place where the Edge Hill Wildlife Sanctuary is today. Much of the ground where the action took place was purchased in 1855 by Russell Smith, a theatrical scenery painter. His children found bullets, buttons, cannon balls, and bayonets. Smith also found the remains of four soldiers and marked the locations with rusty bayonets. When Smith's grandson sold the property to a real estate developer in 1953, the remains of four of Morgan's men were moved to the North Penn VFW post. Thompson, *Whitemarsh,* 62 & 95.

30 Letter, Mordecai Gist to unknown recipient, December 16, 1777; Marshall, *Life of Washington,* 318-319; Chase & Grizzard, eds., *Papers,* vol. 12, 592.

great breach will be made in the line of defence; and this body also will not be able long to maintain their ground; and if they should retreat in disorder, the whole line may be thrown into confusion." Washington agreed.[31]

Unable to hold, Morgan and Gist retired to Washington's main line; some British units pursued. Lieutenant Colonel Robert Abercrombie led the advance with his 1st British Light Infantry Battalion around 3:00 p.m., with "The Grenadiers . . . a hundred Yards distance in our rear," recorded Thomas Sullivan of the 49th Regiment of Foot, "and the rear of third Line at the same distance, from the Grenadiers." Once they arrived along Sandy Run at the base of the Whitemarsh hills, the British "could hear them [Americans] felling the trees to hinder our Cannon from advancing upon them." The enemy, observed Friedrich von Muenchhausen, had "retreated to the very high and wooded hills of their real camp."[32]

The British and Hessian grenadiers had advanced to within pistol shot of the American line. Major Carl von Baurmeister moved in front of the English grenadiers and found the rebels entrenched. Washington's men, he wrote, were "Before and behind their strongest abatis, which went up the slope of the hill, they had dug trenches with embrasures every two to three hundred paces. There were no batteries behind the abatis, but on the entire flank I counted nine uncovered pieces, all of which were manned by French officers and soldiers. . . . They were all determined to wait for whatever might come, but at the same time there was much excitement among them."[33]

Each side spent an uneasy few hours measuring the intentions of the other. "[We] had great reason to fear a general attack," admitted John Laurens. Thinking back later in life, "Light Horse Harry" Lee came to believe the American position "might have been turned by pursuing the old York road; which measure would infalliably have produced battle or have forced retreat." General Washington wrote to Patrick Henry on December 10 that because of the advance, he "expected an attack in the Night or by day break and made disposition accordingly." The Virginian "rode through every brigade of his army, delivering in person his orders respecting the manner of receiving the enemy, exhorting his troops to rely principally on the bayonet, and encouraging them by the steady firmness of his

---

31 Pickering, *Life of Pickering*, 85.

32 Sullivan, *Journal*, 159; von Muenchhausen, *At Howe's Side*, 45. Cannon balls were later found where Hillside Cemetery now sits in Roslyn. Buck, "Battle of Edge Hill," 230.

33 Von Baurmeister, *Revolution in America*, 137-138.

countenance, as well as by his words, to a vigorous performance of their duty," recorded Capt. John Marshall.[34]

"Our army was drawn up in order of battle, in three lines, on a very commanding hill, the brow of which was, at first, strengthened by a formidable abatis," wrote Washington's adjutant general Timothy Pickering. "But we had continued so long on the ground, and the weather had grown so cold, the soldiers had burnt up all the large wood, so that brush only remained. This was gathered into a row, which, however, would have given very little embarrassment to an enemy. The army being thus formed," he concluded, "and a general battle expected on that ground, General Washington rode along, in the rear of the front line, which was posted on the brow of the hill."[35]

William Howe scouted the American position until about 8:00 p.m. In a move reminiscent of Washington, he held a council of war "in order to take the opinion of the general officers respecting an attack upon the lines." They unanimously determined "from the advantageous situation of Mr. Washington, and the extraordinary strength of his intrenchments, it would be unadvisable, and in the highest degree dangerous to attempt to force them." Howe's Hessian aide reported they "found everywhere strong natural and man-made obstacles, which prevented any hope of success." According to a Hessian quartermaster officer, "It was also learned that the enemy sent their heavy baggage to Lancaster, an indicator they were ready to retreat. Therefore, General Howe gave up his plan."[36]

Leaving a strong picket line along Sandy Run, Howe withdrew to Edge Hill and consolidated his gains while the men built campfires. The withdrawal surprised Maj. Benjamin Tallmadge (2nd Continental Light Dragoons). "I thought a general battle was inevitable," he admitted, "but neither General thought it prudent to descend into the plain."[37]

Almost immediately, skirmishes broke out along the picket line. Lieutenant von Feilitzsch recalled being positioned in an open field and "the enemy placed his guards close before mine." December 7 proved a long night for the young jaeger:

---

34 *The Virginia Gazette,* December 26, 1777; Lee, *Memoirs,* 105; Chase & Grizzard, eds., *Papers,* vol. 12, 590; Marshall, *Life of Washington,* 319.

35 Pickering, *Life of Pickering,* 84-85.

36 *Morning Post and Daily Advertiser,* January 19, 1778; von Muenchhausen, *At Howe's Side,* 45; Letter, von Cochenhausen to von Jungkenn, January 19, 1778, 36.

37 Sullivan, *Journal,* 160; Tallmadge, *Memoir,* 25.

Their firing was constant and no sentry could walk up and down. The guards were changed in secrecy. Patrols could not be made. The pickets could not sit by the fire, or walk around it, one could not even get fire for a smoke, because immediately 3-4 bullets would come whizzing into the fire, and because the Jagers finally began to make a joke out of it, I had to forbid it in all seriousness, lest someone were wounded unnecessarily. After I had been standing for half the night, I was very tired and sat down on a dead rebel; the enemy camp was only a cannon shot away from us, and very restless throughout the night.[38]

About an hour after taking their position, the light infantry of the British Brigade of Guards "were very briskly attacked," but "maintained their ground and repulsed the Enemy, with the loss on their side of only one man," wrote Capt. John Andre in his journal. Henry Dearborn of New Hampshire received orders to "attract the Enimys Cavelry, but found them so strongly Posted that I Could Not attack them without too great a Resk." The heavy fighting concluded for the day, wrote John Laurens: "there was nothing more than a little bickering between our pickets."[39]

Men from both armies were exhausted, having been four days into the operation. Captain Jonathan Forman of the 4th New Jersey Regiment complained of being kept "Under Arms 3 or 4 days." Apparently, provisions and rum did not reach all parts of Howe's army before the assault. As Grenadier John Peebles bitterly noted, "no provision today."[40]

As Washington's army bedded down for the night, many anticipated a major engagement the next morning. James McMichael of the Pennsylvania Line wrote in his diary, "the sentries kept up a fire all night and everything presaged a general attack in the morning." Virginian John Marshall wrote after the war, "the dispositions of the evening indicated an intention to attack him [Howe] the ensuing morning." Pennsylvania militia commander John Armstrong reported, "Tomorrow morning, most probably, the general affair comes on." Along the British picket line, few showed concern. "I stood sentry this night where I heard the

---

38 Von Feilitzsch, *Journal*, 142-143.

39 Andre, *Journal*, 69; Brown & Peckham, eds., *Journals of Dearborn 1775-1783*, 116; *The Virginia Gazette,* December 26, 1777.

40 Jonathan Forman, Revolutionary War diary, Fellows Papers, Box 2, Department of Rare Books and Special Collection, Rush Rhees Library, University of Rochester, Rochester, NY; Peebles, *Diary*, 153.

enemy talking very plain," noted Pvt. Jacob Smith of the Queen's Rangers in his diary.[41]

December 8

At dawn on a foggy Monday morning, Washington dispatched scouts, but Howe's army was nowhere in sight because Howe was withdrawing toward Philadelphia. According to the *Journal of the Leib Regiment*, "as General Howe . . . found the enemy too strongly intrenched here and did not wish to sacrifice his army unnecessarily he ordered the troops to march back to their former camp without attacking the enemy." Washington sent out a small detachment of the 4th Continental Light Dragoons and two members of the Philadelphia Light Horse to determine Howe's whereabouts. Around noon, "they found the enemy in motion & sent off one of the horsemen: on proceeding further to their right, they fell in with another body under arms of which they sent off information," recalled militiaman John Donaldson. Howe was moving down Old York Road with his entire force.[42]

"[T]he first certain account that I could obtain of their intentions was that they were in full march towards Philada," explained General Washington in his December 10 letter to Patrick Henry. "I immediately dispatched light parties after them." Militia commander Mordecai Gist was directed to take his Marylanders and some of Daniel Morgan's men and "follow to Harass their Rear but unfortunately," recorded Gist, "their rear Guard had been taken off about an hour before I received these orders notwithstanding I continued my route with an Expectation of picking up some straglers." Gist managed to engage Howe's rearguard near Shoemaker's Mill on Tacony Creek. As Elias Boudinot later wrote, "The light

41 McMichael, "Diary," 156; Marshall, *Life of Washington*, 319; Hazard, ed., *Pennsylvania Archives*, Series 1, vol. 6, 71; Jacob Smith, "Diary of Jacob Smith—American Born," Charles William Heathcote, ed., *The Pennsylvania Magazine of History and Biography*, 128 vols. (Philadelphia, PA, 1932), vol. 56, 261.

42 "Journal of the Remarkable Events Which Occurred to the Hon. Leib Infantry Regiment," Hessian Documents of the American Revolution, letter V, microfiche 312, American Philosophical Society, Philadelphia, PA; Smith, "History of the 1st City Troop." British and Hessian accounts confirm the column moved between noon and 1 p.m. "At one p.m. when we marched back again to Philadelphia." "Journal of the Regiment von Donop 1776-84," Hessian Documents of the American Revolution, Letter E, microfiche no. 40, American Philosophical Society, Philadelphia, PA.

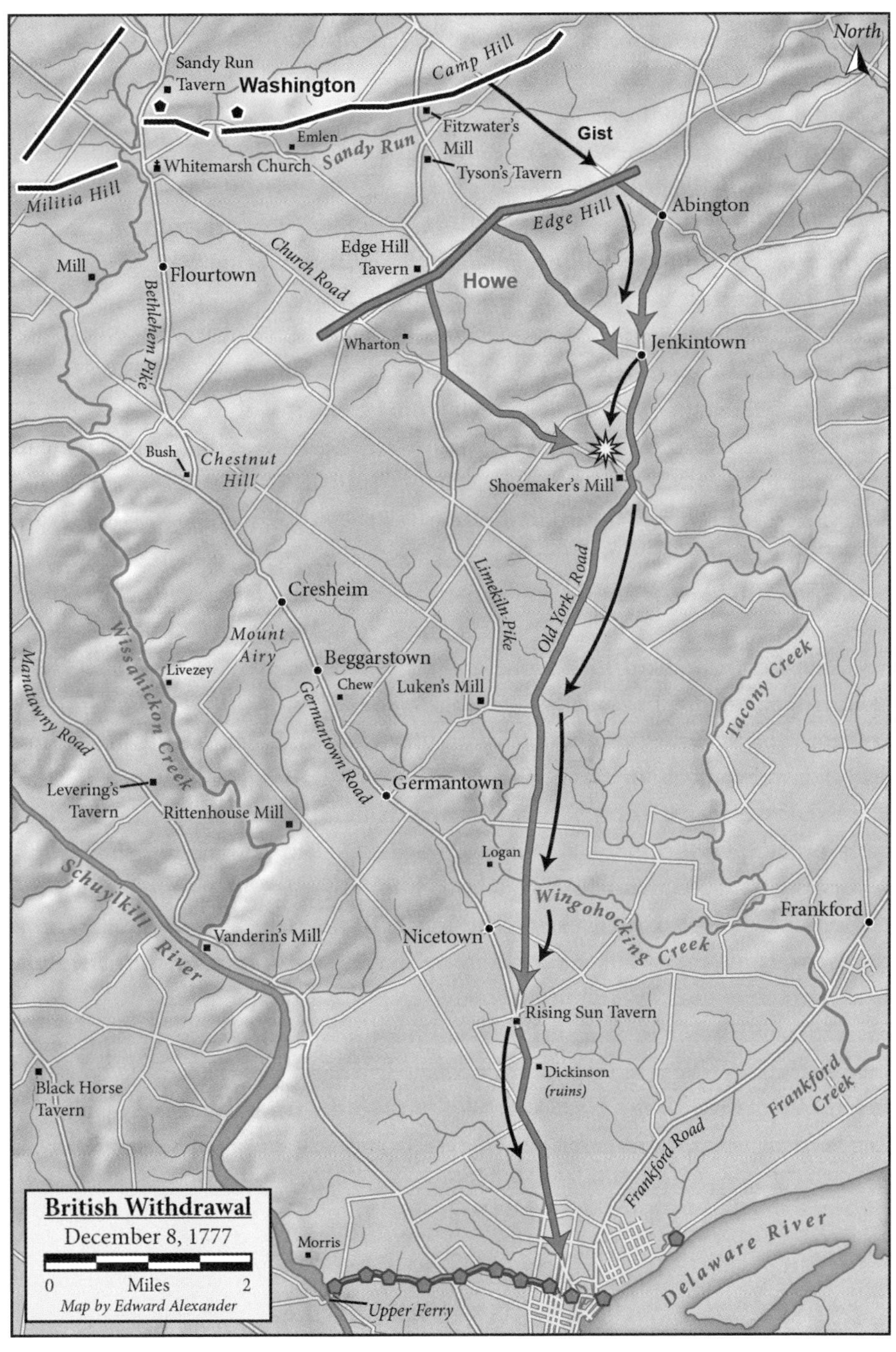
North
Sandy Run Tavern
Washington
Camp Hill
Gist
Fitzwater's Mill
Tyson's Tavern
Emlen
Whitemarsh Church
Sandy Run
Abington
Edge Hill
Militia Hill
Mill
Flourtown
Church Road
Edge Hill Tavern
Howe
Bethlehem Pike
Wharton
Jenkintown
Bush
Chestnut Hill
Shoemaker's Mill
Wissahickon Creek
Limekiln Pike
Old York Road
Tacony Creek
Cresheim
Mount Airy
Manatawny Road
Livezey
Beggarstown
Chew
Luken's Mill
Germantown Road
Levering's Tavern
Rittenhouse Mill
Germantown
Logan
Wingohocking Creek
Frankford
Schuylkill River
Vanderin's Mill
Nicetown
Rising Sun Tavern
Black Horse Tavern
Dickinson (ruins)
Frankford Road
Frankford Creek
British Withdrawal
December 8, 1777
0   Miles   2
Map by Edward Alexander
Morris
Upper Ferry
Delaware River

Horse persued & came up & harassed the rear of the British a few Miles from Philadelphia."[43]

The fight around the mill was a brisk and lively affair. "The Rebels formed to a fence and delivered a very brisk fire," recalled General Grey's aide John Andre. Howe's rearguard Hessian jaegers had somehow failed to cover a hill before descending into the Tacony Creek valley. One jaeger admitted that it was a "bad mistake" to vacate the high ground, and "the enemy took advantage of it right away." Gist's command seized the empty hill and fired down into the withdrawing jaegers. The light infantry of the British Brigade of Guards rushed to their assistance, throwing Gist back. Johann Ewald also put together a force of jaegers and "retook the hill," wrote Heinrich von Feilitzsch. The inexperienced Lt. Friedrich Ebenauer, commander of the rearguard, was reprimanded for his neglect "for permitting his men to run down the hill for buried potatoes," penned von Feilitzsch in his journal. Ewald glossed over the incident in his diary: "I was attacked by a superior party from a wood on the left. . . . The enemy was driven back." The mistake cost the jaegers 21 men and the British light infantrymen 19, all wounded.[44]

That final skirmish marked the end of Howe's move out of Philadelphia. "[T]hese mighty men," bragged George Weedon in a December 17 letter, "retreated back to their strong lines with precipitation, leaving us masters of the Ground, and without attempting the Army which was their object." After the war, "Light Horse Harry" Lee also took a moment to gloat. Howe, he boasted, "returned to Philadelphia, unequivocally acknowledging by his retreat, that his adversary had at length attained a size which forbade the risk of battle on ground chosen by himself." Staffer Joseph Clark agreed with Lee's assessment: "It seems the enemy had waited all this time before our lines to decoy us from the heights we possessed, and thereby get an advantage over us; but finding they could not succeed in this, nor in getting our left flank, they thought best to go off." No one on the American side, of course, was happy that Howe had gotten away. "We were all Chagrin'd at this, as we were willing to Chase them in Rear," complained a Connecticut surgeon. Before we "could expect such a thing from these

<hr>

43 Chase & Grizzard, eds., *Papers*, vol. 12, 590; Letter, Mordecai Gist to unknown recipient, December 16, 1777. This took place near the present Richard Wall Park in Cheltenham Township. Smith, "History of the 1st City Troop"; Boudinot, *Journal*, 53.

44 Andre, *Journal*, 71; von Feilitzsch, *Journal*, 143-144; Ewald, *Diary*, 110.

braggadocios, they were on full march for Philadelphia," declared an anonymous source.[45]

The move out of Philadelphia and back again would be remembered by many, not for the skirmishing or battle that didn't quite come off, but for the trail of destruction Howe left in wake. The British, reported an appalled John Armstrong, "having burnt the new Rising Sun Inn, on their way—whilst they lay on Chestnut Hill they Burnt some good Houses & Barns, and have, it's said, left several familys little more than empty walls." Joseph Reed confirmed the devastation in a letter two days later: "The spirit of ravage and plunder was never more conspicuous, without the least discrimination." Colonel Israel Angell of the 2nd Rhode Island decided to witness the damage for himself and rode into Germantown "to See what Ravages and Destruction the Brittish troops had made, which was Shocking to beholde, as they had destroyd every thing in their power Except the Buildings, and Some of them they had Burnt."[46]

According to Ansbacher Johann Dohla's diary, Howe's long column returned to Philadelphia with "many cattle and provisions that they had taken from the rebels," but mentioned nothing at all about the wanton destruction. Civilian Robert Morton confirmed the British had stolen "about 700 head of cattle," and added that they had also "committed many other depredations, as if the sole purpose of the expedition was to destroy and to spread desolation and ruin, to dispose the inhabitants to rebellion by despoiling their property, and to give their enemies fresh cause to alarm the apprehensions of the people by these too true melancholy facts." Another civilian, Christopher Marshall, also felt compelled to record what he considered appalling British depredations. "It's said they have pillaged and carried with them everything that came in their way and was portable and of any value," he penned in his journal, "besides burning [and] destroying many houses and effects, also taking with them, by force, all the boys they could lay their hands on, above the age of ten years. Thus, this time," Marshall concluded, "has the great boaster

45 Letter, George Weedon to John Page, December 17, 1777; Lee, *Memoirs*, 105. However, at the time, Lee admitted in a dispatch to General Anthony Wayne of his inability to pursue Howe: "I find my men & horses much fatigued." Letter, Henry Lee to Anthony Wayne, December 8, 1777, Anthony Wayne Papers, Historical Society of Pennsylvania, Philadelphia, PA, vol. 4; Clark, "Diary," 108; Rankin, ed., *Narratives of the American Revolution*, 178; Moore, *Diary of Revolution*, 526.

46 Hazard, ed., *Pennsylvania Archives*, Series 1, vol. 6, 71; Reed, *Correspondence of Reed*, 352; Angell, *Diary*, n.p.

[Howe] succeeded in this vainglorious expedition, to the eternal shame of him and of all his boasting Tory friends."[47]

"This expedition has only served to discover the weakness and cruelty of the British army," angrily wrote one anonymous American. "Whenever they marched it was in the night," and

> whenever they halted they took post on the strongest grounds; wherever they came they plundered the miserable inhabitants without respect of persons. Those merciful considerations which should influence us in our treatment of our worst enemies, found no place among them. The poor, the widow, the fatherless children were stripped of their all, even without leaving them bread to eat, or clothes enough to cover them. Did they who talk of British mercy and protection but see those unhappy sufferers![48]

Howe's expeditionary force was back inside its Philadelphia lines by 9:00 p.m. Jacob Smith of the Queen's Rangers recorded he was "glad" that he "got back safe to my former quarters again." Some returned to find that their bunking areas had been ransacked by those left behind. The 71st Highlanders, huffed Grenadier John Peebles, "had taken up our Camp burnt our wood & destroyed our boards & straw." Civilians thought the returning troops looked demoralized. The army, thought Elizabeth Drinker, "carrys no very agreeable appearance with it." Robert Morton discovered, "[T]o the great astonishment of the citizens, the army returned. The causes assigned for their speedy return are various and contradictory." Teenager Sally Wister in Gwynedd Township rejoiced that the British had disappeared from the countryside: "Charming news this. May we ever be thankful to the Almighty Disposer of events for his care and protection of us while surrounded with dangers."[49]

After the fight at Shoemaker's Mill and other minor actions, General Washington recalled his scouts, and the army settled in for the night. A Connecticut man remembered being "remanded back with several draughts of Rum in our frozen bellies, which made us so glad we all fell asleep in our open huts, nor experienced the coldness of the Night 'till we found ourselves much stiffened by it

---

47 Dohla, *A Hessian Diary*, 61; Fellow Anspacher Cpl. Stephen Popp agreed: "Genl Howe returned with a large supply of cattle, provisions . . . captured from the Rebels." Popp, "Journal," 30; Morton, "Diary," 34-35; Marshall, *Extracts*, 148-149.

48 Moore, *Diary of Revolution*, 527.

49 Smith, "Diary," 262; Peebles, *Diary*, 154; Drinker, *Diary of Elizabeth Drinker*, 262; Morton, "Diary," 34; Wister, *Journal*, 118-119.

in the Morning." For most of the army the hours slipped quietly past. As Capt. Paul Brigham of the 8th Connecticut noted in his diary, "Day Passed until Evening and no action."[50]

The absence of "action" notwithstanding, conditions at the front were miserable. Three days earlier Washington had sent away the army's excess baggage with "both tents and kittles and beds," complained Pvt. Elijah Fisher of the 4th Massachusetts. This left the soldiers without "tents nor anything to Cook our Provisions in and that was Prity Poor for beef was very leen and no salt." Meat could only be cooked by throwing "it on the Coles and brile it and the warter we had to Drink and to mix our flower with was out of a brook that run along by the Camps and so many a dippin and washin it which maid it very Dirty and muddy." The army's baggage train was recalled but only reached Trappe on December 8. There, Henry Muhlenberg was forced "to take in the general wagonmaster and his deputee with their horses. Our barn was also filled with marauders who, when begging will not get them far enough, know how to get what they want by pilfering. There is no want of provisions as long as they lie still." Because the woodcutting tools were with the baggage train, his men had great difficulty obtaining firewood and building shelters.[51]

Contemporary Analysis

Although no general action broke out during the Whitemarsh operation, the result elevated American morale. "Thus an expedition, which raised the expectations of every body, and from whence it was thought some great decisive stroke would arise, terminated in degrading the whole British army to a foraging party," boasted John Laurens. "Sir William Howe imagined that on the first appearance of the British army the shivering, half-naked defenders of liberty, would have decamped and left him master of the country." Howe's withdraw, observed a staff officer, "ended that high Threatinings with which the British Army had been filling the Ears of the Citizens of Philadelphia for several Weeks." The British retreat, Henry Dearborn of the 3rd New Hampshire jotted in his journal,

---

50 Rankin, ed., *Narratives of the American Revolution*, 178. Paul Brigham, "A Revolutionary Diary of Captain Paul Brigham: November 19, 1777-September 4, 1778," Edward A Hoyt, ed., *Vermont History*, 92 vols. (January 1966), vol. 34, 15.

51 Elijah Fisher, *Elijah Fisher's Journal While in the War for Independence, and Continued Two Years After He Came to Maine 1775-1784* (Augusta, ME. 1880), 7; Muhlenberg, *Journals*, vol. 3, 111.

"must Convince the world that Mr How Did not Dare to fight us unless he Could have the advantage of the ground." Pennsylvania militia brigade commander James Potter agreed the entire operation had amounted to little when he reported on December 11, "I can't but observe that their mighty boasting may justly be compared to a sudden blast of wind." The Marquis de Lafayette tipped his hat to Howe, who "judged it more prudent to retire during the night, after four days of apparent hesitation." Connecticut brigade commander Jedidiah Huntington agreed with that general assessment. "General Howe came out & took Post on a Range of Hills about two Miles from us . . . with an evident Intention of attacking us or bringing us to an Action," he wrote his brother on December 9. "[W]e wished and expected the former, but his Conduct had convinced us he judged our Ground too strong and that he meant to draw us out of our Lines." Many were disappointed that Howe had not tried Washington's lines. "Had they attacked us here," Elias Boudinot wrote, "I believe, in all human probability, it would have been the last they would have made in America."[52]

Essayist Thomas Paine recorded his thoughts in a letter to Benjamin Franklin on May 16, 1778. "It was a most contemptible affair," scoffed Paine. "The threatening and seeming fury he [Howe] set out with, and the haste and terror the army retreated with, made it laughable. I have seen several persons from Philadelphia, who assure me that their coming back was a mere uproar, and plainly indicated their apprehension of pursuit."[53]

Not everyone agreed with these assessments. Some believed Washington missed an opportunity to defeat Howe by failing to take the offensive. Washington's council of war on December 7 had rejected the idea of a counterattack. "His Excellency expressed the strongest inclination to attack them, as soon as it was known they would not attack us, but his principal officers were utterly opposed to it," complained Joseph Reed. "I think more enterprise in our army would be acceptable." Some members of Congress also voiced concerns. Cornelius Harnett worried that American passivity was inviting disaster: "[W]e shall suffer ourselves to be Attacked instead of attacking. This Conduct I believe has often proved disadvantageous." Elbridge Gerry echoed Harnett's thoughts the

---

52 *The Virginia Gazette,* December 26, 1777; Boudinot, *Letterbook,* 57; Brown & Peckham, eds., *Journals of Dearborn 1775-1783,* 117; Hazard, ed., *Pennsylvania Archives,* Series 1, vol. 6, 83; Marquis de Lafayette, *Memoirs, Correspondence and Manuscripts of General Lafayette: Published by his Family* (New York, 1837), vol. 1, 129; "Huntington Papers," 373.

53 "Military Operations," 294.

same day in a letter to John Adams: "I sincerely wish that our officers would prevent it [British maneuvers] by beginning the Attack, And until such an enterprising Spirit prevails, think that the Enemy will maneuver to Advantage. . . . The American Army are in a better Situation for an Engagement in Point of Numbers than they have been this Campaign," continued Gerry, "may God grant them Fortitude, & crown their Endeavours with Success."[54]

Washington, meanwhile, issued general orders the day after Howe's withdrawal praising Daniel Morgan's efforts. "The Commander in Chief returns his warmest thanks to Col. Morgan, and the officers and men of his intrepid corps, for their gallant behavior in the several skirmishes with the enemy yesterday," read the announcement. "He hopes the most spirited conduct will distinguish the whole army, and gain them a just title to the praises of their country, and the glory due to brave men—They will remember, that they are engaged in the cause of humanity and of freedom, and that the period is probably at hand, when, by their noble and generous exertions, the Liberties & Independence of America shall be firmly established." Washington also heaped praise on the Maryland militia (though in doing so curiously ignored the contributions of the Pennsylvania and Connecticut men). "The General with pleasure has been informed that that the Militia of Maryland under Colonel Gist, shewed in yesterday's skirmishes a spirit becoming freemen, and which claims his sincere acknowledgements."[55]

Washington, who was well aware of the critiques of his generalship, explained his decision not to attack in his final report to Congress. "I sincerely wish, that they had made an Attack, the Issue in all probability, from the di[sposi]ition of our Troops and the strong situ[ation] of our Camp, would have been for[tunate] and happy. At the same time," he added, "I m[ust add,] that reason, prudence, and every principle of policy forbad us quitting our post to attack them. Nothing but success would have justified the measure, and this could not be expected from their position."[56]

Howe's men agreed that attacking Washington's strong position would have been unwise. When asked about that possibility during Howe's testimony to

54 Reed, *Correspondence of Reed*, 352; Smith, et al., eds., *Letters*, vol. 8, 388 & 390.

55 Chase & Grizzard, eds., *Papers*, vol. 12, 571.

56 Ibid., 592. In 1787, Washington recorded in his diary a visit to Whitemarsh. "In company with Mr. Powell [Samuel Powell, Mayor of Philadelphia] rode up to the White Marsh, traversed my old Incampment, and contemplated on the dangers which threatened the American Army at that place." George Washington diary entry, August 19, 1787, www.consource.org/document/diary-entry-by-george-washington-1787-8-18, accessed August 5, 2023.

Parliament, Maj. Gen. Charles Grey replied, "I think an attack of the enemy, so very strongly situated as they were at White-Marsh, would have been highly imprudent." Washington, wrote Lt. William Hale of the British grenadiers on January 20, 1778, "was too strongly entrenched to admit our forcing his lines under the loss of two thousand men, much too great a price at this advanced season." Artilleryman Francis Downman agreed. "Our general saw that they could not be forced without a great loss of men and without any material advantage attending it. A successful blow at this juncture against the rebels," he continued, "would be attended with perhaps no other circumstance than driving them a little further back, which would answer very little purpose."[57]

One month later, an article in the British *Morning Post* mocked Howe's effort. "The History of our American Campaigns must excite Laughter whenever it shall be published. . . . And what must the King of Prussia think of General Howe who drew up his Army in Front of Washington's Lines, looked at him, then wheeled to the Right about and—decamped?"[58]

Others avoided passing judgment. "How far this move of the Army may be considered as good or bad I shall not take upon me to determine, as much maybe said for as against it," concluded engineer Archibald Robertson. Lieutenant Carl von Bueltzingsloewen of the von Mirbach Regiment thought the whole purpose of the expedition was "to determine the positions of the enemy," which was achieved. The entire affair, thought Ambrose Serle correctly, secretary to Richard Howe, "will probably give them [the Americans] fresh Spirits, and encourage them to annoy the Environs of the Town through the winter." Howe soon came to realize the strength of the American position and his inability to maintain his troops in the field at that time of year. He informed George Germain of his unwillingness "to expose the troops longer to the weather in this inclement season, without tents or baggage of any kind for officers or men." In summary, Washington took up a strong position and held his ground, invited a British attack that never came, parried a variety of thrusts and prods, and Howe had little choice but to return to the city.[59]

---

57 *Narrative*, 106; Walter Harold Wilkin, *Some British Soldiers in America* (London, 1914), 233-234; Whinyates, *Services*, 54.

58 Troy Bickham, *Making Headlines: The American Revolution as Seen through the British Press* (DeKalb, IL, 2009), 196.

59 Robertson, *Diaries*, 161; von Bueltzingsloewen, "Journal," 72; Serle, *Journal*, 267; *London Gazette*, January 18, 1778.

The American army was maturing, but it was a motley assemblage. Many of the northern brigades that had served at Saratoga had only recently moved south to join the army. The command structure Washington created just before the Whitemarsh operations was new and untested. The Virginian understandably lacked confidence that this version of his army could be thrown against British veterans with a reasonable chance of success. At a time when rumblings against him were running through Congress, remaining on the defensive may have been politically unwise, but the risk to his army in assuming the offensive was too great to accept. Washington knew it was unlikely that Howe could successfully flank him. Only about 60 percent of Washington's available command was deployed in the front line on the Whitemarsh hills, leaving Lord Stirling's large mobile force in the second line to easily counter any such move.[60]

The British commander apparently wanted to draw Washington into an open field fight. Probes of Washington's right and left, however, demonstrated the formidable strength of the American position. When it became apparent that Washington was not going to leave the high ground to attack him, and that an attack on his lines was too risky, Howe returned to Philadelphia.

If Howe had maneuvered Washington off the hills, the largely untouched Bucks County would have been open to Howe's foragers. He tried his favorite (and usually effective) flanking tactic once for the move to Edge Hill, but did not try it again after December 7. Howe could have continued his flanking move up the Old York Road in an effort to turn Washington's left flank but decided against it—probably because his intention was never to engage in direct heavy combat during the Whitemarsh operation. After nearly four months of hard campaigning, his army was desperately short of provisions. Empty wagons accompanied the expedition for a reason. Howe was so short of food that he had to send back a detachment back to Philadelphia to haul more to his army halfway into the operation. To turn Washington's left flank, Howe would have had to delay at least another day to transport even more food from the city.

The Whitemarsh operation was exactly what it looked like, i.e., a huge foraging expedition with the added hope of catching Washington or a portion of his army at a disadvantage.

60 McGuire, *Campaign*, vol. 2, 256.

Chapter 11

The Roads to Valley Forge

December 9-19, 1777

"I am sick—discontented—and out of humor."[1]

— Albigence Waldo, Connecticut surgeon, December 14, 1777

Continental Decisions

William Howe's return to Philadelphia left George Washington with time to decide his next move. While he continued to harbor hopes of attacking Howe, the need to select a winter encampment site weighed on him. The month or more his Continental Army spent on the Whitemarsh Hills had stripped the surrounding countryside of wood and forage, and Howe's recent excursion demonstrated vulnerability to sudden attacks. Washington needed to relocate the army before his food, clothing, and equipment gave out.[2]

---

1 Rankin, ed., *Narratives of the American Revolution*, 181.

2 McGuire, *Campaign*, vol. 2, 256.

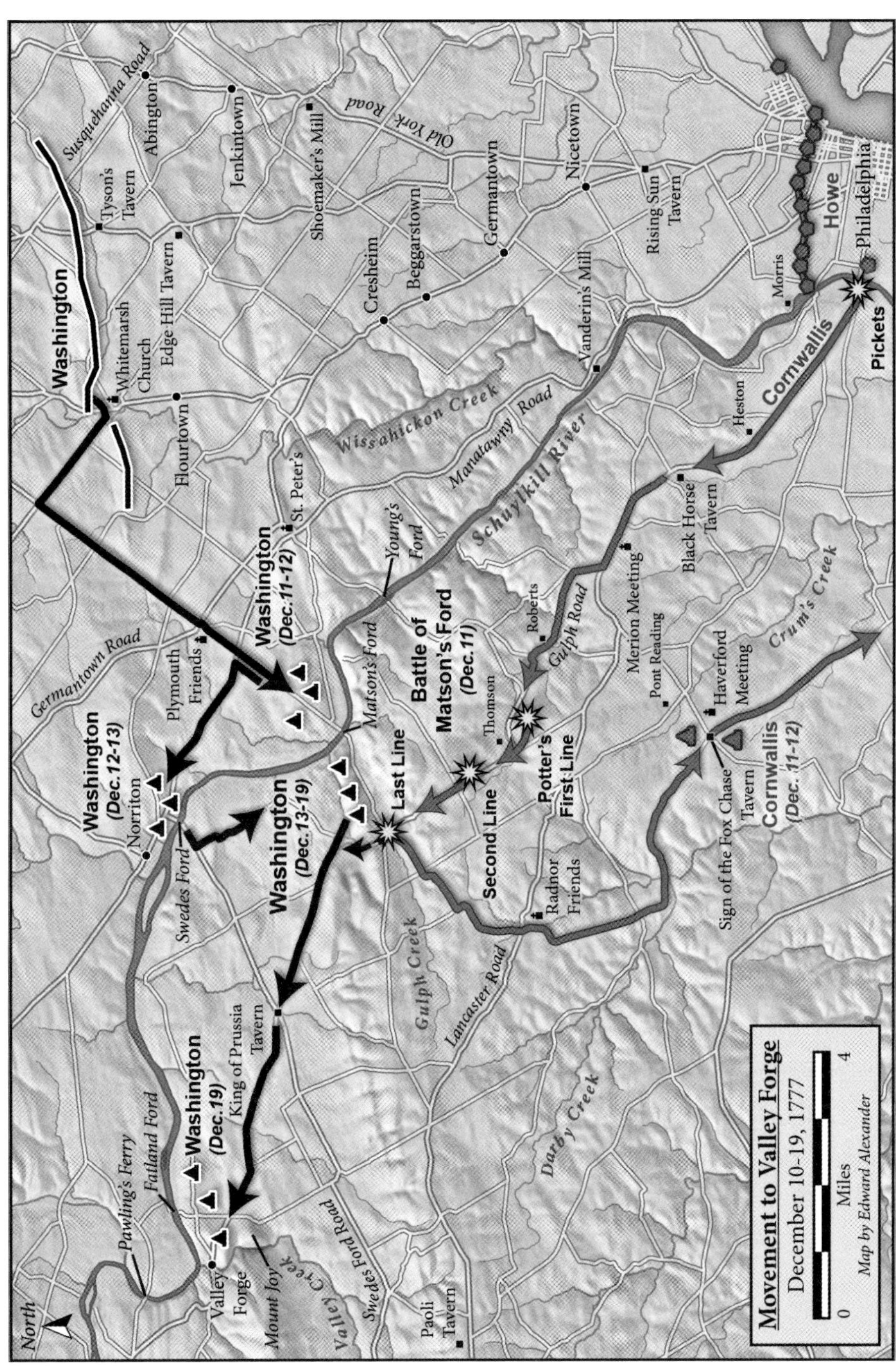
Susquehanna Road
Abington
Tyson's Tavern
Jenkintown
Shoemaker's Mill
Old York Road
Washington
Whitemarsh Church
Edge Hill Tavern
Cresheim
Beggarstown
Germantown
Nicetown
Rising Sun Tavern
Morris
Heston
Howe
Philadelphia
Cornwallis
Pickets
Flourtown
Wissahickon Creek
Manatawny Road
Vanderin's Mill
Schuylkill River
St. Peter's
Young's Ford
Black Horse Tavern
Germantown Road
Plymouth Friends
Washington
(Dec. 11-12)
Matson's Ford
Battle of Matson's Ford
(Dec. 11)
Roberts
Gulph Road
Merion Meeting
Pont Reading
Haverford Meeting
Crum's Creek
Washington
(Dec. 12-13)
Norriton
Swedes Ford
Last Line
Second Line
Thomson
Potter's First Line
Sign of the Fox Chase Tavern
Cornwallis
(Dec. 11-12)
Washington
(Dec. 13-19)
Gulph Creek
Radnor Friends
Lancaster Road
Pawling's Ferry
Fatland Ford
Swedes Ford
King of Prussia Tavern
Swedes Ford Road
Darby Creek
Washington
(Dec. 19)
Valley Forge
Mount Joy
Valley Creek
Paoli Tavern
North
Movement to Valley Forge
December 10-19, 1777
Miles
0   4
Map by Edward Alexander

Action at Matson's Ford

Washington wanted to move the army south of the Schuylkill River to seek new ground. To spearhead the movement and scout the area, Brig. Gen. James Potter crossed the river at Matson's Ford (sight of the Whiskey Scrape back in October) on December 10 with 1,000 Pennsylvania militia. On December 11, Potter reported to President Thomas Wharton of Pennsylvania, "I this day returned to" Chester County "and hope there will be Troops sufficient here in a day or two to keep all the Tories in this County in fear, if not order." Potter expected Washington to follow with the rest of the army "to-morrow if it did not to day." Potter marched his men 11 miles from Whitemarsh and camped three miles from Matson's Ford on the Gulph Road, one of three main roads between Philadelphia and Lancaster. They spent the night on the 500-acre Harriton plantation in sight of the 1704 stone house owned by Charles Thomson, secretary of the Continental Congress.[3]

While Washington planned his shift across the Schuylkill River, Howe envisioned how he was going to stockpile enough supplies for a winter in Philadelphia. He needed to not only feed his army, but the civilian population as well. According to historian John Jackson, "most civilians enjoyed neither plenty nor excellence in their diet." Even though local farmers attempted to sneak their produce into the city at night to avoid Washington's roving patrols, fresh provisions never arrived in abundance. Larger amounts arrived by boat from New Jersey or Delaware, but never enough to satisfy. Detachments of soldiers were sent deeper into the countryside in search of livestock and other provisions.[4]

As Potter's Pennsylvanians settled in for the night at Harriton, Howe issued orders for a massive foraging expedition just two days after his return from Whitemarsh. Charles Cornwallis assembled the column, which included the 2nd Battalion of British Light Infantry (with its two 3-pounders), the 2nd Battalion of British Grenadiers (with its two 6-pounders), the light infantry and grenadiers of the British Brigade of Guards, the 2nd Battalion of the British Brigade of Guards (with its two 6-pounders), the 23rd Regiment of Foot (with two 6-pounders), the 27th, 28th, 33rd and 49th Regiments of Foot, one hundred Hessian jaegers, and the

---

3 Martin, *Campaign*, 165. Matson's Ford is located in present Conshohocken; Hazard, ed., *Pennsylvania Archives*, Series 1, vol. 6, 83; McGuire, *Campaign*, vol. 2, 256 & 259.

4 Jackson, *British Army*, 163.

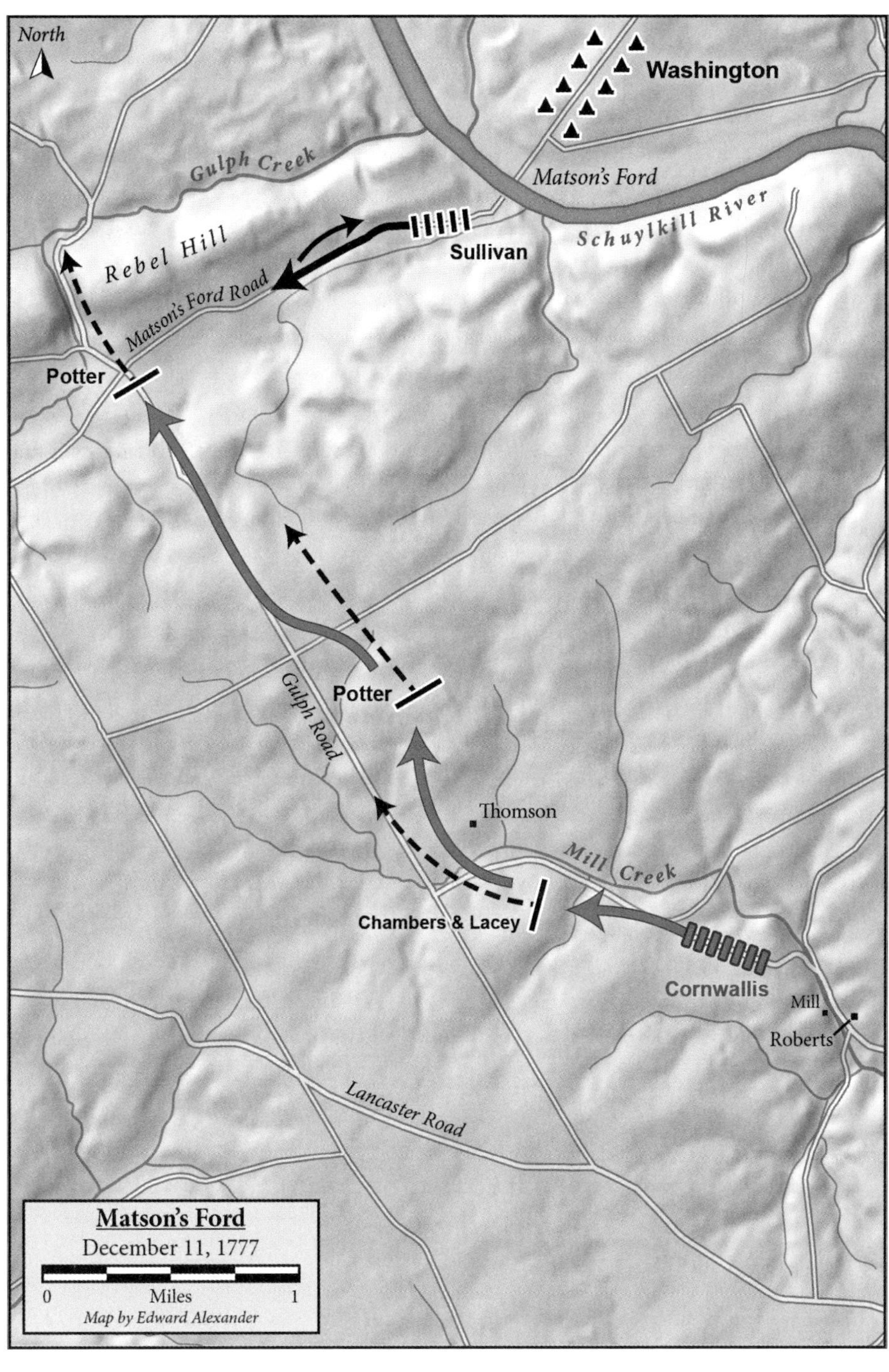

North
Washington
Gulph Creek
Matson's Ford
Schuylkill River
Rebel Hill
Sullivan
Matson's Ford Road
Potter
Gulph Road
Potter
Thomson
Mill Creek
Chambers & Lacey
Cornwallis
Mill
Roberts
Lancaster Road
Matson's Ford
December 11, 1777
0
Miles
1
Map by Edward Alexander

von Lengerke Hessian Grenadier Battalion. These 4,000 men would escort 300 empty wagons to forage wide and far for supplies.[5]

James Irvine's wounding and capture at Chestnut Hill left James Potter as the only brigadier general with the Pennsylvania militia. By the time he awoke the next morning at Harriton, he decided he had had enough and voiced his exhaustion and exasperation to Thomas Wharton. "I hope the Council will appoint some more Brigadiers, that I may for some time be Relieved," he explained. "I am convinced the Council will not expect that I can stand this Winter campaign also, in the last years I have been but three weeks at home, it is time I should go see my family, my affairs call loudly for it." Potter optimistically believed the "fighting is over for some time, I am willing to do any thing in my power to serve my Country, but it is necessary that I should have a little rest." The approach of Cornwallis's large column of foragers abruptly changed Potter's plans for leave.[6]

Cornwallis could not fulfill his mission without defeating or at least scattering Potter's militia, and he knew precisely where they were. "General Washington is said to have detached still more troops to his right across the Schuylkill . . . now under the command of General Potter," noted Howe's Hessian aide Capt. Friedrich von Muenchhausen on December 10. Cornwallis needed a local guide and forced John Roberts, the owner of a mill property along the intended route, to direct his column. The head of Cornwallis's column began crossing the Schuylkill in the early morning hours and easily brushed aside Potter's advanced picket post. The handful of militia retreated up the Lancaster Road to a 100-man reserve at the Black Horse Tavern. Their sprint up the road passed the home of militia officer Lt. Edward Heston, who rode on to alert Potter's main camp back at Harriton that "the British were advancing up the Gulf Road."[7]

Potter rapidly formed the units encamped at Harriton. Two militia battalions and Col. James Chambers's 1st Pennsylvania formed on a slight hill along the Gulph Road, with the rest of his command deployed about half a mile behind

---

5 McGuire, *Campaign*, vol. 2, 257.

6 Hazard, ed., *Pennsylvania Archives*, Series 1, vol. 6, 83.

7 Von Muenchhausen, *At Howe's Side*, 46. The Roberts property still stands near the intersection of Old Gulph Road and Mill Creek Road. When the Americans reoccupied Philadelphia in 1778, they tried, convicted, and hanged Roberts for helping Cornwallis. Reed, *Campaign*, 385. The first skirmish took place near 30th Street Station in Philadelphia. The Black Horse Tavern stood at the intersection of U.S. Route 1 and 54th Street near the St. Joseph's University campus until the 1950s. "Memoirs of Lacey," 108. Local legend states Heston rode naked to warn Potter, but no contemporary document substantiates the tale. Martin, *Campaign*, 165.

them. According to Potter a few days later, he let "the first line Know, that when they were over powered, the[y] must Retreat and form behind the second line."[8]

When Potter's force was discovered, Cornwallis deployed accordingly. The British 2nd Light Infantry Battalion attacked Potter's first line trying to make "a stand in front of a thick wood," according to light infantryman Thomas Sullivan. According to Lt. Col. John Lacey of Potter's militia, the British approached "about two Hundred Yards in Our Front I ordered my men to commence firing, which was continued for three rounds, when the Enemy opened Battery of Cannon with a discharge of small arms." The British light infantry was increasing the pressure on the militia with their two battalion guns. Lacey's militia battalion held the center of the front line. "Both the Regiments to my left as well as on my right gave way and retired on the first Fire, left us exposed on both flanks," complained the officer. The large British numbers easily wrapped around both flanks of Lacey's embattled line. "I ordered a retreat—three or four Men were cut down by the fire of the Enemy whose Bodies [were] left." Lacey withdrew into some low ground "observing the Cannon Balls fired by the Enemy pass over our Heads cutting the Tops of the trees and striking the rising ground in our front."[9]

Sergeant Thomas Sullivan of the British light infantry thought the artillery carried the moment, for "after a few shots being fired from the Guns of the two Battallions, the Enemy retreated about half a mile, taking a second position across the road upon a high hill." It was just as likely that Potter's orders for the first line to withdraw "when they were over powered" triggered the exodus. Either way, the militiamen fought a fighting retreat toward Matson's Ford. "[I]n that manner," recorded Potter, "we formed and Retreated for four miles. . . . on every Hill we disputed the matter with them." Forming retreating veterans to turn and face a superior enemy is always a tall order, but getting militia to do such a thing was nearly impossible. When the Pennsylvanians reached the hill above Matson's Ford, recorded Lieutenant Colonel Lacey, "I tryed, as well as Potter and many of the other officers to rally them but in vain. The Enemy advancing we gave them a fire or two when a Genl. rout insued—every one making the best of his way—many of the men threw away their guns, that they might be less cumbered in running." The actions of the militia disgusted Lacey. When the mounted officer had trouble

---

8 The hill the first line formed on was near the grounds of today's Bryn Mawr College. The second line was approximately where Harriton High School sits today. Hazard, ed., *Pennsylvania Archives*, Series 1, vol. 6, 97.

9 Sullivan, *Journal*, 161; "Memoirs of Lacey," 108.

clearing a fence during the retreat, Lacey's call for help fell on deaf ears, "all being in such a hurry thought of nothing but self preservation, took no notice but left me to get over as well as I could." The officer eventually cleared the fence.[10]

Finding himself alone, Lacey rode into the Gulph Road, where approaching British troops shouted for his surrender. "By a mere machanical movement without time to think I clapt spurs to my Horse and laying flat upon [him] . . . went full speed after" his fleeing men. Galloping down the road, the "Enemy fired their Pistols or Carbines at me—I heard the Bullets wish by me." With mounted British troops closing in, Lacey shouted to his men to fire on his pursuers. The scared militiamen fired several muskets "as the men ran—by firing off their shoulders without stoping or turning about." Friendly fire nearly took out the senior officer—a common occurrence during the campaign. "Conceiving myself in more danger by this mode of firing from my own men than the Enemy," Lacey called upon them "to seace firing or they would shoot me."[11]

Unable to control his mount, one of the redcoat pursuers followed Lacey into the mass of men. The panicked militia shot down both horse and rider. "The event was so sudden, and instantaneous, it was impossible to save either man or Horse, more than twenty guns being discharged at them on the same moment," explained Lacey. Potter later reported, "The Killed don't exceed 5 or 6; taken prisoners about 20; wounded about 20."[12]

Potter's retreat down the Gulph Road exposed the road to Matson's Ford another mile beyond at the Schuylkill. The previous day, the Americans built a floating bridge there to allow Washington to begin crossing behind the screen provided by Potter's bridgehead. The crossing began while Potter was engaging Cornwallis. In a serious lapse of leadership, Potter failed to alert Washington. Whether Potter purposely retreated north away from Washington's column in an effort to draw the British away remains unclear.

John Sullivan's and part of Anthony Wayne's divisions made it safely over the river and moved about a mile beyond when musketry and artillery discharges from atop the hill where Potter's final rout took pace indicated the dangerous position Washington now found himself. Sullivan quickly alerted the commander-in-chief.

---

10 Sullivan, *Journal*, 161-162; Hazard, ed., *Pennsylvania Archives*, Series 1, vol. 6, 97. The final stand took place at the present intersection of Matson Ford Road and Old Gulph Road. "Memoirs of Lacey," 108-109.

11 "Memoirs of Lacey," 109.

12 Ibid.; Hazard, ed., *Pennsylvania Archives*, Series 1, vol. 6, 98.

According to a letter John Laurens wrote to his father on December 15, when Washington arrived, "parties of the enemy were seen on the commanding heights on this side of the river." Timothy Pickering confirmed the news in a letter to his wife on December 13: the head of the column had just crossed the Schuylkill, when "to our surprise . . . the enemy appeared." After dispatching light dragoons to learn the size of the British force, the senior officers present debated the situation. They determined that Cornwallis's "ground was so advantageous, & the passage so difficult, for our bridge would only admit 2 or at most 3 men to go abreast." As Laurens informed his father, "It was considered that our army was near a river to which it had march'd by a narrow road, on each side of which thick woods render'd it impossible for the army to display itself." Washington reasoned that if Howe "shd keep up a show on the opposite side Schuylkil, and at the same march in force from Philadelphia upon us, we must in these circumstances inevitably be ruined." The Virginian decided to pull his forces back across the Schuylkill and remove the bridge.[13]

Washington's adjutant general, Timothy Pickering, found the entire affair upsetting. "If we had gained seasonable intelligence of Cornwallis's being on this expedition," he lamented, "we might probably have taken & destroyed the whole of them. But the first notice we had of them" was the "report of guns in their engagement with" Potter's militia.[14]

Unaware of Washington's decision to make a general withdrawal, Potter heaped anger on John Sullivan in a letter to Thomas Wharton on December 15. "The front of them [Sullivan's and Wayne's divisions] was about one half mill[e] in my Rear, but he [Sullivan] gave orders for them to Retreat and join the army, who were on the other side of the Schuylkill, about one mile and a Half from me."[15]

13 When Washington departed the Whitemarsh hills, the army moved up modern Route 73, turned left on Butler Pike, and followed that road to Matson's Ford. The army marched in the following divisional order: John Sullivan, Anthony Wayne, Lord Stirling, Lafayette, Alexander McDougall (followed by Jethro Sumner's North Carolina brigade), Johann Dekalb, Nathanael Greene, Mordecai Gist's Maryland militia, and Daniel Morgan's rifle corps. Showman, McCarthy, and Cobb, eds., *Papers of Greene*, vol. 2, 239; Simms, *Correspondence of Laurens*, 95-96; Letter, Timothy Pickering to wife, December 13, 1777, Timothy Pickering Papers, Massachusetts Historical Society, Boston, Massachusetts.

14 Letter, Timothy Pickering to wife, December 13, 1777.

15 Hazard, ed., *Pennsylvania Archives*, Series 1, vol. 6, 97-98.

British Foraging

With Potter's militia dispersed and Washington's force fully back on the north side of the Schuylkill, Cornwallis devastated the countryside without interruption. "[T]he enemy Got leave to plunder the Countrey, Whech the[y] have dun without parsiality of favour to any," complained Potter, "leaving none of the Nesscereys of life Behind them that the[y] conveniently could Carrey or destroy." Cornwallis's column turned left on Matson's Ford Road and moved three miles to Radnor Friends Meeting House. Fanning out and sweeping the area for supplies, the redcoats passed the meetinghouse and continued another five miles into Haverford Township. That night they camped around the Sign of the Fox Chase tavern.[16]

Washington moved his command four miles north to Swedes Ford and camped the army on the hills above the river. With the army's baggage still at Trappe, the men bivouacked in the open. Washington wanted to cross the river the morning of December 12, but "the want of provisions—I could weep tears of blood when I say it—the want of provisions render'd it impossible to march," John Laurens informed his father.[17]

With Potter's militia dispersed, Washington sent his own dragoon detachments into Chester County. "Colo [Theodorick] Bland with about 15 horse got intelligence of a party of Hessians on a scout," recorded Adjutant Pickering. "He rushed upon them & made the whole prisoners. The party consisted of a serjeant & ten men, but in the course of the day we lost four of our light dragoons killed & taken prisoners by the enemy."[18]

While Washington marked time at Swedes Ford and dragoon patrols scouted Chester County, two men walked into the Continental camp. Both had used deception to escape from quarters in the Pennsylvania State House. The British had snatched up Capt. David Plunkett of Col. Stephen Moylan's 4th Continental Light Dragoons on October 20 during his attempt to capture a Hessian lieutenant colonel. Moylan's regiment wore red coats faced with blue. Plunkett, explained to

---

16 Ibid., 98. The tavern once stood at the intersection of Darby Road and Eagle Road in Havertown. Cornwallis spent the night in the Pont Reading House near Haverford Meetinghouse. Reed, *Campaign*, 390.

17 Washington moved up Ridge Road to Swedes Ford. Swedes Ford is in Norristown today. The ford was about half a mile below the present bridge to Bridgeport. Reed, *Campaign*, 388; Simms, *Correspondence of Laurens*, 96.

18 Letter, Timothy Pickering to wife, December 13, 1777.

Pickering, "dressed himself clean, put on his regimentals [coat] & powdered his hair, & then marched down from the place of his confinement as if he had been a British officer, the sentries thinking him to be one, & paying him the compliments with their arms [presented arms] as he passed." About 20 officers shared a room with Plunkett, and they were often visited by British officers, "which I suppose was the means of ye sentries being deceived." Once escaped, Plunkett "borrowed the dress of a female quaker with her high heel shoes & so easily obtained a pass. Some woman at the same time brought out his cloaths."[19]

The second man, a Lieutenant Whipple, "escaped in a manner still more extraordinary," continued Pickering. "He one day put on a plain blue coat, and by some accident there was in the room [of confinement] a broad brim'd hat, this also he put on." One of his fellow prisoners remarked he appeared to look like a Quaker. Whipple "walked to another room of our officers, but soon the sentry discovered him, and seeing the young quaker, asked him if he belonged there?" Whipple, not thinking of escaping, "was at first confounded, but recollecting himself, answered, No—he did not belong there." The sentry took Whipple to the captain of the guard, "who examined him strictly, and threatened to send him to the provost for his impudence & presumption in going into the room where the rebel officers were confined; but at length the captain dismissed him & bid him be gone." Whipple simply walked out of Philadelphia "in his Quaker habit."[20]

Around the same time Washington realized he could not recross south of the river as he had intended, Howe ordered Lt. Col. Thomas Stirling's 42nd Highlanders to cross Gray's Ferry from Philadelphia to meet Cornwallis and help escort the plundered supplies. In a cold hard frost, the men crossed the Schuylkill and marched to Cornwallis's camp, where "the waggons dispers'd to get forage & the Troops divided along the Roads to cover" recalled grenadier John Peebles. According to Howe's Hessian aide, Cornwallis had gathered 200 tons of hay and 400 head of cattle. In doing so, admitted John Andre, "great depredations had been committed by the Soldiers on this march. The whole of the cattle which the Troops had procured was stopped at the bridge and delivered to the Commissary, to the disappointment of many people." Cornwallis's plundering had been so widespread

---

19 Ibid.

20 Ibid. The author has not been able to identify "Lieutenant Whipple" or the circumstances of his capture.

and uncontrollable that court-martials would be convened in Philadelphia later in the month.[21]

The British, scolded Timothy Pickering in a letter to his wife,

> have committed, as usual, great devastations; but tis some consolation that these calamities have fallen upon their best friends. . . . . The barborous wretches . . . have plundered them without mercy or distinction. Such was their wantonness, that what they could not carry off they destroyed, as in breaking furniture in pieces, ripping open beds & scattering abroad the feathers, &c. &c. With a sword they ript the cloathes from the back of one woman, & cut off one of her fingers.

"These barbarities," he concluded, "will . . . have their natural effect, to excite the resentment & alienate the affections of these people."[22]

Cornwallis's column returned to Philadelphia that night. British officers, meanwhile, took advantage of the opportunity to secrete livestock from the captured herd for their own regiments. The news enraged both Howe and Cornwallis. According to John Peebles, "the whole return'd with a good hawl of forage, some cattle, & plunder, but old Grizly [Cornwallis] stop'd such cows as had been pick'd by the officers & sent them along wt the public stock." Howe's fury manifested itself in general orders at 10:00 p.m. on December 12: "To his great astonishment inform'd of some Corps having sent their Waggons . . . with it [the seized forage] to Camp; the Commanding Officers of Corps, to be answerable this order is Complied with." Howe had enough trouble struggling to feed his army and civilians without hoarding by his own regiments.[23]

With Cornwallis back in Philadelphia, the Continental Army finally crossed south of the Schuylkill. French engineers and a convoy of wagons loaded with all manner of building materials reached the river and constructed two bridges on the night of December 12. One consisted of a wooden roadbed atop floating rafts. The other involved 36 wagons placed into the ford with wooden rails laid across them. John Laurens described the spans as "Our ancient bridge, an infamous construction which in many parts obliged the men to march by Indian file, was

---

21 Peebles, *Diary*, 154; Von Muenchhausen, *At Howe's Side*, 46; Andre, *Journal*, 71; McGuire, *Campaign*, vol. 2, 263.

22 Letter, Timothy Pickering to wife, December 13, 1777.

23 Peebles, *Diary*, 154-155; William Howe General Orders December 12, 1777, William Howe Orderly Book, 1776-1778, William Clements Library, University of Michigan, Ann Arbor, MI.

restored, and a bridge of waggons made over the Swedes Ford, but fence-rails from necessity being substituted to plank, and furnishing a very unstable footing, this last served to cross a trifling number of troops." The army began crossing at 6:00 p.m., but shifting 20,000 troops across the river was an agonizingly slow endeavor. "The army was 'till Sun Rise crossing the River . . . Cold & uncomfortable," Continental Army surgeon Albigence Waldo scribbled into his diary. Once across, Washington's army moved into "the Gulph" in Upper Merion Township.[24]

"The Gulph" Camp

The camp's odd name, explained Pvt. Joseph Plump Martin of Connecticut, came from "a remarkable chasm in the hills." Martin added that he and his comrades, "encamped for some time, and here we had liked to have encamped forever—for starvation here rioted in its glory." Washington had little choice but to leave the Whitemarsh hills when his army stripped the region of supplies. Unfortunately, the Continentals had just moved into an area picked clean by Cornwallis's recent expedition. "But lest the reader should be disgusted at hearing so much said about 'starvation,'" Martin concluded, "I will give him something [a fist] that, perhaps, may in some measure alleviate his ill humor."[25]

Washington wanted to stay at "the Gulph" just one day and issued general orders on December 13 for the army "to be ready to march precisely at four o'clock to morrow morning." The orders did not specify an intended destination, but the march never took place. Instead, the army remained in this denuded area for six long days. Continued poor weather and uncertainty about Howe's intentions extended the delay from one day to the next. Looking around the new campsite, Surgeon Waldo noted "plenty of Wood & Water . . . few families for the soldiery to Steal from—tho' far be it from a Soldier to Steal . . . [and] warm sides of Hills to erect huts on." On the 13th, Washington ordered "an officer from each regiment is to be sent forthwith to the encampment on the other side Schuylkill [Whitemarsh], to search that and the houses for all stragglers, and bring them up to their corps." The army's adjutant general, Pickering, expressed his ongoing concerns to his wife

---

24 Arthur S. Lefkowitz, "French Adventurers, Patriots, and Pretentious Imposters in the Fight for American Independence," *Journal of the American Revolution: Annual Volume 2022* (Yardley, PA, 2022), 90; Simms, *Correspondence of Laurens*, 96-97; Rankin, ed., *Narratives of the American Revolution*, 180. The camp was in an area known today as Rebel Hill along Gulph Creek.

25 Martin, *Private Yankee Doodle*, 99-100.

that same day: "The weather is too severe to keep the field & our soldiers suffer much. The great difficulty is to fix on a proper" site "for winter quarters, nothing else prevents our going into them."[26]

Conway Cabal

December 13 was a busy day. While Washington tended to his army and dealt with inclement weather, the Board of War promoted Thomas Conway to major general and inspector general of the army. Congress framed the new position such that Conway would not report to Washington but directly to the Board of War. In other words, Washington would not have any direct control over the changes Conway made to the army or how they would be implemented. The bickering and rumblings about Washington's leadership over the previous months had developed into a true cabal: the usurpation of his powers by the Board of War.[27]

"The Gulph" Camp

The Continental Congress also attempted to alleviate supply problems for Washington and issued a resolution to that effect on December 10. "That General Washington be informed, that Congress have observed, with deep concern," began the resolution:

> that the principal supplies for the army under his command have, since the loss of Philadelphia, been drawn from distant quarters, whereby great expence has accrued to the public, the army has been irregularly and [often] scantily supplied, and the established magazines greatly reduced, while large quantities of stock, provision and forage, are still remaining in the counties of Philadelphia, Bucks and Chester, which, by the fortune of war, may be soon subjected to the power of the enemy.

The resolution continued: "That from these considerations, it is the desire and expectation of Congress, that General Washington should, for the future, endeavour as much as possible to subsist his army from such parts of the country as

26 Reed, *Campaign*, 391; Chase & Grizzard, eds., *Papers*, vol. 12, 602; Gary Ecelbarger, "The First Four Days at Valley Forge," https://allthingsliberty.com/2022/12/the-first-four-days-at-valley-firse/#google_vignette, accessed August 20, 2023; Martin, *Campaign*, 166; Rankin, ed., *Narratives of the American Revolution*, 181; Letter, Timothy Pickering to wife, December 13, 1777.

27 Lender, *Cabal!*, 119 & 122.

are in its vicinity, and especially from such quarters as he shall deem most likely to be subjected to the power or depredations of the enemy." Congress directed Washington "to order every kind of stock and provisions in the country above-mentioned, which may be beneficial to the army or serviceable to the enemy, to be taken from all persons without distinction, leaving such quantities only as he shall judge necessary for the maintenance of their families." Lastly, it directed Washington "to cause all provisions, stock, forage, waggons and teams, which may be, at any time, in the route of the enemy, and which cannot be seasonably removed, to be destroyed."[28]

Despite these efforts, "The Army which has been surprisingly healthy hitherto, now begins to grow sickly from the continued fatigues they have suffered," wrote Dr. Waldo in his diary on December 14. "Why are we sent here to starve and Freeze. . . . People who live at home in Luxury and Ease . . . have but a very faint Idea of the unpleasing sensations, and continual Anxiety the Man endures who is in a Camp," he continued. "These same People are willing we should suffer every thing for their Benefit & advantage, and yet are the first to Condemn us from not doing more!" The surgeon was just hitting his stride:

> Mankind are never truly thankfull for the Benefits of life, until they have experience'd the want of them. I am Sick—discontented—and out of humor. Poor food—hard lodging— Cold Weather—fatigue—Nasty cloathes—nasty cookery—Vomit half my time—smoak'd out of my senses—What sweet Felicities have I left at home; A charming Wife—pretty children—Good Beds—good foods—good Cookery—all agreeable—all harmonious. Here all Confusion—smoke & Cold—hunger & filthyness— A pox on my bad luck.[29]

The doctor wasn't finished, "There comes a bowl of beef soup—full of burnt leaves and dirt, sickish enough to make a Hector spue—away with it Boys." The surgeon recalled the plight of "a Soldier, his bare feet are seen thro' his worn out Shoes, his legs nearly naked from the tatter'd remains of an only pair of stockings, his Breeches not sufficient to cover his nakedness, his Shirt hanging in Strings, his hair dishevell'd, his face meagre; his whole appearance pictures a person forsaken

---

28 Ford, ed., *Journals of Congress*, vol. 9, 1013-1015. At the time, Philadelphia County included Montgomery County.

29 Rankin, ed., *Narratives of the American Revolution*, 181-183.

& discouraged. He comes, and crys with an air of wretchedness & despair, I am Sick, my feet lame, my legs are sore, my body cover'd with this tormenting Itch."[30]

British Philadelphia

With the Delaware River about to freeze over, many British and loyalists took hope it was the end of active operations. "This River I expect will be soon shut up so that you will not probably hear from Me, indeed I do not expect to have any thing of importance to tell you for God knows how long," wrote Virginia loyalist James Parker in a letter to a friend on December 17. Washington, he confidently predicted, "will not have the impudence to disturb our winter entertainments."[31]

British patrols wanted to make sure that was the case and continued to probe Washington's outposts in the no-man's-land surrounding Philadelphia. On the night of December 14, a 20-man detachment of Washington's 2nd Continental Light Dragoons took post near Vanderen's Mill. The mill sat on Ridge Road near where the Wissahickon Creek empties into the Schuylkill River. According to a captain from the regiment, "the enemy got intelligence of our strength and situation, and by the help of some infernal tory, were conducted in a bye road till they had marched near a mile in our rear, by this route avoiding our sentinels and patroles." An American vidette positioned half a mile behind Wissahickon Creek on Ridge Road rode into the outpost at 2:00 a.m. with a warning that a large body of British horsemen was approaching. The officer in charge ordered the men to mount, "the horses being kept constantly saddled, and the men accoutered." The vidette was right: 40 British dragoons under Capt. William Cathcart of the 17th Light Dragoons was closing in on the Americans.[32]

Shots ripped through the cold air before the heavily outnumbered American detachment could form. Some of the Continentals negotiated the darkness to escape before the British surrounded the house and barn and took five prisoners: Quartermaster Sgt. Samuel Mills, Pvt. Isaac Brown, Pvt. John Chauncey, Pvt. Naboth Lewis, and Pvt. Ephraim Kirby. The dragoons disarmed and robbed them of their "spurs, watches, &c, &c." With the plunder secure, the officers ordered

---

30 Ibid., 182.

31 Letter, James Parker to Charles Steuart, December 17, 1777, Parker Family Papers.

32 *Hartford Courant*, January 20, 1778. Vanderen's mill was the site of the Hessian jaeger picket outpost during the Battle of Germantown. The British accessed the position's rear in modern Roxborough. Andre, *Journal*, 71.

their men to kill the captives, "notwithstanding the entreaties and prayers of the unfortunate prisoners for mercy." The British fell upon them "and after cutting, hacking and stabbing them till they supposed they were dead, they left them." After mangling Isaac Brown, they shot him and set fire to the barn "to consume any who might be in it." Mills, who was "wounded in several places in the head," was spared and taken prisoner. Brown and Chauncey were killed on the spot, and Kirby and Lewis severely wounded. Major Benjamin Tallmadge broke the news to Washington, adding that the British also killed the property owner, "first cutting & most inhumanly mangling him with their Swords, & then shooting him."[33]

While patrols and skirmishes continued, senior British officers felt confident that campaigning was over for the duration of the winter. On December 16, Lord Charles Cornwallis and other officers boarded the HMS *Brilliant* for the trip home to England for the winter. "Several of the Gentlemen of the Army are goeing home to Britain," was how James Parker put it. The ship departed the next day.[34]

"The Gulph" Camp

Washington was still undecided on a permanent winter camp site when the army's baggage arrived from Trappe. On December 16, the Virginian relented and ordered "the tents to be carried to the encampment of the troops, and pitched immediately." Washington thanked his men in general orders the following day:

> The Commander in Chief with the highest satisfaction expresses his thanks to the officers and soldiers for the fortitude and patience with which they have sustained the fatigues of the Campaign—Altho' in some instances we unfortunately failed, yet upon the whole Heaven hath smiled on our Arms and crowned them with signal success; and we may upon the best grounds conclude, that by a spirited continuance of the measures necessary for our defence we shall finally obtain the end of our Warfare—Independence—Liberty and Peace—These are blessings worth contending for at every hazard—But we hazard nothing. The power of America alone, duly exerted, would have nothing to dread from the force of Britain—Yet we stand not wholly upon our ground—France yields us every aid we ask, and there are reasons to believe the period is not very far distance, when she will take a more active part, by declaring war against the British Crown. Every motive therefore,

33 *Hartford Courant*, January 20, 1778; Chase & Grizzard, eds., *Papers*, vol. 12, 619.

34 McGuire, *Campaign*, vol. 2, 269; Parker Journal, December 10, 1777 entry, Parker Family Papers. The *Brilliant* arrived in Plymouth, England on January 16, 1778.

irresistibly urges us—nay commands us, to a firm and manly perseverance in our opposition to our oppressors.[35]

Five days into the encampment, the army held a national day of praise and thanksgiving. Back in November, Congress had set aside December 18 for the event. The General Orders noted that "Chaplains [are to] perform divine service with their several Corps and brigades." In truth, the men found little to celebrate in their starving condition, as Lt. Col. Henry Dearborn of the New Hampshire Line made clear in his journal: "God knows We have very Little to keep it with this being the third Day we have been without flouer or bread—& are Living on a high uncultivated hill, in huts & tents Laying on the Cold Ground, upon the whole I think all we have to be thankful for is that we are alive & not in the Grave with many of our friends."[36]

Joseph Plumb Martin echoed Dearborn. "But we must now have what Congress said, a sumptuous Thanksgiving to close the year of high living we had now nearly seen brought to a close," he wrote in his postwar memoir. "Well, to add something extraordinary to our present stock of provisions, our country, ever mindful of its suffering army, opened her sympathizing heart so wide, upon this occasion, as to give the world something to stare. And what do you think it was, reader? Guess. You cannot guess, be you as much of a Yankee as you will. I will tell you; it gave each and every man half a gill [2 ounces] of rice and a tablespoonful of vinegar!" The thin helping of rice and vinegar was unevenly distributed. According to Sgt. Ebenezer Wild of the 1st Massachusetts, "we had but a poor thanksgiving— nothing but Fresh beef & flour to eat, without any salt & but very scant of that."[37]

Thanksgiving failed to improve morale. "The army was not only starved but naked," complained Joseph Plumb Martin many years later. "The greatest part were not only shirtless and barefoot, but destitute of all other clothing, especially blankets. . . . But hunger, nakedness and sore shins were not the only difficulties we had at that time to encounter; we had hard duty to perform and little or no strength to perform it with."[38]

---

35 Chase & Grizzard, eds., *Papers*, vol. 12, 613 & 620.

36 Ibid., 621; Brown & Peckham, eds., *Journals of Dearborn 1775-1783*, 118.

37 Martin, *Private Yankee Doodle*, 100; Wild, *Journal*, 30.

38 Martin, *Private Yankee Doodle*, 101-102.

The Move to Valley Forge

Washington and several of his officers set about to determine the location of a winter encampment. Wilmington, Lancaster, and Reading were suggested and considered. Others favored moving west of the Susquehanna River to recruit and rest the army, especially since both armies had picked clean the area around Philadelphia. Moving farther away from the British army, however, opened more of the region to depredations and increased local British support. Staying close to Philadelphia to deter Howe, but far enough away to avoid surprises, was a more probable political and military solution. The army remained a day's march from Howe's command. The hills in the area were steep and rose sharply above narrow valleys, however, which might easily allow Howe to drive them into a confined area not of their choosing.[39]

"It is necessary that an appearance be kept up as much as possible of besieging the enemy, not only to cover the country but to preserve the credit of our currency which will always rise and fall as our army appears superior or inferior to the enemy," argued division commander Nathanael Greene. "By taking Winter Quarters from Lancaster to Reading," opined Chief Engineer Louis Duportail, "we abandon to the Enemy Jersey, and all the Country adjacent to Derby, Chester and Wilmington, one of the richest Tracts in this part of the Continent." Henry Knox suggested that "If the Cover in the range from Lancaster to Reading should be found insufficient, I should be for hutting the whole army about 30 miles distant from Philadelphia in some position which should have the Schuylkill about 10 or 12 miles on the right or left."[40]

Every option had its pitfalls. "Should we retire to the interior parts of the State, we should find them crowded with virtuous citizens, who, sacrificing their all, have left Philadelphia and fled thither for protection," wrote Washington. He continued:

> To their distresses humanity forbids us to add—This is not all, we should leave a vast extant of fertile country to be despoiled and ravaged by the enemy, from which they would draw vast supplies, and where many of our firm friends would be exposed to all the miseries of the most insulting and wanton depredation. . . . These considerations make it indispensably necessary for the army to take such a position, as will enable it most

39 McGuire, *Campaign*, vol. 2, 266-267.

40 Chase & Grizzard, eds., *Papers*, vol. 12, 457-458, 462, 466.

effectually to prevent distress & to give the most extensive security. . . . These cogent reasons have determined the General to take post in the neighborhood of this camp.[41]

Pennsylvania's Executive Council begged Washington to remain in the area for the winter and offered four reasons to the Continental Congress for doing so: moving as far as Wilmington much of Pennsylvania and New Jersey "must be left in the Power of the Enemy"; levied taxes would fail because "nothing but the neighbourhood of the Army keeps them [the people] subject to the Government; the removal of the army will make it "impossible to recruit the Regiments of this State," and; the "Army removing at a Distance from the Enemy must give a fatal Stab to the Credit of the Continental Currency throughout the State." The Council threatened to withdraw its troops from the army should Washington move a significant distance. General Potter of the Pennsylvania militia disagreed with the Council and shared his misgivings with Washington on December 4. "I Assart winter Quarters is not to be found In the State of pennsylvania my Reasons for this Assarteon is, the Capitale is in persesion of the Enemy, and there is such large Numbers fled from it, and the Neighbourhood adjasant, and the Town and Veledges along the River Dalawer, that all the Towns and Velidges Back in the Countey are full of Refugees all Redey. What will be dun with those people[?]" asked Potter. "Turn them out of Dores to make Room for the solders, god for Bid it—that would be cruilly unaxemplyfied by General How himself."[42]

Washington also needed to consider that several villages in the area were used not only as supply depots, but as prisoner of war camps. Both needed to be protected. Easton, as just one example, was becoming overcrowded with prisoners, its jails and other buildings overflowing. When Congress fled Philadelphia earlier in the year, the official papers, documents, and public funds were temporarily stored in Easton. Bethlehem was used as an overflow area for prisoners, though its chief function was as a hospital facility. On December 17, Washington informed the army winter quarters would be established in the immediate vicinity and "he persuades himself, that the officers and soldiers, with one heart, and one mind, will resolve to surmount every difficulty, with a fortitude and patience, becoming their

41 Ibid., 620.

42 Hazard, ed., *Pennsylvania Archives*, Series 1, vol. 6, 104-105; Reed, *Campaign*, 394; Chase & Grizzard, eds., *Papers*, vol. 12, 546.

profession, and the sacred cause in which they are engaged: He himself will share in the hardship, and partake of every inconvenience."[43]

A camp at Valley Forge would keep Washington close enough to Philadelphia to challenge British occupation of the Delaware River valley but compound the Commissary Department's inability to feed the army from an already denuded region. The pressure to remain from Pennsylvania's government, the Continental Congress, and British political threats from Philadelphia, however, were heavy. Washington had few viable options.[44]

Orders on December 18 announced the move to winter quarters. The baggage train would depart "the gulph" at 7:00 a.m. the next morning followed three hours later by the army. To act as a rearguard, Washington left the two Maryland brigades behind under William Smallwood. The roughly 20,000 men trudged seven miles down the Gulph Road to a cone-shaped hill rising above the sky line called Mount Joy. Henry Muhlenberg in Trappe described "stormy winds and piercing cold" that day. Colonel Israel Angell of the 2nd Rhode Island complained the march was "plaged so bad With our waggons as the Roads was Excessive Bad and our horses very poor and weak." Despite popular imagery that bloody footprints in the snow marked Washington's route to Valley Forge, two days of rain prior to the march removed any vestiges of snow.[45]

Lieutenant Samuel Armstrong of the 8th Massachusetts vividly described the day in his diary. "The Sun Shone out this morning being the first time I had seen it for Seven days, which seem'd to put new Life into every thing—We took the Remains of two Days Allowance of Beef, being a Shin and two fowls we had left, of these we made a broth upon which we Breakfasted with a half a loaf of Bread we Begg'd and bought, of which we Shoud have made a tollerable Breakfast, if there

---

43 John B. Frantz and William Pencak, eds., *Beyond Philadelphia: The American Revolution in the Pennsylvania Hinterland* (University Park, PA, 1998), 53-54 & 56. Bethlehem was a German community perched above the Lehigh River. Founded by the Moravians in the 1740s, the population numbered about 600 by 1777. Massive stone buildings dominated a "community dedicated to work and worship." The army had used the community as a general hospital after the Battle of Long Island and was called into service again in 1777. McGuire, *Campaign*, vol. 2, 22; Chase & Grizzard, eds., *Papers*, vol. 12, 620-621.

44 Herrera, *Feeding Washington's Army*, 1.

45 Chase & Grizzard, eds., *Papers*, vol. 12, 628 & 641; Muhlenberg, *Journals*, vol. 3, 114; Angell, *Diary*, n.p.; Ecelbarger, "The First Four Days at Valley Forge." The same day Washington arrived at Valley Forge, the Navy Board ordered the remnants of the Delaware River fleet to move to Bordentown, New Jersey, before ice prevented the move. Jackson, *Navy*, 283. The next day, Washington ordered the two Maryland brigades under William Smallwood to Wilmington, Delaware. Delaware militia was urged to assist Smallwood's defense of the state for the winter.

had been Enough!!" Armstrong believed they got moving at 11:00 a.m., "but did not arrive 'till after Sun Sit. During this march we had nothing to Eat nor to drink."[46]

Washington's legions fanned out on the hills above Valley Creek near where the British had burned an American supply depot three months earlier at the Valley Forge. Eighteen miles from Philadelphia, the five-square-mile region consisted of cleared valleys and hills timbered in hardwood. Joseph Plump Martin complained that "It was dark; there was no water to be found and I was perishing with thirst," when he reached the camp. "I searched for water till I was weary and came to my tent without finding any. Fatigue and thirst, joined with hunger, almost made me desperate. I felt at that instant as if I would have taken victuals or drink from the best friend I had on earth by force. I am not writing fiction, all are sober realities." Those lucky enough to get food ate "like Insatiate Monsters 'till they had some Lilley P. of which we eat 'till our Guts began to Ake," wrote Lt. Samuel Armstrong of the 8th Massachusetts.[47]

With the move to the Valley Forge encampment, the long, bloody, and consequential Philadelphia Campaign came to an end.

---

46 Armstrong, "Diary," 258.

47 In 1701, William Penn set aside 7,800 acres of the future American encampment for his daughter Letitia Penn Aubrey. Phillip S. Greenwalt, *The Winter that Won the War: The Winter Encampment at Valley Forge, 1777-1778* (El Dorado Hills, CA, 2021), 25; McGuire, *Campaign*, vol. 2, 268; Martin, *Private Yankee Doodle*, 103; Armstrong, "Diary," 258. "Lilley P." is possibly a pie made from the jelly of the gillyflower, a clove scented pink or carnation.

The Philadelphia Campaign Considered

"I grow every day more and more disgusted with the folly & iniquity
of the cause in which I am condemned to serve."[1]

— Capt. Richard Fitzpatrick, British Brigade of Guards, January 28, 1778

 arrival of the Continental Army at Valley Forge marked the end of nine months of active campaigning from the Hudson River valley to northeastern Maryland. That timespan included the two major pitched battles of Brandywine and Germantown. Lesser engagements broke out at Short Hills in northern New Jersey, Cooch's Bridge in Delaware, on the South Valley Hill, near Paoli, and along the Whitemarsh hills. Fighting erupted at Billingsport, Fort Mercer, Fort Mifflin, and Gloucester along the Delaware River. Skirmishes rattled the fields and woodlots at Valley Forge, Matson's Ford, and many other places. John Burgoyne surrendered one British army in upstate New York while another marked time occupying Philadelphia.

1 Letter, Richard Fitzpatrick to his brother, January 28, 1778, Richard Fitzpatrick Papers, Miscellaneous Manuscripts 622, Library of Congress, Washington, D.C.

Contemporary American Views

A pair of colonial views cover a broad span of American opinion. Massachusetts congressman and political provocateur Samuel Adams was less than pleased with the results. "Our military Affairs in the middle Department are in such a Situation as to afford us too much Reason to be chagrind," he huffed in a letter to Richard Henry Lee on New Year's Day, 1778. We have indeed sufferd no shameful Defeats, but a promising Campaign has however ended ingloriously." Adams blamed the army's general officers. "For the Sake of our Country, my dear Friend, let me ask, Is our Army perpetually to be an unanimated one; because there is not Fortitude enough to remove those bad Men. We may avoid Factions and yet rid our Army of idle cowardly or drunken officers." The source of his ire, as one might expect, was George Washington. "Is there not Reason to fear that our Commander in Chief may one day suffer in his own Character by Means of these worthless Creatures? At best," Adams continued,

> the unfortunate General has Pity only as the Reward of his Services; and how soon does Pity degenerate into Contempt. Cicero if I mistake not some where tells us, that when a General is fortunate it matters not whether it is ascribd to his being a Favorite of the Immortal Gods, or to certain good Qualities in him which others are incabable of observing. His Soldiers will encounter every Danger under his Conduct. His Enemies will be confounded at his Approach. His Country will revere him.[2]

Other congressmen maintained hope. Two days after Washington's arrival at Valley Forge, Francis Lightfoot Lee wrote to Adams. "This campaign in this quarter has, to be sure, been very disgracefull," he began, "but we have a great many men now inlisted tho scatter'd & disordered. I hope we shall find means to collect them & introduce some . . . if the States will draw the Reins of Governmt. a little tight, check the insatiable rage of avarice, & rouse their people from the present total inattention to public affairs; I make no doubt we shall put a glorious period to the contest next campaign. Our enemy," he concluded, "is not near so strong as heretofore & no prospect of ever becoming so; America in my opinion is stronger then ever." Privately in a diary entry Connecticut surgeon Albigence Waldo maintained, "This then cannot be called an Inglorious Campaign."[3]

---

2 Harry Alonzo Cushing, ed., *The Writings of Samuel Adams*, 4 vols. (New York, 1908), vol. 4, 1-2.

3 Smith, et al., eds., *Letters*, vol. 8, 460; Rankin, ed., *Narratives of the American Revolution*, 192.

The British View

The failure to crush the Continental Army led to a great deal of disgust within the British officer ranks. Captain Richard Fitzpatrick of the Brigade of Guards wrote an extraordinary (and prescient) letter to his brother in late January 1778. "I grow every day more and more disgusted with the folly & iniquity of the cause in which I am condemned to serve, and if the disgraces and disappointments of this year do not somehow or other put an end to the war," he continued,

> I really think I cannot bear to sacrifice every feeling and principle I have to it any longer . . . having been a witness to all the horrors of this war has made me ten times more violent than ever against it, and I hate the Ministry more cordially than ever for having obliged me to become a sort of instrument . . . of injustice, barbarity, and oppression . . . if once America is the ally of France I cannot conceive any salvation for us whatsoever . . . there is a greatness and dignity in all the proceedings of this people that makes us contemptible indeed; I am well convinced they will be the first and greatest people there ever was an example of in the history of mankind; Our only Consolation, as Patriots, must be that they are of English origin.[4]

The newspapers of Great Britain heaped vitriol on William Howe. "The loss of America, the ruin of your country's greatness, an indelible disgrace fixed upon the honour of its arms, the lives of many brave men sacrificed to no purpose," announced a letter printed in the *Caledonian Mercury*. "[T]hese, Sir, form the melancholy catalogue of your achievements." The *Morning Post* mocked the general: "The History of our American Campaigns must excite Laughter whenever it shall be published." The fury toward Howe in England extended to his wife. Citizens easily recognized her coach, which bore the Howe coat of arms. By January 1778 she avoided going out in public and rarely entertained guests.[5]

In the spring of 1778, Lt. William Hale of the 45th Regiment of Foot took a few minutes to summarize the campaign. As far as he was concerned, the patriot cause was beyond repair. "Washington will never attempt to [re]cover Pennsylvania, indeed it is so much exhausted as to be scarcely worth the trouble," he argued. "Figure to yourself two large armies,"

---

4 Letter, Richard Fitzpatrick to his brother, January 28, 1778.

5 Bickham, *Making Headlines*, 196; Julie Flavell, *The Howe Dynasty: The Untold Story of a Military Family and the Women Behind Britain's Wars for America* (New York, 2021), 280.

the one flying from the other and both sweeping all before them, not only the present stock is destroyed, but all the young cattle, the future dependency of the province. Desolation triumphs all around; nor will a century repair the loss America has already sustained in population and commerce, burthened with debt beyond the ability of the most flourishing state in Europe to discharge. . . . Their commerce is almost totally ruined, and what little specie yet remains among them must be sent to foreign Nations for the purpose of prolonging a war every day of which plunges them still further in misery and ruin. The leaders have gone too far to recede, and the people, having parted with the means of freeing themselves from the tyranny of their oppressors, are obliged to submit. Perhaps never was a Rebellion so universal and intense as this; a circumstance which affords in my opinion a most convincing refutation of the patriotic assertion that America was forced into independence. No sudden commotion could have been prepared for, or supported with such obstinacy, so unlooked-for a transition.[6]

The View of History

"Despite another striking victory over the Continentals," concluded historian Donald Johnson, "Howe's occupation of Philadelphia failed to accomplish its tactical objectives." A British historian agreed: "Despite the victories of Brandywine and Germantown, the British once again found themselves in possession of no more territory than they could protect by developed fortifications." James Martin and Mark Lender concluded, "The costs of Howe's delays and Washington's willingness to fight were incalculable for the British cause. Howe had conducted his campaign at the expense of Burgoyne's northern army, which pointed toward formal diplomatic accords between the patriot Americans and France that, in turn, rendered Great Britain's task of winning the war problematic at best."[7]

William Gordon's 1788 history of America declared much the same thing: "Sir W. Howe has plainly the advantage of the American general, but nothing to boast of; for all the fruits derived from his various maneuverings and engagements, from the beginning to the close of the campaign, amount to little besides good winter quarters for his army in Philadelphia, while the troops possess no more of the adjacent country than what their arms immediately command." Ultimately, concluded historian Andrew O'Shaughnessy, "the debacle at Saratoga has

---

6 Wilkin, *Some British Soldiers*, 248-249.

7 Donald Johnson, *Occupied America: British Military Rule and the Experience of the Revolution* (Philadelphia, PA, 2020), 41.

inevitably overshadowed the success of Howe's Pennsylvania campaign against Washington."[8]

Philadelphia campaign historian John Reed added philosophical context into what had transpired. The campaign "was a story of disappointment, but not of failure. The future was to prove that, for the story was only really beginning." Washington's army was "deep in suffering, and would suffer more, but the sun of tomorrow was with them," added Reed. "Then, their suffering would prove worth-while. And from their hearts and souls they hoped, with the deepest of hopes, to communicate their dream, as a fact, to all generations to come."[9]

"The Continental army that marched into Valley Forge," noted another historian, ". . . was very different than the one that had retreated through New Jersey one year earlier. The regiments were now on a permanent footing and formed a larger and more balanced force. . . . While many of the battles of 1777 ended in defeat for the Continental Army, particularly for the Main Army, most of the defeats cannot be attributed to a lack of fighting ability of individual regiments. They came from errors in judgement by generals or from inadequate resources . . . [Washington] knew that his Army could not only fight but also even beat the British under favorable conditions."[10]

Final Analysis

The British began the year with high expectations and the hope of dividing the American colonies. Howe's decision to capture Philadelphia before providing assistance to John Burgoyne's Hudson River campaign doomed those hopes. Howe achieved stunning victories at Brandywine, Germantown, and Fort Mifflin, but was exceedingly lucky at Germantown, failed utterly at Fort Mercer, and accomplished nothing at Whitemarsh.

Wilhelm von Knyphausen and Charles Cornwallis followed their orders but never took initiative when given opportunities to do so. James Grant's bombastic attitude endured in his letters, but nowhere else. Brigade commander Charles Grey

---

8 R. Arthur Bowler, *Logistics and the Failure of the British Army in America* (Princeton, NJ, 1975), 71; Martin & Lender, *"A Respectable Army,"* 83; Gordon, *History*, 12; Andrew Jackson O'Shaughnessy, *The Men Who Lost America: British Leadership, the American Revolution, and the Fate of the Empire* (New Haven, CT, 2013), 118.

9 Reed, *Campaign*, 395-396.

10 Wright, *Army*, 119.

demonstrated inspired leadership at Paoli and Whitemarsh, but remained in the shadows elsewhere. When given the chance to shine and prove Hessian worth, Carl von Donop rashly attacked an American fortification he could not carry and, along with many of his men, died trying.

Ultimately, Howe captured Philadelphia but little else. The Americans maintained control of most of the countryside surrounding the capital. More importantly, Howe's focus on Philadelphia denied him the ability to assist Burgoyne's campaign. The British surrender at Saratoga forced the British government and military to adopt new strategies during the ensuing years of the war.

Howe's plight in the late fall of 1777 can be summarized by Benjamin Franklin's response when informed that the enemy had captured the city: "No Sir, Philadelphia has taken the British," shot back Franklin. The quote reflects Franklin's optimism and wit, i.e., even though the British physically occupied the city, that act could be seen as a strategic disadvantage tying down significant British resources and wasting morale to no overall purpose.[11]

*   *   *

From the outset, Washington needed to maintain the Continental Army while blunting Howe's efforts. While he was always searching for a pitched traditional battle, preserving his army often superseded that desire. By prolonging operations around Philadelphia and sapping British strength, Washington provided Horatio Gates the time and space needed to defeat Burgoyne in New York. Although the Continentals suffered bloody defeats at Brandywine, Paoli, Germantown, and Fort Mifflin, morale remained high. The stunning victory at Fort Mercer and blocking of Howe's thrusts at Whitemarsh helped build confidence.

It was during these crucial months that the senior leadership that would see Washington and America through to ultimate victory at Yorktown began to emerge. Lord Stirling's dependability kept him in Washington's good graces, while Nathanael Greene's solid leadership foreshadowed larger roles ahead. Despite being surprised at Paoli, Anthony Wayne remained a dependable division commander. Lower ranking officers like Samuel Smith, Daniel Morgan, and Christopher Greene showed promise. The Marquise de Lafayette and Johann

---

11 John C. Miller, *Triumph of Freedom, 1775-1783* (Boston, 1948), 220.

DeKalb rose to division command and would help see the army through dark days yet to come.

Thus a confident and unbeaten army marched into Valley Forge that third December of the war. As the cold weeks passed, Congress completed a treaty with France in February 1778, an alliance that would ultimately lead to the Yorktown victory four years later. Following his resignation, Howe returned home in June 1778. In stark contrast, Washington survived a brutal winter and the Conway Cabal, solidified his role as commander in chief, and marched out of Valley Forge with a fresh purpose and renewed hope.

When the British army under Henry Clinton evacuated Philadelphia in June 1778, Washington followed it across New Jersey and fought the enemy to a draw in one of the largest battles of the war at Monmouth Courthouse.

Philadelphia returned to American hands.

The Continental Army

Washington's army comprised Continentals and militia, including Americans, Canadians, and Europeans. Like just about every army in history, women and children marched with it. By the fall of 1777, his army had a mixed bag of veterans and raw recruits. While many of the men and officers invaded Canada, fought in the battles around New York City, and had taken part in the fighting at Trenton and Princeton, just as many others had seen no action at all prior to Brandywine. Most of the first set of enlistments expired the previous year, and it took Washington the entire spring and much of the summer to rebuild his command. Many officers were new to their roles, and many of the regiments did not exist in their current form the previous year. Most of the army learned the lessons of war the hard way at places like Cooch's Bridge, Brandywine, along the South Valley Hills, in the terrifying darkness at the end of a bayonet at Paoli, and in the early morning fog at Germantown. The training and professional transformation at Valley Forge was yet to come. Still, they displayed an amazing amount of grit in the face of the professional legions fielded by the British.

The enthusiasm of the early months of the war could not sustain a long war effort. The grueling campaign of 1776 pushed the men to the limits of what a "highly motivated but short-term, half-trained, insufficiently organized, partly disciplined, and poorly equipped force could accomplish against seasoned regulars," concluded a pair of scholars. Washington needed a well-trained and seasoned army to achieve independence. John Adams, Congressman from Massachusetts, lobbied for a standing army in an August 1776 letter to artilleryman Henry Knox. "I am a constant Advocate for a regular Army, and the most masterly Discipline, because, I know, that without these We cannot reasonably hope to be a powerfull, a prosperous, or a free People, and therefore," he concluded, "I have been constantly laboring to obtain a handsome Encouragement for inlisting a permanent Body of Troops."[1]

During the 1776 campaign, ending in the victory at Trenton, Congress authorized the recruitment of 88 new regiments. The legislators also authorized Washington to raise an additional 16 infantry regiments, three artillery regiments, 3,000 dragoons, and a corps of engineers. At full strength, each regiment contained 35 officers, 32 sergeants, and 640 privates and corporals. By the middle of May 1777, that authorization resulted in 43 regiments averaging 200 men each. The Continentals modeled their regiments after British formations, but they were not exact copies. For example, American regiments lacked grenadier and light infantry companies. British colonels never commanded their regiments in the field, but American colonels did until January 1778. The number of companies and the strength of regiments varied from state to state throughout the long war. Each regiment's high ratio of officers to enlisted men, explained historian Robert Wright, recognized the greater need for control under American conditions. The use of the two-rank battle formation emphasized American faith in musketry rather than shock.[2]

Despite Congressional authorization, the new regiments organized slowly. Only about 1,000 of the 1776 Continental veterans reenlisted. Continental strength did not peak until October 1777 with 39,443 men in the ranks, including militia. Most of the recruits after 1776 came from the lowest rungs of society, and included drifters, unemployed servants, and even slaves. Precious few independent farmers, merchants, and tradesmen enlisted during this period. The latter class of people, if they served in the army at all, usually chose to do so in the militia rather than in the Continental service in order to spend less time away from home. Most recruits were in their late teens and early twenties, but some were under the age of fourteen. Few owned property. Some British and Hessian deserters also found their way into American ranks. With many regiments below strength, Washington issued rank

---

1 Martin & Lender, *"Respectable Army,"* 63; Edmund C. Burnett, ed., *Letters of Members of the Continental Congress*, 7 vols. (Washington, D.C., 1923), vol. 2, 61.

2 Wright, *Army*, 47 & 65; Luzader, *Saratoga*, 226-227. In January 1778, Congress created the rank of Lieutenant Colonel, Commandant to make the exchange of captured regimental commanders easier.

and file muskets to sergeants and junior officers to augment the power of his firing lines.[3]

Much of the strong patriotic ardor exhibited during the war's early months had worn off long ago. The bloody setbacks of 1776 had a direct impact on the readiness of others to join the ranks. Military discipline, high mortality rates, and the rigors of camp life discouraged reenlistment. Paying a cash bounty to induce young men of low economic status with few other options to join the army became common.[4]

Many factors attracted recruits throughout the war. These included boredom, friendship, the excitement of fighting in a war, bounties, a desire to see the world or get away from parental supervision, and support for the political cause of freedom from the home country. As time passed, recruiters found more difficulty locating suitable replacements. After Congress introduced troop quotas for each state in 1777, explained one war historian, "recruiters began to turn a blind eye to race in an effort to get men in the service." British deserters, Africans, and drifters were not accepted for service in 1775. Those exclusions were lifted two years later. "By 1777 a more realistic attitude dictated the acceptance of such undesirables, slaves and convicts," wrote Caroline Cox. "This was often the result of state laws which permitted men called to duty to furnish substitutes, and if the price was right recruiters accepted almost anyone."[5]

When Congress turned responsibility for recruitment over to the individual states, bounties and promises of land helped them meet quotas because a sense of duty alone at that time was simply not enough to get men to enlist or keep them in the ranks. Nearly all the troops maintained stronger ties to their local townships and states rather than to any national cause. That became readily obvious by the end of 1777 when General Washington observed, "we may fairly infer that the country has been pretty well drained of that class of Men, whose tempers, attachments and circumstances disposed them to enter permanently, or for a length of time, into the army; and that the residue of such men, who from different

---

3 Martin & Lender, *"Respectable Army,"* 90-91; Mark Edward Lender & Garry Wheeler Stone, *Fatal Sunday: George Washington, the Monmouth Campaign, and the Politics of Battle* (Norman, OK, 2016), 62-63; Wright, *Army*, 125.

4 Caroline Cox, *A Proper Sense of Honor: Service and Sacrifice in George Washington's Army* (Chapel Hill, NC, 2004), 3.

5 Ibid., 12, 17.

motives," he added, "have kept out of the army, if collected, would not augment our general strength in any proportion to what we require."[6]

By the beginning of 1776, Washington authorized the enlistment of free blacks. The next year, Rhode Island, New York, and Maryland approved enlisting slaves, who were promised freedom in exchange for honorable service. By the fall of 1777, Africans were mixed in among the regiments. Though a black soldier was subjected to the same racial prejudices found elsewhere in eighteenth-century society, the army provided him with food, clothing, and shelter. His service consisted of undesirable duties, such as orderly, cook, teamster, and other forms of laborious work. Given their situation there was little incentive for these men to desert, so they usually served out their full terms of enlistment.[7]

The officers in Washington's army almost all came from the upper social strata. "In the deferential society of eighteenth-century America," explained scholar Robert Wright, "members of the leading families naturally assumed leadership in the regular forces just as they did in the militia, in politics and law, in the church, and in business." While possible for enlisted men to rise to the ranks of the officer corps, "Washington's desire to maintain a distance between officers and men as a disciplinary tool kept most of the latter from rising far."[8]

Just as Washington's troops often lacked discipline, his officers often lacked maturity and leadership skills, which constituted a major discipline problem. Unfortunately for the commander in chief, he spent inordinate amounts of time settling petty problems within the ranks of his officers. Disputes over rank were a typical and thorny issue. Aggrieved officers often submitted requests for permission to resign, which obligated the commander-in-chief to smooth hurt feelings to keep his men together. Officers were guilty of the same offenses as the enlisted men—desertion, gambling, drunkenness, and pillaging. Washington feared mass officer resignations due to complaints of financial hardship, especially amongst his junior officers.

Despite internal squabbling, Washington made strides in turning his officers into a professional cadre. He issued orders for them to use their spare time reading military texts—a sign of growing professionalism within the Continental Army, helped along by numerous foreign observers contributing their time and advice to

6 John D. Fitzpatrick, ed., *The Writings of George Washington from the Original Manuscript Sources 1745-1799* (Washington, D.C., 1933), vol. 10, 366.

7 Pancake, *1777*, 75-76.

8 Wright, *Army*, 184.

the Americans struggling to understand military science. Despite some combat experience, many regiments remained green, and dealing with harsh discipline, the boredom of camp life, long absences from home, combat losses and disease simply proved too much.[9]

While Washington managed long odds to rebuild the army during the winter of 1776-1777, his troops remained new to army life. Even after several months of campaigning, most units lacked discipline. "The men were by nature individually independent, and no officer at hand had the required time, experience and popularity to administer drill with needed severity," one historian observed. "It was only the dream of liberty, and love for the Commander-in-Chief that kept the army in any measure cohesive." Most of these men would have followed Washington anywhere and believed in him. They endured any task required.[10]

Most companies included both a drummer and a fifer. These individuals massed behind their regiments during battle to help signal orders rather than inspire morale. The sound of beating drums carried for miles under good conditions, and when grouped could be heard above the chaos of battle. Musicians also administered corporal punishment, maintained regimental guard rooms, and assisted in evacuating casualties. As early as 1777, many carried firearms.[11]

By regulation, the men were entitled to a substantial daily ration of one pound of beef, ¾ pound of pork, or a pound of salted fish together with a pound of bread or flour. They also received three pints of peas or beans per week to supplement their meat and bread ration. A pint of milk each day was added, along with a half-pint of rice or a pint of "Indian meal" each week. A quart of spruce beer or cider to fight scurvy was also supposed to be issued each day. While the regulations read well on paper, reality was something else entirely. The men were rarely supplied in this manner—especially during active campaigning. Through most of his enlistment, the standard Continental soldier subsisted on bread and meat alone, with the Commissary Department judged upon its ability to supply those two important staples. Sutlers followed the army selling provisions, and Washington allowed farmers to sell products at markets in the camps when time allowed.

A popular misconception has the army uniformly clothed in a blue and off-white uniform, something that was the exception rather than the rule. The

---

9 Wright, *Army*, 140; Lender & Stone, *Fatal Sunday*, 63-64.

10 Reed, *Campaign*, 54.

11 Wright, *Army*, 38.

predominant uniform colors throughout much of the war were green and brown. The Continental Army did not adopt blue as the official color of the uniforms until early October 1779. Only rarely was even a single regiment, let alone the entire army, uniformly clothed. The army's Clothier General, James Mease, attempted in 1777 to uniformly cloth each regiment and left the choice of color to each regimental commander. Stephen Moylan, however, chose scarlet coats for his dragoons, which closely resembled British dragoon uniforms. Washington wisely ordered all red clothing dyed to avoid any confusion in combat, and preferred brown coats with white or buff facings to the enemy's scarlet. By the fall of 1777, obtaining enough quality cloth hampered clothing efforts.[12]

Another misconception has the Continental Army composed of "Indian fighters" and men who spent their lives wielding their deadly muskets or rifles. While some of these men were sprinkled throughout the army, the majority of Washington's men—perhaps as many as nine out of 10—were recruited from the cities and villages east of the Appalachian Mountains and were at least one generation removed from the frontier of today's imagination. Many in his army never saw a Native American nor fired a shot in anger until the Battle of Brandywine. Most, however, had some familiarity with firearms, had hunted game, or defended their livestock from predators, but that was a far cry from combat experience.[13]

Washington armed his army with two basic types of muskets: the .75 caliber British Long Land pattern smoothbore flintlock musket (more commonly called the Brown Bess), and the French Charleville .69 caliber smoothbore flintlock musket. American manufacturers produced muskets patterned on both types. The model 1763 French Charleville was the standard American weapon by 1777. The smoothbore fired a one-ounce lead ball, could be fitted with a 14-inch bayonet, and was more reliable and accurate than the British musket. Professional armies of this age no longer loaded loose ball and powder into muskets. Instead, the men were issued cartridges made of a paper or cloth filled with a single musket ball and gunpowder for one shot. The cartridges were held together with string and stored in cartridge boxes slung around a shoulder for combat. A soldier tore open one end of cartridge with his teeth, dumped the gunpowder down the barrel, and then used a ramrod to seat the round lead ball.

12 Risch, *Washington's Army*, 283, 285-286, 289.

13 Pancake, *1777*, 66.

Washington's men mostly carried smoothbores rather than rifled weapons. Smoothbores took about 30 seconds to reload with accuracy up to 50 yards. Even when fired at a pointblank range of 25 or 30 yards, hitting an enemy soldier was never guaranteed. Organizing men into disciplined ranks so volleys could be "concentrated and controlled" against similarly arranged enemy lines generated effective firepower. Although Washington insisted the Continental Army be trained according to the principles of European military science, the army that fought around Philadelphia lacked such training and would not receive it until the long winter at Valley Forge.

The questionable recruiting practices, the rawness of the recruits, and the diminishing patriotism did not mean these were poor soldiers. Many proved themselves worthy and became the backbone of the army that ultimately achieved victory at Yorktown. Some senior officers fought in the French and Indian War, which made them familiar with British tactics and practices. Much of the organization and logistics Washington attempted to instill built upon British precedents. Many of the junior officers who were too young to serve in the latter war had read British publications and English translations of various French and German studies of military science and tactics. Although the end of enlistments damaged the army's rank and file, many regular and noncommissioned officers had gained significant experience during the prior two years of service and remained.

Camp followers attached themselves to every army in history, and the Continental Army was no exception. Hundreds of hangers-on gathered in the fields outside Philadelphia, including sutlers, women, wives, and children. Washington discouraged the practice and issued orders against their presence, but he realized they helped hold his army together. "He came to accept the followers who helped root the men within the army," explains one historian. "Followers, in turn, further promoted that acceptance through their labor" as laundresses and nurses. They mostly traveled with the baggage train, received partial rations, and were expected to follow camp regulations just like the troops.[14]

---

14 John Resch and Walter Sargent, eds., *War & Society in the American Revolution: Mobilization and Home Fronts* (DeKalb, IL, 2007), 238. The women attached to the army included the wives of soldiers, laundresses, and servants, including others not all of good reputation who performed "a multitude of feminine tasks, good and bad, to ease the lives of soldiers." Men, like teamsters and drivers, and children, were also among them. Camp followers with the Continental Army added approximately 50 percent more people traveling with the armed personnel of the army.

Army Administration

Any analysis of the inner workings of the Continental Army must begin with Washington's personal staff—the men responsible for managing the army's operations. Chief among them were Col. Timothy Pickering, his adjutant general, Brig. Gen. Henry Knox, his chief of artillery, and Maj. Gen. Thomas Mifflin, his quartermaster general. After becoming commander-in-chief in 1775, Congress authorized George Washington to appoint a personal staff of one military secretary and three aides-de-camp. Throughout the war Washington supplemented this authorization with voluntary unpaid aides. Congress authorized generals serving under Washington and commanding divisions or other detachments just two official aides-de-camp each.[15]

Washington was responsible for the army outside Philadelphia, as well as all the other Continental units spread across the colonies. He did all he could to maintain contact with the units he left in the Hudson Highlands, the army under Horatio Gates that dealt the fatal blow to Burgoyne's invading command, and other detached garrisons. Washington was also responsible for maintaining contact with Congress. As a result, he had no choice but to rely "on a small cadre of trusted subordinates—primarily his aides—to help him manage the affairs of the army," concluded historian Arthur Lefkowitz, "and these men quickly found themselves enmeshed in a multitude of critical issues." Washington needed to trust them and relied upon their discretion. They could access sensitive documents "concerning strategy, troop location and movements, the supply situation, unrest in the army, and spy operations," and they often attended councils of war.[16]

---

15 Washington's staff officers included: Col. Henry Emanuel Lutterloh (deputy quartermaster general), Lt. Col. Joseph Thornbury (wagonmaster general), Lt. Col. Benjamin Flower (commissary general of military stores), Charles Stewart (commissary general of issues), Clement Biddle (commissary general of forage), William Buchanan (commissary general), Ephraim Blaine (deputy commissary general), Col. Elias Boudinot (Commissary General of Prisoners), James Mease (Clothier General), Dr. William Shippen (director general of the medical department), Dr. Benjamin Rush (surgeon general of the army), Dr. John Cochrane (chief physician of the army), Lt. Col. John Laurance (Judge Advocate General), Louis Duportail (chief of engineers), Casimir Pulaski (chief of the dragoons), Lt. Col. Robert Hanson Harrison (general military secretary), Lt. Col. Alexander Hamilton (aide-de-camp), Lt. Col. Tench Tilghman (aide-de-camp), Maj. John Fitzgerald (aide-de-camp), John Laurens (volunteer aide), Peter Thornton (volunteer aide), Lt. Col. Richard Kidder Meade (volunteer aide), and Capt. Caleb Gibbs (captain of the guard).

16 Arthur S. Lefkowitz, *George Washington's Indispensable Men: The 32 Aides-de-Camp Who Helped Win American Independence* (Mechanicsburg, 2003), xvi-xvii, 203.

Washington based the Continental Army's logistics on the British model with a Commissary Department looking after food and other supplies. When supplies ran low in the Middle Colonies, flour was transported from the grain plantations along the James, Rappahannock, and Potomac rivers in Virginia. Salted meat was hauled by wagon from New England over a long and inhospitable route.

While quartermaster departments are the mainstay of any army, the Continental Congress failed to adopt regulations for that department until May 14, 1777—just as the summer campaign was getting underway. Highlights of the regulations included a separation of the Forage & Wagon Department and the Quartermaster Department. General Mifflin, the quartermaster general, could appoint a deputy quartermaster for each military department, and each division and brigade of the army was authorized a staff officer to manage such duties. On July 1, Washington announced Col. Emanuel Lutterloh as his deputy quartermaster general for the main Continental Army. Lutterloh's staff included a clerk, paymaster, and assistant deputy quartermaster general, and a second staffer supervised and issued stores assisted by two others. An assistant deputy quartermaster general, with four hostlers, was placed in charge of the Continental horse yards. Pennsylvania housed many supply manufactories, so Mifflin's assistants scattered among them: Robert Lettis Hooper in Easton, Mark Bird in Reading, John Davis in Carlisle, and George Ross in Lancaster. Christopher Ludwick was a German baker from Philadelphia paid 75 dollars a month and two rations a day to superintend the bakers and act as the director of baking for the entire army.[17]

Having enough wagons on hand for the army's needs was a constant problem. Hiring civilian wagons remained the desired method of procurement, but impressment became more common as the army operated in Pennsylvania. The demand for wagons pushed up the cost of hiring them beyond the 30 shillings a day for a wagon, four horses, and driver that Congress authorized. Few civilians worked for such a low rate, and those who did often never received payment, which only compounded the army's supply problem. Impressing wagons, however, angered civilians, who began concealing their wheeled vehicles to keep them away from Washington's army.[18]

17 Risch, *Washington's Army*, 36-38, 195.

18 Ibid., 83.

Support Units

Washington's army included the Light Dragoons Brigade commanded by Brig. Gen. Casimir Pulaski and Brig. Gen. Henry Knox's Artillery Brigade. Congress authorized dragoon regiments on March 1, 1777. The legislation dictated each of the four authorized regiments could have six troops (companies), each comprising a captain, lieutenant, cornet, and 41 enlisted men. Including regimental staff, each prescribed regiment numbered 280. Due to supply shortages, expense, desertion, and occasional outright mutiny, these regiments rarely numbered more than 150 men. After Washington's mounted arm turned in a miserable performance at Brandywine, he assigned Brig. Gen. Casimir Pulaski, an experienced European officer to command his cavalry. The primary purpose of dragoons was reconnaissance, not combat believed Washington. The need to procure enough horses, weapons, and special equipment complicated filling the ranks. The men and the horses needed specialized training.[19]

Three regiments composed the Artillery Brigade. Each consisted of between eight and a dozen companies. Knox attached portions of these companies to each division. By 1777, assigning an artillery company to each brigade of the army was common. Other companies served as part of a general reserve. Two 6-pounders was the ideal armament for each brigade, although this caliber gun required the largest crew—12 to 15 men—of any field piece with the army. The goal was concentrating fire against enemy infantry, so rate of fire and maneuverability were more important than range.[20]

The American Militia

Washington long believed the fledgling country needed a professional army to win a war against Great Britain, and relying on militia was a losing proposition. Congress believed otherwise, and many of its members argued the maintenance of a standing army was one of the chief American complaints against England. Besides, a militia was cheaper and easier to maintain.

The system of rotation practiced by most states was a major sticking point with militia. A portion of eligible men left for the front at a given time, but rotated home after a few weeks or months and were replaced by others. What little discipline and

19 Wright, *Army*, 106-107.

20 Ibid., 104.

training instilled within these men was lost when they rotated back home. Since most of them never saw combat before joining the army, whatever experience they gained during a campaign or battle was lost when they left the front. The vexing cycle taxed the patience of the commander in chief.

Poor reputation preceded the arrival of Pennsylvania's militiamen. Due to the longstanding influence of Quakerism on the Pennsylvania Assembly, the colony had no official militia system prior to or during the early months of the Revolution. Militia was notoriously ill-trained and poorly disciplined, but the problems were compounded in Pennsylvania. The Pennsylvania Militia Act, passed on March 17, 1777, called for obligatory military service for the first time since the French and Indian War. The legislation required service from all white males between the ages of 18 and 53 able to bear arms. The act exempted Congressional delegates, members of the Executive Council, judges of the Supreme Court, masters and faculty of colleges, ministers of the gospel, and servants. Militiamen organized into companies within their respective counties. Eight companies formed a battalion. Under the Act, militia units trained regularly, and when absenteeism became a problem, members were fined for missing training. The Act included a provision allowing the Executive Council to activate portions of the militia during invasion. They limited the period of active duty to a mere 60 days.[21]

These men often came and went on their own, and how many would be in the ranks on a given day proved unpredictable. The Maryland militia battalions were provisional organizations of varying size. Maryland's policy called out several classes from each battalion of a county and assembled them into provisional battalions. Thus, any particular county did not face an undue burden. New Jersey and Pennsylvania had similar policies.

Militia officers were no better trained than their men. They were community leaders, not men of military competence. Their recruiting efforts often led to neighbors and family coming to muster at the local tavern. The fact they were able to withstand any engagement is remarkable.

---

21 Samuel J. Newland, *The Pennsylvania Militia: The Early Years, 1669-1792* (Annville, PA, 1997), 146-7.

The British Army

Great Britain held all the material advantages at the outbreak of the war. The population of the colonies hovered around 2.5 million in 1775, and included 500,000 African Americans, most of them slaves. In contrast, the British home isles housed 11,000,000 souls, 48,000 of whom served in the standing army. The outbreak of war triggered a massive recruiting campaign. The British military establishment emerged as a global bureaucracy. Separate departments existed for barracks, boatmen, commissaries, engineers, hospitals, ordnance, and quartermasters.[1]

Like their American counterparts, most British soldiers joined the army because of its promise of adventure and the supposed attractions that came with a military life. This was not an army of outcasts and criminals, but included farmers, weavers, and laborers with clean records. Prior to 1775, soldiers enlisted for life, and most were veterans of long service in faraway places—every one of them fiercely proud of their regiments. Recruiting during wartime proved difficult, so the British offered three-year enlistments to fill the ranks. When the regiments arrived in North America in 1776, recruiting parties, left behind, forwarded replacements throughout the war.[2]

The basic unit of the British Army was the regiment. "Regiment," however, was an administrative rather than a tactical term. A colonel was the administrative

---

1 Fischer, *Crossing*, 34.

2 Ibid., 39.

commander of a regiment, with whom the King contracted to raise and equip the organization. Except for the Royal regiments, the colonels owned their commands and intended, as one noted historian explained, to "profit financially and socially from that species of property by selling commissions, receiving a bounty for each recruit, negotiating lucrative contracts for uniforms, and retaining for each colonel the captaincy of one company." The financial logistics of running a regiment guaranteed some corruption. The government provided the colonel with an annual sum intended to pay the soldiers, buy clothing for the regiment, and enlist replacements. Any remaining money found its way into the colonel's pocket. In the field, colonels often held the rank of general. Generals did not have a pay scale, so the salary of each general officer depended on his being the colonel of a regiment, which did not have to be within his command.[3]

While "regiment" was the administrative term for British army units, in tactical terms the unit was called a "battalion." The terms are synonymous for purposes of discussing eighteenth-century operations since virtually every British regiment consisted of a single battalion. Because colonels often functioned as generals in field armies, they did not physically command their regiments on campaign. The regiment's lieutenant colonel bore this privilege.[4]

Seventy regiments of foot (infantry) composed the British army prior to the Revolution. With the war's onset, the army expanded by creating new regiments and adding battalions to existing regiments. In October 1775, the British government directed every regiment in America or slated for service there be enlarged to provide stronger units for field service and to "enhance the recruiting and training infrastructure to accommodate wartime attrition." By war's end, 105 regiments were on the rolls.[5]

Every British regiment consisted of eight battalion companies and two flank companies. One flank company included grenadiers, and the other light infantry. On paper each full-strength regiment consisted of a colonel, a lieutenant colonel, a major, nine captains, 14 lieutenants, 10 ensigns, one chaplain, an adjutant, a quartermaster, a surgeon and his mate, 36 sergeants, 36 corporals, 24 drummers,

---

3 Luzader, *Saratoga*, 226. Examples of Royal regiments included the 1st (Royal) Regiment of Foot and 4th (King's Own) Regiment of Foot, as opposed to the non-Royal 10th Regiment and others. Royal regiments bore the names of the monarch or other members of the Royal family.

4 Ibid.

5 Don N. Hagist, comp., *British Soldiers, American War: Voices of the American Revolution* (Yardley, PA, 2012), 11.

two fifers, and 672 privates, all for a grand total of 811 men. Attrition, illness, and other factors left every regiment under strength. Private soldiers wore black shoes with brass buckles, with heavy linen half or full gaiters over the top. Their breeches and waistcoats were of white linen or wool.

Each peacetime company contained three corporals and two sergeants to manage 36 privates. Men rarely rose to the rank of corporal in less than five years. Corporals oversaw a squad, marched soldiers to and from sentry posts, recruiting, carrying messages, and leading small parties on special duties. Corporals performing well eventually became sergeants. Their essential skills included reading, writing, and accounting. Each company also had a drummer, with the grenadier company also having two fifers. Additional corporals, sergeants, and musicians were assigned to recruitment duty. Each company designated a pioneer, equipping him with an axe and saw. Work under the regimental quartermaster included clearing vegetation around encampments, digging latrines and drainage ditches, burying the dead, and shoveling snow.[6]

The need to preserve his army's fighting capacity shaped Howe's decisions. Replacing troops lost in battle proved difficult, especially so far from the home country. The mechanism for replacements in Great Britain was archaic, and the 3,000-mile Atlantic voyage consumed both time and lives. The revulsion Howe experienced as a witness to the bloody frontal assaults against Breed's Hill explains his repeated use of flanking movements thereafter. The difficulty inherent in replacing veteran troops in the eighteenth century caused considerable concern amongst general officers, who strove to avoid unnecessarily losing troops through sickness and desertion, or by exposing them to short rations or inclement weather. This conservative mindset, in turn, limited field mobility, tying armies to magazines, bread ovens, and baggage trains. It also made winter operations impossible.[7]

Battalion Companies

The 10-pound flintlock known as the Brown Bess armed privates in battalion companies. Most British soldiers carried this smoothbore musket, which fired a large .75 caliber lead ball and sported a 17-inch bayonet making it a fearsome

6 Don N. Hagist, *Noble Volunteers: The British Soldiers Who Fought the American Revolution* (Yardley, PA, 2020), 41, 43, 47, 51.

7 Spring, *With Zeal*, 9.

close-quarters weapon but diminished its limited accuracy. Firing the weapon required a dozen separate motions. The soldier ripped away one end of a paper cartridge with his teeth, sprinkled a small amount of black powder into the priming pan, and used his ramrod to seat the cartridge and ball down the muzzle. A well-trained soldier fired at least two and as many as three shots a minute under combat conditions. A mounted bayonet made the loading process more difficult, and many soldiers depended upon a single effective shot per minute. The inaccuracy of the musket made volleys a preferred method of fire delivery, and the difficulty in loading was a reason the British made the bayonet charge their primary assault tactic.[8]

There is a common misconception the British army fought in rigid lines of battle, arrayed shoulder-to-shoulder. Instead, each line of battle consisted of two ranks (with a small interval between each) with the men formed in open order about arm's-length apart. Even in open order, however, the men were not spread out to the extent they operated independently. They presented a solid mass (and thus a ready target) and delivered volleys at a similarly compact enemy formation, often at point-blank range. The first two ranks were responsible for delivering the battalion's firepower. Six paces behind them stood a rank of file closers ready to step up and fill gaps created by the wounded and the dead.

Maintaining fire discipline was essential, since they withheld fire until within 50 yards of an enemy line. The prevailing professional opinion espoused that it was better to receive rather than deliver the initial round of fire, and thus sustaining some level of casualties so that when the fire was returned, one's own men were near enough for every shot to find its mark. This required strict combat discipline, and this type of fire training was the British army's greatest attribute.[9]

British soldiers rarely picked individual targets or fired at their own pace. Instead, the men loaded and fired on command at an enemy line. Smoothbore muskets were inaccurate beyond 50 yards and officers discouraged target practice, since the cost of lead and powder was not worth the expense and time. When a battalion delivered a volley, the "objective was to lay down a curtain of fire ahead of one's troops at the desired rate of one shot every fifteen or twenty seconds, assuring at least two volleys before closing with the enemy," explained one

---

8 Luzader, *Saratoga*, 224.

9 Ibid.

historian. "The men then resorted to clubbing with their muskets or stabbing with the bayonet, with which the British were famously effective."[10]

Specific accuracy may have been superfluous, but organized and controlled speed in both firing and movement was essential. The faster the defenders could load and fire, the more damage they could inflict upon the approaching enemy. The faster the attackers could close with the enemy while simultaneously maintaining unit cohesion, the fewer casualties they would sustain and the stronger they would be when they reached their objective. Since cartridge boxes only held 30 or fewer rounds, uncontrolled fire quickly exhausted the limited ammunition supply. Once firing began, thick black powder smoke enveloped the battlefield making it harder for officers to maintain effective control of their men. The beating drums and tooting fifes, coupled with flags waving above the center of the battalion, could be heard and seen above the chaos, and helped maintain control.[11]

The strict discipline and harsh living conditions made life difficult for the average British soldier. It also molded him into a well-trained and formidable opponent. The monotonous and repetitive drill created soldiers who reacted to orders with predictable speed and precision. British generals lost several battles during the American Revolution, but not because of any lack of discipline in the ranks.

The officers leading these men achieved their positions through either social rank or money. Officers purchased commissions, rising through the ranks from subaltern to colonel, requiring either the death of an officer, an officer's retirement, or the sponsorship of a higher-ranking officer or government patron. Many officers owed their position to someone else. This system created officers devoutly loyal to certain colonels or generals, but who sometimes undermined others within the army. Military competence played little role in the promotion of officers. Officer corps service was a respectable career offering both status and the potential for advancement. Some historians note the purchase system was "institutionalized corruption, but its purpose was to ensure that British officers had a stake in their society and were not dangerous to its institutions." This system, argued David Hackett Fischer, "kept the army firmly in the hands of Britain's governing elite,

---

10 Luzader, *Saratoga*, 224-225.

11 Ibid., 225.

mainly its small aristocracy, who controlled much of the wealth and power in the nation."[12]

Officers rarely criticized their colleagues in public, choosing instead to have political patrons do the dirty work for them, thereby mixing partisan politics with military affairs. Senior commanders often ignored the chain of command and communicated directly with political and government officials.[13]

British officers received no official schooling. Although well-read in military literature, they obtained knowledge of their profession through experience. Senior sergeants supported young subalterns in their companies who were learning the ropes during their teenage years, proving the old adage that sergeants are the backbone of any army. Most officers entered the army as young amateurs and learned to handle their commands in combat. They took their obligations seriously and compiled impressive service records. "Combine purchase rank with political influence, and it should come as no surprise that the system pinned epaulets on its share of fops and blockheads, though it also provided the army with generally competent leadership," argued the historians of the Monmouth campaign.[14]

Flank Companies and Additional Units

The elite soldiers of the eighteenth-century took assignment to the flank companies of their regiments. Throughout most of the Revolution, flank companies rarely served with their parent regiments and instead "brigaded" together to form battalions of light infantry or grenadiers, depriving the regiments of their best men. To offset this practice, the battalion companies supplied reinforcements to the flank companies.

The tallest and strongest men in the regiment made up grenadier companies. Originally, they threw primitive grenades into fortifications, but grenades were no longer in use by the Revolution. The grenadier's uniform included a short sword and a tall bearskin cap instead of the cocked hats worn by the battalion men. The light infantry company included fit men functioning as rangers or scouts. They cut their coats short (for fast movement and to avoid entanglement in rough terrain),

---

12 Martin and Lender, *"A Respectable Army,"* 13; Fischer, *Crossing*, 34.

13 Lender and Stone, *Fatal Sunday*, 55.

14 Pancake, *1777*, 71-72; Ibid., 55-56.

wore leather caps and red waistcoats, and carried small cartridge boxes and hatchets.

Like their comrades, muskets armed grenadiers and light infantrymen, although at least some British light infantry grasped short rifles. The British government sent only a small number of these weapons to North America, and there is evidence that each light company received some, though not enough to arm the entire company. While only a few British light troops were so armed, all the Hessian jaegers (the German equivalent of light infantry) were armed with short jaeger rifles.

A corps of guides and pioneers under Maj. Samuel Holland moved at the front of the marching army to clear obstructions. Axes, saws, and shovels in addition to muskets equipped Holland's corps of 172 men; they wore heavy leather aprons, gloves, and leather caps, and were permitted to grow beards. A significant number were of African descent.[15]

Brigade of Guards

Brigadier General Edward Mathew commanded the British Brigade of Guards—a special composite force consisting of 1,000 men chosen by lottery from the three regiments of Foot Guards. Fifteen men from each of the Guard's 64 companies were selected to serve in America. The army's three regiments of Foot Guards during the eighteenth century included the First Guards (also known as the Grenadier Guards); the Second (the Coldstream Guards); and the Third Guards (the Scots Guards). All three served in London or Westminster as bodyguards for the King. Mathew divided the Brigade of Guards into two battalions of 500 men each and, unlike other British regiments, retained its flank companies while on campaign. The Guards functioned like a light infantry unit in America and used common-sense, flexible tactics when faced with heavy gunfire. All Guards wore uniforms modified for campaign service, including shortened jackets without ornamentation and round hats, under which they wore cropped hair.[16]

15 Thomas J. McGuire, *Philadelphia Campaign: Brandywine and the Fall of Philadelphia* (Mechanicsburg, PA, 2006), Vol. 1, 140.

16 Edward E. Curtis, *The British Army in the American Revolution* (Gansevoort, NY, 1998), 3.

Artillery

The British organized their field artillery into four battalions of eight companies each. Each company consisted of six officers, eight noncommissioned officers, nine bombardiers, 18 gunners, and 73 matrosses (or privates). The British artillery system included enlisted gunners and matrosses, but hired civilian drivers. The 4th Battalion of the Royal Artillery Regiment deployed to the colonies in 1775. Hard service over the next two years reduced the strength of the battalion, and 300 Loyalists recruited from New York supplemented the battalion. Howe took all eight companies to Pennsylvania.[17]

The Royal Artillerymen wore dark blue rather than the traditional red, and artillery officers were promoted through merit rather than through the purchase of commissions. Given the scientific aspects of artillery, its officers were among the most highly trained in the service. The Woolwich Military Academy taught mathematics, engineering, and chemistry to prospective artillery officers. Artillerymen carried carbines—shorter and lighter versions of an infantryman's musket. Fusilier regiments, such as the 23rd of Foot (Royal Welch Fusiliers), were originally formed to escort artillery, but served as infantry in North America.[18]

Field guns ranged in size from large 24-pounders to small 3-pounders. The latter light brass cannons became popular for their mobility in the rough terrain of North America. Developed by William Congreve and James Pattison, these light guns moved by pack horses or by eight men. Since 12-pounders required many horses to haul them, and maintaining horses in North America proved difficult, the British preferred 6-pounders and 9-pounders. Custom allotted two guns (known as "battalion guns") to each infantry regiment. Some officers criticized this practice because it spread the guns out and prevented concentration of fire on a single point, position, or objective.[19]

The maximum range of the most powerful piece in the British artillery was about 2,000 yards, but no field gun was considered effective beyond 1,200 yards

17 Lender and Stone, *Fatal Sunday*, 53-54.

18 Pancake, *1777*, 68; Curtis, *The British Army*, 6-7; O'Donnell, *Immortals*, 43; Fischer, *Crossing*, 37. When matchlocks were common in the British infantry, fusilier regiments were armed with flintlocks, or *fusils* in French.

19 O'Donnell, *Immortals*, 43-44; Fischer, *Crossing*, 37.

(and many of the smaller caliber much less than that). The guns could fire solid shot, grape, or canister.[20]

Most field pieces delivered their fire on a flat trajectory. Howitzers, however, fired projectiles along a high arc, making them effective for lobbing shells over entrenchments or walls. The howitzer's shorter barrel reduced its effective range of fire.[21]

Cavalry

The British had heavy cavalry within its service, but North American terrain precluded its use. As a result, the government dispatched light cavalry in the form of the 16th and 17th Light Dragoons to America. Each regiment consisted of six troops (the equivalent of an infantry company), each containing three officers, four noncommissioned officers, and 38 privates. Few of these units were at full strength though. The dragoons rode large, athletic horses. They wore red jackets with blue trim, white breeches, and black leather helmets with horsehair crests. Each carried a saber, a carbine, and sometimes a pair of pistols. Their officers carried pistols and straight-blade cavalry swords.[22]

Support

Regulations called for provisioning from England for the British army operating in North America. The most important provisions included beef, pork, bread, flour, oatmeal, rice, peas, butter, and salt. Less important provisions, such as cheese, bacon, suet, fish, raisins, and molasses, also found their way to the colonies. Many types of vegetables, including potatoes, parsnips, carrots, turnips, cabbages, and onions, also were dispatched by sea, although they were not always fresh or edible when they reached the men at the front. Most of these vegetables were intended for soldiers recovering in hospitals. Onions, sauerkraut, porter, claret,

---

20 Artillerymen used solid shot against fortifications or opposing artillery. Grapeshot consisted of clusters of iron balls about two inches in diameter, which either devastated infantry or knocked down fence lines or hedges. Canister, a container filled with musket balls, was an effective anti-personnel weapon.

21 Pancake, *1777*, 68-69.

22 Wright, *Army*, 105; McBurney, *Kidnapping the Enemy*, 38.

spruce beer, malt, vinegar, celery seed, and brown mustard seed were used as anti-scorbutics to help ward off scurvy.

Commissary generals complained that moldy bread, biscuits teeming with insects, rancid butter, rotten flour, worm-eaten peas, and maggot-ridden beef arrived from England. Not surprisingly, men frequently attempted to supplement their diet by foraging (or outright looting) in the countryside, which led to depredations against civilians.[23]

By 1777, the British high command hoped the army no longer needed to rely on supplies from Great Britain, but the army's commissary general often noted North America could not be depended upon for supplies. The alternative was a provision train. "No eighteenth-century commander raised in the European tradition would think of taking the field without such a train," explained R. Arthur Bowler, historian of British logistics during the Revolution. "Armies of the period tended to be small and expensive to the point that even victories attended by considerable losses were unacceptable. Aware of the problems of health and morale that accompanied poor and short rations, few commanders willingly trusted the feeding of their armies to the chance that sufficient food could be obtained along the line of march." Simply put, long provision trains became necessary.[24]

Daniel Wier, Howe's commissary general, knew from experience that depending on North American supplies rather than on shipments from England was less than ideal. He served as a commissary official in Germany during the Seven Years' War and in the East and West Indies, where he learned armies could live well off the land in Europe, but the Americas were an altogether different proposition. Rats and other vermin damaged or destroyed much of the food, while careless storage damaged other provisions. Obtaining fresh supplies from the countryside became critical to the health and well-being of Howe's men.

Provision trains required healthy horses in large numbers, which in turn required tons of fodder—a precious commodity the British sought to obtain from the countryside, which in turn required even more horses to haul it. Howe estimated he needed at least 3,662 horses, and all their requisite supplies, for his Philadelphia campaign. Exactly how many horses left New York with him is unknown, but we do know many died and many more became ill during the difficult voyage to the Chesapeake. The mobile workshops of blacksmiths, carpenters, harness-makers, and other tradesmen also required draft horses.

23 Curtis, *The British Army*, 88-93.

24 Bowler, *Logistics*, 49, 55-56.

Foragers roaming the countryside seeking food and horses forced Howe's army to sit idle several times during the campaign.[25]

By the time of the American Revolution, England long had a standing army and long recognized the need for a different kind of support system for it. Each company had an authorized quota of women. The presence of women reduced desertions, and they performed work like mending, cooking, nursing, and laundering. The women who accompanied the army to North America were supposed to be the wives of enlisted soldiers (wives of officers rarely accompanied them on campaign). The marital statuses of these women were questionable, for proof of a legal marriage was not always required. The women traveled with the baggage wagons on the march and did not accompany the men directly.[26]

Every British infantry company had one tailor assigned to fit regimental coats the regiment received annually from contractors. These men also needed to fit new waistcoats and breeches each year, make supplemental clothing when needed, and to keep all garments in repair. Likewise, each company contained a shoemaker.[27]

German Auxiliaries

Attempting to bolster the British war effort, King George III hired German forces to serve with his army. Great Britain was a global empire, with military commitments across the world in places like Gibraltar, India, Canada, the Caribbean, the American colonies, and of course, the home islands. The American Revolution stretched British military manpower to its limits.

The German soldiers sent to North America were not mercenaries in the traditional sense, but rather armies from another country hired for use in the colonies. The soldiers were not paid by Great Britain directly and received nothing more than their regular army pay and rations. Instead, England paid the various German princes for the use of their troops. German officers commanded the German soldiers, and they were not subject to British military discipline.[28]

Six German rulers hired out their soldiers to Great Britain: Frederick II, Landgrave of Hesse-Cassel; William, his son, the independent Count of

---

25 Bowler, *Logistics*, 58.

26 Curtis, *The British Army*, 10-11; Hagist, *British Soldiers American War*, 148-149.

27 Hagist, *Noble Volunteers*, 32.

28 Fischer, *Crossing*, 63-65.

Hesse-Hanau; Charles I, Duke of Brunswick; Frederick, Prince of Waldeck; Charles Alexander, Margrave of Anspach-Bayreuth; and Frederick Augustus, Prince of Anhalt-Zerbst. Because the German troops sent to North America hailed from separate principalities, they were not all "Hessians," though traditionally they have been referred to by that name.[29]

George III's royal house of Hanover was a reason he could acquire these troops. Frederick II (not to be confused with his more famous namesake), of Hesse-Cassel, was married to George's sister. William, the oldest son of Frederick II, not only was the grandson of George II, but was also the ruler of Hesse-Hanau. Duke Charles I of Brunswick had his son, Prince Charles William Ferdinand, marry another of George's sisters. Beyond family obligations, Charles Alexander of Anspach-Bayreuth was so deeply in debt that he felt compelled to supply troops to England. The princes of Waldeck were known to raise soldiers for use by other countries, so providing men to England was merely an extension of an existing program. Frederick Augustus of Anhalt-Zerbst sent only a small number of men, most of whom had to be recruited from other provinces.[30]

The British Parliament lacked enthusiasm for hiring auxiliary troops, and protests erupted in the House of Lords. The arguments expressed the supposed danger and disgrace of the foreign treaties involved, which acknowledged to all Europe that Great Britain was unable, either from want of men or their disinclination toward the intended service, to furnish enough natural-born subjects for the campaign. Others felt it better to send more foreign troops rather than drawing off the national troops and leaving Britain exposed to potential assaults and invasions by powerful foreign nations, particularly France and Spain. There was another side to the argument. "We have, moreover, just reason to apprehend that when the colonies come to understand that Great Britain is forming alliances, and hiring foreign troops for their destruction," came one Parliamentary protest, "they may think they are well justified by the example, in endeavoring to avail themselves of the like assistance; and that France, Spain, Prussia, or other powers

---

29 Edward J. Lowell, *The Hessians and the Other German Auxiliaries of Great Britain in the Revolutionary War* (Gansevoort, NY, 1997), 5-21.

30 Lowell, *Hessians*, 5-21. Brunswick contracted to provide 4,300 men including 336 light dragoons. Hesse-Kassel agreed to provide 12,000 troops. Hesse-Hanau promised 688 men and a 120-man artillery company. Waldeck contracted for 670 soldiers. Lastly, Ansbach-Bayreuth promised a 1,285-man brigade. Friederike Baer, *Hessians: German Soldiers in the American Revolutionary War* (New York, 2022), 12-13.

of Europe may conceive that they have as good a right as Hesse, Brunswick, and Hanau to interfere in our domestic quarrels."[31]

Unlike their British counterparts, Hessian officers were well trained. They attended Collegium Carolinum to study languages, engineering, and mathematics, becoming experts in military cartography, tactics, and logistics. They achieved promotion through merit and often in the field for outstanding service. Many of the officers boasted years of field experience.[32]

Enlisted Hessians were recruited in a process designed to serve the needs of their rulers. Those whose civil occupations were deemed indispensable, including skilled artisans, farmers owning more than 50 acres, and anyone making a major contribution to the economy, were exempted from service. Everyone else was encouraged to enlist, especially the sons of poor peasant families. Jaegers tended to be sons of gamekeepers and foresters, while most artillerymen grew up in the cities as sons of industrial workers. Soldiers were paid more than servants and unskilled farm workers, thus encouraging enlistment. Military families were exempted from onerous taxes. Others, like school dropouts, bankrupt tradesmen, and the unemployed, were all but forced into the army.[33]

Unlike British soldiers, Hessians were eligible for prize money from seizures made while on campaign, which encouraged plundering of the countryside. The need for rations contributed to this practice. If a Hessian ate British-issued rations, money was deducted from his pay. If that same Hessian sought forage in the countryside, his pay was not docked.[34]

Both British and Hessian regiments were short of officers, which affected their command and control in battle. British regiments did not have enough officers partially because of the American habit of targeting officers in battle, but illness and exhaustion associated with campaigning also took a toll. Hessian regiments were organized with a higher soldier-to-officer ratio, which put them at an immediate disadvantage. Replacing both officers and men was difficult at best with more than 3,000 miles separating them from home.[35]

31 Lowell, *Hessians*, 30-31.

32 Fischer, *Crossing*, 55.

33 Ibid., 59-60.

34 Ibid., 64.

35 Ibid., 152.

Unlike British regiments, Hessian regiments typically contained five companies—four line companies and a grenadier company. At full strength, they contained 524 men. At the request of the British, the Hessians were asked to "brigade" their grenadier companies much as the British did. The Hessian Grenadier Brigade for the Philadelphia campaign formed from the grenadier companies of twelve regiments. Two 3-pound artillery pieces supported each grenadier battalion. The grenadiers carried a .72 caliber Prussian-style musket. The Hessian jaeger corps consisted of three Hessian companies, an Ansbach company, and a mounted troop of jaegers. A thirty-man grenadier detachment with two 3-pound artillery pieces served with the jaegers. A 1-pound gun or amusette supported each Hessian jaeger company. Jaegers carried a .65 caliber short-barreled German-made rifle.

Howe's Staff

Much like the staff Washington assembled, a select group of officers served William Howe. Chief among them were Brig. Gen. James Paterson (adjutant general), Brig. Gen. Samuel Cleaveland (chief of artillery), and Brig. Gen. William Erskine (quartermaster general). Managing the army was a difficult proposition. Howe needed to maintain contact with the New York City garrison and other detachments in North America while simultaneously spreading his own army out in the Delaware River valley.[36]

36 Howe's staff also included Lt. Col. Stephen Kemble (deputy adjutant general); Captain Henry Bruen (deputy quartermaster general); Daniel Wier (commissary general); Capt. John Montresor (chief engineer); Capt. Archibald Robertson (engineer); and Capt. Robert McKenzie (military secretary). Six aides served Howe: Majs. Cornelius Cuyler, Nesbitt Balfour, and William Gardiner, and Capts. Henry Fox, Henry Knight, and Friedrich von Muenchhausen.

Appendix C

Jacob Duche & Elizabeth Graeme Ferguson

On October 15, 1777, as Washington's army was recovering from Germantown and the British were preparing batteries before Fort Mifflin, the British arrested Jacob Duche, the former chaplain of the Continental Congress. They released him the next day, and he changed his allegiance. Duche wanted Washington to give up the rebellion and penned a shocking letter to Washington. Now he needed someone to deliver the letter to him.

Washington gave Elizabeth Graeme Ferguson permission to travel from her country home in Horsham (Graeme Park) to Germantown to see her loyalist husband Henry Hugh Ferguson (the former collector of the port of Philadelphia). Henry took refuge with the British in Philadelphia. Since Elizabeth provided linen for shirts for American POWs, Washington granted her request. She and Henry met at Rising Sun Tavern at the intersection of Germantown and Old York roads. Henry asked Elizabeth to deliver Duche's letter to Washington. Elizabeth was a well-known woman in the colonies whose friendships included many influential men, including Jacob Duche and Francis Hopkinson, but her loyalties were confusing at best. Whether she was aware of the letter's purpose or if she agreed with her loyalist husband and Jacob is unknown. Elizabeth delivered the letter.[1]

---

1   The Supreme Executive Council found Elizabeth guilty of treason, confiscated her property, and sold off her land at auction. Her property was later returned and she was acquitted. Francis Hopkinson is considered one of the Founding Fathers and designed Continental paper money and two early versions of American flags. Nagy, *Spies in the Capital*, 54-56; Anne M. Ousterhout, *The Most Learned Woman in America: A Life of Elizabeth Graeme Fergusson* (University Park, PA, 2004), 202.

Duche's letter was a diatribe of evils against the Revolution. "Your most intimate friends at that time shuddered at the thought of a separation from the mother-country; and I took it for granted, that your Sentiments coincided with theirs," he explained. He discussed what he thought of Congress—"The most respectable characters have withdrawn themselves, and are succeeded by a great majority of illiberal and violent men." After urging Washington to consider abandoning the American cause and attacking Congress, Duche vented his thoughts on the Continental Army. "What have you to expect of them? Have they not frequently abandoned even yourself, in the hour of extremity? . . . can you have the least Confidence in a Sett of undisciplined Men, & Officers, many of whom have been taken from the lowest of the People, without Principle, without Courage?" Wherever the army went "the Troops of Britain will pursue, & must compleat the Devastation, which America herself had begun." Duche concluded by appealing to Washington: "Millions will bless the Hero, that left the Field of War to decide this most important Contest, with the Weapons of Wisdom & Humanity." Washington did not reply to Duche, but he did inform Congress about the communication.[2]

In the aftermath of losing the river forts and while dealing with the fallout of Thomas Conway's treachery, Washington wrote to Francis Hopkinson on November 21: "I confess to you, that I was not more surprized than concerned, at receiving so extraordinary a letter from Mr. Duche, of whom, I had entertained the most favorable opinion, and I am still willing to suppose, that it was rather dictated by his fears, than by his real Sentiments; But I very much doubt, whether the great numbers of respectable characters, in the State and Army, upon whom he has bestowed the most unprovoked and unmerited abuse, will ever attribute it to the same cause, or forgive the Man, who has artfully endeavoured to engage me to sacrifice them, to purchase my own safety. I never intended to have made the letter more public, than by laying it before Congress. I thought this a duty which I owed to myself, for had any accident happened to the Army intrusted to my command, and it had ever afterwards have appeared that such a letter had been wrote to, and received by me, might it not have been said that I had in consequence of it, betrayed my Country? and would not such a Correspondence if kept a secret have given good Grounds for the suspicion."[3]

2   Chase and Lengel, eds., *Papers*, vol. 11, 432-435.

3   Chase & Grizzard, eds., *Papers*, vol. 12, 341.

Duche soon fled the country for England. In 1783, Duche wrote to Washington begging to return to the country referencing his "Error of Judgement." Duche would return in 1792 and died two years later. Henry Hugh Ferguson left Pennsylvania with the British and never saw his wife again.[4]

4 Letter, Jacob Duche to George Washington, April 2, 1783, George Washington Papers online, Library of Congress, Washington, DC.

Appendix D

Order of Battle

Delaware River Operations

Continental Forces

Gen. George Washington, Commander in Chief

River Defense Commanders
Brig. Gen. James Varnum
Maj. Gen Nathanael Greene[1]

Fort Mifflin Garrison[2]
Col. Henry D'Arendt[3]
Lt. Col. Samuel Smith
Col. John Durkee[4]
Maj. Simeon Thayer[5]

---

1 Greene superseded Varnum on November 21, 1777.

2 Other units were part of this garrison at times, but it is unclear if they arrived as organized bodies or as volunteers from throughout the entire army.

3 D'Arendt was often absent from the fort due to illness, leaving Smith in command for much of the siege.

4 Durkee replaced the wounded Smith on November 13, 1777.

5 Thayer replaced Durkee on November 14, 1777.

6th Virginia Regiment: Lt. Col. John Green
4th Connecticut Regiment: Col. John Durkee
8th Connecticut Regiment: Col. John Chandler
Continental Battery: Capt. Samuel Treat

Fort Mercer Garrison
Col. Christopher Greene

1st Rhode Island Regiment: Col. Christopher Greene
2nd Rhode Island Regiment: Col. Israel Angell
Continental Battery: Capt.-Lt. David Cook

Reinforcements Arriving after November 20, 1777

1st Virginia Brigade: Brig. Gen. Peter Muhlenberg
1st Virginia Regiment: Col. James Hendricks
5th & 9th Virginia Regiments: Col. Josiah Parker[6]
13th Virginia Regiment: Col. William Russell
German Regiment: Col. Henry D'Arendt[7]
1st Virginia State Regiment: Col. George Gibson

2nd Virginia Brigade: Brig. Gen. George Weedon
2nd Virginia Regiment: Col. Christian Fehiger
6th Virginia Regiment: Col. John Gibson
10th Virginia Regiment: Col. Edward Stevens
14th Virginia Regiment: Col. Charles Lewis
13th Pennsylvania Regiment: Col. Walter Stewart[8]

2nd Connecticut Brigade: Brig. Gen. Jedidiah Huntington
1st Connecticut Regiment: Lt. Col. Samuel Prentiss
5th Connecticut Regiment: Col. Philip Bradley
7th Connecticut Regiment: Col. Heman Swift

---

6 Most of the 9th Virginia was captured at Germantown. The remnants of the unit were consolidated with the 5th Virginia.

7 With D'Arendt assigned to Fort Mifflin, it is unclear who was exercising command of the German Regiment.

8 Originally the Pennsylvania State Regiment, its designation changed to 13th Pennsylvania on November 12, 1777.

2nd Massachusetts Brigade: Col. William Shepard [9]
1st Massachusetts Regiment: Col. Joseph Vose
4th Massachusetts Regiment: Col. William Shepard
13th Massachusetts Regiment: Col. Edward Wigglesworth
15th Massachusetts Regiment: Col. Timothy Bigelow

3rd Massachusetts Brigade: Brig. Gen. John Paterson
10th Massachusetts Regiment: Col. Thomas Marshall
11th Massachusetts Regiment: Col. Benjamin Tupper
12th Massachusetts Regiment: Col. Samuel Brewer
14th Massachusetts Regiment: Col. Gamaliel Bradford

Morgan's Rifle Corps detachment: Lt. Col. Richard Butler

Light Dragoon Troop: Capt. Henry Lee

New Jersey Militia: [10]
Brig. Gen. Silas Newcomb
Brig. Gen. David Forman
Col. Joseph Ellis

Cape May County Regiment: Col. John Mackey
1st Cumberland County Regiment: Col. Elijah Hand
2nd Cumberland County Regiment: Col. David Potter
1st Gloucester County Regiment: Lt. Col. Shute
2nd Gloucester County Regiment: Col. Joseph Ellis
3rd Gloucester County Regiment: commander unknown
Salem County Regiment: Maj. Edward Hall
Eastern Morris County Regiment: Lt. Col. Benoni Hathaway
2nd Burlington County Regiment: Lt. Col. Joseph Haight
Essex County Company: Capt. Myers
Middlesex County Battalion: Maj. Nixon
Monmouth County Regiment: Lt. Col. Lawrence
Somerset County Regiment: Lt. Col. Middagh
Burlington County Light Horse: Capt. Borden

---

9 Brig. Gen. John Glover was not present with his brigade.

10 These units were not present simultaneously, but came and went through the course of the river operations.

Crown Forces

Gen. William Howe, Commander in Chief

Fort Mercer Assault Force

Col. Carl von Donop
Von Minnigerode Grenadier Battalion: Lt. Col. Friedrich von Minnigerode[11]
Von Linsing Battalion: Lt. Col. Otto von Linsing[12]
Von Lengerke Battalion: Lt. Col. George Lengerke[13]
Von Mirbach Regiment: Lt. Col. Justus von Schieck
Hessian Jaegers:[14] Lt. Col. Ludwig von Wurmb

Troops sent to New Jersey November 17

Lt. Gen. Charles Cornwallis

Detachment from Philadelphia garrison

1st Battalion British Grenadiers:[15] Lt. Col. William Meadows
1st Battalion British Light Infantry:[16] Lt. Col. Robert Abercrombie
5th Regiment of Foot (Shiners): Maj. George Harris
15th Regiment of Foot: Maj. Joseph Stopford
27th Regiment of Foot (Enniskillings): Lt. Col. John Maxwell
33rd Regiment of Foot: Lt. Col. James Webster
42nd Regiment of Foot (Royal Highlanders): Lt. Col. Thomas Stirling

---

11 The battalion consisted of the grenadier companies of the Erbprinz, von Ditfurth, von Lossberg, and von Knyphausen regiments.

12 The battalion consisted of the grenadier companies of the 2nd and 3rd Guards regiments and the Leib Regiment.

13 The battalion consisted of the grenadier companies of the von Truembach, von Wutginau, and von Donop regiments.

14 Includes one company Ansbach-Bayreuth jaegers.

15 The 1st British Grenadier Battalion was composed of the following Regiments of Foot's grenadier companies: 4th, 5th, 7th, 10th, 15th, 17th, 22nd, 23rd, 27th, 28th, 33rd, 35th, 37th, 38th and 40th

16 The 1st Light Infantry Battalion was composed of the following Regiments of Foot's light companies: 4th, 5th, 7th, 10th, 15th, 17th, 22nd, 23rd, 27th, 28th, 33rd, 35th, 38th and 42nd.

Von Lengerke Battalion: Lt. Col. George Lengerke
Hessian Jaeger Detachment

Reinforcements from New York garrison: Maj. Gen. Thomas Wilson

7th Regiment of Foot (Royal Fusiliers): Lt. Col. Alured Clarke
26th Regiment of Foot: Lt. Col. Charles Stuart
63rd Regiment of Foot: Col. James Paterson
British Brigade of Guards detachment
17th Light Dragoons: Lt. Col. Samuel Birch
Hessian jaeger detachment
Ansbach-Beyreuth Brigade: Col. Friedrich von Salzburg
1st Regiment Ansbach-Beyreuth: Col. Friedrich von Eyb
2nd Regiment Ansbach-Beyreuth: Col. Friedrich von Salzburg

The Naval Forces

American Ships in the Delaware River (Continental Ships)				
Ship	*Commander*	*Crew*	*Armament*	*Notes*
Delaware	Capt. Charles Alexander	152 men	24 guns	Captured & used by British
Andrea Doria	Capt. Isaiah Robinson		14 guns	
Fly			6 guns	
Washington		18 men		

Pennsylvania State Navy				
Ship	*Commander*	*Crew*	*Armament*	Notes
Montgomery			10 guns	
Convention			4 guns	
Delaware			4 guns	
Chatam				
Speedwell				
Race-Horse			10 guns	Captured British sloop of war off Puerto Rico
Champion				

Pennsylvania State Navy (continued)				
Champion			8 guns	
Repulse			8 guns	
13 row galleys			Carried either 1 or 2 guns	
12 armed boats			1 gun each	
Arnold			12 guns	floating battery
Putnam			14 guns	floating battery
Vesuvius (fire ship)				Scuttled in *cheveaux-de-frise* gap near Billingsport
Strombolo (fire ship)				Scuttled in *cheveaux-de-frise* gap near Billingsport
Hecla (fire ship)				Abandoned by crew Sept. 1777

British Ships in the Delaware River				
Ship	*Commander*	*Crew*	*Armament*	
Eagle	Adm. Richard Howe	500 men	64 guns	flagship
Augusta	Capt. Francis Reynolds	500 men	64 guns	
Somerset	Capt. George Ourry	500 men	64 guns	
Isis	Capt. William Cornwallis	350 men	50 guns	

	British Ships in the Delaware River (continued)			
Roebuck	Capt. Andrew Hamond	280 men	44 guns	
Pearl	Capt. John Linzee	220 men	32 guns	
Liverpool	Capt. Henry Bellew	200 men	28 guns	
Camilla	Capt. Charles Phipps	160 men	28 guns	
Merlin	Capt. Samuel Reeve	125 men	18 guns	
Zebra	Capt. John Tollemache	125 men	14 guns	
Cornwallis	Lt. John Brown	40 men	8 guns	galley
Vigilant	Capt. John Henry	150 men	16 guns	converted merchantman
Fury	Lt. John Botham		3 guns	hulk used as floating battery

The River Forts 1777-Present

Fort Billingsport

Although the Philadelphia Campaign ended in 1777, Billingsport continued to play a role in the Revolution. On April 4 and 5, 1778, Maj Richard Howell's 2nd New Jersey attempted to attack 150 loyalists occupying the British works, but were repulsed. When the British evacuated Philadelphia in June 1778, the loyalists abandoned Billingsport. In September 1778, the Americans reoccupied the site and erected a battery of four 18-pounders to help enforce trade embargoes. Over the next few years, Pennsylvania militiamen periodically garrisoned the battery.

The Marquis de Chastellux visited the battery on December 8, 1780, and described the position in his journal: "As the present situation of affairs does not attract attention to this locality, the fortifications are somewhat neglected. The entire battery consisted only of one rather good brass mortar and five eighteen-pounders. . . . When America has more money and leisure she will do well not to neglect this post, as well as all those which can serve for the defense of the river." Nine months later Comte de Rochambeau made a point of visiting Mud Island and Billingsport enroute to Yorktown.[1]

During the War of 1812, the government occupied the site with 1,000 New Jersey troops under Col. Joshua L. Howell and used the grounds as a militia camp for 1,300 men under Brig. Gen. Ebenezer Elmer. After this war, Billingsport was

---

1 Mooney & Wuebber, "Archaeological Investigations," 17; Dorwart, *Fort Mifflin*, 61, 63; Chastellux, *Travels in North America*, vol. 1, 154.

neglected. On December 29, 1824, army quartermaster Maj. William Linnard reported the site was "free to the ravages of ill disposed persons, who have destroyed the fences etc nearly the whole front on the river and distance back, is broken up by digging for the Breastwork, and embrazures, & would cost more to level it than that part of the ground is worth, the remainder is tolerable good Jersey land, formerly it was an excellent fishing place for shad but the bottom of the [HMS] Augusta drifting on the shore after she was blown up has injured it much." Four months later Linnard reported the tract "a desolate place not a single post or rail of the fences to be seen nor a vestige of any building"[2]

In December 1834, the government sold the tract that once contained Fort Billingsport for $2,000 to a timber business owned by Joseph Gill and John Ford. Six years later Ford bought out his partner. By the early 1850s, Ford began subdividing the property and selling off lots to Philadelphians interested in establishing country retreats. One of the buyers was Charles Dudley Freeman, later president of the Camden and Atlantic Railroad.[3]

Thomas J. Ryan purchased most of the original government tract in 1889 to establish Lincoln Park—a new amusement park. The new owners envisioned a day-trip location similar to Glen Island Resort on the Hudson River. The park opened the next year and annually thereafter from Memorial Day to Labor Day. During the park's heyday, there was a wharf and sea wall, a beer garden facing a large band shell, an ice cream pavilion, a hotel pavilion, a restaurant pavilion, a ladies' cottage, a gentleman's cottage, a refrigeration building, electric light plant, a water tower, and illuminated fountains. Attractions included a carousel, toboggan slide, swings, mechanical horse racetrack, and even a vaudeville show, movie palace, and nightly balloon ascensions. Financial woes forced the park's closure in 1916.[4]

In 1928, a large oil company purchased the remnants of Billingsport. According to a report, "an effort, which may prove successful, has been made to

2 Moffett, ed., *Year Book for 1928*, 39; Mooney & Wuebber, "Archaeological Investigations," 19; Letter, William Linnard to Thomas Jesup, December 29, 1824, "Billingsport, NJ," file, Consolidated Correspondence Files, 1794-1890, Entry 225, Records of the Office of the Quartermaster General, Record Group 92, National Archives, Washington, DC; Letter, William Linnard to Thomas Jesup, April 7, 1825, "Billingsport, NJ," file, Consolidated Correspondence Files, 1794-1890, Entry 225, Records of the Office of the Quartermaster General, Record Group 92, National Archives, Washington, DC.

3 Mooney & Wuebber, "Archaeological Investigations," 21-22.

4 Ibid., 24.

The 1928 Billingsport marker. *Author*

preserve for public park purposes a small piece of the land that shows a deep excavation of the fort. Evidences of trenches and redoubts are widely scattered and apparently nothing can be done to save these remains of great labor of the patriots of the Revolution." In fact, "evidences of trenches and redoubts" were more likely the foundations of the Lincoln Park buildings. A pit near the oil tanks was likely associated with the foundation for a chute-the-shoot ride and not the original fort. Regardless, a marker was erected the same year to note the suspected fort location. During a 1977 lecture, former Marine Corps Brig. Gen. Edwin Simmons recalled growing up in the area in the 1930s and claimed he could "follow the traces of what we called the trenches, but what [others] would call the ditch outlining the main works."[5]

5 Moffett, ed., *Year Book for 1928*, 39; Mooney & Wuebber, "Archaeological Investigations," 46-47.

Standard Oil Company turned the site into a storage tank field in 1952. Twenty-two years later the 1928 marker was moved to its present location in a community park immediately south of the fort's original location.

Fort Mercer

Just as he visited Billingsport, Marquis de Chastellux also visited Fort Mercer in 1781. Captain Thomas du Plessis guided him over the grounds. Taking a boat from Philadelphia, the party landed and du Plessis "proposed conducting us to a Quaker's, whose house is half a musket-shot from the fort, or rather the ruins of the fort; for it is now destroyed, and there are scarcely any reliefs of it remaining," wrote de Chastellux in his journal. Du Plessis stated James Whitall was "a little of a Tory. I was obliged to knock down his barn, and fell his fruit trees; but he will . . . receive us well." Du Plessis was mistaken. "We found our Quaker seated in the chimney corner, busied in cleaning herbs . . . but he did not deign to lift his eyes, nor to answer any of our introducer's discourse, which at first was complimentary, and at length jocose. Except Dido's silence, I know nothing more severe, but we had no difficulty in accommodating ourselves to this bad reception, and made our way to the fort."[6]

After leaving the house and walking toward the fort's remnants, the party "had not gone a hundred yards before we came to a small elevation, on which a stone was vertically placed, with this short epitaph: 'Here lies buried Colonel Donop.'" Du Plessis assured the group they "could not make a step without treading on the remains of some Hessian, for near three hundred were buried in the front of the ditch."[7]

Lafayette's 1824 visit sparked interest in remembering the Revolution and led to the 1829 erection of a blue-veined marble monument about 15 feet tall erected just within the northern line of Fort Mercer's outworks. Because the Whitalls "did not wish it on their ground, because of predatory companies visiting the ground, and using their melons and fruits, &c.," the monument was placed north of the redoubt on the property of the next landowner. As part of the monument dedication, a "sham" battle was held with New Jersey militia holding the fort and

---

6 Chastellux, *Travels in North America*, vol. 1, 156-157. The Whithall Family were victims of the 1798 yellow fever epidemic. Stewart, *Battle of Red Bank*, 13.

7 Chastellux, *Travels in North America*, vol. 1, 157.

Modern view of recreated Fort Mercer trenches. *Author*

Pennsylvanians serving as the attackers. These "battles" continued over the next decade.[8]

On November 27, 1848, Benson Lossing visited Red Bank and left a vivid description of what he found there. "The embankments and trenches are quite prominent, and will doubtless long remain so, for a forest of young pines now covers and protects them from the destroying hand of cultivation, he began. The form of the fort and outworks," he continued,

was easily distinguished, and the serried lines of the soldiers' graves were palpable along the brow of the high bank. . . . They were buried in boxes, and now their remains are often

8 Lossing, *Pictorial Field-Book*, 294-295; Watson, *Annals*, vol. 2, 572; Wade P. Catts, "Memorialization, Reconstruction, Erosion, and Sham Battles: Multiple Ways of Remembering the Battle of Fort Mercer, New Jersey," Paper Submitted for Council for Northeast Historical Archaeology Conference, November 2019, 5. The monument's south side reads: "This monument was erected on the 22d Octo., 1829, to transmit to Posterity a grateful remembrance of the Patriotism and Gallantry of Lieutenant-colonel CHRISTOPHER GREENE, who, with 400 men, conquered the Hessian army of 2000 troops (then in the British service), at Red Bank, on the 22d Octo., 1777. Among the slain was found their commander, Count Donop, whose body lies interred near the spot where he fell." The west side reads: "A number of the New Jersey and Pennsylvania Volunteers, being desirous to perpetuate the memory of the distinguished officers and soldiers who fought and bled in the glorious struggle for American INDEPENDENCE, have erected this monument, on the 22d day of October, A.D. 1829."

The 1906 Fort Mercer monument.
Author

exposed by the washing away of the banks. At the southern line of the fort, close by the bank, are the remains of the hickory-tree which was used as a flag-staff during the battle; and near it are traces of the gateway of the fort. A little below, and in the path leading to the house of Mr. Whitall, is the grave of Count Donop, marked by a small, rough sandstone, about fourteen inches in height. Vandal fingers have plucked relic-pieces from it, and so nearly was the rude inscription effaced that I could only decipher a portion of the words, DONOP WAS LOST. . . . Even his bones have not been allowed to molder in his grave, but are scattered about the country as cherished relics, his skull being in possession of a physician of New Jersey![9]

Fourteen years later, the Whitall family lost their property at a sheriff's sale to Benjamin Heritage for $10,000. In 1866, erosion of the riverbank forced the relocation of the 1829 monument to its present location. The federal government bought the property in 1872 for $25,000. The earthworks were still discernable but overgrown with thickets and brush.[10]

After three decades of ownership, the government put the land and holdings up for public sale. In 1905, the Gloucester County Historical Society was created for the purpose of acquiring the land and commemorating the ground. The society acquired 22 of the original 411-acre property. The next year, a new 60-foot

9 Lossing, *Pictorial Field-Book*, 290.

10 Wade P. Catts, "It Is Painful for me to Lose So Many Good People," Report of an Archaeological Survey at Red Bank Battlefield Park (Fort Mercer), National Park, Gloucester County, New Jersey, June 2017, 15; Catts, "Memorialization," 8.

The 1979 monument to Hugh Mercer, Fort Mercer's namesake. *Author*

monument was dedicated. Tens of thousands came by automobile, steamboat, wagon, and foot to hear the governors of New Jersey and Pennsylvania speak. As part of the dedication, another "sham" battle took place with 400 New Jersey National Guardsmen serving as the Hessians. The fort's defenders were represented by U. S. Marines from League Island, a battalion of Naval Reservists, the Second Troop of Cavalry of New Jersey, and a battery of field artillery from the Third New Jersey Regiment.[11]

As part of the New Deal in the 1930s, the Works Progress Administration excavated the fort's ditches, likely widening and deepening them, which unfortunately damaged the archaeological record.[12]

Annual reenactments began in 1960 accompanied by the Jonas Cattell run, which continues to this day. Gloucester County currently administers the fort and park, which contains 44 acres, about half of which consists of fill along the Delaware River shore. During the summer of 2022, an archaeological team led by Wade Catts unearthed the remains of at least 15 individuals presumed to be Hessians killed on the field and buried in the far northern section of Fort Mercer's abandoned ditch. Archaeological work continues to yield more results.[13]

11 Anderson, *Forty Minutes*, 164; Stewart, *Battle of Red Bank*, 24; Catts, "Memorialization," 6, 9.

12 Catts, "Memorialization," 10.

13 A November 2023 email with archaeologist Wade Catts provided the following: "We do not have bodies, nor is it a grave. We have a burial space. In the space are the remains of at least 15

Fort Mifflin

For the rest of the American Revolution, Fort Mifflin played a key role in the Delaware River's defense. During the late winter and early spring of 1778, the British kept a pilot and a 140-man Marine detachment on the island to guide ships through the *cheveaux-de-frise*. The British repaired the walls of the fort and built a strong redoubt on the southernmost tip of the island. When the British evacuated Philadelphia in June 1778, engineer John Montresor felt Henry Clinton committed a military blunder, "leaving Mud Island and all works standing . . . after being spoke to twice by men respecting blowing them up, for which Chambers were all prepared."[14]

On June 30, 1778, George Washington wrote to Louis Duportail, "The experiment of last campaign points out Mud-Island as a very interesting spot—the trouble it occasioned the enemy, in so imperfect a state as it was then in, is an argument of its being capable of the most effectual defense if judiciously fortified." A two-gun battery was soon erected on the island to enforce trade embargoes. Over the remaining years of the Revolution, Mud Island was periodically garrisoned by Pennsylvania militia and Col. Thomas Proctor's Continental Artillery regiment. By 1779, Mud Island contained two 18-pounders, a 24-pounder, and a 32-pounder mounted on carriages. The Comte de Rochambeau made a point of visiting Mud Island enroute to Yorktown in September 1781.[15]

During the French Revolution in 1793, President George Washington wanted to maintain neutrality. Pennsylvania placed a militia garrison on the island to prevent French privateers from using the port of Philadelphia. Some improvements were made at that time. A year later, the federal government assumed responsibility for coastal defenses after Washington convinced Congress to support a national system of seacoast fortifications. Mud Island figured prominently in that system to protect the American capital. On February 28, 1794, Congress appropriated $11,913.82 to complete works on Mud Island and to establish a garrison. Pierre L'Enfant oversaw the work after Secretary of War

---

individuals. As the various forensic and genetic analyses are ongoing, we can't say definitively that these remains are Hessians, but all the evidence points to that fact. We have body parts, not complete skeletons. Definition of individuals is based on skulls or more accurately skull fragments, such as mandibles and maxilla."

14 Dorwart, *Fort Mifflin*, 54, 58; Montresor, "Journals," 137.

15 Letter, George Washington to Louis Duportail, June 30, 1778, accessed November 19, 2023, George Washington Papers online, National Archives; Dorwart, *Fort Mifflin*, 61, 65.

Henry Knox provided instructions to the engineers. The work became an inexpensive but sturdy earthen structure with parapets properly sloped and sodded with thick grass. Structures included a barracks for 500 men, furnaces to heat shot, and magazines large enough to hold 150 rounds for each of the fort's forty guns.[16]

Fort Mifflin remains an excellent example of the First System of American Fortifications. On April 15, 1795, Pennsylvania passed ownership of Mud Island to the federal government and the post officially became known as Fort Mifflin. The present configuration of the fort's masonry walls was completed in 1797. Mifflin was an enclosed irregular work of masonry defended by bastions and semi-bastions designed for sixty guns. Two brick structures stood on the grounds—a magazine holding 180 barrels of powder and a barracks large enough for 100 men. When the federal government moved to Washington, D.C. and the state government moved to Harrisburg in 1800, Mifflin's importance as a national guardian of the capital ended.[17]

By 1802, the fort held only ten 32-pounders, eighteen 24-pounders, and four 10 ½" mortars. Along the water in a river battery was an additional nine 18-pounders. Five years later, President Thomas Jefferson authorized the second system of American coastal defense. At the dawn of the War of 1812, only 29 guns were mounted within the fort with an additional eight mounted in the river battery.[18]

America's second war with Great Britain proved the inadequacies of her coastal defenses. As a result, the government developed a Third System of defense. Concentrating Philadelphia's defenses downriver at Pea Patch Island became a priority and the construction of Fort Delaware superseded Fort Mifflin's usefulness. The government planned no improvements for forts constructed prior to 1816, which were considered good enough for secondary lines of defense. Once Fort Delaware was completed, Mifflin's garrison would be withdrawn and the fort mothballed. By 1824, no cannon remained at Mifflin.[19]

Due to construction delays at Fort Delaware, Congress appropriated money for Fort Mifflin improvements in 1835. Nine 32-pounders from Fort Monroe were placed in the fort. During the Civil War, the army used Fort Mifflin as a way station

---

16 Dorwart, *Fort Mifflin*, 71; Jackson, *Fort Mifflin*, 116.

17 Dorwart, *Fort Mifflin*, 81. Fort McHenry in Baltimore is another example.

18 Jackson, *Fort Mifflin*, 127.

19 Ibid., 132; Dorwart, *Fort Mifflin*, 97.

Portions of the present eastern wall of Fort Mifflin contain
granite stones from the 1777 fort wall. *Author*

for Union army prisoners awaiting transfer to their respective units for regimental trials or detention in military prisons. By May 1863, Fort Mifflin was processing Confederate soldiers who voluntarily surrendered to the Union army. Most of these deserters claimed they were impressed into Confederate service and were angry over their treatment. The post housed many of these men, where they joined draft dodgers, political prisoners, and other civilians accused of crimes against the government. After the Battle of Gettysburg, more than 5,000 Confederate prisoners were processed at Mifflin prior to being transferred to Fort Delaware. With the end of the Civil War, the post's final garrison was removed in April 1866.[20]

The final improvements made at Fort Mifflin came in 1876. The Endicott System of coastal defenses involved layered defenses for America's major ports. While most of the Delaware River's defenses centered around Fort Delaware by 1876, partial construction took place on land reclaimed from the channel between Hog and Mud Islands south of the original fort. The government planned

20 Jackson, *Fort Mifflin*, 144-145; Dorwart, *Fort Mifflin*, 124.

construction for six gun platforms and two magazines for a high battery as well as a mortar battery. Only two magazines were completed for the mortar battery.

During the Spanish-American War, the privies fouled the terreplain and moat and rainwater sat stagnant in the meadows surrounding the fort. The exterior barrack stairs and dormer windows rotted. Regardless, by 1900 the Grand Army of the Republic held annual reunions there and the Philadelphia Police Department fished around the fort to restock aquariums in their police stations.[21]

In 1904, the government disposed of the fort's remaining ordnance: a 42-pounder went to a Grand Army of the Republic Post in Pittsburgh, two 42-pounders went to the Soldier's Monument Association of Castalia, Ohio, all seven 15-inch Rodmans and the remaining dozen 42-pounders were scrapped. Two years later Congress declared the fort a national monument. The War Department named the fort a national historic monument in 1915.[22]

The fort's buildings saw improvements during World War I when it became a storage facility for the nearby Navy Yard. More significant changes took place in the 1940s. A two-gun anti-aircraft battery was mounted on flatcars and rolled into the fort on old railroad tracks. Despite service through nearly two centuries, the U. S. Army returned the fort to Pennsylvania in 1962, and the state quickly transferred the property to the City of Philadelphia's Recreation Department.[23]

The city hired George Edwin Brumbaugh to oversee restoration and improvements to the fort. Lacking city funds, the Shackamaxon Society, a nonprofit organization of young men who aimed to promote Philadelphia, formed in 1968 to assume responsibility for the restoration. The fort opened to the public the next year and the site became a National Historic Landmark in 1970. For America's Bicentennial, the 79th United States Army Reserves conducted additional fort restoration.[24]

On October 28, 1980, Boy Scouts camping in the fort accidentally set the commandant's house on fire while escaping a storm. In the mid-1980s another major restoration effort took place. Today the fort is administered by a nonprofit formed in 1986 called "Fort Mifflin on the Delaware."[25]

21 Dorwart, *Fort Mifflin*, 134; Jackson, *Fort Mifflin*, 160.

22 Jackson, *Fort Mifflin*, 164. Some of the 42-pounders may have been sent to Fort Monroe.

23 Ibid., 166-167.

24 Dorwart, *Fort Mifflin*, 160; Jackson, *Fort Mifflin*, 169.

25 Dorwart, *Fort Mifflin*, 162-163.

Order of Battle

The Engagement at Whitemarsh

Continental Forces

Gen. George Washington, Commander in Chief

Front Line: Right Wing: Maj. Gen. John Sullivan

2nd Connecticut Regiment Lt. Col. Isaac Sherman[1]

Pennsylvania Militia: Maj. Gen. John Armstrong[2]

1st Pennsylvania Militia Brigade: Brig. Gen. James Potter
Berks County Battalion: Col. Joseph Heister
Chester County Battalion: Maj. David Mackey
Chester County Battalion: Col. Richard Thomas[3]
Cumberland County Battalion: Col. William Chambers

---

1 Sherman's regiment, detached from the 2nd Connecticut Brigade, formed on the right flank of the army.

2 The two brigades of Pennsylvania militia formed to the left of Webb's Regiment with the 1st Brigade to the right of the 2nd brigade. Attached to Armstrong's command were the Philadelphia Light Horse and Col. Jehu Eyre's Philadelphia County Artillery.

3 This battalion was on detached duty patrolling Chester County and not with the army at the time.

Cumberland County Battalion: Col. Samuel Lyons
Northumberland County Battalion: Col. James Murray
York County Battalion: Col. John Andrews
York County Battalion: Col. Joseph Jefferies

2nd Pennsylvania Militia Brigade: Brig. Gen. James Irvine
Berks County Battalion: Col. George Miller
Berks County Battalion: Col. Henry Spycker
Bucks County Battalion: Lt. Col. John Lacey
Chester County Battalion: Capt. Thomas Wilson
Chester County Battalion: Lt. Col. John Bartholemew
Chester County Battalion: Lt. Col. Matthew Boyd
Lancaster County Battalion: Capt. David Whitehill
Lancaster County Battalion: Col. Robert Elder
Northampton County Battalion: Col. George Breinig
Northampton County Battalion: Col. John Rogers
Northampton County Battalion: Col. John Boyd
Philadelphia County Battalion: Col. Siegfrit
Philadelphia County Battalion: Col. Frederick Antes

1st Continental Light Dragoons: Col. Theodorick Bland[4]

3rd Continental Light Dragoons: Col. George Baylor

John Sullivan's Division: Brig. Gen. William Smallwood[5]
1st Maryland Brigade: Col. William Richardson[6]
1st Maryland Regiment: Maj. Levin Winder[7]

---

4 Casmir Pulaski's light dragoon brigade was divided between the left and right wings. The 1st and 3rd Continental Light Dragoons were positioned between the Pennsylvania Militia and the right flank of the Sullivan's wing.

5 With Sullivan commanding the right wing, Smallwood likely held tactical command of the division.

6 With Smallwood commanding the division, William Richardson was the senior regimental commander in the brigade.

7 The colonel and lieutenant colonel of the 1st Maryland Regiment were severely wounded at Germantown and likely recovering at the time of Whitemarsh. Col. John Stone suffered a severe ankle wound and Lt. Col. Uriah Forrest had a leg amputated from wounds.

3rd Maryland Regiment: Lt. Col. Nathaniel Ramsey[8]
5th Maryland Regiment: Col. William Richardson
7th Maryland Regiment: Col. John Gunby
Delaware Regiment: Lt. Col. Charles Pope[9]

2nd Maryland Brigade: Col. Moses Hazen[10]
2nd Maryland Regiment: Col. Thomas Price
4th Maryland Regiment: Col. Josias Hall
6th Maryland Regiment: Lt. Col. Benjamin Ford
2nd Canadian Regiment (Congress' Own) (2 battalions): Col. Moses Hazen

Anthony Wayne's Division: Brig. Gen. Anthony Wayne
1st Pennsylvania Brigade: Col. Thomas Hartley
1st Pennsylvania Regiment: Col. James Chambers
2nd Pennsylvania Regiment: Col. Henry Bicker
7th Pennsylvania Regiment: Maj. Samuel Hay[11]
10th Pennsylvania Regiment: Lt. Col. Adam Hubley
Hartley's Additional Continental Regiment: Col. Thomas Hartley

2nd Pennsylvania Brigade: Col. Richard Humpton
4th Pennsylvania Regiment: Lt. Col. William Butler[12]
5th Pennsylvania Regiment: Col. Francis Johnston
8th Pennsylvania Regiment: Col. Daniel Brodhead
11th Pennsylvania Regiment: Maj. Francis Mentges

Poor's Brigade: Brig. Gen. Enoch Poor[13]
1st New Hampshire Regiment: Col. Joseph Cilley

8 The 3rd Maryland Regiment's colonel—Mordecai Gist—was detached commanding the Maryland Militia.

9 Col. David Hall, the Delaware Regiment's colonel, suffered a severe wound at Germantown and would never rejoin the regiment.

10 No officer was appointed to command of the 2nd Maryland Brigade following the resignation of Brig. Gen. Preudhomme de Borre following the Battle of Brandywine. Hazen likely held tactical command of the brigade as senior colonel.

11 The regiment's colonel, William Irvine, was an unexchanged prisoner-of-war at the time.

12 The regiment's colonel, Lambert Cadwalader, was an unexchanged prisoner-of-war at the time.

13 Poor's brigade was not assigned to a division at this time.

2nd New Hampshire Regiment: Lt. Col. Jeremiah Gilman[14]
3rd New Hampshire Regiment: Col. Alexander Scammell
2nd New York Regiment: Col. Philip van Cortland
4th New York Regiment: Col. Henry Livingston

Front Line: Left Wing: Maj. Gen. Nathanael Greene

Morgan's Rifle Corps:[15] Col. Daniel Morgan

Maryland Militia:[16] Col. Mordecai Gist
Baltimore Battalion: Col. Darby Lux
Prince George Battalion: commander unknown
Montgomery Battalion: Col. John Murdock
Frederick Battalion: Col. Baker Johnson
Ann Arundel Battalion: Col. Thomas Dorsey
Queen Anne Battalion: commander unknown
Caroline Battalion: commander unknown
Kent Battalion: commander unknown

2nd Continental Light Dragoons:[17] Col. Elisha Sheldon

4th Continental Light Dragoons: Col. Stephen Moylan

Nathanael Greene's Division: Brig. Gen. Peter Muhlenberg[18]
1st Virginia Brigade: Col. William Russell[19]
1st Virginia Regiment: Col. James Hendricks

14 The regiment's colonel, Nathan Hale, was captured at the Battle of Hubbardton and not present.

15 Morgan's rifle corps was positioned on the far left flank of the army.

16 The Maryland militia lined up on Morgan's right flank.

17 Casmir Pulaski's light dragoon brigade was divided between the left and right wings. The 2nd and 4th Continental Light Dragoons were positioned between the Maryland militia and the left flank of Greene's wing.

18 With Greene commanding the left wing, Muhlenberg likely held tactical command of the division.

19 With Muhlenberg commanding the division, Russell was the senior regimental commander in the brigade.

5th & 9th Virginia Regiments: Col. Josiah Parker[20]
13th Virginia Regiment: Col. William Russell
German Regiment: Col. Henry Arendt
1st Virginia State Regiment: Col. George Gibson

2nd Virginia Brigade: Brig. Gen. George Weedon
2nd Virginia Regiment: Col. Christian Fehiger
6th Virginia Regiment: Col. John Gibson
10th Virginia Regiment: Col. Edward Stevens
14th Virginia Regiment: Col. Charles Lewis
13th Pennsylvania Regiment: Col. Walter Stewart[21]

Johann DeKalb's Division: Maj. Gen. Johann DeKalb
2nd Massachusetts Brigade: Col. William Shepard[22]
1st Massachusetts Regiment: Col. Joseph Vose
4th Massachusetts Regiment: Col. William Shepard
13th Massachusetts Regiment: Col. Edward Wigglesworth
15th Massachusetts Regiment: Col. Timothy Bigelow

3rd Massachusetts Brigade: Brig. Gen. John Paterson
10th Massachusetts Regiment: Col. Thomas Marshall
11th Massachusetts Regiment: Col. Benjamin Tupper
12th Massachusetts Regiment: Col. Samuel Brewer
14th Massachusetts Regiment: Col. Gamaliel Bradford

4th Massachusetts Brigade: Col. John Bailey[23]
2nd Massachusetts Regiment: Col. John Bailey
8th Massachusetts Regiment: Col. Michael Jackson
9th Massachusetts Regiment: Col. James Wesson

---

20 Most of the 9th Virginia Regiment was captured at Germantown. The remnants of the unit were consolidated with the 5th Virginia Regiment.

21 Originally the Pennsylvania State Regiment, their designation changed to 13th Pennsylvania Regiment on November 12, 1777.

22 Brig. Gen. John Glover was not present with his brigade but in Massachusetts overseeing the Saratoga prisoners.

23 Brigadier General Ebenezer Learned was not with his brigade. He went home on sick leave following the fighting at Saratoga.

Second Line: Maj. Gen. William Alexander (Lord Stirling)

Alexander McDougall's Division: Maj. Gen. Alexander McDougall
Rhode Island Brigade: Brig. Gen. James Varnum
1st Rhode Island Regiment: Col. Christopher Greene
2nd Rhode Island Regiment: Col. Israel Angell
4th Connecticut Regiment: Col. John Durkee
8th Connecticut Regiment: Col. John Chandler

2nd Connecticut Brigade: Brig. Gen. Jedidiah Huntington
1st Connecticut Regiment: Lt. Col. Samuel Prentiss
5th Connecticut Regiment: Col. Philip Bradley
7th Connecticut Regiment: Col. Heman Swift

Marquis de Lafayette's Division: Maj. Gen. Marquis de Lafayette[24]
3rd Virginia Brigade: Brig. Gen. William Woodford
3rd Virginia Regiment: Lt. Col. William Heth
7th Virginia Regiment: Col. Alexander McClanachan
11th Virginia Regiment: Lt. Col. John Cropper
15th Virginia Regiment: Col. David Mason

4th Virginia Brigade: Brig. Gen. Charles Scott
4th Virginia Regiment: Col. Robert Lawson
8th Virginia Regiment: Col. Abraham Bowman
12th Virginia Regiment: Col. James Wood
Grayson's Additional Continental Regiment: Col. William Grayson
Patton's Additional Continental Regiment: Col. John Patton
Virginia Militia: Col. William Rumney

Lord Stirling's Division: Brig. Gen. William Maxwell[25]
3rd Pennsylvania Brigade: Col. William Cooke[26]
3rd Pennsylvania Regiment: Col. Thomas Craig

---

24 Lafayette took command of Adam Stephen's former division on December 4.

25 With Stirling commanding the second line, Maxwell likely held tactical command of the division.

26 Commander of the brigade Thomas Conway had been appointed major general by Congress and made inspector general of the army. Cooke was the senior regimental commander with the brigade.

6th Pennsylvania Regiment: Lt. Col. Josiah Harmar
9th Pennsylvania Regiment: Maj. Francis Nichols[27]
12th Pennsylvania Regiment: Col. William Cooke
Spencer's Additional Continental Regiment: Col. Oliver Spencer
Malcolm's Additional Continental Regiment: Lt. Col. Aaron Burr

New Jersey Brigade: Col. Elias Dayton[28]
1st New Jersey Regiment: Col. Mathias Ogden
2nd New Jersey Regiment: Col. Israel Shreve
3rd New Jersey Regiment: Col. Elias Dayton
4th New Jersey Regiment: Lt. Col. David Rhea

Army Reserve: Col. Jethro Sumner

North Carolina Brigade: Col. Jethro Sumner
1st North Carolina Regiment: Col. Thomas Clark
2nd North Carolina Regiment: Col. John Patten
3rd North Carolina Regiment: Lt. Col. Lott Brewster
4th North Carolina Regiment: Lt. Col. James Thackston
5th North Carolina Regiment: Lt. Col. William Davidson
6th North Carolina Regiment: Lt. Col. William Taylor
7th North Carolina Regiment: Col. James Hogun
8th North Carolina Regiment: Col. James Armstrong
9th North Carolina Regiment: Col. John Williams
Corps of North Carolina Light Dragoons: commander unknown

Unattached Units
Forman's Additional Continental Regiment: Col. David Forman
Lee's Additional Continental Regiment: Col. William Lee
Jackson's Additional Continental Regiment: Col. Henry Jackson
Henley's Additional Continental Regiment: Col. David Henley
Webb's Additional Continental Regiment: Col. Samuel Webb

---

27 The regiment's colonel, Richard Butler served with Morgan's Rifle Corps.

28 With Maxwell likely commanding the division, Dayton was the senior regimental commander in the brigade.

Artillery Brigade: Brig. Gen. Henry Knox[29]
Proctor's Continental Artillery Regiment: Col. Thomas Proctor
Lamb's Continental Artillery Regiment (detached companies):
New York Battery: Capt. Sebastian Bauman
New Jersey Battery: Capt. John Doughty
Continental Battery: Capt. James Lee
Continental Battery: Capt. Andrew Porter
Continental Battery: commander unknown
Crane's Continental Artillery Regiment (detached companies):
New Jersey Battery: Capt. Thomas Clark
Pennsylvania Battery: Capt.-Lt. Gibbs Jones
Continental Battery: Capt. David Cook
Continental Battery: Capt. Thomas Seward

Crown Forces
Gen. William Howe, Commander in Chief

Vanguard: Lt. Gen. Charles Cornwallis

Light Infantry Brigade: Lt. Col. Robert Abercrombie[30]
1st Battalion: Lt. Col. Robert Abercrombie[31]
2nd Battalion: Lt. Col. John Maitland[32]

Hessian Jaegers:[33] Lt. Col. Ludwig von Wurmb

---

29 The artillery brigade did not operate as an independent command. The companies of the three regiments were distributed among various brigades of the army, and some remained as a general reserve under Henry Knox's direct control. However, the records do not indicate which specific batteries were assigned to which brigade or division at Whitemarsh.

30 As the senior officer, Lt. Col. Robert Abercrombie commanded the brigade when it operated independently. The 1st Light Infantry Battalion was composed of the following Regiments of Foot's light companies: 4th, 5th, 7th, 10th, 15th, 17th, 22nd, 23rd, 27th, 28th, 33rd, 35th, 38th and 42nd. The 2nd Light Infantry Battalion was composed of the following Regiments of Foot's light companies: 26th, 37th, 40th, 43rd, 44th, 45th, 46th, 49th, 52nd, 55th, 57th, 63rd, 64th, and two companies from the 71st. Hagist, *Distinguished Corps*, 111, 130.

31 Two 3-pounders were attached to the battalion.

32 Two 3-pounders were attached to the battalion.

33 Includes one company of Anspach-Bayreuth jaegers.

British Grenadier Brigade: Lt. Col. Henry Monckton[34]
1st Battalion: Lt. Col. William Meadows[35]
2nd Battalion: Lt. Col. Henry Monckton[36]

Hessian Grenadier Brigade:[37]
Von Linsing Battalion: Lt. Col. Otto von Linsing[38]
Von Lengerke Battalion: Lt. Col. George Lengerke[39]
Capt. Friedrich von Eschwege[40]
Von Minnigerode Grenadier Battalion: Maj. Carl von Baurmeister[41]

4th Brigade:[42]
33rd Regiment of Foot: Lt. Col. James Webster
37th Regiment of Foot: Maj. James Cousseau
46th Regiment of Foot: Lt. Col. Enoch Mankham
64th Regiment of Foot: Maj. Robert McLeroth

16th Light Dragoons (Queen's Own): 2 squadrons

Artillery: Capt. Thomas Pitts
2 medium 12 pounders, 2 5 ½" Howitzers

34 As the senior officer, Lt. Col. Henry Monckton commanded the brigade when it operated independently. The 1st British Grenadier Battalion was composed of the following Regiments of Foot's grenadier companies: 4th, 5th, 7th, 10th, 15th, 17th, 22nd, 23rd, 27th, 28th, 33rd, 35th, 37th, 38th and 40th. The 2nd Grenadier Battalion consisted of the following grenadier companies: two Royal Marine companies, and the following from Regiments of Foot—26th, 42nd, 43rd, 44th, 45th, 46th, 49th, 52nd, 55th, 57th, 63rd, 64th, and 71st. Hagist, *Distinguished Corps*, 111, 130.

35 Two 6-pounders were attached to the battalion.

36 Two 6-pounders were attached to the battalion.

37 It is unclear who commanded the Hessian grenadier brigade following the death of Col. Carl von Donop at Fort Mercer.

38 The battalion consisted of the grenadier companies of the 2nd and 3rd Guards regiments and the Leib Regiment.

39 The battalion consisted of the grenadier companies of the von Truembach, von Wutginau, and von Donop regiments.

40 Von Lengerke injured his right arm in a fall; von Eschwege held the command on December 7.

41 The battalion consisted of the grenadier companies of Erbprinz, von Ditfurth, von Lossberg, and von Knyphausen regiments.

42 It is unclear who commanded the brigade following the death of James Agnew at Germantown. Four 6-pounders were attached to the brigade.

Main Column: Lt. Gen. Wilhelm von Knyphausen

Leib Regiment: Col. Friedrich von Wurmb

Von Donop Regiment: Lt. Col. Philip Heymell

1st Brigade: Maj. Gen. James Grant[43]
4th Regiment of Foot (King's Own): Lt. Col. James Ogilive
23rd Regiment of Foot (Royal Welch Fusiliers): Lt. Col. Benjamin Bernard
28th Regiment of Foot: Lt. Col. Robert Prescott
49th Regiment of Foot: Lt. Col. Henry Calder

Artillery:
2 light 12-pounders: Capt.-Lt. Charles Wood
2 light 12-pounders: Capt. David Standish

Guards: Brig. Gen. Edward Matthew
1st Battalion: Col. Henry Trelawny[44]
2nd Battalion: Lt. Col. George Ogilvie[45]

16th Light Dragoons (Queen's Own): 1 squadron

17th Light Dragoons: 3 squadrons: Lt. Col. Samuel Birch

Mounted Hessian Jaegers: commander unknown

5th Regiment of Foot (Shiners): Maj. George Harris

7th Regiment of Foot (Royal Fusiliers): Lt. Col. Alured Clarke[46]

26th Regiment of Foot: Lt. Col. Charles Stuart

27th Regiment of Foot (Enniskillings): Lt. Col. John Maxwell

---

43 Four 6-pounders were attached to the brigade.

44 Two 6-pounders were attached to the battalion.

45 Two 6-pounders were attached to the battalion.

46 Four 3-pounders were attached to the Fifth British Brigade. Its unclear if they remained in Philadelphia or accompanied that portion of the brigade on Howe's expedition.

3rd British Brigade: Maj. Gen. Charles Grey[47]
15th Regiment of Foot: Maj. Joseph Stopford
17th Regiment of Foot: Lt. Col. Charles Mawhood
42nd Regiment of Foot (Royal Highlanders): Lt. Col. Thomas Stirling
44th Regiment of Foot: Lt. Col. Henry Hope

Queen's Rangers: Lt. Col. John Simcoe

71st Highlanders: 1 battalion

Philadelphia Garrison:
Brig. Gen. Alexander Leslie

2nd Brigade:[48]
10th Regiment of Foot (Springers): Lt. Col. Francis Smith
40th Regiment of Foot: Lt. Col. Thomas Musgrave
55th Regiment of Foot: Lt. Col. Cornelius Cuyler

Hessian Brigade: Maj. Gen. Johann von Stirn
Von Mirbach Regiment: Col. Heinrich von Borck[49]
Combined Regiment Hessian Battalion:[50] Col. W. von Wollwarth

63rd Regiment of Foot: Col. James Paterson

71st Highlanders: 1 battalion

Artillery: Brig. Gen. James Pattison[51]

47 Four 6-pounders were attached to the brigade.

48 With Maj. Gen. James Grant accompanying the column to Whitemarsh, it is unclear who commanded the 2nd British Brigade. Four 6-pounders were attached to the brigade.

49 Von Borck temporarily commanded the regiment following the death of von Schieck at Fort Mercer and the illness of Maj. Emanuel von Wilmowsky.

50 The unit was composed of the remnants of the regiments that had been decimated at the Battle of Trenton on December 26, 1776. The Combined Hessian Battalion contained the men from the von Lossberg, von Knyphausen, and Rall regiments.

51 Two 3-pounders from the British artillery park remained in Philadelphia.

2nd Battalion, New Jersey Volunteers: commander unknown[52]

17th Light Dragoons: 1 squadron

Ansbach-Beyreuth Brigade: Col. Friedrich von Salzburg[53]
1st Regiment Ansbach-Beyreuth: Col. Friedrich von Eyb
2nd Regiment Ansbach-Beyreuth: Col. Friedrich von Salzburg

Provincial Infantry:
Guides and Pioneers: Capt. Simon Fraser
Roman Catholic Volunteers: Lt. Col. Alfred Clifton
Maryland Loyalists: Lt. Col. James Chambers
Pennsylvania Loyalists: Lt. Col. William Allen

52 This Loyalist battalion was attached to the Royal Artillery during the campaign and presumably was stationed with the heavy artillery in Philadelphia.

53 Von Salzburg was the senior colonel of the brigade.

Bibliography

Manuscripts

American Philosophical Society, Philadelphia, PA

James Pattison Papers
Journal of Officer B. Sol Feinstone Collection, Item No. 409.
Parker Family Papers

Author's Collection

Letter, Robert Rogers to his brother, October 25, 1777

Boston Public Library, Boston, MA

American Revolutionary War Manuscripts Collection

Chicago Historical Society, Chicago, IL

George Weedon letters

William L. Clements Library, University of Michigan, Ann Arbor, MI

Loftus Cliffe Papers
William Howe Orderly Book, 1776-1778

Harlan Crow Library, Dallas, TX

Heinrich Von Feilitzsch, Journal of several Campaigns in America by Heinrich Earl
Philipp von Feilitzsch Prussian Lieutenant of the Ansbach Feldjager. Manuscript journal

Duke University Library, Durham, NC

Ephraim Kirby Papers

Durham University, England

Grey Papers, Lord Cantelupe Diary

First City Troop Archives, Philadelphia PA

Capt. J. H. C. Smith, "History of the 1st City Troop," based largely on the recollections of Trooper John Donaldson

Historical Society of Pennsylvania, Philadelphia, PA

Ferdinand J. Dreer Collection
Anthony Wayne Papers

Library of Congress, Washington, D.C.

Richard Fitzpatrick Papers
George Washington Papers online

Library of Virginia, Richmond, VA

Bounty-land Records
Pension Records

Massachusetts Historical Society, Boston, MA

William Livingston Family Collection
Timothy Pickering Papers

Morristown National Historical Park, Morristown, NJ

Hessian Documents of the American Revolution

National Archives and Records Administration, Washington, D.C.

Revolutionary War Rolls, 1775-1783, Record Group 93. www.fold3.com
Revolutionary War Pension and Bounty-Land-Warrant Application Files (M804) [RWPF], Record Group 15, Records of the Veterans Administration. Accessible at www.fold3.com

National Archives of Scotland, Edinburgh

James Grant Papers

New York Historical Society, New York, NY

Handwritten extract from Journal of Captain Allen McLane, Joseph Reed Papers

New York Public Library, New York, NY

Mordecai Gist Letterbook

Public Records Office, London

HMS Augusta Court Martial Documents. ADM 1/5308
Judge Advocate General Office: Court Martial Proceedings and Board of General Officers' Minutes, War Office. WO71/84, WO71/86
Precis of documents relating to military operations against the revolted colonists

Rush Rhees Library, Department of Rare Books and Special Collections, University of Rochester, Rochester, NY

[Jonathan Forman], Revolutionary War diary, Fellows Papers, Box 2.

Valley Forge National Park, Valley Forge, PA

John Reed Manuscript Collection

Virginia Historical Society, Richmond, VA

David Griffith Letters
Martin Pickett Letters

Wisconsin Historical Society, Madison, WI

Lyman Draper Manuscript Collection

Printed Original Sources

Allen, James. "Diary of James Allen, Esq., of Philadelphia, Counsellor-at-Law, 1770-1778." *The Pennsylvania Magazine of History and Biography*, vol. 9. (Philadelphia, 1887): 424-441.

Andre, John. *Major Andre's Journal: Operations of the British Under Lieutenant Generals Sir William Howe and Sir Henry Clinton. June 1777 to November 1778. Recorded by Major John Andre, Adjutant General.* Tarrytown, NY: William Abbatt, 1930.

Angell, Israel. *Diary of Colonel Israel Angell: Commanding the Second Rhode Island Continental regiment during the American Revolution 1778-1781.* Edward Field & Norman Desmarais, eds. Providence, RI: Preston and Rounds Company, 1899.

Armstrong, Samuel. "From Saratoga to Valley Forge: The Diary of Lt. Samuel Armstrong." *The Pennsylvania Magazine of History and Biography*, vol. 121. (Philadelphia, PA, 1997): 237-270.

Bloomfield, Joseph. *Citizen Soldier: The Revolutionary War Journal of Joseph Bloomfield.* eds., Mark Edward Lender & James Kirby Martin. Yardley, PA: Westholme Publishing, 2018.

Boudinot, Elias. *Journal or Historical Recollections of American Events During The Revolutionary War.* Trenton, NJ: C.L. Traver, 1890.

————. *"Their Distress is almost intolerable:" The Elias Boudinot Letterbook 1777-1778.* Joseph Lee Boyle, ed. Westminster, MD: Heritage Books, 2008.

Brigham, Paul. "A Revolutionary Diary of Captain Paul Brigham: November 19, 1777-September 4, 1778." Edward A Hoyt, ed. *Vermont History*, vol. 34. (January 1966): 3-30.

Brown, Lloyd A. & Howard H. Peckham, eds. *Revolutionary War Journals of Henry Dearborn 1775-1783.* New York: Da Capo Press, 1971.

Browne, William H. *Archives of Maryland, Vol. 16, Journal and Correspondence of Safety/State Council 1777-1778*. Baltimore: Maryland Historical Society, 1897.

Buettner, Johann Carl. *Narrative of Johann Carl Buettner in the American Revolution*. New York: Chas, Fred, Heartmen, 1915.

Burgoyne, Bruce E., ed. *Enemy Views: The American Revolutionary War as Recorded by the Hessian Participants*. Bowie, MD: Heritage Books, Inc., 1996.

Burgoyne, Marie E., and Bruce E. Burgoyne, eds. *Journal of the Hesse-Cassel Jaeger Corps and Hans Konze's List of Jaeger Officers*. Westminster, MD: Heritage Books, Inc., 2008.

Burnett, Edmund C., ed., *Letters of Members of the Continental Congress,* vol. 2. Washington, D.C.: Carnegie Institution of Washington, 1923.

Butterfield, L.H., ed. *The Adams Papers: Adams Family Correspondence*, vol. 2. Cambridge, MA: Harvard University Press, 1963.

———. *Letters of Benjamin Rush*. Princeton, NJ: Princeton University Press, 1951.

Chase, Philander D., and Frank E. Grizzard, Jr., eds. *The Papers of George Washington*, Revolutionary War Series, vol. 12. Charlottesville and London: University Press of Virginia, 2002.

Chase, Philander D., and Edward G. Lengel, eds. *The Papers of George Washington*, Revolutionary War Series, vol. 11. Charlottesville/London: University Press of VA, 2001.

Chastellux, Marquis de. *Travels in North America in the Years 1780, 1781 and 1782 by the Marquis de Chastellux*. Trans. Howard C. Rice. Chapel Hill, NC: The University of North Carolina Press, 1963.

Clark, John. "Memoir of Major John Clark, of York County, Pennsylvania." *The Pennsylvania Magazine of History and Biography*, vol. 20. (Philadelphia, 1896): 77-86.

Clark, Joseph. "Diary of Joseph Clark." *Proceedings of the New Jersey Historical Society* (1855): 93-116.

Clark, William Bell ed. *Naval Documents of the American Revolution*, vol. 3. Washington, D.C.: Naval Historical Center, 1968.

Collin, Nicholas. *The Journal and Biography of Nicholas Collin 1746-1831*. Amandus Johnson, trans. Philadelphia: The New Jersey Society of Pennsylvania, 1936.

Commager, Henry Steele, and Richard B. Morris, eds. *The Spirit of Seventy-six: The Story of the American Revolution as Told by its Participants*. Edison, NJ: Castle Books, 1967.

Crawford, Michael J., ed. *Naval Documents of the American Revolution*, vol. 10. Washington, D.C. Naval Historical Center, 1996.

Cushing, Harry Alonzo, ed. *The Writings of Samuel Adams*, vol. 4. New York: G.P. Putnam's Sons, 1904.

David, Ebenezer. *A Rhode Island Chaplain in the Revolution: Letters of Ebenezer David to Nicholas Brown 1775-1778*. Jeannette D. Black & William Greene Roelker, eds. Providence, RI: The Rhode Island Society of the Cincinnati, 1949.

Dayton, Elias. "Papers of General Elias Dayton." *Proceedings of the New Jersey Historical Society*, vol. 9 (Newark, NJ, 1864).

Dohla, Johann Conrad. *A Hessian Diary of the American Revolution*. Bruce E. Burgoyne, trans. & ed. Norman, OK: University of Oklahoma Press, 1990.

Drinker, Elizabeth. *The Diary of Elizabeth Drinker, vol. 1: 1758-1795*. Elaine Forman Crane, ed. Boston: Northeastern University Press, 1991.

Du Buy, Major Johann Christian to Lieutenant General Wilhelm Maximilian August von Ditfurth. Letter dated October 26, 1777. Donald Londahlsmidt, ed. "German and British Accounts of the Assault on Fort Mercer at Redbank, NJ in October 1777." *Journal of the Johannes Schwalm Historical Association*, vol. 16 (Scotland, PA, 2013).

"Extract of a letter written by a Captain of Lighthorse in the Southern Department to his friend in Connecticut." n.d. *Hartford Courant*. 20 January 1778.

Ewald, Johann. *Diary of the American War: A Hessian Journal: Captain Johann Ewald*. Joseph P. Tustin, ed. and trans. New Haven, CT: Yale University Press, 1979.

Fisher, Elijah. *Elijah Fisher's Journal While in the War for Independence, and Continued Two Years After He Came to Maine 1775-1784*. Augusta, ME: Press of Badger and Manley, 1880.

Fitzpatrick, John C., ed. *The Writings of George Washington from the Original Manuscript Sources 1745-1799*. Washington, D.C.: Government Printing Office, 1931-3.

Ford, Worthington Chauncey, ed., *Journals of the Continental Congress 1774-1789*. Washington, D.C.: Government Printing Office, 1907.

Frazer, Persifor. *General Persifor Frazer: A Memoir Compiled Principally from His Own Papers by His Great-Grandson*. Philadelphia, n.p., 1907.

Freyenhagen, Wilhelm Johann Ernst. "The Journal of Ensign/Lt. Wilhelm Johann Ernst Freyenhagen Jr - 1776-78. Part 2 – 1777-1778." Henry J. Retzer trans., Donald M. Londahl-Smidt, ed. *The Hessians: Journal of the Johannes Schwalm Historical Association*, vol. 14. (Scotland, PA, 2011).

Galloway, Joseph. *Letters to a Nobleman on the Conduct of the War in the Middle Colonies*. London: J. Wilkie, 1779.

Greene, Christopher to James Potter. Letter dated 15 November 1777 *The Pennsylvania Magazine of History and Biography*, vol. 19 (Philadelphia, 1895): 369.

Greene, Zachariah. "Record of my Life and of the Greene Family." *Genealogies of Long Island Families: A Collection of Genealogies Relating to the Following Long Island Families: Dickerson,*

Mitchill, Wickham, Carman, Raynor, Rushmore, Satterly, Hawkins, Arthur Smith, Mills, Howard, Lush, Greene. Charles J. Werner, ed. New York: Charles J. Werner, 1919: 125-130.

Greenman, Jeremiah. *Diary of a Common Soldier in the American Revolution 1775-1782.* Robert Bray & Paul Bushnell, eds. DeKalb, IL: Northern Illinois University Press, 1978.

Hagist, Don N., comp. *British Soldiers American War: Voices of the American Revolution.* Yardley, PA: Westholme Publishing, 2012.

Hamilton, Alexander to Horatio Gates. Letter dated 5 November 1777. https://founders.archives.gov/documents/Hamilton/01-01-02-0335 2 September 2023.

Harcourt, Edward William, ed. *The Harcourt Papers.* Vol. 11. Oxford: James Parker and Company, n.d.

Hazard, Samuel et. al., eds. *Pennsylvania Archives: Selected and Arranged from Original Documents in the Office of the Secretary of the Commonwealth.* Series 1. Harrisburg and Philadelphia, 1853.

Hiltzheimer, Jacob. *Extracts from the Diary of Jacob Hiltzheimer, of Philadelphia. 1765-1798.* Jacob Cox Parson, ed. Philadelphia: n.p., 1893.

Howe, Vice Admiral Richard Viscount to Philip Stephens, Secretary of the Admiralty. Letter dated 25 October 1777. Donald Londahlsmidt, ed. "German and British Accounts of the Assault on Fort Mercer at Redbank, NJ in October 1777." *Journal of the Johannes Schwalm Historical Association,* vol. 16 (Scotland, PA, 2013): 2.

Howe, William to George Germain. Letter dated 13 December 1777. *London Gazette.* 18 January 1778.

"Huntington Papers: Correspondence of the Brothers Joshua and Jedidiah Huntington During the Period of the American Revolution." *Collections of the Connecticut Historical Society,* vol. 20. Hartford, CT: Connecticut Historical Society, 1923.

Hurd, Lewis. "Sergeant Lewis Hurd (Written by Himself)." Dena A. Hurd. *A History and Genealogy of the Family of Hurd in the United States.* New York: Privately Printed, 1910: 69-77.

Inman, George, ed. "List of Officers Killed Since the Commencement of the War 19th April 1775, Regiments Etc. and Officers of Marines Serving on Shore." *The Pennsylvania Magazine of History and Biography,* vol. 27. Philadelphia: The Historical Society of Pennsylvania, 1903: 176-205.

Journal of the Grenadier Battalion von Minnigerode. Donald Londahlsmidt, ed. "German and British Accounts of the Assault on Fort Mercer at Redbank, NJ in October 1777." *Journal of the Johannes Schwalm Historical Association,* vol. 16 (Scotland, PA, 2013): 9-11.

Journal of the Regiment von Mirbach. Donald Londahlsmidt, ed. "German and British Accounts of the Assault on Fort Mercer at Redbank, NJ in October 1777." *Journal of the Johannes Schwalm Historical Association,* vol. 16 (Scotland, PA, 2013) 7-8.

Lafayette, Marquise de. *Memoirs, Correspondence and Manuscripts of General Lafayette Published by his Family*. New York: Saunders and Otley Anne Street, 1837.

Laurens, Henry. *Correspondence of Henry Laurens, of South Carolina*. Frank Moore, ed. New York: Printed for the Zenger Club, 1861.

Laurens, John to Henry Laurens. Letter dated 10 December 1777. *The Virginia Gazette*. 26 December 1777.

Lee, Henry. *Memoirs of the War in the Southern Department of the United States*. Philadelphia: Bradford and Inskeep, 1812.

Lee, Richard Henry. *The Letters of Richard Henry Lee*, vol. 1 *1762-1778*. New York: The Macmillan Company, 1911.

Lesser, Charles H., ed. *The Sinews of Independence: Monthly Strength Reports of the Continental Army*. Chicago: The University of Chicago Press, 1976.

"List of the Killed and Wounded, Prisoners, and Missing of the Officers, Non-Commissioned Officers, and Privates at the storming of the Fort Redbank the 22 October 1777." Donald Londahlsmidt, ed. "German and British Accounts of the Assault on Fort Mercer at Redbank, NJ in October 1777." *Journal of the Johannes Schwalm Historical Association*, vol. 16 (Scotland, PA, 2013): 4.

Marshall, Christopher. *Extracts from the Diary of Christopher Marshall, Kept in Philadelphia and Lancaster, During the American Revolution, 1774-1781*. William Duane, ed. Albany, NY: Joel Munsell, 1877.

Marshall, John. *The Life of George Washington, Commander in Chief of the American Forces, During the War Which Established the Independence of His Country, and First President of the United States*: Philadelphia: C.P. Wayne, 1804.

Martin, Joseph Plumb. *Private Yankee Doodle: Being a Narrative of Some of the Adventures, Dangers and Sufferings of a Revolutionary Soldier*. George E. Scheer, ed. Eastern National, 1962.

Massey, Samuel. "Journal of Captain Samuel Massey 1776-1778." John F. Reed, ed. *Bulletin of the Historical Society of Montgomery Country Pennsylvanvia*, Vol. 20, no. 3. (Fall 1976): 205-251.

McDonald, Hugh. *A Teen-ager in the Revolution: Being the recollections of a high-spirited boy who left his Tory family at the age of fourteen and joined the Continental Army*. Harrisburg, PA: Eastern Acorn Press, 1966.

McMichael, James. "Diary of Lieutenant James McMichael, of the Pennsylvania Line, 1776-1778." William P. McMichael, ed. *The Pennsylvania Magazine of History and Biography*. Vol. 16. Philadelphia: The Historical Society of Pennsylvania, 1892: 129-159.

"A Memoir of General Henry Miller." Henry Miller Watts, ed. *The Pennsylvania Magazine of History and Biography*, vol. 12 (Philadelphia, 1888): 425-431.

"Memoirs of Brigadier-General John Lacey, of Pennsylvania." *The Pennsylvania Magazine of History and Biography*. Vol. 26. Philadelphia: The Historical Society of Pennsylvania, 1902: 101-111.

Minutes of the Provincial Council of Pennsylvania, From the Organization to the Termination of the Proprietary Government, vol. 10. Harrisburg, PA: Theo. Fenn & Co., 1852.

Minutes of the Supreme Executive Council of Pennsylvania, From its Organization to the Termination of the Revolution, vol. 11. Harrisburg, PA: Theo. Fenn & Co., 1852.

Mitchell, S.Weir, ed. "Historical Notes of Dr. Benjamin Rush, 1777." *The Pennsylvania Magazine of History & Biography*, vol. 27. (Philadelphia: The Historical Society of Pennsylvania, 1903): 129-150.

Montresor, John. "The Montresor Journals." G. D. Delaplaine, ed. *Collections of the New York Historical Society for the Year 1881* (1882).

Moore, Frank, ed. *Diary of the American Revolution: From Newspapers and Original Documents*. Vol. 1. New York: C. Scribner, 1860.

Morton, Robert. "The Diary of Robert Morton." *The Pennsylvania Magazine of History and Biography,* vol. 1 (Philadelphia: The Historical Society of Pennsylvania, 1877): 1-39.

Muhlenberg, Henry Melchior. *The Journals of Henry Melchior Muhlenberg*. Trans. By Theodore G. Tappert and John W. Doberstein. Philadelphia: The Muhlenberg Press, 1958.

Murray, James. *Letters from America, 1773 to 1780: Being the Letters of a Scots Officer, Sir James Murray, to his home during the War of American Independence*. Eric Robson, ed. New York: Barnes & Noble, Inc., 1950.

The Narrative of Lieut. Gen. Sir William Howe, in a Committee of the House of Commons, on the 29th of April, 1779, Relative to His Conduct, During His Late Command of the King's Troops in North America: to Which are Added, Some Observations Upon a Pamphlet, Entitled, Letter to a Nobleman. London: H. Bladwin, 1780.

New York Gazette & Weekly Mercury, March 16, 1778.

North Carolina Gazette, October 31, 1777.

Paine, Thomas. Crisis #4. www.ushistory.org/Paine/crisis/c-05.htm 12 April 2022.

————. "Military Operations near Philadelphia in the Campaign of 1777-8." *The Pennsylvania Magazine of History and Biography*, vol. 2. (Philadelphia: The Historical Society of Pennsylvania, 1878): 283-296.

Paullin, Charles Oscar, ed. *Out-Letters of the Continental Marine Committee and Board of Admiralty: August, 1776-September, 1780*, vol. 1. New York: DeVinne Press, 1914.

Peebles, John. *John Peebles' American War: The Diary of a Scottish Grenadier, 1776-1782*. Ira D. Gruber, ed. Mechanicsburg, PA: Stackpole Books, 1998.

Pickering, Octavius. *The Life of Timothy Pickering*. Boston: Little, Brown and Company, 1867.

Popp, Stephen. "Popp's Journal, 1777-1783." Joseph G. Rosengarten, ed. *The Pennsylvania Magazine of History and Biography*, vol. 26 (Philadelphia, 1902): 25-41.

Prechtel, Johann Ernst. *A Hessian Officer's Diary of the American Revolution*. Bruce E. Burgoyne, ed. & trans. Westminster, MD: Heritage Books, 1994.

Rankin, Hugh F., ed. *Narratives of the American Revolution: As Told by a Young Sailor, a Home-Sick Surgeon, a French Volunteers, and a German General's Wife*. Chicago: R.R. Donnelley & Sons Company, 1976.

Reed, William B. *Life and Correspondence of Joseph Reed, Military Secretary of Washington, at Cambridge; Adjutant-General of the Continental Army; Member of the Congress of the United States; and President of the Executive Council of the State of Pennsylvania*. Vol. 1. Philadelphia: Lindsay and Blakiston, 1847.

Remembrancer; or, Impartial Repository of Public Events for the Year 1777. London: J. Almon, 1778.

Report on the Manuscripts of Mrs. Stopford-Sackville, of Drayton House, Northhampshire, vol. 2. London: Hereford Times Co., 1910.

"Revolutionary Pension Records of Morris County." *Proceedings of the New Jersey Historical Society, A Magazine of History, Biography and Genealogy*, New Series, vol. 1 (1916).

Robertson, Archibald. *Archibald Robertson, Lieutenant General Royal Engineers: His Diaries and Sketches in America, 1762-1780*. Harry Miller Lydenberg, ed. New York: New York Public Library, 1930.

Rowland, Kate Mason. *The Life of Charles Carroll of Carrollton, 1732-1832, with His Correspondence and Public Papers*, vol. 1. New York: G.P. Putnam's Sons, 1898.

Rueffer, Carl. "Diary of Second Lieutenant Carl Friedrich Rueffer." Donald Londahlsmidt, ed. "German and British Accounts of the Assault on Fort Mercer at Redbank, NJ in October 1777." *Journal of the Johannes Schwalm Historical Association*, vol. 16 (Scotland, PA, 2013).

Serle, Ambrose. *The American Journal of Ambrose Serle, Secretary to Lord Howe, 1776-1778*. Edward H. Tatum, Jr., ed. San Marino, CA: The Huntington Library, 1940.

Showman, Richard K., Robert M. McCarthy, and Margaret Cobb, eds. *The Papers of General Nathanael Greene*, vol. 2, 1 January 1777-16 October 1778. Chapel Hill, NC: University of North Carolina Press, 1980.

Simcoe, John. *Simcoe's Military Journal: A History of the Operations of a Partisan Corps, Called the Queen's Rangers, Commanded by Lieut. Col. J.G. Simcoe, During the War of the American Revolution*. New York: Bartlett & Wellford, 1844.

Simms, William G., ed. *The Army Correspondence of Colonel John Laurens in the Years 1777-8 Now First Printed from Original Letters Addressed to his Father Henry Laurens President of Congress with a Memoir.* New York: The Bradford Club, 1867.

Smith, George. *A Universal Military Dictionary.* London: J. Millan, 1779.

Smith, Jacob. "Diary of Jacob Smith—American Born." Charles William Heathcote, ed. *The Pennsylvania Magazine of History and Biography*, vol. 56 (Philadelphia, PA, 1932): 260-264.

Smith, John. "Thro Mud & Mire Into the Woods: The 1777 Continental Army Diary of Sergeant John Smith." Bob McDonald, ed. www.revwar75.com/ library/bob/smith.htm 12 September 2021.

Smith, Paul H., et. al., eds. *Letters of Delegates to Congress.* Washington, D.C.: Library of Congress, 1981.

Smith, Samuel to James Varnum. Letter dated 11 November 1777. *The Pennsylvania Magazine of History and Biography*, vol. 19 (Philadelphia, 1895): 238.

Smith, Samuel. "The Papers of General Samuel Smith." *The Historical Magazine and Notes and Queries, Concerning the Antiquities, History and Biography of America*, vol. 7, 2nd series, no. 2 (Morrisania, NY, February 1870): 81-92.

Stirke, Henry. "A British Officer's Revolutionary War Journal, 1776-1778." S. Sydney Bradford, ed. *Maryland Historical Magazine*, vol. 56 (1961): 150-175.

Stockdale, John, ed. *The Parliamentary Register; or, History of the Proceedings and Debates of the House of Commons: Containing an Account of the most interesting Speeches and Motions; accurate Copies of the most remarkable Letters and Papers; of the most material Evidence, Petitions, &c laid before and offered to the House, During the Fifth Session of the Fourteenth Parliament of Great Britain*, vol. 10. London: Wilson and Co., 1802.

Stone, Edwin Martin. *The Invasion of Canada in 1775: Including the Journal of Captain Simeon Thayer, Describing the Perils and Sufferings of the Army Under Colonel Benedict Arnold, in its March Through the Wilderness to Quebec: With Notes and Appendix.* Providence, RI: Knowles, Anthony & Co., Printers, 1867.

Sullivan, Thomas. *From Redcoat to Rebel: The Thomas Sullivan Journal.* Joseph Lee Boyle, ed. Bowie, MD: Heritage Books, Inc., 1997.

Talbot, Silas. *An Historical Sketch to the End of the Revolutionary War, of the Life of Silas Talbot, Esq. of the State of Rhode-Island, Lately Commander of the United States Frigate, the Constitution, and of an American Squadron in the West-Indies.* New York: G & R Waite, 1803.

Tallmadge, Benjamin. *Memoir of Col. Benjamin Tallmadge.* New York: Thomas Holman, 1858.

Taylor, Robert J., et. al., eds. *Papers of John Adams*, vol. 5. Cambridge, MA: Belknap Press, 1983.

Thayer, Simeon to James Varnum. Letter dated 14 November 1777. *The Pennsylvania Magazine of History and Biography*, vol. 19 (Philadelphia, 1895): 248.

Von Baurmeister, Carl. "Journal Installment from Major Carl Leopold Baurmeister." Henry Retzer and Donald Londahlsmidt, eds. "The Philadelphia Campaign, 1777-1778: Letter and Reports from the von Jungkenn Papers. Part 1—1777." *Journal of the Johannes Schwalm Historical Association*, vol. 6, no. 2 (Pennsauken, NJ, 1998): 12-16.

———. Journal of Major Carl Leopold Baurmeister. Donald Londahlsmidt, ed. "German and British Accounts of the Assault on Fort Mercer at Redbank, NJ in October 1777." *Journal of the Johannes Schwalm Historical Association*, vol. 16 (Scotland, PA, 2013): 26-27.

———. *Revolution in America: Confidential Letters and Journals 1776-1784 of Adjutant General Major Baurmeister of the Hessian Forces.* Bernhard A. Uhlendorf, trans. & ed. New Brunswick, NJ: Rutgers University Press, 1957.

Von Bultsingsloewen, Carl. "Journal of Second Lieutenant Carl Wilhelm von Bultsingsloewen." Donald Londahlsmidt, ed. "German and British Accounts of the Assault on Fort Mercer at Redbank, NJ in October 1777." *Journal of the Johannes Schwalm Historical Association*, vol. 16 (Scotland, PA, 2013): 8.

———. "My Journal of the Mirbach Regiment from the Day of Departure in 1776 to the End of 1777." Henry J. Retzer, trans. *Journal of the Johannes Schwalm Historical Association*, vol. 16 (Scotland, PA, 2013): 69-73.

von Cochenhausen, Lieutenant Colonel Johann to Major General Friedrich Christian Arnold Jungkenn. Letter dated 26 October 1777. Donald Londahlsmidt, ed. "German and British Accounts of the Assault on Fort Mercer at Redbank, NJ in October 1777." *Journal of the Johannes Schwalm Historical Association*, vol. 16 (Scotland, PA, 2013): 24.

———. to Friedrich von Jungkenn. Letter dated 28 November 1777. Henry Retzer and Donald Londahlsmidt, eds. "The Philadelphia Campaign, 1777-1778: Letters and Reports from the von Jungkenn Papers. Part 1—1777." *Journal of the Johannes Schwalm Historical Association*, vol. 6, no. 2 (Pennsauken, NJ, 1998): 18-19.

———. to Friedrich von Jungkenn. Letter dated 19 January 1778. Henry Retzer and Donald Londahlsmidt, eds. "The Philadelphia Campaign, 1777-1778: Letters and Reports from the von Jungkenn Papers. Part 2—1778." *Journal of the Johannes Schwalm Historical Association*, vol. 6, no. 3 (Pennsauken, NJ, 1999): 36.

von Dincklage, August. Manuscript Diary. https://orka.bibliothek.uni- kassel.de/viewer/fullscreen/1366290520646/1/, 27 July 2024.

Von Heister, Levin Carl. "Diary of Lieutenant Levin Carl von Heister." Donald Londahlsmidt, ed. "German and British Accounts of the Assault on Fort Mercer at Redbank, NJ in October 1777." *Journal of the Johannes Schwalm Historical Association*, vol. 16 (Scotland, PA, 2013), 14-15.

Von Knyphausen, Lieutenant General Wilhelm to Landgraf Friedrich II. Letter dated 25 October 1777. Donald Londahlsmidt, ed. "German and British Accounts of the Assault on Fort Mercer at Redbank, NJ in October 1777." *Journal of the Johannes Schwalm Historical Association*, vol. 16 (Scotland, PA, 2013): 3.

Von Loos, Colonel Johann August to General von Jungkenn. Letter dated 30 October 1777. Henry Retzer and Donald Londahlsmidt, eds. "The Philadelphia Campaign, 1777-1778: Letters and Reports from the von Jungkenn Papers. Part 1—1777." *Journal of the Johannes Schwalm Historical Association*, vol. 6, no. 2 (Pennsauken, NJ, 1998): 21.

Von Muenchhausen, Friedrich. *At General Howe's Side: 1776-1778: The Diary of General William Howe's aide de camp, Captain Friedrich von Muenchhausen.* Ernst Kipping, trans., and Samuel Steele Smith, ed. Monmouth Beach, NJ: Philip Freneau Press, 1974.

Von Urff, Staff Captain Christian Friedrich to Georg Ernst von und zu Gilsa. 26 October 1777. Donald Londahlsmidt, ed. "German and British Accounts of the Assault on Fort Mercer at Redbank, NJ in October 1777." *Journal of the Johannes Schwalm Historical Association*, vol. 16 (Scotland, PA, 2013): 27-29.

Von Wurmb, Lieutenant Colonel Ludwig Johann Adolph to Major General Friedrich Christian Arnold Jungkenn. Letter dated 25 October 1777. Donald Londahlsmidt, ed. "German and British Accounts of the Assault on Fort Mercer at Redbank, NJ in October 1777." *Journal of the Johannes Schwalm Historical Association*, vol. 16 (Scotland, PA, 2013): 12-14.

———. to General von Jungkenn. Letter dated 7 February 1778. Henry Retzer and Donald Londahlsmidt, eds. "The Philadelphia Campaign, 1777-1778: Letters and Reports from the von Jungkenn Papers. Part 2—1778." *Journal of the Johannes Schwalm Historical Association*, vol. 6, no. 3 (Pennsauken, NJ, 1999): 36-37.

Wallace, James, to Michael Wallace, letter dated 12 October 1777. Horace Edwin Hayden, *Virginia Genealogies: A Genealogy of the Glassell Family of Scotland and Virginia, Also of the Families of Ball, Brown, Bryan, Conway, Daniel, Ewell, Holladay, Lewis, Littlepage, Moncure, Peyton, Robinson, Scott, Taylor, Wallace, and Others, of Virginia and Maryland* (Wilkes-Barre, PA: E.B. Yordy, 1891: 707-708.

Washington, George. Diary entry dated 19 August 1787. www.concsource.org/document/diary-entry-by-george-washington-1787-8-18 5 August 2023.

Watson, John F. *Annals of Philadelphia and Pennsylvania, in the Olden Time; Being a Collection of Memoirs, Anecdotes, and Incidents of the City and its Inhabitants*, vol. 2. Philadelphia, PA: Parry and McMillan, 1855.

Webb, J. Watson. *Reminiscences of Gen'l Samuel B. Webb, of the Revolutionary Army.* New York: Globe Stationary and Printin Co., 1882.

Werner, Friedrich. "Report of First Lieutenant Friedrich Wilhelm Werner, 25 October 1777." Donald Londahlsmidt, ed. "German and British Accounts of the Assault on Fort Mercer at Redbank, NJ in October 1777." *Journal of the Johannes Schwalm Historical Association*, vol. 16 (Scotland, PA, 2013): 5-6.

Whinyates, F.A., ed. *The Services of Lieut.-Colonel Francis Downman, R.A. in France, North America, and the West Indies, Between the Years 1758 and 1784.* Woolwich: Royal Artillery Institution, 1898.

Whittall, Job. "Job Whitall's Diary." Frank H. Stewart, ed. *Notes on Old Gloucester County, New Jersey*, vol. 1 (Camden, NJ, 1917): 255-261.

Wild, Ebenezer. *The Journal of Ebenezer Wild (1776-1781), Who Served as Corporal, Sergeant, Ensign, and Lieutenant in the War of the Revolution.* James M. Bugbee, ed. Cambridge, MA: John Wilson and Son, 1891.

Wilkin, Walter Harold. *Some British Soldiers in America.* London: Hugh Rees, Ltd., 1914.

Wilkinson, James. *Memoirs of My Own Times*, vol. 1. Philadelphia, PA: Abraham Small, 1816.

Willcox, William B., ed. *The Papers of Benjamin Franklin*, vol. 25. New Haven, CT: Yale University Press, 1986.

Williams, Mrs. *Revolutionary Heroes: Containing the Life of Brigadier Gen. William Barton, and also, of Captain Stephen Olney.* Providence, RI: n.p., 1839.

Wister, Sally. *Sally Wister's Journal: A True Narrative Being a Quaker Maiden's Account of her Experiences with Officers of the Continental Army, 1777-1778.* Albert Cook Myers, ed. Philadelphia, PA: Ferris & Leach, 1902.

Wortley, Mrs. E. Stuart, ed. *A Prime Minister and His Son: From the Correspondence of the Third Earl of Bute and Lt. General The Honourable Sir Charles Stuart, K.B.* London: John Murray, 1925.

Secondary Sources

American Quarterly Review (No. 1), March 1827.

Anderson, Lee Patrick. *Forty Minutes by the Delaware: "The Battle for Fort Mercer."* Boca Raton, FL: Universal Publishers, 1999.

Anderson, Troyer Steele. *The Command of the Howe Brothers During the American Revolution.* New York and London: Oxford University Press, 1936.

Baer, Friederike. *Hessians: German Soldiers in the American Revolutionary War.* New York: Oxford University Press, 2022.

Bancroft, George. *History of the United States, Fromm the Discovery of the American Continent.* Boston: Little, Brown, & Co., 1866.

Baule, Steven M. & Stephen Gilbert, *British Army Officers Who Served in the American Revolution 1775-1783*. Westminster, MD: Heritage Books, 2008.

Bickham, Troy. *Making Headlines: The American Revolution as Seen through the British Press*. DeKalb, IL: Northern Illinois University Press, 2009.

Bobrick, Benson. *Angel in the Whirlwind*. New York: Penguin Books, 1997.

Bohrer, Melissa Lukeman. *Glory, Passion, and Principle: The Story of Eight Remarkable Women at the Core of the American Revolution*. New York: Atria Books, 2003.

Botta, Charles. *History of the War of the Independence of the United States of America*. George Alexander Otis, trans. Cooperstown, NY: H & E Phinney, 1845.

Bowler, R. Arthur. *Logistics and the Failure of the British Army in America 1775-1783*. Princeton: Princeton University Press, 1975.

Buck, William J. "The Battles of Edge Hill." *Historical Sketches: A Collection of Papers Prepared for the Historical Society of Montgomery County, Pennsylvania*, vol. 2 (Norristown, PA, 1900): 214-233.

Catts, Wade P. "It Is Painful for me to Lose So Many Good People." Report of an Archaeological Survey at Red Bank Battlefield Park (Fort Mercer), National Park, Gloucester County, New Jersey, June 2017.

————. "Memorialization, Reconstruction, Erosion, and Sham Battles: Multiple Ways of Remembering the Battle of Fort Mercer, New Jersey." Paper Submitted for Council for Northeast Historical Archaeology Conference, November 2019.

Chadwick, Bruce. *The First American Army: The Untold Story of George Washington and the Men Behind America's First Fight for Freedom*. Naperville, IL: Sourcebooks, Inc., 2005.

Chernow, Ron. *Washington: A Life*. New York: The Penguin Press, 2010.

Clement, Justin. *Philadelphia 1777: Taking the Capital*. New York: Osprey Publishing, 2007.

Cotter, John L., Daniel G. Roberts, and Michael Parrington. *The Buried Past: An Archaeological History of Philadelphia*. Philadelphia: University of Pennsylvania Press, 1993.

Cowell, Benjamin. *Spirit of '76 in Rhode Island: or, Sketches of the Efforts of the Government and People in the War of the Revolution*. Boston: A.J. Wright, Printer, 1850.

Cox, Caroline. *A Proper Sense of Honor: Service and Sacrifice in George Washington's Army*. Chapel Hill, NC: The University of North Carolina Press, 2004.

Curtis, Edward E. *The British Army in the American Revolution*. Gansevoort, NY: Corner House Historical Publication, 1998.

Dorwart, Jeffery M. *Fort Mifflin of Philadelphia: An Illustrated History*. Philadelphia: University of Pennsylvania Press, 1998.

Ecelbarger, Gary. "The First Four Days at Valley Forge." *Journal of the American Revolution.* Accessed online www.allthingsliberty.com on 20 August 2023.

———. *George Washington's Momentous Year: Twelve Months that Transformed the Revolution.* Vol. 1. Yardley, PA: Westholme Publishing, 2024.

Edgar, Gregory T. *The Philadelphia Campaign.* Bowie, MD: Heritage Books, Inc., 1998.

Fischer, David Hackett. *Washington's Crossing.* Oxford: Oxford University Press, 2004.

Flavell, Julie. *The Howe Dynasty: The Untold Story of a Military Family and the Women Behind Brtiain's Wars for America.* New York: Liveright, 2021.

Flexner, James Thomas. *Washington: The Indispensable Man.* Bostin: Little, Brown and Company, 1969.

Ford, Worthington Chauncey. *British Officers Serving in the American Revolution, 1774-1783.* Brooklyn: Historical Print Club, 1897.

———. "Defences of Philadelphia in 1777." *The Pennsylvania Magazine of History and Biography,* Vol. 18. Philadelphia: The Historical Society of Pennsylvania, 1894: 1-19.

Frantz, John B., and William Pencak, eds. *Beyond Philadelphia: The American Revolution in the Pennsylvania Hinterland.* University Park, PA: The Pennsylvania State University Press, 1998.

Gillett, Mary C. *The Army Medical Department 1775-1818.* Honolulu, HI: University Press of the Pacific, 2002.

Gordon, William. *The History of the Rise, Progress, and Establishment of the Independence of the United States of America: Including an Account of the Late War, and of the Thirteen Colonies, from Their Origin to that Period.* New York: Samuel Campbell, 1801.

Greene, George Washington. *Life of Nathanael Greene, Major-General in the Army of the Revolution,* vol. 1. New York: G.P. Putnam and Son, 1867.

Greenwalt, Phillip S. *The Winter that Won the War: The Winter Encampment at Valley Forge, 1777-1778.* El Dorado Hills, CA: Savas Beatie, 2021.

Gruber, Ira D. *The Howe Brothers & the American Revolution.* New York: Antheneum, 1972.

Hagist, Don N. *Noble Volunteers: The British Soldiers Who Fought the American Revoution.* Yardley, PA: Westholme Publishing, 2020.

———. *These Distinguished Corps: British Grenadier and Light Infantry Battalions in the American Revolution.* Warwick, England: Helion and Company, 2021.

Hangar, George. *To All Sportsmen, Farmers, and Gamekeepers.* London: J.J. Stockdale, 1814.

Harris, Michael C. *Brandywine: A Military History of the Battle that Lost Philadelphia but Saved America, September 11, 1777.* El Dorado Hills, CA: Savas Beatie, 2014.

————. "The Empire Strikes Back: Philadelphia Campaign 1777." Edward G. Lengel, ed. *The 10 Key Campaigns of the American Revolution*. Washington, D.C.: Regnery History, 2020: 111-28.

————. *Germantown: A Military History of the Battle for Philadelphia, October 4, 1777*. El Dorado Hills, CA: Savas Beatie, 2020.

————. *The Philadelphia Campaign 1777*. Havertown, PA: Casemate, 2023.

Harris, Michael C. & Gary Ecelbarger. "The Numerical Strength of George Washington's Army During the 1777 Philadelphia Campaign." *Journal of the American Revolution*. Yardley, PA: Westholme Publishing, 2022: 112-113.

Hay, Denys. "The Denouement of General Howe's Campaign of 1777." *English Historical Review*, vol. 74 (1964): 498-512.

Heitman, Francis B. *Historical Register of Officers of the Continental Army During the War of the Revolution*. Baltimore: Clearfield Company, Inc., 2003.

Herrera, Ricardo A. *Feeding Washington's Army: Surviving the Valley Forge Winter of 1778*. Chapel Hill, NC: The University of North Carolina Press, 2022.

Heston, Alfred M. "Red Bank: Defence of Fort Mercer." Paper read before the Monmouth County, NJ Historical Association July 26, 1900.

Hibbert, Christopher. *Recoats and Rebels*. New York: W.W. Norton & Company, 1990.

Jackson, John W. *The Delaware Bay and River Defenses of Philadelphia 1775-1777*. Philadelphia: Philadelphia Maritime Museum, 1977.

————. *Fort Mifflin: Valiant Defender of the Delaware*. Norristown, PA: James and Sons, 1986.

————. *The Pennsylvania Navy, 1775-1781: The Defense of the Delaware*. New Brunswick, NJ: Rutgers University Press, 1974.

————. *Whitemarsh 1777: Impregnable Stronghold*. Fort Washington, PA Historical Society of Fort Washington, 1984.

————. *With the British Army in Philadelphia*. San Rafael, CA: Presidio Press, 1979.

Johnson, Donald. *Occupied America: British Military Rule and the Experience of the Revolution*. Philadelphia, PA: University of Pennsylvania Press, 2020.

Katcher, Philip R.N. *Encyclopedia of British, Provincial, and German Army Units 1775-1783*. Harrisburg, PA: Stackpole Books, 1973.

Ketchum, Richard M. *Saratoga: Turning Point of America's Revolutionary War*. New York: Henry Holt and Company, 1997.

Knouff, Gregory T. *The Soldiers' Revolution: Pennsylvanians in Arms and the Forging of Early American Identity*. University Park, PA: Pennsylvania State University Press, 2004.

Lefkowitz, Arthur S. "French Adventurers, Patriots, and Pretentious Imposters in the Fight for American Independence." *Journal of the American Revolution: Annual Volume 2022.* Yardley, PA: Westholme Publishing, 2022: 80-91.

———. *George Washington's Indispensable Men: The 32 Aides-de-Camp Who Helped Win American Independence.* Mechanicsburg, PA: Stackpole Books, 2003.

———. *George Washington's Revenge: The 1777 New Jersey Campaign and How General Washington Turned Defeat into the Strategy that Won the Revolution* Blue Ridge Summit, PA: Stackpole Books, 2022.

Lender, Mark Edward. *Caball: The Plot Against George Washington.* Yardley, PA: Westholme Publishing, 2019.

Lender, Mark Edward & Garry Wheeler Stone. *Fatal Sunday: George Washington, the Monmouth Campaign, and the Politics of Battle.* Norman, OK: University of Oklahoma Press, 2016.

Lengel, Edward. *General George Washington: A Military Life.* New York: Random House, 2005.

———. *Inventing George Washington: America's Founder, in Myth & Memory.* New York: Harper, 2011.

Lossing, Benjamin J. *The Pictorial Field-Book of the American Revolution.* New York: Harper and Brothers, 1852.

Lowell, Edward J. *The Hessians and the Other German Auxiliaries of Great Britain in the Revolutionary War.* Gansevoort, NY: Corner House Historical Publications, 1997.

Luzader, John F. *Saratoga: A Military History of the Decisive Campaign of the American Revolution.* New York: Savas Beatie, 2008.

Mackesy, Piers. *The War for American: 1775-1783.* Lincoln, NE: University of Nebraska Press, 1964.

Mahon, Lord. *History of England from the Peace of Utrecht to the Peace of Versailles: 1713-1783.* Vol. 6. London: J. Murray, 1858.

Martin, David G. *The Philadelphia Campaign: June 1777-July 1778.* Conshohocken, PA: Combined Books, Inc., 1993.

Martin, James Kirby, & Mark Edward Lender. *"A Respectable Army": The Military Origins of the Republic, 1763-1789.* West Sussex, United Kingdom: Wiley-Blackwell, 2015.

Mayer, Holly A. *Belonging to the Army: Camp Followers and Community during the American Revolution.* Columbia, SC: University of South Carolina Press, 1996.

McBurney, Christian. *George Washington's Nemesis: The Outrageous Treason and Unfair Court-Martial of Major General Charles Lee during the Revolutionary War.* El Dorado Hills, CA: Savas Beatie, LLC, 2020.

————. *Kidnapping the Enemy: The Special Operations to Capture Generals Charles Lee & Richard Prescott.* Yardley, PA: Westholme Publishing, 2014.

McGeorge, Wallace. *The Battle of Red Bank, Resulting in the Defeat of the Hessians and the Destruction of the British Frigate Augusta, Oct. 22 and 23, 1777.* Camden, NJ: Sinnickson, Chew & Sons Co. Printers, 1905.

McGuire, Thomas J. *Battle of Paoli.* Mechanicsburg, PA: Stackpole Books, 2000.

————. *The Philadelphia Campaign: Brandywine and the Fall of Philadelphia.* Mechanicsburg, PA: Stackpole Books, 2007.

————. *The Philadelphia Campaign: Germantown and the Roads to Valley Forge.* Mechanicsburg, PA: Stackpole Books, 2007.

McIntyre, James R. *A Most Gallant Resistance: The Delaware River Campaign September – November 1777.* Point Pleasant, NJ: Winged Hussar Publishing, 2022.

Mickle, Isaac. "Reminiscences." *The Constitution, and Farmers' and Mechanics' Advertiser.* 10 March 1846.

Moffett, Louis B., ed. *Year Book for 1928: The New Jersey Society of Pennsylvania* (1929).

Moomaw, W. Hugh. "The Naval Career of Captain Hamond, 1775-1779." PhD dissertation. University of Virginia, 1955.

Mooney, Douglas B. & Ingrid Wuebber. "Archaeological Investigations of Revolutionary War Fort Billingsport: Paulsboro, Gloucester County, New Jersey." Burlington, NJ: URS Corporation, May 2009.

Morning Post and Daily Advertiser, 19 January 1778.

Morrisson, Mary Foulke. "Reminiscences of the Year 1776." *The Pennsylvania Magazine of History and Biography,* vol. 90 (Philadelphia, 1966): 517-523.

Nagy, John A. *Rebellion in the Ranks: Mutinies of the American Revolution.* Yardley: Westholme Publishing, PA, 2008.

————. *Spies in the Continental Capital: Espionage Across Pennsylvania During the American Revolution.* Yardley, PA: Westholme Publishing, 2011.

Neff, Jacob. *The Army and Navy of America: Containing a View of the Heroic Adventures, Battles, Naval Engagements, Remarkable Incidents, and Glorious Achievements in the Cause of Freedom.* Philadelphia: J.H. Pearsol & Co., 1845.

Newland, Samuel J. *The Pennsylvania Militia: The Early Years, 1669-1792.* Annville, PA: Commonwealth of Pennsylvania, The Department of Military and Veterans Affairs, 1997.

O'Donnell, Patrick K. *Washington's Immortals: The Untold Story of an Elite Regiment Who Changed the Course of the Revolution.* New York: Atlantic Monthly Press, 2016.

O'Shaughnessy, Andrew Jackson. *The Men Who Lost America: British Leadership, the American Revolution, and the Fate of the Empire.* New Haven, CT: Yale University Press, 2013.

Ousterhout, Anne M. *The Most Learned Woman in America: A Life of Elizabeth Graeme Fergusson.* University Park, PA: Penn State University Press, 2004.

Pancake, John S. *1777: The Year of the Hangman.* Tuscaloosa, AL: The University of Alabama Press, 1977.

Peckham, Howard H., ed. *The Toll of Independence: Engagements & Battle Casualties of the American Revolution.* Chicago: The University of Chicago Press, 1974.

Rankin, Hugh F. *The North Carolina Continentals.* Chapel Hill, NC: The University of North Carolina Press, 1971.

Reed, John F. *Campaign to Valley Forge: July 1, 1777-December 19, 1777.* Philadelphia: Pioneer Press, 1965.

Resch, John, and Walter Sargent, eds. *War & Society in the American Revolution: Mobilization and Home Fronts.* DeKalb, IL: Northern Illinois University Press, 2007.

Risch, Erna. *Supplying Washington's Army.* Washington, D.C.: Center of Military History, 1981.

Rosswurm, Steven. *Arms, Country, and Class: The Philadelphia Militia and the "Lower Sort" during the American Revolution.* New Brunswick, NJ: Rutgers University Press, 1989.

Ruppert, Bob. "Fortifying Philadelphia: A Chain of Redoubts and Floating Bridges." *Journal of the American Revolution,* 18 February 2015, www.allthingsliberty.com, accessed 21 April 2023.

Scheer, George F., and Hugh F. Rankin. *Rebels & Redcoats: The American Revolution Through the Eyes of Those Who Fought and Lived It.* New York: Da Capo Press, 1957.

Sellers, Charles Coleman. *Charles Willson Peale: Early Life: 1741-1790,* vol. 1. Philadelphia: The American Philosophical Society, 1947.

Smith, Charles R. *Marines in the Revolution: A History of the Continental Marines in the American Revolution 1775-1783.* Washington, D.C.: U.S. Marine Corps, 1975.

Smith, Samuel Steele. *Fight for the Delaware 1777.* Monmouth Beach, NJ: Philip Freneau Press, 1970.

Spears, John R. *Anthony Wayne, Sometimes Called "Mad Anthony."* New York: D. Appleton and Company, 1903.

Spring, Matthew H. *With Zeal and With Bayonets Only: The British Army on Campaign in North America, 1775-1783.* Norman, OK: University of Oklahoma Press, 2008.

Stewart, Frank H. *History of the Battle of Red Bank: With Events Prior and Subsequent Thereto*. Woodbury, NJ: Board of Chosen Freeholders of Gloucester County, 1927.

Stone, Garry Wheeler & Paul W. Schopp. *The Battle of Gloucester 1777*. Yardley, PA: Westholme Publishing, 2022.

Stryker, William S. *The Forts on the Delaware in the Revolutionary War*. Trenton, NJ: The John L. Murphy Publishing Co., 1901.

Sullivan, Aaron. *The Disaffected: Britain's Occupation of Philadelphia During the American Revolution*. Philadelphia: University of Pennsylvania Press, 2019.

Thompson, Ray. *Washington at Whitemarsh: Prelude to Valley Forge*. Fort Washington, PA: The Bicentennial Press, 1974.

Trevelyan, George Otto. *The American Revolution*. Vol. 4. New York: Longmans, Green, and Company, 1912.

Trussell, John B.B. *The Pennsylvania Line*. Harrisburg, PA: Commonwealth of Pennsylvania, Historical and Museum Commission, 1993.

Wainwright, Nicholas B. *Colonial Grandeur in Philadelphia: The House and Furniture of General John Cadwalader*. Philadelphia: Historical Society of Pennsylvania, 1964.

Ward, Christopher. *The War of the Revolution*. 2 vols. New York: Macmillan Company, 1952.

Ward, Harry M. *Charles Scott and the "Spirit of '76."* Charlottesville, VA: University Press of Virginia, 1988.

————. *General William Maxwell and the New Jersey Continentals*. Westport, CT: Praeger, 1997.
Wood, W. J. *Battles of the Revolutionary War: 1775-1781*. Cambridge, MA: Da Capo Press, 1990.

Wright, Robert K., Jr. *The Continental Army*. Washington, D.C.: Government Printing Office, 1983.

Chapter 13

The British Assault Birmingham Hill:
Afternoon, September 11, 1777

"The line moving on exhibited the most grand and noble sight imaginable.
The grenadiers beating their march as they advanced contributed
greatly to the dignity of the approach."[1]

— Lt. Frederick Augustus Wetherall, September 11, 1777

The British Advance Guard

By the middle of the afternoon on September 11, Gen. Howe's
veteran troops under the steady hand of Gen. Cornwallis were
poised to deliver the crowning blow of Howe's flanking strategy.

Sometime after 3:00 p.m., Capt. Johann Ewald "caught sight of some
infantry and horsemen behind a village on a hill in the distance, which was
formed like an amphitheatre." A short time later, Capt. Alexander Ross,
General Cornwallis's aide-de-camp, delivered an order to Ewald to take the
advance guard and attack the American infantry and cavalry spotted up ahead.
The capable Hessian captain organized the advance guard with the 17th
Regiment of Foot's light company deployed on the left, the light company of
the 42nd Highlanders deployed on the right, and the mounted jaegers

---

1   Wetherall, *Journal of Officer B.*

positioned on the road in the center. The foot jaegers moved out front in skirmish order while the main line formed.[2]

The Americans spotted by Ewald and targeted for attack were not, as the Hessian believed, "behind a village," but near the Samuel Jones farm buildings and Birmingham Meetinghouse, which the captain mistook for a small community. The patriots were elements of Col. Thomas Marshall's 3rd Virginia Regiment, part of Brig. Gen. William Woodford's brigade of Maj. Gen. Adam Stephen's division, together with some of Col. Theodorick Bland's light dragoons. The Virginians had deployed on the Jones property south of the Street Road - Birmingham Road intersection east of the latter road about one mile below Osborn's Hill. Southeast of the intersection was the Jones woodlot. His brick farmhouse (which Ewald had also spotted) was another 150 yards farther south along Birmingham Road, and just south of the house was the family orchard. The Americans, first positioned in the woodlot and later in the orchard, enjoyed a slight advantage in elevation over the light troops immediately confronting them.

The British advance guard extended its line eastward as it advanced toward the American position in an effort to outflank Colonel Marshall's 3rd Virginia Regiment. The regiment, explained one American officer in his memoirs, "having been much reduced by previous service, did not amount to more than a battalion; but one field officer, the colonel, and four captains were with it."[3] The Virginians opened a long-range small arms fire. Captain William Scott of the 17th Regiment of Foot's light company recalled the effort to get around the American right. His company, he wrote, "received a fire from about 200 men in the orchard, which did no execution."[4]

After watching Cornwallis's men march through Sconneltown and returning home to check on his family, young Quaker Joseph Townsend passed through the moving British Army as he walked south down the Birmingham Road to Osborn Hill and down its southern slope toward Street Road. "We reached the advanced guard, who were of the German troops," recalled Townsend. "Many of them wore their beard on their upper lips." The youth,

---

2   Ewald, *Diary*, 84; McGuire, *Philadelphia Campaign*, vol. 1, 200.

3   Lee, *Memoirs*, vol. 1, 16.

4   William Scott, *Memoranda on the Battle of Brandywine and The Battle of Germantown*, in the Sol Feinstone Collection of the David Library of the American Revolution, Washington Crossing, PA, item no. 111.

who was unaware that British troops also comprised the advance guard, recalled the opening moments of the battle after the Virginians had fired upon Ewald's command: "The attack was immediately returned by the Hessians, by their stepping up the bank of the road alongside the orchard, making the fence as a breast work through which they fired upon the company who made the attack."[5] If Townsend's recollections are accurate, some of the jaegers pushed far enough beyond Street Road to use the eastern embankment of the Birmingham Road as protection to fire into the Jones orchard.

Townsend continued, "From the distance we were from them (though in full view until the smoke of the firing covered them from our sight) I was under no apprehension of danger [from the American fire] especially when there was such a tremendous force coming on [Cornwallis's division] and ready to engage in action." Townsend observed the approaching British and German formations with deep interest: "[W]e had a grand view of the army as they advanced over and down the south side of Osborne's Hill and the lands of James Carter, scarce a vacant place left. . . . [A]lmost the whole face of the country around appeared to be covered and alive with these objects." By this time the novelty of examining the British Army had worn off and it dawned on the youngster that he had walked directly into the middle of a growing battle: "I concluded it best to retire, finding that my inconsiderate curiosity had prompted me to exceed the bounds of prudence." The Quaker turned northward, and walked back alongside the Birmingham Road.[6]

The opening and wildly inaccurate American fire hit but two of his men, which in turn allowed Ewald to push ahead and reach one of the buildings on the Jones property with both his foot and mounted jaegers. At that point the firing intensified. "Unfortunately for us," explained Ewald, "the time this took favored the enemy and I received extremely heavy small-arms fire from the gardens and houses." The sharp fire and firm stand offered by the Virginians, who may have been more numerous than Ewald originally believed, convinced the captain to pull his jaegers and the two British light companies back to the fence line along Street Road. The Americans let them fall back without advancing in return.[7]

---

5   Townsend, *Some Account*, 24.

6   Ibid., 24-25.

7   Ewald, *Diary*, 85.

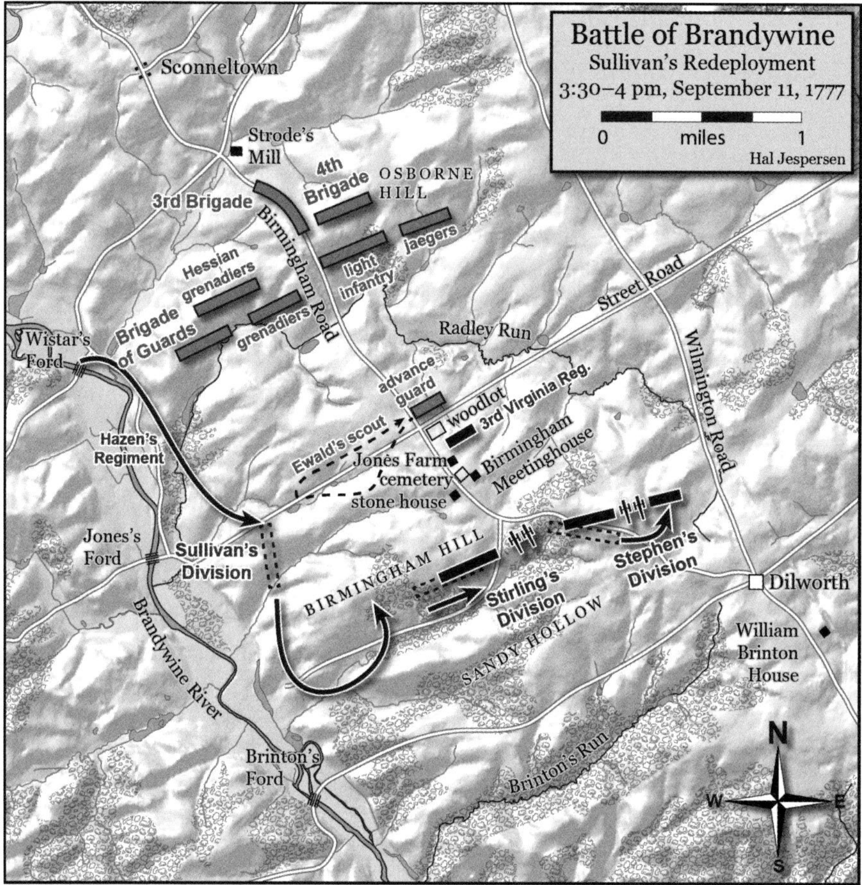

It was at this time that Ewald realized his advance guard was more than living up to its name. Indeed, it was now much too far in advance of the balance of Cornwallis's division. "They [the other members of the advance guard] shouted to me that the army was far behind, and I became not a little embarrassed to find myself quite alone with the advanced guard," reported the Hessian. "But now that the business had begun, I still wanted to obtain information about these people who had let me go so easily."[8]

Once he was satisfied with his new fallback position, Ewald took three men and rode well to the right (west) in an effort to better scout the American position. His initial route carried him to the top of a small hill southwest of the

8   Ewald, *Diary*, 85.

Street Road-Birmingham Road intersection. What he beheld stunned the veteran officer: "I gazed in astonishment when I got up the hill, for I found behind it—three to four hundred paces away—an entire line deployed in the best order, several of whom waved to me with their hats but did not shoot. I kept composed, examined them closely, rode back, and reported it at once to Lord Cornwallis" via a mounted jaeger named Hoffman. Ewald's reconnaissance discovered Lord Stirling's division in line less than one-half mile farther south on Birmingham Hill. Lieutenant William Keugh of the 44th Regiment of Foot, who was far behind Ewald at this time, would recall the strength of this American position and describe the terrain as "Hills which Nature Unassisted, had abundantly fortified." Lieutenant Colonel Ludwig von Wurmb remembered Cornwallis receiving Ewald's report back on Osborn's Hill: "Captain Ewald of the advance guard reported the enemy was approaching and they were forming up on a hilltop and that another column was approaching on the right." Captain Scott, whose company of the 17th Regiment of Foot was part of the advance guard that afternoon, took note of additional American troops when he observed, "it was evident tho' the enemy fell back they were well supported."[9] The "additional" troops were the now very visible divisions of Stephen and Stirling forming farther south along Birmingham Hill.

Ewald was one of the first to see and realize the formidable nature of the American position, and that the Virginians on the Jones farm were not a small picket or advance force, but part of much larger command. It is likely that both Howe and Cornwallis believed the Americans were by this time retreating from their former position east of the Brandywine, their exposed flank turned and a strong force under Gen. Wilhelm von Knyphausen pressing their rear. Now they learned the truth: the Americans had simply maneuvered northward with a strong force to blunt Howe's flanking effort. The British would not be dropping into Washington's rear area without a fight.

After sending his report to Cornwallis, Ewald continued his reconnaissance by riding down the hill and then west along Street Road toward Jones's Ford. He spotted more American troops as he approached the crossing—"a whole enemy column with guns marching through the valley in which Lord Cornwallis's column had been marching for some time, a quarter or half an hour away to the right." The "enemy column" was Moses Hazen's regiment

---

9 Ibid.; Von Wurmb to von Jungkenn, October 14, 1777, 10; McGuire, *The Philadelphia Campaign,* vol. 2, 280, reproduces the entire letter; Scott, *Memoranda.*

marching south to link back up with the rest of Maj. Gen. John Sullivan's division, which was approaching Street Road on its march from Brinton's Ford. Hazen would fall in with the division and continue the march to unite with the divisions on Birmingham Hill. "[T]he Enemy headed us in the Road about forty Rods from our advance Guard," reported Sullivan. "I then found it necessary to turn off to the Right to form & to get nearer to the other two Divisions [Stirling's and Stephen's] which I that moment Discovered Drawn up on an Eminence both in the Rear & to the Right of the place I was then at."[10]

Sullivan's change of direction moved his division onto the same hill Ewald had used just minutes earlier to observe Stirling's position. The other two American divisions were deployed on Birmingham Hill about one-half mile to Sullivan's right and rear. His division was the last major piece of the American blocking force, which was now aligned, by division, from left to right as follows: Sullivan, Stirling, and Stephen, with Sullivan in command of all three. Although most of three divisions had succeeded in shifting north at the last moment to meet Howe's substantial flanking column, argues one historian, "these hurried alterations were liable to dent inexperienced troops' confidence."[11]

Ewald, meanwhile, returned to the advance guard still pinned down along the fence line near the Street Road-Birmingham Road intersection. His hurried ride had discovered Stirling's division to his right front, and the arrival of more enemy troops in that quarter. Cornwallis had been duly informed. Now back with his men, the Hessian oversaw the fitful skirmish fire for which his men were famous, and awaited orders. He would not have long to wait. With the information from Ewald's reconnaissance in hand, Howe directed Cornwallis to "to form the line." Within minutes the columns of soldiers redeployed into crisp, heavy lines of battle. It was time to brush aside the incompetent Americans and drive into the rear of Washington's imperiled army.[12]

END OF EXCERPT

<hr>

10 Ewald, *Diary*, 85-86; Hammond, ed., *Papers of Sullivan*, vol. 1, 463.

11 Spring, *With Zeal*, 64.

12 Von Wurmb to von Jungkenn, October 14, 1777, 10.

Chapter 11

Marching to the Attack

October 3-4, 1777

"We had not above two hours notice of their advancing,
& then gave no credit to it."[1]

— Capt. Richard Fitzpatrick, 1st British Foot Guards, October 28, 1777

George Washington concocted an ambitious plan for assaulting the British force at Germantown. His young Continental Army had a long night of marching ahead of it.

No lights, noise, or talking were permitted along the way. Clouds blocked the moonlight and the temperatures dropped into the fifties. "The night was dark and it looked like rain, but it remained dry," recorded Rev. Henry Muhlenberg in his journal. Stark darkness greeted the men as they tramped southeast in silence. To shorten the march and arrive in the proper order "to attack the different parts of the Enemy's lines," wrote an anonymous American officer to George Clinton, the governor of New York, the day after the battle, "Conway, Sullivan & Wayne followed by the Reserve marched down one Road, Green Stevens & McDougall another, Armstrong a third, & Smallwood & Foreman a fourth Road."[2]

---

1 Letter, Fitzpatrick to his Brother, 28 October 1777.

2 Muhlenberg, *Journals*, vol. 3, 82; McGuire, *Campaign*, vol. 2, 53; *Public Papers of George Clinton, First Governor of New York, 1777-1795 — 1801-1804*, 10 vols. (New York, 1900), vol. 2, 367-368.

Smallwood's Column

As it had the longest march of anyone that night, William Smallwood's Maryland and New Jersey militia column was the first to leave the American camp. The militia descended Methacton Hill using the Morris Road (a mile to the left of Skippack Road), turned right onto Bethlehem Pike, and headed for the Whitemarsh Church intersection, where they turned left down Church Road heading farther east to the Old York Road intersection. After crossing Tacony Creek, the militiamen turned right onto Old York Road a quarter mile south of Jenkin's Tavern. With a little luck Smallwood's men would then approach Germantown and come out on the right rear of the British camp. Old York Road was fifteen miles from camp, and they would need to march another three or four miles before encountering the enemy. According to Smallwood, he left "about 6 o'clock in the evening of the 3rd." James Vance of New Jersey's Hunterdon County militia remembered "they fixed pieces of white paper on their hats by which to know one another" in the darkness. Another New Jerseyman, Aaron Hageman of the Somerset County militia, recalled how they "Marched all night, halted in the road about break of day so as not to be there too soon." It was Smallwood's task to drive the Queen's Rangers away at daybreak.[3]

Three miles after turning onto Church Road the head of Smallwood's column approached Limekiln Road, down which some of the flankers marched in error. Each step down the wrong road moved them closer to the camp of the British 1st Light Infantry Battalion. Later, the capture of one of these flankers provided an early warning to the British that the enemy was near.[4]

Greene's Column

Nathanael Greene, who commanded the largest column in the Continental Army, had to wait for Smallwood to clear out before getting his own men on the road. Sources claim Greene was moving by 6:00 p.m., but with Smallwood using the same narrow road and claiming to have left about the same time, it is more likely

---

3 Morris Road took Smallwood's men to the Bethlehem Pike, where they would turn right. Just down the road was the Skippack Road intersection at Whitemarsh Church. Church Road is modern Route 73. Letter, William Smallwood to unknown recipient, October 9, 1777, reproduced in *PMHB* (Philadelphia, 1877), vol.1, 401; RWPF, files S4697 and S819.

4 McGuire, *Campaign*, vol. 2, 62.

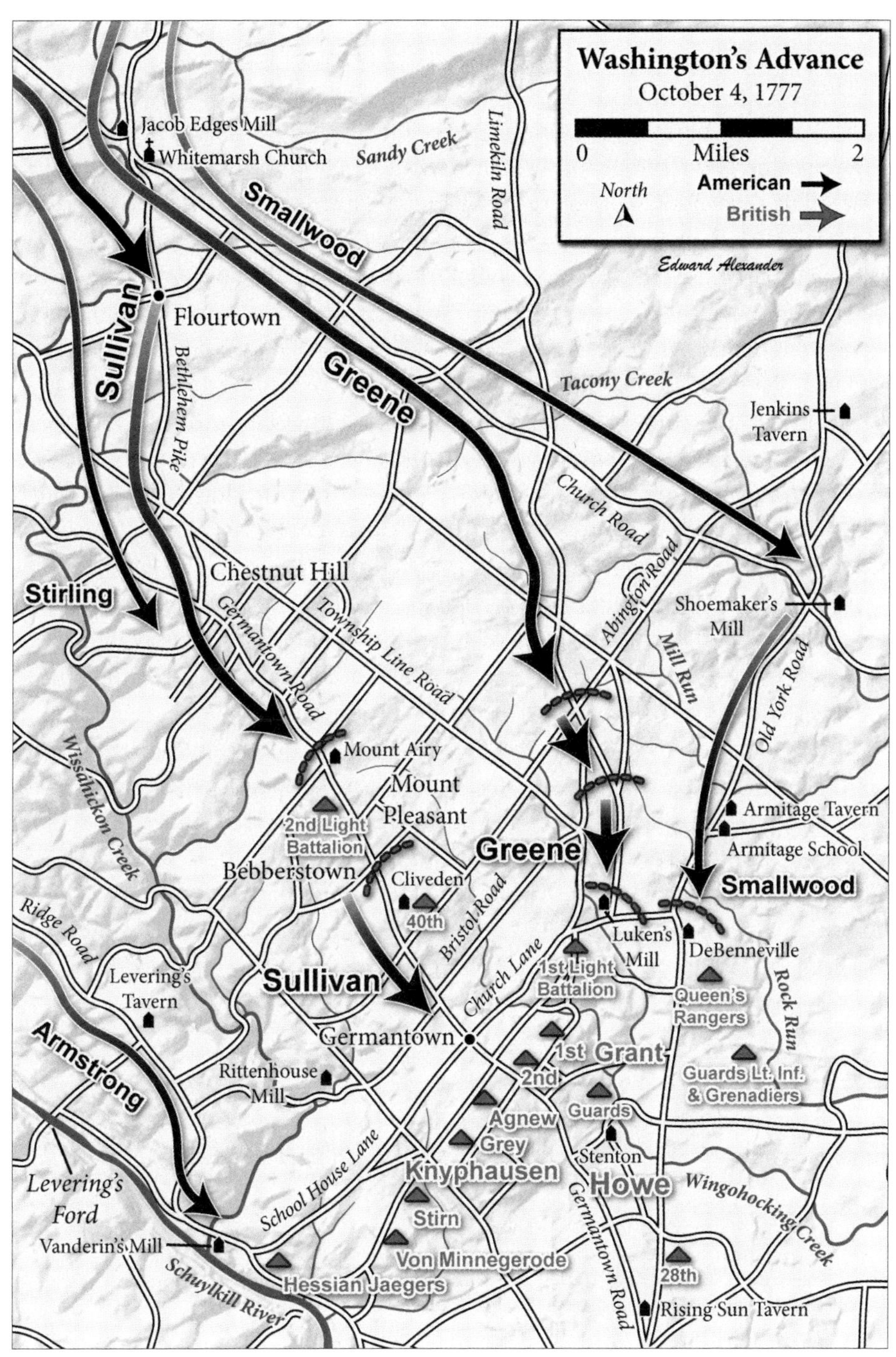

Washington's Advance
October 4, 1777
0   Miles   2
North
American
British
Edward Alexander

Jacob Edges Mill
Whitemarsh Church
Sandy Creek
Limekiln Road
Smallwood
Sullivan
Flourtown
Bethlehem Pike
Greene
Tacony Creek
Jenkins Tavern
Church Road
Stirling
Chestnut Hill
Germantown Road
Township Line Road
Abington Road
Shoemaker's Mill
Mill Run
Old York Road
Wissahickon Creek
Mount Airy
Mount Pleasant
2nd Light Battalion
Bebberstown
Cliveden
40th
Greene
Armitage Tavern
Armitage School
Smallwood
Ridge Road
Levering's Tavern
Sullivan
Bristol Road
Church Lane
Luken's Mill
DeBenneville
Rock Run
1st Light Battalion
Queen's Rangers
Armstrong
Germantown
Rittenhouse Mill
1st Grant
2nd
Guards Lt. Inf. & Grenadiers
Agnew
Guards
Grey
Stenton
Levering's Ford
Vanderin's Mill
School House Lane
Knyphausen
Howe
Wingohocking Creek
Germantown Road
Stirn
Schuylkill River
Von Minnegerode
Hessian Jaegers
28th
Rising Sun Tavern

that Greene did not get started until at least 6:30 p.m. or thereafter. Alexander McDougall's Connecticut brigade led the movement followed by Greene's own division, with Adam Stephen's Virginia division bringing up the rear. Like Smallwood, Greene tramped down Church Road but turned right onto Limekiln Road three miles past Whitemarsh Church. (Smallwood had marched farther out Church Road to get to Old York Road.) The movement to Limekiln Road separated Greene from Sullivan's column to the northeast by more than two miles. If all went as planned, Greene would slam into the British 1st Light Infantry Battalion just after sunrise beyond Luken's Mill. The roads were poorly marked and the night dark, so the march was slower than desired. Greene arrived in position about half an hour later than Sullivan's men off his right flank.[5]

"I left my baggage and my Bible which my father bought for me when I was six years old, in my trunk," recalled Lt. James Morris of the 5th Connecticut Regiment, McDougall's brigade. "I marched with only my military suit, and my implements of war, without any change of dress or even a blanket." Morris also took note of "Samuel Stannard my waiter," a servant he described as "a strong athletic man [who] carried my blanket and provisions with a canteen of Whiskey." Ensign Jonathan Todd of the 7th Connecticut Regiment of the same brigade remembered moving all night "without so Much as speaking A Loud word. Just at day we arriv'd within a Mile from Town Where we formed." The 4th Connecticut's Joseph Plumb Martin made it clear that specific instructions for the attack had been withheld from the men when he observed that he "naturally concluded something serious was in the wind. We marched slowly all night. In the morning there was a low vapor lying on the land which made it very difficult to distinguish objects at any great distance." Similarly, Col. Charles Webb, the commander of the 2nd Connecticut, recalled "marching the whole night" and arriving "at the day dawn . . . at Germantown."[6]

---

5 McGuire, *Campaign*, vol. 2, 55; Reed, *Campaign*, 220-221; Edgar, *Campaign*, 57. It is important to note that commanders' watches were not synchronized. Greene has been criticized for being misled by his guide down the Morris Road. Had Greene taken the Skippack Road with Sullivan's column, however, more than three-quarters of Washington's army would have been using the same road to approach the Whitemarsh Church intersection. Despite later criticism by such campaign historians as Thomas McGuire and John Reed, it was wise for Greene to utilize Morris Road to spread the army out over multiple routes. Some writers claim this change of roads forced his troops to countermarch to return to his intended route, but no contemporary accounts from Greene's column mention any such needless marching.

6 Letter, Jonathan Todd to his Father, October 6, 1777, Jonathan Todd Letters, Revolutionary War Pension Files, reel 2396, National Archives, Washington, DC; Martin, *Yankee Doodle*, 72; Ryan, ed.,

Lieutenant James McMichael of the Pennsylvania State Regiment, part of George Weedon's Virginia brigade marching behind the Connecticut men, recorded a curious order he received as the column passed Whitemarsh Church. "Major J[ohn] Murray, Capt. [John] Nice and I were ordered at the head of 80 men to feel their advance pickets, and if we conveniently could to attack. Owing to the picket being within a mile of their main body, we were unsuccessful, and rejoined our regiment at daybreak." These Pennsylvania troops represented the only locals in Greene's entire column, and using them to probe ahead of the column on the dark night made sense.[7]

Few accounts agree on the distance marched that night, which is not surprising since the men were moving in column along strange roads in the dark, uncertain of their destination. Brigade commander Weedon believed his men marched about "22 miles to the Ground, did not arrive so soon as we Expected so that it was near six in the Morning" by the time they reached their jump-off point. Morris of the 5th Connecticut echoed Weedon's estimate when he recorded the march covered "a distance of about twenty miles." Sergeant Charles Talbot of the 6th Virginia, Weedon's brigade, however, thought the march much shorter, covering just "12 or fourteen miles," as did Col. Walter Stewart of the Pennsylvania State Regiment, who wrote that he and his men marched "about 12 miles; on account of the darkness of the night and badness of some Roads we did not arrive at our appointed place until past 6 O'Clock." The shorter estimates were in fact the most accurate gauges of the distance from the American camps to the point designated for the opening of the attack.[8]

Adam Stephen's division moved out behind Weedon's brigade at the end of Greene's column. Like the rest of the recorded departure times, when it did so is

---

Salute to Courage, 103; "Contemporary Account of the Battle of Germantown," *PMHB* (Philadelphia, 1887), vol. 11, 330. Greene's march was conducted well and without serious incident. The record shows that one officer, Lt. Joseph Fish of the 4th Connecticut, was charged with "Leaving the regiment and platoon, he belonged to, while on the march towards the enemy . . . and also with being much disguised with liquor." After the battle he was tried and acquitted of the first charge but found guilty of being inebriated "and sentenced therefore, to be reprimanded, by the Brigadier General, in the presence of the officers of the brigade." Chase and Lengel, eds., *Papers*, vol. 11, 605.

7   McMichael, "Diary," 152.

8 Letter, George Weedon to John Page, 4 October 1777, original in Weedon Letters, Chicago Historical Society, Chicago, IL; Charles Talbot, "Letters of Charles Moile Talbot to Charles Talbot," Mrs. J. B. Friend and Elizabeth V. Gaines, eds., *The William and Mary Quarterly* (Williamsburg, VA, 1931), vol. 11, 318; Letter, Walter Stewart to General Gates, October 12, 1777, reproduced in *PMHB* (Philadelphia, 1877), vol. 1, 400.

END OF EXCERPT

About the Author

Michael C. Harris is a graduate of the University of Mary Washington and the American Military University. He has worked for the National Park Service in Fredericksburg, Virginia, Fort Mott State Park in New Jersey, and the Pennsylvania Historical and Museum Commission at Brandywine Battlefield. Mike conducts tours and staff rides of many east coast battlefields and enjoys speaking with audiences about all things military, and especially about the American Revolution and Civil War.

His first book in the Philadelphia Campaign series was the bestseller *Brandywine: A Military History of the Battle that Lost Philadelphia but Saved America, September 11, 1777* (2017), which was awarded the American Revolution Round Table of Richmond Book Award (2015) and was a finalist for the Army Historical Foundation Distinguished Book Award. His second in the series, also a bestseller, was *Germantown: A Military History of the Battle for Philadelphia, October 4, 1777* (2020). *Fighting for Philadelphia* completes the trilogy.

Mike is certified in secondary education and currently teaches in the Philadelphia region. He lives in Pennsylvania with his wife Michelle and son Nathanael.